PEARLS, PEOPLE, AND POWER

Indian Ocean Studies Series

Richard B. Allen, series editor

Richard B. Allen, *European Slave Trading in the Indian Ocean, 1500–1850*

Erin E. Stiles and Katrina Daly Thompson, eds., *Gendered Lives in the Western Indian Ocean: Islam, Marriage, and Sexuality on the Swahili Coast*

Jane Hooper, *Feeding Globalization: Madagascar and the Provisioning Trade, 1600–1800*

Krish Seetah, ed., *Connecting Continents: Archaeology and History in the Indian Ocean World*

Pedro Machado, Steve Mullins, and Joseph Christensen, *Pearls, People, and Power: Pearling and Indian Ocean Worlds*

ADVISORY BOARD

Edward A. Alpers
  University of California, Los Angeles, Emeritus

Clare Anderson
  University of Leicester

Sugata Bose
  Harvard University

Ulbe Bosma
  International Institute of Social History, Leiden

Janet Ewald
  Duke University

Devleena Ghosh
  University of Technology Sydney

Engseng Ho
  Duke University

Isabel Hofmeyr
  University of the Witwatersrand

Pier M. Larson
  Johns Hopkins University

Om Prakash
  University of Delhi (emeritus)

Himanshu Prabha Ray
  National Monuments Authority, India

Kerry Ward
  Rice University

Nigel Worden
  University of Cape Town

Markus Vink
  SUNY at Fredonia

Pearls, People, and Power

Pearling and Indian Ocean Worlds

EDITED BY

Pedro Machado,
Steve Mullins, and
Joseph Christensen

OHIO UNIVERSITY PRESS
ATHENS, OHIO

Ohio University Press, Athens, Ohio 45701
ohioswallow.com
© 2019 by Ohio University Press
All rights reserved

To obtain permission to quote, reprint, or otherwise reproduce or
distribute material from Ohio University Press publications,
please contact our rights and permissions department at
(740) 593-1154 or (740) 593-4536 (fax).

Cover image: The pearl fisheries, Tuticorin, southern India, c. 1680.
Source: Johan Nieuhof, *Zee en lant-reize door verscheide gewesten van
Oostindien* (Amsterdam: Van Meurs, 1682).

Printed in the United States of America
Ohio University Press books are printed on acid-free paper ∞ ™

29 28 27 26 25 24 23 22 21 20 19   5 4 3 2 1

Library of Congress Cataloging-in-Publication Data
Names: Machado, Pedro, 1970- editor. | Mullins, Steve, 1952- editor. |
Christensen, Joseph (Postdoctoral Fellow), editor.
Title: Pearls, people, and power : pearling and Indian Ocean worlds /
edited by Pedro Machado, Steve Mullins, and Joseph Christensen.
Description: Athens : Ohio University Press, 2019. | Series: Indian Ocean
studies series | Includes bibliographical references and index.
Identifiers: LCCN 2019040671 | ISBN 9780821424025 (hardcover) | ISBN
9780821446935 (pdf)
Subjects: LCSH: Pearl industry and trade--Indian Ocean Region--History.
Classification: LCC HD9678.P42 I536 2019 | DDC 338.3/724091824--dc23
LC record available at https://lccn.loc.gov/2019040671

Contents

Acknowledgments ix

Introduction Indian Ocean Pearling Worlds
PEDRO MACHADO 5

PART I: COMMODIFICATION

Chapter 1 The Pearl Commodity Chain, Early Nineteenth Century to the End of the Second World War
Trade, Processing, and Consumption
WILLIAM G. CLARENCE-SMITH 31

Chapter 2 Tea, Pearls, and Pearl Shell
Cross-Cultural Trade, Slave Raiding, and the Transformation of Material Worlds—The Sulu Zone, China, and the West, 1349–1898
JAMES FRANCIS WARREN 55

PART II: REGULATION, RESOURCE MANAGEMENT, AND SCIENCE

Chapter 3 An Uncertain Venture
Pearling Labor and Imperial Political Economy in South India and Sri Lanka, ca. 1790–1840
SAMUEL M. OSTROFF 85

Chapter 4   The Pearler's Problem
             *Management, Markets, and the Marine
             Environment in the Shark Bay Pearling
             Industry*
             JOSEPH CHRISTENSEN   118

Chapter 5   Early Pearling on the Indian Ocean's
             Southeast Fringe
             MICHAEL MCCARTHY   147

             PART III: REGIONALIZATION AND GLOBALIZATION

Chapter 6   Shell Routes
             Exploring Burma's Pearling Histories
             PEDRO MACHADO   183

Chapter 7   Pearl Fishing, Migration, and Globalization
             in the Persian Gulf, Eighteenth to Twentieth
             Centuries
             ROBERT CARTER   232

Chapter 8   Enslaved Africans and the Globalization
             of Arabian Gulf Pearling
             MATTHEW S. HOPPER   263

Chapter 9   Torres Strait in the Moluccas
             *The Transformation of Pearling in the
             Residency of Ambon, Netherlands Indies,
             1890s–1942*
             STEVE MULLINS   281

             PART IV: LIFE-STORIES, MEMORY, AND EXPERIENCES

Chapter 10   Pearling Fortunes
             *Recovering 'Alī al-Nahārī, a Legendary Red Sea
             Magnate in the Early Twentieth Century*
             JONATHAN MIRAN   313

Chapter 11 Pearling Women in North Australia
           Indigenous Workers and Wives
           JULIA T. MARTÍNEZ   344

Chapter 12 "Pearly Shells," a "Perfect Pearl," and a
            Guitar in a Pillowcase
            *Australian Pearling Industry Songs
            as Community and Personal Memories*
            KARL NEUENFELDT   364

            Selected Bibliography   401

            Contributors   413

            Index   419

Acknowledgments

A collective endeavor of multisited research and writing, this book has its seeds in an Australian Research Council grant that brought several specialists—established and emerging scholars—together to consider the place of pearling in the histories of the Indian Ocean. We would therefore like to acknowledge the Australian Research Council for the award of Discovery Project DP150103124, and acknowledge and thank the project's lead chief investigator, Professor James Francis Warren, for his oversight and leadership of this multifaceted international collaboration. Project members and collaborators also benefited from the support of the organizers of the Seventh International Congress of Maritime History held at Murdoch University, Perth, Western Australia, in mid-2016, where the papers upon which this volume is based were first presented. Questions from audience members at all of the pearling sessions helped sharpen analyses and were useful in thinking through the larger publication project. The detailed and generous critical engagement with the manuscript by Ohio University Press's anonymous readers contributed significantly to its quality as the project moved through the stages of becoming a book. The editors would also like to thank all of the organizations and individuals who contributed images and/or gave permission for the reproduction of copyrighted material, as well as Theresa Quill, Alexander Brown, and Julian Tyne for their invaluable help in producing the maps that will orientate the reader in locating the pearling sites discussed in the following pages.

For his steadfast belief in the project from its earliest inception and guidance in shepherding an ambitious proposal through various phases of the publication process, the editors and contributors collectively express their thanks to Richard Allen, editor of the Indian Ocean Studies Series at Ohio University Press and longtime friend. Richard has been a proponent of Indian Ocean scholarship for over two decades now and it is testament to his generosity of spirit and fierce intellectual inquiry that the press established a new series with him at the helm. Others at Ohio University Press, from its recently retired director, Gillian Berchowitz, who shared Richard's enthusiasm for the project, to Rick Huard and Sally Welch, are deserving of our sincerest thanks for bringing the project to fruition. Under their leadership, the series no doubt will continue to thrive as a home for Indian Ocean scholarship.

Map I.1. Pearling sites across the Indian Ocean discussed in the book. Map by Theresa Quill.

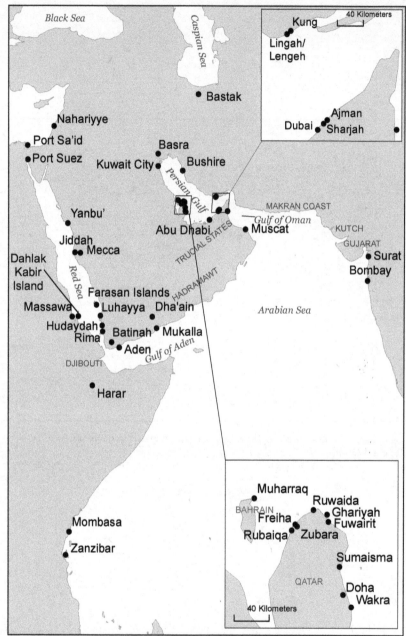

Map I.2. Arabian and Red Seas. Map by Theresa Quill.

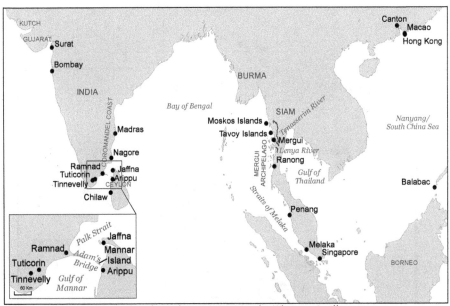

Map I.3. Bay of Bengal and Southeast Asia. Map by Theresa Quill.

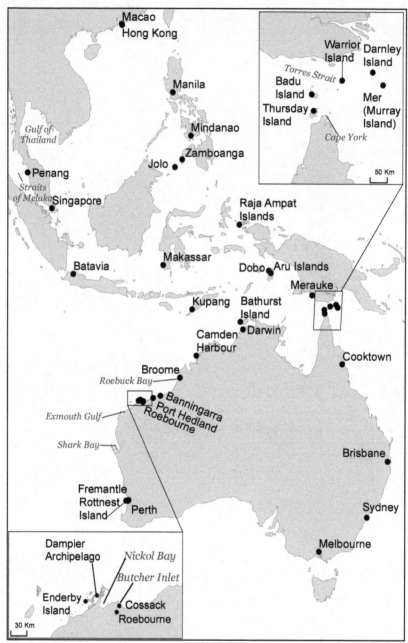

Map I.4. Insular Southeast Asia and Australia. Map by Theresa Quill.

INTRODUCTION

Indian Ocean Pearling Worlds

PEDRO MACHADO

PEARLS HAVE long held a fascination in the imaginations and lives of people across much of the world. Since their earliest uses, pearls—and pearl shell from the bivalve molluscs that produce them—both reflected and shaped sociocultural and adornment practices defining aesthetic contours of taste and bodily practice, and in so doing reinforced, challenged, or expanded the possibilities for self-fashioning for a range of people and groups. From spiritual appreciation and worship of pearls in the Americas, to Aboriginal collection of shell along Australia's vast northwest coast and Moken pearlers of the Mergui archipelago in the far south of coastal Burma, Mughal emperors of north India, Ming Chinese merchants, and American and European women and men on the streets of London, Paris, Amsterdam, New York, and Florence, pearls and mother-of-pearl (the commodity derived from pearl shell) have fulfilled desires and satisfied spiritual, bodily, and other needs.[1]

Pearls often served as repositories of value and were important in generating, mediating, and managing wealth not only for Asian and European royal households but equally for the merchants, traders, and jewelers who handled them as they were transacted along local and global circuits of commercial exchange in early global modernity and beyond.[2] Early modern European painting contains numerous examples of the depiction of pearls as symbols of material wealth, while engravings on shell became a popular form of expressive art in the seventeenth-century Netherlands, where artisans were also increasingly incorporating mother-of-pearl into objects such as fans from the growing shipments of shell that Verenigde Oostindische Compagnie (Dutch East India Company) ships were bringing to Amsterdam at this time.[3] Similarly, *riji*, or shell decorated with engraving, was also a feature among Aboriginal societies of the Kimberley region of Australia, but their importance lay in their ritual use in ceremonies and dances that were performed as part of the maintenance of complex social relationships.[4] Sartorial elegance was articulated and displayed in the Persian Safavid period (1502–1736), partly through turbans worn by rulers and noblemen that were laced with strings of pearls, and these were a fashionable item too in Mughal India from the sixteenth century, as they were throughout central Islamic lands. In the Sung (960–1279), Yuan (1280–1368), and Ming (1368–1644) eras, elaborately decorated headdresses festooned with pearls were worn by Chinese empresses in displays of courtly opulence and wealth. *Materia medica* from a range of periods attest, moreover, to the widespread medicinal usage of pearls—ingested in either powdered form or dissolved in liquid—to treat a variety of ailments such as eye afflictions and hemorrhages.[5]

Pearls have thus encompassed a wide variety of meanings and have been associated with a range of uses for numerous people throughout different parts of the world. Early accounts of pearl use both reflected these variations, and influenced perceptions and understandings about pearls. For Europeans, the lengthy discussions about the origins and genesis of pearls and their formation in Pliny the Elder's first-century *Natural History* (*Historia Naturalis*)—including an elaboration of the idea that pearls were formed by rain or dew—was important in helping shape how people came to think about and understand the jewel.[6] Chroniclers elsewhere wrote extensively about pearls. In the tenth century, the experienced Arab traveler al-Masᶜūdī of Baghdad also discussed the origins of pearls, noting the existence of two schools of thought on the matter—those who believed that pearls were produced by rain and those who did not. But al-Masᶜūdī, like his contemporary, al-Bīrūnī, in likening the pearl oyster and pearl to a mother and child, or alternatively to a mother and the fetus in her womb, also made explicit an ancient linkage with female sexuality and a certain idea of feminine virtue that would endure long after these accounts.[7] In Arabic and Persian poetry and literature, too, pearls assumed a symbolic importance that was matched by few other objects, epitomizing for instance all that was excellent and noble in word, thought, and deed. By contrast, Chinese mythology reflected the association of pearls with a variety of animals, and in Chinese-Buddhist legend the luminous and vitalizing pearl had an intimate association with the moon.[8]

In all of these cases, pearls and shell were key objects expressing particular social, cultural, religious, and moral values according to which societies and peoples organized their lives and made sense of the world in which they lived.

A major source of these pearls and shell were the waters of the Indian Ocean. Home to many of the great pearl fisheries and pearl-shell collecting zones of the world—several dating back at least to classical times—harvesting of these marine resources had taken place for centuries in the shallow subtropical and tropical seas of this vast ocean stretching from the Red Sea and Persian/Arabian Gulf to the Palk Strait and Gulf of Mannar located between India and Sri Lanka, the Andaman, Sulu, and Celebes Seas in insular Southeast Asia, and Australia's northern seaboard.[9] Pearl-bearing oysters were found in significant quantities across all of these regions in the warm waters that gave rise to the monsoon system which for centuries had been critical to social, religious, and commercial intercourse across the Indian Ocean. Communities in these regions relied on the harvesting of pearl oysters and the collection of other shell species for a variety of medicinal, subsistence, and other purposes, and ultimately were linked through medium- and long-distance trade, migration, kinship, and networks of political and economic power to centers of wealth and authority often far removed geographically from the pearling waters themselves. Pearls and pearl shell represent among the earliest objects exchanged across the ocean and formed an integral part of larger commercial worlds of goods from the fifteenth and sixteenth centuries, as their extraction and the local and interregional circuits along which they were traded became constitutive elements of a growing global economy.

Pearls, People, and Power examines the multifaceted and multinodal exchange, trade, distribution, and commodification of pearls and mother-of-pearl in the Indian Ocean over more than five centuries.[10] It seeks to highlight the importance of the dynamics of this particular marine-product extraction to both the broader historical rhythms of the ocean and to the creation of a maritime space defined as much by its circuits of human movement as by its distinctive ecologies. If, as recently argued, the Indian Ocean was a "peopled" space, it was also a space of marine environmental life and activity.[11]

Part of larger sea-product exchange structures and economies (involving, among others, tortoise shell, shark's fin, and trepang, or sea cucumber), pearl-oyster harvesting was critical in shaping the social, political, economic, labor, and environmental histories of the Indian Ocean in fundamentally important ways. The process of acquiring pearls and shell was embedded historically within complex circuits of social and financial arrangements that involved South Asian, Arab, European, American, Chinese, and other mercantile interests that in turn were connected to far-flung markets, a variety of distribution channels, and manufacturing and consumer nodes located often many thousands of miles from the waters where these marine products had first been taken from the ocean.

This work of harvesting pearl shell was often done by slave and unfree labor drawn from a range of local communities whose ties to the ocean may or may not have been of longstanding duration. African slaves brought from the East African interior many miles from the coast, for instance, made up a significant proportion of the diving labor used during the expansion of pearling in the Gulf in the nineteenth century, while in the pearling waters of the Sulu Zone, located between the southern and western boundaries of the Philippines and the northeast coast of Borneo, slave raiding by the Iranun and Balangingi along these coasts and in the Celebes and Malay Peninsula resulted in the capture of local sea peoples with deep histories tied to the ocean.[12] In all of these cases, the labor and productive aspects of pearl and shell extraction were critically implicated in the broader movement of these products around the shores of the Indian Ocean and to global markets, fostering commercial connections and structuring the complex linkages across maritime spaces that the exchange of pearls and shell enabled.

As several chapters in the volume demonstrate, pearling connected the "small," seemingly inconsequential histories of localized shell collecting—too often occluded or marginalized by scholars and therefore left in the shadows—with the broader currents of regional and global exchange with which they were inextricably linked and whose structures they helped mold. The long histories of shell extraction in the ocean and the myriad uses to which pearls and pearl shell were put by a diversity of groups, from royal households in northern India and Muslim sultanates in Southeast Asia to Aboriginal groups in Australia and Arab merchants, reflect the richness of experience with this marine product and offer a compelling window into how the lives of individuals involved in the extractive process were intimately tied to the purchasers, financiers, and consumers of pearls and shell.

While the importance of pearling to the social, cultural, and economic practices of coastal and other areas of the ocean—and their communities—has been noted by scholars, the overwhelming majority of these works have confined themselves to highly localized or at best regional studies of pearling.[13] This has resulted in a segmented and therefore incomplete view of the ocean's pearl fisheries. *Pearls, People, and Power* recognizes that the dynamics of the surrounding maritime zones of these fisheries were indeed important in shaping how communities and groups approached their extraction and "managed" this resource, but stresses the imperative of moving beyond their treatment as discrete entities; rather, the volume stresses how the extraction, collection, and exchange of pearls and shell were interrelated processes binding the ports, islands, and coasts of the ocean to one another, and to more distant markets. An integral part of the increasingly global transactional worlds of goods that flowed across the Indian Ocean with greater intensity from the sixteenth century and shaped its variegated economic, social, political, and urban landscapes in the periods covered by this book, pearls and shell left deeply complex imprints on the histories of the ocean. This volume seeks to identify and examine the precise nature of their contours and to locate the ocean's fisheries in relation to broader histories of empire, labor, marine extraction, maritime ecology, and global exchange.

Possessing particular qualities as objects and things onto which different meanings could be inscribed, pearls and mother-of-pearl were in persistent demand and established widely dispersed markets as commodities and cargoes of note that were shipped over short, medium, and long distances throughout the many waterways of the Indian Ocean and beyond as they were transported to markets in such places as China,

Europe, and America.[14] The movement of pearls and shell remind us therefore that the ocean was not a bounded geographical entity but part of trajectories animating global commerce. Consumers used these marine products in highly original ways as markers of identity and prestige, for medicinal remedies, in elements of ritualized cultural and bodily practice, and for the adornment of elite and domestic spaces. Manufacturing processes associated with growing industrialization in the nineteenth century increased European demand for the high-quality pearl shell *Pinctada maxima*, which became a mainstay, especially of the Australian pearling industry, for the manufacture of everyday objects such as buttons, cutlery, personal grooming items, and musical instruments, reflecting increasingly changing notions of taste among burgeoning urban middle classes who were establishing identities as purveyors of "modern" sensibilities and aesthetics.

In being attentive to the materiality of pearls and shell—and to their diverse biographies across the Indian Ocean and more broadly—*Pearls, People, and Power* draws insights from the work of Arjun Appadurai, who showed how the life cycles of objects are revealed in the transitions between their social forms, including the commodity, ritual object, gift, and so forth.[15] Several of the essays in the present volume focus on one social form, the commodity, with pearls and mother-of-pearl regarded as "objects of economic value," where value is determined by a "judgement made about them by subjects."[16] Pearls, especially, were perceived to have special qualities and thus were associated with distinctive characteristics that were implicated in their transformation from things into commodities. In the nineteenth century, for instance, the sheen and light associated with pearls—what Natasha Eaton terms "pearlesence"—became important to modes of representing and understanding the British colonial economy in South Asia. Pearls thus offered the possibility of "transforming the magic of their thingness into a commodity."[17]

But, just as importantly, like all things and objects, pearls and shell also accumulated layers of meaning as they moved through various stages of extraction, exchange, ownership, and transformation.[18] Pearls and shell did not have fixed or stable meanings or value but assumed meanings and could fluctuate in value in relation to particular commercial, cultural, and social contexts. They thus offer a compelling material window into the historical trajectories of things and objects and their enduring influences on the contours of the commodification of the ocean's natural resources.[19]

Equally, though, because they were mobilized increasingly through imperial networks and structures in the nineteenth century, pearls and shell can be identified as circulating within "empires" of goods. This idea, elaborated recently by Kate Smith, draws on insights from political economy that stress the power and violence inherent in the governance, processing, trade, and consumption that produces goods.[20] Pearl harvesting became a focus of imperial investment and control as officials sought to rationalize various aspects of the extractive process or redirect the distribution of pearls and shell away from vernacular networks and into the hands of colonial shippers and merchants.

However, as local merchants and rulers sought to supply ever-expanding imperial and metropolitan markets, in addition to robust Asian markets in India, China, and elsewhere, they were themselves implicated often in violent and exploitative practices that were focused on control over labor. As several of the book's essays demonstrate, the work of locating pearl beds and extracting their bounty in the Indian Ocean was in many cases the work of unfree and slave divers whose recruitment involved a range of labor arrangements of varying complexity and substance. Because pearling was marked by rapid labor turnover, the result mostly of high rates of morbidity and mortality among pearl divers drawn from the ocean's local and translocal maritime labor, expanding marine extraction and production caused the heightened and often violent coerced movement of people to and across pearling zones. These included slaves and indentured laborers who formed an integral feature of the ocean's deeper histories of migration and contributed significantly to the multilingual and multiethnic communities traversing its waters and populating its coastal and littoral zones.[21] Yet, while this process created as a consequence more ethnically complex communities whose movements were part of the ocean's crisscrossing migratory flows of free and unfree peoples, it also subjected many to increased levels of violence and displacement from kidnapping, raiding, and the drudgery of dismal labor conditions.

For those communities in the Indian Ocean involved in pearl harvesting that were not subjected to the violence and privation of aggressive labor recruitment, they competed with local rulers and imperial powers over rights to trade in pearls and shell as they shaped debates regarding jurisdiction over marine resources. With growing European and especially British territorial conquest in the Indian Ocean by the late nineteenth century, and related sovereign claims over territorially defined colonial space, pearling beds became subject to similar pressures as their potential as a source of imperial revenue heightened their importance and stimulated further contestations over who could manage the ocean's marine-product extraction and in which particular ways. Their location along or near (mainland and island) coasts—they were the "narrow bands, or corridors" where empires attempted to establish sovereignty and exercise control that Lauren Benton has described in her work—challenged notions of space that had been primarily territorially defined and raised questions about how to conceptualize and delimit boundaries that were fluid, and how to understand "terraqueous" histories involving the frequent movement of people, boats, and pearl shell across the waters of the Indian Ocean.[22]

Pearl-oyster beds thus constituted coastal frontiers that, in inviting questions about maritime jurisdiction, exposed the anxieties of European colonial states struggling to solidify porous maritime boundaries as they sought the formalization of the reach of imperial rule over ocean and sea spaces that were in many ways, however, defined by their permeability.[23] These fluid frontiers came to encompass both a lateral and vertical dimension, as the colonization of oyster beds reached greater depths and new ecological strata with the development of new technologies in the eighteenth and especially nineteenth centuries. Pearl harvesting required not only colonization and the establishment of sovereignty across space but also reached downwards, beneath the waves, to reef floors and pearl beds, requiring changing conceptualizations of territory. It was precisely at these coastal margins, constituted by a "fluid ontology," that "forms of law [and] government . . . [were] crystallized."[24] The search for pearls and shell—and the contestations over how, where, and by whom they could be extracted from ocean beds—highlights vital questions about the spatial dimensions of empire, labor mobility, resource use, and their entangled political, cultural, and social histories. Even with the application of technologies to diving in the nineteenth century that pushed the bathymetric frontier of pearling into deeper coastal waters (most visibly in the form of the so-called diving dress), new challenges emerged over control of the industry and the establishment of territorial waters whose scale reached unprecedented depths.

While the pearling waters of the Indian Ocean were sites of competing jurisdictions and sovereignties, they were also sites of an extraordinary assault on their marine ecosystems during the period covered in this book. The relentless harvesting of pearls and shell that the aforementioned forms of industrialized extraction represented by the end of the nineteenth century highlight the importance of incorporating environmental and ecological histories into studies of the ocean. Despite the growth of scholarship that a renewed interest in the Indian Ocean has generated in the past decade, there has been a dearth of work addressing the marine environmental aspects of the ocean itself.[25] The coastal and island ecosystems from which pearl oysters were extracted formed part of the larger ecological seascape of the ocean, where the interplay between marine and maritime actors shaped lives above and below the waterline. Pearling waters, the present volume emphasizes, were critical sites to capture the dynamics of these processes, and their study contributes to efforts—as articulated by Jeffrey Bolster—to bring the ocean into studies of oceanic history, and thereby grant it recognition not only as a blank space across which goods, people, and ships moved but as a living organism.[26] A focus on pearls and shell, moreover, expands the burgeoning field of marine environmental history from its established and still dominant focus on whaling and capture fisheries.[27]

In focusing on pearls and shell in the Indian Ocean, the essays in *Pearls, People, and Power* do not necessarily treat the ocean as a coherent whole or as an "integrated" singular world, but rather recognize its plural worlds with their own dynamics and particularities, including microclimatic and environmental conditions.[28] Thus, the pearling waters of the Persian Gulf, South India and Sri Lanka, the Red Sea, the Bay of Bengal, and the northern Australian and insular Southeast Asian coasts were shaped by local factors and historical currents that were the product of the interplay between specific actors, contexts, and conditions. Yet, this disaggregation of the ocean into its constituent parts—what Sujit Sivasundaram has recently termed "revisionist pluralism"—should not result in the reinforcement of an idea of regional or national compartmentalization that obscures patterns of interaction or processes of connection across the Indian Ocean.[29] Instead, while being attentive to the distinctiveness of each of the regions discussed in the book, the contributors endorse an approach—as previously mentioned—that teases out the spatial and historiographical linkages across the ocean as they seek to establish the ways in which peoples, regions, and areas were brought into relation with one another along the many seascapes of pearl and shell harvesting throughout the Indian Ocean.

Moreover, while several of the contributors to the volume discuss consumption of pearls and mother-of-pearl, they do so in ways that do not privilege the changing habits of Europe or the United States, significant as these were as markets, especially in the nineteenth and twentieth centuries. This remains the case in the literature on pearls, where the focus is on the use, display, and sartorial incorporation of pearls into new styles and fashions in Euro-American contexts. The essays in this book challenge this narrative and consider new geographies and markets that remained robust and in certain instances grew for the marine products of the Indian Ocean.

ORGANIZATION OF THE VOLUME

Pearls, People, and Power brings together leading scholars and younger researchers to offer the first dedicated and multidisciplinary study of pearling across the entire Indian Ocean. For such a vast and multidimensional topic, approaching it from the vantage point of different disciplinary practices is imperative to enhancing and deepening our understanding of its complexities. The volume thus echoes recent calls to cultivate approaches for the study of the Indian Ocean that draw on a range of disciplines and foster collaborative research between scholars.[30] Such joint endeavors are increasingly necessary if we are to enrich our studies of the past with the multiplicity of perspectives that it warrants.

The chapters collected here range widely in spatial and temporal scales, providing detailed studies of the circulation of people and ideas and of the complex processes through which pearls and shell became commodities of value across the ocean and beyond. Historical research on the Indian Ocean has moved increasingly toward "connective comparison," and this book draws on extensive work by an international group of scholars in an effort to encompass the geographical, cultural, and thematic diversity of Indian Ocean pearling.[31] The authors make significant contributions to our understanding of the impact of European imperialism and industrialization on regional and local communities, and illustrate the permeability of political boundaries and the fluid nature of sociocultural maritime borderlands. They show, also, how local actors frequently asserted themselves in controlling the trajectories of pearl-shell exchange in ocean spaces never entirely dominated by imperial capital and authority. Further, by locating pearl harvesting within a wider historiographical framework, the volume aims to contribute to understandings of the interdependent links between global and local histories, furthering our appreciation of the many strands that brought seemingly disparate worlds of the Indian Ocean into dialogue with one another, and in turn with the global arenas with which they were inextricably enmeshed.

The volume is organized around five themes that reflect the contributors' interests but are also thematic foci that have increasingly attracted the attention of scholars of the ocean: state regulation and resource management; technology; extraction and consumption; globalization; memory and experiences. Within these broad categories, the authors discuss fine-grained questions related to labor and slavery, migration, gender, European and Asian financial investment in pearling, cultural and musical expression, taste as an aesthetic expression, marine environments, and indigenous forms of diving practice. Together and in their scope, the chapters thus capture a range of experiences and histories that defined pearling in the Indian Ocean as a transregional and global endeavor.

A central logic of the extractive processes involved in the harvesting of pearl oysters was consumer use and demand for its marine products. The first part of the volume, "Commodification," opens with a wide-ranging essay by William G. Clarence-Smith, who examines the global history of modern pearling from a commodity-chain perspective, focusing his analysis on the final links in the chain. There has been much research on local production, he maintains, but less on commerce, transport, processing, and consumption, processes that are critical for a fuller understanding of the pearling cycle. Looking closely at these, Clarence-Smith suggests that two significantly different commodity chains evolved over the nineteenth and first half of the twentieth centuries. Diasporas, or "communities of reputation," were supremely important in marketing pearls, but were strikingly less prominent for mother-of-pearl. Steamers transformed the economics of mother-of-pearl, but not of pearls. Factory workers increasingly processed mother-of-pearl, especially into buttons, whereas artisans continued to prepare pearls for the market. Finally, highlighting often poorly understood and therefore overlooked markets, Clarence-Smith makes a compelling case that while European and American consumers did more to stimulate the mother-of-pearl sector, it was in South and East Asia that demand for pearls continued to be fundamental to global trade. In short, pearls seem to have remained a largely ancien régime commodity, contrasting with the modernity of mother-of-pearl.

The processes of commodification are developed further by James Francis Warren, but in specific contexts in insular Southeast Asia. Explicitly utilizing a commodity-history approach, the chapter investigates global trade, a system of bondage and dependency, and patterns of consumption and desire at a specific moment in regional time—a span of 130 years—and a specific place: the Sulu Zone. Warren links the worlds of the latter to China and the West, and raises questions regarding the nature of the transitions and transformations of the Sulu Zone as a particular Indian Ocean micro-zone and its emerging "global character" as it became more firmly embedded within the global economy. Locating pearling and the exchange of shell within particular social, economic, and political structures, the chapter maps out the connections of various peoples in relation to the production, circulation, and consumption of other commodities within the confines of the Sulu Zone and beyond. Underscoring the need to consider the interconnections of pearls and pearl shell, on the one hand, and tea, ceramics, textiles, opium, and firearms on the other, Warren makes the critically vital intervention that their interrelation both illustrates and signifies how the structure and function of money, markets, and cross-cultural trade, and a repertoire of practices in contemporary life, were shaped by the material turn and its negotiation during a period of significant European imperial encroachments and growing colonial control in Southeast Asia.

In the second part of the book, "Regulation, Resource Management and Science," authors address a host of distinct but interlinked themes that were crucial to pearl and shell harvesting: labor, technologies of extraction, and resource management. Focusing on the production side of the Indian Ocean pearl trade, Samuel M. Ostroff examines the elaborate security apparatuses that were designed to discipline labor and curb theft at the pearl fishery of the Gulf of Mannar between southeastern India and northwestern Sri Lanka in the late eighteenth and early nineteenth centuries. In 1796, the English East India Company secured managerial rights over the human and natural resources of the pearl fishery through its annexation of Dutch Ceylon, a territory that included settlements on mainland India, and in 1802 the island became a formal colony of the British state. Thus, as Ostroff shows, Ceylon—with one of the world's most abundant sources of natural pearls—became located along a geographical and political borderland, managed by the Company on the India side of the Gulf and the Crown on the Ceylon side. During this period of regime change, the governments of Madras and Ceylon increasingly turned their attention to attenuating the financial, physical, and environmental hazards of the pearling industry through intensively regulative and monopolistic practices. A particular focus, Ostroff argues, was on divers and other laboring groups, which armed vessels at sea and police forces on shore, together with native mercantile elites, subjected to extraordinary levels of oversight during pearling operations, as boats fished beyond demarcated boundaries, divers palmed pearls, and washers skimmed product. We are reminded that the physical qualities of pearls—small, valuable, and fathoms underwater—heightened anxieties about theft, but Ostroff is able to demonstrate that measures to control labor and prevent theft mapped onto wider concerns about the circulation of bodies, contraband, and disease through seasonal marketplaces such as the pearl fishery. The Company and Crown governments brought an assemblage of political and economic ideas to bear on the management and governance of people and oysters that sought not only to increase productivity but also fundamentally reshape the social, economic, and political foundations of the industry. However, as Ostroff underscores, attempts by British officials to disembed the pearling industry from local networks and institutions were fraught with contradictions and seldom delivered on the promise of radical change.

Questions regarding the control over and management of pearl fisheries in the Indian Ocean were a frequent concern for imperial authorities imbued with notions of depletion and sustainability of a natural resource. While the topic of sustainability is taken up elsewhere in the volume, Joseph Christensen examines it most fully in his chapter on the "pearler's problem" in the Shark Bay pearling industry, a small but historically important center for the production of pearls and mother-of-pearl on the Western Australian coastline between the 1860s and 1930s. Although separate from the larger pearling grounds of the northwest Australian coast, Shark Bay shared similarities with other pearl and mother-of-pearl fisheries, including those in the waters separating India and Sri Lanka, in terms of the nature of its marine environment, and, crucially, the management regime adopted by Western Australia's colonial government during the latter decades of the nineteenth century, which was based on principles developed in waters under the control of British authorities elsewhere in this period. Against this backdrop, Christensen draws on biology, economics, and history to explore the pearler's problem as a variant of the familiar concepts of the fisherman's problem and the tragedy of the commons, referring to the perennial challenges of maintaining viable annual harvests within a context of rigid social and political goals underpinning resource management strategies, fluctuating global markets for pearls and mother-of-pearl, and the changing and unpredictable dynamics of the marine environment. Offering a textured discussion and analysis, Christensen bases the chapter around a dispute over resource management arrangements at Shark Bay between English marine biologist (and one of the English-speaking world's foremost experts on pearl fisheries in the late nineteenth century) William Saville-Kent and the Austrian pearling master Ludwig Stross, a pearler with practical experience in several Indian Ocean pearling grounds. Remarkably, in the early twentieth century, both men moved into manufacturing pursuits—Stross in the international plastics industry and Saville-Kent in the artificial culture of pearls—that helped undermine the industry in Shark Bay that they had done much to develop.

The final essay of the second part of the book explores shifts in collecting shell that profoundly transformed the industry in Australia's northwest coast. Michael McCarthy shows how Aboriginal clans in the area had gathered pearl shell for food, ornamentation, ritual, and trade for millennia, and that, before British colonization, "dry shelling," walking in shallows to collect pearl shell at low tide, had been sufficient to create patterns of distribution that extended as far as central Australia. When in the late 1860s colonists grasped the commercial potential of the northwest pearl-shell beds, according to McCarthy, Aboriginal men and women were recruited to wade and then "skin dive" (diving without the use of any kind of breathing apparatus) for pearl shell that was aimed at the international market. Thus, over a short period of time, northwest coast Aborigines became renowned for their underwater prowess and the ability to see shell on the bottom without visual aids. But the industry became marked by physical coercion and the extreme exploitation of labor, resulting in pearlers seeking to supplement their workforce in the mid-1870s by recruiting indentured "Malays" from the nearby islands of Indonesia, a pattern that would recur in other parts of Australia's pearling waters. Together, Aboriginal and "Malay" skin divers proved an effective workforce, and, consequently, as McCarthy argues, industrial "hard hat" diving and its attendant technology was not introduced to the northwest until the mid-1880s, more than a decade later than it was in Torres Strait (located at the far northeastern point of Australia), where Australian pearling had a prominent presence. Examining especially detailed records that documented the progression from dry shelling to skin diving, the chapter uses this valuable material to provide insights into the development of the early phases of pearl fisheries elsewhere in the Indian Ocean, most of which had reached the free-diving stage of pearling well before being described by outside observers.

Indian Ocean pearling was defined by its transregional and global linkages, topics that are the focus of the third part of the book, "Regionalization and Globalization." The movement of pearls and shell across waters and coasts that today are seen to fall into one or another "Area" challenges us to rethink the geographies of Area Studies. Pedro Machado opens this section of the book by examining the Mergui archipelago off the southern Burmese coast and the shell collecting areas to its north as located geographically within an interstitial space that in traditional Area Studies frameworks would place Burma in Southeast Asia. Yet, the archipelago's pearling histories saw it maintain connections with India, Sri Lanka, Penang, and other parts of what became the Straits Settlements, and with China and eventually Australia in the nineteenth century.[32] Mergui pearling, Machado notes, thus reflected the broader circuits in which it was embedded as a node in wider marine-products trade. The chapter discusses early pearling practices and ways of collecting shell by local divers, and stresses the participation early on in its development of Chinese merchants with interests in such commercial pursuits as the esculent bird's-nest trade. While Mergui pearling has been associated often with the late nineteenth-century expansion of Australian colonial interest in the shell that was available among its hundreds of islands—resulting in the development of management strategies and attempts at boundary-making that shared similarities with other pearling zones that had come under British suzerainty—Machado makes the important point that this interest was ephemeral and reflective of a singular moment in the archipelago's history. Rather, it was the sustained involvement of Chinese, Indian, and other local merchants that, together with local markets, animated pearling in Mergui over the long decades of its existence. Some of these, notably Ebrahim Ahmed, became prominent pearlers and utilized their position to diversify their commercial undertakings into areas such as mining.

The following two essays in this section of the book focus on the Persian Gulf, where for centuries pearls and shell had been extracted for local, regional, and global markets. Recognizing the deep histories of pearling in the Indian Ocean that his own work has helped uncover, Robert Carter uses the archaeological record to understand the Gulf's pearling pasts. Long before the coming of oil, the urban and political configuration of the Persian Gulf coalesced around its pearl-fishing settlements, many of which survive as the capitals of the Gulf states that exist today. The foundation and existence of these towns depended heavily, and in many cases exclusively, on the region's highly productive pearl fishery. Although the history of pearling in the Gulf is of immense antiquity, going back to the sixth millennium BCE, it was not until the eighteenth and nineteenth centuries CE that the fishery began to exert a strongly formative role. As Carter makes clear, local and regional political conditions intersected with increasing integration into the world's markets and globally increasing pearl prices to trigger an unprecedented boom in migration and economic specialization in pearl fishing. Families arrived from inland Arabia, Oman, Persia, Iraq, and India to supplement the existing coastal populations, a process that increased dramatically in the last decades of the nineteenth century and first decades of the twentieth, as the effects of globalization accelerated. Most of these people constitute the bulk of the national population of today's emirates on the Arabian shore. The process is clearly revealed in the region's archaeological record, in terms of changing settlement patterns, the expansion of the towns through time, and the excavated material culture, for example in the excavated sequence in Doha. The latter, the chapter shows, displayed sharp increases in the quantity and proportion of global commodities, chiefly ceramic trade wares and glass, coinciding precisely with documented increases in pearling revenues. Thus, demographics, settlement distribution, economic behavior, and consumption patterns became increasingly stimulated by and dependent on the global economy.

That this phenomenon is part of global patterns is demonstrated by contemporary trends toward specialization and intensification of production in other regions of the world, for instance in the pearling industry of Australia. Where economic and demographic data is available, distant regions dependent on the production of completely different products also show similar and simultaneous transformations under the impact of processes of globalizing exchange patterns. Importantly, the pearling boom in the Gulf demonstrates the local effects of global integration, a theme also taken up Matthew Hopper but steered in new directions. Like Carter, he underlines the massive expansion in the late nineteenth century of the Arabian Gulf's leading industry, pearling. Although pearls from the region had circulated regionally to markets in India and the Middle East for centuries, in the late nineteenth century a global pearl craze ignited a surge in pearl production that transformed the Gulf economy. As demand for pearls in Europe and North America soared, the value of pearl exports, especially from Bahrain—the Gulf's primary export center—increased more than eightfold in the twenty years between 1885 and 1905, and then nearly doubled again in the following ten years. Crucial to this expansion, an element that is discussed throughout this volume, was labor. Many of the divers who made this transformation in production possible, however, were enslaved Africans or free Africans of slave descent. Africans accounted for between a quarter and half of the annual diving crews, and the pearl boom accompanied a growth in the African diaspora in the Gulf. By the close of the nineteenth century, slave ships from East Africa carried an overwhelming majority of young males, many ultimately destined for Gulf pearl banks. In a period of attempts by Great Britain to control the Gulf littoral, officials and officers struggled to reconcile abolitionism with the region's dependence on slave labor for a commodity with high consumer demand in London and elsewhere. Yet, as suddenly as the Gulf pearl boom emerged, it collapsed when confronted with Japanese cultured pearls and the Great Depression in the 1930s. Consequently, as Hopper demonstrates, many of the enslaved divers who had been instrumental in the Gulf's pearl boom between the 1880s and 1920s were then cast out to fend for themselves, the casualties of global forces that they had helped shape but that were beyond their control.

The regionalization of pearling as an aspect of a global economy of extraction of marine products brought many parts of Australia's northern coasts into close relation with nearby Indonesian islands. After the commencement of industrial pearling in northern Australia in the 1870s, a pearling zone developed that encompassed the islands of the Indonesian archipelago, with some of these becoming significant sources of labor for the Australian industry. The connections between these two areas were not only defined by labor exchanges, however, for as Steve Mullins shows in the final essay of the third part of the book, some of the traditional pearling regions adopted the technologies and techniques of Australian-style pearling. This transformation commenced and was most pronounced in the Aru Islands, in the Residency of Ambon, one of the ancient pearling grounds of the Indian Ocean world. It was facilitated by a new mode of production initiated by pearlers in the mid-1880s in Torres Strait: the floating-station system, in which a schooner of about one hundred tons served as tender to a fleet of pearling luggers, a uniquely Australian type of vessel from which full-dress helmet divers worked in deep water. Floating stations ranged widely and could remain at sea for months at a time, and in the early 1890s they began to encroach on the Aru Islands. Mullins's chapter traces the influence of Australian-style industrial pearling in the Residency of Ambon through to 1942, when the Pacific War brought it to an end, exploring how it affected the administration of the industry, assessing its impact on indigenous pearling, reflecting on its internal power relations, and examining how it responded to the perennial challenges of resource depletion and a radically fluctuating market. Moreover, it also identifies regional commonalities and contrasts that bring these issues into sharper focus in Torres Strait, the Kimberley Coast of Western Australia, and other pearling regions of the Indian Ocean.

The fourth and final part of the book sheds light on the often-neglected lives of the many individuals who were involved in the harvesting, processing, and exchange of pearls and shell. While we may know a fair amount about some of the European and American merchants and investors involved in the trade from the Persian Gulf, India, and Southeast Asia in the eighteenth and nineteenth centuries, we know very little about the local men and women who traded in pearls or worked in harvesting shell. Adopting an approach that marries biography with commodity histories, Jonathan Miran reconstructs multiple dimensions of the life and business activities of the most prominent Red Sea pearl merchant of the early twentieth century, Sayyid ʿAlī ʿAbd al-Raḥmān al-Nahārī (1851–1931). The grandson of a Yemeni who moved from Hudaydah to Massawa, ʿAlī al-Nahārī came to dominate the pearling industry in the Dahlak archipelago off the Eritrean coasts during the heyday of the global pearling boom in both the Red Sea and Persian Gulf. In the process—and like some of his counterparts in the Arabian Gulf—ʿAlī interacted directly with some of the most prominent global pearl dealers in Paris who sourced pearls from the Red Sea to satisfy French fashion demands, such as Léonard Rosenthal and Jacques Bienenfeld, and in 1907 and 1924 traveled to France to sell pearls and invest his profits in real estate holdings. He also, it appears highly likely, maintained relationships with merchants in Bombay, to which Red Sea and Gulf pearls and shell were also shipped. With so few biographical accounts of Arab mercantile involvement available to us, the reconstruction of ʿAlī al-Nahārī's story—made possible through the creative use of a set of disparate sources that include Islamic court records, Italian colonial materials and official publications, entries in the published diary of the governor of Eritrea (Ferdinando Martini), oral data, family papers, and diary entries—is particularly valuable. It demonstrates in compelling detail that the efflorescence in pearling experienced by the Persian Gulf in the late nineteenth and early twentieth centuries was not an isolated moment in the region nor defined by the logics of British, American, French, or other European capital. Additionally, Miran addresses a further dimension of this story, one that traces the intersection of commodity histories, changing consumption habits in Europe, and cultural production in France in the 1930s. This is done through a discussion of a classic in the genre of French travel and adventure literature, *Les secrets de la mer Rouge*, written by the eccentric adventurer and prolific author, Henry de Monfreid, and published in France in 1931. As discussed by Miran, one of the main protagonists in this fictionalized version of Monfreid's experiences in the Red Sea as a one-time smuggler, pearler, and gunrunner, "Said Ali," is based on ʿAlī al-Nahārī, whom Monfreid had met briefly in late January 1914 in the Dahlak archipelago, underscoring how ʿAlī al-Nahārī's life offers a compelling picture for exploring new spaces between microhistory, transregional Indian Ocean history, and global history.

Among studies of pearling, women as a social category and gender as an analytical framework are seldom examined to understand the complexities of social relations in the industry. Julia Martínez seeks to remedy this by focusing on northern Australia and examining how, during the 1860s, when the frontier pearl-shell industry was in its infancy, Aboriginal women were the first choice for European pearling masters seeking labor. Their employment was controversial, and accusations of slavery led to the Western Australian government banning women's employment in 1871. Instead, as has been well established, pearling masters came to rely on male indentured labor from Japan, the Philippines, and the Malay archipelago. Martínez shows that very few women came from Asia, apart from several hundred Japanese *karayuki-san*, whose immigration into the sex industry was tolerated but not sanctioned. The pearling ports of north Australia were male-dominated, and Aboriginal women remained closely associated with pearl-shell workers, both as sexual and working partners. For immigrant pearling workers, all temporary formal and informal relationships with local women were subject to government censure; their "mixed relations," as Regina Ganter has termed them, being imagined as a threat to White Australia.[33] Despite generalized discourses of moral and racial panic, we know very little about the actual lives of women who were connected to the pearl-shell industry, nor is it clear how many male workers had wives at home. Martínez thus makes a singular contribution to these questions by casting light on the lives of pearl-shell women, considering their roles as workers, as sexual partners, and as wives.

Although also often overlooked, pearling and its social experiences produced rich cultural traditions that were expressed in music and song. Pearl divers' songs (*fjeri*) in the Gulf, for instance, were performed as a form of entertainment beyond the domain of work and expressed emotions attached to departure, sorrow, and divine love.[34] Karl Neuenfeldt, an ethnomusicologist and performer, builds on this work to explore the music and pearling songs of communities of Torres Strait. For generations, from the mid-nineteenth century until approximately the 1970s, the multicultural communities of this area were heavily involved in the pearling industry, and while it declined from the 1930s with the advent of Japanese cultured pearls and the widespread use of plastics, memories of the pearling era remain alive and are captured in unique songs and dance forms. Neuenfeldt analyses some of these and the community memories that inform them as instructive examples of how music can embed social history within a popular art form that continues to be practiced and performed today. Although almost all the pearling boats are gone, and many of the men who worked on them have died, the songs commemorate what was an economic, social, and cultural mainstay of the region for decades. To provide audio and visual evidence of the key role of music in helping recall and preserve community memories of the pearling era, the chapter explores examples of professional recordings done in collaboration with Torres Strait Islander communities and artists who enjoy significant popularity in the area.

NOTES

1. The classic work by George Frederick Kunz and Charles Hugh Stevenson, published over a century ago, captured some of this history: *The Book of the Pearl: The History, Art, Science, and Industry of the Queen of Gems* (New York: Century, 1908). See also Nicholas J. Saunders, "Biographies of Brilliance: Pearls, Transformations of Matter and Being, c. AD 1492," *World Archaeology* 31, no. 2 (October 1999): 243–57.

2. Nuno Senos, "The Empire in the Duke's Palace: Global Material Culture in Sixteenth-Century Portugal," in *The Global Lives of Things: The Material Culture of Connections in the Early Modern World*, ed. Anne Gerritsen and Giorgio Riello (New York: Routledge, 2016), 128–44, discusses the extraordinarily large sixteenth-century Portuguese inventory of the fifth Duke of Bragança—one of the largest of this period in Europe—whose most valuable item, exceeding all others by a large degree, was a pearl necklace highly prized as a royal possession. See also Molly A. Warsh, *American Baroque: Pearls and the Nature of Empire, 1492–1700* (Chapel Hill: University of North Carolina Press, 2018).

3. W. H. van Seters, "Oud-Nederlandse parelmoerkunst: Het werk van leden der familie Belquin, parelmoergraveurs en schilders in de 17de eeuw," *Nederlands Kunsthistorisch Jaarboek* 9 (1958):185–237; Daniëlle Kisluk-Grosheide, "Dirck van Rijswijck (1596–1679), a Master of Mother-of-Pearl," *Oud Holland* 111, no. 2 (1997): 77–94.

4. Kim Akerman and John E. Stanton, *Riji and Jakuli: Kimberley Pearl Shell in Aboriginal Australia* (Darwin: Northern Territory Museum of Arts and Sciences, 1994).

5. This is based on R. A. Donkin, *Beyond Price: Pearls and Pearl-Fishing: Origins to the Age of Discoveries* (Philadelphia: American Philosophical Society, 1998), which discusses the uses of pearls in great detail across a range of periods.

6. As discussed by Pliny in *Historia Naturalis*, cited in Donkin, *Beyond Price*, 3–4.

7. Donkin, *Beyond Price*, 5. Elisabeth Strack discusses the actual process of pearl formation in *Pearls* (Stuttgart: Rühle-Diebener-Verlag, 2006).

Pearls would continue to have gendered associations of female virtue and vice into later centuries, as noted recently by Warsh, *American Baroque*.

8. Donkin, *Beyond Price*, 12.

9. The terms "Persian Gulf" and "Arabian Gulf" are used interchangeably by authors throughout the book. Mexican and Caribbean pearl fisheries also enjoyed a global importance, especially in the sixteenth and seventeenth centuries, for which see Warsh, *American Baroque*.

10. "Mother-of-pearl" is defined in the volume as the commodity derived from pearl shell.

11. Kerry Ward, *Networks of Empire: Forced Migration in the Dutch East India Company* (New York: Cambridge University Press, 2009), 31–32.

12. For the African diaspora in Arabia, see Matthew S. Hopper, *Slaves of One Master: Globalization and Slavery in Arabia in the Age of Empire* (New Haven, CT: Yale University Press, 2015). For the Sulu Zone, the classic work of James Francis Warren is indispensable: *The Sulu Zone 1768–1898: The Dynamics of External Trade, Slavery, and Ethnicity in the Transformation of a Southeast Asian Maritime State*, 2nd ed. (Singapore: National University of Singapore Press, 2007).

13. In many instances, these have been focused on production and especially labor allocation in the harvesting of pearls and shell.

14. The connections of the Indian Ocean to other oceans is also noted recently by Krish Seetah and Richard B. Allen in their introductory chapter, "Interdisciplinary Ripples across the Indian Ocean," in *Connecting Continents: Archaeology and History in the Indian Ocean World*, ed. Krish Seetah (Athens: Ohio University Press, 2018), 1–29.

15. Arjun Appadurai, "Introduction: Commodities and the Politics of Value," in *The Social Life of Things: Commodities in Cultural Perspective*, ed. Arjun Appadurai (Cambridge: Cambridge University Press, 1986). See also Amiria J. M. Henare, Martin Holbraad, and Sari Wastell, *Thinking through Things: Theorising Artefacts Ethnographically* (Abingdon, UK: Routledge, 2006).

16. Appadurai, "Introduction," 3.

17. Natasha Eaton, "In Search of Pearlesence: Pearls, Empire and Obsolescence in South Asia," *Journal of Material Culture* 21, no. 1 (March 2016): 30, drawing on the work of Michael Taussig, "Redeeming Indigo," *Theory, Culture and Society* 25, no. 3 (May 2008): 1–15.

18. Anne Gerritsen, "Domesticating Goods from Overseas: Global Material Culture in the Early Modern Netherlands," *Journal of Design History* 29, no. 3 (August 2016): 228–44; Gerritsen, "From Long-Distance Trade to the Global Lives of Things: Writing the History of Early Modern Trade and Material Culture," *Journal of Early Modern History* 20, no. 6 (November 2016): 526–44.

19. Interest in the study of things and objects, as reflective of particular social and cultural meanings, and the material worlds that were constituted through and by them has grown dramatically. See, for example, Craig Clunas, *Superfluous Things: Material Culture and Social Status in Early Modern China* (Honolulu: University of Hawai'i Press, 1991); John Brewer and Roy Porter, eds., *Consumption and the World of Goods* (Abingdon, UK: Routledge, 1993); Susan B. Hanley, *Everyday Things in Premodern Japan: The Hidden Legacy of Material Culture* (Berkeley: University of California Press, 1997); Suraiya Faroqhi, "Moving Goods Around, and Ottomanists Too: Surveying Research on the Transfer of Material Goods in the Ottoman Empire," *Turcica* 32 (February 2000): 435–66.

20. Kate Smith, "Amidst Things: New Histories of Commodities, Capital, and Consumption," *Historical Journal* 61, no. 3 (September 2018): 841–61.

21. For recent work highlighting the translocal dynamics of the histories of pearl trading, see Julia Martínez and Adrian Vickers, *The Pearl Frontier: Indonesian Labor and Indigenous Encounters in Australia's Northern Trading Network* (Honolulu: University of Hawai'i Press, 2015).

22. Alison Bashford, "Terraqueous Histories," *Historical Journal* 60, no. 2 (June 2017): 253–72; Lauren Benton, *A Search for Sovereignty: Law and Geography in European Empires, 1400–1900* (New York: Cambridge University Press, 2010), 2.

23. John R. Gillis and Franziska Torma, eds., *Fluid Frontiers: New Currents in Marine Environmental History* (Cambridge, UK: White Horse, 2015); and J. C. Heesterman, "Littoral et intérieur de l'Inde," in *History and Underdevelopment: Essays on Underdevelopment and European Expansion in Asia and Africa*, ed. Leonard Blussé, H. L. Wesseling, and George D. Winius (Leiden: Leiden University Press, 1980), 87–92.

24. Sujit Sivasundaram, Alison Bashford, and David Armitage, "Introduction: Writing World Oceanic Histories," in *Oceanic Histories*, ed. David Armitage, Alison Bashford, and Sujit Sivasundaram (Cambridge: Cambridge University Press, 2018), 19.

25. Indian Ocean scholarship has featured work on various aspects of the environmental histories of coasts and islands—such as the development of ideas tied to colonial botany or deforestation—for which see, for example, the classic work by Richard H. Grove, *Green Imperialism: Colonial Expansion, Tropical Island Edens and the Origins of Environmentalism* (Cambridge: Cambridge University Press, 1995); and also Haripriya Rangan, Judith Carney, and Tim Denham, "Environmental History of Botanical Exchanges in the Indian Ocean World," *Environment and History* 18, no. 3 (August 2012): 311–42.

26. W. Jeffrey Bolster, "Putting the Ocean in Atlantic History: Maritime Communities and Marine Ecology in the Northwest Atlantic, 1500–1800,"

American Historical Review 113, no. 1 (February 2008): 19–47. For an elaboration, see Bolster, *The Mortal Sea: Fishing the Atlantic in the Age of Sail* (Cambridge, MA: Harvard University Press, 2012).

27. "Fisheries" is defined here as involving fishing that yields food for human consumption, with whaling having enjoyed an especially prominent focus in marine environmental history. I thank Joe Christensen for highlighting this point for me.

28. This volume is thus writing somewhat against the notion, most fully expressed by K. N. Chaudhuri, of the Indian Ocean as a unified space or "system" expressed in structuralist terms. See Chaudhuri, *Trade and Civilisation in the Indian Ocean: An Economic History from the Rise of Islam to 1750* (Cambridge: Cambridge University Press, 1985).

29. Sujit Sivasundaram, "The Indian Ocean," in Armitage et al., *Oceanic Histories*, 31–61. Richard Allen has regularly cautioned against the "tyranny of the particular" when approaching the histories of the Indian Ocean, specifically in studying the global traffic in chattel labor across the ocean. See Richard Allen, "Ending the History of Silence: Reconstructing European Slave Trading in the Indian Ocean," *Revista Tempo* 23, no. 2 (May–August 2017): 295–313.

30. See, for instance, Seetah and Allen, "Interdisciplinary Ripples"; and Pedro Machado and Sarah Fee, "Introduction: The Ocean's Many Cloth Pathways," in *Textile Trade, Consumer Cultures, and the Material Worlds of the Indian Ocean: An Ocean of Cloth*, ed. Pedro Machado, Sarah Fee, and Gwyn Campbell (New York: Palgrave Macmillan, 2018), 1–25.

31. This mode of analysis was proposed and applied fruitfully by the Modern Girl Around the World Collective, for which see Alys Eve Weinbaum, Lynn M. Thomas, Priti Ramamurthy, Uta G. Poiger, Madeleine Yue Dong, and Tani E. Barlow, eds., *The Modern Girl around the World: Consumption, Modernity, and Globalization* (Durham, NC: Duke University Press, 2008).

32. Some of my thoughts about Area geographies have been prompted by Jonathan Saha, "Is It in India? Colonial Burma as a 'Problem' in South Asian History," *South Asian History and Culture* 7, no. 1 (2016): 23–29.

33. See Regina Ganter, with contributions by Julia Martínez and Gary Lee, *Mixed Relations: Asian-Aboriginal Contact in North Australia* (Crawley: University of Western Australia Press, 2006).

34. Nassar Al-Taee, "'Enough, Enough, Oh Ocean': Music of the Pearl Divers in the Arabian Gulf," *Middle East Studies Association Bulletin* 39, no. 1 (June 2005): 19–30. See also Laith Ulaby, "On the Decks of Dhows: Musical Traditions of Oman and the Indian Ocean World," *World of Music*, n.s., 1, no. 2 (2012): 43–62; as well as Ulaby, "Performing the Past: Sea Music in the Arab Gulf States" (PhD diss., University of California, Los Angeles, 2008).

PART I

Commodification

ONE

The Pearl Commodity Chain, Early Nineteenth Century to the End of the Second World War
Trade, Processing, and Consumption

WILLIAM G. CLARENCE-SMITH

THE POTENTIAL PROFITS to be made in pearls attracted the attention of the booming West. Natural pearls suitable for jewelry only occurred in very few molluscs, whether saltwater or freshwater. Their high price stimulated experiments in aquaculture from the 1890s, through both farming and artificially seeding molluscs. These trials came to fruition, mainly in Japan, in the interwar years.

Pearls remained for the most part an Asian business, which long displayed marked premodern features. Asian artisans continued to dominate processing, serving a luxury market that was still largely situated in Asia. Asian diasporas effectively resisted competition in marketing from mainly Jewish Western networks. Japanese entrepreneurs received a boost from the emergence of cultured pearls, although this was a markedly more modern business.[1]

THE GLOBAL TRADE IN PEARLS

Statistical information for pearls is poor, as they were easy to conceal and often untaxed, so that transactions bypassed official channels.[2] Scholars have generally relied on the estimates given by Kunz and Stevenson for 1906 (table 1.1), though these figures probably underestimate the value of freshwater pearls destined for Chinese and Russian markets.

Table 1.1. Estimated value of world output of pearls in 1906

	Local prices, converted to US$
Persian, or Arabian, Gulf	4,000,000
Red Sea, Gulf of Aden, East Africa	200,000
Ceylon, or Sri Lanka	1,200,000
India	100,000
Southeast Asia	300,000
South Pacific	125,000
Australia	450,000
China, Japan, Inner Asia (partly freshwater)	400,000
Latin America and Caribbean	600,000
North America (freshwater)	650,000
Europe (freshwater)	115,000
TOTAL	8,140,000

(Source: Kunz and Stevenson, *Book of the Pearl*, 80)

Asia, including the Middle East, probably remained the largest market for pearls of gem quality throughout the period.[3] Demand was enhanced because wealthy elites of both sexes wore pearls.[4] Many Asian consumers at this time preferred golden colors, whereas Europeans tended to go for white shades.[5]

Descriptive evidence repeatedly portrays South Asia as the great global sink for pearls, right through to the Second World War.[6] Initially, the chief mart was the Gujarati port of Surat, but newly founded Bombay (Mumbai) had become the prime center by the 1830s.[7] Bombay not only imported pearls, but also processed and redistributed them, within India and far beyond.[8] India even imported freshwater pearls from Europe and North America, typically small, cheap specimens. As such, they served to embellish embroidery, and, crushed, they were consumed for medicine or added to betel quids for chewing.[9]

Other Asian lands imported significant quantities. China relied chiefly on its own saltwater and freshwater output.[10] However, the empire also imported marine pearls from Japan, the South Pacific, Australia, Southeast Asia, and India, many of the latter being re-exports from the Middle East.[11] Persia (Iran), with its close cultural ties to India, stood out among Middle Eastern buyers.[12] The Ottoman Empire and its successor states were also significant purchasers.[13]

Nevertheless, the consumption of pearls in the West was probably growing faster. Stimulated by role models such as Empress Eugénie in France and Queen Victoria in Britain, women's necklaces were to the fore.[14] Unlike in previous centuries, however, Western men at best wore few and small pearls to avoid being perceived as effeminate.[15] As pearl prices rose to giddy heights in the early twentieth century, accumulated stocks were released onto Western markets. Owners in Asia, Latin America, and peripheral parts of Europe obtained up to twenty times the purchase price of their gems.[16] Most famously, many of the Ottoman imperial family's jewels were sold at auction in Paris in 1911.[17]

Western pearl marts shifted in the nineteenth century, away from Seville, Lisbon, Venice, Amsterdam, Vienna, and Leipzig.[18] Initially, London enjoyed a major advantage through its imperial connections.[19] However, it was Paris, the fashion capital of the West, which gradually established itself as the premier center for pearls.[20] Russia remained a largely self-contained market for its own freshwater pearls, centered on Saint Petersburg, until the Bolshevik Revolution of 1917.[21] New York's role grew from the 1880s, reflecting the increasing wealth of the United States.[22] Indeed, New York took center stage during the First World War and kept a significant part of the business thereafter, although London and Paris recovered to some degree in the interwar years.[23]

From 1914 to 1945, the world pearl market became more volatile and less profitable. The First World War almost closed down European markets, although demand in the United States persisted.[24] A "democratization" of consumption occurred in the 1920s, stimulated by the availability of cheaper Japanese cultured pearls.[25] But the Great Depression and the Second World War were periods of severe slump.[26]

THE PROCESSING OF PEARLS

Tasks were overwhelmingly carried out by hand, and some required very high levels of skill. Pearls needed to be cleaned, dried, sorted, and sometimes peeled or cut to remove imperfections. Color might be enhanced or altered, though this was frowned upon, before polishing and matching by size and color. Some pearls were drilled right through and strung and knotted for necklaces, with clasps added. Others were partly drilled, or left whole, and set in jewels. The risks were immense, especially when peeling or drilling valuable specimens, which could be destroyed by one false move.[27]

Asian artisans continued to carry out many of these operations, exporting semi-processed or finished goods to the West.[28] Jain and Hindu Vaniya "of the poorer class" specialized in such work in Bombay.[29] They employed "fine bow-drills" to pierce the pearls.[30] Drilling was more expertly done in India than in the West, with straighter and narrower holes.[31] Even Venezuelan wholesalers sent pearls to India for drilling and stringing in the 1930s, partly for cost reasons.[32] Bombay, the great center for this kind of work, exported both strung bunches and finished necklaces.[33] Much processing was also carried out on the Sri Lankan coast.[34] "A troop of Indian artisans" who charged "moderate" fees arrived annually to carry out this work.[35] Artisans were not only in ports. In Hyderabad, inland in the lands of the Nizam in southern India, pearl processing dated from the eighteenth century.[36]

For all that, Sugata Bose wrongly repeats an allegation in a Gulf report that drilling was "an Indian monopoly."[37] Chinese workers were reputed to drill even smaller holes than their Indian colleagues, at least in half-pearls.[38] However, the Chinese practice of drilling twin holes to sew pearls onto garments was not appreciated in Western markets.[39] Kobe workers also drilled and strung pearls.[40] Although Bose contends that drilling was not carried out in the Middle East, a Jeddah artisan was reported to be making pearl necklaces in 1858.[41]

Other processing also occurred outside South Asia, with Canton as the center in China.[42] Chinese artisans often set undrilled pearls in jewels, with clasps.[43] Expatriate Chinese also peeled pearls in Sulu.[44] A Kobe entrepreneur, Todo Yasui, pioneered a new technique to bleach pearls, imparting the whiteness desired by some customers.[45]

Mikimoto Kokichi, the leading seller of cultured pearls, even established factories. From around 1908, one in Tokyo made jewelry for his Ginza store. By 1911 it employed sixty-five workers, and it was subsequently enlarged.[46] Mikimoto also had a pearl factory in Toba by the 1930s "for sorting, drilling, and stringing into necklaces," partly for export.[47] However, processes in these factories are not described in available sources, and they may have consisted of collections of artisans under one roof.

Processing in the West was essentially artisanal.[48] This was especially true of the luxury trade. Some machines were used for *demi-luxe* products, but more for treating metals than gems.[49] Although mechanical drills could pierce an average of fifteen hundred pearls per day, compared to an artisan's forty to fifty, they were little used.[50] Jacques Bienenfeld, a major trader in pearls, invented a drilling machine in Paris, but apparently with indifferent success.[51]

Skilled artisans remain shadowy figures. At the beginning of the nineteenth century, many worked in Vienna, but by the end of the century Paris was the principal center, followed by London.[52] Kornitzer noted that an "Indian pearl-doctor," a "Hindu," worked in Paris around the 1890s.[53] Jewelry workshops in the Marais (third arrondissement), the heart of the business in Paris, never employed more than fifty workers, and subcontracted much of the work. Employment plummeted in times of economic crisis.[54] Payments were strongly correlated to skills, even in performance of the same task.[55]

PEARL TRADING

The pearl trade benefited from improved security and insurance, speed and reliability of transport, and communications by telegraph and post. However, the value of pearls simultaneously attracted specialized criminals, who occasionally pulled off spectacular coups. One gang stole a valuable necklace, sold by the Ottoman sultan, which was in transit between Paris and London in 1913. The insurance company offered a reward, and nearly all the pearls were eventually recovered.[56]

Mercantile intermediaries in the wholesale trade in pearls fell into various categories.[57] Commission agents acted for distant sellers.

Brokers (*courtiers*) matched sellers and buyers, taking a commission from both parties if a sale went through. Dealers (*négociants*) owned pearls, borrowed money on the security of pearls, and gave credit. They also paid agents to purchase pearls in production zones.[58]

Pearl merchants were generally men belonging to diasporic entrepreneurial communities.[59] Trust and reputation were extraordinarily important, as pearls were extremely valuable and judging them required great expertise. Men typically operated as individuals, or as members of small family firms, inheriting both skills and reputation.[60] Women appeared only exceptionally in this man's world, seemingly through quirks of inheritance, although more research would be needed to investigate this.[61]

ARABS, PERSIANS, AND "BANIANS" IN THE WESTERN INDIAN OCEAN

Banians were the premier pearl traders of the world. They were of the Vaniya *jati*, a caste within the Vaishya *varna* of traders, who had long held a commanding position in the trade of the western Indian Ocean. By religion, they were either Hindu or Jain.[62] Formerly based in Gujarat, Sindh, or Rajasthan, they increasingly moved to the new British imperial center of Bombay.[63] Dealers in pearls were highly specialized, and the profession often passed from father to son.[64]

In 1909, the bulk of the pearl trade of Bombay was firmly in the hands of some forty Jains.[65] Many of the Jains who flocked to the city in the late nineteenth century were jewelers, such as Amîchand Pannâlâl, "the personal jeweller of the Nizam of Hyderabad," who donated most of the money for a large Jain temple erected in Bombay in 1904.[66] However, dealing in pearls should have posed an ethical problem for Jains, as the killing of molluscs violated the principle of *ahimsa*, or nonviolence.[67] Jains appear to have evaded this dilemma by claiming that they were not directly involved in the deaths of molluscs. This was also the case for their substantial trade in ivory.[68]

Hindu Vaniya, often originating in Kachchh (Kutch), dominated purchasing for export in the pearling zones of the western Indian Ocean.[69] They provided local traders with credit or trade goods and purchased their pearls for export.[70] Legends associating Vishnu and Krishna with wearing pearls morally facilitated Hindu participation in the business.[71] A few Bombay-based pearl traders were Muslim, notably Khoja from the Isma'ili community, or Parsi Zoroastrians.[72]

Arab and Persian Muslims in the western Indian Ocean began as local agents of Banians.[73] However, they gained market share from their former patrons from around the 1870s.[74] Increasing numbers traveled regularly to Bombay to sell pearls, and a few set up businesses there.[75] However, Arab pearl merchants in Bombay continued to depend on close relations with Banians.[76] Moreover, during the 1930s depression, the deep pockets of a few South Asians enabled them to survive more effectively in the business than Arabs and Persians.[77]

ASIAN RIVALS IN SOUTH INDIA AND SRI LANKA

The pearl fisheries of South India and Sri Lanka (Ceylon) were riven by rivalry between diasporas. Marakkayar, Tamil Muslims who claimed Arab ancestry, had long dominated the sector.[78] From the late eighteenth century, however, astute Nattukottai Chettiars, from a dynamic Tamil Hindu banking caste, seized control of the business, chiefly by obtaining licenses from the newly powerful British.[79]

The Marakkayar fought back with considerable success, aided by growing British unease about monopolistic licenses.[80] Some Marakkayar entrepreneurs also financed illegal pearl diving.[81] The formerly dominant "Moormen" thus regained much of their old position over time, although no exact balance sheet exists of shares in the trade.[82] Chettiars were certainly not entirely driven out of the business.[83]

Indians and Arabs based in Bombay also expanded their pearl-trading operations to the area. Parsis were pioneers, as early as the 1820s adding pearls as a sideline to the goods that they sold in China, such as raw cotton and opium.[84] In the 1900s, the great Parsi firm of Tata, which also had Chinese interests, was a major buyer of pearls in Tuticorin, on the Indian side of the Straits.[85] By around 1900, Bombay Arabs and northwestern Indians, including some Jains, financed and marketed a significant proportion of the output of these pearl banks.[86]

THE CHINESE AND THEIR COMPETITORS IN SOUTHEAST ASIA

From Burma to the Philippines, Chinese entrepreneurs were initially the foremost pearl traders. Hokkien merchants had monopolized eighteenth-century exports of pearls from the Sulu archipelago (southern Philippines) to Canton.[87] They were similarly prominent in eastern Indonesia.[88]

At the other end of the region, they dominated the Mergui archipelago of southern Burma by the 1820s, bartering for pearls with local fishermen.[89]

Trading patterns were affected significantly by the British foundation of Singapore in 1819. Many Chinese traders in marine products, including pearls, set up their commercial headquarters in the port.[90] They developed a satellite center in Makassar after the Dutch had liberalized trade there.[91] However, it is unclear where they sold the pearls that they amassed, and under what conditions.

What is clear is that there was growing competition from other Asian diasporas. Tamil Muslim Marakkayar merchants were in the Mergui archipelago of Burma by the late nineteenth century, gaining commercial advantages by taking out British pearling licences.[92] This community was also active in retailing pearls in Penang.[93] They went as far as Sulu to buy pearls, albeit not in any numbers.[94]

Hadrami Arabs, from what is today eastern Yemen, engaged in production to control trade. Their strengths in shipping helped them to enter pearling in eastern Indonesia and to overshadow the Chinese.[95] (Sjech) Sa'id bin 'Abdullah Baädilla, born in the Banda archipelago, came to be known locally as the *raja mutiara*, or pearl king, even though his main business was dealing in the shells of molluscs.[96]

Japanese individuals and companies similarly gained market share through investing in production. By 1913, Japanese interests owned the largest number of pearl luggers in Sulu.[97] However, the most effective strategy was to develop cultured pearl production. The Fujita brothers, backed by the powerful Mitsubishi *zaibatsu*, first attempted to set up a pearl farm near Zamboanga, in the southern Philippines, in 1916. Fearing political uncertainty there, they moved their operations to Buton, in southeastern Sulawesi, in the early 1920s. They enjoyed modest success, sending cultured pearls back to Japan for marketing.[98]

CHINESE, JAPANESE, AND INDIANS IN EAST ASIA AND THE PACIFIC

Chinese traders branched out from their internal market, crossing the Pacific.[99] They enjoyed undisputed control over the marketing of imported and local natural pearls, with Hong Kong, Canton, and Shanghai as major centers in the 1900s.[100] Traders were especially successful in French Polynesia, despite vigorous attempts by settlers to have them expelled.[101] They reached as far as Baja California in Mexico, where they were reported to be exporting the dried flesh of pearl oysters.[102] In Australia, early Chinese success in Shark's Bay and elsewhere was undone by policies discriminating against Asian immigrants.[103]

Japan was a hard nut to crack for Chinese traders until Japan acquired Taiwan in 1895. After that date, small Chinese traders, claiming to be Taiwanese or acquiring Japanese nationality after a short period of residence, found it relatively easy to set up shop in Japan. They moved especially to Kobe, where they traded in pearls among other goods.[104]

Northwestern Indians developed a presence quite early in East Asian pearl markets. On the back of exports of raw cotton and opium to China, Parsi merchants dabbled in exporting pearls to Canton.[105] In Kobe, Japan, "Bombay Indians" began to arrive soon after the Meiji Restoration of 1868, with Parsis as pioneers.[106] Over time, Jains became the chief South Asian pearl traders in Kobe, so that there is now a Jain temple in the city.[107]

The main break for Japanese merchants, outside their home market, came with the successful development of cultured pearls. This allowed Japanese firms to enter the Chinese market, with Mikimoto targeting Western tourists in Shanghai from 1906.[108] In Palau, part of Japan's South Pacific Mandate after the First World War, Japanese firms went into cultured pearl production from 1920, with pearls sent to Japan for marketing.[109]

WESTERN PEARL MERCHANTS AND JEWISH NETWORKS

Western pearl merchants were also mainly drawn from diasporic communities of trust, with Jews of widely varying origins commanding a disproportionately large share of the business. Their prior entrenchment in the jewelry trades probably explained this, reflecting a long Christian tradition of restricting their economic activities to niche occupations.

Many Jewish pearl dealers came from peripheral areas, attracted by economic opportunities in large Western cities. One of two men called the "pearl king" of Paris, Jacques Bienenfeld was from Austrian Galicia. Arriving in Paris around 1889, he also dealt in diamonds. The Great Depression bankrupted him in 1933, but his cousin David kept the firm going.[110] The other "pearl king" of Paris, Léonard Rosenthal, also known as the "Napoleon of pearls," came to France at around the same time.[111] From a community of Mountain Jews in Daghistan, North

Caucasus, Rosenthal spoke a Judaeo-Arabic dialect, which proved useful for his pearl business.[112] Rehavia Moussaieff, another major Parisian dealer, was born in Jerusalem of Jewish parents from Bukhara, and held Russian nationality.[113] Indeed, the non-Western origins of many Jewish pearl traders blurred the rather facile distinction between "the West and the Rest," even if these men tended to portray themselves as Westerners.

The pearl trade clustered strongly in certain quarters of great Western cities. In London's Hatton Garden, merchants traded in both pearls and diamonds. The same was true of Maiden Lane in Lower Manhattan's financial district. In Paris, dealers and brokers haunted the cafés around the Rue La Fayette in the ninth arrondissement.[114] This Paris location was conveniently close to the Grand Synagogue in the Rue de la Victoire.

Other groups in the West dealt in pearls, and Jewish predominance was fading by the interwar years. Kornitzer already noted the presence in Paris in the 1890s of "Armenians, Syrians, Arabs, Parsees, Hindus, with a sprinkling of Neapolitans and Catalans, and an odd Frenchman or two."[115] More significantly, large jewelry companies consolidated their hold over retailing in the 1920s and moved upstream into wholesale pearl dealing. Of the "big three," Tiffany was based in the United States and Cartier and Chaumet in France.[116] None of the families behind these firms seem to have been Jewish.[117]

WESTERN PEARL MERCHANTS IN THE GLOBAL SOUTH

Pearl dealers based in the West experienced great difficulties in breaking into marketing networks in pearl-producing lands. A condition of success was to enter into partnership with Asian rivals, who may have been the main beneficiaries of such alliances. This again blurred the simple distinction between Western and non-Western networks of traders.

The Gulf was the crucial battleground, as the producer of nearly half the world's pearls by value (see table 1.1). British residents warned Western capitalists that they were no match for Banians, Arabs, and Persians.[118] Nevertheless, Western-based Jewish firms attempted to purchase pearls directly from the 1860s, and with renewed vigor from the 1890s.[119] Some of these men appear to have been "Oriental Jews," or Mizrahim, and thus Arabic-speaking.[120] Indeed, the Rosenthal brothers themselves were in this position, despite their Ashkenazi-sounding name.[121]

Léonard Rosenthal made the bombastic claim that the 1907 financial crisis resulted in a massive transfer of the Gulf's pearl trade from Asian hands to those of his firm and associates.[122] Historians have repeatedly taken him at face value.[123] And yet, Rosenthal failed to get a pearl diving concession in the Gulf in 1911, and circumstantial evidence indicates that Bombay continued to be the word's "pearl capital."[124] Moreover, a much more serious financial crisis, from 1929 to 1934, favored Bombay.[125]

In the Red Sea, representatives of Western firms struggled to make headway. The Bienenfeld family of Trieste, perhaps related to the Paris pearl trader, did better than most, but dealt mainly in shell rather than pearls.[126] Monfreid's literary account plays up the roles of Rosenthal's Tunisian Jewish pearl buyer, together with a malevolent Greek from Mytilene. However, reading between the lines, their success was no more than partial.[127]

The record was equally mixed elsewhere. The Ceylon Company of Pearl Fishers Ltd., based in London, obtained a twenty-year monopolistic lease on the Sri Lankan banks from the British authorities, which commenced in 1907.[128] However, the venture proved to be a financial disaster.[129] In Sulu, Louis Kornitzer, a Viennese Jew, claimed to have been the most successful pearl dealer before 1914. And yet, his own account suggests that his Chinese and other rivals were scarcely cowed.[130] Émile Lévy, from Paris, offered spirited competition to entrenched Chinese pearl buyers in French Polynesia, but did not overcome them.[131]

In terms of cultured pearls, various Westerners bought some in Kobe, but they were clearly far from elbowing aside Japanese or foreign Asian merchants.[132] One somewhat ambiguous example was Elias Antaki, an Aleppan Jew by origin, who came to Kobe after settling in Alexandria, Egypt. He became prominent in the 1930s in purchasing cultured pearls for sale in the West. Antaki presented himself as a member of the Western community in Kobe, despite his non-Western origins.[133]

In contrast, Western pearl merchants prevailed in lands where Asian diasporas were weak, notably in Latin America. In Venezuela, the two greatest Jewish firms of Paris had agents from at least 1901.[134] In 1925, Rosenthal and Bienenfeld headed the list of six main pearl dealers in Venezuela. Two had possibly Syrian names and two Spanish ones.[135] Of the four main pearl traders in Panama in the 1890s, two were definitely Jewish, and a third one probably was.[136] In Baja California, western

Mexico, Russian pearl traders arrived from the 1830s. Probably Ashkenazim, they sold Mexican pearls to Jewish firms in Paris.[137]

Excluding Asian traders from Australia by legislative fiat left the field artificially clear for Western rivals.[138] In the 1900s, the chief buyer of pearls in Broome, the northwestern center of the industry, was Roth, a Jew.[139] Later, Russian-born Mark Rubin, who came to Melbourne as a jeweler in the 1890s and was also Jewish, took over this position. Owning a pearling fleet, his commercial connections were with London and Paris.[140]

ASIAN PEARL MERCHANTS IN THE WEST

A number of Asian pearl dealers themselves moved to the West, notably Paris, for varying lengths of time. In some cases, a Western firm allied with a family in a pearling zone would provide succor to members of that family on their travels. Such arrangements were particularly found with Arabs.

Gulf Arabs were the most numerous. The Kuwayti pearl merchants Jasim and 'Abd al-Rahman al-Ibrahim went to Paris in 1910, staying in a hotel close to the Rue La Fayette. They bought some pearls auctioned by the Ottoman sultan in 1911, but their main purpose was to scout out possibilities for selling pearls directly in Europe. Two well-known Western pearl merchants, Joseph van Praag and Albert Habib, with business in the Gulf, assisted them in Paris.[141] Other Kuwayti dealers came to both Paris and London into the early 1930s. They hoped to obtain better prices for their pearls than in Bombay, though they found the cost of living high.[142] Some Kuwayti went to lesser centers, such as Marseilles and Milan.[143]

Merchants from other coastal areas in the Gulf did likewise in the interwar years.[144] 'Abd al-Rahman bin Hasan al-Qusaybi, from Bahrayn, first went to Paris and London around 1922. He was followed by about a dozen others, from Bahrayn, Sharjah, Lingah (Lengeh), and Bastak, the latter two towns being in Persia. Muhammad Faruq bin Muhammad 'Aqil, a Bastaki, married a Frenchwoman.[145]

Muhammad 'Ali bin Zaynal 'Alireza stood out among these migrants. His family was originally Persian and had settled in Jeddah. However, Muhammad made his fortune in Bahrayn pearls, to support ambitious educational plans, and he set up shop in Bombay. He then established offices in the Rue La Fayette in 1920, with the intention of cutting out middlemen in Europe. He shuttled back and forth between Paris and Bombay, and purchased a house in the prestigious Champs-Élysées.[146] He also had offices in London, Dubai, and Karachi.[147] In 1927, he took some £600,000 worth of pearls to Paris.[148] Four years later, he was one of the "four great lords of the pearl in Paris."[149] And yet, he owed much of his position to his close, even intimate, relations with the Bienenfeld family.[150] Yet again, boundaries between East and West were fudged.

Other Arabs went to the West. Sayyid 'Alī al-Nahārī, originally from al-Hudaydah on Yemen's Red Sea coast, arrived in Paris in 1906. Accompanied by a Rosenthal agent, he brought pearls from Massawa with him. It is not clear how long he stayed, but he purchased three buildings in Paris as an investment.[151] Sa'id bin 'Abdullah Baädilla, from Indonesia, traveled round the world to sell his pearls.[152] In the Netherlands, he presented some of his finest gems to different Dutch queens in 1896 and 1909, and was made a knight of the Oranje Nassau Order on the second occasion.[153]

South Asians in the West left only fragmentary traces. They seemed reluctant to partner with Western merchants, although Bombay dealers had commission agents in Western centers.[154] By the 1890s, there were a few Parsis and Hindus dealing in pearls in Paris.[155] Around 1900, some Indians of unspecified background were in McGregor, Iowa, buying small, cheap river pearls for export to India.[156]

Bombay Jains were seemingly to the fore in interwar Paris. Thakordas Nemchand went to the city in 1920 to sell Gulf pearls, and he lived there "in style" to 1928.[157] A Bombay Jain firm, Premchand Roychand & Sons, intervened in Paris lawsuits on Japanese cultured pearls in 1925.[158] A Kuwayti in Paris in 1931 reported, perhaps with surprise, "We have found some Banian traders" who sold the pearls of Arabs on commission. This arrangement led to a long dispute in the 1930s with Chandulal Shah, who owned a large store in Bombay and had dealings in Gulf pearls.[159] Shah is a common Jain name.

The Japanese moved to the West with the advent of cultured pearls. Mikimoto Kokichi may have been alone in venturing out in this manner, but he did so on quite a scale, employing a number of Japanese abroad. Initially, he exhibited jewels at foreign events and consigned pearls to commission agents. To cut out middlemen, he then founded stores from 1904 in London, Paris, New York, Chicago, Los Angeles, and San Francisco. The emphasis was on North America, which proved less resistant than Europe to purchasing cultured pearls.[160]

THE PEARL COMMODITY chain tended to remain early modern in nature in this period, and strongly focused on Asia. Many historians have succumbed to a narrative of modernization and Western domination in these years, for which the evidence is, at best, partial. To be sure, the story was different for the shells of the molluscs. However, even in this case, it is easy to exaggerate the extent to which Western interests dominated the field.[161]

Moreover, the rise of Japanese cultured pearl production from the end of the nineteenth century actually reinforced the Asian focus of the business, notably after the First World War. Indeed, in the period after the Second World War it was Kobe that took over Bombay's former title as "pearl capital of the world." And Kobe has retained this sobriquet till our own day, despite the mounting challenge from Hong Kong.

NOTES

1. For overviews, see Edwin W. Streeter, *Pearls and Pearling Life* (London: George Bell and Sons, 1886); Wallis R. Cattelle, *The Pearl: Its Story, Its Charm, and Its Value* (Philadelphia: J. B. Lippincott, 1907); George F. Kunz and Charles H. Stevenson, *The Book of the Pearl: The History, Art, Science and Industry of the Queen of Gems* (New York: Century, 1908); W. J. Dakin, *Pearls* (Cambridge: Cambridge University Press, 1913); Micheline Cariño and Mario Monteforte, *Une histoire mondiale des perles et des nacres: Pêche, culture, commerce* (Paris: L'Harmattan, 2005); Elisabeth Strack, *Pearls* (Stuttgart: Rühle-Diebener-Verlag, 2006); Atsumi Yamada, *Shinju no sekaishi* [World history of pearls] (Tokyo: Chuokoron-Shinsha, 2013).

2. Cariño and Monteforte, *Une histoire mondiale*, 208.

3. Kunz and Stevenson, *Book of the Pearl*, 31; Cariño and Monteforte, *Une histoire mondiale*, 219–20.

4. Cattelle, *The Pearl*, 83; Léonard Rosenthal, *Au royaume de la perle* (Paris: Payot, 1919), 162–63; Cariño and Monteforte, *Une histoire mondiale*, 211.

5. William Milburn, *Oriental Commerce* (London: Black, Parry, 1813), 119, 359; Lewis Pelly, "Remarks on the Pearl Oyster Beds in the Persian Gulf," *Transactions of the Bombay Geographical Society* 21 (1868): 34–35; John Gordon Lorimer, *Gazetteer of the Persian Gulf, Oman and Central*

Arabia, vol. 1, pt. 2 (Calcutta: Superintendent Government Printing, 1908), 2236; Jonathan Miran, *Red Sea Citizens: Cosmopolitan Society and Cultural Change in Massawa* (Bloomington: Indiana University Press, 2009), 105.

6. Streeter, *Pearls and Pearling Life*, 208; Kunz and Stevenson, *Book of the Pearl*, 124, 357; Cariño and Monteforte, *Une histoire mondiale*, 211.

7. Robert Carter, *Sea of Pearls: Seven Thousand Years of the Industry That Shaped the Gulf* (London: Arabian, 2012), 169; Chhaya Goswami, *Globalization before Its Time: The Gujarati Merchants from Kachchh* (Gurgaon: Portfolio-Penguin, 2016), 98–99.

8. Streeter, *Pearls and Pearling Life*, 208; Guillemette Crouzet, *Genèses du Moyen-Orient: Le Golfe Persique à l'âge des impérialismes, vers 1800–vers 1914* (Ceyzérieu, France: Champ Vallon, 2015), 381–82.

9. Strack, *Pearls*, 199, 233–34, 245.

10. Milburn, *Oriental Commerce*, 119, 359; D. T. McGowan, "Pearls and Pearl-Making in China," *Journal of the Society of Arts* 2, no. 56 (1853): 72–73; Kunz and Stevenson, *Book of the Pearl*, 298; Derek J. Content, "Reflections on the Geography and History of the Pearl Trade in China, Vietnam, India and the Near East," in *The Pearl and the Dragon: A Study of Vietnamese Pearls and a History of the Oriental Pearl Trade*, ed. Derek J. Content (Houlton, ME: Outset Services, 1999), 41; Neil H. Landman et al., *Pearls: A Natural History* (New York: Harry N. Abrams, 2001), 118–19; Strack, *Pearls*, 176.

11. James Steuart, *An Account of the Pearl Fisheries of Ceylon* (Cotta, Ceylon: Church Mission Press, 1843), 18; Harry Emmanuel, *Diamonds and Precious Stones: Their History, Value, and Distinguishing Characteristics*, 2nd ed. (London: John Camden Hotten, 1867), 193; Kunz and Stevenson, *Book of the Pearl*, 212; Rosenthal, *Au royaume de la perle*, 95; Louis Kornitzer, *The Pearl Trader* (New York: Sheridan House, 1937), 10; Robert Eunson, *The Pearl King: The Story of the Fabulous Mikimoto* (London: Angus and Robertson, 1956), 168–69; Dorothy Shineberg, *They Came for Sandalwood: A Study of the Sandalwood Trade in the South-West Pacific, 1830–1865* (Melbourne: Melbourne University Press, 1967), 27; Michael Greenberg, *British Trade and the Opening of China, 1800–42* (Cambridge: Cambridge University Press, 1969), 79; James Francis Warren, *The Sulu Zone, 1768–1898: The Dynamics of External Trade, Slavery and Ethnicity in the Transformation of a Southeast Asian Maritime State* (Singapore: Singapore University Press, 1981), 8, 43; Strack, *Pearls*, 176; Goswami, *Globalization before Its Time*, 99.

12. James E. Alexander, *Travels from India to England: Comprehending a Visit to the Burman Empire, and a Journey through Persia, Asia Minor, European Turkey, Etc., in the Years 1825–26* (London: Parbury, Allen, 1827), 207; Kunz and Stevenson, *Book of the Pearl*, 336–37;

Rosenthal, *Au royaume de la perle*, 162; Cariño and Monteforte, *Une histoire mondiale*, 211.

13. Pelly, "Remarks on the Pearl Oyster Beds," 34–35; Kunz and Stevenson, *Book of the Pearl*, 360; Saif Marzooq al-Shamlan, *Pearling in the Arabian Gulf: A Kuwaiti Memoir* (London: London Centre of Arab Studies, 2000), 71; Goswami, *Globalization before Its Time*, 98–100.

14. Kunz and Stevenson, *Book of the Pearl*, 30–31; Henri Vever, *La bijouterie française au XIXe siècle, 1800–1900*, vol. 2, *Le Seconde Empire* (Paris: H. Floury, 1908), 100–104; Rosenthal, *Au royaume de la perle*, 118, 122–23, 170–71; Jacqueline Viruega, *La bijouterie parisienne, 1860–1914: Du Second Empire à la Première Guerre Mondiale* (Paris: L'Harmattan, 2004), 30, 207–8; 300; Crouzet, *Genèses du Moyen-Orient*, 374, 383, 387.

15. Cattelle, *The Pearl*, 73, 83–84; Kornitzer, *Pearl Trader*, 327–30; Viruega, *La bijouterie parisienne*, 64.

16. Rosenthal, *Au royaume de la perle*, 94, 132.

17. Hans Nadelhoffer, *Cartier: Jewelers Extraordinary* (London: Thames and Hudson, 1984), 126; Content, "Reflections," 67 (citing auction catalogue); Yacoub Y. al-Ibrahim, *Les relations koweito-françaises à partir de 1778* (Kuwait: Alqabas, 2012), 21, accessed September 10, 2016, http://www.ambafrance-kw.org/Livre-Les-relations-koweito.

18. Jannetaz et al., *Diamant et pierres précieuses* (Paris: J. Rothschild, 1881), 537; Rosenthal, *Au royaume de la perle*, 50; Cariño and Monteforte, *Une histoire mondiale*, 205, 212–13, 220–22; Molly A. Warsh, "Adorning Empire: A History of the Early Modern Pearl Trade, 1492–1688," (PhD diss., Johns Hopkins University, 2009), 70, 92–93.

19. Gedalia Yogev, *Diamonds and Coral: Anglo-Dutch Jews and Eighteenth-Century Trade* (Leicester, UK: Leicester University Press, 1978), 133–34, 254–55, 298n41; Cariño and Monteforte, *Une histoire mondiale*, 212–13.

20. Jannetaz et al., *Diamant*, 530, 537; Viruega, *La bijouterie parisienne*, 55–58.

21. Fred Woodward, *The Scottish Pearl in Its World Context* (Edinburgh: Diehard, 1994), 101–2; Strack, *Pearls*, 8.

22. *US Consular Reports: Commerce, Manufactures, Etc.* (Washington, DC: Government Printing Office, 1896), 1:622–24; George F. Kunz, "The Fresh-Water Pearls and Pearl-Fisheries of the United States," *Bulletin of the United States Fish Commission for 1897* 17 (1898): 373–426; Kunz and Stevenson, *Book of the Pearl*, 361; Rosenthal, *Au royaume de la perle*, 170; Matthew S. Hopper, *Slaves of One Master: Globalization and Slavery in Arabia in the Age of Empire* (New Haven, CT: Yale University Press, 2015), 97–100.

23. Rosenthal, *Au royaume de la perle*, 104–5, 134; Eunson, *Pearl King*, 165; Nadelhoffer, *Cartier*, 134.

24. Rosenthal, *Au royaume de la perle*, 104–5, 134.

25. Crouzet, *Genèses du Moyen-Orient*, 400–401; Eunson, *Pearl King*, 165; Cariño and Monteforte, *Une histoire mondiale*, 237.

26. al-Shamlan, *Pearling in the Arabian Gulf*, 166; Sugata Bose, *A Hundred Horizons: The Indian Ocean in the Age of Global Empire* (Cambridge, MA: Harvard University Press, 2006), 84–9; Crouzet, *Genèses du Moyen-Orient*, 401.

27. Kunz and Stevenson, *Book of the Pearl*, 371–89; Herbert H. Vertrees, *Pearls and Pearling* (New York: Fur News Publishing, 1913), 190–93; Rosenthal, *Au royaume de la perle*, 49–58; Louis Boutan, *La perle: Étude générale de la perle: Histoire de la méléagrine et des mollusques producteurs de perles* (Paris: Gaston Doin, 1925), 68–70, 87–88; Strack, *Pearls* 296–98; Shigeru Akamatsu, *Pearl Book* (Tokyo: Japan Pearl Promotion Society, 2015), 124–34.

28. J. S. Wright, "The Jewellery and Gilt Toy Trades," in *The Resources, Products, and Industrial History of Birmingham and the Midland Hardware District: A Series of Reports*, ed. Samuel Timmins (London: Robert Hardwicke, 1866), 459; Kunz and Stevenson, *Book of the Pearl*, 375–76.

29. *The Gazetteer of Bombay City and Island*, vol. 1 (Bombay: Times Press, 1909), 454n1.

30. Richard L. Bowen Jr., "The Pearl Fisheries of the Persian Gulf," *Middle East Journal* 5, no. 2 (Spring 1951): 177.

31. Emmanuel, *Diamonds and Precious Stones*, 198.

32. Cariño and Monteforte, *Une histoire mondiale*, 220.

33. Rosenthal, *Au royaume de la perle*, 56, 67–68, 91–92; Cariño and Monteforte, *Une histoire mondiale*, 205–6, 212; Crouzet, *Genèses du Moyen-Orient*, 382.

34. Milburn, *Oriental Commerce*, 358–59; Steuart, *Account of the Pearl Fisheries*, 87, 93–94; Streeter, *Pearls and Pearling Life*, 189.

35. Charles Williams, *Silver-Shell; or The Adventures of an Oyster* (London: Ward and Lock, 1856), 86–87.

36. Strack, *Pearls*, 156.

37. Bose, *A Hundred Horizons*, 89.

38. Kunz and Stevenson, *Book of the Pearl*, 381, 391.

39. Strack, *Pearls*, 174–75.

40. Kjell D. Ericson, "Nature's Helper: Mikimoto Kokichi and the Place of Cultivation in the Twentieth Century's Pearl Empires" (PhD diss., Princeton University, 2015), 261–62.

41. Bose, *A Hundred Horizons*, 89; Philippe Pétriat, *Le négoce des lieux saints: Négociants hadramis de Djedda, 1850–1950* (Paris: Publications de la Sorbonne, 2016), 93.

42. Strack, *Pearls*, 174.

43. Cattelle, *The Pearl*, 79.
44. Streeter, *Pearls and Pearling Life*, 119–20; Kornitzer, *Pearl Trader*, 283–90.
45. Ericson, "Nature's Helper," 261–62; Akamatsu, *Pearl Book*, 131.
46. Eunson, *Pearl King*, 150–52, 193.
47. Ericson, "Nature's Helper," 232, 328–29.
48. Wright, "Jewellery and Gilt Toy Trades," 452–59; Kornitzer, *Pearl Trader*, 147–48, 294–95.
49. Viruega, *La bijouterie parisienne*, 8, 33–40, 83–84, 141–42.
50. Kunz and Stevenson, *Book of the Pearl*, 378–82.
51. Nadelhoffer, *Cartier*, 298n27.
52. Rosenthal, *Au royaume de la perle*, 49, 56.
53. Kornitzer, *Pearl Trader*, 148–49.
54. Viruega, *La bijouterie parisienne*, 319–23.
55. Kornitzer, *Pearl Trader*, 147–49, 281–90, 295–96.
56. Christmas Humphreys, *The Great Pearl Robbery of 1913: A Record of Fact* (London: William Heinemann, 1929).
57. For an overview of roles, see J. A. Slater, *Pitman's Business Man's Guide: A Handbook for All Engaged in Business*, 2nd ed. (London: Sir Isaac Pitman & Sons, [ca. 1902]).
58. For the West, see *US Consular Reports 1896*, 1:635; Kunz and Stevenson, *Book of the Pearl*, 358, 371; Rosenthal, *Au royaume de la perle*, 115–24; Boutan, *La perle*, 60–62; Humphreys, *Great Pearl Robbery*, 36–41, 46–50, 85–87, 100–101; Kornitzer, *Pearl Trader*, 135–37, 143–46, 157–60, 165–66, 243–45, 349; Cariño and Monteforte, *Une histoire mondiale*, 212–14. For other areas, see al-Shamlan, *Pearling in the Arabian Gulf*, 165–66; Goswami, *Globalization before Its Time*, 101; Dionisius Agius, *Seafaring in the Arabian Gulf and Oman: The People of the Dhow* (London: Routledge, 2005), 152.
59. For an overview of diasporas, see Robin Cohen, *Global Diasporas: An Introduction*, 2nd ed. (London: Routledge, 2008).
60. Rosenthal, *Au royaume de la perle*; Humphreys, *Great Pearl Robbery*.
61. Kornitzer, *Pearl Trader*, 141–42; Carter, *Sea of Pearls*, 168.
62. Pedro Machado, *Ocean of Trade: South Asian Merchants, Africa, and the Indian Ocean, c. 1750 to 1850* (Cambridge: Cambridge University Press, 2014).
63. Christine Dobbin, *Urban Leadership in Western India: Politics and Communities in Bombay City, 1840–1995* (London: Oxford University Press, 1972); William G. Clarence-Smith, "Indian Business Communities in the Western Indian Ocean in the Nineteenth Century," *Indian Ocean Review* 2, no. 4 (1989): 18–21.
64. Rosenthal, *Au royaume de la perle*, 66, 87–92.

65. *Gazetteer of Bombay City*, 1:454n1.

66. John E. Cort, *Jains in the World: Religious Values and Ideology in India* (Oxford: Oxford University Press, 2001), 39–40.

67. Cort, 149.

68. Goswami, *Globalization before Its Time*, 142.

69. Goswami, 100–101.

70. For East Africa and Madagascar, see Kunz and Stevenson, *Book of the Pearl*, 154, 156; G. Petit, *L'industrie des pêches à Madagascar* (Paris: Société d'Éditions Géographiques, Maritimes, et Coloniales, 1930), 134, 136; Boutan, *La perle*, 116. For the Red Sea, see Henry de Monfreid, *Les secrets de la mer Rouge* (Paris: B. Grasset, 1932), 108–9; Richard Pankhurst, "The 'Banyan' or Indian Presence at Massawa, the Dahlak Islands and the Horn of Africa," *Journal of Ethiopian Studies* 12, no. 1 (January 1974): 190, 198–99; Miran, *Red Sea Citizens*, 101, 104, 107, 141–42. For the Gulf, see Bose, *A Hundred Horizons*, 79–81, 84, 89; Fahad Bishara, "A Sea of Debt: Histories of Commerce and Obligation in the Indian Ocean, c. 1850–1940," (PhD diss., Duke University, 2012), 72–73; James Onley, "Indian Communities in the Persian Gulf, c. 1500–1947," in *The Persian Gulf in Modern Times: People, Ports, and History*, ed. Lawrence G. Potter (Basingstoke, UK: Palgrave Macmillan, 2014), 231–66; Goswami, *Globalization before Its Time*, 91–94, 203.

71. N. A. Thoothi, *The Vaishnavas of Gujarat* (Calcutta: Longmans, Green, 1935), 335, 338–40; Kornitzer, *Pearl Trader*, 316; Strack, *Pearls*, 18.

72. Onley, "Indian Communities," 236, 241–45, 249–51.

73. See references in note 70.

74. Lorimer, *Gazetteer of the Persian Gulf*, vol. 1, pt. 2, 2236.

75. Kunz and Stevenson, *Book of the Pearl*, 98; Rosenthal, *Au royaume de la perle*, 66, 87–90; Nadelhoffer, *Cartier*, 134–35; Michael Field, *The Merchants: The Big Business Families of Saudi Arabia and the Gulf States*, 2nd ed. (Woodstock, NY: Overlook, 1985), 21–24, 183, 188; al-Shamlan, *Pearling in the Arabian Gulf*, 94–95, 164–67; Miran, *Red Sea Citizens*, 105; al-Ibrahim, *Les relations koweito-françaises*, 15, 17; Carter, *Sea of Pearls*, 170; Pétriat, *Le négoce des lieux saints*, 186–88, 213.

76. *Gazetteer of Bombay City*, 1:454n1.

77. Mahdi A. al-Tajir, *Bahrain 1920–1945: Britain, the Shaikh and the Administration* (London: Croom Helm, 1987), 124–25; Bose, *A Hundred Horizons*, 87, 89.

78. Susan Bayly, "Islam in Southern India: 'Purist' or 'Syncretic'?," in *Two Colonial Empires: Comparative Essays on the History of India and Indonesia in the Nineteenth Century*, ed. C. A. Bayly and D. H. A. Kolff (Dordrecht: Martinus Nijhoff, 1986), 37–47; Sanjay Subrahmanyam, "Noble Harvest from the Sea: Managing the Pearl Fishery of Mannar, 1500–1925," in *Institutions and Economic Change in South Asia*, ed. Burton Stein and

Sanjay Subrahmanyam (Delhi: Oxford University Press, 1996); J. Raja Mohamad, *Maritime History of the Coromandel Muslims: A Socio-historical Study on the Tamil Muslims, 1750–1900* (Chennai: Government Museum, 2004), 199–204.

79. Steuart, *Account of the Pearl Fisheries*, 28–30, 83, 87, 90; Streeter, *Pearls and Pearling Life*, 208; David W. Rudner, *Caste and Capitalism in Colonial India: The Nattukottai Chettiars* (Berkeley: University of California Press, 1994), 58, 259n8; Subrahmanyam, "Noble Harvest," 157–58, 161.

80. Subrahmanyam, "Noble Harvest," 162–63; Raja Mohamad, *Maritime History*, 211.

81. Raja Mohamad, *Maritime History*, 204–10.

82. Ali Fouad Toulba, *Ceylon: The Land of Eternal Charm* (London: Hutchinson, 1926), 116–17; Harry Williams, *Ceylon: Pearl of the East*, 2nd ed. (London: Robert Hale, 1963), 215–16.

83. Kunz and Stevenson, *Book of the Pearl*, 121; Subrahmanyam, "Noble Harvest," 139.

84. Jamsheed K. Choksy, "Iranians and Indians on the Shores of Serendib (Sri Lanka)," in *Parsis in India and the Diaspora*, ed. John R. Hinnels and Alan Williams (Abingdon, UK: Routledge, 2008), 189.

85. Arnold Wright, *Twentieth Century Impressions of Hong Kong, Shanghai, and Other Treaty Ports of China* (London: Lloyd's Greater Britain Publishing Co., 1908), 228.

86. Kunz and Stevenson, *Book of the Pearl*, 128; Subrahmanyam, "Noble Harvest," 139; Cariño and Monteforte, *Une histoire mondiale*, 218.

87. Louis Kornitzer, *Trade Winds* (London: Geoffrey Bles, 1933), 54, 63–65, 98–100; Warren, *Sulu Zone*, 8, 43, 74, 127–29.

88. Roy F. Ellen, *On the Edge of the Banda Zone: Past and Present in the Social Organization of a Moluccan Trade Network* (Honolulu: University of Hawai'i Press, 2003), 105–8, 123.

89. "The Conquered Provinces of Ava," *Asiatic Journal* 22, no. 129 (1826): 513. See Machado chapter in this volume.

90. Kunz and Stevenson, *Book of the Pearl*, 134–36, 149; Eric Tagliacozzo, "A Sino–Southeast Asian Circuit: Ethnohistories of the Marine Goods Trade," in *Chinese Circulations: Capital, Commodities, and Networks in Southeast Asia*, ed. Eric Tagliacozzo and Wen-Chin Chang (Durham, NC: Duke University Press, 2011), 435, 437, 439, 446.

91. Cariño and Monteforte, *Une histoire mondiale*, 56–57.

92. Felix Potter, *Myeik Heritage Walking Tour* (Alta California, CA: James & Hook Books, 2016), stops 9, 16.

93. Salma Nasution Khoo, *The Chulia in Penang: Patronage and Place-Making around the Kapitan Kling Mosque 1786–1957* (Penang: Areca Books, 2014), 418–19, 426n7.

94. Kornitzer, *Pearl Trader*, 41–42, 77.

95. William G. Clarence-Smith, "The Economic Role of the Arab Community in Maluku, 1816 to 1940," *Indonesia and the Malay World* 26, no, 74 (1998): 32–49.; Clarence-Smith, "The Rise and Fall of Hadhrami Shipping in the Indian Ocean, c. 1750–c. 1940," in *Ships and the Development of Maritime Technology in the Indian Ocean*, ed. David Parkin and Ruth Barnes (London: RoutledgeCurzon, 2002), 227–58.

96. Hugo Merton, *Forschungsreise in den südöstlichen Molukken (Aru- und Kei-Inseln)* (Frankfurt am Main: Senckenbergischen Naturforschenden Gesellschaft, 1910), 13, 18; R. Broersma, "Land en volk in Molukken-Zuid," *Koloniaal Tijdschrift*, vols. 24 and 25 (1935–1936): 66; Des Alwi, *Friends and Exiles: A Memoir of the Nutmeg Isles and the Indonesian Nationalist Movement*, ed. Barbara S. Harvey (Ithaca, NY: Southeast Asia Program, Cornell University, 2008), 11–18. See also the chapter by Steve Mullins in this volume.

97. Kornitzer, *Pearl Trader*, 111–12.

98. Strack, *Pearls*, 492, 500; Akamatsu, *Pearl Book*, 93; Ericson, "Nature's Helper," 247–49.

99. Cariño and Monteforte, *Une histoire mondiale*, 219.

100. Gilberte Gautier, *La saga des Cartier, 1847–1988* (Paris: Michel Lafon, 1988), 174–75.

101. Pierre-Yves Toullelan, *Tahiti colonial, 1860–1914* (Paris: Publications de la Sorbonne, 1984), 101–3, 280–81; Claus Gossler, *Die Société Commerciale de l'Océanie (1876–1914): Aufstieg und Untergang der Hamburger Godeffroys in Ost-Polynesien* (Bremen: MontAurum, 2006), 70.

102. Kunz and Stevenson, *Book of the Pearl*, 250.

103. Kornitzer, *Pearl Trader*, 6, 14, 24; J. P. S. Bach, *The Pearling Industry of Australia: An Account of Its Social and Economic Development* (Canberra: Department of Commerce and Agriculture, 1955), 50–51.

104. Man-houng Lin, "Taiwanese Merchants, Overseas Chinese Merchants, and the Japanese Government in the Economic Relations between Taiwan and Japan, 1895–1945," in *The Chinese Overseas*, vol. 4, ed. Hong Liu (Abingdon, UK: Routledge, 2006), 263, 265; Stephen G. Bloom, *Tears of Mermaids: The Secret Story of Pearls* (New York: St. Martin's, 2009), 61; Ericson, "Nature's Helper," 261.

105. Choksy, "Iranians and Indians," 189; Goswami, *Globalization before Its Time*, 99; Rusheed Wadia emails June 12 and August 10, 2016 (citing Jamsetjee Jejeebhoy Letterbooks in Bombay).

106. Visit to Kobe Foreign Cemetery, December 28, 1988.

107. Cort, *Jains in the World*, 40.

108. Ericson, "Nature's Helper," 289–92.

109. Strack, *Pearls*, 462; Ericson, "Nature's Helper," 240–42, 248–51; Akamatsu, *Pearl Book*, 97.

110. Nadelhoffer, *Cartier*, 298n27; Yves Abel, comp., "Souvenirs de la Villa Léa et la famille Bienenfeld à Suresnes," *Bulletin de la Société Historique de Suresnes* 11, no. 51 (1997): 24–32; David Bellos, *Georges Perec: A Life in Words*, 3rd ed. (London: Harvill, 1999), 15, 18–21, 25.

111. al-Ibrahim, *Les relations koweito-françaises*, 15, 18–20.

112. "Léonard Rosenthal, roi de la perle et jardinier des gemmes," n.d., accessed March 14, 2016, http://histoire.villennes.free.fr/Pages/Extension44.htm.

113. Crouzet, *Genèses du Moyen-Orient*, 391.

114. Humphreys, *Great Pearl Robbery*; Kornitzer, *Trade Winds*, 2–3; Kornitzer, *Pearl Trader*, 135; Strack, *Pearls*, 293.

115. Kornitzer, *Pearl Trader*, 136.

116. Cariño and Monteforte, *Une histoire mondiale*, 215.

117. Nadelhoffer, *Cartier*; Gautier, *La saga des Cartier*; John Loring, *Tiffany Pearls* (New York: Abrams, 2006).

118. Goswami, *Globalization before Its Time*, 95–96.

119. al-Ibrahim, *Les relations koweito-françaises*, 26; Carter, *Sea of Pearls* 168; Crouzet, *Genèses du Moyen-Orient*, 388–89.

120. Field, *The Merchants*, 188; al-Shamlan, *Pearling in the Arabian Gulf*, 166; al-Ibrahim, *Les relations koweito-françaises*, 15–16. Possibly among them were Albert Habib, Jacob Sofer/Sufir, and Rehavia Moussaieff.

121. "Léonard Rosenthal."

122. Léonard Rosenthal, *Faisons fortune* (Paris: Payot, 1924), 98–103.

123. Cariño and Monteforte, *Une histoire mondiale*, 213; Carter, *Sea of Pearls*, 169; Crouzet, *Genèses du Moyen-Orient*, 389–91.

124. Carter, *Sea of Pearls*, 169.

125. al-Tajir, *Bahrain*, 124; Bose, *A Hundred Horizons*, 85–86, 89.

126. Miran, *Red Sea Citizens*, 73, 104–5.

127. Monfreid, *Les secrets*, 135–44, 201, 218, 224.

128. James Hornell, "The Pearl Fishery," in *Twentieth-Century Impressions of Ceylon: Its History, People, Commerce, Industries, and Resources*, ed. Arnold Wright (London: Lloyd's Greater Britain Publishing Co., 1907), 229.

129. Subrahmanyam, "Noble Harvest," 167–71.

130. Kornitzer, *Trade Winds*, 67–68, 77, 94–96, 141–47, 188.

131. Gossler, *Die Société Commerciale de l'Océanie*, 356–57.

132. Ericson, "Nature's Helper," 260–61.

133. Kobe Port Festival Association, *Kobe, the Premier Port of Japan, Illustrated* (Kobe: Kobe and Osaka Press, 1933), 7, 152.

134. "Léonard Rosenthal, roi de la perle"; Bellos, *Georges Perec*, 18.

135. Ericson, "Nature's Helper," 193n429, citing *La Perle* 2, no. 9 (1925): 2.

136. For the list, see *US Consular Reports 1896*, 1:632. See also Dennis Sasso, "A History of the Panama Jewish Community," *Indiana Jewish Post and Opinion*, July 14, 1978, 2, for Brandon and Piza; Grupo Calesa, "History," n.d., accessed August 17, 2017, http://grupocalesa.com/en/history, for Herbruger.

137. Cariño and Monteforte, *Une histoire mondiale*, 222–24.

138. Bach, *Pearling Industry of Australia*, 50–51.

139. Kornitzer, *Trade Winds*, 13, 20–22.

140. Robert Lehane, *The Pearl King* (Brisbane, Australia: Boolarong, 2014), 281–83, 312.

141. al-Ibrahim, *Les relations koweito-françaises*, 13–14, 21.

142. al-Shamlan, *Pearling in the Arabian Gulf*, 169–72; Carter, *Sea of Pearls*, 169; al-Ibrahim, *Les relations koweito-françaises*, 22.

143. al-Shamlan, *Pearling in the Arabian Gulf*, 168–69.

144. Field, *The Merchants*, 184.

145. al-Shamlan, *Pearling in the Arabian Gulf*, 164–69.

146. Field, *The Merchants*, 24, 184; al-Shamlan, *Pearling in the Arabian Gulf*, 171.

147. al-Shamlan, *Pearling in the Arabian Gulf*, 164.

148. Bose, *A Hundred Horizons*, 86.

149. Albert Londres, *Pêcheurs de perles* (Paris: Albin Michel, 1931), 214.

150. Field, *The Merchants*, 24, 188; Bellos, *Georges Perec*, 25–26.

151. Miran, *Red Sea Citizens*, 134–35.

152. R. Broersma, "Koopvaardij in de Molukken," *Koloniaal Tijdschrift* 23 (1934): 325.

153. Willard A. Hanna, *Indonesian Banda: Colonialism and Its Aftermath in the Nutmeg Islands* (Philadelphia: Institute for the Study of Human Issues, 1978), 125; Alwi, *Friends and Exiles*, 13; Julia Martínez and Adrian Vickers, *The Pearl Frontier: Indonesian Labor and Indigenous Encounters in Australia's Northern Trading Network* (Honolulu: University of Hawai'i Press, 2015), 59.

154. Goswami, *Globalization before Its Time*, 101.

155. Kornitzer, *Pearl Trader*, 136, 148–49.

156. Strack, *Pearls*, 233–34.

157. Gira Shroff Gratier, "A Shroff Family: From Indigenous Bankers to Cosmopolitans," in *Cooperation and Competition, Conflict and Contribution: The Jain Community, Colonialism, and Jainological Scholarship, 1800–1950*, ed. Andrea Luithle-Hardenberg, John E. Cort, and Leslie C. Orr (Berlin: EB-Verlag, forthcoming). My thanks to the author for letting me see this.

158. Cariño and Monteforte, *Une histoire mondiale*, 232n79, spelling the name as Preichand-Raichand. For the family, see Sharada Dwivedi, *Premchand Roychand, 1831–1906: His Life and Times* (Bombay: Eminence Designs, 2006).

159. al-Shamlan, *Pearling in the Arabian Gulf*, 166, 169, 172–75.

160. Eunson, *Pearl King*, 154–7, 170, 176–77; Ericson, "Nature's Helper," 148–72, 195–97, 288–98, 305, 310.

161. See the chapter by Pedro Machado in this volume for the importance of local and regional economies within the Indian Ocean for the trade in pearl shell.

TWO

Tea, Pearls, and Pearl Shell
Cross-Cultural Trade, Slave Raiding, and the Transformation of Material Worlds—The Sulu Zone, China, and the West, 1349–1898

JAMES FRANCIS WARREN

THIS CHAPTER utilizes a commodity-based history approach to investigate global trade, a system of bondage and dependency and patterns of consumption and desire at a specific moment in regional time and a specific place—the Sulu Zone. I trace the connections that various peoples and the production, circulation, and consumption of particular commodities had with one another within the confines of the Sulu Zone, and beyond. The interconnectedness of pearls and pearl shell, on the one hand, and, on the other, tea, opium, wine, chocolate, textiles, ceramic, and firearms both illustrates and signifies how the structure and function of money, markets, and cross-cultural trade, and a repertoire of practices in contemporary life, were determined by their negotiation within a borderless world in an age of empire.

THE SULU ZONE

In the eighteenth century, the Sulu archipelago bridged two worlds and lay at a most strategic point for the maritime trade of the nineteenth century. China, the Philippines, and Mindanao were situated to the north, Borneo to the southwest, and, to the southeast, the Celebes and Moluccas. At the end of the eighteenth century, the emergence of Jolo, the capital of the Sulu Sultanate, as the focal point of a broad system of trade and a center for the marketing of slaves, outfitting of marauders, and defiance of Spanish incursion was in large measure attributable to its location astride the arterial trade routes near the center of the Eastern Seas. The geopolitical and commercial advantages inherent in the Sultanate's location were both enviable and unique.[1]

In contemporary ethnohistorical studies of Southeast Asia, the "zone" and/or "border" have become chosen metaphors for theorizing the historically complex and contradictory ways in which cultural difference and ethnic diversity have been articulated in social relations and in political and economic practice across time. My emphasis here is on a "zone" created through the intersections of geography, culture, and history centered around the Sulu and Celebes seas, as well as China's and the West's complicated role within it.[2] The Sulu Zone constituted a Southeast Asian economic region with a multiethnic precolonial Malayo-Muslim state, and an ethnically heterogeneous set of societies of diverse political backgrounds and alignments that included tribal swidden agriculturalists, maritime nomadic fishers and forest-dwelling hunter-gatherers. A basic interpretation of the history of pearls and pearl shell in the Sulu Sultanate, the heart of the Zone, must focus, then, on the decisive importance of maritime peoples and the slave in the functioning of Sulu's economy and society.[3]

MOMENT IN REGIONAL TIME

I now want to speak briefly about "regional time." The creation of a "zone," whose evolution and development occurred with the spread of commodities, technology, ideas, and practices of the world capitalist economy and western imperialism, is demarcated by both space and time, which signify two halves of the same historical process. The Sulu Zone as a regional "spatial" system and social order, like the economy it represented, was not atemporal. My framing and interpretation of the "zone" as a spatial system rests on the axiom that it was "inherently unstable and generally dynamic." And, that it was thrust on to the global stage at a specific moment in "regional time." Edmund Leach's classic work on state and community structures in highland Burma traced the pattern of the shifting balance between two representations of political order and social phenomena over 150 years.[4] Similarly, the Sulu "Zone" was also "a process in time": a recognition that all ethnic groups and communities were being shaped and changed by the interplay between internal social and cultural forms and external courses of action. In a sense, the peoples of the "zone" were "products" of large-scale processes of global socioeconomic change that made them what they were and would continue to make them what they would become in response to the uncontrollable and rapid impact of these forces.[5]

Fernand Braudel's time of "geohistory," "a history of constant repetition, ever-recurring cycles," was essential for the creation of the regional "space" or "zone," but it was the second time, *l'histoire conjoncturelle*, which is relevant here, concerned as it was with historical changes to economic, political, and social structures.[6] For example, the economic, social, and environmental ramifications of Sulu and China's inextricable involvement in a dynamic global-regional economy was a harbinger of the momentous changes beginning to occur in Eastern Asia between 1768 and 1848. With explosive speed, Europeans spread out to trade and colonize various regions and states of Southeast Asia. When English traders and explorers like Alexander Dalrymple, James Rennell, Thomas Forrest, and others first came to Sulu in the 1760s, they recognized that the "zone" was a potentially valuable source of natural commodities like pearls and pearl shell for trade on the Chinese market. They soon learned that Taosug *datus* (chiefs) and other leading inhabitants of the Zone would exchange these marine products for manufactured industrial goods. Eager to obtain these natural resources from this virtually undiscovered area, European merchants extended their international trade network and knowledge of the world to the Sulu Zone after 1768.

The speed of historical change is important here. The reverberations from the shock waves of Braudel's time of "economic systems and states" caused by events on the southeast coast of China, due to the intersections of the world capitalist economy, were felt early in the Sulu

Zone. It was an insatiable demand for tea that initiated European, but especially British, interest in the Sulu Zone's pearl banks. During the eighteenth century, tea replaced ale as the national beverage in England and was particularly popular among the poorer classes. China was the major supplier of tea to England. The incessant demand for tea opened China to a wider regional trade involving both the Indian subcontinent and Southeast Asia. Asian, European, and American merchants based in Calcutta and, later, Manila, Macao, and Salem, were unable to deliver suitable commodities for the burgeoning Canton market. However, these merchants were quick to recognize the potential of participation in the established Sino-Sulu trade as a means of redressing the flow of silver from the West. Pearls and pearl shell, highly valued in China and the West, were needed to stem it.[7]

The commercial interests of the English East India Company and private country traders in India provided the initial catalyst for the transformation of Sulu in the late eighteenth century. It was from the trade in tea with China that the Company derived the bulk of its profits. English commodities did not sell in China, and the drain of silver to purchase the Chinese tea threatened financial ruin for the Company administration. This predicament drove officials and merchants in Calcutta and Europe to look at the islands of Southeast Asia as a vast new market for English manufactures and India's trade commodities, especially opium and piece goods, in exchange for natural commodities like pearl and pearl shell.[8]

The establishment of European and Asian commerce at Sulu in the late eighteenth century on a hitherto unprecedented scale caused dramatic increases in commodity production and the demand for labor. Slave and dependent labor in the pearl fisheries provided the commodities introduced into the international trade circuits. Power was predicated on personal following. The competitive activities of ambitious datus now forced the demand for additional labor up and swelled the flow of international trade.[9]

Critical regional transitions began with Britain's involvement in the intra-Asian trade. British merchants in search of wealth bartered arms, textiles, opium, and specie for an enormous variety of natural commodities, but especially pearls and pearl shell, to redress the economic imbalance and drain of their China trade. As British naval power increased in the late eighteenth century, trading settlements and outposts in Southeast Asia developed rapidly and, in places like Penang and Balambangan, the search for profitable commodities for the China trade began in earnest. This quest for pearls and pearl shell was to have a profound impact upon the various peoples of the Zone and their ways of life, as well as the rest of the eastern archipelago, constituting one of the most fascinating episodes in the history of China's tea trade and the world capitalist economy.[10] The Sulu Sultanate's ascendancy toward the end of the eighteenth century developed out of global economic interconnections and interdependencies of the world capitalist economy between British India, Southeast Asia, and China. Equally significant, commercial and tributary activity became directly linked with long-distance maritime slave raiding and the incorporation of captured people in a redistributive economic system that made Jolo the principal entrepôt for the large-scale delivery of pearls and pearl shell for the China tea trade.[11]

COMMODITY-BASED HISTORY APPROACH

The commodity-chain methodology is linked to approaches variously called commodity systems, commodity circuits, commodity networks, value chains, and production networks, to which the word global is often attached. The Sulu Zone project is concerned with commodity chains due to the social embeddedness of pearls and pearl shell, and their procurement, production, distribution, and consumption, forming trajectories and circulations that transcended national borders where the globalizing processes of the modern world system were influential.[12] Tea, gunpowder, weapons, opium, and textiles were some key trade items that closed this commodity chain.[13]

Inspired by the work of Arjun Appadurai and Igor Kopytoff on the social and cultural biographies of "things," my intent is to investigate particular commodities—pearls and pearl shell—as if they "are like persons; they have social lives and move in and out of different regimes of value in discrete space and time. The 'total trajectory' of commodities—that is, from the course of their production, through their exchange and distribution, to their eventual consumption—involves different stages, and is enmeshed in complex intersections of economic, political, and cultural factors."[14] In other words, it is important to look at the complete life cycle of these commodities when possible to do so.

Jean Comaroff and John Comaroff note in their discussion of the "history" of a commodity and its impact on social and cultural life that, from the analysis of the journey or "biography" of valued everyday objects and goods, we can comprehend the nature and evolution of complex social processes and individual intention and action.[15] Ideas about fashion, work, property, value, class, and authority all changed and were transformed by the relationship between specific commodities like pearls and pearl shell and economic and political events and developments in the Zone, China, and the West.[16] Considerable work based on the commodity-history model has been done for the Atlantic world by Sidney Mintz and Elizabeth Abbott on sugar, Mark Pendergrast on coffee, Giorgio Riello on cotton, and Mark Kurlansky on cod and salt, as well as the University of Warwick's project on global commodities after 1400, which includes ceramics.[17] However, except for my earlier work on the Sulu Zone, Matthew Hopper's work on the Persian Gulf pearl fishery, and Steve Mullins's work on the Torres Strait, there has been relatively little work done on pearls and pearl shell for the Indian Ocean world.[18]

The commodity-based history approach is significant because it links the worlds of the Sulu Zone, China, and the West, due to its geographical scope and temporal span from the fourteenth century onwards, posing important questions about the nature of the transitions and transformations in the Sulu Zone and its emerging global character and integration within the modern world system. Important research material can be pulled together and chronologically ordered on these circulations and the farther ends of the pearl and pearl shell commodity chains across this increasingly integrated economic landscape and world. From the fourteenth century onwards the Chinese and subsequent European arrivals begin to provide a consistent comparable picture, one which provides a rich source of data on pearls and pearl shell—precious commodities—that were present in various areas of the Sulu Zone.

A fundamental principle of this commodity-based history approach is that it does not allow the boundaries of contemporary nation-states to shape the way I frame or study the complexity and diversity of the Sulu Zone. Instead, the kinship and trade connections of various peoples and the production, circulation, and consumption of these entangled commodities must be linked and mapped out across the oceans and seas of the globe. Such an approach offers a local historical perspective toward a reframing of the insular and nationalist perspectives of Indonesian, Malaysian, and Philippine historiography. Consequently, I utilize the concept of the Zone and a commodity-based history approach as a methodological way of exploring larger-scale systemic processes of socioeconomic change linking the Sulu Zone with a borderless history of a broad-ranging maritime trading network oriented toward China, Singapore, Europe, and the United States.

This commodity-history orientation ties in perfectly with an object-centered biographical approach, which serves to link the disciplines of history, ethnography, and archeology. In the overall context of this chapter, the object-centered biographical approach, which foregrounds pearls and pearl shell, is a fundamental organizing method and way to think about linking the history of the Sulu Zone, China, and the West over the centuries. This approach advocates a material culture orientation, in order to tell us something about the regional peoples that procured pearls and pearl shell and the individuals and cultures who desired and consumed them, especially at the further ends of the commodity chain. This globalized history explored through objects can reveal a separate but related story that complements the narrative history written largely through documents and the use of ethnographic data. The entwined approaches argue for thinking and speaking about how pearl and pearl-shell-related things have historically underpinned various people's economies, and shaped their sense of identity, cultures, and landscapes.

THE MARINE GARDENS: THE CULTURAL-ECOLOGICAL SETTING

The sea played a major role in the Sulu Sultanate's commodities trade. The Taosug drew heavily upon the resources of the Zone's fisheries for classes of commodities most sought after in China and the West, especially pearls and mother-of-pearl shell. The task of diving for pearls and pearl shell, of immense importance to the Taosug aristocrats, fell to their retainers, slaves, and the "sea people" or Samal Bajau Laut.[19] Indeed, the pearl fisheries were the hub of community life for the majority of Sulu Samal, and the procurement of pearls and pearl shell was their main subsistence task.

The pearling grounds of the Sulu Zone are located in the area between the southern and western boundaries of the Philippines and the northeast coast of Borneo. The Sulu archipelago comprises three groups of islands generally of volcanic or coral formation, surrounded by waters

Figure 2.1. The Samal Bajau Laut, maritime nomadic boat-dwelling fishers of the Sulu Zone. Photograph by author, taken near Dinawan Island, northeast coast of Sabah, Malaysia, May 1968.

of diveable depth. These groups are Sulu, Tapul, and Tawi-Tawi. They comprise 140 islands, many large enough to be of geographical importance, and are scattered over a sea surface of 173 miles (282 kilometers) long by from 30 to 75 miles (48 to 120 kilometers) wide. The Tapul group was early noted for the quantity and excellence of its mother-of-pearl output. One of its islands, Siassi, was the most productive shell island in the archipelago.[20] In the inter-island waters of the Sulu Sea the depths seldom exceed 60 feet (18 meters), and average about half that depth. There were few pearl shell beds in Sulu waters beyond 54 feet (16.5 meters) in depth. This meant comparatively shallow waters for the industry that linked China to the West. Expert testimony from the eighteenth and nineteenth centuries revealed that the pearl and pearl-shell fishery of the Sulu Zone, both in quality of product and potential for development, compared extremely well with the ancient grounds of Ceylon and the Persian Gulf, as well as the grounds of northwestern Australia and the Torres Strait discovered in the second half of the nineteenth century.

Sulu's pearl fisheries were renowned in Asia for centuries. Chinese records as early as 1349 mention the pearls found in the "marine gardens" of the Sulu archipelago as important objects of trade.[21] Alexander Dalrymple's 1760s account of Taosug trade and society provides a detailed overview of Sulu's pearl fisheries. The East India Company agent was amazed by the richness and extent of its pearl banks—in places over 25-miles (40 kilometers) wide. Numerous pearling sites in the Laparan, Pangutaran, and Pilas groups were recorded by him, in addition to the pearl beds near Balabac and Maratua. Dalrymple noted that the southern shoals and reefs in the environs of Tawi-Tawi "were extremely intricate and narrow," but invaluable to the trade of the Sultanate linked to China. He wrote, "These guts [the intricate and narrow channels] are the most valuable pearl fishery in the world," and they attracted countless Taosug- and Samal-speaking people, their kindred and slaves.[22]

Sultan Bantilan (Muizz un-Din) furnished Dalrymple with a list of thirty-seven products of Sulu and its immediate dependencies that English country traders could purchase at Jolo. Among the more important items from the sea, which were in constant demand in China, were "pearls, mother-of-pearl, *tripang*, tortoise shell, and shark's fin."[23] For country traders these commodities were to remain stock-in-trade items in their traffic between Sulu and Canton. This search for pearls and pearl shell, so highly desired in China and the West, was to have a profound impact upon various peoples of the Zone and their traditional way of life, as well as upon vast stretches of coastal Southeast Asia, constituting one of the most dramatic episodes in the history of the region's integration into the world capitalist economy.[24]

In 1883, another Englishman, Edwin Streeter of Bond Street, a London-based Victorian jeweler and a leading authority on pearling, also recognized that the waters of the Sulu Zone comprised one of the most valuable pearl fisheries in the world. He wrote that "the islands constituting the 'Sooloo Archipelago' . . . [produce] the greater number of the finest round Pearls" to commerce.[25] An official turn-of-the-century American report compiled by Major O. J. Sweet stated, "The pearl fishing is very important in this [Sulu] Archipelago, not so much on account of the great number and value of the pearls but for the great abundance and large production of mother-of-pearl shell which supplies the markets of Singapore and Manila."[26]

However, the pearls that lay at the bottom of the sea in the Sulu Zone were early discovered by the Chinese to be more beautiful than those found in the Persian Gulf. The Sulu waters produced the finest type of the *Maleagrina margaritifera*, the very best of the pearl-bearing molluscs. The translucent shell of this oyster, known as *selisip*, was also ground up as powder for use in Chinese pharmacopoeia.[27]

The pearling grounds of the Zone brought early fame to the islands of the Sulu archipelago. Jolo became the center for this pearl trade with China, which increased at the end of the eighteenth century with European ships passing through the Zone in search of pearls and pearl shell on their way to trade with China.[28]

LABOR AND THE FINDING OF PEARLS AND SHELL

Thousands of pairs of shells could be opened without finding a single valuable pearl. Most molluscs secrete mother-of-pearl, but few yield pearls. But the best and most reliable bearer of both was found in the waters of the Sulu Zone. The experience of Sulu pearl fishers showed that shells of irregular shape, stunted in growth, and bearing excrescences and honeycombed with boring parasites were most likely to yield pearls. But they also believed a perfectly healthy oyster might contain a pearl of great price. Some oysters could contain a dozen pearls, some more, some just one, and hundreds none at all. The pearls yielded by the *Maleagrina margaritifera* were often large and if black were considered to be very rare. Sultan Badar ud-Din I, who reigned from 1718 to 1732, was reputed to have received a shell containing twelve pearls.[29]

The Samal, strand dwellers with close ties to the sea, who possessed well-developed boatbuilding skills and sometimes practiced simple garden agriculture, were the most widely dispersed of all ethnolinguistic groups in the Sulu Zone.[30] Manifesting the greatest degree of internal linguistic and cultural differentiation, Samal communities predominated on the coralline island clusters of the northern and southern parts of the Sulu archipelago, as well as on the coasts of north Borneo and Celebes. The Samal distinguished among themselves by dialect, locality, and cultural-ecological factors (principally between sedentary Muslim shore-dwellers and nomadic animistic boat-dwellers).[31]

Samals tended to identify themselves with a particular island, island cluster, or regional orbit. In the late eighteenth and early nineteenth centuries, they comprised a number of groups who occupied noncontiguous territories along the south Mindanao shore, on the south coast and in the near interior of Basilan, and on the islands of the Tapian Tana group, Cagayan de Sulu, and the Balangingi cluster. Expert voyagers at sea, particular groups had fixed bases of operation on a series of low coral-and-sand islands flanking the northeastern side of Jolo. This group of islands, named Los Samales by the Spanish, was a springboard for launching seasonal raids against coastal villages from Luzon to Celebes. The most important island was Balangingi, dwelling place and organizational center of a major slaving group of the Sulu Sultanate in the first half of the nineteenth century.[32]

In the Sulu archipelago, pearling activity involving Samal boat people and slaves was seasonal—stipulated by the rhythm of the semiannual monsoon. There were two collecting periods: the first began with the end of "dirty" weather at the close of the southwest monsoon and lasted from the middle of September to the middle of December, when the sea was frequently calm; the second covered February to May. But at Tawi-Tawi, where the surrounding sandy islands, shoals, and reefs created an inland sea, pearl fishing was a year-round pursuit.[33]

Divers were called *panglooroorak* or *tan maksak*; the art of diving, *maklurop*; the pearl, *muchia*; and pearl shell, *tipie*.[34] Diving trips, entailing hundreds of small *vinta* (sailing craft) and lasting several months at a time, were organized by Taosug datus and their kindred. In 1880, a Spanish naval officer noted the size of these groups employed in Jolo's mother-of-pearl fisheries: "In order to collect mother-of-pearl shell, they [the Taosug] assemble innumerable expeditions which are often led by a datu (I guarded one [expedition] of 2,200 fishermen and 3 datus)."[35] Customarily, the crew of a vinta numbered up to ten.

The greatest depth at which Samal Bajau retainers and slave divers could work was 25 fathoms (150 feet or 46 meters). The pressure of the water was so great at that depth that such activity could not be sustained for more than five minutes, after which the diver had to return to the surface for rest and recuperation, requiring at least 30–45 minutes for this purpose. Because of the obvious danger and limited results at this great depth, the shell beds most sought after and exploited were from 15 to 20 fathoms (120 to 160 feet or 27.5 to 36.5 meters) deep. At this depth, pearling work could be conducted for up to an hour without rest, with only 15 to 20 minutes above water necessary to restore the divers for further work.[36] On a rich pearling ground, for example in the waters and reefs around Siassi Island, a diver could procure enough shell in five or six dives to support a family for a month.[37]

Pearl diving was difficult and dangerous work. Occupational hazards included sight impairment, as "even professed divers have, after diving, their eyes much inflamed; in some this goes off, but in others it always remains," and injury and death from the large sharks and giant stingrays that infested the Sulu Sea.[38] The reluctance of the Samal Bajau Laut to exploit some of Sulu's richest pearl banks stemmed from their dread of sharks. In 1812, J. Hunt, an East India Company agent, wrote of the Sangboy Islands.

> The tepoy (mother-of-pearl shell) is of remarkably large size. There are also pearls of a large size and extremely valuable, but from want of Bajows, the depth of water and innumerable sharks and sea monsters, the fishery is not carried to that extent its importance would warrant.[39]

The diver took a knife with him on his descent, with which he dislodged the shells, and a basket, in which he gathered them and sent them up to the boat.

Edwin W. Streeter, in *Pearls and Pearling Life*, described the prowess of the Samalan-speaking divers of the Sulu Zone in the 1880s as follows:

> The Sooloo and Tawi-Tawi men are principally divers, those from the town of Parang and the little island of Secubun, especially attaining great depths.... The average time they remain below the surface is from a minute to eighty seconds.... On one occasion a dive lasted... two and a half minutes. The greatest depths [sic] that Mr. Haynes has seen accomplished is seventeen and a half fathoms (105 feet) and the same man did fifteen and a half fathoms in the presence of the captain and officers of H.M.S. "*Champion*."... But there is little doubt that there are divers in Sooloo who can do their twenty fathoms and even more.[40]

By then, they were arguably the most expert divers in the world engaged in pearl-shell fishing.[41]

In the nineteenth century, the *palit*, a bamboo dredge, was used by some divers to minimize the risks involved in collecting mother-of-pearl.[42] This rake-like instrument, which was weighted with a stone, was employed extensively by the Taosug, who "do not practice diving at all . . . and only comprehend the slow method of dredging for the tipy, with a thing like the fluke of a wooden anchor."[43]

The Sultan and datus claimed any pearl of value. In return for a large pearl a slave diver was entitled to his freedom, and they rarely delivered any to their masters without some form of compensation.[44] Forrest noted that if a diver attempted to defraud his master and sold a pearl of great worth to the Chinese traders, he received more, but never its full value.[45] All pearls under a pennyweight belonged to the divers, and to evade the customary rights of their datus, the *panglooroorak* "frequently rub off the outer coats of the pearl, till they reduce them to the size to which they are entitled."[46]

It can be roughly estimated from trade statistics that some forty-eight thousand fishers (men) were engaged in diving for pearls and mother-of-pearl by hundreds of Taosug datus and Samal headmen during the 1830s.[47] But, by the first quarter of the nineteenth century, the finding of pearls was already becoming less important than the development of the mother-of-pearl industry. However, single pearls were valued up to 25,000 pesos, and the overall value of pearls sold to European buyers alone still amounted to one million pesos in the early twentieth century.[48]

RELATIONS OF PRODUCTION: SLAVERY
The Boat People

The Samal Bajau Laut were distinguished as pariahs from the larger sedentary population under the Sulu Sultanate, by their boat-dwelling way of life, animistic beliefs, and certain physical features which directly derived from their unique lifestyle. Scattered in small flotillas throughout the Sulu archipelago and along the Celebes rim, they were often found near the strand, in inlets, and on the sea among the reefs close to Taosug and Samal communities.[49]

Sea nomadism, an age-old ecological adaptation, which characterized the Samal Bajau Laut as a people and from which they derived their sense of identity, tended to inhibit the development of cohesive kinship groups. The nuclear family was the only kinship unit recognized by these nomadic fishers. Each boat household comprised a family. These families formed temporary alliances when residing at traditional mooring sites. A *panglima*, generally an older man, assumed a nominal degree of authority over the boat clusters or "family alliance units" within the moorage only when an arbiter was required.[50]

Scorned by land-dwelling Taosug and Samal and considered physically and socially repugnant, their pariah status was signified by the pejorative terms *luwaan* and *pala'u* and denigrating etiological myths.[51] The Samal Bajau Laut possessed neither a territorial base nor the political structures necessary to weld localized kindred groups into viable political communities. Landless and destitute, these nomadic fishers were dependent on Taosug and strand-dwelling Samal for their security and meager material circumstance. However, reliance on flight, or the capacity to shift their allegiance and services to another political overlord in the face of unreasonable authority, prevented their absolute subordination and distinguished them from slaves.[52] These maritime nomadic fishers had limited scope for interaction with the majority of Sulu's population and played only a marginal role in the daily life of the Zone. But, as expert fishers and gatherers of marine commodities, they performed an indispensable service to the sultanate. Among the very best pearl divers, they were mobilized as clients of coastal Taosug and Samal to procure pearls and mother-of-pearl for Sulu's overseas markets.[53]

While most sedentary Samal speakers procured mother-of-pearl shell, *trepang*, tortoise shell, and agar-agar, the collection of pearls demanded the exceptional diving skills of the Samal Bajau boat-dwellers and trained slaves. They spent their lives afloat in their vintas and *lipa-lipa*, and, as expert divers and fishers, exchanged their pearls and shell with Jolo's aristocrats for rice, Chinese earthenware, and coarse cotton cloth from China and India.[54] The majority of these Samal Bajau boat people were the direct subjects of the Sultan of Sulu and his kindred.[55]

Banyaga

But who else, beside the Samal Bajau Laut, collected the pearls and mother-of-pearl shell traded at Jolo? A major argument of this chapter is that the economy of Sulu's rich pearling grounds depended on the labor of people, captured by Iranun and Balangingi saltwater raiders, who were put to work in the Zone as *banyaga*, or slaves. As John Butcher notes, "In short, the people collecting tripang, pearl shell, and other products in various parts of the Sulu Zone were part of a larger economic system along with the Sultan and his chiefs, slave raiders, powerful merchants in London and India, country traders, and consumers of opium and fine food in China."[56] Consequently, slaves and nomadic fishers, on the one hand, and cross-cultural traders, mariners, and court consumers, on the other, were linked together by product and fate with regional-global practices of predation, production, and consumption.

In the late eighteenth and nineteenth centuries, the population of Sulu was heterogeneous and changing—socially, economically, and ethnically. This was a direct result of the Sultanate's external trade with China and the West. The populating of the Sulu Zone by banyaga from the Philippines and various parts of the Malay world and their role in the redistributional economy centered upon Jolo cannot be underestimated. At the bottom of the Sulu hierarchy were the banyaga. However, the testimonies of fugitive slaves and historical accounts leave no doubt that slavery was the essential element determining the economic, military, and social patterns of the Sulu state. In large measure it was the banyaga who held the social fabric of Taosug society, as well as the political economy of the pearling grounds, together.[57]

Slaveholding was the primary form of investment for the Taosug. As a form of wealth, slaves were a tangible asset in readily transferable form. They played a major role in the economy both as a unit of production and as a medium of exchange. The accumulation of wealth and the transmission of power and privilege in Taosug society was facilitated by the ownership of slaves. This was even more the case after the external trade in pearls and mother-of-pearl intensified with China and the West in the latter part of the eighteenth century.[58]

It is important here to emphasize again the crucial role of slave production in the evolution of this trade-process, commodity-driven system involving the circulation of pearls and mother-of-pearl shell. The relationship between external trade and slavery in Sulu was reciprocal. Power depended on control of persons (slaves and retainers), which in turn depended on disposable wealth to maintain and attract them. Escalating competition for wealth and status further fuelled the demand for labor power (more slaves and retainers) to procure commodities like pearls and pearl shell so highly desired in China.[59]

The need for a reliable supply of manpower was met by the Iranun and Balangingi slave raiders. They annually captured thousands of people to be trained to work alongside the Samal Bajau Laut in the pearl fisheries.[60] More than anything else, it was this source and use of labor power that gave Sulu its distinctive predatory character in the eyes of Europeans in the nineteenth century as a "pirate and slave state."[61]

The Sulu archipelago now witnessed the appearance of Iranun communities that specialized in slave-raiding. These Iranun settled on the north and east coasts of Jolo and on Basilan and established client relationships with Taosug. The terror associated with the sudden harsh presence of these well-armed raiders live on in the oral recollections, reminiscences, popular folk epics, and drama of the victims' descendants in the Philippines, Indonesia, and Malaysia to this day.[62] To the Europeans of the late eighteenth and nineteenth centuries, the Iranun and Balangingi were like the spawn from hell.[63]

ENTANGLED COMMODITIES: THE NATURE OF THE TRADE OVER TIME

A fundamental principle of this chapter about pearls and pearl shell is that historians must not allow the boundaries of contemporary nation-states to shape the way they view the past. Instead, they must map out the actual connections people had with one another and the circulations of material objects. Thus, nomadic fishers and slaves, on the one hand, and merchants, sailors, and court consumers, on the other, are linked together with practices of depredation, production, and consumption, and with commodities such as pearls, pearl shell, tea, opium, firearms, ceramics, and textiles.[64]

Jolo was the site of repeated complex cultural exchanges linked to the China tea trade that highlighted the ways cultural difference and diversity were increasingly blurred. From documents, journals, and illustrations left by traders and travelers we can learn about how particular commodities, such as pearls and pearl shell and opium, tea, and guns bridged two worlds and changed people's cultural attitudes and practices toward daily life. My emphasis here, as we follow various commodities and trade objects with their readily defined characteristics as "modern," with their singular "magicalities and enchantments," from China, Europe, and India to the Sulu Zone, is on the complicated role they played in the modern world system, creating and breaking down the "borders" of cultures across Asia—cultures usually regarded as noncapitalist and "traditional."[65]

By the beginning of the nineteenth century, the Jolo market offered British manufactured brassware, glassware, Chinese earthenware and ceramic, fine muslins, silk and satin garments, Spanish tobacco and wines, and opium from India. There was a constant increase not only in the variety but in the quality of these trade commodities. Luxury goods for personal adornment and pleasure and for the household were translated into power and prestige symbols by the aristocracy to form the material basis of their social superiority.

Let me close this discussion about the history of the China tea trade, material culture, and cultural transformation by tracing the journey, albeit briefly, of two commodities—a pearl and a steel knife—between the worlds of the Sulu Zone and Europe. The journey of the pearl began in the late 1700s; at the bottom of a reef, an expert Samal Bajau diver collected it for shipment back to Europe. The pearl was exchanged for a steel knife manufactured in Sheffield by a master smith.[66] The Sulu pearl was sent across the globe to a London jeweler—a priceless commodity of the China tea trade—to be placed in an exquisite necklace or ring that would become a symbol of royal authority and the European class system.

The Sheffield knife brought by an English country trader to Jolo did not at once change the Taosug and Samal's life, as, for example, opium would do in the nineteenth century. Instead, as a local object in the expert hands of boat builders and sea raiders, this steel blade improved both their artisan skills and fighting methods. Things alien to their way of life and of little practical value were rarely exchanged or bought. The handcrafted, dependable steel knife represented the highest-quality merchandise that Sheffield technology could manufacture. There was prestige involved in owning such a tool and/or weapon and its use became habit-forming. However, the knife now served different needs than either the English manufacturer or Bengal country trader envisaged. The knife now became a Taosug or Samal, not European, weapon used on maritime slave raids, one of many new trade commodities that were responsible for the expansion of Taosug power and culture throughout the region. In this context, the Sheffield knife and the pearl necklace or ring became strikingly ironic, albeit oppressive, symbols both of the material ties between two worlds and of the market-driven forces of the world-capitalist economy responsible for their creation and circulation.[67]

The mingled commodities served not only as motors of change but as realized signs, signifying that two or more worlds had met. This encounter between commodities and peoples highlighted in various ways the interconnectedness of the modern world. These commodities led to a continuous redefinition of belonging to a place as either "here" or "there" and of markers of social identity, status, and power. Lives and cultures blended wherever such commodities changed hands in the Zone. The Sultanate's trade in pearls and pearl shell had started in the seas and along the coasts of the Sulu Zone when the Chinese, Europeans, and Taosug found that each had key items of global commerce the other desired. The Sulu and Samal wanted European firearms, knives, and kettles and Chinese silk and cotton textiles and ceramics. The Chinese and Europeans valued the Zone's marine commodities, especially pearls and pearl shell. They traded, and both parties frequently thought they were getting a bargain. But their worlds and lives had been altered in the process, sometimes irrevocably so. After 1768, the consequence of "globalization," accelerated by the world capitalist economy, and the opening of China was that areas, encompassing remote maritime villages and tribal longhouses in the Zone to entire continents, were "caught up in processes which linked them to events that, though geographically distant, [were] culturally, economically, politically, strategically, and ecologically quite near [and] the distinction between 'here' and 'there' [broke] down."[68]

DEMISE OF THE TRADE

The Chinese of the Sulu Sultanate, despite their earlier disadvantage as resident traders, exercised a profound influence on events between 1870 and 1898. The Taosug's loss over the redistributive trade of the Sulu Zone to the Chinese was not a gradual process; rather, it was the sudden consequence of a combination of factors: the Spanish cruising system and naval blockade, and large-scale immigration of Chinese from the Straits Settlements. The Sultanate's political autonomy and economy after 1870 increasingly depended upon the loyalty and trade of its Chinese inhabitants.[69]

The Straits Chinese paid the Sultan for the right to procure pearls and pearl shell in this crucial period of transition and transformation at the end of the nineteenth century. Pearling agreements with the Sultan were authorized and signed under the auspices of the Spanish authorities. They gave the Chinese the exclusive rights to fish the pearling grounds of the Zone.

Despite the Spanish blockade, the Straits Chinese were able to establish a wide range of trade contacts that linked Singapore and Jolo with Zamboanga, the interior of Mindanao, and the outer islands of the Sulu archipelago. Prior to 1870, Jolo's Chinese traders had visited Singapore and Labuan every year and occasionally chartered schooners for trading ventures between Singapore and Sulu.[70] Once the Spanish began the calculated destruction of Sulu shipping in the 1870s, Chinese merchants freighted their goods from Singapore on European-owned vessels through family and business associates, while continuing to operate their sailing *prahus* between certain parts of the archipelago. In this manner they came to occupy the pivotal redistributive position in the trade of the Sulu Zone.[71]

> The trend was to continue. Shortly before the American invasion of the Philippines in 1898, the Chinese had come to control the trade between northeast Borneo, the Sulu archipelago, and Mindanao, and were spread over the pearling grounds of the Zone. By the end of the Spanish period, Najeeb Saleeby observed the dramatic transfer of economic power that had taken place: "Chinese merchants have complete control of the trade of the Sulu Archipelago. They are found everywhere and command all the avenues of commerce. The Sulus [Taosug] have abandoned commerce as a trade and apparently have no inclination to resume it on any large scale. This is due mainly to the decline of their power and the present abeyance of their national life."[72]

THE COMMODITY-BASED historical approach enables the investigation of various systems of labor allocation, production, exchange networks, and circulations on a transhistorical and transcultural basis, both within the Sulu Zone and beyond its borders, in changing patterns that reflect trajectories of consumption, tastes, and desires within the world of the Zone and beyond. As Heather Sunderland notes, the advantage of a commodity-chain approach is that it "places relationships within an explicitly commercial context, in which a complementary search for profit transcends divisions between political entities and ethnic groups."[73]

After 1768, the forces of the global capitalist economy and western imperialism pushed into the worlds of Asia, giving rise to a set of interconnected and increasingly interdependent societies: on the one hand, strong core states and/or empires, and, on the other, mid-level or weak peripheral ones, with their relative position in this modern world system being set either on the global stage or in a local-regional setting. During the late eighteenth century, a powerful Malayo-Muslim state with rich pearling grounds emerged within the Sulu Zone—an extensive economic region encompassing the southern rim of the Sulu Sea and the whole of the Celebes basin. My understanding of and discussion here about global economic-cultural interconnections and interdependencies between the Sulu Zone and the China tea trade is based on the premise that these intersections were governed by particular economic systems and set in a specific era and locality. The Taosug and Samal Bajau Laut lived in a singular time, and time meant change. The Zone was a place where borders were becoming ever more porous, less bounded, less fixed, stimulated in large measure by global-regional flows of commodities, people, and ideas, a kind of powerful magnet whose force European and Chinese traders were attracted to because that was where a great deal of the pearls and pearl shell for the Canton market was being collected and processed. The Zone was fast becoming a vitally important Southeast Asian economic region at a periphery of the world system that both reflected and transcended its locality. The Zone as a spatial system rested on the historically contingent axiom that it was inherently unstable and generally dynamic, and that it had been thrust on the global stage at a specific moment or era in "regional time."

A key factor in the Taosug's ascendancy was Europe's globalizing trade with China. The West's search for suitable commodities to exchange for Chinese tea is the most convincing explanation of the origin of the Sulu Sultanate's startling regional expansion.[74] Since the West primarily wanted pearls and pearl shell for the trade in China tea, the issue of the nature of productive relations in Sulu—slavery—suddenly became primary. Slave labor in the pearl shell fisheries provided the key commodities introduced into the external trade with China and the West. Power in the Sulu Zone was predicated on personal followings. The competitive commercial drive of ambitious datus forced the demand for additional coerced and dependent labor up, and swelled the flow of external trade.[75] In this globalizing context, tea was more than simply a crucial commodity in the development of trade between China and Britain. Tea was also an evergreen shrub that was instrumental in the stunning systematic development of commerce, power, and population in the Sulu Zone—an economic and demographic transformation which altered the regional face and history of insular Southeast Asia.

The individuals involved in this system of cross-cultural trade changed one another's lives by means of tens of thousands of transactions conducted over more than a century, involving commodities—objects and goods—that reflected the interests of the people who collected or manufactured them and the global economic imperatives that bridged two worlds to facilitate a trade in them. When they traded commodities like pearls or pearl shell and gunpowder weapons, Europeans and Chinese exchanged part of the signs and practices of their societies, which could turn out to have complex, devastating social consequences in the world of the Zone, as in the case of firearms and opium. Increasingly, particular objects played a role, albeit a critical one, as a bridge between their respective cultures and worlds. The impact of these unanticipated "marrying" processes could be discerned in a myriad of everyday choices over such things as appropriate language and speech, fashion, interior decoration, and the characteristics of food and eating habits. The importance of stratification symbols brought luxuries from Europe and China like Sheffield knives, Waterford crystal and bone china, and Ming earthenware to trading enclaves in the tropical wilderness of the Zone. The Sultan of Sulu and leading datus had their own stocks of wine, chocolate, brandy, and cigars and served their guests on Chinese porcelain. In terms of what Michael Mann calls a "history of power," many of these commodities and objects were outward symbols of hierarchy and social distinction among the Taosug, and critically important to the self-maintenance of the pearl fisheries and the trading world of the Zone.[76] For Sulu's scions of "royal blood," wealth and leadership ability were essential to attain political office. They established themselves in the political sphere and attracted and retained followers through vigorous participation in the marine commodity-procurement trade and in the promotion of slave raiding.[77]

It is worth emphasizing again the powerful economic forces that were pushing the Taosug aristocracy in the direction of acquiring more and more slaves. In the first place, their desire for all kinds of new products coming in from external trade had to be satisfied—demands that were constantly increasing. These desires and demands were both a consequence and cause of slavery. In order to trade, it was necessary for the Taosug to have something to exchange. Hence the collection and redistribution of pearls and pearl shell was dominated by those datus with the largest number of slaves; that is, by the Sultan and certain datus on the coast who were most directly involved in Sulu's global trade. Second, the more dependent Sulu's economy was on the labor power of slaves, the larger loomed the question of its supply of slaves. The only way for the Taosug to obtain the pearls and mother-of-pearl shell that formed the basis of their cross-cultural commerce was to secure more slaves by means of long-distance raiding. In the early nineteenth century, the rate of growth of the Sultanate's population had not kept pace with its expanding trade economy. Since it was the labor of slaves that made possible global-regional trade, slavery rose markedly from this time and became the dominant mode of production. This also explains why Jolo quickly became the principal entrepot in the Zone for the importation of slaves and the outfitting of marauders.[78]

The Iranun and Balangingi scoured the coasts of the Philippines, Borneo, Celebes, and the Malay Peninsula in search of their prey; they were an integral part of the whole economic system because they procured the pearling labor on which the system depended. Understanding these circumstances does not make "their brutality any more palatable, but it goes a long way towards explaining it."[79] One extraordinary feature of the interconnections between Sulu slave raiding and the advent of the world-capitalist economy was its rapid movement across the entire region, as one Southeast Asian coastal population after another was hunted down or driven away from the coasts.[80]

Certain lessons and examples from history about global economic-cultural interconnections and interdependencies also tend to explain patterns and events that have been formally glossed over. For example, sugar "demanded" slaves and the Atlantic slave trade. Similarly, tea was inextricably bound to sugar as product and fate, and pearls and pearl shell would also "demand" slaves in the Sulu Zone and thus lead to the advent of Iranun-Balangingi long-distance, saltwater slave raiding. However, in a comparative diasporic context, the statistics on this extraordinary displacement, and on the widespread pearling activities that occurred in the Sulu Zone to satisfy patterns of consumption and desire spanning continents and two empires, are still small when compared to the eleven million Africans who endured the middle passage to the New World during the three and half centuries of the Atlantic slave trade.

NOTES

1. James Francis Warren, "The Sulu Zone, the World Capitalist Economy and the Historical Imagination: Problematizing Global-Local Interconnections and Interdependencies," *Southeast Asian Studies* 35, no. 2 (September 1997): 177–222.

2. James Francis Warren, *The Sulu Zone, the World Capitalist Economy and the Historical Imagination* (Amsterdam: VU University Press/CASA, 1998), 177.

3. James Francis Warren, *The Sulu Zone 1768–1898: The Dynamics of External Trade, Slavery, and Ethnicity in the Transformation of a Southeast Asian Maritime State* (Singapore: National University of Singapore Press, 2007), xviii.

4. Edmund Ronald Leach, *Political Systems of Highland Burma: A Study of Kachin Social Structure* (London: London School of Economics and Political Science, 1954).

5. Warren, *The Sulu Zone, the World Capitalist Economy*, 183–84.

6. The characterization of geohistory is from Fernand Braudel, *The Mediterranean and the Mediterranean World in the Age of Philip II*, vol. 1, trans. Siân Reynolds (Berkeley: University of California Press, 1995), 20. The term *"conjoncture"* does not refer to a conjuncture, but rather to either phase (the rising or the declining phase of a cyclical process), one half, so to speak, of a bell-shaped curve on a chart. See Immanuel Wallerstein, *Unthinking Social Science: The Limits of Nineteenth-Century Paradigms* (Philadelphia: Temple University Press, 2001), 136.

7. Warren, *The Sulu Zone 1768–1898*, 3.

8. Warren, 17.

9. Warren, 252.

10. Warren, *The Sulu Zone, the World Capitalist Economy*, 190.

11. Warren, 189.

12. James Francis Warren, "Metaphorical Perspectives of the Sea and the Sulu Zone, 1768–1898," in *The Sea: Thalassography and Historiography*, ed. Peter N. Miller (Ann Arbor: University of Michigan Press, 2013), 149.

13. Warren, 149.

14. Wen-Chin Chang and Eric Tagliacozzo, "Introduction: The Arc of Historical Commercial Relations between China and Southeast Asia," in *Chinese Circulations: Capital, Commodities, and Networks in Southeast Asia*, ed. Eric Tagliacozzo and Wen-Chin Chang (Durham, NC: Duke

University Press, 2011), 2. See Arjun Appadurai, "Introduction: Commodities and the Politics of Value," in *The Social Life of Things: Commodities in Cultural Perspective*, ed. Arjun Appadurai (Cambridge: Cambridge University Press 1986); and Igor Kopytoff, "The Cultural Biography of Things: Commoditization as Process," in Appadurai, *Social Life of Things*.

15. John L. Comaroff and Jean Comaroff, *Ethnography and the Historical Imagination* (Boulder, CO: Westview, 1992), 14.

16. Warren, "Metaphorical Perspectives," 162.

17. Sidney W. Mintz, *Sweetness and Power: The Place of Sugar in Modern History* (New York: Penguin, 1986); Elizabeth Abbott, *Sugar: A Bittersweet History* (London: Duckworth, 2008); Mark Pendergrast, *Uncommon Grounds: The History of Coffee and How It Transformed Our World* (New York: Basic Books, 1999); Giorgio Riello, *Cotton: The Fabric that Made the Modern World* (Cambridge: Cambridge University Press, 2013); Mark Kurlansky, *Cod: A Biography of the Fish that Changed the World* (London: Vintage, 1997); and Kurlansky, *Salt: A World History* (London: Vintage, 2003).

18. See, particularly, the chapter "Pearls, Slaves, and Fashion," in Matthew S. Hopper, *Slaves of One Master: Globalization and Slavery in Arabia in the Age of Empire* (New Haven, CT: Yale University Press, 2015), 80–104; Steve Mullins, *Torres Strait: A History of Colonial Occupation and Culture Contact, 1864–1897* (Rockhampton: Central Queensland University Press, 1995).

19. Warren, *The Sulu Zone 1768–1898*, 67.

20. Major G. J. Sweet, "Report Pearl Fisheries in the Philippines," United States National Archives and Record Administration (NARA), Record Group 350, Bureau of Insular Affairs, File 642. 5.

21. Ching-Hong Wu, *A Study of References to the Philippines in Chinese Sources from Earliest Times to the Ming Dynasty* (Quezon City: University of the Philippines, 1959), 110; also in Warren, *The Sulu Zone 1768–1898*, 71–72.

22. Alexander Dalrymple, *Oriental Repertory*, 2 vols. (London: Ballintine and Law, 1808), 2:525.

23. Alexander Dalrymple, "A Memoir on the Sooloogannan Dominion and Commerce," February 26, 1761, Public Records Office, Egremont Papers, 30/47/20/1. See also Helen Follet, *Men of the Sulu Sea* (New York: Charles Scribner and Sons, 1945), 8.

24. Warren, "Metaphorical Perspectives," 151.

25. Edwin W. Streeter, *Pearls and Pearling Life* (London: George Bell and Sons, 1886), 127.

26. Sweet, "Report Pearl Fisheries in the Philippines," 5.

27. Warren, *The Sulu Zone 1768–1898*, 80.

28. Helen Follett, *Men of the Sulu Sea* (New York: Charles Scribner and Sons, 1945), 8.
29. Warren, *The Sulu Zone 1768–1898*, 73.
30. Warren, 252.
31. Warren, xlii.
32. Warren, xlii.
33. Warren, 72.
34. Streeter, *Pearls and Pearling Life*, 51.
35. Warren, *The Sulu Zone, the World Capitalist Economy*, 217.
36. Streeter, *Pearls and Pearling Life*, 138.
37. Streeter, 139.
38. Warren, *The Sulu Zone 1768–1898*, xxxv–xxxvi.
39. Warren, 73.
40. Streeter, *Pearls and Pearling Life*, 138.
41. Sweet, "Report Pearl Fisheries in the Philippines," 153.
42. Alexander Dalrymple, "Account of Some Natural Curiosities at Sooloo," in Dalrymple, *An Historical Collection of the Several Voyages and Discoveries in the South Pacific Ocean*, vol. 1 (London: J. Nourse, 1770), 12; Thomas Forrest, *A Voyage to New Guinea and the Moluccas from Balambangan: Including an Account of Magindano, Sooloo and other Islands* (London: G. Scott, 1779), 328.
43. J. Hunt, "Sketch of Borneo or Pulo Kalamantan, communicated by J. Hunt Esq. in 1812 to the Honorable Sir T. S. Raffles, Late Lieut. Governor of Java," in *Notices of the Indian Archipelago and Adjacent Countries*, ed. J. H. Moor (London: Cass, 1967), 21.
44. Dalrymple, "Account of Some Natural Curiosities at Sooloo," 11.
45. Forrest, *Voyage to New Guinea*, 328.
46. Dalrymple, "Account of Some Natural Curiosities at Sooloo," 11.
47. Warren, *The Sulu Zone 1768–1898*, 74–75.
48. Sixto Y. Orosa, *The Sulu Archipelago and its People* (Yonkers, NY: World Book Company, 1963), 18.
49. See Harry Arlo Nimmo, "The Structure of Bajau Society" (PhD diss., University of Hawai'i, 1969), 49; Nimmo, *The Sea People of Sulu: A Study of Social Change in the Philippines* (San Francisco: Chandler, 1972).
50. Harry Arlo Nimmo, "Social Organisation of the Tawi-Tawi Badjaw," *Ethnology* 4, no. 4 (1965): 436.
51. Thomas Kiefer notes that the word *luwaan* literally means "that which is spat out," referring to God's rejection of their way of life. See Kiefer, *The Tausug: Violence and Law in a Philippine Moslem Society* (New York: Holt, Rinehart and Winston, 1972), 22. *Pala'u* is a pejorative term with no commonly accepted definition used by land-dwelling Samal to describe the Samal Bajau Laut, most likely derived from *perahu*, the

Malay word for "boat." See Carol Warren, *Ideology, Identity and Change*, Southeast Asia Monograph Series 14 (Townsville: James Cook University of North Queensland, 1983), 7–8.

52. For an excellent discussion of the Samal Bajau Laut see Keifer, *The Tausug*, 22–24; and Clifford Sather, "Sulu's Political Jurisdiction over the Bajau Laut," *Borneo Research Bulletin* 3, no. 2 (1971): 58–62.

53. Warren, *The Sulu Zone 1768–1898*, 69.

54. Victor Hurley, *Swish of the Kris* (New York: E. P. Dutton, 1938), 38.

55. Warren, *The Sulu Zone 1768–1898*, 72. The remnant of these nomadic subsistence fishermen, approximately 2 percent of Sulu's population, are found today, still clients of land-dwelling Taosug, near the major islands of Jolo, Pata, Lungus, Siassi, and Tapul, but are particularly concentrated in the Tawi-Tawi region (68).

56. John Butcher, "Foreword," in Warren, *The Sulu Zone 1768–1898*, xviii.

57. Warren, xlvi. There are no statistics on the overall number of slaves imported into Jolo between 1768 and 1878, except the estimates of European observers and local informants. In *The Sulu Zone 1786–1898*, I have argued that slave imports to the Sulu Sultanate during the first sixty-five years probably averaged around 2,000 to 3,000 annually. The steepest rise in the estimated number of slaves annually brought to Sulu—from 3,000 to 4,000—occurred in the period 1836 to 1848, and this number slackened considerably in the next several decades, with imports ranging between 1,200 and 2,000 slaves a year until the external trade collapsed in the 1870s. The figures appeared formerly to show that between 200,000 and 300,000 captives were transported in Iranun and Samal Balangingi vessels to become slaves in the Sulu Sultanate in the period from the late eighteenth to late nineteenth centuries. However, earlier estimates of the scale of the slave traffic described and analysed in *The Sulu Zone* now have to be revised further upward for the first half of the nineteenth century, especially as the trade with China reached its zenith in the decades from the 1820s to the 1840s. In July 2004, I discovered a hitherto unknown confidential report on the number of slaving vessels entering the port of Jolo, with detailed data provided by a Spanish merchant captain on the numbers captured and brought to be sold there. The stunning findings of the confidential log or "census" suggests that between 4,000 to 6,000 Visayans—expert divers and seafarers—alone were being enslaved on an annual basis by the Iranun and Balaningi by 1845. See Warren, *The Sulu Zone 1768–1898*, xxxv.

58. Warren, 201.

59. Warren, 253. Fernand Braudel's work on material life and

capitalism in early modern times, Philip D. Curtin's formulations about economic change in precolonial Africa in the era of the slave trade, and my own study of change over more than a century which focuses on the seafaring populations of a Southeast Asian economic region all owe an intellectual debt to the economic theory and ideas of Karl Polanyi about modes of exchange. See Karl Polyani, Conrad M. Arensberg, and Harry W. Pearson, eds., *Trade and Market in the Early Empires: Economies in History and Theory* (Glencoe, IL: Free Press, 1957); and Polyani, *Dahomey and the Slave Trade* (Seattle: University of Washington Press, 1966). One important mode was "reciprocity," another was "redistribution." It is important to note, too, that in Polanyi's view these two types of transactions, as historical modes of organizing economies, were neither mutually exclusive of one another nor of the market economy. Polanyi's system of redistribution depends on social hierarchy and a tributary mode of production and exchange where goods flow into the "center" of an empire, state, or "zone," engendering distinctions of rank, privilege, and patronage among tribute takers, and flow out again to the producers of tribute on the "periphery," in the provinces, hinterlands, or frontiers. The mobilization of social labor to reproduce the dynamic and social conditions for the proliferation of a political system based on redistribution gives rise to military and political competition between contending social groups and segments of society, to control trade with the outside world and labor power. See Eric R. Wolf, *Europe and the People without History* (Berkeley: University of California Press, 1982), 386.

 60. A. J. F. Jansen, "Aanteekeningen omtrent Sollok en de Solloksche zeeroovers," *Tijdschrift voor Indische Taal-, Land- en Volkenkunde* 7 (1858): 217.

 61. Warren, "Metaphorical Perspectives," 153.

 62. See Charles Frake, "Abu Sayyaf: Displays of Violence and the Proliferation of Contested Identities among Philippine Muslims," *American Anthropologist*, n.s., 100, no. 1 (March 1998): 41–54; Benedict Sandin, *The Sea Dayaks of Borneo before White Rajah Rule* (London: Macmillan, 1967), 63–65, 127; Esther Velthoen, "'Wanderers, Robbers and Bad Folk': The Politics of Violence, Protection and Trade in Eastern Sulawesi, 1750–1850," in *The Last Stand of Asian Autonomies: Responses to Modernity in the Diverse Worlds of Southeast Asia and Korea, 1750–1900*, ed. Anthony Reid (London: Macmillan, 1997); Warren, *The Sulu Zone, The World Capitalist Economy*.

 63. Warren, "Metaphorical Perspectives," 156.

 64. Peter N. Miller, "Introduction: The Sea Is the Land's Edge Also," in *The Sea: Thalassography and Historiography*, ed. Peter N. Miller (Ann Arbor: University of Michigan Press, 2013), 12.

 65. Warren, "Metaphorical Perspectives," 160.

66. It is interesting to note that, according to Streeter, at one time "about 100 tons of Mother-of-Pearl were consumed annually by the Sheffield cutlers." See Streeter, *Pearls and Pearling Life*, 103.

67. James Francis Warren, *The Global Economy and the Sulu Zone: Connections, Commodities and Culture* (Quezon City, Philippines: New Day, 2000), 29.

68. Kenneth Prewitt, "Presidential Items," *Items* (Social Science Research Council) 50, no. 1 (1996): 15; see also Warren, *The Global Economy and the Sulu Zone*, 71–72.

69. Warren, *The Sulu Zone 1768–1898*, 126.

70. Statement of Chinese trader Ko Pic to Hugh Low, December 3, 1872, in the Earl of Derby to Lord Odo Russell, February 12, 1876, CO, 144/46.

71. Warren, *The Sulu Zone 1768–1898*, 129.

72. Najeeb M. Saleeby, *The History of Sulu*, vol. 4 (1905; repr., Manila: Filipiniana Book Guild, 1963), 21.

73. Heather Sutherland, "A Sino-Indonesian Commodity Chain: The Trade in Tortoiseshell in the Late Seventeenth and Eighteenth Centuries," in *Chinese Circulations: Capital, Commodities, and Networks in Southeast Asia*, ed. Eric Tagliacozzo and Wen-Chin Chang (Durham, NC: Duke University Press, 2011), 187.

74. Warren, *The Global Economy and the Sulu Zone*, 9–10.

75. Warren, *The Sulu Zone 1768–1898*, 252.

76. Michael Mann, *The Sources of Social Power* (Cambridge: Cambridge University Press, 1986), 490.

77. Warren, "Metaphorical Perspectives," 159.

78. Warren, *The Global Economy and the Sulu Zone*, 32.

79. Butcher, "Foreword," xiv.

80. James Francis Warren, "The Iranun and Balangingi Slaving Voyage: Middle Passages in the Sulu Zone," in *Many Middle Passages: Forced Migration and the Making of the Modern World*, ed. Emma Christopher, Cassandra Pybus, and Marcus Rediker (Berkeley: University of California Press, 2007), 53.

PART II

Regulation, Resource Management, and Science

THREE

An Uncertain Venture
Pearling Labor and Imperial Political Economy in South India and Sri Lanka, ca. 1790–1840

SAMUEL M. OSTROFF

IN 1833, as members of British parliament debated the contentious issue of the renewal of the East India Company's royal charter, Harriet Martineau, a young British theorist and activist, gained notoriety for what would become her nine-volume series, published collectively as *Illustrations of Political Economy*.[1] Martineau's magnum opus combined bleeding-heart fiction with the science of political economy and the language of utilitarianism, translating the academic esoterica of Adam Smith, Jeremy Bentham, Thomas Malthus, and other intellectual giants into narrative form to educate the general public about the hidden barbarity of British colonialism. She identified British Ceylon as an ideal setting for her intellectual project because the island was "more thoroughly and ingeniously beggared than any dependency."[2] Scottish jurist Alexander Johnston championed Martineau and encouraged her to write about the island and its pearling industry. She remarked that Johnston was "more thoroughly acquainted with the Cingalese than perhaps any other man then in England."[3] During his tenure as chief judge and president of the Royal Council in Ceylon, Johnston visited the pearl fisheries on numerous occasions. In March 1814, for instance, he and his wife joined the governor of Ceylon at Arippu to watch the divers.[4] While posted overseas, Johnston collected materials on "fisheries, geology, and natural history," and in a report on the natural history of Ceylon to British Secretary of State of the Colonies the Marquis of Londonderry, Johnston prescribed a "survey of the whole of that Gulf by able and scientific men, who could procure on the spot... such information relative to the history, the winds, the currents, the marine productions, and the coral formations of every part of the gulf, as might enable them to form a scientific and a deliberate opinion upon all the questions connected with the Pearl and Chank fisheries."[5] He later facilitated publications about pearling in the journal of the Royal Asiatic Society, an organization that he helped found with the renowned orientalist Henry Thomas Colebrooke in 1823. Colonial engagements with the pearl fishery provided the backdrop to a key chapter of *Illustrations* set in a fictional nineteenth-century Sri Lankan pearling village that Martineau used to promote a rational, scientific, and public-spirited agenda.

"Cinnamon and Pearls" in *Illustrations* tracks a series of unfortunate events in the lives of an aspirational pearl diver named Rayo and his fiancée Marana.[6] Rayo and Marana are caught pilfering marine animal products like pearls and conch shells over which the British colonial government asserted monopolistic control. An ill-fated dive one moonlit night sets this course of events in motion. Rayo believes that obtaining a pearl, by any means, is "the proper payment of his labour, considering that strangers carried away all the profit from the country people." Rayo desperately wants to become a skilled and successful pearl diver, and he plies his trade as the season approaches. "No circumstance had ever produced so happy an effect on him as his advancement to be a pearl-diver, an advancement in dignity, if not in gain," Martineau remarks.[7] On the first day of the season, Rayo bobs in the water, and the glimmer of a bright white pearl that has slipped from an open oyster catches his eye. He furtively snatches the pearl and swallows it in one swift motion. Despite his best efforts to avoid detection, Rayo is immediately apprehended. He is abused and flogged. The authorities then issue a mysterious substance to induce vomiting, expelling the pearl from his gut and recovering the contraband. The couple is then banished from the community in humiliating and shameful fashion and forced to live among strangers in the upland cinnamon fields.

Martineau used the tragic tale of Rayo and Marana to advance a rather awkward vision of reform based upon economic freedom, moral uplift, and personal fulfillment. She blamed government monopolies and colonial negligence for weakening the material and spiritual states of the local population. Even though pearl divers were "the natural owners of the native wealth of their region," they had been "kept bare of almost the necessaries of life" by an overbearing and extractive colonial regime.[8] In the coda to "Cinnamon and Pearls," a section given the anodyne title "Summary of Principles," Martineau wrote that monopolies were "disadvantageous as impairing the resources of the dependency, which are a part of the resources of the empire, and the very material of the trade which is the object of desire."[9]

PEARLING AND THE POLITICAL ECONOMY OF EMPIRES

The Gulf of Mannar—the shallow body of water between present-day India and Sri Lanka—was once one of the most abundant sources of natural pearls in the world. Dozens of fertile pearl oyster beds located along the shores of both the island and mainland attracted the attention of merchants and travelers for millennia. The geography of the region was particularly attractive to mariners during the age of sail. Adam's Bridge, a chain of low-lying shoals and islands, and the island of Mannar off the western coast of Sri Lanka create a narrow passageway between the Gulf of Mannar and Palk Bay known as Palk Strait, which afforded safeguarded passage and reduced travel time between the Bay of Bengal and the Arabian Sea.[10] Jorge Manual Flores has characterized the Gulf of Mannar and Palk Strait as a discrete "microworld" of the Indian Ocean.[11] Rather than capital-intensive trades across vast oceanic spaces, Flores highlights "substantially more discrete" trades between merchants of modest means in staple commodities such as rice. Mannar, according to Flores, is a "gold mine for the historian who enters the scope of the small change."[12] Indeed, pearls sourced from the fertile waters of Mannar had been trucked and trafficked by land and sea within the microworld of Mannar for centuries. This tiny, natural gem also ventured in the slipstreams of the movement of people, things, ideas, and biota to shape the contours of the early modern world, one of the many currents that formed the "connected histories" of the era.[13] At the turn of the sixteenth century, the pearl trade materialized into a truly global enterprise, as European expansion across the Atlantic Ocean opened Caribbean pearling grounds to the world, and the buying and selling of precious gems facilitated the integration of oceanic economies and imperial systems across and between the Atlantic, Indian, and Pacific Ocean worlds. Pearls from American fisheries mingled with "oriental" pearls from Persia and Ceylon in the metropolitan gem markets of Lisbon, Madrid, Antwerp, Amsterdam, Paris, and London.[14] India held its place as a de facto clearinghouse of the global gem trade, as pearls and precious stones from around the world arrived at emporia such as Goa and Madras for sorting and grading by merchants and jewelers of diverse backgrounds.[15] As historian Molly Warsh writes in *American Baroque*, a rich historical study of pearls and pearling in the Iberian Atlantic, "the stories generated by this unusual, organic jewel range globally, crossing geographic and imperial boundaries and, perhaps more importantly, moving across scales, linking the bounded experiences of individuals to the legacy of imperial bureaucratic elaboration."[16]

Historian Sanjay Subrahmanyam surveys how the Portuguese, Dutch, and English, one right after the other, were directly involved with managing the human and natural resources of the pearl fishery of Mannar from the early Portuguese period at the turn of the sixteenth century through the end of British rule and the birth of independent Indian and Sri Lankan states in the mid-twentieth century. He writes, "One can scarcely find an enterprise then that encapsulates the phases of European 'expansion' in Asia better than the fishery, which passed through the hands of each of the great colonial powers in Asia of the early modern and modern periods."[17] The Portuguese Estado da Índia was involved with the pearling industry in different capacities from around the turn of the sixteenth century to the mid-seventeenth century. With the support of the Kandyans of Sri Lanka, the Dutch East India Company (Verenigde Oostindische Compagnie, or VOC) drove Iberian forces from maritime Ceylon and the Fishery Coast in 1658.[18] The Dutch East India Company claimed control over much of this territory and managed the pearling industry until 1796, when the VOC was ousted by its English rivals. A confluence of local and global dynamics in the context of the Napoleonic Wars led to the transference of control over the pearling industry from the Dutch to the British during the second half of the eighteenth century. The VOC pivoted to Southeast Asia and the British East India Company emerged as the predominant European power in South Asia. Subsequent political reorganizations in the region further patterned the regulatory environment of the pearling industry. In 1802, the East India Company transferred its Ceylon territories to the British Crown, which established the island as a formal colony of the British state, while the coastal districts of southeastern India remained under Company rule. The Company Raj accordingly superintended the pearl fishery on the India side of the Gulf of Mannar and British Ceylon took care of the banks off the western coast of the island. Dozens of rich pearl oyster beds were thus located in the domains of two different British political entities, forming a maritime borderland between the Crown's island and the Company's mainland.[19] At the precise moment when the East India Company consolidated its position in Madras and British Ceylon was founded as a crown colony, administrators on both sides of the Gulf turned their attention to the people, animals, and ecosystem that not only produced a precious marine commodity, but also held considerable political and cultural value for a fledgling colonial government apparatus.

The eighteenth century witnessed the growth and development of liberalism as a political theory and philosophical system that articulated with imperial expansion. Liberalism was a hefty branch of the tree of imperial governance in India and shared a knotty trunk with the science of political economy, utilitarianism, and Christian evangelism.[20] Historians have examined the relationship between the discourse of political economy in early colonial India, yet the focus has been mainly on agrarian systems and private property regimes.[21] Many of the issues that motivated the introduction of land tenancy systems in Bengal and Madras reverberated through the management schemes that officials imposed on the pearling industry.[22] A contradictory state of affairs emerged. Company Madras and British Ceylon introduced regimes of private property in the agrarian economy while asserting monopolistic control over the production of pearls, conch shells, and other such marine animal products. The vicissitudes of colonial and imperial rule in India and Sri Lanka created pathways for the introduction of new ideas about governing the humans, animals, and environments along the littorals in British-occupied areas. Indeed, as the strands of Pax Britannica came together, a major intellectual shift occurred in the realm of economic thought, as liberalism wrestled with mercantilism for a position as the preferred framework of political economy.[23] Economic and intellectual historians have shown that the rise of free-trade ideology emerged alongside the birth and development of a British global imperial order.[24] In *Empire of Free Trade*, Sudipta Sen shows that British commercial entanglements with Indian economies and territorial expansion in eastern India joined together to create a blunt instrument with which the East India Company disrupted regional politics, economy, and society.[25] Sen demonstrates through district-level archival sources that markets in the abstract, classical economic sense, as well as physical spaces like marketplaces and bazaars, in early colonial eastern India were sites of competing authority. Across eastern India, European theories of markets rooted in the science of political economy converged with a substantive Indian system that was operationalized not by the logic of the invisible hand but by honors, titles, and gifts and embedded in social and political systems. Sen finds evidence of such historical phenomena in the political and symbolic economies of certain "prestige goods," such as betel, salt, and tobacco.[26]

The pearl fishery of Mannar was the source of one such prestigious commodity that generated debate between political economists on either side of the divide between mercantilists and free-trade hawks. Scottish political economist John Ramsay McCulloch—an acolyte of David Ricardo and editor of Adam Smith's *The Wealth of Nations*—wrote that "these [pearl fishery] monopolies are of no value." Lifting them would bring an end to "some very oppressive regulations" and breathe "fresh life into the fishery." He reasoned that "the sum for which the fishery is let equal the expenses incurred in guarding, surveying, and managing the banks."[27] Instead of leasing the pearl fishery to a local commercial magnate or harvesting the crop on its own, McCulloch recommended that the government sell licenses to all interested parties, thereby opening the industry to the dynamics of the free market. Naturally, there were those on the other side of the debate who advanced arguments in favor of a government monopoly. James Steuart served as the master attendant and chief inspector of the pearl banks for British

Ceylon in the 1820s and 1830s and authored one of the first single-subject works on the pearl fishery of Mannar. In *An Account of the Pearl Fisheries of Ceylon* (1843), Steuart wrote, "the Gulf of Manaar pearl fisheries can only be made of general benefit to the community, by their being protected and preserved, or in the language of political economists, monopolized by Government." For men like Steuart, the British colonial state and company-state ought not be high-handed proprietors but should instead assume the role of a "trustee," managing the pearling industry for the benefit of the local population. He wrote, "it is the duty of the Trustees or Guardians of the interests of the community to adopt measures calculated to increase the revenue obtained from it, in order, that the taxes which bear directly upon the people may be lightened."[28] Yet this was not a blanket endorsement of monopolies: "We would not be supposed to be favourers of monopoly, or of exclusive rights and privileges of some of the community to the injury of others; nor do we approve of trading Government."[29] He added, "when a beneficent Providence blesses a country with a peculiar benefit, it is right in the Government of that country jealously to preserve and monopolize such natural advantage for the good of its people."[30] Jonathan Forbes, the author of an early nineteenth-century study of Ceylon, also voiced support for a government monopoly: "Theorists have called for the abolition of what they are pleased to term 'the pearl-fishery monopoly,' and have had the hardihood to assert, that to throw it open would benefit the inhabitants of Ceylon; but it is to be hoped that neither vague theory, nor the sound of a word—monopoly, will triumph over common sense and justice, to deprive the public of Ceylon of this unexceptionable source of revenue." Forbes feared that the lack of government oversight would ruin the pearl oyster banks. He continued, "If the pearl-fisheries of the island were thrown open to all speculators, a very short period would suffice to annihilate this mine of wealth."[31] Monopolists such as Steuart and Forbes advanced arguments that government control over the pearl fishery was the most effective method to protect and manage pearl oyster populations and the marine ecosystem of Mannar. Antimonopolists like McCulloch dismissed these arguments wholesale: "The fears of exhausting the banks is quite ludicrous. The fishery would be abandoned as unprofitable long before the breed of oysters had been injuriously diminished; and in a few years it would be as productive as ever."[32]

British officials were far more engaged with the managerial aspects of the pearling industry than with the actual buying and selling of precious gems. This bias for management is further reflected in the historiography of the pearl fishery, focusing primarily on the years and dates in which fisheries were held and the revenue that each generated for treasuries.[33] The pearl fishery constituted small corners of the overall revenue pictures of Company Madras and British Ceylon, as taxes collected from agricultural lands, as well as cash crops such as cinnamon and tea, represented deeper and more predictable revenue streams. British officers differentiated pearls from other commodities to further rationalize monopolistic policies. Pearls and the nature of their production were viewed through a special lens that allowed British officials to experiment and tinker with existing policies and practices. In the first instance, pearling was seasonal, an intermittent activity that required skilled labor, large-scale mobilization of resources, and massive infusions of local capital. Officials also argued that the unique nature of the product, and the fragility of the ecosystem in which it was produced, rendered pearl oyster populations particularly vulnerable to overfishing. Officers of the Company and Crown averred that only the capable hands of a strong government could modulate use, protect persons and property, and provide the proper inducements to attract labor and capital. It was thus incumbent upon the Madras and Ceylon governments to turn the pearl fishery from, as one official wrote, an "uncertain venture" into a "state of regular and rich annual reproduction."[34]

Preexisting social, political, cultural, and economic conditions circumscribed European engagements with the pearl fisheries during the eighteenth and nineteenth centuries and, like the industries that produced the "prestigious commodities" of eastern India identified by Sen, these spaces did not closely align with the ideal political and economic models used by colonial administrators. Indian royal courts, such as Arcot and Ramnad, and temples claimed certain privileges at the pearl fishery.[35] Claims to *mauniam* (Tamil, *māniyam*), or tax-free boats, and shares of the revenue by local polities and religious institutions were not only concerned with the material benefits derived from the industry but also motivated by the need to have "traditional" rights and honors recognized by the Company Raj and British Ceylon during a period of political tumult. However, during the course of the late eighteenth and early nineteenth centuries, both Madras and Ceylon sought to erode the preexisting economy of gifts and honors that undergirded the pearl fishery. For example, in March 1828, two agents of Avudaiyarkoil, a Shaivite temple also known as Tirupperunturai located in present-day Pudukkottai, led a six-person party across the Gulf of Mannar to Arippu. Sundaralingam Pillai, Muttu Pillai, and four peons set out from their hometown through Rameswaram and continued by boat to Kondachi Bay. The group ventured across land and sea to receive *māniyam* boats and diving stones on behalf of the temple. However, they encountered an unforeseen roadblock. Governor Edward Barnes of British Ceylon reversed decades of precedent by refusing to deliver boats and divers usually allocated for Indian religious institutions. Sundaralingam Pillai, Muttu Pillai, and representatives from four other rights-bearing temples—Rameswaram, Thirupallani, Thiruchendur, and Uthirakosamangai—made repeated appeals to government officials with the help of professional scribes. They also scheduled a series of face-to-face meetings through local go-betweens to plead their case to government officials. The temple agents petitioned Governor Barnes in what they described as a "polite manner" and attached "ancient [documents] given in the time of [Tirumalai Nayak] and [the Setupati of Ramnad]," which, Sundaralingam Pillai and Muttu Pillai maintained, would "prove the enjoyment" of Avudaiyarkoil and demonstrate "much of the holiness of the Pagodas."[36] They presented copper-plate inscriptions awarded to the temples by the Nayakas of Madurai and Setupatis of Ramnad alongside government-issued certificates and passports from the Dutch and British to substantiate their claims that tax-free boats and divers were protected rights conferred by former sovereigns of India and subsequently recognized by European powers. Sundaralingam Pillai and Muttu Pillai also suggested that government officials solicit the opinions of "the other Gentlemen and the great Merchants" attending the pearl fishery who "will Certify the truth of our allegation."[37] Despite a mountain of evidence before them, Governor Barnes and his colleagues maintained that the government was under no obligation to recognize such claims to tax-free boats and divers. Sundaralingam Pillai, Muttu Pillai, and representatives of the other temples returned home empty-handed. Reports about the confrontation at Arippu then streamed into the Madras government.

The events at Arippu in 1828 set off a decade-long debate between the East India Company and British Ceylon about rights and authority at the pearl fisheries. British Ceylon officer George Lee, former postmaster general at Colombo, who "undertook laborious examination of a large and very interesting mass of Documents" concerning the claims of the "Indian Pagodas," issued a report in 1838.[38] He delivered the results of his investigation to Governor J. A. Stewart Mackenzie at the Queen's House in Colombo in August 1838. The Lee Report on the "Claim of Indian Temples on the Pearl Fisheries" came at the end of a period in which the pearling industry had been the object of targeted governmental reform and improvement. Drawing on the power of monopoly, Governor Barnes and his colleagues proposed abolishing the renting system and implementing a type of direct management in which the pearl banks would be fished each season as a government enterprise. What appeared to be an innovative reform was actually the return to an older system of management. The Portuguese and Dutch had both managed the pearl fishery along the same lines until the mid-eighteenth century when VOC officials introduced the renting system. British Ceylon and the Company Raj elaborated this mode of management in the late eighteenth and early nineteenth centuries, but the rights of religious institutions at the pearl fishery had not been stripped away. British Ceylon tried to decouple the claims of religious institutions to tax-free boats and divers from the wider political economy of the pearl fishery, which went hand in hand with efforts to disembed local networks and institutions from the industry more generally. The work of Governor Barnes and his colleagues came at the precise moment when the British colonial office in London appointed commissioners W. M. G. Colebrooke and C. H. Cameron to bring liberal-minded and reform-orientated perspectives to the political, economic, and social structures of the island.[39]

At the turn of the nineteenth century, the Company and Crown governments inherited two primary modes of managing the human and natural resources of the pearling industry. A direct mode of management was known as *amani*, a system in which the government proprietor assumed all the risk and fished the banks on its own account. The other system was renting. In the mid-eighteenth century, Dutch VOC governor Gustaav Willem Baron van Imhoff shifted from amani to revenue-farming, a renting system that been employed in various sectors of the premodern and early modern economies of India and Sri Lanka.[40] The Madras and Ceylon governments continued to experiment with renting and amani and decisions about how to best manage the pearl fisheries were regular features of administrative proceedings during the British period. For instance, Governor Frederick North of Ceylon advanced an argument in favor of amani. He wrote, "At all Events I intend to conduct it myself in Amannee, as I shall any other Pearl-Fishery which may take Place during my stay on this Island. Every Reason both of Calculation & Experience has convinced me that there is no mode of carrying on that Business, either so economical, so productive, so certain, or so little liable to abuse."[41] Debates over the best mode of management continued through the nineteenth and early twentieth centuries, yet no concrete government-wide policy emerged.[42] Most of the pearl fisheries in the late eighteenth and early nineteenth centuries were conducted under the renting system. By the 1830s, however, British Ceylon officials wanted to turn away from the renting system and reintroduce a system of direct management, and by the mid-nineteenth century officials such as George Vane remarked that the renting "had given much trouble at former fisheries so conducted, and led to abuses of the rights of the divers and boatmen (also, as believed, to the over-fishing of the banks)."[43]

The protean ideas that Company Madras and British Ceylon brought to bear on the management and governance of people and oysters produced fields of "state intervention" that sought not only to increase profits and productivity by attenuating the financial and physical risks of pearling, but also fundamentally reshape the social, economic, and political foundations of the industry.[44] British officials targeted the breakup of "traditional" economic relationships to turn the pearl fishery from an industry embedded in local economy and society to one operationalized by the logic of markets and protected by the rule of law. Numerous local people and institutions had a pivotal role to play in the success of the pearl fishery, which marked key stakeholder groups as *the* objects of governmental reform and improvement.[45] However, attempts to extricate local networks and institutions from pearling operations were fraught with contradictions and seldom delivered on such promises. Efforts to open labor markets or promote certain types of economic behavior were paradoxically undergirded by fiercely guarded government monopolies and enforced by naked violence. Many of the policy proposals and management schemes forwarded by government officials that imagined radical change were unevenly realized at best and met with considerable resistance from local laborers and experts.

BETWEEN REFORM AND RESISTANCE: DISCIPLINING PEARLING LABOR

Company and Crown officials, often in concert with local mercantile elites, identified the workforce—pearl divers in particular—as an object of governmental reform. Drawing on medieval and early modern travelogues as well Portuguese and Dutch records, British officials and their contemporaries invested pearling labor with an idealized, unchanging character. George Turnour, an East India Company military officer who superintended pearl fisheries in the late 1790s, wrote that diving was "prescribed by ancient usage" and that "no degree of richness of the Banks, or value of the Pearls, would induce [the divers] to deviate one *Iota* from what their Fathers did before them."[46] Problematizing "ancient" pearling practices dovetailed with broader concerns about theft and security to provide space for the emergence of a disciplinary regime that targeted labor. British traveler James Cordiner described the extent of the problem: "The divers, the boat-men, the persons employed in washing the oysters and sifting the sand, leave no expedient untried to accomplish frauds. Even the peons, employed as a check upon the labourers, have been known to attach a viscous substance to the end of their canes, and extract from the washing-troughs valuable pearls, with the very instrument used to punish such delinquencies."[47] Likewise, military officer Jonathan Forbes believed that proclivities for theft were not only endemic among the local population but also reflected a moral defect: "Where thefts are so easily made, and a valuable article like a pearl is so easily secreted, incessant watchfulness is necessary . . . but I believe their utmost endeavours are ineffectual, as the moral character of most of those assembled . . . affords no check to their inclinations. . . . Their only principle and pursuit is how to make money, and if successful, the end to them would sufficiently sanctify the means."[48] The physical qualities of pearls—small, valuable, and easily kept out of sight—and the nature of extraction—miles from the coast and fathoms under water—heightened anxieties about unsupervised labor and theft. To minimize risks, British officials and local merchant-investors assembled a multifaceted security apparatus designed to protect people and pearls from physical dangers and financial loss that directed the flow of colonial governmental power through the lives and work of pearl divers and other laborers.

A central concern was the unchecked circulation of merchants, capital, labor, information, diseases, and goods that moved along the coasts of India and Sri Lanka and through the Gulf of Mannar during the pearling season. Sugata Bose's *A Hundred Horizons* conceptualizes the Indian Ocean as an "interregional arena" rather than a coherent cultural and economic unit, one that lies somewhere between a totalizing "world-system" and hyper-locality.[49] Pearling in the Gulf of Mannar was one such horizon of the Indian Ocean over the *longue durée*. The circulation of people and things animated by seasonal pearling activities created patterns of movement that constituted part of a wider "circulatory regime" of South India and Sri Lanka and beyond.[50] Sujit Sivasundaram argues that policies and practices of British colonialism effectively splintered Sri Lanka from India during the course of the nineteenth century. Through geographic knowledge production, policing strategies, legal power, administrative organization, and numerous other governing tactics, British colonialism remade the island into a "unit in the Indian Ocean" separate and apart from the wider regional sphere of South Asia.[51] The movement of people and things through the Gulf of Mannar during the pearling season, however, suggests that the process of "islanding" Sri Lanka from the Indian subcontinent was always a work in progress. From seasonal migration and smuggling to disease outbreaks and poaching, circulatory patterns related to the pearl fishery compromised the ability of Madras and Ceylon to solidify the "porous" maritime borderlands of the region.[52] Indeed, the frontier has been a useful geographic and conceptual construct in South Asian historiography to understand environmental, economic, political, cultural, and social change and interaction.[53] Jan Heesterman identifies the coastlines as such a space, writing that "the Littoral forms a frontier zone that is not there to separate or enclose, but which rather finds its meaning in its permeability."[54] In other words, the fertile pearl oyster beds of Mannar formed a "fluid frontier," a space between *terra* and *mare*, humans and animals, island and mainland, Company and Crown, and Europe and Asia.[55]

Most divers and boatmen came from southeastern India and the western and northern districts of Ceylon. As one contemporary eyewitness observed, "The boats with their crews and divers come from Manaar, Jaffna, Ramisseram, Nagore, Tutakoreen, Travancore, Kilkerry, and other parts on the coast of Coromandel. They arrive completely equipped, and furnished with every thing necessary to conduct the business of the fishing."[56] Seasonal migration and the movement of goods and capital were mediated and far from routine phenomena. The Portuguese and Dutch had relied on local intermediaries to facilitate the recruitment and mobilization of labor. Maintaining relationships with local Parava, Marakkayar, and Lubbai communities through the extension of patronage and protection was critical for the success of the pearl fishery and broader political and economic agendas. British Ceylon and Company Raj officials expanded the scope of this work and turned to the medium of print to spread information about the pearl fishery. Published in English, Tamil, Sinhala, and sometimes even Dutch, advertisements contained important information about the pearl fishery, such as the dates and location of particular events, as well as the number of boats that an event would admit. An advertisement for the 1803 pearl fishery at Chilaw contained the following passage: "Notice is hereby given that a Pearl Fishery will take place at Chilaw, in the Island of Ceylon, in the Ensuing season—the Number of Boats employed will be from Eighty, to one hundred, and the fishery will commence on the 20th February 1803, by which day, it is requested that the Boats, and Divers, intending to seek employment for the usual Reward of one fourth part of the Oysters taken, may be at Chilaw that [season] being peculiarly favorable for the operations."[57]

High-ranking government officials like governors and district collectors regularly furnished the lead supervisor of the pearl fishery with instructions to "facilitate the intended Enterprize [sic] [by] sending over the Boats and Divers."[58] In some instances, officials on the island and mainland coordinated the inward and outward flows of labor, goods, and capital each season. In March 1800, for example, Governor North volunteered pearl appraisers and other laborers, provided information about the value and class of pearls, and suggested sending over an old Dutch sloop that could be used for examining and patrolling the pearling grounds.[59] The following year, Fort St. George returned the favor when it furnished Collector Lushington of Ramnad with instructions to enable the movement of boats and divers from his district to pearling grounds off the western coast of Ceylon. North requested that Lord Clive at Fort St. George instruct Collector Lushington to "facilitate the intended Enterprise" by "sending over the Boats and Divers in his District."[60]

One idea that was regularly entertained to address the problem of seasonal migration was the forced settlement of specialized pearling labor along the western coast of the island. These proposals, which had been floated by European officers engaged with the industry from at least the seventeenth century, specifically concerned Tamil Paravas. The Dutch VOC had considered coercing Parava divers and others skilled in the art of pearling to relocate. For instance, Anthony Paviljoen, Dutch commander at Jaffnapatnam, recommended that "four good pearl divers with their tools and implements" be spirited away to as far as the Banda Islands in Southeast Asia.[61] In the late eighteenth and early nineteenth centuries, British administrators spun a new rationale for forced migration. Officials from various corners of the company-state and colonial state administrations believed that offering incentives to members of the Parava community to settle near Arippu would not only provide the pearl fishery with a regular and fixed supply of labor, but also facilitate the development of irrigation and agriculture. For instance, Cordiner wrote, "The ruins of a large tank or reservoir, capable of watering ground sufficient to produce one hundred thousand parrahs of paddee, afford one proof of its former prosperity. It might be highly beneficial to the interest of the pearl fishery, if settlers were again encouraged to reside there; and it ought especially to be rendered the head-quarters of the pilots, divers, and other persons necessary to be employed in conducting the concern."[62] Establishing a permanent community of divers near the site of the pearl fishery was also meant to reduce seasonal traffic. John McDowall, one of the commissioners of the 1799 pearl fishery at Arippu, wrote to his colleague George Turnour a few months before the start of the event that Governor North "will apply to the Bombay Government for the protection you have suggested and will direct the Superintendent of the Fishery to guard against an evil, which threatens to [serve as an] inconvenience to the Divers on the Pearl Banks. It is certainly much to be wished that some of these should settle at Arreppo, and every means should be used during the Fishery to induce them thereto."[63] British officer Davey Roberson proposed that the government induce Parava communities to settle on the island by granting them tax-free lands.[64] Likewise, Anthony Bertolacci wrote: "It becomes, therefore, in every way, an object of great importance to protect the interests of the Ceylon divers; and to induce those of the opposite coast, who accumulate wealth in the Ceylon fisheries, to settle in it, by granting them lands, and such advantages as may make them comfortable in it."[65]

Heavy seasonal migration animated by the pearl fishery was also seen as a security problem and mapped onto wider colonial concerns about the circulation of bodies, contraband, and disease through areas in which European powers claimed sovereignty. For instance, an 1811 legislative act extended the maritime boundaries of British Ceylon beyond three miles from shore—the distance then accepted by international law—and invested the state with the authority to arrest any boats and crews that ventured onto the pearling grounds throughout the year.[66] According to the Act, "depredations are committed in the Pearl Banks of this Island by Boats and other Vessels frequenting those places in the calm season without any necessity or lawful cause."[67] The specters of illicit fishing and trading were not limited to those few weeks of the pearling season between late February and early April when tens of thousands of people gathered on the shores of southeastern India or western Ceylon. Both Portuguese and Dutch officials had recognized that various smuggling and poaching operations were often linked with pearl fishing. For instance, Dutch commander Paviljoen wrote in a 1665 memorandum, "The prospects for next year are better than they have ever been since our possession. Next January the banks must be carefully inspected, and a good sloop must be made to sail coastwise with a view to keep away Moors and other thieves, or to otherwise capture them so that they may be punished."[68] British officials were also wise to the "notorious fact that the banks are extensively robbed" between the end of the examination and start of the pearl fishery.[69] Governor Barnes of British Ceylon wrote in March 1821 that this interlude "affords the season for the dhoneys [boats] to pass from the Southern Coast of Coromandel to this Island, anchoring as they do on our pearl oyster banks and their crews are all divers!"[70] Officials also expressed concern that unauthorized pearling occurred during the off-season under the pretense of fishing for conch shells. Collector Huddleston of Tirunelveli called attention to this problem in 1822: "It is strongly suspected that the chank divers are in the habits of poaching upon the Pearl banks and in Ceylon a Guard vessel is for some time before a fishery employed to protect the Banks. The greater value of the produce of the Pearl fishery on that Coast may require more watchful attention [than] there is necessary for the Tinnevelly Banks but totally exposed as they have hitherto been it is highly probable that they have not [escaped] depredation."[71]

The workforce was subjected to additional forms of oversight during the pearling season. The Dutch VOC had issued rules and edicts that dictated lawful conduct through *plakkaaten*, placards that contained various codes and regulations. A *plakkaat* from 1665 expressly forbade all Muslim divers, boatmen, and merchants from traveling to the pearl banks because officers had "received information" that "many Muslims are not afraid to steal or pilfer." The VOC claimed "sovereign jurisdiction" and identified this class of subjects as "enemies of the state and general public." VOC intelligence maintained that members of Muslim seafaring communities robbed the sea of pearl and oysters under "the pretense that they are making a trip or sailing somewhere else."[72] Likewise, British officials issued edicts that established certain rules and laid down penalties for violating them, which ranged from petty fines to heavy flogging. As a list of regulations posted at the 1800 pearl fishery at Tuticorin read, "In case it should happen that a smuggling Dony be found amongst the others with Design to fish Oysters under pretence [*sic*] of wind and Currents and of being driven away by night, and other unfortunate Circumstances, it shall be immediately seized and the parties threatened as the Circumstances shall require."[73]

Concerns about security and mobility remained as the divers and boatmen assembled at the location of the pearl fishery and the superintendent and members of his administrative team undertook an extensive registration process. A similar system was in place during the Portuguese era.[74] There are also references in the Dutch records to the practice of registering pearling crews (*uitschrijving*) at the start of the season. Dutch governor Hendrick Becker wrote to his successor in 1716, "The names of all the divers with their number of stones, each under his Pattangatyn, must be carefully entered by the Commissioners, and each individual must receive a certificate signed on behalf of the Company, while a number of sloops must constantly cruise about the scene of the pearl fishery, to examine every vessel and to see that it has no unauthorized divers or stones on board."[75] These practices continued into the British period. Each boat was assigned a number and issued a passport, complete with a passenger manifest that provided the exact number and names of the divers, pilots, and other crewmen.[76] A copper plate inscribed with both Roman and Tamil numerals that corresponded to the superintendent's logbook was then tied to the boat with coir rope.[77] The registration process, assignment of number, and issuing of passports was also meant to deter illicit fishing, as pearling boats, government agents, and other participants were given the tools to monitor the boats. If there was any behavior deemed suspicious or illegal, an informant could identify the boat by number and notify the authorities. Guard vessels also regularly checked that each boat carried proper documentation. According to a public announcement released during the 1799 pearl fishery at Arippu, it had been decreed that "a Certificate containing the No. of the Boat and the Names of the Tindals, Crew, and Divers [shall] be open for inspection, and that a general Register of the same [shall] be kept by the Commissioners."[78] If the crew did not have its paperwork in order, carried a phony passport, or employed over and above the assigned number of divers and stones, then government officials were empowered to mete out punishment, which ranged from fines and the confiscation of property to arrest and corporeal punishment.[79]

Another mechanism through which European officials tried to police the movement of boats and divers was the placement of wooden buoys and canvas flags to demarcate the boundaries of the pearling grounds. Cordiner offered a description of the flag-and-buoy system: "The buoys are rafts of wood of a triangular shape, having flags of different colours raised upon them, and are fixed to the place by a cable and wooden anchor, with two large stones attached to it. Drawings of the flags are inserted in a book, and a particularly description is given of the quality, age, and denomination of the oysters found where they are laid."[80] In the late seventeenth century, Dutch VOC governor Gerrit de Heere instructed an *opperkoopman* (senior merchant) at Jaffnapatnam that "four buoys should be made as beacons for the vessels, each having a chain of 12 fathoms long, with the necessary adaptations in the links for turning."[81] This system was not only meant to deter theft by keeping all the pearling boats within a specially marked area, but also functioned as a mode of resource management. Governor North wrote to Fort St. George in 1800 that the Company had an interest "in preserving the Banks from premature exhaustion & the Power which it has of restraining the Divers on the spot from fishing in improper Places, & of immediately punishing any Irregularity in that Respect."[82] North proposed that pearling fleets sweep the entire area so that no oysters went undetected.[83] The superintendent and his assistants, with the help of local authorities such as the *jati talaivan*, marked the boundaries of the pearling grounds at the start of the season with wood, rope, paint, and other supplies shipped to the camp.[84] Formal contracts with the renter further stipulated that it was incumbent upon the government to undertake this work. Rules posted for public viewing at the superintendent's makeshift office also contained information about the perimeter of the pearling grounds.[85]

By the 1820s and 1830s, instead of wooden buoys and colored flags, British Ceylon officials recommended the installation of solid columns in the water. Cordiner underscored the problem: "The buoys are not allowed to continue permanent, as they would either require a vessel constantly to guard them, or, if not watched, would leave the beds exposed to the ravages of pirates."[86] Steuart also expressed a similar concern. In the mid-1820s, Governor Barnes moved forward with plans to erect permanent columns. After his team of engineers and experts identified the best location of the markers, according to Steuart, "plans and estimates were prepared, and the requisite number of bricks ordered to be made of some clay found in the neighbourhood of Condatchy."[87] Yet these experiments yielded no actionable results and British officials continued to search for ways to improve the flag-and-buoy system through the nineteenth century without much success. In 1862, Superintendent George Vane thought iron buoys might be a suitable replacement, but officials instead used "large, heavy, clumsy, iron, coal, tar drums" with insufficient cables and "small anchors."[88] Predictably, "owing to the bungholes not having been properly soldered," the metal buoys immediately sank to the bottom of the ocean, after which the commanding officer "reverted to the old triangular wooden buoys."[89]

At sea, security forces were placed on board pearling boats to detect and deter any frauds or thefts by the crew. As naturalist Henry Le Beck wrote around the turn of the nineteenth century, "the boat owners, and purchasers, often lose many of the best pearls while the [boat] is returning from the bank; for, as long as the animal is alive, and untouched, the shells are frequently open near an inch; and if any of them contain a large pearl, it is easily discovered, and taken out by means of a small piece of stiff grass, or bit of stick, without hurting the pearl fish. In this practice they are extremely expert. Some of them were discovered whilst I was there, and received their due punishment."[90] There were reports of divers swallowing pearls who, if caught, were given "strong emetics and purgatives," echoing the story of Rayo and Marana.[91] Guardsmen were also employed by the proprietor of the boat, a merchant who purchased the boat at auction or subleased it from the principal renter. Cordiner wrote that to the crew was "added a peon on the part of the renter, to guard against fraud."[92] Likewise, government officials placed a servant in their employ on board to ensure that the day's catch was accurately measured. This was sometimes written into the contract of the renter. For instance, the contract between the East India Company and Manali Chinniah Mudaliar, renter of the 1805 pearl fishery at Tuticorin, stipulated "a servant belonging to the Superintendent shall be placed in each Boat to take an account of the Number of Oysters fished in the Course of each Day."[93]

Government officials deployed guard vessels to keep pearling fleets within demarcated boundaries, check passports and licenses, and look for any other signs of illicit fishing. The Portuguese and Dutch had used naval forces for such purposes. Governor Joan Gideon Loten of Dutch Ceylon, for instance, referenced the use of a guard vessel to suppress "fraud" in a report to his successor in 1757.[94] Hiring of guard vessels was an essential part of managing and protecting the treasures (and persons) in the water. In a report submitted to the Madras Board of Revenue in January 1807, Collector James Hepburn provided a rationale for the use of armed vessels: "It has always been customary for the Government when this Bank was fished to station a Vessel on it at its own expense with some respectable person on board to regulate the Boats while fishing and to alter the Buoys when required and to inspect the License of each Boat daily." He continued, "It may at first appear that these concerns belong more properly to the Renter, yet I am told that it is so necessary for the security of Government to limit the Divers to a particular part of the Bank and not to allow them to leave till it is compleatly [sic] cleaned of Oysters, otherwise the whole could be ransacked in the course of a few days to a probable serious loss and protest from the renter that he had been deceived in the report of the state of the Banks."[95] The guard vessels were granted authority not only to patrol the pearling grounds but also board the boats and enforce the rules.[96] If boats ventured beyond the flags and buoys, a warning shot straight from the barrel of a cannon was often fired. A set of regulations posted at the 1800 pearl fishery contained the following clause: "Those Donies which begin Fishing before the signal is given, and those that continue to fish after the signal is shown for leaving off shall be fired into from the Guard sloop or otherwise punished."[97] Guns, cannons, and other types of heavy artillery were transported from various forts and garrisons to the location of the season's event. For instance, in 1822, the Madras government hired a bullock train to transport a gun from Palamcottah to Tuticorin, and one of the delivery men was even retained by the collector because he needed security reinforcements.[98]

Company Madras and British Ceylon also sought to modify the actual practices and techniques of pearl diving. From at least the medieval period onward, pearl diving was one of the most commented-on features of the industry, and some of the earliest descriptions of diving are found in medieval travelogues.[99] Divers used pyramid-shaped stone with loops to help accelerate their descent to the bottom of the ocean floor. The diver placed his foot in a stirrup-like loop made from coir and carried a basket, formed by a wooden or iron hoop and coir netting and about eighteenth inches in diameter, in which he placed the oysters. Each reddish granite stone weighed about twenty to thirty pounds, a hefty load to handle for the crew of rudimentary craft navigating rough water. Pearling boats usually contained five stones and ten divers, as two divers shared each stone. Divers worked at a breakneck pace, alternating between resting and diving for hours on end from the early morning till late in the afternoon. As Robert Percival wrote, "the diver thus prepared, seizes another rope with his right hand, and holding his nostrils shut with the left, plunges into the water, and by the assistance of the stone speedily reaches the bottom."[100] When the diver reached the bottom of the ocean, a depth of anywhere between one and ten fathoms, he released the stone from his waist for his partners on board to haul up. For as long as his lungs would allow, no more than a minute or two, the diver collected oysters and other marine products like coral, often aided by stones tied around the waist. When the diver came to the surface, a group of men helped haul the baskets on board the boat. The productivity of the divers is astounding by any measure, as a crew of around twenty to thirty people would bring thousands of oysters per day and, over the course of thirty days of fishing, tens and hundreds of thousands.[101] Aside from diving stones, coir nets, and other tools, the boats used during the pearl fishery were often seen as simple, primitive craft.[102] By the late 1830s, British Ceylon started to experiment with the use of steamships during the examination instead of traditional coastal craft with sails and oars.

The use of steamships was not limited to pearling. For instance, Governor Stewart Mackenzie of British Ceylon wanted to use a steamboat to patrol the pearl banks, convey "treasure," and transport personnel.[103] In 1840, a steamer named the *Seaforth*, built for the express purpose of pearling, arrived at Colombo from Bombay, which a superintendent of the Ceylon pearl fishery in the late nineteenth century described as an "important change and improvement."[104]

Contemporary observers were also impressed by the simple dress and tools used by pearl divers.[105] The general absence of special clothes, nose clips, oils, and other diving aids at the pearl fishery of Mannar struck writers from the medieval period onward.[106] There were coordinated efforts by the governments of Madras and Ceylon to update and modernize the diving process during the early nineteenth century. Historian C. R. de Silva suggests that the Portuguese did not introduce any game-changing technologies.[107] The Dutch brought diving bells to pearling centers in the Indian Ocean without much success.[108] A report by French naturalist Eudelin de Jonville mentions the use of diving bells at the Mannar fishery during the Dutch period but notes that such equipment was "not found to answer the purpose expected."[109] Yet following a series of unsuccessful fisheries in the late 1810s and early 1820s, Governor Barnes "resolved to leave no stone unturned to investigate the subject."[110] As he prepared to assume the governorship of Ceylon in 1823, Barnes had two diving bells shipped from England. The first was a wooden diving bell constructed by the Royal Staff Corps and the second a more sophisticated type made of cast iron that arrived at Colombo around June 1825. As master attendant of Colombo and chief inspector of the pearl banks, Steuart used diving bells during an examination in March the following year. Men like Barnes believed that the introduction of new technologies and equipment would revolutionize pearling. The use of diving bells, according to this logic, would deter illicit fishing, provide officials with a more precise assessment of the state of the banks, and prevent the formation of secret agreements among divers and merchants to misrepresent the size of the season's harvest.[111]

Not all officials in British Ceylon involved with the management of the pearl fishery at that time fetishized the diving bell. Revenue officer Robert Boyd wrote, "The inapplicability of the Diving Bell to fishing for oysters, arises from the difficulty of working such a Machine and from the small surface included within its circumference."[112] There were also those who voiced concerns about the environmental impact of such equipment. Captain James Crisp, described as "the most intelligent Master Attendant at Ceylon," wrote that the diving bell "may answer very well at first; but it will ultimately be the means of destroying the oysters." Crisp believed that the marine environment of Mannar and its pearl oyster population was far too fragile. A diver in heavy equipment tramping along the ocean floor would severely damage the marine environment. The diving bell "must crush a great many [oysters]; which will putrefy; and so extremely delicate is the nature of the oysters, that it will spread like a plague, gradually extending its vortex, and destroying all within."[113] Nonetheless, colonial powers and enterprising prospectors continued to introduce new technologies such as diving bells and dredging machines at pearling centers across the globe, from Mexico and the Caribbean to the Persian Gulf and Australia.[114]

CONCLUSION: LOCAL LABOR, VERNACULAR CAPITAL, GLOBAL COMMODITY

The history of the pearl fishery during the early years of British management might best be written as a history of failure. Each season, tens of millions of oysters were harvested from the shallow waters of the Gulf, yet only a fraction yielded pearls and only a handful of those were of any significant quality and value. Vexed officials found the pearl fishery nearly impossible to predict, as revenue and produce often fell short of expectations. British officials proposed fundamental change to labor markets, economic organization, and diving practices, yet seldom realized such visions. In many ways, this project was bound to fall short, as government officials drew upon a contradictory set of discourses and practices drawn from liberal political economy and other emergent sciences that failed to work their magic on a stubborn workforce. As Warsh argues, "the political economy of pearls gave rise to a productive tension between vernacular, small-scale understandings of wealth management (in which nature and expert labor played a major role, as did pearls' particular qualities) and developing imperial understandings of the same." The tension Warsh identifies between vernacular and imperial practices vis-à-vis the political economy and nature resource management of pearling in the early modern Iberian Atlantic resonates with the situation in late eighteenth-century and early nineteenth-century Sri Lanka and India. Indeed, as Warsh writes, "these vernacular customs limited the success of familiar early modern governing mechanisms to extend control over wealth production, such as patents, monopolies, technology, and joint-stock companies." She adds, "in the case of pearls, these mechanisms failed because of the expert human knowledge needed to mediate the interaction between nature and the state."[115] The governing effects of Company and Crown rule during this period of political flux left impressions of varying depths on the people, institutions, and environment of the pearling industry, the evidence of which are found in the spaces between success and failure. Pearling in the Gulf of Mannar was nevertheless a source of a tremendous amount of discursive energy for Company and Crown officials. European powers in the region—whether company-states such as the Dutch and English East India Companies or formal colonial governments like British Ceylon—devoted considerable attention to the pearling industry and committed substantial resources to the management of people and oysters. Yet interest in the people, institutions, animals, and environment that constituted the pearling industry far exceeded the hunt for gems and profits. The "uncertain nature" of the pearl fishery did not hinder but rather enabled European engagements with the human and natural resources of the industry. The peculiar logic of colonial rule and governance meant that people and oysters were always in need of improvement. As marine biologist William Herdman wrote in the early twentieth century, "there is no reason for any despondency in regard to the future of the pearl fisheries, if they are treated scientifically." In other words, he added, "the material exists, ready for man's operations."[116] Pushing for change, but unable to impose regulatory oversight over the vernacular customs, practices, and understandings of pearling in the Gulf of Mannar, the British, like their European predecessors, failed to realize a vision of widespread reform based on the principles of liberal political economy and scientific management. But, alas, this was the nature of the beast.

NOTES

1. Harriet Martineau, *Illustrations of Political Economy*, 9 vols. (London: Charles Fox, 1832–34).

2. Harriet Martineau, "Cinnamon and Pearls," in vol. 7 of Martineau, *Illustrations of Political Economy*, 22. See also Deborah Logan, *Harriet*

Martineau, Victorian Imperialism, and the Civilizing Mission (Farnham, UK: Ashgate, 2010), 108.

3. Harriet Martineau, *Harriet Martineau's Autobiography*, ed. Maria Weston Chapman (Boston: J. R. Osgood, 1877), 1:245–46. See also Logan, *Harriet Martineau*, 105.

4. *Ceylon Government Gazette*, no. 653, March 23, 1814, United Kingdom National Archives (UKNA), Colonial Office, CO 58/1.

5. James Steuart, *An Account of the Pearl Fisheries of Ceylon* (Cotta, Ceylon: Church Mission Press, 1843), 2.

6. For a complete synopsis of this episode, see Logan, *Harriet Martineau*, 105–11.

7. Martineau, "Cinnamon and Pearls," 33, 23.

8. Martineau, 21.

9. Martineau, 124.

10. Jean Deloche, "Le chenal de Pāmban et le route de pèlerinage de Rāmēśvaram: Un exemple d'aménagement ancien," *Bulletin de l'École Française d'Extrême-Orient* 74, no. 1 (1985): 167–82; Kenneth McPherson, "Paravas and Portuguese: A Study of Portuguese Strategy and Its Impact on an Indian Seafaring Community," *Mare Liberum* 13 (1997): 69–82.

11. Jorge Manuel Flores, "The Straits of Ceylon and the Maritime Trade in Early Sixteenth Century India: Commodities, Merchants and Trading Networks," *Moyen Orient et Océan Indien* 7 (1990): 27–58. For more on the connections between India and Sri Lanka, see Michael Roberts, "From Southern India to Sri Lanka: The Traffic in Commodities, Bodies, and Myths from the Thirteenth Century Onwards," *South Asia* 3, no. 1 (June 1980): 36–47; Roberts, *Caste Conflict and Elite Formation: The Rise of a Karāva Elite in Sri Lanka, 1500–1931* (Cambridge: Cambridge University Press, 1982); Sinnappah Arasaratnam, *Merchants, Companies and Commerce on the Coromandel Coast, 1650–1740* (Delhi: Oxford University Press, 1986); Sanjay Subrahmanyam, *The Political Economy of Commerce: Southern India, 1500–1650* (Cambridge: Cambridge University Press, 1990); Eric Meyer, "Labour Circulation between Sri Lanka and India in Historical Perspective," in *Society and Circulation: Mobile People and Itinerant Cultures in South Asia, 1750–1950*, ed. Claude Markovits, Jacques Pouchepadass, and Sanjay Subrahmanyam (Delhi: Permanent Black, 2003); Ronit Ricci, *Islam Translated: Literature, Conversion, and the Arabic Cosmopolis of South and Southeast Asia* (Chicago: University of Chicago Press, 2011).

12. Flores, "Straits of Ceylon," 28.

13. Sanjay Subrahmanyam, "Connected Histories: Notes Towards a Reconfiguration of Early Modern Eurasia," *Modern Asian Studies* 31, no. 3 (1997): 735–62.

14. Molly A. Warsh, *American Baroque: Pearls and the Nature of Empire, 1492–1700* (Chapel Hill: University of North Carolina Press, 2018).

15. George D. Winius, "Jewel Trading in Portuguese India in the XVI and XVII Centuries," in *Studies on Portuguese Asia, 1495–1689* (Aldershot: Ashgate, 2001); João Teles e Cunha, "Hunting Riches: Goa's Gem Trade in the Early Modern Age," in *The Portuguese, Indian Ocean, and European Bridgeheads, 1500–1800: Festschrift in Honour of Prof. K. S. Mathew*, ed. Pius Malekandathil and Jamal Mohammed (Tellicherry: Institute for Research in Social Sciences and Humanities of MESHAR, 2001). For Madras, see Gedalia Yogev, *Diamonds and Coral: Anglo-Dutch Jews and Eighteenth-Century Trade* (Leicester, UK: Leicester University Press, 1978); Søren Mentz, *The English Gentleman Merchant at Work: Madras and the City of London 1660–1740* (Copenhagen: Museum Tusculanum Press, University of Copenhagen, 2005). For a recent study, see Francesca Trivellato, *The Familiarity of Strangers: The Sephardic Diaspora, Livorno, and Cross-Cultural Trade in the Early Modern Period* (New Haven, CT: Yale University Press, 2009).

16. Warsh, *American Baroque*, 9.

17. Sanjay Subrahmanyam, "Noble Harvest from the Sea: Managing the Pearl Fishery of Mannar, 1500–1925," in *Institutions and Economic Change in South Asia*, ed. Burton Stein and Sanjay Subrahmanyam (Delhi: Oxford University Press, 1996), 135.

18. Markus P. M. Vink, *Encounters on the Opposite Coast: The Dutch East India Company and the Nayaka State of Madurai in the Seventeenth Century* (Leiden: Brill, 2015); Zoltán Biedermann, *The Portuguese in Sri Lanka and South India: Studies in the History of Diplomacy, Empire and Trade, 1500–1650* (Wiesbaden: Harrassowitz Verlag, 2014).

19. Some high-ranking officials proposed bringing the management of the entire pearl fishery under the collective authority of Madras and Colombo. Alexander Johnston wrote to the British secretary of state for the colonies in 1809 with a "plan for changing the system observed by the Ceylon Government, in the management of the Pearl and Chank fisheries on the North West Coast of Ceylon, for placing all the Pearl and Chank Banks in the gulf of *Manaar*, as well those belonging to the East India Company as those belonging to the Crown, under one and the same management." Steuart, *Account of the Pearl Fisheries*, 2.

20. Thomas R. Metcalf, *Ideologies of the Raj* (Cambridge: Cambridge University Press, 1994).

21. Eric Stokes, *The English Utilitarians and India* (Oxford: Clarendon, 1959); Ranajit Guha, *A Rule of Property for Bengal: An Essay on the Idea of Permanent Settlement* (Durham, NC: Duke University Press, 1996); Jon E. Wilson, *The Domination of Strangers: Modern Governance in Eastern India, 1780–1835* (Basingstoke, UK: Palgrave Macmillan, 2008).

22. Subrahmanyam writes that "the spirit of *raiyatwari*, so much in the air in these years, could not leave the fishery's administration untouched." Subrahmanyam, "Noble Harvest from the Sea," 158.

23. Keith Tribe, *Land, Labour, and Economic Discourse* (London: Routledge, 1978); Sudipta Sen, *Empire of Free Trade: The East India Company and the Making of the Colonial Marketplace* (Philadelphia: University of Pennsylvania Press, 1998).

24. Bernard Semmel, *The Rise of Free Trade Imperialism: Classical Political Economy, the Empire of Free Trade and Imperialism, 1750–1850* (Cambridge: Cambridge University Press, 1970); William J. Barber, *British Economic Thought and India, 1600–1858: A Study in the History of Development Economics* (Oxford: Clarendon, 1975); S. Ambirajan, *Classical Political Economy and British Policy in India* (Cambridge: Cambridge University Press, 1978); Sen, *Empire of Free Trade*; Philip Stern and Carl Wennerlind, eds., *Mercantilism Reimagined: Political Economy in Early Modern Britain and Its Empire* (Oxford: Oxford University Press, 2013).

25. Sen, *Empire of Free Trade*.

26. Sen, *Empire of Free Trade*.

27. John Ramsay McCulloch, *A Dictionary, Practical, Theoretical and Historical of Commerce and Commercial Navigation*, rev. ed. (London: Longmans, Green, 1871), 1044.

28. Steuart, *Account of the Pearl Fisheries*, 30

29. Steuart, 30–31; see Subrahmanyam, "Noble Harvest from the Sea," 159.

30. Steuart, *Account of the Pearl Fisheries*, 31.

31. Jonathan Forbes, *Eleven Years in Ceylon*, 2 vols. (London: R. Bentley, 1840), 1:258

32. McCulloch, *Dictionary*, 1044.

33. Chandra R. De Silva, "The Pearl Fisheries of Ceylon, 1796–1837," *Ceylon Literary Register* 2, no. 10 (1932): 433–42; Colvin R. De Silva, *Ceylon under the British Occupation, 1795–1833*, 2nd ed., 2 vols. (Colombo, Ceylon: Colombo Apothecaries' Co., 1953–62), 2:501–10; Lennox A. Mills, *Ceylon under British Rule, 1795–1932* (London: Oxford University Press, 1933); G. C. Mendis, *Ceylon under the British* (Colombo, Ceylon: Colombo Apothecaries' Co., 1946); U. C. Wickremeratne, *The Conservative Nature of the British Rule of Sri Lanka* (New Delhi: Navrang, 1996).

34. UKNA, CO 54/7, 10v.

35. See chap. 4, "The Most Sovereign Commodity," in Samuel Ostroff, "The Beds of Empire: Power and Profit at the Pearl Fisheries of South India and Sri Lanka, c. 1770–1840" (PhD diss., University of Pennsylvania, 2016).

36. Tamil Nadu Archives (TNA), Board of Revenue (BOR) Proceedings, vol. 1168, 11458 (November 6, 1828).

37. TNA, BOR Proceedings, vol. 1168, 11459 (November 6, 1828).

38. UKNA, CO 54, 166.

39. *The Colebrooke-Cameron Papers: Documents on British Colonial Policy in Ceylon, 1796–1832*, ed. G. C. Mendis (Oxford: Oxford University Press, 1956); David Scott, "Colonial Governmentality," in *Refashioning Futures: Criticism after Postcoloniality* (Princeton, NJ: Princeton University Press, 1999).

40. *Memoir Left by Gustaaf Willem Baron Van Imhoff, Governor and Director of Ceylon, to his Successor, Willem Maurits Bruynink, 1740*, trans. Sophia Peters (Colombo, Ceylon: Government Press, 1911), 53; Colvin R. De Silva, *Ceylon under the British Occupation*; K. M. De Silva, *A History of Sri Lanka*, rev. ed. (New Delhi: Penguin, 2005); Wickremeratne, *Conservative Nature of the British Rule*.

41. UKNA CO 54/7, 10v.

42. Subrahmanyam, "Noble Harvest from the Sea," 157.

43. George Vane, "The Pearl Fisheries of Ceylon," *Journal of the Ceylon Branch of the Royal Asiatic Society* 10, no. 34 (1887): 17.

44. Scott, "Colonial Governmentality."

45. Scholars have considered the extent to which scribes, bankers, merchants, fixers, landed elites, and other native intermediaries enabled colonial state formation and conquest. C. A. Bayly, *Empire and Information: Intelligence Gathering and Social Communication in India, 1780–1870* (Cambridge: Cambridge University Press, 1996); Bernard S. Cohn, *Colonialism and Its Forms of Knowledge: The British in India* (Princeton, NJ: Princeton University Press, 1996); Nicholas B. Dirks, *Castes of Mind: Colonialism and the Making of Modern India* (Princeton, NJ: Princeton University Press, 2001); Muzaffar Alam and Sanjay Subrahmanyam, "The Making of a Munshi," *Comparative Studies of South Asia, Africa, and the Middle East* 24, no. 2 (August 2004): 61–72; Bhavani Raman, *Document Raj: Writing and Scribes in Early Colonial South India* (Chicago: University of Chicago Press, 2012). Another line of inquiry has focused on the place of intermediaries in knowledge production. For instance, see Phillip B. Wagoner, "Precolonial Intellectuals and the Production of Colonial Knowledge," *Comparative Studies in Society and History* 45, no. 4 (October 2003): 783–814; Kapil Raj, *Relocating Modern Science: Circulation and the Construction of Knowledge in South Asia and Europe, 1650–1900* (London: Palgrave Macmillan, 2007); Michael S. Dodson, *Orientalism, Empire, and National Culture: India, 1770–1880* (London: Palgrave Macmillan, 2007).

46. British Library (BL), India Office Records (IOR) F, 4, 129, 2401, 132.

47. James Cordiner, *A Description of Ceylon*, 2 vols. (London: Longman, Hurst, Rees, and Orme, 1807), 2:58–59.

48. Forbes, *Eleven Years in Ceylon*, 1:254–55.

49. Sugata Bose, *A Hundred Horizons: The Indian Ocean in the Age of Global Empire* (Cambridge, MA: Harvard University Press, 2006).

50. Claude Markovits, Jacques Pouchepadass, and Sanjay Subrahmanyam, "Introduction: Circulation and Society under Colonial Rule," in Markovits, Pouchepadass, and Subrahmanyam, *Society and Circulation*.

51. Sujit Sivasundaram, *Islanded: Britain, Sri Lanka, and the Bounds of an Indian Ocean Colony* (Chicago: University of Chicago Press, 2013), 322.

52. Eric Tagliacozzo, *Secret Trades, Porous Borders: Smuggling and States along a Southeast Asian Frontier, 1865–1915* (New Haven, CT: Yale University Press, 2005).

53. For example, see Richard Maxwell Eaton, *The Rise of Islam and the Bengal Frontier, 1204–1760* (Berkeley: University of California Press, 1993); Jos Gommans, "The Silent Frontier of South Asia, c. A.D. 1100–1800," *Journal of World History* 9, no. 1 (Spring 1998): 1–23.

54. J. C. Heesterman, "Littoral et intérieur de l'Inde," in *History and Underdevelopment: Essays on Underdevelopment and European Expansion in Asia and Africa*, ed. Leonard Blussé, H. L. Wesseling, and George D. Winius (Leiden: Leiden University Press, 1980). Quoted in Michael Pearson, *The Indian Ocean* (London: Routledge, 2003), 38.

55. John R. Gillis and Franziska Torma, eds., *Fluid Frontiers: New Currents in Marine Environmental History* (Cambridge, UK: White Horse, 2015).

56. Cordiner, *Description of Ceylon*, 2:41.

57. TNA, Tinnevelly District Records (TDR), vol. 3562, 8 (January 10, 1803).

58. TNA, BOR Proceedings, vol. 268, 10303–10 (December 11, 1800).

59. TNA, BOR Proceedings, vol. 247, 2161–87 (March 6, 1800).

60. TNA, BOR Proceedings, vol. 268, 10303–10 (December 11, 1800).

61. *Instructions from the Governor-General and Council of India to the Governor of Ceylon, 1656–65* (Colombo, Ceylon: H. C. Cottle, 1908), 121. Paviljoen continued, "If asked to go no one will consent to do so, and should they hear of our plans they will all conceal themselves for a time. Four of them must therefore be secretly pointed out by the Patangatyn and be taken on board. Fair promises must be held out to them, and they may be told that they will be required to stay away one year only and will receive high wages. This must also be told to those who remain behind, with a view to prevent any general discontentment among them with regard to our action, which apparently would seem rather hard" (122).

62. Cordiner, *Description of Ceylon*, 2:36.

63. BL, IOR, F, 4, 129, 2401, 76–77.

64. BL, IOR, G, 11, 54.

65. Anthony Bertolacci, *A View of the Agricultural, Commercial, and Financial Interests of Ceylon* (London: Black, Parbury and Allen, 1817), 269.

66. *A Collection of Legislative Acts*, Ceylon Government, Regulation No. 3 of 1811, 130. For more, see Thomas W. Fulton, *The Sovereignty of the Sea: An Historical Account of the Claims of England to the Dominion of the British Seas, and of the Evolution of the Territorial Waters: With Special Reference to the Rights of Fishing and the Naval Salute* (Edinburgh: William Blackwood and Son, 1911); David Armitage, *The Ideological Origins of the British Empire* (Cambridge: Cambridge University Press, 2000); Armitage, "The Elephant and the Whale: Empires of Land and Sea," *Journal for Maritime Research* 9, no. 1 (2007): 23–36.

67. *A Collection of Legislative Acts*, 130.

68. *Instructions from the Governor-General*, 112.

69. UKNA, CO 54, 79; Chandra R. De Silva, "Pearl Fisheries of Ceylon," 440.

70. UKNA, CO 54, 79; Chandra R. De Silva, "Pearl Fisheries of Ceylon," 440.

71. TNA, TDR, vol. 4364, 122 (April 8, 1822).

72. Lodewijk Hovy, *Ceylonees plakkaatboek: Plakkaten en andere wetten uitgevaardigd door het Nederlandse bestuur op Ceylon, 1638–1796* (Hilversum: Verloren, 1991), 117.

73. TNA, BOR Proceedings, vol. 248, 2879 (April 3, 1800). Similar terms and conditions governed the 1815 pearl fishery at Tiruchendur. The superintendent received Tamil translations of rules from a previous year. TNA, BOR Proceedings, vol. 672, 3168–69 (March 30, 1815).

74. Chandra R. De Silva, "The Portuguese and Pearl Fishing off South India and Sri Lanka," *South Asia: Journal of South Asian Studies* 1, no. 1 (1978), 24.

75. Hendrick Becker, *Memoir of Hendrick Becker, Governor and Director of Ceylon, for His Successor, Isaac Augustyn Rumpf, 1716* (Colombo, Ceylon: H. C. Cottle, 1914), 13.

76. Collector Drury of Tirunelveli wrote to the master attendant of the 1822 pearl fishery at Tuticorin, "You will ascertain at the time of examining the Passes every day that no Boat contains [more] people, divers, or stones than the Number specified in its Pass. Any deviation from this you will report with the number of the boats for my information." TNA, TDR, vol. 4717, 117–18 (March 18, 1828). For similar instructions sent by Drury to a certain "Mr. Coq.," see TNA, TDR, vol. 4719, 240–41 (March 13, 1830). For instructions from Collector Huddleston to Meyer at Tuticorin, see TNA, TDR, vol. 4696, 391–92 (February 3, 1822).

77. Collector Lushington of Tirunelveli reported from Tuticorin in 1800, "A Copper Plate with the number of the Boat Marked upon it in

English and Malabar with several yards of Cord attached to it." TNA, BOR Proceedings, vol. 249, 3099 (April 10, 1800).

78. BL, IOR, F, 4, 130, 2402, 190.

79. According to the regulations posted at the 1799 pearl fishery at Arippu, "And if any person or persons shall presume the employment of a Boat on the Pearl Oyster bank, not fairly purchase[d] at the Public Outcry, and as such bearing a Certificate signed by the Commissioner, such Boat shall on proof of such fraudulent fishing be instantly confiscated, and the persons so employing it, shall be punished [with] fine, imprisonment, and Corporal punishment as the Commissioners shall Judge the offence to deserve, as well as the Tindall Crew and Divers who are employed on board such boat, and the letter to discover and to bring to punishment such offenders the commissioners hereby promise a reward of 200 St. Pagodas to any person or persons as may give such information as shall convict those employed in such fraudulent transactions." BL, IOR, F, 4, 130, 2402, 190–91.

80. Cordiner, *Descriptions of Ceylon*, 2:42.

81. Zwaardecroon, *Memoir of Hendrick Zwaardecroon, Commandeur of Jaffnapatam (afterwards Governor-General of Nederlands India), 1697* (Colombo, Ceylon: H. C. Cottle, 1911), 121.

82. UKNA, CO 54/7, 196–6v.

83. TNA, BOR Proceedings, vol. 247, 2165 (March 6, 1800).

84. TNA, TDR, vol. 3582, 220 (August 8, 1807). For the 1815 pearl fishery, see TNA, BOR Proceedings, vol. 670, 2134–36 (February 23, 1815).

85. According to rules and regulations at the 1800 pearl fishery at Tuticorin, "Proper Buoys will be laid down to mark the space to be fished by the Boats daily and the Tindals will be held answerable not to pass the Boundary prescribed [and] no excuse will be admitted for a disregard of this order but such a transgress[ion] . . . will invariably [be] punished with severity." TNA, BOR Proceedings, vol. 248, 2874–80 (April 3, 1800).

86. Cordiner, *Description of Ceylon*, 2:43.

87. Steuart, *Account of the Pearl Fisheries*, 21.

88. W. C. Twynam, *Report on the Ceylon Pearl Fisheries, 1899* (Colombo, Ceylon: Government Press, 1902), 15.

89. Twynam, *Report on the Ceylon Pearl Fisheries*, 15.

90. Henry J. Le Beck, "An Account of the Pearl Fishery in the Gulph of Manar, in March and April, 1797," *Asiatick Researches* 5 (1807): 404–5. See also Cordiner, *Description of Ceylon*, 2:59.

91. "Those fellows who are employed to search among the fish also commit many depredations, and even swallow the pearls to conceal them; when this is suspected, the plan followed by the merchants is to lock the fellows up, and give them strong emetics and purgatives, which have frequently the effect of discovering the stolen goods." Robert Percival, *An Account of*

the Island of Ceylon, Containing Its History, Geography, Natural History (London: C. and R. Baldwin, 1803), 70.

92. Cordiner, *Description of Ceylon*, 2:42.

93. TNA, TDR, vol. 3565, 39 (March 22, 1805).

94. Joan Gideon Loten, *Memoir of Joan Gideon Loten, Governor of Ceylon, Delivered to His Successor Jan Schreuder on February 28, 1757*, trans. E. Reimers (Colombo, Ceylon: Government Press, 1935), 18. For more on Loten, including mentions of his involvement with the pearl fishery, see Alexander J. P. Raat, *The Life of Governor Joan Gideon Loten (1710–1789): A Personal History of a Dutch Virtuoso* (Hilversum, Neth.: Verloren, 2010).

95. TNA, TDR, vol. 3582, 6–7 (January 8, 1807).

96. TNA, TDR, vol. 4717, 117–18 (March 18, 1828).

97. TNA, BOR Proceedings, vol. 248, 2878 (April 3, 1800).

98. He wrote, "I have thought it advisable to detained [sic] the escort who accompanied the gun in order to avail myself of their service during the fishery for the protection of the valuable Property which will be collected here under the hope that no inconvenience will result to your arrangements from the measure, but should you particularly require the presence of the men in question they will of course be sent at Palamcottah as you had previously detached a Guard hither on the duty." TNA, TDR, vol. 4696 (February 3, 1822), 408–9.

99. R. A. Donkin, *Beyond Price: Pearls and Pearl-Fishing: Origins to the Age of Discoveries* (Philadelphia: American Philosophical Society, 1998), 158–61.

100. Percival, *An Account of the Island of Ceylon*, 64.

101. At the 1807 pearl fishery at Tuticorin, for instance, over seventy-one million oysters were fished over a thirty-day period. TNA, TDR, vol. 3582, 153–57 (May 14, 1807).

102. Steuart, *Account of the Pearl Fisheries*, 9–10; James Hornell, *Report to the Government of Madras on the Indian Pearl Fisheries in the Gulf of Mannaar* (Madras: Government Press, 1905); Hornell. *Fishing in Many Waters* (Cambridge: Cambridge University Press, 1950).

103. Steuart, *Account of the Pearl Fisheries*, 11, 26.

104. Twynam, *Report on the Ceylon Pearl Fisheries*, 13.

105. Cordiner, *Description of Ceylon*, 2:50.

106. Donkin, *Beyond Price*, 159. The use of such devices and substances was more common among pearl divers in the Persian Gulf. An account of the Persian Gulf pearl fishery by British Lt. H. H. Whitlock, for instance, contains the following description: "When diving they make use of a piece of horn to close the nostrils, to enable them to breath longer, which likewise prevents the water from getting up the nose; this is about the size and form of a common wine bottle cork, with a notch at one end cut in the centre, so

as to fit remarkably well." Quoted in Steuart, *Account of the Pearl Fisheries*, 68; George Frederick Kunz and Charles Hugh Stevenson, *The Book of the Pearl: The History, Art, Science, and Industry of the Queen of Gems* (New York: Century, 1908), 114.

107. Chandra R. De Silva, "Portuguese and Pearl Fishing," 14.

108. For studies of pearling in the Persian Gulf that contain discussions of Dutch experiments with diving bells, see Willem Floor, "The Bahrain Project of 1754," *Persica* 11 (1984), 129–48; Floor, "Pearl Fishing in the Persian Gulf in 1757," *Persica* 10 (1982): 209–22. There are also references in Dutch sources to the use of diving bells as diplomatic gifts to the Shogun of Japan in 1833. See *Hoge Regering te Batavia*, Nationaal Archief, The Hague, Netherlands, 1.04.21, ff. 1466a.

109. Steuart, *Account of the Pearl Fisheries*, 51.

110. Steuart, 10; Twynam, *Report on the Ceylon Pearl Fisheries*, 14.

111. According to Steuart, "It had been believed by many persons, that the native divers employed by Government at the examination of the banks, were subject to the improper influence of certain wealthy natives, who were suspected of employing boats and divers to rob the oysters [*sic*] beds, and that therefore the reports given by the divers could not be depended upon. It had also been said that the oyster beds were at some periods overwhelmed with drifted sand, which at other times passed away. To clear up these doubtful reports, appears to have been one, if not the only use of the diving bells;—for one native diver at a pearl fishery, would collect more oysters in a day than could be obtained by all the men that could work in a diving bell." Steuart, *Account of the Pearl Fisheries*, 20. It is worth noting also that, beyond its intended commercial use, the diving bell supported nineteenth-century marine science studies. For example, Austrian naturalist Eugen Ransonnet-Villez used a diving bell to render the "submarine scenery" of coral gardens on the floor of the Gulf of Mannar in vivid detail and brilliant color. Ransonnet-Villez, *Sketches of the Inhabitants, Animal Life and Vegetation in the Lowlands and High Mountains of Ceylon* (Vienna: published by the author, 1867).

112. Steuart, *Account of the Pearl Fisheries*, 52.

113. John Bennett, *Ceylon and Its Capabilities: An Account of Its Natural Resources, Indigenous Productions, and Commercial Facilities* (London: W. H. Allen, 1843), 206, 205.

114. Matthew S. Hopper, *Slaves of One Master: Globalization and Slavery in Arabia in the Age of Empire* (New Haven, CT: Yale University Press, 2015), 100.

115. Warsh, *American Baroque*, 8, 10–11.

116. William A. Herdman, *Report to the Government of Ceylon on the Pearl Oyster Fisheries of the Gulf of Manaar*, 5 vols. (London: Royal Society, 1903–6), 1:8.

FOUR

The Pearler's Problem
Management, Markets, and the Marine Environment in the Shark Bay Pearling Industry

JOSEPH CHRISTENSEN

IN THE MID-1930S, the pearlers of Shark Bay formed an isolated and almost forgotten community on one of the most barren stretches of Australia's coast. With their industry in terminal decline, their plight was captured by Ernestine Hill in her widely read travelogue, *The Great Australian Loneliness* (1937). "Toilers of the sea to the third and fourth generation," she wrote, they inhabited a village of merely 250 people, "so remote from the world that sometimes neither a stranger nor a daily newspaper is seen here in a period of years." The village, Denham, was a relic of pearling's multiracial workforce that Hill viewed as a curiosity in the era of the White Australia Policy: "In fifty years of seclusion there has been such interbreeding among the coloured races and intermarriage of the whites that to-day the population is variegated indeed, and mostly related—a Pitcairn in Australia."[1] Like the Japanese divers and Malay boatmen of the pearling fleets of Broome, further along the Western Australian coast, the position of these pearlers was uncertain. Markets for pearls and mother-of-pearl (or pearl shell) had collapsed in the Great Depression, before the rise of cultured pearls and plastics in the 1930s dampened hopes for recovery. The problem was laid bare when, in 1939, the Western Australian government ordered an investigation into Shark Bay. After prices flattened in the early 1930s, many pearlers had resorted to overfishing in an effort to maintain profits, leaving the pearl oyster banks badly depleted. Now the outbreak of World War II threatened to finish them off altogether. Hardly any boats were still working because of uncertainties in the market, reported the inspector John Gregory, and the industry was at its lowest ebb in living memory.[2]

Hill sensed this decline, and her observations became a requiem for a unique form of pearling. "I watched them securing their pearls and pearl shell by a method curious and very primitive. Pegging the shallow bay into leases from 500 to 1,000 acres, fenced off like poultry-yards, the pearlers travel across it a week at a time in tiny cutters, dragging the ocean bed with hand-dredges of wire, sails set to some three miles an hour. At the weekend they return with the haul, each ship bringing from ten to twelve bags."[3] This was the manner of harvesting the Shark Bay pearl oyster, *Pinctada albina*, a smaller and less lucrative alternative to the larger *Pinctada maxima* or Silver-lipped pearl oyster that supported the larger pearl-shelling industry based at Broome. Once ashore, the shell was opened in "tumble-down tin shacks known as pearling-pits," although, as she noted, only "the first quality is eligible for auction in London." Pearls were then obtained by shucking the oysters into large cauldrons known as "pogey-pots," where "they are left to putrefy into a vile and liqueous mass, and when putrefaction can go no further, are boiled to a seething and even more evil-smelling scum, in which the sediment of pearls sinks to the bottom."[4] As Hill hinted at, this was a mode of operation that had not changed in decades.

By the late 1930s, such a picture of decline was a familiar scene across the Indian Ocean and its adjoining seas. In *Sons of Sinbad* (1940), Alan Villiers captures the last days of pearling in the Arabian Gulf, when a vast fleet lay neglected on the beaches of Kuwait "as thick as the discarded shells of empty oysters on a pearling beach—big ships and little ships, jalboots, sambuks, belems, shewes."[5] Between India and Sri Lanka, the pearl fishery of Palk Strait and the Gulf of Mannar had become a shadow of its former self.⁶ At Broome, government assistance had been required since the Depression to maintain a handful of luggers from what had been, before the First World War, the largest pearl-shelling fleet on Earth. When Hill arrived, continuing her travels from Denham, she found "its population has been reduced from 6,000 to 1,000, white and coloured, and its fleet from 400 to 50 ships."⁷ Yet Broome's slump also helps to place Shark Bay in perspective. Whereas the Silver-lipped oyster still sold for £180 a ton and its pearls realized as much £8,000 each, the best Shark Bay shell yielded only £14–35 per ton and its pearls "rarely touch the £100 level," Hill recorded.⁸ When Gregory investigated, he found that it was only through the sale of these pearls that the bay's pearlers had remained solvent during the 1930s. But the outbreak of war in Europe meant this trade was now closed, and most leases had since been abandoned. The industry, he found, "is practically non-existent today."⁹

To Gregory, however, the causes of Shark Bay's decline ran far deeper than these inescapable realities of global commerce. To explain it he highlighted the system of individual or exclusive leases that Hill had observed, only a few years earlier, in its last days of operation. This form of governance had "divided the industry against itself," he suggested, "and prevented the development of the cooperative spirit essential to any industry. Each pearler worked his bank in his own way, and in the isolation of Shark Bay he came to regard himself as a self-sufficient cosmos."¹⁰ In 1956 the historian John Bach reached a similar verdict on Australian pearl shelling at large. Like Gregory, Bach was commissioned to report on an industry that was failing amidst competition from overseas competitors and the rise of plastics and cultured pearls as substitutes. "In theory, the causes of the recurrent crises in pearling are simple," he argued. Restricted demand, high labor costs and a tendency to combat falling prices with increased production "all contribute to the precarious state of mother-of-pearl fishing. The pearlshell market has always been one with which liberties cannot be taken, and the need for a degree of organisation has been increasingly evident. Australian pearlers, however, have lived from day to day, and have shown themselves incapable of understanding the basic character of their industry."¹¹ To both observers, the explanation for pearling's demise therefore lay not in the marketplace but with the pearlers themselves. Although in late 1939 Gregory's assessment had been quietly filed away, Bach's report to the

Commonwealth government, the first detailed study of Australian pearling's long-term development, remained influential for decades to come.[12]

This chapter is based upon the predicament that Gregory exposed in 1939—a confluence of resource depletion, management failure, and economic collapse that I refer to as "the pearler's problem." This metaphor is borrowed from Arthur E. McEvoy's model of "the fisherman's problem," as developed in his seminal history of the California fisheries. McEvoy's insight is to take the "tragedy of the commons" concept, which holds that a resource owned in common will inevitably be over-exploited because there is no incentive for individual users to act in the long-term interest of all, and argue instead that resource management involves the complex interaction of legal processes and policymaking, the ecology of natural resources, and the behavior of harvesters. The fisherman's problem, he concludes, is that unstable relationships between industry and resources is the unavoidable outcome of environmental variability, the autonomy of fishers, and forms of social organization built around capitalist economic expansion.[13] As Sanjay Subrahmanyam suggests, this framework can be usefully applied to the history of Indian Ocean pearling, particularly in the imperial or capitalist age.[14] Following McEvoy's example, my aim is to use Shark Bay as a case study for exploring the pearler's problem through the interplay of the politics of resource management, the fluctuating global market for pearls and mother-of-pearl, and changes in the marine environment.

Much of what follows focuses on two figures who were central to the development of the management system observed by Hill and criticized by Gregory in the late 1930s. The first is a well-known figure in Australia's maritime history. The English marine biologist William Saville-Kent (1845–1908), who came to Western Australia after working as an applied biologist and fisheries manager in Tasmania and Queensland, was instrumental in designing the Sharks Bay Pearl Shell Fishery Act (1892) and thereby establishing the system of exclusive leases that remained the hallmark of the industry's organization thereafter.[15] The second is comparatively unknown. Ludwig Stross (1858–1913), a master pearler in the 1880s and 1890s, is best remembered as a founding partner of the Viscoloid Company, one of the world's earliest plastic manufacturers.[16] Born in Bohemia to a family of prominent textile manufacturers, Stross was a merchant in Cairo and Alexandria before branching into the pearl shell trade in the Red Sea and Arabian Gulf in the 1880s.[17] He then entered into Shark Bay's pearling industry, where he emerged as a leading spokesman for the pearlers and Saville-Kent's foremost critic. In their engagement with each other and in the industry's reform, sustainability, and future, these two figures shed light on the historical background to Gregory's verdict, and, beyond this, to the complexity of the pearler's problem itself.

FROM BOOM TO BUST IN SHARK BAY'S PEARLING INDUSTRY

Pinctada albina occurs widely throughout the central Indo-Pacific, its range corresponding broadly to the distribution of *Pinctada maxima*, but at Shark Bay (known as Sharks Bay in the nineteenth century) it is unusually prolific, thriving on the sandy banks that make up large parts of the bay's shallow waters (Figure 1). It differs from its larger cousin in that its small pearls occur more frequently, and the color of its nacre varies considerably, ranging from pure white to the shades of yellow and gold of so-called "oriental" pearls. Historically, only the whitest shell was competitive on international markets, but pearls were different, with whites preferred in Europe or North America and colored pearls favored in India and China.[18] Although William Dampier observed pearl-bearing oysters at Shark Bay as early as 1699, commercial exploitation began only after the colony of Western Australia was established in 1829, with the export of three tons of shell in 1850 effectively inaugurating the Australian pearl-shelling industry.[19] However, as there was not yet an established market for the shell, early interest focused instead on pearls. In the late 1860s the forays of colonial speculators made way for a more settled industry, particularly after rich banks were discovered inside Dirk Hartog Island and Useless Inlet. By 1871 more than forty vessels worked the bay: small cutters (of no more than five tons) suited to shallow waters were the most common craft in use, oyster dredges were being widely employed, and the practice of shucking oysters into pogey pots was widely practiced.[20] The colony's Pearl Shell Fishery Act of 1873 introduced a license fee for vessels engaging in pearl fishing, helping to offset the cost of supervising the employment of Aboriginal labor in the industry.[21]

During 1873 Shark Bay shell reentered the global market as a competitor to the Lingah shell of the Arabian Gulf, causing production to surge. Men and boats were reported to be flocking to pearling grounds, and at least 380 tons of shell, worth £3,800, were exported for the year. The population of the pearling camps peaked at around four hundred men. At the start of 1874 an exodus took place after fever spread through the camps and the banks in Useless Inlet became depleted.[22] *Pinctada albina* is a fast-growing species, typically reaching maturity within three years, but dredging was a destructive practice that removed not only marketable shell but also juvenile oysters and the dead shell, seagrasses, and other materials that spat adheres to. For a time, the discovery of new banks further inside the bay allowed yields to keep on increasing, and some 476 tons of shell valued at £3,335 were exported in 1879.[23] Yet the industry remained unregulated from a conservation standpoint, so with persistent demand for both pearls and shell the industry faced an inevitable collapse. In 1880 an inquiry by the Western Australian government confirmed an emerging view that "the Fishery is being very seriously injured by the reckless and exhausting system of dredging

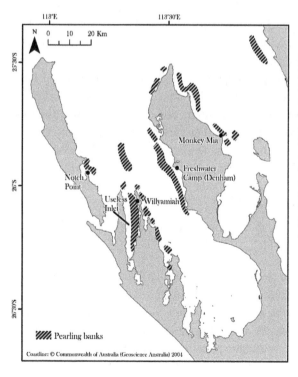

Figure 4.1. Shark Bay, showing the main pearling banks and pearling camps, ca. 1892. Source: Adapted from map in D. A. Hancock, *A Review of the Shark Bay Pearling Industry*, Fisheries Management Report no. 27 (Perth: Fisheries Department of Western Australia, 1989).

continuously." A legal size for the *Pinctada albina* shell was accordingly introduced, alongside a system of rotating closures to dredging to allow stocks on the main pearling banks to regenerate.[24] The banks in Useless Inlet were initially closed for five years, but when it was found in 1884 that stocks had recovered, a reduced period was introduced.[25]

This system lasted until 1886, when conflict between European and Chinese pearlers forced further reforms. Chinese laborers had been present at Shark Bay since the early 1870s, but with the advent of a regular steamship service between Western Australia and Singapore in 1884, new operations were established in direct competition to established pearling masters. A movement to expel them soon developed. Anti-Chinese sentiment had been building in the colony's mining and agricultural districts during the mid-1880s, and amidst fears the Chinese would overrun the banks restored under the system of closures, the government passed the Sharks Bay Pearl Shell Fishery Act (1886), giving it the power to grant an exclusive license for the entire fishery. A consortium of European pearlers was then awarded the license for an annual fee of £1,000, thus excluding their Chinese rivals, who were promptly compensated by the government before departing the colony.[26] The consortium in turn sublet fishing rights exclusively for a fee of £8 per vessel. For a time, the new system appeared to work. As shell prices surged in the late 1880s, reaching as high as £60 per ton for the highest grades, men and boats had flocked to Shark Bay. In 1890, when more than 80 boats worked the banks, the harvest of 534 tons of shell valued at £16,020 was the most lucrative year on record. After another 760 tons were taken in 1891, the industry was once more in trouble. The practice of rotating closures had been abandoned by the consortium in order to derive the maximum in license fees, and the banks were again on the brink of exhaustion.[27]

A "HARDY MARINE POPULATION": THE ENCLOSURE OF SHARK BAY

It was at this juncture that Stross and Saville-Kent emerged as influential figures at Shark Bay. After departing the Red Sea (where he was, for a time, the Austrian consul in Jeddah) due to ill health, Stross arrived in Western Australia at the beginning of 1890. Acquiring a fleet of three cutters along with shore facilities at Monkey Mia, one of the main pearling camps, he was soon established as one of the bay's most prominent pearlers. At this stage Saville-Kent was midway through his term as commissioner of fisheries in Queensland, during which period resource depletion in the pearl-shelling grounds of Torres Strait was a major preoccupation. As with Stross, this earlier experience would help to shape his approach to the reform of pearling at Shark Bay. By the start of 1896 both figures had departed Western Australia for good, but not before they had decisively shaped the management regime that would remain in place for the next half-century.

Stross signaled his concern for the industry when, in June 1891, he wrote to the *West Australian* newspaper to warn against the looming failure of the Sharks Bay Pearl Shell Fishery Act passed only a few years earlier. "In the last two years the number of boats has increased from about fifty to more than ninety, while no new banks have been discovered," he wrote. "None of the banks have been closed for the last two years or so, but all the Bay has been thrown open. No control whatever is exercised over the quality of shells that is taken off the banks. . . . It is evident that if this state of things is allowed to go on for any length of time (to my belief within two years) Sharks Bay will be ruined forever." The pearlers had since split into opposing factions and were now at odds with each other. To avert all of this, Stross called for centralizing control via a government-industry partnership when the consortium's lease expired at the end of 1891. The colony would grant exclusive rights to the current group of pearlers together with a loan of £6,000; the pearlers would then elect a board of management that would be empowered to disburse the loan in buying out established operators to reduce the number of boats by half, and to fix regulations for working the banks, before authorizing dredging to resume. Profit would be restored under this "business-like management of the Bay" through the reduced competition among pearlers, generating revenue for the colony through repayment of the loan and a duty of ten shillings per ton of shell exported. "What I propose is practically a sort of monopoly for a few, but there is no other way left," Stross wrote. "That Sharks Bay is overstocked with boats is clearly proved by the present state of affairs. Any other method the Government may adopt will ruin either the Bay or the pearlers."[28]

The merit of this scheme was that it combined sound economic principle with a measure of ecological caution. The British intervention in Ceylon's pearl fishery in the mid-nineteenth century had been based upon a similar approach, combining a limit on boats (and thus, fishing effort) with a catch share arrangement to generate revenue for the treasury.[29] Like the waters of Palk Strait or the Red Sea grounds he had previously worked, Stross also understood that the productive areas within Shark Bay were limited in extent. "There is a sort of legend amongst the pearlers that big undiscovered banks still exist, but if any of them is asked the whereabouts of these mythical banks he will reply with a vague move of the hand, which comprises half the horizon," he wrote in June 1891. "After talking the matter over with almost all the people who pretend to know Shark's Bay, I have come to the firm conviction that this is all empty talk."[30] In October, a second letter to the press expanded on this point.

> Sharks Bay is not the open sea. It is a comparatively small area and the banks are limited, and it is not logic that the number of boats should not be limited too. Sharks Bay can be compared to a paddock that is overstocked with sheep. There is no food for all, and the weakest will have to die, while the others are starving. Doubtless things will find their own level in some way, but if legislation does not provide, new boats will flock in as soon as the banks are re-opened, and after some time the same starvation story will repeat itself. I think Sharks Bay has been worked like a mine up to the present, and it will have to be worked like a farm in the future. People will have to sow and to wait for their harvest. Artificial banks will have to be created, and shells grown systematically. But as long as nobody is sure of getting the fruits of his labour, as long as at any time any number of boats can flock in and work wherever they choose, nobody can be expected to take any special interest or trouble.[31]

This is a fine example of the "tragedy of the commons" scenario, expressed in terms that anticipate Garret Hardin's famous metaphor of farmers grazing cattle on a common pasture.[32] Stross illustrated it so as to underline the rationale behind his proposal. "It is by monopoly only, in one form or another, that Shark's Bay will ever be brought into more settled conditions and a more prosperous state. The monopoly will have to be created either by gradually reducing the number of licensed boats to a certain limit, approximate to the carrying capacities of the Bay, or by letting the Bay in portions, which practically comes to the same thing."[33]

Yet Stross had erred in one key regard. Insisting on a "monopoly" was politically risky, for reasons that extended beyond the debacle of the arrangements established in 1886. A democratic and egalitarian ethos hostile to monopolies, oligopolies, or cartels had taken hold in Western Australia, coinciding with the advent of Responsible Government in 1890 and fueled by the nascent labor movement, the rapid growth of the working class following the opening of new goldfields, and economic depression in the eastern colonies, from which many new migrants came. It had a subtle and yet profound impact on public policy, shaping, for example, support for prospectors and small miners against the encroachment of London-based mining companies, or homesteading legislation to promote closer agricultural settlement ahead of extensive pastoral leases.[34] In the Northwest pearl-shelling industry, the imperative of assisting small-scale capital fostered the rise of the lugger-based system in place of the "floating stations" that were predominant in the 1880s and early 1890s, cementing Western Australia's reputation for being, in Steve Mullins's words, a "bastion of the small-time operator."[35] Stross barely had time to see his proposal in print before this same orthodoxy rendered it impractical. On June 30, 1891, a deputation of Shark Bay pearlers called upon the Western Australian premier, Sir John Forrest, to implore that the lease granted in 1886 not be renewed and that the colony instead resume direct control over the industry. Forrest's response made the government's position plain.

> It came to this—that an inspector might be appointed, some banks closed—and in that the Government would have to be guided largely by the views of those persons who were on the spot, and were disinterested enough to give them their opinion as to the boundaries of the areas to be closed. They had to deal with that portion not closed, and to frame regulations in order to have it worked. There were several ways they might follow. They might divide it, as blocks of land were divided, and lease them to individuals who might have some interest in maintaining them in an efficient way, or they might allow all persons who had licenses to go on them, but he [Forrest] could not say which way they would choose. But they must get it out of their minds that the Government would grant a monopoly.[36]

In presenting their case, the pearlers had echoed Stross's letter in suggesting that "in framing by-laws, the carrying capacity of the Bay must be made the first principle." But Forrest, who "could see no reason why the people there should have a monopoly over the pearling banks," now ruled out any centralized form of ownership and control.[37]

The government's plans centered instead upon the appointment of Saville-Kent. Shortly after the deputation called, Forrest initiated his recruitment to Western Australia upon the expiry of his engagement in Queensland.[38] In December 1891, when a new bill to replace the 1886 act was put before the parliament, the government's intentions became clear. "We propose to obtain the services of Mr. Saville-Kent," the Attorney General explained, "who is an expert, and a very capable and scientific man . . . the time has arrived when we should no longer go on in the haphazard and indefinite way we have been, but obtain some scientific information, and profit by it."[39] Early the following year, the Sharks Bay Pearl Shell Fishery Act (1892) was passed. Framed according to Saville-Kent's recommendations and modelled on similar legislation introduced in Queensland, the new act allowed the fixing of minimum legal size for *Pinctada albina*, the closure of specified areas, and the appointment of an inspector to enforce regulations, as well as introducing a new system of "exclusive leases" which gave sole access (that is, property rights) to specified areas for fourteen-year terms, and "general leases" granted on an annual basis and giving access to any part of the bay not held under exclusive lease.[40] Revenue would accrue from rental of leases and duty on exports of shell. An inspector was duly appointed and in May 1892 a proclamation issued to close the main pearling grounds to dredging (see Figure 2). Saville-Kent arrived in the colony in March 1893 to commence a two-year term as commissioner of fisheries. In addition to restoring Shark Bay's pearling industry, he was to promote resource conservation in the Northwest pearl-shelling industry, investigate the potential for developing other fisheries, and acclimatize "British fish" in the rivers and lakes of the colony's temperate districts.[41]

In April 1893, Saville-Kent made the first of three visits to Shark Bay. Finding the industry at a standstill and the pearlers in acute financial hardship, but the banks only partially recovered, he resolved to allow the industry to resume on a limited basis and under the supervision of the new inspector. The deeper banks lying off Fresh Water Camp were thus opened to dredging, and hand collection permitted

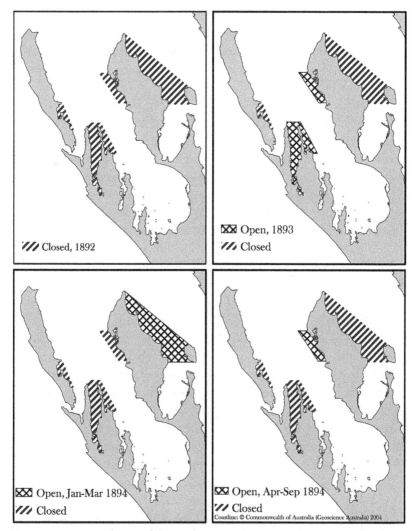

Figure 4.2. Rotating closure of the pearling grounds, 1892-94. Source: Adapted from map in D. A. Hancock, *A Review of the Shark Bay Pearling Industry*, Fisheries Management Report no. 27 (Perth: Fisheries Department of Western Australia, 1989).

on the shallowest "pick-up banks" in Useless Inlet.[42] A longer-term plan to restore the bay's productivity was also developed. This comprised two strategies. The first was to encourage systematic cultivation of *Pinctada albina*. The Shark Bay pearl oyster, Saville-Kent determined, "grows under conditions almost precisely identical" to the table oysters of Moreton Bay, near Brisbane on Australia's east coast, "and like that species is equally capable of highly profitable cultivation." This could be done by first seeding selected banks with broken and discarded shell, and then replanting immature oysters brought up by dredging and transplanting "dwarf" or smaller oysters from the eastern reaches of the bay to the main pearling grounds, where they typically reached their largest size. The second strategy was to acclimatize the more valuable *Pinctada maxima* within the bay. Saville-Kent had found corals and tropical fishes occurring in waters near Notch Point on Dirk Hartog Island, similar to species found in the pearling grounds of the northwest coast and Torres Strait, and he believed this meant that the larger Silver-lipped variety could also be introduced and cultivated as well. His recommendation to Forrest was therefore for the establishment of exclusive leases under the new legislation, "to be granted for taking up areas of shallow water, or pick-up banks, in Sharks' Bay, of the dimensions of ten acres and upwards, for the purpose of cultivating pearl shell and planting the immature shell obtained during dredging and collecting operations."[43]

Saville-Kent's visit therefore led not only to the industry's resumption but also to the beginning of the bay's enclosure. This was just as Forrest had foreshadowed, and although it had taken nearly two years to materialize, Saville-Kent's proposal met with a positive response. The idea of farming *Pinctada maxima* was lauded by the *West Australian*.

> Sharks Bay, it would appear is admirably adapted for this industry, and it is now suggested that the Government, which is always being urged to settle people on the land, should take steps to settle some of our population on the water. Under the Premier's homestead scheme, 160 acres were the least with which it was thought advisable to endow a settler, but on the oyster farms as proposed by Mr. Saville-Kent, ten acres of bank is regarded by him as amply sufficient to bring in to the holder an income of £250 per year. If this system can be established we shall have a hardy marine population at Sharks Bay, engaged in growing oysters, just as in other parts of the colony there are farmers employed in raising sheep and cattle, wheat, fruit, and potatoes.[44]

Such platitudes are explicable in light of the region's development to this point in time. In the 1870s and 1880s, Shark Bay had been a lawless and often violent frontier, with cases of "blackbirding," or the enslavement of Aboriginal labor by pearlers, several murders in the pearling camps, some well-publicized outrages committed by Malays and Chinese against European women, and the conflict that culminated in the exclusion of Chinese pearlers.[45] This was characteristic of social relations across the colony's vast and thinly settled northern districts, yet the bestowal of Responsible Government came with an expectation that the colony could control and develop this remote region.[46] A pathway to achieving this for one such district had now been presented. Having been favorably received, Saville-Kent's report to Forrest became a blueprint for the remainder of his term as commissioner of fisheries.

Saville-Kent returned to Shark Bay in October 1893 with live *Pinctada maxima* oysters in special tanks fitted to a coastal steamer traveling southward from Broome. These were laid down in cages at Dirk Hartog Island among the corals he had found on his first visit. He also carried out a further inspection of the banks and, finding sufficient improvement in their condition, he recommended reopening Useless Inlet to dredging in the latter part of 1893, followed by the banks at Monkey Mia in early 1894.[47] To his mind, there was no doubt that the industry was now on the path to recovery. Rotating closures would allow the deeper banks to replenish, and shallow banks would be steadily taken up under lease for the cultivation of both varieties of oyster. His strategy, he advised Forrest, "had saved the fishery, and there was every prospect of it producing a few years hence as rich an annual yield of shell as in any former years."[48]

It was this confidence, however, that drove Stross's dispute with Saville-Kent. During 1894 the pearlers became frustrated with the pace of reform, and in September a petition organized by Stross raised their concerns with the government. "Experience has now shown that pearling in rotation does not answer, as the banks are in so impoverished a state as not to allow the fleet to work on any of these banks for time sufficient to let other banks recover," it asserted, adding that "the system of cultivation introduced by Mr. Saville-Kent has not produced the results which might have reasonably been expected" because there was insufficient shell within the bay to plant upon them anyway.[49] Stross had earlier raised other doubts when, in June 1894, he wrote to the press to question Saville-Kent's claim that transplanted shell was alive and propagating at

Shark Bay. "It will take years and generations of shells to obtain such a result, if any result is obtained at all," he argued, and with cultivation of *Pinctada albina* also not working as predicted, the pearlers were hardly convinced of their future prosperity.[50] By September these failings had led the pearlers to request the extension of exclusive licenses into deeper banks reserved for dredging. "After all the different unsuccessful experiments of the past the community has come to the conclusion that the only way to save the place is the dividing of it into blocks and leasing them to the pearlers," the petition concluded. "Shark's Bay has amply proved that it cannot exist as a ground open to all and that common ground means nobody's ground. While divided into private blocks it is natural that the owners will look after their property, and do all in their power to make their grounds valuable and reproductive. It is only by private ownership and the stimulus of self interest that the place can ever expect to regain its ancient fertility." The banks should be surveyed at once, they pleaded, and divided among them.[51]

Saville-Kent's third visit brought matters to a head. Meeting with the pearlers, he defended both his scheme and additional charges of negligence brought against the inspector; as he reported to Forrest; "I may state that l have found that many of the assertions contained in the above-named petition are misleading, and in certain instances inaccurate, being based upon unreliable and unsupported evidence."[52] There was, however, one vital concession to be made. The question of extending leaseholds into the deeper-water banks was taken up, and, on "fully discussing this question with the pearlers at Sharks Bay, the decision was arrived at, that an area of say one square mile, 640 acres, would represent an appropriate allotment from off which, by collection and cultivation, a [lessee] might reasonably expect to derive a profitable income. Such a superficial area of one square mile in Useless Inlet or elsewhere, would not, it is maintained, contain more than 100 acres of good shell-bearing ground."[53] This was of course a much larger size than the ten-acre allotments he had originally proposed, and its implementation would ensure that extensive tracts of the best shell-bearing banks within the bay would be subsumed under exclusive leases.

In 1896 a surveyor was sent to mark out leases, or "blocks." At Useless Inlet, some twenty-nine leases extending across 14,725 acres were delineated with wooden posts driven into the seabed (Figure 4), with others similarly laid out near Monkey Mia.[54] The pearlers had got what

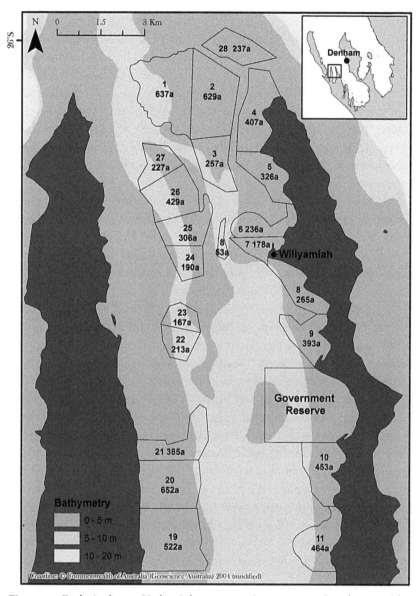

Figure 4.3. Exclusive leases, Useless Inlet, ca. 1901. Leases are numbered 1–27, with bathymetry size in acreage also shown. Source: Adapted from Fisheries Department file 1901/0602, "Exclusive licenses Sharks Bay: Opening of pearling banks," Cons. 477, State Records Office of Western Australia.

they wanted, although it came too late for some. At the start of 1895, Stross had written a final letter from Shark Bay: "One year ago about 60 boats were at work, now there are 16 or 17. In the last twelve months fully one-third of the male adult population—white and coloured—has left the place, and in another six months another third will have gone, myself included."[55] With his investment of £1,500 in boats and equipment no longer worth even a tenth of its original value, Stross kept his word, leaving Western Australia before the end of 1895.[56] Profit from shell in that year amounted to only £1,088, hardly any higher than when the fishery was closed for most of 1892, while in 1896 it was a mere £53, the lowest since regular sales began.[57]

Those who remained soon experienced a recovery of sorts. During 1897, the best shell fetched between £25 and £30 at auction, and pearls averaging £15 per ton of shell harvested were obtained. Reporting for the year, Western Australia's new, permanent chief inspector of fisheries, Charles Frederick Gale, prophesised a bright future: "Over 15,000 acres are at present held under exclusive lease, and the industry gives every promise of increase."[58] In 1898, Fresh Water Camp was gazetted as the townsite of Denham, and after a school, police station, and public jetty were built most pearlers relocated their camps there, lending the town a sense of prosperity.[59] Saville-Kent had already claimed his vindication. His *The Naturalist in Australia* (1897), a chronicle of his work in Western Australia, outlined the basis of his scheme: "the restriction of the fishery to the taking for sale of mature shell only, the closing of overworked banks until such time as they had recovered sufficiently to permit of moderate but not exhaustive fishing, and more particularly the encouragement of the establishment of systematically cultivated private fisheries, as represented by the leasing by the Government of banks of varying dimensions to private individuals." Only time was required to prove its success. "Notwithstanding the circumstance that some years must necessarily elapse before this fishery recovers its former prosperity, the measures adopted have already begun to yield highly satisfactory results."[60]

REASSESSING THE "FISHERIES SAVANT"

Had the industry been saved? Figure 4 shows revenue derived from pearls and shell between the mid-1880s (when exports began to be regularly recorded) and the Great Depression (when the inspector was withdrawn and statistics ceased to be kept). Some caution is needed with these figures. To begin with, the trade in pearls was notoriously secretive, at Shark Bay as elsewhere. Rumors of illegal sales, often to buyers on passing steamships, were persistent throughout the early twentieth century, so that true profit was probably greater than acknowledged because only sales to licensed pearl dealers were recorded.[61] Secondly, the figures on shell record sales rather than production. Significant quantities of shell were fished only to be discarded, and, as we will see, the pearlers were obliged to be highly selective over what was consigned to market. Nevertheless, some observations can be made. One is that although the industry did resume after the Sharks Bay Pearl Shell Fishery Act (1892) and associated reforms, it was never as profitable as it had been in the late 1880s and early 1890s. Another is that pearls, and not pearl shell, accounted for the bulk of profits after 1900. At the conclusion of his appointment Saville-Kent had anticipated "the early renewal of the formerly prosperous condition of the Shark's Bay Pearl Shelling industry," but the reality proved different.[62]

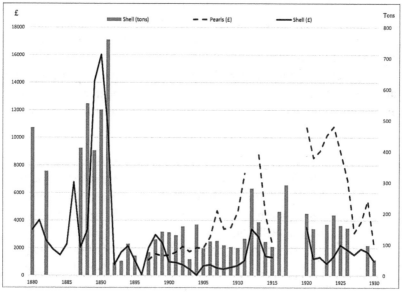

Figure 4.4. Output in the Shark Bay Pearling Industry, 1887–1930. Source: *Western Australian Yearbook* (Perth: Government Printer, 1887–1902 inclusive) and *Statistical Register of Western Australia* (Perth: Government Printer, 1903–30 inclusive).

The most obvious explanation for this lies in the failure to acclimatize *Pinctada maxima*. Saville-Kent maintained his experiment had succeeded, even publishing photographs in *The Naturalist in Australia* purporting to show the spat of juvenile oysters affixed to transplanted shell at Dirk Hartog Island. In 1904, Gale inspected the site and, with the aid of a marine glass, "was particularly struck with the quantity of young shell, apparently healthy and thriving well, some considerable distance from where the parent shells were laid down."[63] But when Gale's successor, Fred Aldrich, returned to the area in 1911, he was not able to locate any of this larger variety of oysters, and neither was Gregory when he searched in 1939. As early as 1894, Stross had suggested that spat from *Pinctada albina* had become caught in the cages holding *Pinctada maxima* to refute the commissioner's claims that the introduced shell had begun reproducing. In a 1912 study of the application of biological science in global pearling industries, the British zoologist Lyster Jameson reached a similar verdict, suggesting that Saville-Kent had mistaken *Pinctada maxima* spat for another *Pinctada* species that had propagated naturally in surrounding waters.[64] This seems a plausible explanation for the confusion that once existed. Given that the ranges of Silver-lipped and Shark Bay pearl oysters overlap closely on a wider bioregional scale, *Pinctada maxima* would almost certainly occur naturally in the bay if the conditions within it were already suitable for its propagation and growth.

The reliance upon cultivating *Pinctada albina* also exposes the shortcomings of Saville-Kent's scheme. In advocating it, he was attempting to overcome what Stross had identified in October 1891 as one of the industry's chief limitations.

> Sharks Bay contains almost as many different sorts of shell as there are banks. In some instances, banks that are only a few miles distant from each other produce completely different shells, not only in size but in shape and colour, and even the barnacles attached to these shells show altogether different formations. . . .
>
> Near Dirk Hartog island are a few patches of shells weighing as much as 6 to the pound. Collecting shells there that weigh 12 to the pound, means therefore collecting immature shell, while on the east shore 24 to the pound is excellent weight. Owing to the depth of water, the difference of food (seaweed), the greater or

lesser exposure to the sun during low tides in summer, the difference of the sea bottom (sand, mud, coral, &c), almost every bank produces a different and, in some instances, most distinct species of shells.[65]

The implications were twofold: that uniform legal sizes were impracticable in light of such diversity; and the whitest shell, which commanded the highest prices, was restricted in abundance. Saville-Kent had believed that this latter constraint would be overcome by transplanting small and yellow shell to Useless Inlet and Dirk Hartog Island, where it would grow naturally to the largest size and best condition. Stross had questioned this assumption in 1895, but left the verdict open: "the Commissioner has started experiments on a large scale with East Shore shells, and another couple of years will show if his theory is correct, and a practical success with these shells will go immensely to his credit, as it will solve one of the great difficulties in replanting some portions of the place."[66] Time would bear out his skepticism. Aldrich found little cultivation being practiced during his visit: "with one or two exceptions the necessary work is not carried out. Nature is allowed to take her own time in re-stocking the areas. The bank may be worked this season, allowed to rest a few months, perhaps a year, and again worked."[67]

What this suggests is that Saville-Kent placed undue trust in his principles of scientific management. Such conviction in the amenability of the natural world was the hallmark of professional biologists in the late Victorian era, of course, and, in fairness to him, his experiments with cultivating table oysters in Tasmania and Queensland had each produced promising results.[68] On the other hand, as Stross had alluded to, Shark Bay is a complex marine environment. The bay is known today to be characterized by distinct temperature gradients and salinity regimes that are shaped by its shallow hydrography and which give rise to highly specialized faunal assemblages.[69] Reports from the early decades of the twentieth century also point to a dynamic ecosystem, revealing fluctuations in *Pinctada albina* stocks caused not only by over-exploitation but also through the impact of tropical cyclones, plagues of echinoderms (or starfish) and other predators, or the spread of seagrasses across the banks.[70] The successful cultivation of pearl oysters certainly proved elusive in other comparable environments. The experience of the Ceylon Company of Pearl Fishers in the early 1900s is a case in point. Its attempt to systematically farm the Indian pearl oyster was, in Subrahmanyam's verdict, both naïve and greedy, ignoring as it did the accumulated knowledge of the pearlers themselves, who continued to practice harvesting, as opposed to cultivation, in concert with the natural variability of the wild stock.[71]

There is also the question of the market. Mullins shows that the lesson of Saville-Kent's attempt to promote systematic cultivation of *Pinctada maxima* in Queensland is that only the largest of Australian pearl shellers, James Clark's "Clark Combination," had the wherewithal to take up and develop leases.[72] In promoting small-scale cultivation at Shark Bay on leases as small as ten acres, Saville-Kent could only have presumed the high prices prevailing in the late 1880s and early 1890s would hold indefinitely. But this was not to be the case. As early as June 1891, Stross had signaled the advent of more challenging times: "To add to the gloomy prospects for Sharks Bay, shells have lately fallen more than 50 per cent in price, and pearls are almost unsaleable. I may add that Sharks Bay shells were almost exclusively worked in Austria for a low class button, called the Tertia button, and exported to the United States. . . . Now the McKinlay [sic] Bill has ruined this trade."[73] The McKinley tariff had lasting effects, supporting the development of the Mississippi clamshell button industry at the same time as obstructing imports into the Unites States of cheaper buttons manufactured in Europe.[74] By 1901, Gale was reporting that the high prices of the late 1890s had been temporary, as Shark Bay shell again "found the level of the Persian Lingah shell, at present the lowest in the English market" at around £5–£8 per ton.[75] A decade later, Aldrich revealed how insecure the industry's position had become. Although "the industry at the present time is considered to be in a flourishing condition," he reported, "I am of the opinion that the principal contributing feature towards this satisfactory condition can be traced to the fact that keen competition exists between the two pearl buyers doing business at Denham, and as a consequence, full market value is realised for all pearls found." Prices for shell had been adequate of late, he noted, and yet, "there is no guarantee that they will continue to do so. The product of an industry of this description, pearls in particular, cannot be classed as an absolute necessity of life and prices or market values are regulated or governed by the prevailing financial conditions, locally, at 'home' [i.e., Great Britain], and abroad."[76]

Periodically, shell even became unsaleable. The most dramatic instance came in 1904 when one of the major European shell traders, Albert Ochse and Co., dumped a stockpile of second-grade (or yellow-tinged) Shark Bay shell on the London market, causing prices to crash and rendering the most recent consignments worthless. As Gale reported, "The present state of affairs has to a very great extent been caused by a neglect to grade and classify shells before shipment in the past, and judging from reports received from London, buyers are fighting shy of Shark Bay parcels."[77] Although Western Australia's agent general formally investigated the issue, the most illuminating evaluation came directly from Stross, who had taken up a position in Ochse's New York office after leaving the colony. "Times have changed immensely in the past ten years and the thin class of shells such as Sharks Bay and Persian Gulf mussels have almost entirely been driven out of the market by the competition of other shells, which are not only cheaper but produce also a better button," he advised his old friends at Denham. "There are today Trocas which produce a beautiful and cheap button, and there are furthermore the Mississippi Clams in America which produce a thick button which is not very brilliant as far as colour goes, but which is entirely white, and therefore, preferred for underwear by the consumer. . . . I am sorry that I cannot hold out any great hope for better times to you, at least certainly not for the immediate future."[78] Only twenty-one boats and forty-five men worked in the industry at the time, and numbers fluctuated around this level until the First World War, when the shell price collapsed again. High pearl prices helped to sustain the pearlers during the 1920s, but when this market also crashed after 1929, they were indeed caught in a fraught position.

While Stross had not succeeded as a master pearler, he also helps to expose Saville-Kent's shortcomings as commissioner of fisheries. And yet for both, departure from Shark Bay heralded a change in fortunes. Stross had prospered in New York with Ochse, albeit by trading in horn rather than mother-of-pearl. American cattle were being increasingly dehorned, creating opportunities to meet demand from herds in Australasia and South America, for which he had the right contacts. By 1901 he accumulated enough to invest in the Sterling Comb Company, a first step toward the creation of the Viscoloid Plastics Company, which became highly successful at manufacturing consumer products imitating goods previously made from shell, horn, bone, tortoiseshell, amber, and other natural products.[79] He died a wealthy man in 1913. Saville-Kent returned to England before resuming his career in the early 1900s through a contract to experiment with the culture of pearls at the Cook Islands. He then formed his own company and went back to Torres Strait to work on pearl culture again. According to his biography, *Savant of the Australian Seas* (1997), it was here that he reached the pinnacle of his career by becoming the first biologist to successfully seed oysters to produce pearls.[80] By these most remarkable twists, both Stross and Saville-Kent had major hands in establishing the very industries—the manufacture of plastics and the artificial culture of pearls—that brought about the demise of pearling across the wider Indian Ocean. Together, it seems, they achieved as much to bring about the ruin of Shark Bay's industry as they ever had to develop it.

CONCLUSION: UNDERSTANDING THE PEARLER'S PROBLEM

By 1935, the situation for the bay's pearlers had become untenable. Most could no longer afford the rental of one shilling per acre for their leases, and the government was asked to remit all arrears and reduce exclusive license fees in the future.[81] Their request was granted, in the same way that Broome's pearl shellers received government aid to support their industry during these years of decline. In practice, most pearlers now combined work on their leases with seasonal labor as sandalwood cutters or on nearby pastoral stations, although one Denham resident had acquired a fish freezer in the late 1920s and several boat owners now made their living by beach seining in the same shallows where they once dredged *Pinctada albina*. All of this was observed by Gregory during his inspection. And yet he still found the pearlers at fault for their industry's demise: "I believe the cause of this and the other depressions in the Shark Bay pearling industry during the past forty years have arisen largely from what I might call the illogical method of working the banks, and the illogical supervision and marketing methods accruing to, or arising from this method of working." It was illogical, he continued, because rather than encouraging "capitalistic enterprise," exclusive leases had left the industry divided, unorganized, and lacking sophistication. "The Shark Bay pearler simply waited for what the gods would send him, and the industry, far from being stimulated and stabilised by individual initiative was left entirely to the fluctuation of the market and nature's uncertain bounty of shell and pearls."[82]

Gregory did at least advance his own solution for the bay's salvation. It was reminiscent of what Stross had outlined in 1891, even if it was probably inspired more by contemporary belief in the need for government intervention to restructure Australia's struggling primary industries. The government should cancel exclusive leases and seize ownership of the industry, he proposed, before monopolizing the marketing of shell and employing pearlers as wage laborers to work the banks as directed: "The whole of the Shark Bay pearlshell area is to be considered as one unit and worked under one control," he urged.[83] Amidst the war, however, this recommendation went nowhere. "I should like to add," Gregory concluded, "as a parting slap at the *Shark Bay Pearling Act*, that it was the government who provided for my investigation into the causes for the present depression in the industry, and that with one exception the pearlers of Shark Bay showed little interest in my work or the developments which might arise from it."[84] Hill had been hardly any more flattering. "Pursuing its sleepy destiny for half a century in a world of cataclysmic change, Shark Bay still slumbers on," she had written in the mid-1930s.[85]

Hill's imagery in *The Great Australian Loneliness* harkens back to pearling's history as a frontier industry in the colonization of Western Australia's vast northern districts, if not to the antiquity of pearl fishing across the Indian Ocean at large. What lay hidden in the mode of pearling she found so curious, if not backward, was the residual memory of an early cycle of boom and bust and the legacy of the economic and political contexts in which Saville-Kent had devised his plans for the industry's reform. Insofar as his scheme failed, it was because neither the market nor the marine environment allowed it, just as Stross had predicted. Crucially, what both Hill and Gregory also misunderstood was that, just as the *jalboots* and *sambuks* were being laid up in their hundreds on the beaches of Kuwait, the bay's small fleet of cutters was opening a new fishery. Beach seining would be the mainstay of Denham for another half-century, before the advent of tourism remade the town and its economy.[86] As they became net fishers instead, it was the pearlers themselves who alone had grasped the true nature of their industry's problem—an unstable global market, a dynamic marine environment, and a system of resource management that could not be reconciled with either of these realities.

ACKNOWLEDGMENTS

I am grateful for the assistance of Elisabeth Strack, for sharing biographical information on Ludwig Stross, and to Steve Mullins, Malcolm Tull, Michael McCarthy, and the anonymous reviewers for their comments on earlier drafts of this chapter. All errors and omissions are the responsibility of the author.

NOTES

1. Ernestine Hill, *The Great Australian Loneliness*, 2nd ed. (Sydney: Angus and Robertson, 1963), 24.
2. John Gregory, "Shark Bay Pearlshell Investigation," 17, in Fisheries Department file 1939/103, "Fisheries. Shark Bay. Pearl shell investigation," Cons. 1510, State Records Office of Western Australia.
3. Hill, *The Great Australian Loneliness*, 25–26.
4. Hill, 26.
5. Alan Villiers, *Sons of Sinbad: An Account of Sailing with the Arabs in Their Dhows, in the Red Sea, around the Coasts of Arabia, and to Zanzibar and Tanganyika: Pearling in the Persian Gulf, and the Life of the Shipmasters, the Mariners and Merchants of Kuwait* (1940; repr., New York: Charles Scribner's Sons, 1968), 350.
6. Sanjay Subrahmanyam, "Noble Harvest from the Sea: Managing the Pearl Fishery of Mannar, 1500–1925," in *Institutions and Economic Change in South Asia*, ed. Burton Stein and Sanjay Subrahmanyam (Delhi: Oxford University Press, 1996), 134.
7. Hill, *The Great Australian Loneliness*, 78; see also Joseph Christensen, "Their Inescapable Portion? Cyclones, Disaster Relief, and the Political Economy of Pearlshelling in Northwest Australia, 1865–1935," in *Natural Disasters and People in the Indian Ocean World: Bordering on Danger*, ed. Greg Bankoff and Joseph Christensen (New York: Palgrave Macmillan, 2016).
8. Hill, *The Great Australian Loneliness*, 26.
9. Gregory, "Shark Bay Pearlshell Investigation," 17.
10. Gregory, 17.
11. J. P. S. Bach, *The Pearling Industry of Australia: An Account of Its Social and Economic Development* (Canberra: Department of Commerce and Agriculture, Commonwealth of Australia, 1955), 180.
12. See, for example, Steve Mullins, "To Break 'the Trinity' or 'Wipe Out the Smaller Fry': The Australian Pearl Shell Convention of 1913," *Journal for Maritime Research* 7, no. 1 (2005): 215–44.

13. See Arthur F. McEvoy, *The Fisherman's Problem: Ecology and Law in the California Fisheries, 1850–1980* (New York: Cambridge University Press, 1986), 3–16.

14. Subrahmanyam, "Noble Harvest from the Sea." Another to have applied this to pearling is Regina Ganter, *The Pearl-Shellers of Torres Strait: Resource Use, Development and Decline, 1860s–1960s* (Melbourne: Melbourne University Press, 1994), 5–6.

15. James Bowen and Margarita Bowen, *The Great Barrier Reef: History, Science, Heritage* (Cambridge: Cambridge University Press, 2002), 156–58; Anthony J. Harrison, *Savant of the Australian Seas: William Saville-Kent (1845–1908) and Australian Fisheries* (Hobart: Tasmanian Historical Research Association, 1997).

16. Bernard W. Doyle and Perry Walton, *Comb Making in America: An Account of the Origin and Development of the Industry* (Boston: n.p., 1925), 112–14.

17. Biographical information supplied by Elisabeth Strack in possession of the author.

18. Elisabeth Strack, *Pearls* (Stuttgart: Rühle-Diebener-Verlag, 2006), 50–51.

19. Bach, *The Pearling Industry of Australia*, 4.

20. *Inquirer* [Perth], September 9, 1871. The early history of Shark Bay's pearling industry is chronicled in Mike McCarthy, *Xantho and the Broadhursts* (Carlisle, Western Australia: Hesperian, 2017), 64–73.

21. Ronald Moore, "The Management of the Western Australian Pearling Industry, 1860 to the 1930s," *The Great Circle: Journal of the Australian Association for Maritime History* 16, no. 2 (1994): 121–38.

22. See *Inquirer* [Perth] for the following dates: August 27, 1873; October 8, 1873; October 29, 1873; December 13, 1873; February 25, 1874. This period is covered in D. A. Hancock, *A Review of the Shark Bay Pearling Industry: Fisheries Management Report no. 27 (April 1989)* (Perth: Fisheries Department of Western Australia, 1989), Annex A, "Chronological History of the Shark Bay Pearl Fishery," 97–105.

23. Hancock, *A Review of the Shark Bay Pearling Industry*, 9–12 and 97–105.

24. "Report of the Commission Appointed by His Excellency the Governor to Report on the Pearl Shell Fisheries of the Colony," *Votes and Proceedings of the Western Australian Legislative Council* A2 (1880): 4.

25. "Report of the Select Committee Appointed to Consider and Report upon His Excellency the Governor's Message No. 22, Relative to the Expediency of Opening the Closed Pearling Ground at Sharks Bay," *Votes and Proceedings of the Western Australian Legislative Council* A25 (1884).

26. Anne Atkinson, "Placing Restrictions upon Them: Controlling 'Free' Chinese Immigrants and Capital in Western Australia," *Studies in Western Australian History* 16 (1995): 70–89.

27. *Western Australian Parliamentary Debates, 1891–1892*, vol. 2, December 18, 1891, 139.

28. Ludwig Stross, "Sharks Bay Pearl Fishery: To the Editor," *West Australian* (Perth), June 29, 1891, 4.

29. Subrahmanyam, "Noble Harvest from the Sea," 158–62.

30. Stross, "Sharks Bay Pearl Fishery," *West Australian*, 4.

31. Ludwig Stross, "The Sharks Bay Pearl Fishery: To the Editor," *Western Mail* (Perth), October 10, 1891, 16.

32. Garret Hardin, "The Tragedy of the Commons," *Science*, n.s., 162, no. 3859 (1968), 1243–48.

33. Stross, "The Sharks Bay Pearl Fishery," *Western Mail*, 16.

34. For a general discussion of this period, see F. K. Crowley, *Australia's Western Third* (London: Macmillan, 1960), 112–55

35. Mullins, "To Break 'the Trinity,'" 237.

36. *West Australian*, July 1, 1891, 5.

37. *West Australian*, July 1, 1891, 5.

38. Sir John Forrest to Sir Samuel Griffiths, July 29, 1891, in Fisheries Department file 108/1952, "Appointment of Mr Saville-Kent Commissioner of Fisheries," Cons. 477, State Records Office of Western Australia.

39. *Western Australian Parliamentary Debates*, vol. 2, December 18, 1891, 139–40.

40. See the discussion in Joseph Christensen, "Shark Bay 1616–1991: The Spread of Science and the Emergence of Ecology in a World Heritage Area" (PhD diss., University of Western Australia, 2008), 132–45.

41. *West Australian*, March 29, 1893, 4.

42. *West Australian*, May 10, 1893, 2. Saville-Kent's report to Forrest is kept in Fisheries Department file 202/1949, "Pearling—Sharks Bay—Pearl Shell Fishing—Report by W. Saville-Kent," Cons. 477, State Records Office of Western Australia.

43. *West Australian*, May 10, 1893, 2.

44. *West Australian*, May 13, 1893, 4.

45. Hugh Edwards, *Shark Bay through Four Centuries, 1616–2000* (Perth: Shark Bay Shire Council, 2001), 144–78; See also the chapter by Michael McCarthy in this volume.

46. See Joseph Christensen, "'A Patch of the Orient in Australia': Broome on the Margin of the Indo-Pacific, 1883–1939," in *Subversive Sovereigns across the Seas: Indian Ocean Ports-of-Trade from Early Historic Times to Late Colonialism*, ed. Kenneth R. Hall, Rila Mukherjee, and Suchandra Ghosh (Kolkata: Asiatic Society, 2017).

47. *West Australian*, December 27, 1894, 6.
48. *West Australian*, November 14, 1893, 7.
49. *Western Mail*, September 29, 1894, 2.
50. *West Australian*, June 25, 1894, 7
51. *Western Mail*, September 29, 1894, 2.
52. Saville-Kent's reports to Forrest (invariably reproduced in the press) are kept in Fisheries Department file 1949/202, "Pearling—Shark's Bay Pearlshell Fishery—Report by W. Saville-Kent (1894) and Regulations Enacted," Cons. 477, State Records Office of Western Australia.
53. *West Australian*, December 27, 1894, 6.
54. *West Australian*, June 11, 1896, 3; and the correspondence in Fisheries Department file 3246/1894, "Surveys in Shark Bay," Cons. 477, State Records Office of Western Australia.
55. *West Australian*, January 16, 1895, 6.
56. *West Australian*, January 16, 1895, 6.
57. *West Australian*, April 7, 1898, 3.
58. *West Australian*, April 7, 1898, 3.
59. *Western Mail*, April 11, 1903, 55.
60. William Saville-Kent, *The Naturalist in Australia* (London: Chapman and Hall, 1897), 210.
61. See correspondence in Fisheries Department file 1080/1913, "Shark Bay: Confidential Telegrams," Cons. 477, State Records Office of Western Australia.
62. *West Australian*, December 27, 1894, 6.
63. Report of Charles F. Gale, Chief Inspector of Fisheries, October 10, 1904, in Fisheries Department file 1156/1904, "Report of Mr. Gale's Trip to Shark's Bay: Pearling, Trawling and Spongeing," Cons. 477, State Records Office of Western Australia.
64. H. Lyster Jameson, "Biological Science and the Pearling Industry," *Knowledge* 35, no. 532 (November 1912), 421–31.
65. *Western Mail*, October 10, 1891, 20.
66. *West Australian*, January 16, 1895, 6.
67. Report by Fred Aldrich, Chief Inspector of Fisheries, October 31, 1911, 9, in Department of Aborigines and Fisheries file 1911/1624, "Reports of C.I.F. on Pearl and Pearl Shell Oyster Fisheries at Sharks Bay," Cons. 652, State Records Office of Western Australia.
68. William Saville-Kent, *The Great Barrier Reef of Australia: Its Products and Potentialities* (London: W. H. Allen, 1893), 258–65.
69. Christensen, "Shark Bay 1616–1991," 132–55.
70. See, for example, the annual inspector's reports for 1921 (file 1922/002); 1922 (file 1923/0019), 1923 (file 1924/0003), and 1924 (1925/007) in the files of the Fisheries Department, Cons. 477, State Records Office of

Western Australia; see also Hancock, *A Review of the Shark Bay Pearling Industry*, 9–12.

71. Subrahmanyam, "Noble Harvest from the Sea," 171

72. Mullins, "To Break 'the Trinity,'" 222.

73. *West Australian*, June 29, 1891, 4.

74. George Frederick Kunz and Charles Hugh Stephenson, *The Book of the Pearl: The History, Art, Science, and Industry of the Queen of Gems* (New York: Century, 1908), 200.

75. *Western Mail*, July 6, 1901, 84.

76. Report by Fred Aldrich, 1–2.

77. Report of Charles Gale, in Fisheries Department file 1904/1156, State Records Office of Western Australia.

78. Ludwig Stross, c/o Albert Ochsé, London, to J. Barnard, Shark's Bay, W.A, May 9, 1904, in Fisheries Department file 1949/0200, Shark Bay—Inspector's Reports on Pearling Industry and State of Markets (1904–05), Cons. 477, State Records Office of Western Australia.

79. Doyle and Walton, *Comb Making in America*, 112–14.

80. Harrison, *Savant of the Australian Seas*; see also "Saville-Kent, William (1845–1908)," *Australian Dictionary of Biography*, National Centre of Biography, Australian National University, http://adb.anu.edu.au/biography/saville-kent-william-13185/text23869.

81. *West Australian*, October 28, 1937, 18; Christensen, "Their Inescapable Portion," 298–303.

82. Gregory, "Shark Bay Pearlshell Investigation," 17.

83. Gregory, 18.

84. Gregory, 17. Gregory is referring here to the Sharks Bay Pearl Shell Fishery Act (1892).

85. Hill, *The Great Australian Loneliness*, 26.

86. Roy Jones, Joseph Christensen, and Tod Jones, "Global Ecologies and Local Moralities: Conservation and Contention on Western Australia's Gascoyne Coast," in *Moral Ecologies: Histories of Conservation, Dispossession and Resistance*, ed. Carl Griffin, Roy Jones, and Iain Robertson (New York: Palgrave, 2019), 64–65.

FIVE

Early Pearling on the Indian Ocean's Southeast Fringe

MICHAEL MCCARTHY

THE ONE PLACE in the world where pearl-shell harvesting methods, ranging from ancient Indigenous practices right through to the modern day, have been fully documented is the northwest coast of Australia.[1] Given that most of the detailed descriptions of the world's fisheries date only from the fourteenth century, in examining the genesis and development of the Australian industry we can gain insights into what might have transpired elsewhere prior to European overseas expansion. One example is Ibn Battuta's description of the methods used in the Persian Gulf near Bahrain.

> When the months of April and May come, numerous boats arrive on the spot carrying pearl fishers and merchants. . . . The divers put a shield of tortoise shell in front of their faces whilst an object of the same material, something like a pair of scissors serves to clip their nostrils. When they are ready the divers attach a cord to their waists and dive into the sea . . . the diver finds oyster shells

amongst the stones. He picks them up with his hand, or prises them loose with the knife he carries with him, putting them into a leather bag suspended from his neck.[2]

Clearly, in referring to the use of "nose clips," the leather bag, and "a shield of tortoise shell," Ibn Battuta was describing a relatively mature industry, for a great deal of experience and learning must have preceded these innovations. Other fisheries existed in the Persian Gulf, the Red Sea, the Gulf of Aden, the Gulf of Mexico, Panama, Sri Lanka, India, China, Japan, Korea, and Thailand. Many of these were also in operation for many generations before the arrival of outsiders.

Each fishery probably developed some specific harvesting characteristics as a result of many factors, including the prevailing physical conditions. Methods used in the open sea might differ from those used in the shallows or enclosed waters and factors such as wave action, currents, tidal patterns, water temperature, depth, and underwater visibility all would have influenced the specific techniques used. As one example of locational variation, shell was also found in many river systems throughout the world, and in this detailed seventeenth-century illustration harvesters are shown wading and using tools to obtain it from a riverbed (figure 5.1).[3]

Other examples of regional differences in harvesting method are provided by the seventeenth-century French traveler J. B. Tavernier, who stated that in Ceylon (Sri Lanka) "fishing goes on at depths of between 4 and 12 fathoms and it takes place on beds over which there are up to 250 boats at a time."[4] And in the eighteenth century in the Sulu archipelago in the southwest Philippines, Alexander Dalrymple noted that

> The greatest part of the divers are slaves to the Sultan, &c. They are entitled to their freedom in consideration of their finding a very large pearl for their masters. . . . [They] commonly go down in the depths of 7 or 8, to 12 or 15 fathom; but though a few can dive in 20 fathom, that is too great a depth for the fishery. They swim to the bottom, tumbling when they first plunge into the water, and then making long strokes, get out of sight in three or four. . . . They generally remain from one to two minutes, but in warm sunshine they can stay, perhaps, longer. . . . A boat, with two or three persons will, in a day, get about 40 or 50 shells, sometimes even 100, and sometimes scarce any.[5]

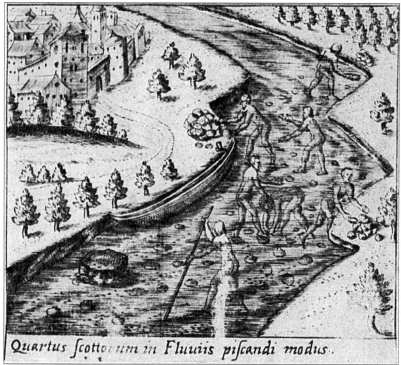

Figure 5.1. Wading for shell in the Seventeenth Century. Source: "Four Methods of Pearl Fishing," Malachias Geiger, *Margaritologia* (Munich: Leysser, 1637).

A form of mother-of-pearl harvesting using what commentators and researchers have variously called free diving, swimming diving, skin diving, and breath-hold diving was recorded by the author in 1989 in the Indonesian trochus shell industry around offshore islands in the Kimberley region of Australia.[6] In this instance they were diving out of canoes in a similar fashion to that described by Dalrymple. Their only diving aids were a pair of hand-carved wooden goggles with glass insert and shorts and a shirt for protection against marine stingers, the sun, and the cold.

Though not present in every fishery, women are reputed to be better able to withstand the cold, and in one instance the famous "Ama" of Japan dive to the exclusion of their men. One woman was recorded in the 1970s diving more than twenty meters over the course of fifty dives conducted in one afternoon, with each dive lasting for around sixty seconds. Her aids were goggles, simple protective clothing, and a weight

Early Pearling on the Indian Ocean's Southeast Fringe   149 with which to hasten her descent.[7] Stones were also used for the same purpose in the ancient Panama and Sri Lanka fisheries, where divers often made forty to fifty descents in one day. By this means, divers sped up their progress to the bottom, reducing the effort required to get to the seabed and thereby markedly improving their efficiency in locating and harvesting shell.

There are many factors affecting dive times and the depths attained, such as the recompense or incentive on offer or, if diving as a slave, the forms and severity of the coercion used by their masters. Not everyone was suitable for diving, however, for there were personal factors such as fear and the ability to withstand pain and discomfort. Pressure in the ears and other air spaces, notably the sinuses, causes severe pain in depths exceeding around two meters, requiring "compensation," i.e., forcing of air back through the nasal passages to the inner ear. While this was apparently the reason for Ibn Battuta's nose "clip," some divers would pinch their nose to achieve the same effect. It was common practice neither to use clips nor pinch the nose and compensate, however, and many would continue on downwards, despite great pain, until the eardrums burst. This allowed the ingress of water into the inner ear, releasing pressure on the eardrum, thereby easing the pain. According to E. W. Streeter, the late nineteenth-century jeweler and author, divers from the Sulu islands, following a "lay off," experienced "great pain" in the ears, which was slightly alleviated by "oil and laudanum," but once their "ears were broken," the divers did "fairly well."[8] This same phenomenon was reported in the Sri Lankan account cited above, in which on being brought on board, divers are said to have discharged "water from their mouths ears and nostrils, and frequently even blood."[9] Burst eardrums were also evident in the Indonesian trochus shell fishery. Thus, for the free-diving pearl, pearl shell, and trochus shell fishers, pain, discomfort, and hardship were features of their industry.

ADVENT OF COMPRESSED AIR IN THE PEARLING INDUSTRY

During the nineteenth century, when compressed air first appeared in pearling industries around the world, a great deal of experimentation with and development of diving equipment—and learning how to use it safely—took place. After being proved viable in salvage operations around 1830, "diving apparatus" involved (in most cases) a hand-driven compressor forcing air down a hose to a diver dressed in a fully enclosed, waterproof protective suit topped with a copper or copper-alloy helmet fitted with viewing ports. Buoyant air in the helmet and suit needed to be offset with lead boots and chest weights, with valves allowing the diver to control the ingress or exit of air. By this means a skilled operator was able to control movement on the seabed and in the water column. The best-known forms of diving apparatus in the nineteenth century were the English Siebe Gorman, the German Heinke, and the French Cabirol and Denayrouze systems, and all began appearing in the world's salvage operations and in its sponge, coral, and pearl fisheries. Being very similar in appearance and operation, the British forms were also sometimes referred to as "standard dress," the divers as "dress divers," and diving itself as "helmet diving" or "dress diving."[10]

Though revolutionizing the salvage industry, in many instances diving apparatus was resisted in the fisheries. Its lines, compressor, equipment, and suit were expensive and bulky, and, in addition to the diver, required an attendant to act as "tender" for the air hose and lines and at least one operator to work the hand-operated pump. All this took a good deal of space on board the parent vessel and contrasted markedly with the deployment of numerous free divers from small boats. There were other disadvantages. The apparatus diver was necessarily tethered to the boat by the air lines and could only move slowly by walking across the seabed. Though blessed with the ability to see more clearly underwater, stay on the bottom for greater lengths of time, and to an extent be protected from the cold and marine life, the seabed that could be covered by the diver, especially if the boat was at anchor, was limited by the length of the hoses and lines. If the parent vessel's crew were sufficiently skilled, they could follow the diver, but it was difficult. Any speed greater or less than that of the diver caused severe problems, especially as communication between the seabed and the boat was rudimentary, normally being by signals relayed by the safety line that ran along the air hoses. If a strong current was flowing, the diver also had trouble staying upright or in the desired position on the bottom due to the drag on the suit and lines.

This contrasted with free divers, who, though limited of vision and in the time that could be spent on the bottom, were able to move wherever they pleased. If in a current, they could also cover much greater ground by using the flow to their advantage. In strong tidal flows, diving apparatus proved especially impractical and even dangerous for the diver. As a result, diving normally occurred at slack tide or in relatively still conditions with little or no current. To the practiced eye, many of these problems can be seen from a close examination of figure 5.2. With tenders needed to handle the line and air hose and even more crew to operate the bulky air pump, there is a clear lack of space on board.

Opposition to diving apparatus in all its forms was not just a rejection of change or the result of economic or logistical concerns, for there were many unexplained accidents and deaths with the new technology. In 1867 for example, of twenty-four divers involved in the sponge fishery in the Aegean Sea using Siebe Gorman apparatus, ten died.[11] While some would have been caused by gear failure or operating errors, many deaths were the result of the lack of understanding of nitrogen narcosis and the dangers of the progressively greater retention of dissolved nitrogen in the blood at depths in excess of ten meters. In the first instance, divers became disoriented and confused, sometimes severely, and on ascending rapidly to the surface, or after a

Figure 5.2. The deck of a small vessel with a European diver preparing to descend, showing the space occupied by the equipment and those operating the gear. Source: *Australian Town and Country Journal*, July 14, 1888, 3.

long deep dive, nitrogen was released as bubbles into the blood stream. These bubbles could, if large enough, occlude blood vessels and cause pulmonary and respiratory disorders. These often resulted in what were at the time inexplicable symptoms, often followed by paralysis and death.

Few linked the malaise to the use of compressed air under pressure, and as a result the condition also inexplicably killed those operating an American Civil War–era submarine converted for use in the Panama pearl fishery. Using compressed air to clear its ballast and supply air to its crew, in 1869 the *Sub Marine Explorer* descended to depths up to thirty meters for up to four hours and recovered shell by allowing access to the seabed through hatches in its bottom. These also allowed free divers to exit and reenter the vessel, though deep underwater. Attributed to yellow fever, the deaths were not linked to decompression sickness until recently.[12] Thus, decompression sickness as it is now known became a problem in the nineteenth-century pearl fisheries and it has been claimed that, until the adoption of staging and recompression in the early twentieth century, 10 percent of all apparatus divers died from diver's paralysis, or the "bends," as it was also called. Over a fifty-year period, of a total of 274 deaths recorded in the apparatus pearling industry on the northwest Australian coast, 158 men died of the bends, 33 of heart failure, 24 of asphyxiation, and 59 of beriberi.[13] Thus, from the safety aspect alone, there was initially good reason to avoid diving apparatus, for in its very success in allowing more time at greater depth lay one of its chief flaws.

UNDERSTANDING PREVIOUSLY UNRECORDED STAGES IN HARVESTING PEARLS AND SHELL

Clearly each of the relatively sophisticated methods described above, including harvesting from a shallow riverbed, are indicative of a relatively mature fishery. This leads to some conjecture about the methods that preceded the stages described. An opportunity to fill this void presents itself with the study of the transition from centuries-old Indigenous "dry" harvesting methods on the northwest Australian coast through many, sometimes overlapping, stages to apparatus diving following the arrival of European pastoralists on those shores in the early 1860s.

Being the last of the world's great pearl fisheries, the stages in the development of the northwest Australian fishery are also among the most copiously documented. This was primarily because from 1865 onwards newspapers avidly carried detailed accounts of what was to prove an entirely fortuitous, and for some pastoralists a very lucrative, seasonal "sideline." That these records are so detailed lies in the fact that the chief primary source for the news was the district's resident magistrate Robert Sholl. A well-educated and keen observer, Sholl was uniquely placed among the world's pearling commentators, being not only a former newspaper owner and an avid diarist, but effectively the regional pro-consul.[14] Isolated from his superiors in Perth, with wide-ranging freedoms and powers, Sholl made it his business, in the official, personal, and financial senses, to know and record what was going on. All official dispatches and information flowed through his office, adding further to Sholl's unique position. In providing official dispatches and accounts on an almost-weekly basis, he inadvertently documented the transition from dry shelling through wading, on to diving without aids and then all the failed experiments with compressed air, as pearlers jostled to gain an advantage over their competitors.[15] Sholl and the newspapers feeding on him also documented the various labor sources, the transition from small rowing boats to progressively larger sailing craft, and then to the "mother boats" carrying a number of smaller vessels. Sholl, other diarists, and the press also record that, in proving very efficient, naked diving (as it was then called) remained the norm in the northwest fishery right through to the mid-1880s, when diving apparatus began to prove its full worth out of Roebuck Bay in the Kimberley region further north.

Finally, it needs be explained that, throughout what follows, the term "naked diving" will be used to the exclusion of other common terms such as "free diving," "skin diving," "swimming diving," or "breath-hold" diving, partly due to its contemporary use on the northwest coast, but also to differentiate its form from those types using aids such as stones, nose clips, and rudimentary goggles as described above. While any who have dived without aids such as masks, fins, weights, and snorkels can learn to descend and find camouflaged shell underwater, those who have not might consider naked diving almost impossible. In fact, the method proved so efficient that it continued to be used alongside diving apparatus through to the end of the nineteenth century, as figure 5.3 shows.[16]

Figure 5.3. Naked divers and an apparatus diver at work together. Source: E. E. Morris, ed., *Cassell's Picturesque Australasia*, vol. 2 (New York: Cassell & Company, 1888).

ANCIENT INDIGENOUS PEARLING AND EUROPEAN ENTRY INTO THE PEARLING INDUSTRY

The use of shell for Aboriginal ceremonial and religious purposes and the patterns of trade across northern and inland Australia is well documented.[17] One facilitating feature of that ancient industry was the huge tidal range on Australia's northwest coast (sometimes in excess of six meters at low-water spring tides).[18] This saw vast areas of usually inundated seabed exposed for a few hours, revealing numerous shell species, including pearl shell (*Pinctada maxima*). These were utilized for utilitarian, decorative, and religious purposes, for which shell was regarded as an "emblem of life in its own right" and was worn on the chest in a decorated form as *riji*. To some Aborigines, "Pearl shell is 'water'; its flashing the lightning that precedes the summer storms.... Water, rain, lightning, factors in the seasonal re-awakening of the land after long dry periods, are all embodied in the shell."[19]

When the tide was in, shell was difficult to see through the water, for it was often completely hidden in sediment or marine growth with only the lip visible. Refraction, murky water, and wave action added to the problem in seeing the shell. Over generations in a culture known for its ability to pass learning down through the ages, coastal Aborigines became very proficient at recognizing the shapes of the camouflaged or buried shell and the beds that the shells preferred. When shell beds were completely exposed at regular intervals, especially during low-water spring tides, the Aborigines were easily able to recover shell from the sediment. Being found in relative abundance, trade was extensive and widespread, with shell from the Kimberley region found well over six hundred miles away in central and south Australia.[20] There also appears to have been a form of oceangoing trade in shell, bêche-de-mer (trepang), and turtles in exchange for rice, tobacco, axes, and other goods beginning around the late seventeenth century with the visits of the Makassan trepangers to the northern coasts.[21]

In 1699, William Dampier reported *Pinctada maxima* on the shores of the northwest coast of New Holland and a smaller form, *Pinctada albina*, further south at Shark Bay. He was followed by other Europeans, including the French under Nicolas Baudin, and by some visiting American whalers. The evidence for this appears in the form of northwest shell found in the wreck of the American whaling-sealing barque *Cervantes*, lost about 120 nautical miles north of Fremantle in 1844.[22] F. T. Gregory, based in Australia in the nineteenth century, gleaned £500–£600 worth of *Pinctada maxima* shell and a pearl worth £25 while he was exploring in the hinterland of the Nickol Bay region (near present-day Cossack) in 1861. Gregory was thus led to comment on the commercial possibilities, and within a month of his return one colonial entrepreneur sent a schooner from Fremantle to Nickol Bay, but found the beds too scattered to be commercially viable. As a result, the development of the industry had to await the influx of pastoralists to the region after 1864. In the following year, after seeing Aboriginal men wearing riji, two station hands went to Nickol Bay, where they were successful in finding around one hundred "pairs" of shell (as the complete bivalve was called) in two days. While one left the district soon after, quite disappointed with the prospects, the other, a former mariner, took a small derelict boat once belonging to a defunct pastoral company and with two other men searched along the coast as far east as Depuch Island. Sholl's report for July 1866 was published in the Perth press and, in apparently direct reference to the efforts of the mariner (a Mr. Darling and his associates), noted that a group who had "fitted out a boat for the pearl fishery" failed in discovering a "defined bank," but had obtained a ton and a half of good shell.[23]

In contrast, W. F. Tays, a Nova Scotian, proved especially successful in dry shelling along the shore. He and his associate vastly extended their range by expanding their partnership to include another well-established pastoralist who had earlier obtained a boat from a visiting American whaleship. They ranged east as far as Banningarra (near present-day Port Hedland), a distance of nearly 150 nautical miles (240 kilometers).[24]

By November 1866, after only three months at sea, they had amassed around nine tons of shell that they hid in heaps along the coast. A prominent Perth-based merchant, shipowner, and northwest pastoralist then sent what was described as a "large boat" to a pearling partnership led by pastoralist John Withnell, who with his wife Emma (they were the first Europeans to settle in the region) had established very friendly and mutually supportive relations with the Aborigines.[25] In order to fit on the 26-meter-long *Emma* on which it was carried, this boat must have been relatively small, however, and was perhaps not much larger than Tays's vessel. Given its origin, it was presumably of the common whaleboat type: open boats, generally up to 10 meters long and 1.8 meters broad, ideal for rowing and sailing and with a good carrying capacity.

Boats of any form placed Darling, Tays, Withnell and their partners a step ahead of their contemporaries. Though shell could be obtained by anyone beachcombing from the shore, utilizing the huge rise and fall of the tide, boats facilitated the transport of harvesters and the shell around the often difficult, mangrove-lined shores and to the offshore beds. They also enabled the harvesters to move around the vast areas of shallows exposed by the receding tide with their "catch" or "take" (as it was called) on board. Those with access to numerous Indigenous assistants were also at a clear advantage. Given the superior visual skills of the coastal Aborigines and their knowledge of what one commentator referred to as the "fishes habits," all the nascent pastoralist-pearlers soon realized that "one black fellow is worth 20 white men in this occupation."[26] Initially, these men and women would have been from the local Ngarluma, Martuthunira, and Jaburrara coastal groups.[27]

Concerned about increasing competition, in March 1867 Tays took passage south on the *Emma* with a cargo of shell and with the intention of using his success to gain backers and thereby obtain a larger boat. Though the *Emma* and all on board disappeared without trace, the stage was set for the arrival of larger boats and more capital. The first, the *Morning Star*, commenced pearling within months of Tays's departure, and though it initially proved unsuccessful it was the portent of things to come.

By June 1867, the 33-ton, two-masted broad schooner *Mary Ann* recovered 4 tons of shell.[28] In the following month, a Mr. Tuckey joined three pastoralists in a partnership in the *Morning Star* and this combination (pastoralists assisted by compliant Indigenous labor and an experienced mariner) proved successful, with 5 tons of shell recovered. As an indication of the sudden growth of the industry, the catch for the twelve months up to October 30, 1867, was 32 tons, which at an estimated £80 per ton landed in Fremantle represented a £2,560 return. By this time, between eight and ten craft left Fremantle bound for the fishery.[29] Another two or three were in the process of being fitted out and advertisements, such as that for the 17-ton cutter *Gazelle*, which was claimed to be "well adapted for the pearl fishery," appeared in the press.[30] As each ton represented a 100 cubic feet capacity (2.8 cubic meters), the largest of these vessels were capable of both accommodating their harvesters and crew and storing the shell. This would prove to be the next step up in the industry.

In a record of arrivals and departures that he kept throughout his tenure, Sholl recorded that between December 1867 and January 1868 the *Lone Star*, *Little Eastern*, *Pearl*, *Sophia Jane*, and *Saucy Lass* arrived at Butcher Inlet (later called Cossack). He also noted the arrival of the 48-ton schooner *Nautilus*, a vessel large enough to carry a number of small boats. In January 1868 the *Ariel*, the first of many losses on the pearling grounds, sank near the Ashburton River with all hands and around a ton of shell. Undeterred, other boats arrived in this busy period, including the 18-ton *Medora*, the 23-ton *Albert*, the *Fairy*, and the *Charon*.[31] Even those who could not afford these larger vessels were doing well, and one pearler/pastoralist received "£800 for shells collected in a small boat that did not cost him £50."[32] At the time it was observed that two or three men in a single open boat could, over the space of one tide, gather "over one ton" of shell and that it was fetching £80–100 per ton at Fremantle, which was the equivalent of a mid-level government servant's annual salary.[33] As a result, there were "swarms of small boats on the coast."[34]

Despite the number and size of the boats involved, dry shelling remained the norm throughout this period. It continued as the sole means of harvesting from 1865, when Aborigines showed the first Europeans to arrive on their shores the pearl-shell oysters, right through to January 1868, when it was stated that "at present it can scarcely be called a fishery as at best all that is done is to prowl along the coast and *gather as many as can be seen at low water.*"[35]

Though copying Indigenous harvesting methods, the Europeans had actually introduced some forms of new technology, the first in the form of containers such as hessian sacks allowing individual harvesters to carry far more shell than had been traditional to that time. The many open boats and larger vessels, some big enough to carry a number of open boats, eventually caused overharvesting of those shallows lying in close proximity to the European settlement at Roebourne (which was gazetted as a town in 1866) and its port in Butcher Inlet (Cossack). The shortage of shell inexorably led the industry into its second stage. A transition from dry shelling to wading in the shallows had occurred by the following April, as noted in a newspaper account: "The pearl and the shells which have been secured up to the present have been only, so it seems, those which could *be had by wading on the banks at low tide.*"[36]

From there, Aboriginal harvesters and their European colleagues quickly advanced to wading in waters up to the armpits. There the shell was of a better quality, partly because it did not dry so often, as the following comment made in June 1868 shows: "The best shells are those not exposed. . . . [The] great secret is to gather those in the water. . . . [To do this it was] *necessary to wade up to the armpits.*"[37] In wading up to their armpits, collectors may have initially been feeling with their feet and then loosening the shells either with their feet or using implements such as that shown in figure 5.1 above. In that illustration the harvesters are also shown in waters up to their armpits with some bending down to pick the shell up. A close examination of the image shows that one harvester has located the shell with a foot and the other has bent down using the body and hands of the other as a guide in order to retrieve the shell. Anyone prepared to try knows that shapes and some colors can be recognized even underwater when the water is relatively clear. It is a process of learning, as indicated earlier, albeit an uncomfortable one in the beginning. The experience earlier gained in a dry environment or in recognizing the often camouflaged or buried shell while dry shelling and wading, when combined with the Aborigines' exceptional eyesight and knowledge of the ground oysters preferred and how they were camouflaged, led to the ability to see through the water with the head fully submerged. It is at this point that productive diving became possible. In fact, it soon became necessary, as all the shell in shallow water was quickly being taken up: "We must expect however soon to hear that all the shell has been gathered that is obtainable under the *present system of simply gathering as much as may be obtained by wading at low tides. After which diving must be resorted to.*"[38] The northwest Aborigines were excellent swimmers, known to have covered great distances over water when the occasion demanded it, but they had no cause to dive for shell where the tidal range provided all they needed.[39] As recorded in the Withnell family history and as supported by the news accounts above, it was "another skill learnt with the coming of the white man."[40]

What the northwest industry provides in these instances is a clear account of how the transition from gathering on the drying beds to wading occurred. At this same time (1868), there was another turning point when, as the fleet expanded, the requests for assistance from the once compliant Aborigines turned, in many cases, to demands and coercion. As one newspaper account observed, "The thirst for shells, for pearls, for success, brutalizes ... the pearling speculator or diver. ... No day is respected, no dark man's life is valued ... but the utmost of diving must be sucked out of them, killing them or not."[41]

There were exceptions. Blurton of the *Medora*, for example, recovered a "magnificent pearl" and was apparently the most successful of all in this period, due to the good relationships he established with a tribe of island people who were defended by his crew from a marauding mainland group and in return became willing harvesters. With the advantage of an enthusiastic labor force, *Medora* was able to utilize the short time and few days allowed by the best tides. The press also noted the better success of Blurton, who, in using "conciliation instead of Colt's revolver or short rations has enlisted their [the Aborigines'] services and done better."[42]

Local knowledge, sympathetically applied, was clearly one of the keys to the early success. With the aid of Aboriginal guides and a fellow pastoralist, Charles Harper examined the coast from the Ashburton to the De Grey Rivers and found good beds. They also realized that a suitable boat was required and they built the 11-meter-long *Amateur* from timbers native to their station—the hull from "mahogany," as eucalypt timber was then called, with knees and timbers of "cadjeput" (paperbark). Like Blurton, Harper also treated his divers well and found himself suffering in consequence. Robert Sholl's son Robert engaged Harper in "fisticuffs" over the desire of his Aborigines to work for Harper, and the latter subsequently received "an awful face."[43]

Despite these and other instances of cooperation, the newspaper reference to the use of "Colt's revolver" and Robert Sholl's assault on Harper are clear indication that at this time others felt justified in using force and abducting Aborigines. To make matters worse, in April 1868 the resident magistrate entered the industry. Finding most boats "too slight and small for the service," he first attempted to purchase a share in the *Morning Star*. On arrival he found that he had been beaten to the sale, but soon became owner of the 7.5-ton cutter *Pilot*, which he purchased in December 1868 for £130. By being thus engaged in the industry, Sholl found that in matters involving Aborigines and in disputes over their welfare, such as that involving Harper and his own son, or more seriously on the occasion of the infamous "Flying Foam Massacre" in 1868, he was unable to act entirely in accordance with his brief as resident magistrate.[44] In supporting a clearly excessive punitive raid in response to an attack, which attack was itself in response to the rape of an Aboriginal woman, Sholl was, however, reflecting the prevailing European attitudes of the time. Those who objected often found themselves ostracized, as the widely publicized "Gribble affair" attests.[45] In fact, Sholl came to be much praised (often with great justification in other matters) by his European colleagues for his wisdom and for his untiring efforts in the North.

THE SECOND PHASE: THE NAKED DIVING ERA

As the demand for shell grew, Aborigines progressed from wading up to the armpits to diving. Soon after the beginning of the warm weather in September 1868, the shell harvesters were operating in depths of around 10 meters. Then, inured to hardship, supremely fit in their native state, and with their visual abilities above water transferred to this new submerged environment, Aborigines began to emulate the feats of others already engaged in the industry elsewhere throughout the world. As one newspaper put it, "The powers of the natives in diving, especially the females, are spoken of as something wonderful. They go down to depths of 7 fathoms [ca. 13 meters] and remain below a time that astonishes their white employers."[46] The methods used in diving in this period are described in two chief primary sources, the diaries and official dispatches of Robert J. Sholl and those of Edwin W. Streeter, author of the much-cited *Pearls and Pearling Life*. From these two sources we learn that the harvesters operated from dinghies, the largest containing six to eight divers. When it was running, they went up against the tide, and, when ready, the divers went overboard. The leader, most often a white man standing in the stern of the dinghy, drifted along with the divers until good beds were found. There he would try to hold the boat in position over the divers with sails and/or oars or make repeated "runs" over the bed. Everyone worked hard and traveled great distances, for they could end up miles from the mother boat and had to return to it at the end of the day. The tides were an advantage in this instance, allowing the divers to be carried relatively effortlessly across far more ground than they could ever cover on their own. The majority entered the water feet first, turning toward the bottom as their head submerged. A "fair day's work" was considered to be the recovery of ten to twenty-five pairs, at a general rate of one "pair" of shells in eight dives. Two to three pairs were frequently brought up in one dive.[47]

Figure 5.4. A contemporary illustration showing diving out of an open boat with the "mother boat" in the distance. Source: H. P. Whitmarsh, "Fishing for Pearls in Australia," *Century Illustrated Magazine* 21 (April 1892).

UNSUCCESSFUL EXPERIMENTATION WITH DIVING APPARATUS

Experimentation, mainly with the Siebe Gorman and Heinke systems—which were very similar in appearance, principle, and operation—occurred alongside naked diving in the northwest. For example, when the ill-fated *Emma* carrying Tays and his shell was finally found and examined by this author in recent times, a crushed Siebe Gorman diving helmet was found in the wreck and was clearly on board when the ship disappeared in mid-1867.[48] It has not been ascertained whether the *Emma*'s owner kept it on board for his own purposes, or whether it had been sent up on speculation to one of the wealthier pearlers, for secrecy is to be expected in an industry where gaining access to hitherto unharvested deepwater beds was crucial.

In contrast, the colonial pastoralist and entrepreneur C. E. Broadhurst and his partners made no secret of their June 1868 operations with the Heinke diving system and a 25.6-meter, two-masted schooner at the rich beds in the Flying Foam Passage to the west of Nickol Bay. It was known for its strong currents and, soon after they anchored in the tide and sent him down, their diver was swept off his feet, to be hauled back on board in an understandably distressed state.[49] In the meantime, Sholl recorded that the much smaller *Pearl, Fairy, Industry, Nautilus, Albert,* and Chapman's *Mary Ann* all used naked diving, dry shelling, and/or wading techniques, with very successful results.

Undaunted, Broadhurst purchased the diving gear from his partners and entered into a loose partnership with Allan Hughan, who had just arrived from the east in the 73-ton schooner *Pilot* with his wife and two children on board. According to Sholl, Hughan was experimenting with French equipment "differing somewhat from Broadhurst's," yet seeming in "every way adapted for the design purpose."[50] He then spent a morning "attempting to translate Hughan's French instructions for use of the diving apparatus." On this evidence, there is a possibility that the gear was not Cabirol's or Denayrouze's diving apparatus, the French equivalent of the British standard dress helmet diving systems, but the Aérophore, the unacknowledged forerunner to the modern aqualung. It had recently been invented by Rouquayrol and Denayrouze and was being used in the sponge, coral, and pearl fisheries in the Mediterranean.[51] All that is definitely known, however, is that Hughan's system was a different form of diving apparatus to that used by the others, and along with it Hughan also operated forty small open boats, each with three Europeans and six Aboriginal divers on board.[52] Though their apparatus divers were deployed on the seabed, they advised Sholl upon returning that it had become "too cold for the natives to work" and that they had been unsuccessful, despite having traveled far afield in pursuit of shell. An examination of the plant specimens collected by Mrs. Hughan show that they ranged as far as Camden Harbour in the Kimberley region, calling in at many places en route.[53] Hughan and his family then left the colony, bound for Melbourne.

Others were also traveling great distances, and the 33-ton *Argo* went as far north as Camden Harbour with Aborigines whose home was at the Robe River area near Cossack. Though reporting good pearling beds, nine divers absconded at Camden Harbour, rendering the expedition fruitless.[54] Although their fate is unknown, any attempt to return overland would have risked conflict with other Aboriginal groups over transgression on their land.

In August 1870, when the season opened with the onset of warmer weather, the pastoralist-turned-pearler F. McRae noted that "almost everyone has gone out pearling. . . . [There are] satisfactory wool prices but the cost of getting it out eats up the profit. . . . The pearl shell fishery looks much better now than it ever did before as pearlers have got the natives to dive in deeper water for the shells."[55]

SEARCH FOR OTHER LABOR SOURCES

Around this time there were "some 300 natives employed on approximately thirty boats by sixty-two whites."[56] With so many boats in competition for their services, combined with the ravages of introduced diseases, neglect, and physical abuse, there was a growing lack of coastal Aboriginal labor. This produced wide-ranging hunts further along the coast and miles inland, heralding the era of the illegal acquisition of Aboriginal labor and experiments with imported labor sources. In late August 1869, two large Sydney-based boats, the 72-ton *Coquette* and the 133-ton *Melanie* with a crew of sixty Pacific Islanders, worked as far north as Roebuck Bay.[57] All lived on board while not wading and diving out of smaller boats, and for unstated reasons they also clashed with the local Aborigines on an earlier visit.[58]

Perhaps believing they were all natural swimmers and would therefore become good divers, and because there was a prohibition on the use of European convicts in the north district, Charles Broadhurst obtained the services of twenty Aboriginal convicts from the Rottnest Island prison. Despite being "volunteers," there was a considerable outcry at them being sent for pearling, because by then the industry was gaining a poor reputation in Perth, the colony's capital. Nonetheless, they left in the schooner *Adur* and proceeded on to Cossack. From there they went east to Banningarra, where Broadhurst had established a base. For the remainder of the 1870–71 season, Broadhurst employed both Aborigines and a European apparatus diver, together or separately as the conditions suited. The weather was against them, and to make matters worse many of "his" Aborigines attempted to escape both en route and while pearling. Sholl had the police inquire into their discontent, finding from their warder that they were "determined on escaping. . . . The cause of their absconding is fear of the water." Providing considerable insight into what transpired, Broadhurst wrote to the colonial secretary in Perth, recording his "deep regret" that the Aboriginal convicts had "turned out perfectly useless as far as diving for shell goes. I have tried every plan that kindness or ingenuity could suggest but all to no purpose.... Some of them can dive well enough. They appear to be thoroughly frightened of salt water. I must say, I am sorely disappointed for having found them so useful on shore and believing them to have more courage and energy in them than the natives of this coast I had great hopes."[59]

Apparently, Broadhurst also tried to shame them by working them together with six local Aborigines from the same boat. Though the convicts were severely ridiculed by the locals and thereby encouraged to prove their worth, the stratagem failed, and he prepared to leave the north as the season came to a close in late April. He had failed while others proved remarkably successful, for they recovered nearly forty tons of shell, which represented a return of £6,000–7,000 and between £1,000 and £1,500 worth of pearls.[60]

Those using apparatus alongside naked divers were able to send the dressed diver down to assess the seabed before the naked divers joined him on the bottom, as shown in figure 5.3. Other than that, the only real advantage at the time of having an apparatus diver appears to have been the protective suit.[61] In the colder months, naked divers would have rapidly succumbed to hypothermia, and the pearling season in the northwest became effectively limited to the period between October of one year and April of the next. As Streeter observed, "during these months [May–September] the temperature of the water and atmosphere is so low that naked diving cannot be carried on."[62]

Some pearlers did try to extend the season nonetheless, and as Aboriginal women were apparently better able to withstand the cold they would have been much sought after. The accompanying sexual abuse proved worrying to some, and in 1869, soon after some of Hughan's party were threatened by the natives of Enderby Island, Sholl noted that "Broadhurst told me that some of the pearlers were in the habit of taking native women away and he named Coppido as the principal offender. He said the natives were so exasperated that loss of life would be the result."[63] In his official dispatches, Sholl claimed that "Native Women, as a rule are not employed as divers," intimating that they were generally employed in other capacities such as shelling, wading, cleaning, and packing.[64] While that was often the case, the use of the phrase "as a rule" and the earlier reference to the "powers of the natives in diving, especially the females" suggest convincingly that women did indeed work in that capacity. As disquiet built in Perth government circles, legislation prohibiting their employ was enacted in 1871, specifically entitled "An Act to Regulate the Hiring and Service of Aboriginal Natives in the Pearl Shell Fishery and to Prohibit the Employment of Women Therein."[65]

As further indication of the range of abuses requiring action, this act was followed by the Pearl Shell Fishery Regulation Act of 1873, by subsequent amendments, and by the promulgation of regulations. Apart from prohibiting Aboriginal women from diving, these regulations codified the provision of minimum rations, a requirement for all Aborigines to enter service voluntarily through a written agreement signed or marked in front of an official, a prohibition of the use of force or fraud, provisions regarding remuneration in kind (generally food, tobacco, and clothing), a ban on involvement in the fishery until the onset of puberty, prohibition of diving in the cold months of April through September, and protections against working on a Sunday. Again attesting to the abuses that saw them enacted in the first place, the regulations also required that divers be allowed a suitable time to recover, and that all Aborigines were to be returned to their home regions at the end of their involvement.[66] Clearly, the opposite had been occurring. In respect of the requirement that service was to be voluntary, recent research and fieldwork have added further to the understanding that Aborigines were marooned on islands far offshore, attesting to hidden but apparently endemic brutality in the northwest Australian pearling industry.[67]

Government oversight was almost impossible and abuses continued essentially unabated. While there was little mention of this in the contemporary records, hints emerge from private correspondence, such as the letters of the McRae brothers to their family from 1870. One from George McRae at the Ashburton River, for example, refers to "a good many fellows travelling up and down" hunting for Aborigines for use in the industry, while another penned at Cossack from Duncan McRae reports, "Busy getting my darkies together for pearling. I have got a very good crowd this season nearly 40 and would have done a good thing if it had not been for the new regulations which will throw us back a good bit. . . . Jack has been out after his darkies. I make a start for the eastward pearling grounds tonight."[68]

Attempts were made to water down the proposed legislation. Dispatches from the governor in Perth to the secretary of state for the colonies in London advised, though, that strict legislation was required, "since many Aborigines in the north west were in a condition little short of slavery."[69] This would continue to be a concern for some officials.

INTRODUCTION OF "MALAY" DIVERS

By the early 1870s, with thirty-one large vessels and fifty-two small boats active on the coast, there was an increased demand for labor, but—more and more, due to the spread of disease—an inadequate supply of workers. Given the failure of the Pacific Islanders, the notorious "blackbirder" (abductor of native labor) Francis Cadell and others experimented with the introduction of people from overseas then generally but incorrectly called "Malays." These were initially brought from the islands to the north of Australia, including present-day Indonesia, Singapore, and Timor, and from Malaysia itself. Initially, Cadell brought forty-four men from Alor and Solor and set them to work at his base at Condon near Banningarra.[70]

Being experienced divers, these "Malays" initially proved more efficient than the local Aborigines in being prepared to dive in the colder months and able to work in deeper water for longer periods.[71] Heartened by the results, other vessels went to Kupang, Batavia, Makassar, and Singapore.[72] The recruits included 140 boys aged between twelve and fourteen brought over on the SS *Xantho*.[73] A 35-meter-long iron-hulled, schooner-rigged screw steamship, it was part of C. E. Broadhurst's plan to use a steamer capable of sailing against wind and tide in transporting laborers, boats, and shell along the northwest coast. On paper it was a grand strategy, for the winds and tides on the northwest coast were notoriously difficult and navigation in and out of the mangrove-lined pearling bases very challenging. Broadhurst also planned to use it as a "tramp steamer," picking up passengers and cargo when free from pearling duties.[74]

The new labor force fed a surge in the industry. In February 1873, Sholl recorded that at the Flying Foam Passage alone there were 24 "large boats," 47 smaller boats, and 291 Aborigines and 134 "Malays" at work, with 50 unspecified "camp followers" ashore. These would have been women and children and perhaps some Chinese laborers. Their combined efforts resulted in the recovery of around three tons of shell per day, with one boat returning 134 pairs of shell in four hours.[75]

The divers worked for about four hours each day. Most entered the water feet first, as described earlier, though "two or three plunge head first." Apparently, these were divers from the Sulu Islands. This indicates that there were regional differences in the methods used by the labor force wrongly homogenized as Malays. Broadhurst's experiences with the "Malays" at Flying Foam Passage and his comparison of them with the Rottnest Island convicts (above) and northwest Aboriginal divers highlight this issue: "There were some good divers among the Malays, but many of them either could not or would not bring up shells. On the whole the natives were superior. Their eyesight is more keen, their knowledge of the ground is better, they are better swimmers and are more cool and collected."[76]

Of importance also is Sholl's observation that the "Malays" were "tractable... quick to learn [and] pleasant," but they were not the equal of the Aborigines, who he said "cannot be beaten" for finding shell and who were "unequalled in the world for powers of endurance."[77]

With such evident underwater capacity and with so many boats in operation, large amounts of shell were recovered. As they were inevitably overfished, previously rich beds were abandoned and the pearlers moved elsewhere, some west to Exmouth Gulf, others east to Condon (both rich sources of shell). All along the coast, many were succeeding with "Malays," barring Charles Broadhurst at Banningarra and Flying Foam Passage. He proved an exceptional failure with his "Malays" and in hindsight it appears, on the basis of their age alone, that they were far too young and physically immature for the rigors of pearl diving.[78]

Notwithstanding Broadhurst's failures, the use of "Malays" in the industry grew dramatically in this period and reached its peak around the beginning of the 1875–76 season, when twenty-two large vessels arrived in the north of Western Australia, mainly from Kupang and Macassar. On board the vessels were around 75 white men, about 770 "Malays," an unspecified number of Port Essington Aboriginals, 17 Chinese, 24 women, and a few children.[79]

PEARLING AT SHARK BAY AND ITS IMPACT ON THE USE OF "MALAY" LABOR

In November 1872, SS *Xantho* abruptly sank, destroying Broadhurst's vision of linking his far-flung bases in the northwest fishery with a vessel that was also able to take laborers and shell from there to Batavia and the Straits Settlements directly. Meanwhile, Aborigines and "Malays" in his employ had proved singularly unsuccessful as naked divers. As a result, Broadhurst took "Malays" to what the Malgana people in Shark Bay called Wilyah Miah (place of the pearl), where they had harvested shell at low tide. Cadell also had a base there.

Harvesting at Shark Bay was for an oyster noted for the quantity of pearls contained within it rather than for the size and thickness of the shell, as was the case further north. These pearls were small and of varying shades of gold or of a dark hue rather than white and were called "oriental" or "golden" pearls.[80] After some experimentation with wading at low tide and with diving, the shell was gathered almost entirely using wire-covered dredges towed behind a small sailing vessel. The resultant "catch" was taken ashore to be broken down in pots, where the contents rotted to the point that the pearls could be easily sorted from the shell and marine detritus. The shell was initially discarded, being considered worthless, and hundreds of tons of it once lined the beaches. The local Malgana people also helped form the workforce and often were found on the growing fleet of pearling boats. As in the northwest, the initial successes were remarkable, with the most successful, Charles Broadhurst, famously taking over 200 ounces of pearls in October 1873. This haul was worth in excess of £2,500. The influx of gold-rush proportions—at one stage there were 50 Europeans, 80 Aborigines, and 110 "Malays" just at Wilyah Miah—ensured that the beds were soon fished out.[81] A downturn inevitably occurred and labor problems became endemic.

In mid-1874, Broadhurst's manager (his nephew Daniel) and Cadell became embroiled in a scandal over the abuse, nonpayment, and nonrepatriation of their "Malay" laborers. It affected others seeking to recruit "Malays." In September 1874, for example, an English vessel was forced back to Singapore after finding it impossible to obtain divers in the neighboring islands. Other boats encountered similar problems at Solor and Alor and British vessels generally were being shunned everywhere. To make matters worse, Cadell had also left twenty-seven "Malay" men marooned on Barrow Island while he went back for more. Word of these activities soon spread and while there were a number of investigations and calls for action from the authorities in London, the Dutch governor general at Batavia decisively resolved the matter by enacting what a Western Australian administration unable to control the excesses on its own coast recognized as "wise and humane" regulations.[82] Requiring a minimum wage, a deposit as surety, and a commitment to repatriate, these regulations also led to the near abandonment of the use of "Malays" on the northwest coast. In 1874 there were 225 "Malays" employed in the northwest fishery, in 1875 there were 989, in the following year (after the governor stepped in) 13, in 1877 none, and in 1878 there were 24. In contrast, the number of Aborigines in the industry remained relatively steady, being 493 in 1875, 344 in 1876, then 434 the next year, and in 1878 there were 497.[83]

The Dutch government's actions forced northwest pearlers and their recruiters to seek alternative sources, extending their activities to include the Philippines. Though known as "Manilamen" in the records, they were also referred to as "Malays," making the statistics and descriptions unreliable. As conditions improved, "Malays" gradually made a reappearance right along the coast, though the reporting processes were too unreliable to be able to fix their source. In the period 1879–83, for example, the official statistics do not show "Malays" in the northwest at all, though they were certainly at Shark Bay.[84] A census there in 1886 showed that of the 200 people involved in the industry there, 68 were "Malay" and 60 European. A growing number of Chinese had also slowly become involved at Shark Bay as the industry picked up and an overseas market was found for the shell. As was the case in the northwest pastoral and pearling industries, the Chinese proved very industrious and capable and by 1886 there were 102 at Shark Bay. While most were land-based, some also "controlled" 7 of the 68 vessels in the fishery.[85] Concerned at the number of "Asiatics" involved, a "European Association" of pearlers lobbied the colonial government, resulting in the proclamation of the 1886 Shark Bay Pearl Fishing Act restricting the number of leases and granting them favorably to the Europeans. The inevitable unrest at the major Chinese camp at Notch Point was bloodlessly quelled by a show of force with "fixed bayonets." Peace was restored and the industry continued to pick up, such that by 1890 there were 300 people operating 89 vessels out of the four major centers of Wilyah Miah, Monkey Miah (now spelled "Monkey Mia"), Dirk Hartog Island, and Fresh Water Camp (later called Denham).

DECLINE OF NAKED DIVING AND USE OF ABORIGINAL LABOR

While naked diving methods using Aborigines and the "Malays" continued well into the 1882–83 season, when nineteen vessels manned by

539 divers raised 250 tons of shell, a decline inevitably set in at Cossack and the other major naked diving centers at Condon, Banningarra, and Exmouth Gulf. As this occurred, the industry became centered on Roebuck Bay in the Kimberley region. There shell was being found in waters that were becoming progressively out of reach, such that pearlers were slowly being forced to utilize diving apparatus. Introduced in 1883, in the next year there were "five successful dress-diving boats"; in the 1885–86 season, with an influx of Darwin and Torres Strait–based vessels, 34 of the 54 vessels were using the apparatus, and in 1887 there were only 8 "native diving boats" among the 30 in the pearling fleet.[86]

These developments also resulted in a number of changes to the makeup of the workforce. Recruitment of divers became focused specifically on those who, from experience and experimentation, had proved the most capable of handling the new technology. This did not include the Aborigines, and in explaining the reason apparatus diver Hubert Phelps Whitmarsh observed that "during the three years [from 1885] I spent on the coast of Western Australia I never knew of an instance where an aborigine was broken in to work in a diving-dress, their objection to it arising from some superstition."[87] Though remaining on the boats as tenders, deck hands, and shell packers, between 1886 and 1888 Aboriginal numbers fell from 528 to 16.[88] In this manner, Aboriginal divers "disappeared from the industry almost overnight."[89] Of the former "Malay" naked divers who remained, "Manilamen" came to be preferred over those less capable of handling the bulky, restrictive, and often claustrophobic gear. The others who stayed on thereafter worked as shell packers and tenders.

Apparatus diving out of Roebuck Bay with Europeans, "Manilamen," and then almost exclusively with the Japanese proved a great success and is the subject of many other works.[90] With some Chinese remaining in the support and service industries, by the end of the nineteenth century the port of Broome had a population of around a thousand Europeans and twice that of other groups (Malays, Chinese, Japanese, and Aborigines). It was also a haven to around three hundred "luggers," as the distinctive Broome-era pearling boats soon came to be called. As defined in the *International Maritime Dictionary*, the term "lugger" in the pearling sense is a "local name given in northwest Australia to small ketch-rigged boats employed in the pearl fisheries."[91] Its design informed by the lessons learned earlier about the best manner in which to house and transport a crew, to carry equipment, supplies, and shell, and, equally importantly, to effectively deploy an apparatus diver who needed to move about the seabed in search of shell, the lugger was an agile, relatively easily managed, gaff ketch-rigged type that evolved specifically for the industry. A separate yet equally distinctive strain of pearling cutter also evolved at Shark Bay.[92]

IBN BATTUTA, one of the first travelers ever to describe a pearl fishery, arrived when that fishery was relatively mature, leaving us to wonder about what went on before that time. Subsequent commentators have been similarly disadvantaged, including those modern scholars seeking to trace the origins of other fisheries throughout the world.

Clues to what may have transpired before (and during) the advent of technology in the form of nose clips, tortoise-shell goggles, boats, stones, ropes, levers, bags, and then diving apparatus are copiously provided in the northwest Australian pearl fishery, arguably the world's best documented. Central was the former newspaper owner, pearler, and senior government official in the region, Robert J. Sholl. Though clearly compromised in his brief to protect the Aborigines upon whom the industry depended, and who regularly worked in abject slavery, through his official dispatches and the unashamed personal diaries on which they were based Sholl nonetheless inadvertently opened a window on early pearling, one that might also provide glimpses of what transpired well beyond the southeastern shores of the Indian Ocean.

NOTES

1. This chapter, incorporating some new research, is synthesized from a number of my earlier works on the beginnings of the pearling industry in Western Australia. These include Michael McCarthy, "Charles Edward Broadhurst (1826–1905), a Remarkable Nineteenth-Century Failure" (MPhil diss., Murdoch University, 1990), chap. 4; McCarthy, "Before Broome," *The Great Circle: Journal of the Australian Association for Maritime History* 16, no. 2 (1994): 76–89; and McCarthy, "Naked Diving for Mother-of-Pearl," *Early Days: Journal of the Royal Western Australian Historical Society* 13, no. 2 (2008): 243–62.

2. Ibn Battuta, *Voyages d'Ibn Batoutah dans la Perse et l'Asie centrale* (Paris, 1848), cited in Pierre de Latil and Jean Rivoire, *Man and the Underwater World* (London: Jarrolds, 1956), 192–93.

3. Latil and Rivoire, *Man and the Underwater World*, chap. 10, "Margaritology, or the Science of Pearls," 193, 218.

4. Latil and Rivoire, 196.

5. Alexander Dalrymple, "Account of Some Natural Curiosities at Sooloo," in *An Historical Collection of the Several Voyages and Discoveries in the South Pacific Ocean*, vol. 1 (1770; repr., New York: Da Capo, 1967), 11–13.

6. Michael McCarthy, "Indonesian Divers in Australia's Northern Waters," *The Great Circle: Journal of the Australian Association for Maritime History* 20, no. 2 (1998): 120–37.

7. Louis Marden, "Ama Sea Nymphs of Japan," *National Geographic* 140, no. 1 (July 1971): 122–35.

8. Edwin William Streeter, *Pearls and Pearling Life* (London: George Bell and Sons, 1886), 177.

9. Latil and Rivoire, *Man and the Underwater World*, 197.

10. John Bevan, *Another Whitstable Trade: An Illustrated History of Helmet Diving* (Gosport, England: Submex, 2009). In tropical waters divers sometimes used only the helmet and corselet.

11. Latil and Rivoire, *Man and the Underwater World*, 178.

12. Michael McCarthy, "Report on the Wreck of the *Sub Marine Explorer* (1865) at Isla San Telmo, Archipielago de las Perlas, Panama, and the 2006 Fieldwork Season," Western Australian Museum, Department of Maritime Archaeology, Report no. 221 (2007), 7, quoting the *New York Times*, August 29, 1869; available at http://museum.wa.gov.au/maritime-archaeology-db/maritime-reports/report-wreck-sub-marine-explorer-1865-isla-san-telmo-archipielago-de-las-perlas-pan.

13. For a detailed examination of early free diving and apparatus diving, together with a full list of references, see McCarthy, "Charles Edward Broadhurst," chap. 4.

14. Sholl was editor of the Perth *Inquirer* from 1849 to 1855, when he left to establish the *Commercial News and Shipping Gazette*.

15. For Sholl's dispatches and accounts, see Robert John Sholl, Diaries and Occurrence Books, RJS QB Sho, Battye Library, State Library of Western Australia (SLWA).

16. Edward E. Morris, ed., *Australia's First Century 1788–1888* (Sydney: Child and Henry, 1980), 354; this volume consists of facsimiles "from the pages devoted to Australia appearing in Cassell's *Picturesque Australasia* [1888]," edited by Morris. The illustration of diving in the Torres Strait and on the northeast coast of Australia mirrors the methods used on the northwest coast of Australia.

17. Kim Akerman and John E. Stanton, *Riji and Jakuli: Kimberley Pearl Shell in Aboriginal Australia* (Darwin: Northern Territory Museum of Arts and Sciences, 1994), 19.

18. Estimates vary on the extent of the shore uncovered at low tide, which would obviously be greatest in spring tides. The maximum range recorded at Port Walcott was 5.8 meters. *Australian National Tide Tables 1989* (Canberra: Australian Government Publishing Service, 1988), 192.

19. Akerman and Stanton, *Riji and Jakuli*, 19.

20. Ronald M. Berndt and Catherine H. Berndt, eds., *Aborigines of the West: Their Past and Their Present* (Perth: University of Western Australia Press, 1979), 247.

21. Campbell C. MacKnight, *The Voyage to Marege': Macassan Trepangers in Northern Australia* (Carlton: Melbourne University Press, 1976).

22. Graeme Henderson, *Unfinished Voyages: Western Australian Shipwrecks 1622–1850*, 2nd. ed. (Perth: University of Western Australia Press, 2007), 273–75.

23. *Perth Gazette and West Australian Times* (Perth), August 6, 1866, 3.

24. Spelled in many ways in the records. The name would be Aboriginal and the variety found in the spelling is an indication of this. "Banningarra" is used here, as it is the spelling most used by Sholl.

25. Nancy E. Withnell Taylor, *Yeera-Muk-A-Doo: A Saga of the North-West: An Authentic History of the First Settlement of North-West Australia Told Through the Withnell and Hancock Families, 1861 to 1890* (Carlisle, Western Australia: Hesperian, 1987).

26. *Herald* (Fremantle), June 6, 1868.

27. Many other northwest coastal and inland groups, such as those shown in the *Encyclopaedia of Aboriginal Australia* and other works, later became involved. David Horton, ed., *The Encyclopaedia of Aboriginal Australia* (Canberra: Aboriginal Studies Press, 1994).

28. As the ton and the tonne are within 0.02 kg of each other, the ton (which also represents 100 cubic feet capacity) is used throughout.

29. Sholl, Diaries and Occurrence Books.

30. *Inquirer* (Perth), January 29, 1868, and January 1, 1868.

31. Details are found in Rod Dickson, comp., "Ships Registered in Western Australia from 1856 to 1969: Their Details, Their Owners and Their Fate" (October 1996), available through the website of the Maritime Heritage Association of Western Australia, http://www.maritimeheritage.org.au/documents/Shipping%20Register.pdf.

32. A. McRae to his sister, February 24, 1868, Battye Library, SLWA.

33. A report in the Perth *Inquirer* of May 6, 1868, notes that the Nickol Bay trade was opening up just as that based in Ceylon was in the decline and gives a range of prices from £140 to £180 per ton, for the best and largest class, down to £35–45 per ton for the smallest class of shell, with an intermediately priced variety worth £45–50 per ton. For a schedule of wages and salaries at the time see McCarthy, "Charles Edward Broadhurst," Appendix 1.

34. A. McRae to his sister, February 24, 1868, Battye Library, SLWA.

35. *Perth Gazette and Western Australian Times*, January 31, 1868; emphasis added.

36. *Perth Gazette and Western Australian Times*, April 24, 1868; emphasis added.

37. *Herald*, June 6, 1868; emphasis added.

38. *Perth Gazette and Western Australian Times*, June 19, 1868; emphasis added.

39. As a by-product of what became the not uncommon practice of marooning Aborigines and others on offshore islands, records of Aborigines' long-distance swimming commenced when they started to escape from islands on which they had been marooned, as appears in numerous works such as Mary Albertus Bain, *Full Fathom Five* (Perth: Artlook, 1982). See also McCarthy, "Before Broome." There is a reference to an Aboriginal man who swam from Delambre Island on the northwest coast of Western Australia to escape imprisonment by pearlers, a distance in excess of ten nautical miles.

40. Withnell Taylor, *Yeera-Muk-A-Doo*, 115.

41. *Inquirer* (Perth), April 28, 1875.

42. *Inquirer* (Perth), December 2, 1868.

43. F. R. Mercer, *The Life and Times of Charles Harper* (Perth: Westralian Farmers Co-operative Printing Works, 1958), 34–36; and Sholl, Diaries and Occurrence Books, February 10, 1869.

44. By being a participant in the pearling industry, Sholl severely compromised his public position, as occurred with others, such as in the well-known case of Frank Jardine in the Torres Strait, who in 1873 was stood down and then brought before a commission of inquiry for similar behavior. Although in this case no charges were laid, Jardine had to leave the service.

45. J. B. Gribble, *Dark Deeds in a Sunny Land, or blacks and Whites in North-West Australia* (1886; repr., Perth: University of Western Australia Press with Institute of Applied Aboriginal Studies, Western Australian College of Advanced Education, 1987).

46. *Perth Gazette and Western Australian Times*, September 25, 1868.

47. Streeter, *Pearls and Pearling Life*, 151–60.

48. See Michael McCarthy, "*Emma* 1867," in *Shipwrecks of the Ningaloo Reef: Maritime Archaeological Projects from 1978–2009*, ed. Jeremy N. Green (Fremantle: Australian National Centre of Excellence in Maritime Archaeology, 2011); available at http://museum.wa.gov.au/maritime-archaeology-db/sites/default/files/no._14_shipwrecks_of_ningaloo_reef.pdf.

49. *Perth Gazette and Western Australian Times*, September 25, 1868, and November 11, 1868.

50. *Inquirer* (Perth), February 24, 1869.

51. Bevan, *Another Whitstable Trade*, 91–92.

52. *Inquirer* (Perth), March 31, 1869.

53. Tim Willing to G. Henderson, letter in SS *Xantho* File, 9/79, Department of Maritime Archaeology, Western Australian Museum.

54. Colonial Secretary Records (CSR), Battye Library, SLWA, 646/173.

55. CSR, Battye Library, SLWA, 697/110; see also 678/54.

56. *Inquirer* (Perth), March 31, 1869. See also B. W. Sheperd, "A History of the Pearling Industry off the North-West Coast of Australia from its Origins until 1916" (MA thesis, University of Western Australia, 1975). Robert Sholl's account in "Report by the Government Resident at Roebourne on the Pearl Shell Fishery of the North-West Coast," July 31, 1880, Legislative Council, Votes and Proceedings, SLWA, 471–72, shows that there were no official records until 1875, when 493 Aborigines were involved.

57. Sholl, Diaries and Occurrence Books, June–August 1869, reproduced in the *Inquirer* (Perth), January 27, 1869, and September 29, 1869.

58. *Perth Gazette and Western Australian Times*, April 24, 1868.

59. CSR, Battye Library, SLWA, 697/110. According to anthropologist Dr. Ian Crawford, "There is debate about the extent to which the Aborigines of the South took to the water and on the whole it seems that it was not part of their cultural tradition." Crawford, pers. com., to M. McCarthy, 1990.

60. Sholl, Diaries and Occurrence Books, April–May 1871; and *Inquirer* (Perth), May 31, 1871.

61. The average sea temperatures for the Dampier region do not vary much more than 6°C over the year. In summer they are around 29° and in winter they drop to around 23°. There was, however, a marked drop in ambient temperature from a mean average (over the twelve years 1881–99, night and day) at Cossack of around 87°F (30°C), in summer to around 67°F (19°C). W. Ernest Cooke, comp., *The Climate of Western Australia from Meteorological Observations Made during the Years 1876–1899* (Perth: Wm. Alfred Watson, Government Printer, 1901). From this evidence, it can be seen that the onset of hypothermia would have been rapid in those months in winter when the ambient temperature was low.

62. Streeter, *Pearls and Pearling Life*, 147.

63. CSR, Battye Library, SLWA, 646/141.

64. CSR, Battye Library, SLWA, 646/165.

65. CSR, Battye Library, SLWA, 646/165.

66. Guy Wright and Leonie Stella, *Pearling in the Pilbara 1860s–1890s* (Perth: National Native Title Tribunal, 2003[?]), 27–30; and "Early Legislation" and "Western Australia," chap. 4 and 5, esp. 28–40, in J. P. S Bach, *The Pearling Industry of Australia: An Account of Its Social and Economic*

Development (Canberra: Department of Commerce and Agriculture, Commonwealth of Australia, 1955).

67. See Wright and Stella, *Pearling in the Pilbara*, 2, paraphrasing a number of sources, including Bain, *Full Fathom Five*, 41, and Wright and Stella, "Aboriginal Women," in *Pearling in the Pilbara*, 31–32, based on several sources. See also Alistair Paterson, "Unearthing Barrow Island's Past: The Historical Archaeology of Colonial-Era Exploitation, Northwest Australia," *International Journal of Historical Archaeology* 21, no. 2 (June 2017): 346–68.

68. Letters from the McRae brothers to their family, August 2, 1870–April 12,1883, Battye Library, Acc. Nos. 286–89, SLWA.

69. Bach, *Pearling Industry of Australia*, 7.

70. Peter J. McGann, "'Malays' as Indentured Labour: Western Australia 1870–1900" (BA Hons diss., Murdoch University, 1988), 55.

71. *Inquirer* (Perth), May 24,1871.

72. Peter J. McGann, "'Malays' as Indentured Labour," 2.

73. Broadhurst to Colonial Secretary, January 3, 1873, CSR, Battye Library, SLWA, 752/31.

74. See McCarthy, "Charles Edward Broadhurst," chap. 4.

75. Scholl, Diaries and Occurrence Books, February 6–9, 1873.

76. CSR, Battye Library, SLWA, 752/58–63; See also Streeter, *Pearls and Pearling Life*, 76.

77. Streeter, 76.

78. As one visitor commented, "I visited Broadhurst's Malays at their camp. . . . I looked through the various rooms and found them very clean. . . . The Malays have not the slightest idea of either swimming or diving being completely out of their element in water." CSR, Battye Library, SLWA, 714/57, 168.

79. CSR, Battye Library, SLWA, 809/183.

80. McCarthy, "Charles Edward Broadhurst," 222–45.

81. For a detailed examination of the Shark Bay industry generally, see McCarthy, *Charles Edward Broadhurst*, and for its best-known encampment see Sally McGann, "Wilyah Miah" (MSc thesis, University of Western Australia, 1999).

82. Correspondence Relative to the State of Affairs on the North West Coast and the Treatment of Malay and Other Labourers Employed in the Pearl Fishery, Legislative Council, Votes and Proceedings (1875–1876), 250.

83. "Report by the Government Resident at Roebourne," 471–72.

84. Peter J. McGann, "'Malays' as Indentured Labour," 65–66; and Christine Choo, "The Impact of Asian-Aboriginal Australian Contacts in Northern Australia," *Asian and Pacific Migration Journal* 3, nos. 2–3 (June 1994): 295–310.

85. Michael McCarthy, "Pearling at Shark Bay: The Early Beginnings and Ross Anderson Survey of the Notch Point Pearling Site," in *Report on the 2006 Western Australian Museum, Department of Maritime Archaeology, Cape Inscription National Heritage Listing Archaeological Survey*, ed. Jeremy Green, Department of Maritime Archaeology, Western Australian Museum, Report no. 223, Special Publication no. 10 (Fremantle: Australian National Centre of Excellence for Maritime Archaeology, 2007), 157–61; available at http://museum.wa.gov.au/maritime-archaeology-db/maritime-reports/report-2006-western-australian-museum-department-maritime-archaeology-cape-inscript.

86. Compiled from Bach, *Pearling Industry of Australia*, 84, referencing Legislative Council, Votes and Proceedings, 1886. See also Streeter, *Pearls and Pearling Life*, 160; *West Australian* (Perth), September 28, 1887. Bach, who examined the industry across Australia in considerable detail—covering many elements and the linkages to the Darwin, Torres Strait, and other fisheries—references the "confused nature" of some contemporary reports. For instance, Streeter claims he was the first to use apparatus "on a large scale" (47), while modern scholars reference the Darwin-based pearlers Erikson and Wood and the Northern Australian Pearling Company (Biddle et al.) as also being early successes. Personal communication, Michael Gregg, Western Australian Museum.

87. Hubert Phelps Whitmarsh, "Fishing for Pearls in Australia," *Century Illustrated Magazine* 21 (April 1892): 906.

88. Rachel Miller, "From Dark Hands to White Pockets: A Chronology of Aboriginal and Non-European Involvement in the Pearling Industry," unpublished paper, 3.

89. Peter J. McGann, "'Malays' as Indentured Labour.", 71.

90. See, for example, John Bailey, *The White Divers of Broome: The True Story of a Fatal Experiment* (Sydney: Pan Macmillan Australia, 2001); and Hugh Edwards, *Port of Pearls: A History of Broome*, 2nd ed. (Swanbourne, Western Australia: published by the author, 1988).

91. René de Kerchove, *International Maritime Dictionary*, 3rd ed. (New York: Van Nostrand, 1961), 575.

92. Bill Leonard, *In Search of Fish and Fortune along Australia's West Coast* (Welshpool: Western Australian Museum, 2017), chap. 1 ("Broome Vessels") and chap. 2 ("Shark Bay Vessels").

PART III

Regionalization and Globalization

SIX

Shell Routes
Exploring Burma's Pearling Histories

PEDRO MACHADO

THE BAY OF BENGAL has emerged in recent years as an important subregion of the plural Indian Ocean, its crisscrossing circuits of migration tracing the human movements that linked southern India to Ceylon, Burma, and Malaya and shaped their ecologies in particular ways in the nineteenth and early decades of the twentieth century. These circuits involved a wide array of actors whose experiences of navigating the bay's waterways mapped maritime trajectories that stitched Nagapatnam and Nagore on India's Coromandel coast together with Penang, Melaka, and Singapore (and beyond) within a context of highly commercialized exchanges of goods and the movement of significant numbers of people—most especially South Asian laborers to work in the plantations, mines, and agricultural economies of the burgeoning regional global economy—around its shores, hinterlands, and interiors.[1]

If the Bay of Bengal's oceanic histories were shaped by the migrations and labor movements of South Asians across the bay and involved also the well-studied exchanges in tea, opium, and textiles, it was influenced in no less important ways by robust marine goods economies that were underpinned by Chinese, Indian, British, American, and Australian commercial interests. The pearling economies of coastal Burma, including, importantly, those of the Mergui archipelago that were located in its southern reaches, were primary sites of marine extraction and trade that represented vital nodes in the many flows of commodities linking the Bay of Bengal and parts of South India to Southeast Asia and the South China Sea, and ultimately also to pearling's globalizing markets of the nineteenth and early twentieth centuries. Marine product extraction, involving a sustained search for pearls—but more significantly, in terms of quantities fished and their consumption, for shell—was a critical dimension in shaping the complex waterways around which the varied contours of the Indian Ocean took shape. The pearl-shell exchange and commerce of the Mergui islands, involving the shipment of significant quantities of shell (*Pinctada maxima*) in the second half of the nineteenth century to and through Penang, Singapore, the northern Australian coast, and particularly southeast China, illuminate the vitality of the role of vernacular networks in sustaining intra-Asian trade.[2] While these networks operated from the late eighteenth and especially in the nineteenth century through ports such as Singapore that had been established by an expanding British imperium in Southeast Asia and along the coast of China, they were structured around self-sustaining circuits traversing the waterways of the Straits of Malacca and the southern reaches of the Malay Peninsula. If the place of Chinese merchant networks cannot be overemphasized, of course, there has been a tendency, as noted recently, to focus on their interactions in insular Southeast Asia with regard to the marine goods trade, or, when considering their place in the eastern Bay of Bengal, to privilege Upper Burma and cities such as Rangoon and Moulmein and their involvement in areas like the rice and tin trades. Chinese activities along coastal Burma, by contrast, have been given little attention, especially those in the nineteenth century.[3]

Equally, European and Australian involvement in Mergui pearling has been privileged, while the participation of Chinese and South Asian capital and labor has been marginalized or largely occluded in the scholarship. That much of the pearl shell extracted from the Mergui archipelago was shipped to Chinese markets is undeniable, but it is important to recognize the multiple circuits through which shipments reached the latter, and also the broader significance of other regional consumer markets for Burmese shell in the nineteenth and early twentieth centuries.

This chapter shines a light on the Mergui archipelago and Burma's pearling histories, locating them at the interstices of translocal and transregional dynamics that connected them to commercial interests operating within the Bay of Bengal and across insular Southeast Asia and coastal China. These included, especially from the early decades of the nineteenth century, the Straits Settlements and northern Australian pearling areas like the Torres Strait as they became embedded within the expanding circuits of pearling's globalizing currents.

EARLY PEARL TRADING AND MARINE PRODUCT EXTRACTION

The Mergui archipelago comprises a vast area of over eight hundred islands of varying size scattered over an extensive maritime area of roughly eleven thousand square miles. An early twentieth-century visitor captured the diversity of their topography in vivid detail: "a cluster of islands and islets, with bays and coves, headlands and highlands, capes and promontories, high bluffs and low shores, rocks and sands, fountains, streams, and cascades, mountain, plain and precipice unsurpassed for their wild and picturesque beauty."[4] Many of the islands, some as small as just a few square miles, had rich fishing waters but few coral reefs, the result likely of the "enormous quantity" of mud carried to the coast and sea by the Tenasserim and Lenya Rivers. These deposits, not unlike those that flow down the Brahmaputra River to the coast of Bangladesh and are discharged regularly into the Bay of Bengal, created sizeable deltas that stretched out to nearby islands, filling the channels between them and the mainland. Islands closest to the coast thus gradually became "absorbed into the mouths of the rivers and [were] only separated from one another by narrow creeks and mud-flats."[5] The coral reefs that were to be found existed in the southern reaches of the archipelago and were especially rich in pearl oyster banks, despite their being "thickly populated with rich alcyonaria and black corals (*Antipathes arborea* and *A. spiralis*)" that made the pearl oysters "none too easy to find."[6] Still, shell was found throughout these reefs at reachable depths of thirty-three to forty-six feet without the use of diving equipment, enabling their extraction with relative ease. Many of the archipelago's outer islands, while not necessarily possessing coral reefs, contained abundant pearl banks at depths that allowed for their collection without the aid of any kind of diving apparatus.

Shell extraction had been the work historically of the Moken, fisherfolk and sea people whose lives were intimately bound to the waterways of the archipelago's maze of small and medium-sized islands. They made their living from year-round fishing along the shores and around the reefs of the islands' disparate maritime geography. These fisherfolk lived in small communities of several dozen boats that were integral to social life and labor structured around tightly knit family units and kin. Most appear to have kept to this maritime life, while some others built stilt houses over the mud flats that became exposed at low tide. During the southwest monsoon from May to September, when the heavy rains and rough waters made sailing in the archipelago challenging if not highly dangerous, Moken erected temporary dwellings on platforms along the beach and waited out the return of the northeast monsoon (September to May), during which time the weather made it possible for them to resume their maritime activity.

Moken had historically utilized most of their energies in food collection for their own subsistence needs, gathering fish, crustaceans, and oysters from the sea. According to Jacques Ivanoff and Thierry Lejard, anthropologists and ethnographers who conducted extensive fieldwork in the Mergui archipelago over several decades, "several thousand" Moken had been living among its islands "for at least two centuries," or roughly from no later than the eighteenth century. They may have been at the forefront of a coastal migration from the shores of the Malay Peninsula, "colonizing the Tenasserim region from the south," sailing in small vessels known as *kabang* that were designed to navigate and maneuver through the tight channels and tidal flows of the islands but robust enough to withstand some of the vagaries of the monsoon rains and tidal changes throughout the archipelago.[7]

If not a mainstay of their maritime existence, the collection of shell was certainly a feature of a broader economy of extraction for the Moken that combined subsistence (oysters in particular, a key dietary element) and trade in marine products. Gathering was done in shallow waters but experienced and skilled divers could go down to depths of up to forty-six feet or so in search of shell. It is unclear how much of what was collected remained in the archipelago, but, even from the earliest days of shell collection, it is likely that significant quantities were not leaving the islands. Overall, then, for the Moken, the gathering of shell and crustaceans was integrated into a routinized search for what they could gather in food collection from the sea for their livelihood and to supply the local economy.

This began to change dramatically, however, from the early decades of the nineteenth century as the Mergui archipelago became integrated as a node in the larger Chinese marine goods economy that dominated insular Southeast Asia, with demand for shell from the islands also attracting Australian pearlers later in the century supplying primarily European and American demand for shell. What appears to have drawn Chinese commercial interests most keenly to coastal southern Burma in the first decade or so of the nineteenth century, though, was not initially pearl-shell extraction per se but an intensified search for esculent birds' nests or *yen-wo*.[8] A translucent edible delicacy made from the glutinous secretion of swallows and swifts, birds' nests were highly sought after in China and also among overseas Chinese communities and settlements throughout Southeast Asia for their perceived restorative and therapeutic qualities. Although their consumption was regarded at times as an "ancient Chinese custom," references to birds' nests appear in the historical record no earlier than the fourteenth century. These were sporadic throughout the Ming dynasty (1368–1644), however, and it was only with the publication in 1765 of the supplement to the well-known encyclopedia of Chinese herbal medicine, *Pen-ts'ao kang-mu* (*Compendium of Materia Medica*), that bird's nest was extensively discussed and its healing effects noted with greater regularity. Its growing prominence became evident especially during the Qing dynasty (1644–1912), when bird's nest was mentioned, for instance, as a taxable commodity and sent among royal tributes from Southeast Asian polities.[9]

Growing demand drove the trade beyond the Gulf of Thailand and Straits of Melaka and into the eastern Bay of Bengal, too, where these nests were found in coastal rocky crags and were abundant among the hilly islands of the Mergui archipelago and Tavoy Islands along the southern Burmese coast. Seeking to exploit this abundance, the governor of Cochinchina (southern Vietnam) sought permission from the Burmese court in 1820 specifically to purchase nests on the Tenasserim coast in order to sell them in China and thereby increase his personal wealth. According to Michael Charney, that the embassy encountered several traders involved in the esculent bird's nest trade when it stopped en route in Penang, by this time an important redistribution center for maritime products in the region, points to how entrenched it had become in commercial exchange by the early nineteenth century.[10]

Chinese merchants were thus able to monopolize the trade in such important commodities as esculent birds' nests in the Mergui archipelago and elsewhere in the region in part by establishing cooperation with royal courts and securing supplies through payments to these courts for the farms (the right to collect products in a given area in exchange for the payment of an agreed-upon rent for a specified period of time) of gathering and trading in these avian products whose extraction was labor-intensive due to the significant challenges of where the nests were located.[11] It is likely that it was the expanding trade in bird's nest conducted on several of the Mergui islands and elsewhere that brought the potential of their pearling waters to the attention of Chinese merchants in the eighteenth and early nineteenth centuries. Moreover, farms included all products from the Mergui archipelago and pearl shell would, of course, have been among these. Its extraction was done by Moken divers working from their own vessels and harvesting shell for specific Chinese traders, who appear mostly to have paid for these hauls in kind.[12] The structure of these relationships endured well into the twentieth century, by which time they encompassed a robust exchange of shell (and other marine products) in Ranong, a Siamese border town that later in the century would operate as a collection point for marine exports from Thailand.[13] I discuss this later in the chapter.

Although Moken may also have been involved in the esculent bird's nest trade, possibly contributing the labor required to climb up the rocky crevices where the nests were to be found, evidence suggests that they focused their emerging translocal exchange economy primarily on pearl and pearl-shell extraction. We find, therefore, a *Peranakan* or locally born Chinese merchant in Mergui, U Shwe I, establishing commercial relationships with Moken for the collection of shell "and other valuable products to be found in the sea or upon the islands." He appears to have generally worked within these relationships to exploit the pearl grounds of several islands, relying on the experience and diving skills of the Moken, who could undertake several dives a day.[14] In addition to pearl shell, the Moken also collected trochus shell and *trepang*—edible holothurians, also known as *bêche-de-mer* in French, sea cucumbers in English, and *haishen* in Chinese—for foreign traders in a marine goods economy that was expanding dramatically from the 1820s. The dynamics of this economy encompassed esculent bird's nest and a host of other products from the sea, drawing on both natural resources and the human resources of the Moken.[15]

This expansion both reflected broader (and earlier) regional trends and was part of a larger intensification in the search for marine products from the world's oceans that unfolded over the course of the nineteenth century. Trepang and other sea products such as tortoiseshell had been valued imports into China from a variety of areas of insular Southeast Asia since at least the time of the Song dynasty, stimulating the dispersal of Chinese commercial networks in the region for centuries. In the eighteenth century, for instance, in places such as Makassar—an important trading center on the southwest peninsula of Sulawesi (Celebes) connected to local, regional, and imperial Dutch networks and Maluku (the Moluccas or Spice Islands)—growth in the trepang trade drove Chinese commerce there amidst rising levels of consumption in China for this particular marine animal.[16] Considered a culinary delicacy and a potent medicine with extraordinary healing properties, Chinese doctors used its dried body wall to treat such conditions as kidney disorders, impotence, and high blood pressure. Such was the scale of Chinese demand for trepang that its zones of extraction extended across the Pacific, incorporating islands such as Fiji into its reach.[17] China's markets and consumption patterns were thus a core feature of the vast networks of marine exchange that braided widely dispersed supply areas in the Indian and Pacific Oceans. Mergui pearls and shell were a small yet fastening link in these expansive networks of marine product extraction and trade that not only hinted at rapidly expanding global commercial currents, but also at transformative interventions and depletions of marine environments.

IMPERIAL MANEUVERINGS

Interest in Mergui pearls and shell did not, however, only come from China. Growing British imperial state and private capital interest in its marine products in the nineteenth century responded also to Chinese logics of demand. These were shaped in significant ways by the compulsions of increasing—and increasingly complex—imperial territorial and maritime commitments in the Bay of Bengal and throughout many parts of insular and mainland Southeast Asia.

In Burma, tensions had been rising from the late eighteenth century between the Konbaung under Alaungpaya, who in defeating Pegu had reunited Upper and Lower Burma, and the East India Company. Involving also the region of Arakan that the Burmese had conquered in 1784, which bordered Company-administrated Chittagong, several cross-border incidents reflected the heightened state of agitation that had come to define the relationship between these two adversaries by the early nineteenth century. Indeed, the rising antagonism between them resulted in the Company declaring war in March of 1824, a costly and destructive affair for both sides that lasted almost two years. The conclusion of this First Anglo-Burmese War with the Treaty of Yandabo in 1826 gave the Company not only the relatively recently acquired Burmese provinces of Assam and Manipur, and Arakan in the southwest, but also Tenasserim in the far south of the empire. Together with control over the districts of Mergui and Tavoy that had been occupied by the British a year before the signing of the treaty, the colonial presence thus experienced a significant expansion in Lower Burma and brought the Mergui archipelago under nascent British imperial jurisdiction.[18]

British imperial reach into coastal southern Burma reflected and in some ways helped reinforce the reality and idea of imperial acquisition then taking place in the region. It was concurrent with the deepening commercial commitments of British merchant capital that had been developing markedly since the final decades of the eighteenth century. This was perhaps nowhere more clearly visible, as argued by Eric Tagliacozzo, than in the volume of East India Company trade, which rose rapidly in the 1770s and 1780s, especially once the Commutation Act of 1784 was passed, lowering import duties on tea—by this time widely consumed in ever greater quantities in Britain—from 119 percent to a very favorable 12.5 percent. As a result, British trade with China exploded.[19]

However, the challenge of how to pay for Chinese exports was a pressing concern (the opium boom was still some years in the future), and one—albeit provisional—answer was marine products. A key part of this strategy was the acquisition of the offshore island of Penang from the Sultan of Kedah in 1786 with the explicit aim of operating as a marine products mart along the sea route to Canton. Within a few years, Penang was attracting an increasingly greater share of regional and transregional shipping, with even Malay and Bugis *prahus* from South Sulawesi that had once gone to Junk Ceylon (Phuket Island) for ocean produce (trepang and tortoise shell, among many others), sailing rather to Penang for their cargoes.[20]

Likewise, the value of the Mergui archipelago for the emergent British colonial state lay precisely in its potential to contribute to the costs of administration and commercial expansion in southern Burma, as a site of expanding interests in the Bay of Bengal and Southeast Asia.[21] British officials thus encouraged the marine products trade and sought the continued involvement of Chinese (Hokkien) merchants already active along coastal Burma, as well as those trading from Penang, which would remain a key node for the Mergui marine products trade. Chinese continued to control the farming of birds' nests at Tavoy in the early years of the British takeover of Tenasserim, with an unnamed merchant owning it for the five years between 1835 and 1840.

The Mergui farm for birds' nests was separated from the Tavoy farm, however, and, as a demonstration of the cosmopolitan nature of the interest that the marine goods trade was attracting in these years, was contracted out to an Armenian merchant called "Sarkies" (an abbreviated form of Sarkesian) who may have held it for a year or so before the full assertion of British control over the islands. Notably, the farm also awarded him the right to trade in all marine products from the Mergui archipelago, and this would have included pearls and pearl shell. Armenian merchants, with long histories of involvement in Indian Ocean commerce, were active also in its pearl trading. For instance, only a few decades before Sarkies was awarded the farm, another Armenian merchant named Gregory Baboom, with connections in Bengal, Madras, and Canton, invested in 1800 in the pearl fishery at Tuticorin, long a site of pearling in the Gulf of Mannar, which divided the southeastern coast of India from northwestern Sri Lanka.[22] And, reflecting the length of their pearling involvement, in the 1690s during a six-year stay in Lhasa as a result of the extension of trade networks in Bengal and areas to its north, the Julfan merchant Hovhannes traded in pearls—along with textiles and amber—from India.[23] Sarkies was but the most recent embodiment of the extensive involvement of Armenian commercial networks in the Indian Ocean's many and diverse trades.

Before it could develop, though, and for reasons that remain unclear, Sarkies's right to the Mergui farm was ended by the first British commissioner of Tenasserim, A. D. Maingy. The fact that Maingy expected the farm to be purchased by "the Chinese" after he departed for

Tavoy suggests strongly that he may have sought to maintain Chinese involvement in this commerce due to its well-established structures and its prominence at Penang as well as throughout the Straits.[24] This decision was prompted by the understanding that Chinese merchant networks were beneficial to the growing British imperial presence through the duties that were generated from their regional commerce. Moreover, it behooved British officials to promote Chinese commerce in order to avoid an adverse response from the Qing state—and therefore threaten their interests in Canton—if they were regarded as actively opposing the prospects of Chinese mercantile investments by favoring other competing groups.

Yet, it appeared that Chinese merchants were not necessarily guaranteed the farm. Indeed, there was some discernible concern from certain officials that there were "few practical means of protecting the farm if it were to be rented out" in the Mergui archipelago during the early years of British rule, because the archipelago was considered something of a "no man's land"; in other words, in these early years, it was seen as a space over which British jurisdictional control had not been formalized or secured.[25] As if to emphasize and expose the limitations of this rule, Malay "poachers" and "pirates" from Penang sailed to the islands to collect bird's nest and other marine products, resulting in repeated entreaties from Maingy in the 1830s for British naval intervention, which, despite the heightened concern, was never forthcoming. Instead, vessels from Penang continued to arrive in Mergui. Perhaps recognizing that these attempts to establish firmer control over the islands in the early years of British rule were likely to fail, the farm was granted eventually to Malay traders by the end of the decade.[26] The growing scope of Chinese involvement in the economy of Burma—for instance, in tin mining in the northwest and in the rice trade that brought Chinese junk fleets to Burma in the 1840s—meant ultimately, however, that Chinese commerce in esculent bird's nest and pearl shell in the Mergui islands was never displaced.[27]

What did change in these decades, nonetheless, was that many of those Chinese active along the Burmese coasts were more often than not either based in Penang or settled in southeast Burma, and that the junks plying these waters were made up of Malay (and not Chinese) crews.[28] Some of the traders were Peranakan Chinese, as was the case of U Shwe I, whose father had come to Mergui as a pilot on one of the ships that brought British troops across to Burma in the Second Burmese War of 1852–53. At the end of the war, his father settled in Mergui and "lived by trading." U Shwe I also became involved in commercial exchange in the islands, forging close relationships with several Moken for the purchase of pearls and pearl shell.[29]

Quite what the quantities of pearl shell being traded in the Mergui archipelago in the first half of the nineteenth century were is unclear. According to Kunz and Stevenson's classic work published in 1908, *The Book of the Pearl*, shell was collected by Moken divers at depths of between eleven and fifteen meters, an estimate that is consistent with the accounts of travelers and observers of the pearl fisheries in the nineteenth century.[30] The increasing activity of Chinese and other vessels in and around the islands of the archipelago—notwithstanding their focus on esculent birds' nests—suggests that the collection of shell was occurring regularly as Mergui became more deeply integrated into the regional marine products commercial economy. And from the second half of the century, increasingly, its pearling waters became subject to intensified extraction that eventually industrialized the process in the 1890s but did not entirely undermine local harvesting methods of the Moken.

These changes are attributed often in the (limited) literature on pearling in the Mergui archipelago to the "discovery" of deepwater beds by British imperial interests as well as the involvement of Australian pearlers in the final decade or so of the nineteenth century, as they expanded their search for pearl shell that was targeted primarily at European markets. While it would be hard to deny the impact that these developments had on the islands and other pearling zones of the Burmese coast, as indeed elsewhere in the region, we should be careful not to overstate them. The importance of the establishment of the Straits Settlements in 1826 is clear, as an imperial arrangement that subsumed Penang, Singapore, and Malacca into a single administrative unit, resulting, for instance, in the marine goods trade passing increasingly through Penang and, from the 1820s, Singapore as it emerged as a prominent transshipment port for pearl shell along with a variety of other marine products. However, local associational networks of commercial exchange that included Chinese merchants and South Asian entrepreneurial capitalists remained vital to the financing and movement of these goods across the waterways of the eastern reaches of the Indian Ocean.[31] Indeed, while East India Company vessels and particularly English country traders from the late eighteenth and the first decades of the nineteenth century carried significant quantities of marine products from Asia to China, many of these country traders actually included Armenians and Indians, among whom Parsis appear to have been dominant. They owned several large vessels and, in sending them to Canton, were responsible for revitalizing the trade of merchants in Indian-owned and operated vessels, which had been dormant for many decades.[32]

It is worth remembering that the junk trade was also of considerable significance. By 1835, half the value of Singapore's trade with China was carried by these vessels, which, in redirecting their commerce increasingly away from ports in the Nanyang to which they had traded extensively beforehand (such as Batavia and the inter-island shipping of the Philippines), added decisively to the vitality of the British port. Indeed, overall, as noted recently, the "real energy" for the transportation of marine products from Southeast Asia to China—a trade involving several source areas dispersed over a large maritime space—was provided by a range of Asian shippers, bankers, and financiers. It was they, with detailed knowledge, access to financial capital, and commercial structures and mechanisms, who were largely responsible for organizing the purchase, transportation, and sale of marine products in the Chinese market.[33] In the Mergui archipelago, therefore, it is not surprising that Chinese and Malay merchants continued to play a prominent role in the procurement of pearl shell in the 1840s and 1850s and over the next few decades, working extensively and exclusively with Moken diving families as they had in the earlier years of the century.

At the end of the diving season, pearl shell was exported to Penang, and in some cases to Singapore, before being shipped on to coastal China. Perhaps due to its proximity to the Mergui archipelago, Penang remained an important transshipment and financial center for the movement south of pearl shell from the coast of Burma, notwithstanding the clear dominance of Singapore as a port of call for junks and prahus (and, of course, European shipping) by the 1830s. Although at times overshadowed in the literature by Singapore, Penang maintained significant regional connections through its commercial networks to ports and towns of the northern Burmese littoral and along the Coromandel coast in southeastern India.[34] I discuss this in greater detail below.

There was one other important transshipment node through which pearl shell—and a host of other marine products such as green snails—

reached markets in China: Ranong. Although its beginnings are unclear, Moken vessels sailed there sometime in the latter half of the nineteenth century to deliver cargoes of shell to specific Chinese merchants with whom they maintained regular and long-lasting relationships. These were then transported either directly to China or, as seems to have occurred in the majority of cases, were shipped first through Penang before being transported further east. Ranong would remain a significant node through which the marine products of the Mergui archipelago would reach Chinese markets into and throughout the twentieth century.[35]

It was this level of activity in the Mergui pearling waters—along with their aforementioned revenue-generating potential—that drew and sustained British interest, and a likely source of the first information received by imperial officials about the archipelago was Chinese merchants. Indeed, almost as soon as the British formalized their presence in Mergui in the 1820s, they began to take practical measures to exploit the pearl banks. For instance, in July 1827, A. D. Maingy—the first British commissioner of Tenasserim, whom we met earlier—wrote to the assistant commissioner to inform him that pearl divers "from Madras" had been imported into Mergui, presumably recruited from among the diving labor working in the Tuticorin or other pearl fisheries of South India.[36] Clearly, without adequate appreciation of Moken divers or their skills, the British drew on a labor pool with which they were familiar from decades of managing the various pearl fisheries under the governments of Company Madras and Crown Ceylon, and whose labor they had sought to discipline since assuming control over these fisheries from the late eighteenth century. The aim behind the shipment of the unspecified number of divers from Madras to the Mergui archipelago was to search specifically for pearls rather than pearl shell, a strategy that once again was informed by prior imperial experience. Pearl harvesting in South India and Sri Lanka had historically produced significant yields of this valuable marine product and their fisheries remained vibrant in the early decades of the nineteenth century. British administrators sought to emulate what they believed to have been great Dutch success in the collection of pearls in the Gulf of Mannar in the eighteenth century, once the VOC (Dutch East India Company) had withdrawn from the region after their defeat by British forces in the late eighteenth century.

However, it was established by the British administration early on in Mergui that, as only "seed-pearls were secured" there, the banks would yield but "an insignificant revenue," and thus the interest in developing the fisheries through further imperial endeavor or finance was initially abandoned.[37] This is surprising, if we assume that British officials were thinking about the possibilities of pearl exports to European markets. Seed pearls—small pearls less than two millimeters in diameter and often unevenly shaped—had been utilized in European jewelry from at least the seventeenth century and by the late eighteenth were becoming quite popular, as seen, for instance, in contemporary portraiture and in the adornment practices of royal households.[38] This intensified especially in the nineteenth century, as Victorians came to favor the delicate look of pieces made with seed pearls and often associated them with purity. Perhaps Maingy and his colleagues were unaware of this growing taste for seed pearls in Europe or considered the particularities of the Mergui varieties to be of low quality and therefore ill-suited to English markets. Whichever might have been the case, they did not pursue or encourage the exploitation of the Mergui pearl banks at first and appear to have been relatively satisfied with their continued extraction by Chinese capital and Malay and South Asian merchants amidst the robust vibrancy of Asian markets for pearls, pearl shell, and seed pearls.

"MANAGING" EXTRACTION

These Asian capitalists operated through a system structured around the farming of rights to collect shell, a model and practice that the British inherited from the Burmese court in its dealings with traders operating along coastal southeast Burma. Given the seemingly modest nature of the trade in pearl shell and other marine products, it appears that the imperial authorities were content with maintaining the status quo. Farming generated enough revenue to subsidize the cost for the British of superintending the Mergui archipelago as part of a territory—Burma—that was becoming increasingly part of broader imperial ambitions in the Indian Ocean and particularly insular and mainland Southeast Asia.

This changed from the 1870s, though, with the revival of interest among British officials in the potential of the Mergui archipelago's pearl banks as an integral area in the administration of Lower Burma, and other areas of the burgeoning colony such as the Bassein coast and rivers, and the Arakan coast, as European and American consumption of pearls and pearl shell in the late nineteenth century continued to expand.[39] Herbert Warrington Smyth, a British naval officer and mining engineer who visited the Mergui archipelago for an extended period during his five-year stay in Siam between 1891 and 1896, dated the "investigation" of the pearl fisheries by British officials to 1874, after which interest in establishing another productive fishery possibly to match or surpass that of the Gulf of Mannar grew quickly.[40] Some success in collecting pearls in the gulf in the 1850s seems also to have revived the belief in the potential of the Mergui archipelago to be at least equally productive. Nonetheless, it was difficult to escape the reality that, as had been the case in the 1820s, even when pearls were found (about one in every fifteen shells, according to Warrington Smyth), they were relatively small, and that therefore it was unlikely that Mergui would be as greatly a profitable source as the other pearling zones in the Indian Ocean with which the British were becoming increasingly involved in the nineteenth century.

In pearling areas beyond Mergui, equally, the reality for British officials and private interests seeking to profit from Burmese pearl banks was equally disappointing, if nonetheless important to local imperial revenue and an element of imperial governance.[41] In Bassein district, northwest of the Mergui archipelago, despite the belief among some officials that "large pearls [were] to be found and in abundance in deep water off Diamond Island," no such finds were ever reported. Instead, large amounts of "small pearls" were being extracted from hundreds of thousands of oysters that were annually being taken from the sea.[42] These seed pearls, like those found in the Mergui archipelago, were among the most readily available and abundant marine products of coastal and riverine Burma. Along with other marine products such as green snails, bêche-de-mer, and particularly pearl shell, which continued to supply Chinese and Indian markets and from the final quarter of the century was increasingly being shipped west to meet rising European demand for objects fashioned from or incorporating mother-of-pearl, they essentially constituted the backbone of Burma's marine trade. Seed pearls, it was noted, "always [found] a ready sale,"[43] and, as such, the revenue that their export generated was an integral component of British fiscal concerns that local authorities could do little but accept. Additionally, the pearl banks represented another site for the projection of imperial authority amidst growing British terraqueous ambitions in the

Bay of Bengal and beyond, and were thus of importance to the project of colony-making.[44]

If Warrington Smyth's dating of heightened British interest is correct, it was not until the 1890s, after Burma had been incorporated administratively as a province of British India, that efforts to rationalize extraction actually took shape.[45] European and Australian pearlers had begun to appear on the Lower Burmese coast in search of pearls and pearl shell by this time, concentrating their operations around the imperially named Malcolm and Page Islands while, in a reflection of the continued importance of Chinese pearlers to the Mergui marine economy, the latter concentrated their collection further north, "with Ross island as headquarters, and the neighbourhood of Ross, Elphinstone, and Grant islands as their fishing-grounds."[46]

The rights to fish in these waters were now sold by public auction at the court of the deputy commissioner at Mergui, and in the decade of the 1890s, if not earlier, included trepang and green snails.[47] Auctions, similar to farming but with an openly competitive element where bidders would go up against one another, also represented speculative opportunities for these individuals to pay a sum of money on what they predicted future hauls would yield in the following pearling season. This created a variable—but at least regular—source of income for the imperial authorities that also had the advantage for the colonial state of deflecting the risk associated with the extraction of marine products away from itself and onto the winning bidder.[48] The auction-lease system was a variant of the farming of esculent birds' nests from previous decades and echoed the renting of the right to the pearl beds of South India and Ceylon that became the predominant form of regulation for waters the British authorities had been managing since the late eighteenth century. The inclusion of green snails and bêche-de-mer in the public auction, the latter having likely formed part of the farm for birds' nests as one of the marine goods merchants were given the right to collect in the 1820s, as previously noted, indicated further the extent to which the British considered the waters of the Mergui archipelago a source of marine goods and not exclusively a site of pearl-shell extraction.

In Bassein, where the collection of pearls and shell was taking place both along the islands dotting the coast and along its riverbanks, the right to do so was also structured around the lease system. There were, though, some distinguishing features that differentiated Bassein pearling from that of the Mergui archipelago, notably that leases were to be granted for only one year and that the "right to collect pearls be put to auction with and at the same time as the right to work the turtle banks."[49] As with Mergui, that the collection of turtle eggs was included in the "Fishing Directions for the Disposal and Regulation of the Pearl Fisheries in the Bassein District" underscores how the harvesting of pearls and shell in Burma was inextricably bound up with a larger marine products economy of which it had always formed an integral part.[50]

Being guided by an administrative praxis of "managing" Burma's pearl banks as a particular "environment" and resource over which government sought to exert authority and mediate use and access, reflecting notions of liberal improvement, resulted, though, in further intervention in how extraction of pearls and shell would be organized. Thus, in the case of the Mergui archipelago, the Burma provincial government set about dividing the pearl banks that they believed to be scattered across its vastly dispersed islands into five "blocks" or "districts" that were sold, either singly or in groups, at public auction (figure 6.1).[51] A winning bid guaranteed unrestricted access to that particular block's banks—some extending over extraordinarily vast areas—for an extended period of time. For instance, Block 3 comprised 1,800 square miles scattered along the southern Burmese coast.[52] Each block was understood as "an area of sea within which the exclusive right of pearl fishing is leased."[53] These were defined along demarcated maritime lines of division that brought particular islands together into one or another discrete grouping that nonetheless was to be managed as part of a larger ecological whole. The block system thus retained leases as the mechanism through which rents were collected from the pearl banks, with the deputy commissioner able to "grant a lease of a pearl fishery for one year, or with the previous sanction of the Financial Commissioner, for any number of years not exceeding five." At least one month before the auction, information on the terms of the lease would be advertised in English and Burmese in Mergui and throughout the "principal ports" of Burma and the Straits Settlements. Once a successful bid had been secured—and an earnest-money payment of 10 percent of the rent deposited into the treasury—the "auction purchaser or successful tenderer" would be given a marked chart indicating "the limits of every block [and therefore] the limits within which pearl-fishing is permitted by the lease."[54]

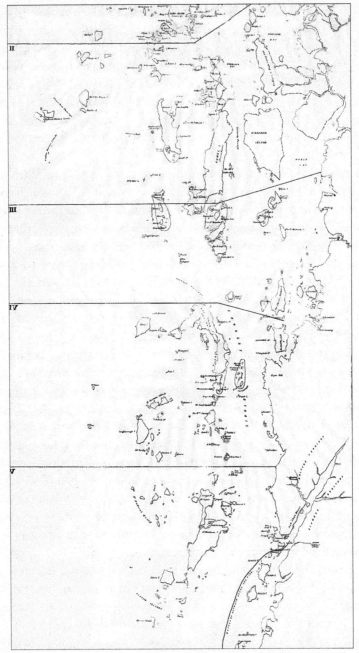

Figure 6.1. Blocks II, III, IV, and V, Mergui Archipelago. Source: R. N. Rudmose Brown and James J. Simpson, *Report to the Government of Burma on the Pearl Oyster Fisheries of the Mergui Archipelago and Moskos Islands* (Rangoon, 1907).

Coinciding with the establishment of the block system, and a likely contributing factor, was the intensification of colonial Australian interest in Burma's shell. Pearlers working especially in the Torres Strait were drawn overwhelmingly—if not exclusively—to the islands of the Mergui archipelago as a "comparatively new pearling ground" because of their potential as a source particularly of mother-of-pearl, from which pearling merchants had been making considerable profits since the 1870s from shell exports from Australia to London and other European markets as consumption began to rise sharply.[55] Britain alone at this time imported around 1,500 tons of shell that was ultimately re-exported to the button industries of France and Austria.[56] Prominent Australian pearlers thus began to arrive in Mergui, especially in the 1890s, and most notably Frank Jardine, a magistrate and cattle station owner who had been a pioneering figure in the Torres Strait pearling industry.[57] Reflecting the intensification of Australian interest in the archipelago's pearl banks, Jardine had come to Burma at the invitation of the British Indian government, which had commissioned a report from him on the fisheries in order to gauge their commercial viability in pearl shell. Others "who had experience of the pearl banks of Queensland" also arrived in Burma to gain access to Mergui's banks—in 1892, for instance, a Mr. Chill had purchased the lease for Centre Block for a three-year period, and would attempt also to collect shell in islands off coastal Upper Burma.[58]

Though dominated by South Asian, Chinese, and other non-Australian capital, the imperial logic informing the block system in Mergui was applied, equally, to Bassein and its pearling banks—with the qualification that "the river or estuary area and the open sea area shall not be included in the same block" (figure 6.2).[59] The reason for this qualification was, as previously noted, that pearling in Bassein district was carried out both in the estuaries and along the banks of its rivers, and among the islands that dotted its coast. The district commissioner of Bassein, writing to the deputy commissioner in 1895, noted however that it was "not essential that each block should be of the same value" and that it would be "more convenient" to award specific river banks to single lessees.[60] But with the failure of the auction that year—when not a single bid was made after a disappointing previous year—and the competitive petitions that followed in its wake, in which petitioners were requesting monopoly rights over specific islands and coastal points, Bassein's pearling waters were divided into a total of three blocks.[61] While turtle banks

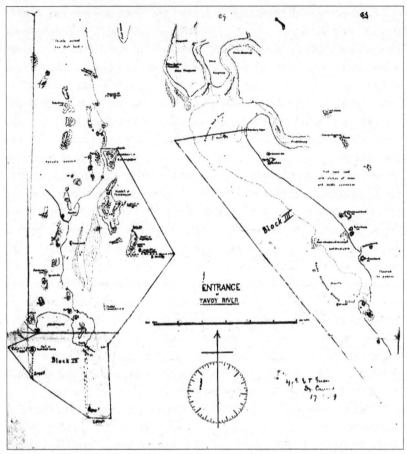

Figure 6.2. Sketch of the division into blocks of the estuary of the Tavoy River. National Archives of Myanmar, 1/7/67.

that were already leased when this change was made were excluded from the blocks, in future it was thought that "the right to collects turtle's eggs and pearls on these banks should . . . be auctioned together."[62] The judiciousness of parceling the pearling waters into three blocks was seemingly demonstrated when the rights to them were sold successfully for the following year, even if their purchase was made by a single merchant, Hajji Shah Mahomed Ali, of Rangoon.[63]

With the block system, British authorities had devised an extractive structure that could meet the revenue needs and governance aims of the incipient colonial state. Rights to each of the blocks in Mergui and

Bassein could be leased either separately or together and, especially when there were several interested parties, could generate competitive bidding that would thus drive up the price of the rent on the banks. When, as occasionally though rarely happened, no bidders presented themselves at an auction, monopoly rights for each of the blocks could be awarded to any bidder whose price the district commissioner deemed appropriate for that particular block.

Moreover, rights to each or all blocks could be transferred to third parties in what became, essentially, a subleasing arrangement. Thus, in 1892, when Mr. Chill had purchased the rights to Centre Block, as noted above, he transferred them to the Mergui Pearling Company, whose directors and "most of the shareholders" were based in Singapore.[64] Other companies entered Mergui pearling in this manner in the late nineteenth century. One of their challenges, of course, was to estimate the volume of a particular block's oyster yield so as not to overpay and thereby risk losing money should the banks prove to have far less shell than had been anticipated—or, as happened to the Mergui Pearling Company in 1894, losing money because the price of pearl shell on the London market, where it was focused, had fallen from £110 to £55 per ton. As a newspaper reported dryly, "the price for the company's concession is now discovered to have been too high," the company suffering a loss of almost £10,000.[65] Despite the risks, another company (the Pearling and Trading Company) sent part of its fleet to the islands, and its "example has been followed by several individual owners of schooners."[66] In this manner, the companies and schooners were allowed largely unrestricted access to their particular block or blocks. To help spread their financial risk, companies effectively "instituted a system of sub-leasing, or rather granting a permit to would-be constituents to fish for pearl-shells on their leaseholds."[67]

The block system served a further critical purpose in the dynamics of colonial governance—the consolidation of claims to maritime space. Indeed, the territorialization of ocean space had become an increasingly dominant feature of British and other European imperial claims from around the middle of the eighteenth century, particularly throughout the many islands and coastal areas of insular Southeast Asia. The idea of extending imperial jurisdiction over maritime space was, of course, one with a very long history in the expansionist trajectory of European empire.[68] In the nineteenth century, the territorialization of oceanic space and all that lived within it resulted in the incorporation of islands and coastal areas into an imperial legal framework that would also expose unresolved tensions and lay bare the limits of imperial jurisdiction.

A case in 1893 illustrates the contours of these limits. It involved a legal challenge to the government of Burma from an Australian pearler active in the Mergui archipelago after it had granted "a concession of the exclusive right of fishing on these banks." This unnamed Australian (possibly Thomas Henry Haynes, a prominent pearler and trader with interests also in Southeast Asia, or one of his associates) claimed through his legal representatives that he had a right to operate in these waters because he considered "them to be in the high seas outside the territorial waters" controlled by the government of Burma, and that it was therefore acting unlawfully in granting monopoly rights. This kind of oppositional stance had been adopted equally by pearlers in Australia and surrounding waters who claimed that the colonial government could claim no jurisdiction over operations taking place beyond the three-mile limit of its territorial waters.[69]

In Burma, the government responded with the contention that "its jurisdiction extend[ed] to a distance of three miles beyond the outer edge of the archipelago," arguing further that this jurisdiction "include[ed] all waters lying between that line and the mainland." The three-mile distance was what was then accepted by international law, which British authorities in Ceylon had codified equally to extend the maritime boundaries of their island territory in 1811 through a legislative act investing the state with the authority to arrest any boats and crews that ventured into the island's pearling waters throughout the year.[70] This approach and thinking informed colonial logic in Burma "to support their concession of an exclusive right of fishing."[71]

But in seeking to establish definitively where its territorial waters lay and thus what it could claim as its maritime jurisdiction in relation to control over the Mergui archipelago's pearling banks, the government of Burma sought the intervention of the Crown's law officers in establishing the legitimacy of its position vis-à-vis claims to the contrary. The matter, as far as they were concerned, turned on "whether the jurisdiction of the government of Burma and its power to grant exclusive fishing rights extends over all waters lying between the mainland of Burma and a distance of three miles beyond the outer edge of the Mergui archipelago, or whether it is limited in the manner stated by the legal advisers of the Government of India, or otherwise." It will come as no surprise, perhaps, that the law officers agreed that the government had correctly stated its territorial jurisdiction and thus it followed "that the government [had] no power to grant exclusive fishery rights except in waters *within* the extent of the jurisdiction so described." In making this determination, and in a statement replete with imperial hubris, they also essentially denied the possibility of the existence of any rights or claims to the banks by Moken fishermen by stating presumptively that "we assume that in the case of the pearl fisheries in the Mergui archipelago, there has not been as in the case of the Ceylon fisheries, an immemorial claim to the pearl oyster fishery."[72] The reference to Ceylon was an invocation of the customary rights to pearl fishing that groups such as Tamil Paravas had negotiated and protected historically as perquisites from local and foreign rulers in the Gulf of Mannar. In the eyes of the colonial state, Moken claims were nonexistent.

The case had additional significance, though. In raising questions of territoriality and maritime jurisdiction, it exposed further anxieties of an incipient colonial state struggling to solidify the porous maritime boundaries of the region.[73] Coastlines represented amorphous spaces, however, where, as Jan Heesterman reminds us, "the littoral forms a frontier zone that is not there to separate or enclose but which rather finds its meaning in its permeability." As we find also with the pearl oyster beds of Mannar, those of the Mergui archipelago constituted a fluid frontier and found their meaning in the permeability of their surrounding waters and coastlines.[74]

It was precisely this permeability, however, that was the source of considerable British imperial anxiety. These found voice specifically in the concern expressed by the secretary to the government of India in correspondence with the chief commissioner of Burma over the existence of "no clear proof . . . of the Mergui islands having been at any time officially declared to be part of Tenasserim [Lower Burma] and under the administration of the Chief Commissioner of Burma." Calcutta thus urged that a "draft notification" be submitted, "bringing them formally into the province of Tenasserim and under the Chief Commissioners' administration."[75] The urgency for such a notification related also to the larger imperial project of boundary-making that had deepened in the late 1860s around the demarcation of space between Tenasserim, as the southernmost region of Burma, and Siam. Emerging from attempts earlier in the century to establish boundaries with the court of Siam after the British conquest of southern Burma had turned it into Tenasserim Province—and reflecting particular notions of space that differed from local understandings of the constitution of borders—the delineation of frontiers became increasingly key to imperial visions.[76] Given the uncertainty over the status of the islands of the Mergui archipelago, there was thus great concern at the end of the nineteenth century that they be included "with the British government."[77]

Moreover, in the face of competing French imperial interests in Siam, border-making was an integral strategy in consolidating a notion of imperial boundedness and incorporation that was seen both to reflect and engender the power of the state and render this power visible through its enforcement.[78] The indeterminacy and permeability of the southern border would, however, remain a fact of life for British authorities, with Moken regularly sailing to Ranong to deliver prearranged cargoes of pearl shell to Chinese merchants into the 1920s and 1930s. "Siamese" poachers would also sail to certain blocks regularly to fish for pearls and shell, both undermining the rights of the lessees and jeopardizing the future revenue of colonial income because "a lower price would be paid for this monopoly in future and Government therefore will also lose."[79] With limited policing of the blocks—lessees were actually asked to contribute to their surveillance in 1898 and 1899—there was little chance of preventing this coastal activity that had been ongoing since at least the early nineteenth century, well before the establishment of British interest in the Mergui archipelago.[80]

If the block system signaled deepening European and Australian participation in the Mergui archipelago and helped solidify British attempts at establishing maritime borders in Burma, it also encouraged the involvement of local and regional merchants and pearl entrepreneurs. In Bassein and Arakan, those most active in the extraction of pearls and shell were a mix of ethnic Burmese, locally born Chinese, and Tamil-speaking South Indian traders.[81] The extent of Tamil involvement in the fisheries was reflected in a colonial notification issued in 1903 in Mergui announcing that a pearl fishery was to take place in Ceylon that year; apart from the copies that were published in English and distributed throughout the region, the majority were published in Tamil.[82] South Asian interest in Bassein's pearl banks was not confined to Tamil-speaking traders, though, with Bombay merchants and "Surati traders," who may have been residing in Rangoon and were not necessarily based in Surat, purchasing leases for the fisheries. As with the Bombay merchants, these were likely Gujarati Khojas with connections to the small coastal state of Kutch (Kachchh), whose transnational circulations in the Indian Ocean in the nineteenth century assumed extensive proportions, with merchants active from the 1850s and 1860s in areas such as East Africa, Madagascar, and the opium trade to China.[83] Mergui represented for Khojas further opportunities to diversify their commercial involvement in the Indian Ocean.

In the Mergui archipelago, as in other areas of Burmese pearl and shell harvesting, ethnic Burmese continued to be active in the extraction of shell by purchasing licenses from government or as subleasers.[84] Malay traders, in an extension of their long participation in pearling, as noted earlier, were also active in Mergui, particularly through the maintenance of relationships that were established over the years with Moken divers and collectors of shell.[85] But among the most prominent merchants in the islands were Penang-based Chinese, many of whom were by the end of the nineteenth century locally born or Peranakan Chinese. As I have noted previously, despite the clear importance of Singapore in the marine goods trade, Penang remained a significant regional port and intra-Asian commercial node throughout the nineteenth century and into the twentieth for the flow of marine products and other goods between Burma and the rest of Southeast Asia and China. Indeed, many of the Malay traders seeking shell in the archipelago were themselves shipping it through Penang on to other destinations. Peranakan or Straits Chinese in particular transported pearl shell from Mergui to Penang regularly, where their value was often double what it was in Burma, before their cargoes were transshipped on to China. Some Burma-born Chinese also participated in this commerce but they appear to have been outnumbered by Chinese merchants operating from Penang in the late nineteenth century.[86] This was a time when Chinese investments in Burma and throughout many parts of Southeast Asia were expanding into such areas as tin mining and the rice trade, and included continued participation in the regional marine goods economy.[87] Much like Chinese syndicates such as the Khaw Group, active in Penang and Siam, these merchants demonstrated "the connections between marine produce and efficient forms of Chinese business organization," and the purchasing, sorting, packaging, and shipping of pearl shell from Burma, among a variety of marine products, remained a significant part of the local economy of Penang into the early twentieth century, before being overtaken by the larger movement of goods during the high colonial era.[88]

At least as important in Mergui were South Asian merchants who subleased rights to harvest pearls and shell in the blocks. Many of these merchants were India-born but included a small but growing number of locally born Indians from the early twentieth century. And once the lease system was abolished (discussed below), South Asian traders also purchased permits from the Mergui Pearling Company, among others, and financed investments in boats and equipment at several of the blocks.[89] Like Chinese merchants, Indian financiers also invested in advanced pearling technologies, especially in suited divers to reach greater depths in the islands.[90] Notable among South Asian participation in pearling in Mergui and elsewhere were Nattukottai Chettiar capitalists who may have arranged for the shipment of divers with South Indian diving experience to labor in the waters of the Mergui archipelago. One of a number of South Asian groups to migrate to Burma in the nineteenth century, Chettiars arrived in growing numbers in Lower Burma from the 1850s following the British occupation in 1852. Their role as providers of credit in the expansion of rice cultivation from the 1870s in the fertile Irrawaddy delta is well known, but less well understood is their participation in pearling.[91] While never encompassing their primary involvement in Burma, investment in the collection of shell was nevertheless an area of interest for several Chettiar merchants. Nakarattar commercial activities in South India earlier in the nineteenth century had seen these merchants gain control of the pearl fisheries in the Ceylon Strait and Gulf of Mannar at the expense of Muslim Marakkayar (Chulia) merchants until around the 1830s. Participation in the Mergui archipelago's pearl fisheries, for some at least, was an extension of earlier family involvement in Ceylon and India, with Chettiar merchants thus among those who purchased, or financed the purchase of, permits to sublease rights to pearl fishing.[92]

More significant than Chettiar involvement in Burma's pearling economy, however, were Tamil Marakkayar Muslim merchants with ancestral ties to South India but who in Mergui by the late nineteenth century were hailing from Penang as Jawi Peranakan. These were hybrid Malay–South Indian communities whose members would play prominent roles in the political life of Penang and lead the Malay-Muslim reform movement there in the 1920s.[93] In Mergui, there was no more important Jawi-Peranakan family than the Ahmeds, whose head and founding member of the family's business interests in Burma, Ebrahim Ahmed, was described in 1909 as "the largest pearler in Mergui."[94] Although Ebrahim had been born in Mergui, the family had come to Burma from Penang sometime in the second half of the nineteenth century and its members maintained close commercial relationships with the city. Among the "principal . . . lessees of the pearling grounds at Mergui," the Ahmeds were regarded favorably by British officials because, according to one assessment of the family's involvement in pearling, "they have invested time, and money, very largely in boats and diving gear."[95] The family forged close relationships not only with European pearl-shell buyers, through contacts with London financiers, and Bombay and Singapore merchant houses, but also arranged for the regular shipments of shell to Penang and northwest across the Bay of Bengal to Calcutta.[96] They did not, though, confine themselves to pearling, diversifying their investments through ownership of a rice mill and wolfram and tin mines—areas of investment that attracted also other Asian merchants—that saw the family accumulate considerable wealth and political influence. Ebrahim Ahmed, for instance, became the first member from Mergui to serve in the Legislative Council for Burma. Their wealth and influence extended also to religious patronage, the family financing the construction of a large mosque (still standing today) and madrasa that drew Muslim children from the region.[97] The Ahmeds' involvement in pearling would be a mainstay of the Mergui archipelago's shell extraction economy into the late 1920s and 1930s, as the family consolidated its position as the most influential commercial actors of Burma's southern region.

SHIFTING SANDS

While the block system became the dominant structural apparatus through which the colonial state sought to manage—and profit from—the extraction of pearls and shell from Burma's banks by all interested parties, it did not go unchallenged. Within a few years of its implementation, misgivings began to be expressed in Mergui about certain aspects of its extractive effects, specifically related to questions about the regeneration of oyster stocks and the impact this could have on yields.

Thus, while "all the fishing rights" to the archipelago were sold again for a three-year period in 1895, when this ended in 1898 they were sold for only two years, as government officials worried about overfishing.[98]

As concerns began to grow, there were some who nonetheless remained unconvinced of this threat. Frank Jardine, for instance, whom the British Indian government had commissioned to produce a report on the fisheries and who was therefore in a position to exert considerable influence on officials, was firm in the belief that "although several of the first-worked beds have been temporarily abandoned they are not in anything approaching a worked out condition." He was convinced, for instance, that "the whole of the north-eastern corner of the concession lying between Sir John Malcolm, Ravenshaw, Paway [sic] Islands, and the southern boundary of No. 2 Block, is one immense bed of pearl shell."[99] Jardine's optimistic view no doubt inspired an idea more broadly that the archipelago's waters held great and untapped potential for large-scale exploitation by pearlers. This appeared to be confirmed by the dramatic rise in the volume of shell collected as a result of the creation of the block system: whereas only 26 tons had been extracted in the 1891–92 season, this grew to 294 tons in 1893–94 and by the 1894–95 season had increased markedly to 315 tons.[100] But, at least according to official figures, there was a steady decline in yields after this period, dropping down to 111 tons in 1899–1900 and 66 tons in 1900–1901.[101] This prompted R. N. Rudmose Brown and James J. Simpson, authors in 1907 of an official report on the archipelago, to claim that the block system "was undoubtedly detrimental to the pearl banks, inasmuch as individuals of companies leasing these blocks recklessly exploit them."[102]

Other, arguably more vocal, concerns were voiced among government officers beyond the Mergui archipelago concerning the deleterious effects of granting monopoly rights over pearl banks. District officers were concerned over how the extraction of shell along the Bassein and Arakanese coasts was depriving local populations of a valuable food source through intense searching for seed pearls. Some expressed dismay that, in the former, the search for seed pearls resulted in the oysters being discarded in great number, "the flesh of the oyster [being] allowed to rot [and consequently] the amount of food thrown away must have been many thousands of tons."[103] And in response to inquiries that had been made regarding the collection of pearl shells on the banks of the Byetma and Athabya Islands in the Myebon township of Kyaukpyu District in

Arakan in 1896, it was noted that the "local officers were averse from [sic] the creation of any monopoly with regard to such shells chiefly on the grounds that the shell fish in question are to a considerable extent used as food by the people who live near where they are found."[104] They were, in addition, part of a local food economy in which oysters were shipped and sold in Akyab, thus providing a source of valuable income for maritime families and of protein for local consumers.[105]

With these considerations in mind, several pearling merchants were denied access to the banks "because in order to obtain any quantity of pearls, a number of oysters out of proportion to the value of the pearls found would have to be opened which would cause considerable waste and deprive the people, resident in the vicinity, of food."[106] As examples, Maung Tun U, a broker from Rangoon, and Taing Shwe Hla, of Akyab, were not permitted to access the banks in 1896 and 1904, respectively, because their actions had belied their stated aims. It appears, while Maung Tun U had declared that what he was "desirous of doing was not to take pearl shells from the sea but to collect the shells of the dead fish taken by natives for food and discarded on the shore as useless," that he had actually sought "the tiny pearls [seed pearls] sometimes found in these pearl oysters and used for medicine and that the shells were discarded as useless." The wasteful nature of this process, it was argued, "would deprive the people of a source of food." By the same token, Taing Shwe Hla allegedly "really wanted the pearls in the oysters and not the mother-of-pearl shells."[107]

There was further questioning about the depletion of oyster stocks and its consequent effect on pearling in the region. According to one estimate for Bassein made in 1896, the number of oysters extracted from the banks may have amounted to a remarkable figure: F. D. Maxwell, the deputy commissioner of Bassein, claimed that, as "2000 *tolahs* [a unit of measure used in colonial South Asia] of small pearls were taken from two stations, as about 20,000 oysters produced only 1 *tolah* . . . the number of oysters taken must have been about 40 millions."[108] Even allowing for a degree of exaggeration in this staggering figure, it crystallized for the administration an idea of a scale of oyster collection in Bassein that could have been disastrous for the local industry. Perhaps not surprisingly, officials recommended that, with the exception of the taking of oysters for "home consumption," the banks should remain "unworked" for a few years until around 1900 when, despite uncertainty over how quickly stocks would replenish, it was hoped that the collection of oysters could be resumed in areas where it was possible to do so.[109]

Yet, even as concerns over overfishing remained a consistent theme in imperial correspondence, there was also an unwavering commitment to finding all possible ways of making the collection of shell as profitable as possible in Bassein and Arakan. This is perhaps best captured by the continued attempts in Arakan—despite the acknowledgement of the vibrant local commerce in oysters that formed part of coastal economies—to establish whether the oysters taken along its coast were "really a mother-of-pearl oyster of which the shell has a commercial value."[110] Even when allowing that the oysters were, from the point of view of the colonial administrators and their "scientific" advisers, "not of very high value," it was nonetheless maintained that "it is worthwhile considering that if the shell were proved to have commercial value it might be taken with profit without any diminution of food supply to the people." Furthermore, in a statement that reflected less an expectation than a hope that the beds were viable as an exploitable maritime resource, there came a request from the office of the financial commissioner that an "inquiry might be held as to the extent of the banks where these oysters are found, as to the depth of water, and whether operations with diving apparatus would render available, banks closed to the present methods of taking them; and whether the kind of pearl found is such as to grow to a marketable size in favourable conditions."[111] The application of new technology in the form of the diving "dress" held the prospect of locating and colonizing yet-to-be-discovered banks at greater depths than had previously been possible.

By the same token, in Bassein, while there was an appreciation that seed pearls were primarily what was extracted from its maritime and riverine waters, there remained interest in establishing whether there was the possibility of greater profitability from its beds. There was thus a request, in 1910, for "specimens of various kinds of pearl oyster shell" and for more precise information on where banks were located, the depth of the water, and their "pearl producing qualities." This included the shells of the seed-pearl-producing oysters that were to be found in the Bassein and Thetkethaung Rivers, though it was "impossible to say what the pearl producing qualities of these particular shells was—the bank is of sand so that about 6,000 oysters produce about one *tolah* of seed pearls."[112] Some of these shells appear to have been from the "windowpane" oyster (*Placuna placenta*), whose translucent qualities were to make them ideal as a substitute for the use of glass in windows; they were used also for lime burning. No doubt influenced by the successful extraction of pearls and especially shell in the Mergui archipelago, colonial administrators sought similar gains from the Arakan and Bassein fisheries, and this aspirational thinking would continue to influence their approach to pearling in these northern Burmese waters well into the twentieth century.

So, despite the ambivalence of colonial administrators toward the block system as an institutional structure for managing Burma's pearl fisheries as a marine resource, it remained in place into the first decades of the twentieth century. There was, though, one significant change of fundamental importance, implemented to ameliorate concerns of overfishing and guarantee continued revenue from the fisheries in the Mergui archipelago: the auction system, whereby blocks were put up to public auction, was abolished in the late 1890s and replaced by one of fees or licenses on each of the pumps being used by pearlers on diving vessels.[113] Pumps, as the next section will elaborate, were an integral apparatus of the new technology that had been introduced into the Mergui archipelago toward the end of the nineteenth century, the so-called "diving dress" or "suit" that required the use of pumps to provide air to divers who were going down to far greater depths than was possible through naked diving, in which none of this technology was utilized to extract shell. Indeed, the introduction of a licensing system on individual pumps was also a move to accommodate the elaborated use of the diving suit in Mergui pearling, while the rights to collect shells, green snails, and trochus shell "without apparatus" continued to be sold by auction.[114]

Not embraced by all in the colonial administration—some thought that there would be great difficulty in fixing the fee and that it "would be liable to attract the scum and dregs of the two hemispheres"—licenses were generally agreed to be the most expedient way forward for government, especially in light of the decline of European and Australian involvement in the archipelago by the end of the nineteenth century.[115] Moreover, with the auction system, the rights to collect pearl shell, green snails, trochus, and other marine products had been sold together as part of a block, but now they were being sold separately. The new system, it was thus noted, "brought an increase of revenue which [is attributed] chiefly to the fact that pearling with machinery and diving for g.s. [green snails] are carried on by entirely different classes of people and need a different kind of knowledge, so that to sell them together was manifestly wasteful."[116]

But the change was not only positively endorsed by the Revenue Department—local pearlers welcomed it, too, claiming in a letter to the lieutenant governor of Burma in 1900 that it would "induce more people taking up [sic] the concern."[117] With the fee set at Rs 400 per pump, the result of careful calculations that were based on how much the blocks had been leased for in previous years, the license system was understood to broaden the involvement of local pearlers and establish continued revenue for local government offices.[118] At the same time, though, it raised serious questions about diving as a physical and labor practice—fundamental to the overall functioning of the entire industry—in which the colonial state sought to intervene increasingly from the late nineteenth century.

GOING DEEP

Diving for and collecting pearls and shell, as noted earlier, had for years before the consolidation of British rule in Burma in the nineteenth century been mostly carried out by Moken divers in a coastal economy that combined subsistence with the exchange of marine products. Divers could reach impressive depths of well over thirty-three feet in their search for shell, with some claiming that the Moken had actually "cleared" the banks of the Mergui archipelago "nearly all down to a depth of six fathoms."[119] Moken divers maintained relationships with Chinese merchants as these called at the islands with greater frequency from the late eighteenth and especially first decades of the nineteenth centuries in search of shell and other marine products. Moken appear to have been paid according to the number of shells they collected, which could be at a rate of roughly twelve per hour. They worked for one or two hours at a time and at the lowest spring tides, which amounted roughly to five or six days of labor per month. During the southwest monsoon, with its heavy rains and strong currents, diving became impossible "owing to the thick condition of the water during that season."[120]

As British interests in Burma grew from the 1820s, the prospect of exploiting pearling waters through the use of the same rationalized labor force that had been employed in the banks over which the East

India Company and Crown had exerted control in the Gulf of Mannar resulted in Tamil divers being shipped to the archipelago. The details of this endeavor are not available, but it would appear that it did not develop as a government scheme. Rather, in the first half of the nineteenth century, the extraction of shell was undertaken predominantly by Moken diving labor that continued to be engaged by Chinese and also Malay traders on a seasonal and sustained basis, as they were also by Penang-based merchants. This did not change substantially in the following decades, as Moken divers continued to labor among the islands' oyster beds for specific traders.

The colonial state's introduction of the block system in the early 1890s, with its overt attempt at rationalizing pearl fishing in the archipelago and elsewhere in the colony, did not necessarily alter these arrangements in its initial years. Blocks were sold in their entirety or together at auction, and the rights thereby granted the lessee to exploit their banks did not encompass the labor that was actually required to collect shell. The assumption on the part of colonial officers seems to have been that the use of Moken divers, going down to collect shell without utilizing any of the equipment of dress diving, would persist with lessees. And, indeed, this appears to have been the case.

However, the introduction of the diving suit into the Mergui archipelago by European and Australian pearling capital around 1894 as an element of "modern" maritime technology created, as it would elsewhere in the pearling world, the separate and distinct category of "naked" diving. In Burma as more generally throughout Southeast Asia, divers were capable of attaining depths of around thirty-nine to forty-six feet prior to the introduction of the dresses, spending a limited amount of time searching for and collecting oysters before having to return to the surface. Divers were thus restricted to work in relatively shallow water, "even though they knew that pearl oysters were often abundant in deeper waters."[121] Having been developed through different stages over the course of the nineteenth century, the diving dress—consisting of a helmet, corselet, a suit made of waterproof canvas, and weighted boots—allowed divers to go down to far greater depths than was otherwise possible. The associated use of a hand pump and hose through which air was carried to the helmet and a rope attached to the diver to enable, by tugging at it, the conveying of different signals to the crew completed the diving ensemble. Despite its cumbersome and somewhat restrictive nature, the dress meant that divers were able to reach depths over twice that of diving without the apparatus and that their time under water was also greatly extended. Any technological advantage that would allow divers to reach these greater depths was, of course, an extremely attractive if costlier proposition for pearlers, who, unsurprisingly, embraced the adoption of the diving dress. And for the colonial state, it introduced a vertical dimension to the territorialization of oceanic space by making it possible to claim and exploit beds at unprecedented depths.

Never fully supplanted as a labor mode, though, naked diving continued to exist, often as a complementary form for the extraction of pearl shell as well as an array of marine products. In the Mergui archipelago (the dress was not used elsewhere in Burma), naked diving remained a vibrant endeavor practiced exclusively by Moken divers who were engaged by merchants, including in blocks where pumps and dress diving were being utilized simultaneously, to collect shells, green snails, and trochus shell found in shallower waters. But, after considerable debate about its merits and demerits, the agreement on the part of colonial officers to introduce the licensing system comprised of "fees on pumps being used" brought to the fore the question of "diving without apparatus."[122] Specifically, the question centered on how the *right* of collecting the aforementioned marine products should be apportioned—in other words, should the right to collect shell without the use of diving equipment be sold separately "along with the other rights," or should naked diving be somehow incorporated into a fee structure that was associated with what was levied on pumps. Revenue department officials, in particular, were concerned that the latter had actually rendered naked pearling "free," and therefore sought a resolution to an activity in which there continued to be considerable interest among pearl shell and marine product traders in the Mergui archipelago.[123]

Although urged by these traders, even before the auction-lease system had been abolished, that it would indeed be desirable to sell the "right of collecting m.o.p. [mother-of-pearl] shells without diving apparatus . . . along with the other rights," government officers were hesitant—at least initially—to grant this change. Some, fully cognizant that naked diving was in the hands of Moken seafarers, believed that these divers "might benefit by the fact of such pearling being free."[124] But this was dismissed as untrue, according to the Mergui revenue officer, for the

Moken "hardly get fair play at the hands of the licensees, to whom they look for food and what clothing they need." The notion that Moken divers were being exploited by "individual Chinese and Malays" reflected colonial stereotyping of groups with whom Moken divers and families had cultivated relationships over many decades of pearl fishing in the archipelago's waters. This notion was a guiding principle, nonetheless, and resulted in revenue officials and the financial commissioner jointly endorsing that the "exclusive right of working without diving apparatus in the various blocks of the pearling area . . . be leased separately."[125] Its inclusion in the 1905 Burma Fisheries Act enshrined what had already become commonly accepted by Burma's local colonial officers.[126]

This did not entirely resolve matters from the government's standpoint, however, for "free" diving remained widely practiced among the archipelago's islands. Several Chinese merchants operating in Mergui in the first two decades of the twentieth century "employ[ed]" Moken divers "without licence for pearling."[127] Clearly driven by an imperative to derive as much taxation as possible from the collection of any and all marine products in the region's waters, this concern also reflected ongoing efforts to define maritime borders that were, as noted earlier, indeterminate and traversed constantly by the movement of goods, boats, and people. Moken divers thus continued to either dive for traders who sailed to the archipelago or, as seems to have been more common, to sail the relatively short distance to Ranong, where they delivered their cargoes of assorted marine products to specific Chinese—and in some cases Malay—traders with whom they had prearranged agreements. Understanding little of the dynamics of these relationships, colonial officers sought the criminalization of this behavior, with imprisonment a possibility or large fines being issued to traders who, upon inspection, could not produce the license that had to be kept onboard vessels.[128] It is difficult to get a sense of how successful this approach was, but the almost total absence of colonial naval patrol vessels meant that local officials were forced to rely on the logic, applied as much to the idea of Moken naked diving as to the extraction through dress diving, that the "holders of licences would . . . inform against any unlicenced pumps who would be competing unfairly with them."[129] Quite to what degree this may have been true is hard to discern. But even with the complaints of some prominent merchants—like those made by Ebrahim Ahmed in the 1920s—about Moken trading to Ranong in marine products fished from areas to which these merchants had been granted de facto exclusive rights, this economy continued to thrive as an irrepressible feature of the exchange of marine products in Burma's coastal waters.

Pearling and shell harvesting in the Mergui archipelago, then, was characterized at the turn of the century by the coexistence of naked and dress diving. The number of pumps being used in the islands had grown from around sixty in the mid-1890s to possibly as many as eighty by the early years of the twentieth century, but does not appear to have grown much beyond this number. Indian and Chinese merchant investments, noted earlier, contributed to this number of pumps through significant investments in boats and dresses. Schooners employed mostly Filipino, Malay, and Japanese divers in the small boats that actually carried the pumps and that sailed to the pearl banks before returning to the larger vessel operating as a "floating station" where their hauls were discharged. While Australian involvement in Mergui had been prominent until around the turn of the century, many of the dress divers had been brought to the islands from the pearling grounds of the Torres Strait and Aru Islands. Thereafter, while the number of Australian or European-owned pumps dropped significantly, dress diving remained a feature of pearling in the archipelago, with growing numbers of Japanese divers—as would be the case beyond Burma, of course—laboring to collect shell at great depths.

In areas "outside the open pearling grounds"—the blocks into which the islands of the archipelago continued to be divided—diving was organized through leases and not the pump system, with divers working in waters where "exclusive rights of pearling and taking of green snails etc [were granted] within a definite area."[130] This was, a government official wrote in Moulmein in 1908, so as not to "interfere with persons diving for pearls under licences in the public pearling area."[131] This appears to have been part of efforts to allow the exploration of waters that could contain pearl banks, specifically around the Moskos Islands that lay to the north of the Mergui archipelago.[132]

The complementarity of dress and naked diving, coupled with the investments in equipment and boats by Asian traders and merchants and the ongoing relationships of Moken divers and mariners with Chinese traders, created a thriving pearling economy in the transregional Burmese waters. The bustling cosmopolitan town of Mergui, which served as the capital of the pearling industry for the archipelago—it was where pearlers in many instances brought their haul of pearl shell and other marine products for sale and where prices were negotiated—reflected its dynamism, as a visiting journalist described in 1913:

> Nestling between river and jungle . . . half hidden until one comes abreast of it . . . Mergui is not the sleepy place that it looks from the sea; there is plenty of life and stir in its streets and market places. Its bazaar is alive with a glowing panorama of half the races of the East—Chinaman and Burman jostle one another; Madras coolies, Malays and Siamese are all to be seen . . . while among them move Japanese and Filipinos. . . . Mergui is a thriving town, which is growing year by year.[133]

Pearling remained a mainstay of local and transregional economies into the 1920s and 1930s, where, even for those with broader investments in, for instance, tin mining, it remained a significant part of their portfolio. Also, part of the appeal of pearling in the coastal and island waters of Burma may well have been that, as pointed out by John Butcher, "a much higher proportion of the pearl oysters in the Mergui Archipelago contained pearls [when they did] than in some other pearling areas such as the Aru Island and the Torres Strait."[134] There was thus always the possibility that a pearler might strike it lucky, despite the odds that they would not.

IF THE PROSPECT of discovering an oyster among the many shells that divers were bringing to the surface was enough to induce investment in Burma's pearl banks, it appears that the industry—like others in the Indian Ocean—suffered from the competition from cultured pearls by the 1930s and the effects of that decade's economic depression.[135]

Yet, in another sign of its resiliency, investors turned increasingly to pearl cultivation in the 1950s, when the Burma Pearl Fishing and Culture Syndicate (BPFCS), a private Japanese-Myanmar joint-venture farm, began cultivating pearls at Domel Island.[136] This had already been attempted in the early years of the century, when an unnamed syndicate that had been in operation for a decade cultivated pearls that had "reached a commercial basis."[137] It would appear that the development of the cultured-pearl industry occurred primarily in the postwar years under the influence of the BPFCS. After moving to Sir J. Malcolm Island in 1956, the country's revolutionary government (brought to power by the military coup in 1962) nationalized the joint-venture farm in 1963; after some reshuffling over the years, it was eventually transformed into a separate enterprise in 1989 under the Ministry of Mines and renamed the Myanmar Pearl Enterprise (MPE). Since the introduction of economic reforms from this time, three joint-venture companies—"both local and foreign"—began white South Sea Pearl production in addition to the government-owned MPE.[138] Investments from Japanese, Australian, Tahitian, and Thai companies, in partnership with MPE, stimulated an expansion of the industry that was grounded in seeding techniques developed locally, after Japanese knowledge had been successfully transferred in the 1950s. Yields of mother-of-pearl fluctuated over the thirty years between 1967–68 and 1995–96, from 20–30 metric tons to 90 metric tons, while production of cultured South Sea Pearls was equally uneven over the same period. Sales revenue, generally relatively modest, could reach significant levels, as it did in 1990 when a little over $5 million worth of pearls were sold.

These efforts reflect a continuity of interest in the potential of the Mergui archipelago as a maritime zone of extraction. More broadly, in the last two decades of the twentieth and first few years of the twenty-first century there has been a resurgence in the shipment of ocean products between Southeast Asia and China. Spurred by record economic growth since the 1980s, ocean commerce in traditional conduits of trade between the two regions has revitalized an exchange that had never really disappeared, but that had existed in the shadow of other, more important lines of commerce for much of the twentieth century. Encompassing different sets of actors and networks of business organization, the marine goods economy (including a variety of fish, too, of course) has flourished along the coasts of the Southeast Asian mainland and throughout its islands, as varying ethnic subgroups have shipped cargoes of shellfish from the Indian Ocean coast of southern Thailand (astride the Andaman Sea), dried fish from Cambodia's Tonle Sap (the country's great lake), edible sea cucumbers collected throughout the region from Taipei, Taiwan, and shark fins from Manila in the Philippines to discerning Chinese markets. From Burma, too, traditionally sought marine goods "are shuttling en masse to China," and include very expensive holothurians, among other items.[139] Harvesting the ocean, as much now as in the past, represents an enduring arena of business for a range of interested parties and will likely continue to do so in the future.

NOTES

1. Sunil S. Amrith, *Crossing the Bay of Bengal: The Furies of Nature and the Fortunes of Migrants* (Cambridge, MA: Harvard University Press, 2013).

2. For a general discussion of pearls and shell, see Elisabeth Strack, *Pearls* (Stuttgart: Rühle-Diebener-Verlag, 2006).

3. Michael Charney, "Esculent Bird's Nest, Tin and Fish: The Overseas Chinese and Their Trade in the Eastern Bay of Bengal (Coastal Burma) during the First Half of the Nineteenth Century," in *China and Southeast Asia*, vol. 4, *Interactions from the End of the Nineteenth Century to 1911*, ed. Geoff Wade (London: Routledge, 2009).

4. "Traveller—The Salones," *Wingham Chronicle and Manning River Observer*, June 18, 1904.

5. R. N. Rudmose Brown, "The Mergui Archipelago: Its People and Products," *Scottish Geographical Magazine* 23, no. 9 (1907): 464.

6. Rudmose Brown, 467.

7. Jacques Ivanoff and Thierry Lejard, *A Journey through the Mergui Archipelago* (Bangkok: White Lotus, 2002), 3; Jacques Ivanoff, "Moken Boats," *Nest*, no. 22 (2003): 91.

8. Bien Chiang, "Market Price, Labor Input, and Relation of Production in Sarawak's Edible Birds' Nest Trade," in *Chinese Circulations: Capital, Commodities, and Networks in Southeast Asia*, ed. Eric Tagliacozzo and Wen-Chin Chang (Durham, NC: Duke University Press, 2011), 409. See also Leonard Blussé, "In Praise of Commodities: An Essay on the Cross-Cultural Trade in Edible Birds' Nests," in *Emporia, Commodities and Entrepreneurs in Asian Maritime Trade, c. 1400–1750*, ed. Roderich Ptak and Dietmar Rothermund (Stuttgart: Franz Steiner Verlag, 1991).

9. Chiang, "Market Price, Labor Input," 410–11.

10. Charney, "Esculent Bird's Nest." The holder of the Burmese royal bird's nest farm for southeast Burma, Thiwa-Kyawthu-Nawratta, paid 20,000 ticals (or perhaps their value in kind) for the right of collection and exchange for Tavoy Islands and the Mergui archipelago, a right he appears to have held for several years.

11. See, for instance, discussion of the considerable time and trouble it took to identify caves with viable nests, including asking local villages for information and having to confront the presence of large bat populations, in National Archives of Myanmar (NAM), 1/7/37, "Diary of Maung Ba Hein," February 12, 1894.

12. *Selected Correspondence of Letters Issued from and Received in the Office of the Commissioner, Tenasserim Division, for the Years 1825–26 to 1842–43* (Rangoon: Superintendent, Government Printing and Stationery, Burma, 1928).

13. Eric Tagliacozzo, "A Sino-Southeast Asian Circuit: Ethnohistories of the Marine Goods Trade," in Tagliacozzo and Chang, *Chinese Circulations*, 441.

14. For a description of U Shwe I and his relationship with the Moken, see Walter Grainge White, *The Sea Gypsies of Malaya* (London: Seeley Service, 1922).

15. Trepang was an important marine good connecting Southeast Asia to China through the South China Sea, for which see Heather Sutherland, "Trepang and Wangkang: The China Trade of Eighteenth-Century Makassar, 1720s–1840s," *Bijdragen tot de taal-, land- en volkenkunde* 156, no. 3 (2000): 451–72; and James Francis Warren, *The Sulu Zone, 1768–1898: The Dynamics of External Trade, Slavery and Ethnicity in the Transformation of a Southeast Asian Maritime State* (Singapore: Singapore University Press, 1981), who discusses the slaving expeditions of regional sea-peoples for the collection of trepang that Taosug *datus* (princes) organized in the nineteenth century.

16. Heather Sutherland, "A Sino-Indonesian Commodity Chain: The Trade in Tortoiseshell in the Late Seventeenth and Eighteenth Centuries," in Tagliacozzo and Chang, *Chinese Circulations*, 179.

17. Edward D. Melillo discusses how, amidst the expansion of whaling in the Pacific from the end of the eighteenth century, mariners from Nantucket and New England merchants from Salem Harbor forged close connections to Fiji and became involved extensively in the export to China of sea cucumbers that were found in abundance throughout the island's warm coastal shoals. Taking advantage of different valuation systems, North American entrepreneurs with connections to Canton (and also Manila) exchanged trepang for Chinese silks, jade, tea, porcelain, and lacquered goods that were becoming increasingly popular in Euro-American markets. See Melillo, "Making Sea Cucumbers Out of Whales' Teeth: Nantucket Castaways and Encounters of Value in Nineteenth-Century Fiji," *Environmental History* 20, no. 3 (July 2015): 449–74; and also Gregory T. Cushman, *Guano and the Opening of the Pacific World: A Global Ecological History* (Cambridge: Cambridge University Press, 2013).

18. Ashley Wright, *Opium and Empire in Southeast Asia: Regulating Consumption in British Burma* (Basingstoke, UK: Palgrave Macmillan, 2014), 22.

19. Eric Tagliacozzo, "A Necklace of Fins: Marine Goods Trading in Maritime Southeast Asia, 1780–1860," *International Journal of Asian Studies* 1, no. 1 (2004): 23–48.

20. Tagliacozzo, 28.

21. Charney, "Esculent Bird's Nest"; Daw Win and Loh Wei Leng, "Regional Links: Yangon, Penang, and Singapore," *Journal of the Malaysian Branch of the Royal Asiatic Society* 82, no. 2 (December 2009): 68.

22. Samuel Ostroff, "Between Promise and Peril: Credit and Debt at the Pearl Fisheries of South India and Sri Lanka, c. 1800," in *The Cultural History of Money and Credit: A Global Perspective*, ed. Chia Yin Hsu, Thomas M. Luckett, and Erika Vause (Lanham, MD: Lexington Books, 2016), 3. There are further details of Baboom's commercial activities in Carl T. Smith and Paul A. Van Dyke, "Four Armenian Families," *Review of Culture* (international ed.), no. 8 (October 2003), 40–50.

23. Sebouh Aslanian, *From the Indian Ocean to the Mediterranean: The Global Trade Networks of Armenian Merchants from New Julfa* (Berkeley: University of California Press, 2011), 53.

24. Charney, "Esculent Bird's Nest," 211–12.

25. Charney, 212; A. D. Maingy to E. A. Blundell, Assistant Commissioner, Mergui, July 21, 1827, in *Selected Correspondence of Letters*.

26. A. D. Maingy to E. A. Blundell, Mergui, August 14, 1828, in *Selected Correspondence of Letters*; Charney, "Esculent Bird's Nest," 212.

27. For an examination of Chinese junk trade with Siam around this time, see Jennifer Wayne Cushman, *Fields from the Sea: Chinese Junk Trade with Siam during the Late Eighteenth and Early Nineteenth Century*, Studies on Southeast Asia no. 12 (Ithaca, NY: Cornell University, Southeast Asia Program Publications, 1993).

28. Tagliacozzo, "Necklace of Fins," 42–43.

29. White, *Sea Gypsies*, 67–68.

30. George Frederick Kunz and Charles Hugh Stevenson, *The Book of the Pearl: The History, Art, Science, and Industry of the Queen of Gems* (New York: Century, 1908).

31. According to Eric Tagliacozzo, Singapore's advantages included that it was geographically better positioned than Penang to major collecting areas for marine goods located in insular southeast Asian waters, and its status as a "free" port. See "Necklace of Fins," 29–32.

32. Tagliacozzo, 38.

33. Tagliacozzo, 43, where the author provides further details of these changes.

34. Loh Wei Leng, "Penang as Commercial Centre: Trade and Shipping Networks," *Journal of the Malaysian Branch of the Royal Asiatic Society* 82, no. 2 (December 2009), 29. See also Nordin Hussin, *Trade and Society in the Straits of Melaka: Dutch Melaka and English Penang, 1780–1830* (Singapore: National University of Singapore Press, 2006); and, for a later period, Chiang Hai Ding, *A History of Straits Settlements Foreign Trade, 1870–1915* (Singapore: National Museum, 1978).

35. NAM, 1/7/1219, E. Ahmed to Deputy Commissioner, September 10, 1926; E. Ahmed to Deputy Commissioner, October 16, 1926.

36. A. D. Maingy to E. A. Blundell, Assistant Commissioner, Mergui, July 21, 1827, in *Selected Correspondence of Letters*.

37. Kunz and Stevenson, *Book of the Pearl*, 134.

38. See, for instance, the collections of royal Portuguese jewelry at the Museu Nacional de Arte Antiga in Lisbon.

39. This was prompted not only by the accumulated wealth of Euro-American industrialists but also by the broadening markets that a nascent middle class was creating for a variety of pearls and especially products made from mother-of-pearl.

40. H. Warrington Smyth, *Five Years in Siam, from 1891 to 1896* (London: John Murray, 1898).

41. Office of Indian and Oriental Collections (OIOC), British Library, Political and Secret Department Records (P&S), 1874; *Report on the Administration of Lower Burma during 1886–87* (Rangoon: Superintendent, Government Printing, Burma, 1888), 97.

42. NAM, 1/15(e)/14238, Capt. F. D. Maxwell, Deputy Commissioner, Bassein, to Commissioner, Irrawaddy Division, Bassein, August 31, 1896, and Reporter on Economic Products to the Government of India to the Revenue Secretary to the Chief Commissioner, Burma, July 21, 1896; NAM, 1/15(e)/16259, R. F. Greer, Secretary to the Financial Commissioner, Burma, to Commissioner, Irrawaddy Division, Bassein, March 24, 1910.

43. NAM, 1/15(e)/13922, Secretary to Financial Commissioner, Burma, to Commissioner, Irrawaddy Division, Bassein, March 2, 1895.

44. Alison Bashford, "Terraqueous Histories," *Historical Journal* 60, no. 2 (June 2017): 253–72.

45. Michael W. Charney, *A History of Modern Burma* (Cambridge: Cambridge University Press, 2009); Thant Myint-U, *The Making of Modern Burma* (Cambridge: Cambridge University Press, 2001).

46. William Sutherland, "South Tenasserim and the Mergui Archipelago," *Scottish Geographical Magazine* 14, no. 9 (1898), 451.

47. Sutherland, 451.

48. The "intermittent character of the fisheries," i.e., the variable nature of the availability of oysters along pearling banks from one season to the next, was well established and commented upon in a report by W. A. Herdman on the Gulf of Mannar fisheries: *Report to the Government of Ceylon on the Pearl Oyster Fisheries of the Gulf of Manaar* (London: n.p., 1903), 3.

49. NAM, 1/15(e)/13922, Secretary to the Financial Commissioner, Burma, to the Commissioner, Irrawaddy Division, Bassein, February 8, 1895, issuing "Fishing Directions for the Disposal and Regulation of the Pearl Fisheries in the Bassein District."

50. For other instances of the regulation of turtle egg collection in other parts of coastal Burma, see, for example, NAM, 1/7/1072, Deputy

Commissioner, Tavoy, to Deputy Commissioner, Mergui, May 10, 1900; and NAM, 1/7/1094, Deputy Commissioner, Mergui, to Deputy Commissioner, Tavoy, May 29, 1902. Other marine products, such as green snails and bêche-de-mer, continued to be included with pearl-shell collection, as they were at times with the extraction of bat guano and bird's nest.

51. Robert N. Rudmose Brown and James Jenkins Simpson, *Report to the Government of Burma on the Pearl Oyster Fisheries of the Mergui Archipelago and Moskos Islands* (Rangoon: Office of the Superintendent, Government Printing, Burma, 1907), 3; NAM, 1/7/67, H. L. Tilly to Deputy Commissioner, Tavoy, July 4, 1908.

52. OIOC, P/4769, Pro. No. 1–5, "Report," February 16, 1894; NAM, 1/7/67, G. E. T. Green to Commissioner, Tavoy, July 13, 1908.

53. NAM, 1/15(e)/14231, "Rules Regulating the Pearl Fisheries of Lower Burma, 1896," 1.

54. "Rules Regulating the Pearl Fisheries of Lower Burma, 1896," 1–2.

55. "The Mergui Pearl Fisheries," *Northern Territory Times and Gazette* (Darwin), May 31, 1895, 3.

56. Julia Martínez and Adrian Vickers, *The Pearl Frontier: Indonesian Labor and Indigenous Encounters in Australia's Northern Trading Network* (Honolulu: University of Hawai'i Press, 2015), 30.

57. Martínez and Vickers, *Pearl Frontier*, 30. The fourth chapter of the book further discusses Jardine's relationship with James Clark, the major pearling figure in northern Australia.

58. This would have necessitated coming to an "arrangement with the turtle bank lessees," an arrangement that Chill was ultimately unable to secure. See NAM, 1/15(e)/13699, Secretary to the Financial Commissioner, Burma, to the Commissioner, Irrawaddy Division, April 17, 1894; 1/15(e)/13699, Secretary to the Financial Commissioner, Burma, to Mr. Chill, May 14, 1894; 1/15(e)/13699, Mr. Chill to Secretary to the Financial Commissioner, Burma, May 25 1894; NAM, 1/15(e)/13435, Secretary to the Financial Commissioner, Burma, to the Commissioner, Irrawaddy Division, Bassein, August 31, 1893.

59. NAM, 1/15(e)/13922, "Fishing Directions for the Disposal and Regulation of the Pearl Fisheries in the Bassein District, 1895."

60. NAM, 1/15(e)/13922, District Commissioner, Bassein, to Deputy Commissioner, Bassein, February 16, 1895.

61. NAM, 1/15(e)/13922, Secretary to the Financial Commissioner, Burma, to the Commissioner, Irrawaddy Division, Bassein, October 3, 1895. Although not entirely clear, there was some discussion among certain officers that the reason for the failure of the auction was that its date had not been properly and widely advertised. See, for instance, NAM,

1/15(e)/13922, District Commissioner, Bassein, to Financial Commissioner, Bassein, August 26, 1895.

62. NAM, 1/15(e)/13922, District Commissioner, Bassein, to Financial Commissioner, Bassein, November 29, 1895.

63. NAM, 1/15(e)/13922, District Commissioner, Bassein, to Financial Commissioner, Bassein, October 3, 1895.

64. National Archives of India (NAI), Shimla Records, No. 66C-2F-13, Revenue Secretary to Government of Burma to Secretary to Government of India, May 26, 1906.

65. "Notices to Correspondents," *Queenslander* (Brisbane), November 24, 1894.

66. "West Kimberley Notes," *Daily News* (Perth), September 1, 1894. The company had been founded by the well-known figure, Edwin Streeter (though run by Thomas Haynes), a prominent jeweler with interests in pearling across Australian and Southeast Asian waters. See, for instance, Steve Mullins, "Australian Pearl-Shellers in the Moluccas: Confrontation and Compromise on a Maritime Frontier," *The Great Circle: Journal of the Australian Association for Maritime History* 23, 2 (2001): 3–23; and Mullins, "James Clark and the Celebes Trading Co.: Making an Australian Maritime Venture in the Netherlands East Indies," *Great Circle* 24, 2 (2002): 22–52.

67. OIOC, P/4769, Pro. No. 1–5, "Report," February 16, 1894.

68. Philip E. Steinberg, *The Social Construction of the Ocean* (Cambridge: Cambridge University Press, 2001); see also Lauren Benton, "Legal Spaces of Empire: Piracy and the Origins of Ocean Regionalism," *Comparative Studies in Society and History* 47, no. 4 (October 2005): 700–24.

69. See, for instance, Mary Albertus Bain, *Full Fathom Five* (Perth: Artlook, 1982); J. P. S. Bach, *The Pearling Industry of Australia: An Account of Its Social and Economic Development* (Canberra: Department of Commerce and Agriculture, Commonwealth of Australia, 1955); and Mullins, "Australian Pearl-Shellers."

70. *A Collection of Legislative Acts of the Ceylon Government from 1796, Distinguishing Those Now in Force,* vol. 1 (Colombo: W. Skeen, Government Printer, 1853), Regulation No. 3 of 1811, 130.

71. NAI, Home Department, Public B, June 1894, Nov. 1/3, "Enclosure—Mergui Pearl Fisheries," December 19, 1893.

72. NAI, Home Department, Public B, June 1894, Nov. 1/3, "Opinion of the Law Officers," December 19, 1893; emphasis added.

73. More recently, postcolonial anxieties led the Indonesian state to declare in the late 1950s that it had "absolute sovereignty" over the waters lying within straight baselines drawn between the archipelago's outermost islands. For the international outrage and alarm that this caused, and the

ultimate recognition by the United Nations Convention on the Law of the Sea that Indonesia fell under a new category of states known as "archipelagic states" with sovereignty over the "archipelagic waters," see John G. Butcher and R. E. Elson, *Sovereignty and the Sea: How Indonesia Became an Archipelagic State* (Singapore: National University of Singapore Press, 2017). I thank Eric Tagliacozzo for bringing this work to my attention.

74. J. C. Heesterman, "Littoral et intérieur de l'Inde," *Itinerario* 4, no. 1 (1980): 89; John R. Gillis and Franziska Torma, eds., *Fluid Frontiers: New Currents in Marine Environmental History* (Cambridge, UK: White Horse, 2015). See also the chapter by Samuel M. Ostroff in this volume.

75. NAI, Sir E. C. Buck KT, CSI, Secretary to the Government of India, to Chief Commissioner of Burma, May 23, 1894.

76. In a reflection of changing notions of space, the Siamese court sought also by the end of the nineteenth and beginning of the twentieth century to solidify its frontiers as it strove to maintain the integrity of the geo-body of Siam, for which see Thongchai Winichakul, *Siam Mapped: A History of the Geo-Body of a Nation* (Honolulu: University of Hawai'i Press, 1994); and also Eric Tagliacozzo, "Ambiguous Commodities, Unstable Frontiers: The Case of Burma, Siam, and Imperial Britain, 1800–1900," *Comparative Studies in Society and History* 46, no. 2 (April 2004): 354–77.

77. NAI, Secretary of State for India, May 2, 1894.

78. Eric Tagliacozzo has explored these dynamics in relation to illegality and the establishment of borders in Southeast Asia in the context of imperial rivalries between the British and Dutch. See Tagliacozzo, *Secret Trades, Porous Borders: Smuggling and States along a Southeast Asian Frontier, 1865–1915* (New Haven, CT: Yale University Press, 2005).

79. NAM, 1/7/1190, Deputy Commissioner, Mergui, to District Superintendent of Police, March 8, 1924.

80. See various letters in NAM, 1/7/1060.

81. This information is derived from several files in NAM, such as 1/7/1219; 1/7/1190; 1/15(e)/16175; and 1/15(e)/13922.

82. NAM, 1/15(e)/15301, Secretary to the Financial Commissioner, Burma, to Commissioner, Irrawaddy District, Bassein, February 3, 1903. While the publication of this notification in Tamil may also have reflected the larger realities of the migratory movement of South Indian laborers to Burma that was taking place at this time, the majority of these came to work in rubber plantations and were not therefore participating in the pearling economy.

83. NAM, 1/15(e)/14231, Deputy Commissioner, Bassein, to Commissioner, Irrawaddy Division, Bassein, June 29, 1896; NAM, 1/15(e)/14448, Deputy Commissioner, Bassein, to Commissioner, Irrawaddy Division, Bassein, May 5, 1897; Claude Markovits, "South Asian Business in the Empire

and Beyond, c. 1800–1950," in *Routledge Handbook of the South Asian Diaspora*, ed. Joya Chatterji and David Washbrook (Abingdon, UK: Routledge, 2013).

84. See, for instance, the "Revenue Chalans [receipts]" detailing purchasers of pearling licenses in the 1920s in NAM, 1/7/1190.

85. NAM, 1/7/1094, Revenue Department, Mergui, to Commissioner, Moulmein, June 24, 1902.

86. Smyth, *Five Years*, 296; Wei Leng, "Penang as Commercial Centre," 29.

87. Rajeswary Brown, "Chettiar Capital and Southeast Asian Credit Networks in the Inter-War Period," in *Local Suppliers of Credit in the Third World, 1750–1960*, ed. Gareth Austin and Kaoru Sugihara (London: Palgrave Macmillan, 1993).

88. Tagliacozzo, "A Sino-Southeast Asian Circuit," 436. See also J. W. Cushman, "The Khaw Group: Chinese Business in Early Twentieth-Century Penang," *Journal of Southeast Asian Studies* 17, no. 1 (March 1986): 58–79.

89. Markovits, "South Asian Business," 75. See also Amrith, *Crossing the Bay of Bengal*; Sunil S. Amrith, *Migration and Diaspora in Modern Asia* (Cambridge: Cambridge University Press, 2011).

90. Micheline Cariño and Mario Monteforte, *Une histoire mondiale des perles et des nacres: Pêche, culture, commerce* (Paris: L'Harmattan, 2005), 56. I thank William G. Clarence-Smith for this reference. I discuss the entry of suited diving into Burma later in the chapter.

91. Markovits, "South Asian Business," 73; Brown, "Chettiar Capital"; Michael Adas, *The Burma Delta: Economic Development and Social Change on an Asian Rice Frontier, 1852–1941* (Madison: University of Wisconsin Press, 1974). See also Amrith, *Crossing the Bay of Bengal*, particularly chap. 4.

92. OIOC, British Library, P&S, Burma, 1898; David West Rudner, *Caste and Capitalism in Colonial India: The Nattukottai Chettiars* (Berkeley: University of California Press, 1994), 58.

93. See Helen Fujimoto, *The South Indian Muslim Community and the Evolution of the Jawi Peranakan in Penang up to 1948* (Tokyo: Gaikokugo Daigaku, 1989); and Su Lin Lewis, *Cities in Motion: Urban Life and Cosmopolitanism in Southeast Asia, 1920–1940* (Cambridge, UK: Cambridge University Press, 2016).

94. OIOC, P/8242, Pro. No. 9–13, April 1909.

95. NAM, 1/7/83, F. C. Colomb, Rangoon, to Deputy Commissioner, Mergui, September 20, 1912.

96. *Who's Who in Burma* (Calcutta and Rangoon: Indo-Burma Publishing Agency, 1926), 3

97. *Who's Who in Burma*, 3.

98. NAI, Shimla Records, No. 66C-2F-13, Revenue Secretary to Government of Burma to Secretary to Government of India, May 26, 1906.

99. "The Mergui Pearl Fisheries," 3.

100. NAM, 1/7/1063, "Statement Showing Quantity and Value of M.O.P. shell exported from Mergui during 5 years," January 3, 1900.

101. NAM, 1/7/1063, "Statement Showing Quantity and Value of M.O.P. shell exported from Mergui during 5 years," January 3, 1900; Rudmose Brown and Simpson, *Report to the Government of Burma*, 4 and 23. Cited also in John G. Butcher, *The Closing of the Frontier: A History of the Marine Fisheries of Southeast Asia c. 1850–2000* (Singapore: Institute of Southeast Asian Studies, 2004), 127.

102. Rudmose Brown and Simpson, *Report to the Government of Burma*, 3.

103. NAM, 1/15(e)/14238, Deputy Commissioner, Bassein, to Commissioner, Irrawaddy Division, Bassein, August 31, 1896.

104. NAM, 1/15(e)/16175, I.A. Offg. Commissioner, Arakan Division, to Secretary to the Financial Commissioner, Burma, October 18, 1909.

105. NAM, 1/15(e)/16175, I.A. Offg. Commissioner, Arakan Division, to Secretary to the Financial Commissioner, Burma, October 18, 1909. "The Deputy Commissioner, Akyab," it was claimed, had established "that the people dwelling on the coasts depend to a great extent on oysters as their food and also on the sale of these fish in Akyab."

106. NAM, 1/15(e)/16175, I.A. Offg. Commissioner, Arakan Division, to Secretary to the Financial Commissioner, Burma, October 18, 1909

107. NAM, 1/15(e)/16175, Secretary to the Financial Commissioner, Burma, to the Revenue Secretary to the Government of Burma, November 11, 1909. For the denial of the applications of other merchants, such as Ain Wein Hein, see NAM, 1/15(e)/16175, I.A. Offg. Commissioner, Arakan Division, to Secretary to the Financial Commissioner, Burma, October 18, 1909.

108. NAM, 1/15(e)/14238, Deputy Commissioner, Bassein, to Commissioner, Irrawaddy Division, Bassein, August 31, 1896.

109. NAM, 1/15(e)/14569, Deputy Commissioner, Bassein, to Commissioner, Irrawaddy Division, Bassein, January 26, 1898; and Secretary to Financial Commissioner, Burma, to Commissioner, Irrawaddy, Bassein, February 11, 1898. In at least one area of Bassein District, the pearl fishery "from Pyinkayaing Cape to the Thekke thaung creek," this proved not to be possible and the fishery was abolished in 1908 after languishing for the previous four years. It had been put up for auction "but there were no purchasers . . . [and] it is not likely that the fishery can ever be sold as there are no signs of any living oysters." See NAM, 1/15(e)/16088, Deputy Commissioner, Bassein, to Commissioner, Irrawaddy Division, Bassein, May 20, 1908.

110. NAM, 1/15(e)/16175, Secretary to the Financial Commissioner, Burma, to the Revenue Secretary to the Government of Burma, November 11, 1909.

111. NAM, 1/15(e)/16175, Secretary to the Financial Commissioner, Burma, to the Revenue Secretary to the Government of Burma, November 11, 1909.

112. NAM, 1/15(e)/16259, Secretary to the Financial Commissioner, Burma, to Commissioner, Irrawaddy Division, Bassein, March 24, 1910.

113. NAM, 1/7/1094, Revenue Department to Commissioner of Tenasserim Division, Moulmein, June 24, 1902.

114. OIOC, P/4769, Pro. No. 1–5, "Report," February 16, 1894; Kunz and Stevenson, *Book of the Pearl*, 136.

115. NAM, 1/7/1063, Secretary to the Financial Commissioner to the Commissioner, Tenasserim Division, March 6, 1900. This concern that the licensing system would attract "undesirables" was dismissed on the grounds that approximately Rs 5,000 in capital was required by anyone seeking "to start pearling operations."

116. NAM, 1/7/1094, Revenue Department to Commissioner, Tenasserim Division, Moulmein, June 24, 1902.

117. NAM, 1/7/1063, Ebrahim Ahmed, Mohamed Salim, et al. to Lieutenant Governor of Burma, Mergui, February 22, 1900.

118. NAM, 1/7/1063, Secretary to the Financial Commissioner to the Commissioner, Tenasserim Division, March 6, 1900.

119. Smyth, *Five Years*, 295.

120. Smyth, 296.

121. Butcher, *Closing of the Frontier*, 124.

122. NAM, 1/7/1094, Revenue Department to Commissioner, Tenasserim Division, Moulmein, June 24, 1902.

123. NAM, 1/7/1094, Revenue Department to Commissioner, Tenasserim Division, Moulmein, June 24, 1902.

124. NAM, 1/7/1094, Revenue Department to Commissioner, Tenasserim Division, Moulmein, June 24, 1902.

125. NAM, 1/7/83, Secretary to the Financial Commissioner, Burma, to Colonel K. M. Foss, Rangoon, September 23, 1908.

126. NAM, 1/7/67, Offg. Commissioner of the Tenasserim Division, Moulmein, to the Deputy Commissioner, Tavoy, July 4, 1908.

127. NAM, 1/7/1094, "Salon Diving," n.d.

128. NAM, 1/7/1063, "Draft Pearling Licencing Form," January 31, 1901.

129. This and the previous detail from NAM, 1/7/1063, Secretary to the Financial Commissioner to the Commissioner, Tenasserim Division, March 6, 1900.

130. NAM, 1/7/83, Secretary to the Financial Commissioner, Burma, to Colonel K. M. Foss, London, September 23, 1908.

131. NAM, 1/7/67, Offg. Commissioner of the Tenasserim Division, Moulmein, to Deputy Commissioner, Tavoy, July 4, 1908.

132. See, for instance, the proposal put forward in 1912 by a London "partnership" to extend the size of a lease that had already been granted earlier in the Moskos Islands for the purposes, among others, of extending "the pearl and shell industry by opening up new areas" and of "restocking denuded banks." NAM, 1/7/83, F. C. Colomb to Deputy Commissioner, Tavoy, November 5, 1912.

133. "The Mergui Archipelago," *Oamaru* [New Zealand] *Mail*, April 22, 1913.

134. Butcher, *Closing of the Frontier*, 128.

135. The development of cultured pearls by Kokichi Mikimoto, a Japanese noodle-shop owner who perfected the ancient Chinese practice of inserting a spherical piece of mother-of-pearl into oyster shells to induce the oyster to produce a pearl, is well known. See, for instance, Robert Eunson, *The Pearl King: The Story of the Fabulous Mikimoto* (Tokyo: Charles E. Tuttle, 1963)

136. Tint Tun, "Myanmar Pearling: Past, Present and Future," *SPC Pearl Oyster Information Bulletin*, no. 12 (December 1998), 3.

137. "Nutshell Interviews," *Observer* (Adelaide), February 26, 1910.

138. Tint Tun, "Myanmar Pearling," 3.

139. Quoted in Tagliacozzo, "A Sino-Southeast Asian Circuit," 441.

SEVEN

Pearl Fishing, Migration, and Globalization in the Persian Gulf, Eighteenth to Twentieth Centuries

ROBERT CARTER

THIS CHAPTER examines the growth of the pearling industry in the Persian Gulf during the eighteenth to twentieth centuries. It takes the pearl fishing communities of Qatar as a detailed case study, especially focusing on migration into and within Qatar, and examines historical and archaeological evidence for changing patterns of consumption and integration with global markets.

Space precludes a detailed account of the long history of pearl fishing in the region, which goes back at least seven thousand years.[1] Organized and intensive exploitation is evident by the last centuries BCE and first centuries CE, particularly feeding a voracious demand in the Roman west, not to mention booming markets nearer to home in the Middle East. Following this, pearl fishing remained a mainstay of the regional economy during the Late Antique, Early Islamic, and Medieval periods, and subsequently attracted the interest of the Portuguese overlords of the Gulf.[2]

Pearl fishing thrived during a protracted period of instability between the late seventeenth and early nineteenth centuries, when competing tribal Arab groups vied for control of the fisheries, some newly arrived to the Gulf from inland Arabia, and some long-term residents of the Arabian and Persian shores. This process was accompanied by the foundation of numerous small and medium-sized towns which were largely or wholly dependent on the pearl fishery for their existence, particularly on the Arabian shore, where the influence of regional and European imperial powers was weak. I have argued elsewhere that this process was stimulated by increasing pearl revenues due to growth of global and particularly Western markets.[3]

I begin this chapter with an account of the fishery at its peak in the nineteenth and early twentieth centuries; then follow with an overview of the process of migration and coastal settlement foundation, using Qatar as a case study; and finish with an exploration of detailed economic and archaeological data from Bahrain and Qatar, which demonstrate the impact of the pearling boom on the towns, their people, their material culture, and their engagement with global patterns of trade and consumption.

Archaeological work supplies a significant portion of the core data in this analysis, particularly regarding changes in material culture, settlement patterns, and settlement size. Excavated sites and finds provide detailed data which are absent from historical sources, particularly in areas (such as the Persian Gulf) which have relatively scant written documentation. To take an explicit example used in this chapter, while historical economic sources tally the import of "chinaware and porcelain," the quantified finds from excavations in Bahrain, Qatar, and elsewhere reveal precisely what wares were imported, as well as their origins and in what proportions. Moreover, if the site is well-stratified, so that separate levels (and their associated finds) can be isolated and closely dated, then changes in material culture though time can be identified. In the examples used below, changes in the proportion of imported ceramics are noted and used as a proxy measure of engagement in trading activities and wealth levels. Other classes of find, and sometimes architectural characteristics, can be similarly used. Archaeological data also provide a valuable means of testing historical assumptions. For example, Qatar in the late nineteenth and early twentieth century is historically characterized as a relatively isolated area within a region (the Gulf) that was already considered remote to Western eyes, whereas the archaeological record reveals the direct impact of an intimate engagement with global markets.

Archaeological methods are also used to identify changes in settlement patterns, numbers, and size. Archaeological sites, including both deserted and occupied urban settlements, are identified either by systematic ground survey or by remote survey (often using a combination of aerial imagery and historical cartography, in the case of the Gulf towns), which is then followed by foot survey. They can be dated by their surface remains (dateable ceramics, coins, glassware, etc.). These techniques can also sometimes reveal the size of sites at any given time. In the case studies mentioned below, the expansion of certain towns is traced using a combination of historical maps, early aerial photographs, historical descriptions, architectural features, and archaeological work. Regarding the latter, excavations in those parts of a living town with surviving archaeological deposits will reveal approximately when that part of town was first occupied. In areas where historical documentation is limited or absent, this can provide good evidence for the physical extent of settlements at given points in time.

PEAK OF THE PEARL FISHERY

In the early twentieth century the Gulf was overwhelmingly the largest supplier of pearls to global markets, contributing 65–80 percent of the world's supply. The region had been one of the world's major suppliers of pearls for centuries, and usually the chief supplier, on account of the relative predictability of its harvest, the abundance and apparent inexhaustibility of its pearl banks, and the widely acknowledged superior quality of its pearls.[4] Pearling revenues in the Gulf peaked in 1912, when the value of Bahrain's exports stood at over Rs 30,500,000 (over £2,030,000). The value for the whole Gulf would have been around twice that, according to Bahrain's usual proportion of the Gulf fishery.[5] Just thirty-four years previously, in 1878 the value of Bahrain's exports stood at Rs 1,520,000—one-twentieth of the 1912 value. Although strenuous attempts were made to increase the harvest by expanding the range of banks exploited and employing ever-increasing numbers of pearlers to fish them, it is clear that much of this value increase was due to price inflation. According to J. G. Lorimer, using data gathered in 1905–7, the prices of various classes of pearl "are subject to change, and there is no doubt that during the last half century they have risen enormously; between 1852–53 and 1877–78 they doubled, and since 1877–78 they have more than doubled again."[6]

Figure 7.1 shows how the value of exported pearls spiked between 1886 and 1912, after which a series of geopolitical events and market corrections took prices back down to 1870s levels. After 1929, the combined force of the Great Depression and the advent of cultured pearls (first appearing commercially around 1925) caused the effective demise of the industry, though it lingered into the 1960s in those areas which were late to obtain direct oil revenues.[7]

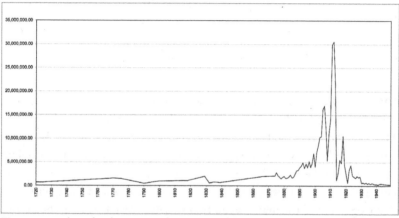

Figure 7.1. Value of Bahrain's pearl exports, 1723–1949. Chart by Robert Carter.

Regarding the available statistics on the value of the fishery, Bahraini data is used as a proxy for the Gulf-wide fishery in this chapter. Estimates of the value of Bahrain's exports are available for the seventeenth to the mid-twentieth century, occasionally at first but then annually from 1873. In contrast, estimates for the entire Gulf fishery are more sporadic, and missing after 1904.[8] Figure 7.2 shows the values for the Bahrain and the "Whole Gulf" fisheries together. These indicate that Bahrain accounted for the vast majority of the Gulf's pearl exports up to around 1829, when a localized collapse occurred, after which a significant share of the regional output came from or via other localities. Bahrain's share settled at around 50 percent of the whole Gulf output from the late 1860s onwards. The chart demonstrates that the figures for Bahrain are a good proxy indicator for the whole region between 1866 and 1904, and one can expect that they continued to be so into the 1910s, 1920s, and 1930s.

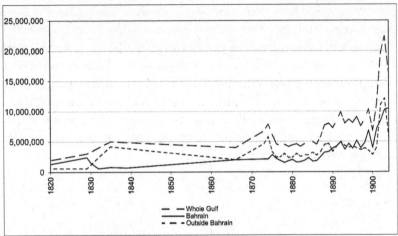

Figure 7.2. Value of the pearl exports in Bahrain, outside Bahrain, and for the whole Gulf, 1818–1904. Chart by Robert Carter.

Around 50 percent of the male population of the Arabian littoral was directly engaged in the fishery in the first decade of the twentieth century.[9] Many of the towns and sheikhdoms, especially those which lacked agricultural land or major concerns in the carrying trade, were entirely reliant on the pearl fishery for their existence. For example, out of a total population of 27,000 in Qatar, nearly 13,000 men went pearl fishing, implying that 95 percent of the male population was directly engaged in the fishery, on the assumption that half the population was male and of employable age (but see below for clarifications). More than 74,000 men worked the banks annually, mostly from the Arabian shore (over 65,000 individuals).

Numerous observers emphasized the overwhelming importance of the industry during the nineteenth century. Up to and during the eighteenth century, observers had tended merely to note the major importance of the pearl fishery, particularly with regard to Bahrain, but by the 1820s the total reliance of the population of the Arabian littoral on pearling was being noted. For example, in 1823 Captain McLeod wrote of the Qawasim in the Lower Gulf (based in what is now the northern UAE) that "they possess no articles of export, since their pearls are generally purchased by merchants on the spot, and the produce of their country is not even sufficient for their maintenance. Their only employment is fishing, diving for pearls, and importing dates, grain and other necessities of life, which they purchase with the price of those pearls. Their dates are chiefly brought from Bahrein and Bassora [Basra], grain and cloth from Muskat and the Persian ports."[10] Ten years later, the British resident in the Gulf, Colonel Wilson, observed the same, that the pearl fishery "produces the means of subsistence for nearly the whole population of the Arabian shore of this sea. The land produces little else besides dates, but they even are not in sufficient quantities to support the whole of the population; supplies therefore must be imported."[11] This reliance on a pearl-based monetary economy meant that the Arabian littoral supported a population well beyond its carrying capacity in terms of food production, that had been attracted to the new towns by the proceeds of the pearl fishery. This was a formative shift in the settlement patterns and economic structure of the region.

Lorimer's opening paragraph to his unequalled survey of the fishery as it stood in 1905–7 is still the most eloquent testimony to its importance in the early twentieth century.

> Pearl fishing is the premier industry of the Persian Gulf; it is, besides being the occupation most peculiar to that region, the principal or only source of wealth among the residents of the Arabian side. Were the supply of pearls to fail, the trade of Kuwait would be severely crippled, while that of Bahrain might—it is estimated—be reduced to about one-fifth of its present dimensions and the ports of Trucial 'Omān, which have no other resources, would practically cease to exist; in other words, the purchasing power of the inhabitants of the eastern coast of Arabia depends very largely upon the pearl fisheries.[12]

Table 7.1. Lorimer's counts of men engaged in pearl fishing against total population of each sheikhdom or region. The percentage of the male workforce is notional, based on a 50-50 gender division in the resident population.

	Total Pop.	Men in Pearling	% Pop.	% Males
Kuwait	37,000	9,200	25	50
Bahrain	100,000	17,633	18	35
Qatar	27,000	12,890	48	95
Trucial States (west coast, i.e., Gulf side only)	72,200	22,045	31	61
Coastal Al-Hasa *sanjaq*, i.e., Qatif villages, Tarut villages, Jinnah and Musallamiyah Islands	26,000	3,444	13	26
SUM	262,200	65,212	25	50

Table prepared by Robert Carter

In one sense these figures underestimate the percentage of resident adult males employed in the fishery, as all males are included in the total population figures of each sheikhdom (which count "souls"), including infants and children below employable age (around ten). On the other hand, the percentages involved in the fishery are likely inflated by the influx of labor from outside the sheikhdoms, such that a much greater number of males took part in a fishery than the total male population. One of the Trucial States, Ajman, is a case in point: this small coastal settlement had a permanent population (of both genders) of only about 750 people, yet 780 men went pearling. Here we must assume that males came in to participate from outside the territory of Ajman. In the case of Qatar, 95 percent of the male population is estimated to have taken part in the fishery. We know that this included many *bedu* residents of the peninsula (i.e., full-time pastoral nomads, who are included in Qatar's population figures, comprising 22 percent of Qatar's population), but it probably also included people from outside Qatar, particularly given the strong ties of Qatar's urban Huwala population with relatives on the Persian shore and the representation of Qatar's major bedu tribes in Saudi Arabia, Bahrain, and elsewhere.[13]

The pearling ports themselves varied in size considerably, and some of those considered towns were no bigger than villages, as was the case with Ajman (see also below for comments on the Qatari towns). At the larger end, the population of Kuwait City numbered 37,000 in 1908, while that of Manama was 25,000, with Muharraq the third biggest in the region at 20,000. Sharjah numbered 15,000, Doha had 12,000, with Dubai counting 10,000 inhabitants, and the town of Abu Dhabi just 6,000. Significant proportions of the population of the bigger towns (Kuwait, Manama, Muharraq) were engaged in trading concerns and services other than rather direct engagement in the pearl fishery. For example, in Muharraq, Lorimer lists general merchants, shopkeepers, sailors, fishermen, boatmen, bakers, barbers, butchers, tailors, shoemakers, masons, carpenters, tin-workers, water-sellers, and washermen.[14]

In the medium-sized and smaller towns, however, practically the whole male population participated directly in the pearl fishery. Thus, for four months of the year the towns were almost empty of adult and adolescent males. Remarking about the "Pirate Coast" (i.e., the Trucial States, now UAE), James Wellsted noted in 1838 that "during the season every person who can procure a boat himself, or obtain a share in one, is thus employed, and their villages have no other occupants than children, females, and men who are too aged to follow this pursuit."[15]

The main fishing season, the *Ghaws al-Kabir* (Great Dive) ran from early June to the end of September, during which time the water was warm and comparatively clear, and the strong northwesterly winds (the *shamal*) had abated. This was preceded by earlier and later dives (the *Ghaws al-Barid*, or Cold Dive, and the *Ridda*, or Return), in which not all boats and personnel participated.[16] Many of the boats stayed at sea throughout the season, except for a brief break in the middle, while some of the larger ones spent the whole four months at sea, being provisioned by maritime pearl merchants known as *tawawish* (s. *tawwash*), who also sought the best pearls at sea and who were often paid in pearls for their provisions. At the end of the season, the boats, which tended to travel and fish in fleets belonging to each sheikhdom (or, in the case of Qatar, each pearling town), would rush for home, entering the home port simultaneously to great celebration and ululations from the families. During the following days and weeks, the bulk of pearls were sold in a frenzy of haggling, first passing from the captains to the tawawish or other merchants, then usually on to greater merchants with bases in Bahrain, Lengeh, or Dubai, and Bombay. At the same time, the debts between merchants, captains, and pearl fishers were settled, or carried over in the case of a poor harvest (see below for an account of the pearling debt chain and its implications).

Most of the pearls from the Central and Upper Gulf were pooled in Bahrain before being shipped to Bombay. The wealthier local merchants maintained offices in Bombay and took the pearls there themselves or via agents (often family members), while others sold to those merchants or to Indian ("Banian") traders who had long operated in the Gulf.[17] Pearls from the Lower Gulf (the Trucial States) and the Persian shore were taken to Lengeh rather than Bahrain from the mid-eighteenth century onwards, before being carried or sold on to Bombay. During the first decade of the twentieth century, the merchant families of Lengeh relocated, mainly to Dubai, along with much of the pearl fishing population and other Arab and Persian families, and Dubai took on the role of pearl emporium of the Lower Gulf.[18] From Bombay, the pearls radiated outwards to London, Paris, and eventually New York, as well as many other destinations in South Asia, the Middle East, the Russian empire, and the Far East, at each point gaining value.

The fishery itself was conducted using a variety of different kinds and sizes of boat, ranging from very small vessels with as few as two pearlers (diver and hauler) to very large vessels with more than a hundred operatives, the majority of whom were the divers and haulers, the latter doubling as crew. There was also an assortment of spare hands, cooks, apprentices, boys, and singers, along with captain and first mate on board. In the first decade of the twentieth century, the typical size of the crew was ten to forty, averaging around sixteen.[19] Nearly 4,500 pearling boats went to sea annually from both shores of the Gulf (just under 3,600 from the Arabian shores), with the biggest fleets being based in Bahrain (917 boats, with the largest contribution being from Muharraq, at 282) and Qatar (817 boats, with Doha providing 350). The largest fleet belonging to a single town was from Kuwait (461 boats), followed by Abu Dhabi (410), Doha, Dubai (335), and Muharraq.[20] These figures were gathered five years *before* the peak of the pearling boom in 1912, so it is possible that numbers then were higher still.

Diving was undertaken without goggles, with a paired diver and hauler, using a weighted rope to take the diver to the pearl bed (usually between six and fifteen fathoms deep), with a second rope used to pull up the diver and his basket of oysters after a minute or two of collection.[21] In cold weather, and on larger boats during phases of intensive work, divers would work in shifts and the ratio of divers to haulers was higher, i.e., a hauler would work with more than one diver. Unless it was cold, a diver would normally make fifty to sixty descents each day, but sometimes up to a hundred or more. It was the responsibility of the captain (*nokhada*, also *nākhuda*) or leader of the sheikhdom or port's fleet (*amir al-ghaws*, or *sardal*) to find the best pearl beds, the most productive varying from year to year within the stretch of banks customarily fished by the fleet of a given port or sheikhdom, though technically a "native" boat was permitted to fish on any pearl bed in the Gulf. Typically, the fleets of a given town or sheikhdom traveled and fished together, but they were permitted to split up according to the will of the amir.[22]

Some of the pearl-fishing townsfolk had other sources of income or subsistence during the off-season: for example, the bedu returned to their herding, many Kuwaitis pursued the carrying trade around the western Indian Ocean outside the diving months, and many with ties to farming communities around the Gulf retreated to the date groves and oases to work. The majority in most sheikhdoms, however, found only occasional work in the town or spent much of the year without employment, awaiting the next pearling season. For example, in 1836 Henry Whitelock, speaking of the inhabitants of what is now the UAE, recounted how, "having no agricultural labours to take to at this time, they are reduced to a total state of idleness." Around seventy years later, Lorimer said the same: "in winter some of the pearl diving class take part in the ordinary sea fisheries, but the majority of them spend the season at home in idleness, supported by boat owners and contractors who thereby acquire, under the stringent rules of the industry, an indefeasible lien on their services for the next pearling season."[23]

The majority of the pearl fishers therefore relied entirely or almost entirely on their share of the profits from the sale of pearls at the end of the diving season. This, however, was frequently insufficient for them to support themselves and their families for the year, for which reason it was standard practice to take loans from their captains, who in turn took loans from the merchants, themselves usually borrowing from greater merchants or financiers. Customarily three loans were taken during the year, being the *salaf* taken prior to the start of the season, the *kharjiyya* taken during the season, and the *tisqam* taken two months after the close of the dive, to support the families during the off-season.[24] The captains used the salaf loans to repair, equip, and provision their boats for the pearling season, as well as to advance loans to their crew. The entire system therefore relied on a chain of debt that bound the participants together in the industry, from the wealthiest to the poorest.

One ramification was that most pearl divers were permanently indebted to their captains (and likewise the captains were indebted to the merchants, who were generally indebted to greater merchants), leading to a situation analogous to bonded labor whereby indebted personnel were obliged to remain in employment with the same captain in the next season, unless special arrangements were made between creditors to transfer an individual and his debts. Likewise, an indebted captain was obliged to maintain his business relationship with his merchant creditor year after year, until the debt was cleared (by all accounts a rare occurrence). It followed that a man's property, including his home and even his wife and family, could be forfeit to the creditor (a situation considered abusive by British authorities, who tried to stamp it out), and also that he could be obliged to work for free for the creditor during the off-season, a problem mentioned above in the quotation from Lorimer.

Despite its evident problems and abuses, the loans system provided resilience to the pearling communities after a poor harvest, or a run of poor harvests, provided the merchants at the top of the debt pyramid had the liquidity to keep lending. It was wholly accepted that debts could mount year after year until a particularly good harvest or high market prices provided redress. However, it also meant that at the death of the industry in the late 1920s and 1930s, investment continued year after year in the face of a collapsing market, until even the great merchants were impoverished. This even affected sheikhly families, who themselves relied on the great merchants for loans in times of contingency. Thus, to a great extent the political economy and social fabric of the region were knitted together by relations of labor and debt that also provided the economic structure for the pearl fishery.

MIGRATION, DEMOGRAPHICS, AND THE FOUNDATION OF THE PEARLING TOWNS

Although the peak of the fishery evidently occurred in the late nineteenth and early twentieth centuries, this was the culmination of a process stretching back to the eighteenth century. As noted in several previous publications, the economic basis of the new towns of the eighteenth century, and sometimes explicitly the rationale for their founding, was predicated upon intended profit from the pearl fishery, including Kuwait (around 1716), Abu Dhabi (around 1762), and Zubara (around 1766).[25] The process continued into the early and mid-nineteenth century with the foundation of numerous other new towns, including Doha, Dubai, Muharraq, and many others by the 1820s.

In some areas, particularly Qatar, a large number of adjacent small towns sprang up, often little more than walled villages, though Palgrave's condescending description indicates that the Qataris had no doubt as to their urban status: "little clusters of wretched, most wretched, earth cottages and palm leaf huts, narrow, ugly and low; these are the villages, or rather the 'towns' (for so the inhabitants style them) of Ḳaṭar. . . . For the villages of Ḳaṭar are each and all carefully walled in, while the towns beyond are lined with towers."[26] Guy and Brucks's 1824 map of northern Qatar illustrates this proliferation of small towns very clearly (figure 7.3).

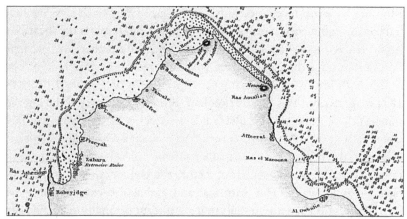

Figure 7.3. Guy & Brucks's map of northern Qatar of 1824. Leaving aside geographical features, the place names are more usually transcribed today (from west to east) as Rubaiqa, Zubara, Freiha, Khor Hassan (later known as Khor Khuwair), Yusufiyya (perhaps here conflated with Ruwaida), Jumail, Abu Dhuluf, Ruwais (not shown here as a town, but recently abandoned at the time of drawing), Fuwairit, Huwaila. Source: "Trigonometrical Survey of the Arabian or Southern Side of the Persian Gulf by Lieutenants J. M. Guy & G. B. Brucks H.C. Marine. 1824. Drawn by Lieutt. M. Houghton Draughtsman H.C.M. Engraved by John Bateman. Sheet 3rd," British Library Map Collections, IOR/X/3630/20/5, in Qatar Digital Library <https://www.qdl.qa/archive/81055/vdc_100024174406.0x00000e> [accessed 15 January 2019].

None of these towns are clearly attested historically before the 1760s, and, as far as can be ascertained archaeologically, only one or two of these show signs of habitation during or before the early eighteenth century. A supposed reference to Freiha in an Ottoman document of 1701 is actually a reference to Deylam, on the Persian coast. This tells of fighting in the vicinity of Bahrain between the 'Utub (a confederation from interior Arabia that had recently migrated to the Gulf coast), the "Khalifat" (a tribe then based at Deylam, probably the same as the Kholaifat found today in Qatar and Bahrain), and unnamed Huwala tribes from around Kung, also on the Persian shore (see note 13).[27] Excavations at Freiha have nonetheless revealed a largely early-eighteenth-century sequence, with possible evidence of earlier occupation.[28] Another site that has revealed remains which are perhaps older than the eighteenth century is Ruwaida. This site is in the same place as a town named Yusufiyya on the early nineteenth century maps (e.g., figure 7.3), but this appears to be a separate settlement.[29] Excavations at

Pearl Fishing, Migration, and Globalization in the Persian Gulf 243

Ruwaida have produced a ceramic assemblage likely to date to the first half of the eighteenth century, while the initial phase of its fortifications is constructed in a manner to support cannon and is therefore perhaps Portuguese (and therefore dating to the sixteenth or first half of the seventeenth century). Regarding the other towns on Guy and Brucks's 1824 map, excavations at Rubaiqa have revealed occupation during the nineteenth century, while Zubara has a sequence dating from the late eighteenth to the nineteenth century.[30] Significant excavation has not occurred at the other sites of the other towns, but surface collections so far do not indicate an occupation before the eighteenth century, except perhaps at Huwaila. The historical and archaeological geography of northern Qatar therefore reveals that significant occupation began only in the eighteenth century, with a minority of sites displaying possible seventeenth- or perhaps sixteenth-century settlement.

It is clear that the region saw a major influx of people from many different directions and of diverse ethnicities. The leading Arab families of some of the new towns and a significant portion of their populations originated from settled and semi-settled communities in inland Arabia, particularly the vast Nejd region of central Arabia, most prominently the families of the 'Utub alliance (who provided and still provide the leadership of Kuwait and Bahrain, and also founded Zubara) and their followers, but also many other tribes and families. The Dhafra region and Liwa oases provided the rulers and founding tribes of Abu Dhabi and Dubai.[31] Other sources of leadership and significant urban population included Huwala families from the Persian coast; occasionally bedu families (just one town, Ajman, was ruled by a bedu lineage); tribes originally from Oman; perhaps a component from Iraq or Arabistan (the portion of southwestern Iran adjoining southern Iraq, now Khuzestan); and tribes present on the coast before the eighteenth century.[32]

As well as the tribal and Huwala Arab component, the population of these towns included, to varying degrees and regardless of their origin of their ruling elites, Baharna (indigenous Shi'a Arabs of Bahrain and Al-Hasa); Persians ('Ajam) of both Shi'a and Sunni persuasions; Baluch tribesmen, often hired as guards and mercenaries in the Lower Gulf; slaves and freed slaves, mainly of African origin but also Baluch; and a minority of Indian merchants and their families, with even smaller numbers of Jewish, Armenian, and other residents. By definition, bedu did not live in the towns, though sometimes they camped for long periods outside them, and neither does it appear that many of the townsfolk were of recent bedu origin.[33] The slave component was important and numerous in most Gulf towns, sometimes contributing a quarter to a third of the population. The increasing labor demands of the pearl fishery were a significant driving factor behind the slave trade of the nineteenth and early twentieth century, and a major cause of inward enslaved population migration.[34]

As an example (which should not be automatically extrapolated to other Gulf towns), the population of Doha in 1908 was 54.5 percent from named Arab tribes of various or uncertain origin; 30 percent African (slave and freed slaves); 8.5 percent Huwala; 2.5 percent Baharna; 2.5 percent Persian; and 2 percent miscellaneous Nejdis. Of the Arab tribes, the most numerous was the Suluta (at 3,250 residents, nearly 28 percent of Doha's total population). A large Arab tribe which was considered to have founded Doha around a century before, the Al Bu 'Ainain, were no longer resident in the town but lived in the nearby town of Wakra; unknown to the census-taker, they were about to leave Qatar permanently, to migrate in 1909 to Qasr Al-Subaih (now Jubail, on the coast of Saudi Arabia).

Such tribal movements underline the irony that the settled population of Qatar was highly mobile. This was most notable in the movement of the Arab tribes, whose mobility was often en masse, with the whole tribe or significant segments traveling more or less simultaneously. Such losses or additions of population, with concomitant losses or gains in tax revenue, prestige, and military strength, were highly significant to local rulers and therefore also salient to, and recorded by, the British authorities. In 1845, Kemball outlined some motivations and examples of such tribal movements.

> It is by no means uncommon for one of the branches of a tribe, to the number sometimes of several hundred individuals, in order to escape excessive taxation and oppression, or with a view to secure to themselves greater immunities and advantages, to secede from the authority and territory of their lawful and acknowledged chief into that of another [*note in original:* the Boo Muhair, at Shargah, are an example of the former], or to establish themselves and build a fort on some other spot [*note in original:* the Boo Felasa, of Debaye, of the latter], and assert and maintain independence; nor is it a matter of great moment that the chief they are about to

join, or whose friendship and countenance they must in the first place command, is a rival at implacable feud with their own: the advantages attending any numerical increase of subjects ensure them welcome asylum and protection. It will not escape observation, that the facilities thus mutually offered to seceders on the one hand, and the loss of authority and revenue consequent on their secession on the other, act, *vice versâ*, as a salutary check to the tyranny and oppression of the respective chiefs.[35]

These migrations were still significant up to the twentieth century, and it appears that few Qatari tribes stayed long in one town, though some were more strongly associated with certain towns than others. To take just one example, a major branch of the Al Bu Kuwara, a large Qatari tribe of long standing, attempted to leave their town of Fuwairit (northern Qatar) to follow the Bu 'Ainain to Qasr Al-Subaih in 1912, but were rebuffed by all parties on that shore at the urging of the British, who had a history of antagonism toward their leader, Nasr bin Shahin al-Towar. The travels of the Bu Kuwara must be given in detail in another publication, but they had a long history of movement around northern Qatar (Jumail, Fuwairit, Ghariyah), eastern Qatar (Sumaisma, Dha'ain, Doha, perhaps Wakra), as well as sojourns in Bahrain and on the Persian coast (Lengeh).[36] Sometimes they divided into two or three sections, sometimes they coalesced back into a single settlement. At times they moved out of choice, usually following disagreement with their overlords of the time, and at other times they were forced to relocate. Of particular note is a letter from Lt. Manners in 1850, who had been sent from Bahrain to deliver a letter to the sheikh of Fuwairit. He reported that he "found the town almost entirely deserted, there being about a dozen Arabs who were left for the purpose of pulling down the houses for the rafters. The inhabitants I am informed as also those of Wukrah have located themselves at El Biddeh."[37]

Here we see the fundamental reason underlying the mobility of the people of the region: their specialization in the pearl fishery and orientation to the sea freed them from permanent ties to place. Lacking agricultural and legal bonds to the land, they could relocate (or be made to do so) at short notice and with a minimum of effort, simply requiring their boats, access to the pearl banks, and a relatively reliable source of fresh water. Cash from the pearl fishery was necessary to obtain the basic staple foods (dates and grain), while wood was the other most important commodity, being required not only for the boats (the wood for these being obtained mainly from India) but also for the roofing of their homes (mangrove poles from East Africa). The most serious punishment that could be inflicted by the British, more damaging than fines, imprisonment, and the shelling of towns, was the burning of offending boats or fleets.[38]

It is worth underlining that despite the tribal status assigned to many of them, these highly mobile pearl-fishing townspeople were not bedu, but were considered settled (hadar) by themselves and others. Nonetheless, bedu did participate in the pearl fishery, coming into the towns from the desert at the start of the summer to embark on the boats. According to some observers, the proportion of bedu taking part in the dive in Qatar was higher than elsewhere, though this claim was also made of other regions.[39]

TRADE AND CONSUMPTION

The income derived from the pearl fishery, particularly at its peak, directly impacted the material culture of its participants. Of particular note is the increased consumption of hardware manufactured outside the Gulf, which demonstrably peaks in the archaeological record during the late nineteenth and early twentieth century CE. Here we may take as a measure the combined percentage of European "China" and Far Eastern porcelains within the excavated ceramic assemblage of Doha, Qatar.[40] Joint excavations by University College London Qatar and Qatar Museums produced a phased sequence running from the early nineteenth century to the mid-twentieth century CE, the best-preserved levels of which date from the 1890s to the 1950s. In one excavated area (Area D), their occurrences (combined into the category "Global Ceramics," as opposed to wares understood to have been manufactured in the Gulf region) can be calculated over six phases. Each phase is dated according its coins, ceramic, and glass type-fossils, and (in the later stages) evidence from aerial imagery. When the percentage of Global Ceramics in each phase is lined up according to its date range above the Bahrain record of the value of the pearl harvest (a reliable proxy for the region, as noted above), a remarkable correlation is evident (figure 7.4).

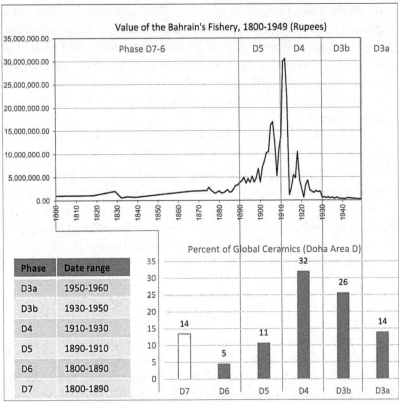

Figure 7.4. Percentage of "global ceramics" (European chinaware and Far Eastern porcelains) in the ceramic assemblages of each phase in Area D, Doha, lined up chronologically with the value of Bahrain's Pearl Fishery.

This chart shows that the percentage of ceramics of distant origin increased dramatically during the last decades of the nineteenth century, peaking during and just after the time of maximum pearl revenues, and dropping again once the pearling industry had collapsed.[41] Archaeologists consider that changes in material culture reflect economic change, often specifically linking increases in long-distance trade goods to increased wealth. This correlation suggests that in some cases the assumption is justified.

Corroborative evidence can be found in the trade figures for Bahrain, where the annual level of import of such ceramics ("chinaware and porcelain" in the trade reports) quite precisely tracks annual pearl revenues (figure 7.5). Indeed, after 1906 it can be shown that a rise or

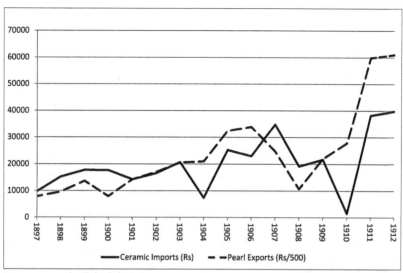

Figure 7.5. Value of Global Ceramic Imports (Porcelain and Chinaware) into Bahrain, 1897–1912, alongside value of pearl exports/500. Data derived from the Persian Gulf Administration Reports of those years.

drop in the pearl fishery was tracked a year or two afterwards by the level of import of such commodities. Thus, it appears that the level of pearling revenues translated directly into expenditure on consumer goods. This was noticed in 1910 by the British political agent in Bahrain, Captain Mackenzie: "the increased use of luxuries during the last few years has been noticeable in the town of Manama and among the richer inhabitants of Bahrein, no doubt consequent upon their visiting Bombay in connection with pearl transactions. Among the poorer classes no such symptoms are visible (except perhaps as regards food)."[42]

The Global Ceramics of European origin consist of transfer-printed bowls and dishes in various patterns and painted-and-sponge-printed bowls and dishes, nearly all of Dutch manufacture (from the Petrus Regout and Société Céramique factories of Maastricht).[43] These appear to become common around the 1890s, but typologically some could be as early as the 1870s or 1880s; the most frequent transfer patterns in the Doha assemblage were named Toko, Goudkust, and Tancrede (figure 7.6), but there were others (Awa, Bali, Cenis, Rhine). Willow pattern is present but rare, perhaps because of local discomfort with figurative imagery. The painted-and-sponge-printed vessels generally bore variants of the so-called "Adam's Rose" decoration, and a minority appear to be British in origin (figure 7.6, top left). From the 1920s, Japanese copies of the Maastricht transfer-printed bowls and dishes appear, as well as a distinctive Lion and Palm Tree pattern (figure 7.6, bottom right), eventually supplemented by saucers. Teapots also appear in the 1920s or slightly earlier, including Japanese and Russian products (not illustrated).

One of the most striking and frequent elements of the assemblage is a limited range of coffee cups with fluted bodies and "birdsfoot" spray decoration of differe nt colors, sometimes with a motto printed in gold inside (figure 7.6, top right). Their origin is unknown but it is likely to be Japan.[44] These are common from the 1890s through to the 1930s (with developed variants appearing thereafter into the 1950s or

Figure 7.6. European and Japanese trade wares from the Qatar National Museum Collection (all bowls and dishes), from excavations at the Radwani House, Doha (coffee cup, top right), and from excavations in Muharraq (coffee cup with red crook decoration, middle right).

1960s). They are accompanied by another variety of coffee cup with finer flutes and red crook pattern decoration, possibly older in origin, most likely of various origins (including Japanese) but perhaps originally Meissen.[45] From the 1930s onwards, coffee cups with wide flutes and complex transfer-printed designs appear, and from the 1950s unfluted varieties with smooth sides and transfer-printed designs become common, some of which are stamped to indicate Japanese manufacture (not illustrated).[46] The birdsfoot pattern remains common but painted sprays are replaced by transfer-printed sprays by the 1950s, or perhaps earlier.

Accompanying this relatively new range of ceramics are much older varieties of porcelain from China, including low- to medium-quality blue-and-white wares, and some polychrome enameled wares. The Dehua kilns of Fujian provide most of the porcelain (both blue-and-white and enameled wares), with a minority from the Jingdezhen kilns.[47] Polychrome enameled porcelain appears to be rare compared to the eighteenth- and earlier nineteenth-century assemblages (though we await quantified analyses), and we speculate that these were largely replaced in the last quarter of the nineteenth century by the more colorful (and perhaps cheaper) European sponged and transfer-printed ceramics.

Here only ceramics imported from distant manufacturing centers have been singled out for study, but other classes of trade goods followed the same pattern in the Doha sequence, including glassware (the quantity and variety of which appears to increase in step with the ceramic assemblage), and metalwork (especially padlocks from India). Some likely imported items do not show up well in the archaeological record, including imported woodwork (Indian chests and other furniture, sometimes attested by their brass fittings), and no doubt textiles of Indian and British origin. Further work needs to be conducted on the detailed trade returns of the Gulf to assess changes in the annual value of traded goods, both overall and in specific commodities.

POPULATION EXPANSION AND URBAN SPRAWL

A final correlate of the pearling boom, related to the processes of migration and settlement discussed earlier, can be found in the physical expansion of the towns and the growth in their populations. Here we again take Doha as a case study: population estimates show a broad trend of increase from the early nineteenth century, starting at an estimated 2,000, peaking at 12,000 at the height of the pearling boom, and then falling again as the industry collapsed and sections of the population left for work in regions and towns with more diversified economic opportunities (figure 7.7).[48] Counterintuitively, but not unique to Doha, there was then a brief population recovery in the 1930s, owing to migration from Persia.[49]

The area covered by Doha can also be calculated through time using a combination of historical maps, written accounts of the town's urban geography and districts, and early aerial photography.[50] Here we see the size of the town increasing steadily until the 1890s, when it begins to level off (figure 7.7). With this curve we note that potential fluctuations in occupied area would be flattened out by the paucity of data points and rudimentary nature of some of the data.

The two curves (for population and area through time) can be laid over the proxy record of pearling revenues derived from Bahrain, to

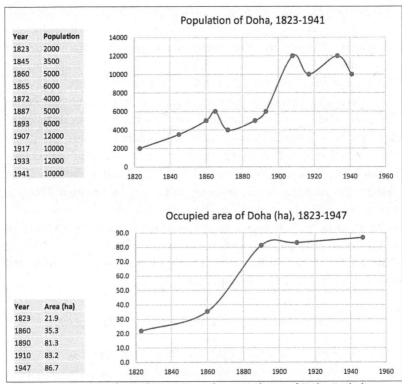

Figure 7.7. Estimates of population size and occupied area of Doha (including Bida') from the early nineteenth to the mid-twentieth century.

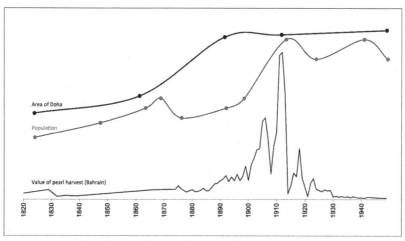

Figure 7.8. Overlay of curves for population and area of Doha with value of Bahrain's pearl exports (as a proxy for the Qatari pearl fishery).

illustrate clearly how demography and urban growth marched in tandem with income from pearl fishing, particularly in terms of population (figure 7.8).

THE SOURCES REVEAL how the pearl fishery underpinned not merely the subsistence base of the people of the Gulf littoral, but also its settlement patterns, history of migration, and political economy. Although this intimate involvement with pearl fishing was extremely ancient, the impact of the fishery became increasingly formative from the eighteenth century onwards, its effects accelerating as the industry peaked in the last decades of the nineteenth and first decades of the twentieth centuries CE.

Here we see a true process of economic integration taking place, though it may not have been obvious to its participants. The historical evidence for economically driven migration to coastal settlements, and the archaeological evidence for changing consumption patterns, underline the reflexive nature of the nineteenth- to early twentieth-century globalization process: while rises in the price of pearls in the West stimulated settlement and intensification of production in the pearling area, the resulting economic acceleration in the latter region created an (archaeologically demonstrable) demand for Western consumer products and an overall increase in the volume of trade.

The global forces behind these region-specific and product-specific developments are relatively well known, and were founded upon lowering freight costs and journey times during the nineteenth century, combined with the removal of trade restrictions on a global scale. According to data gathered on Atlantic, eastern Mediterranean, and Black Sea shipping, reductions in freight costs were dramatic from the 1870s onwards, and in tandem the value of grain exports climbed steeply. Both the transport revolution and the opening of free trade also had dramatic ramifications for East Asia, including China and Japan.[51] The opening of the Suez Canal in 1869 was critical in this regard for the western Indian Ocean region, as cargoes (including but not restricted to mass-produced ceramics) no longer had to make the lengthy journey around Africa to reach Arabia and Asia. Of similar impact was the opening of the steamer trade in the Gulf from the early 1860s onwards, which not only tied the region more closely to European (and thence American) markets, but connected India, the Gulf, Iran, and Iraq into a predictable and rapid bulk transport system.[52] Within the Gulf, the increase in the volume and range of imported goods was connected not merely to falling transport costs, but also increased spending power due to the booming pearl fishery.

Finally, on the matter of global processes, it must be underlined that while the developments seen in the Gulf are contextual and regionally specific, in this case focused on pearls, simultaneous examples of economic specialization and intensification, and changes in consumer behavior, are not difficult to find elsewhere. In Zanzibar, for example, a similar range of mass-produced European ceramics appears in abundance at the same time that they become common in the Gulf; in this case, the local economy is based on cloves, not pearls.[53] Similarly, the towns of the grain-producing regions of the Black Sea saw a dramatic increase in both production and population during the "long nineteenth century," in a process analogous to that of the Gulf.[54]

This study therefore demonstrates the transformative impact of the pearl fishery on a local scale, but also reveals how it was part of a wider process that connected Qatar, its small pearling towns, and its people to the global economy. Moreover, mass migration, explosive urban growth, and consumer behavior are not new products of the oil economy, but were deeply embedded in local experience for two and half centuries before the coming of oil, particularly since the late nineteenth century CE.

NOTES

1. Robert Carter, "The History and Prehistory of Pearling in the Persian Gulf," *Journal of the Economic and Social History of the Orient* 48, no. 2 (2005): 139–209; Vincent Charpentier, Carl S. Phillips, and Sophie Méry. "Pearl Fishing in the Ancient World: 7500 BP," *Arabian Archaeology and Epigraphy*, no. 23 (2012): 1–6.

2. Robert Carter, *Sea of Pearls: Seven Thousand Years of the Industry That Shaped the Gulf* (London: Arabian, 2012), 3–21, 69–70; R. A. Donkin, *Beyond Price: Pearls and Pearl-Fishing: Origins to the Age of Discoveries* (Philadelphia: American Philosophical Society, 1998).

3. Robert Carter, "The History and Prehistory of Pearling": 150–58; Carter, "How Pearls Made the Modern Emirates," in *New Perspectives on Recording UAE History*, ed. Jayanti Maitra (Abu Dhabi: Centre for Documentation and Research, 2009).

4. Carter, *Sea of Pearls*, 175–80; Léonard Rosenthal, *The Kingdom of the Pearl* (1920; repr., London: Hodder and Stoughton, 1984), 65; George Frederick Kunz and Charles Hugh Stevenson, *The Book of the Pearl: The History, Art, Science, and Industry of the Queen of Gems* (New York: Century, 1908).

5. Between 1873 and 1904, when we have annual figures for both Bahrain and the whole Gulf, the mean proportion of Bahrain's contribution was 46 percent, though it broadly climbed during this period, notwithstanding short-term fluctuations. See Carter, *Sea of Pearls*, Appendix 2, for the data sources. The annual figures are derived from Appendix C in Lorimer's Historical volumes: John Gordon Lorimer, *Gazetteer of the Persian Gulf, Oman and Central Arabia*, vol. 1, *Historical* (Calcutta: Superintendent Government Printing, 1915), 2220–93.

6. Carter, *Sea of Pearls*, 157, for an account of attempts to increase the harvest in the late nineteenth/early twentieth century; and Lorimer, *Gazetteer*, vol. 1, *Historical*, 2239, for the increase in rates.

7. Carter, *Sea of Pearls*, 260–69, for stages in the collapse of the pearl fishery.

8. Carter, *Sea of Pearls*, Appendix 2, for the full list of data sources.

9. The total population figure, and other detailed statistics, are derived from John Gordon Lorimer, *Gazetteer of the Persian Gulf, Oman and Central Arabia*, vol. 2, *Geographical and Statistical* (Calcutta: Superintendent Government Printing, 1908), by adding the figures he gives for each coastal "principality," except for the area corresponding to the coastal area of the Ottoman *sanjaq* of Al-Hasa, for which I took the population of the coastal zone (Qatif, Tarut, and adjacent areas). The population figure therefore includes the coastal and inland territories roughly corresponding to the modern territory of Kuwait, Bahrain, Qatar, UAE, and the littoral of Saudi Arabia's Eastern Province.

10. McLeod (sometimes MacLeod) was cited by Lt. Arnold Kemball in 1845, who noted that "the same holds good for the tribes in general to the present day, except that their own boats are now engaged in the Indian trade." Kemball's report, entitled "Memoranda on the resources, localities and relations of the tribes inhabiting the Arabian shores of the Persian Gulf," can be found in Robert Hughes Thomas, *Arabian Gulf Intelligence: Selections from the Records of the Bombay Government*, n.s., no. 24 (1856; repr., Cambridge: Oleander, 1985), 92–119.

11. D. Wilson, "Memorandum Respecting the Pearl Fisheries in the Persian Gulf," *Journal of the Royal Geographical Society* 3 (1833), 283–86. For eighteenth-century observers, see Carsten Niebuhr, *Travels through Arabia and Other Countries in the East*, trans. Robert Heron (Edinburgh: R. Morison and Son, 1792); Guillaume-Thomas-François Resnal, *A Philosophical and Political History of the Settlements and Trade of the Europeans in the East and West Indies*, trans. J. Justamond, 4 vols. (Dublin, 1776); Abraham Parsons, *Travels in Asia and Africa* (London: Longman, Hurst, Rees, and Orme, 1808); and the report by Manesty and Jones in Jerome A. Saldanha, *The Persian Gulf Précis*, vol. 1, *Selections from State Papers, Bombay, Regarding the East India Company's Connections with the Persian Gulf, with a Summary of Events, 1600–1800* (1908; repr., Gerrards Cross, UK: Archive Editions, 1986).

12. Lorimer, *Gazetteer*, vol. 1, *Historical*, 2220.

13. Most Gulf towns included a significant population known as *Huwala*, being Sunni Arab families and tribes who had been long settled on the Persian shore, frequently with branches on the Arabian coast. Ties and movement between the communities on both coasts remained very significant until the mid-twentieth century. Major Qatari bedu tribes with sections outside the peninsula include the Bani Hajir and the Murrah, who were both very numerous in inland Saudi Arabia; the Na'im, who were present in all neighboring states; as well as smaller representations by the Manasir, Ka'aban, Dawasir, and others. For details, see individual entries in Lorimer, *Gazetteer*, vol. 2, *Geographical and Statistical*.

14. Lorimer, *Gazetteer*, vol. 2, *Geographical and Statistical*, 1271.

15. James Wellsted, *Travels in Arabia*, vol. 1 (London: John Murray, 1838), 264.

16. These dives all had several other names, according to the locality, and in addition there could be a further late dive potentially running into November (*al-Rudaida*, meaning the Little Return), as well as off-season oyster collection by wading (*al-Mujanna*). For full details, timing, and terminology of the dives see Carter, *Sea of Pearls*, 201–4; and Anie Montigny, "Évolution d'un groupe bédouin dans un pays producteur de pétrole: Les Al-Na'im de Qatar" (PhD thesis, Université de Paris V, 1985), 250.

17. Saif Albedwawi, "Pearl Merchants of the Gulf and Their Life in Bombay," *Proceedings of the Seminar for Arabian Studies* 47 (2017): 1–7; Carter, *Sea of Pearls*, 169–75, 233.

18. Lengeh (in full, Bandar-e Lengeh, also Lingah) held this importance under the rule of the Qawasim sheikhs of Ras Al-Khaimah and Sharjah, but previously Kangan (in the early eighteenth century) and Kung ("Congo" to the Portuguese, important in the seventeenth century) had fulfilled this role on the Persian shore. The population of Dubai doubled from 10,000 to 20,000 between 1908 and 1933 as it supplanted Lengeh.

Carter, *Sea of Pearls*, 156; Lawrence Potter, "The consolidation of Iran's frontier on the Persian Gulf in the nineteenth century," in *War and Peace in Qajar Persia*, ed. Roxane Farmanfarmaian (London: Routledge, 2008), 140 and n. 96; Lorimer, *Gazetteer*, vol. 1, *Historical*, 774–5; Lorimer, *Gazetteer*, vol. 2, *Geographical and Statistical*, 455; 1098.

19. Lorimer, *Gazetteer*, vol. 1, *Historical*, Appendix C, esp. 2227–28.

20. Lorimer, *Gazetteer*, vol. 1, Appendix C, Annexure 3, 2256–62; Carter, *Sea of Pearls*, 181.

21. Carter, *Sea of Pearls*, 185. Al-Hijji puts the typical depth at 5–13 fathoms: Yacoub Yusuf Al-Hijji, *Kuwait and the Sea: A Brief Social and Economic History* (London: Arabian, 2010), 35. The comfortable limit for repeated dives for a normal diver was said to be 12 fathoms, ca. 22 m.

22. Carter, *Sea of Pearls*, 204–17.

23. Henry H. Whitelock, "An Account of Arabs Who Inhabit the Coast between Ras-el Kheimah and Abothubee in the Gulf of Persia, Generally Called the Pirate Coast," *Transactions of the Bombay Geographical Society (1836–1938)* 1 (1844): 32–54; Lorimer, *Gazetteer*, vol. 2, *Geographical and Statistical*, 1438.

24. Carter, *Sea of Pearls*, 192–94.

25. Carter, *Sea of Pearls*, 110–22; Carter, "The History and Prehistory of Pearling"; Carter, "How Pearls Made the Modern Emirates."

26. William Gifford Palgrave, *Personal Narrative of a Year's Journey through Central and Eastern Arabia (1862–1863)* (London: Macmillan, 1866), 386.

27. With thanks to Dr. Nora Barakat of NYU Abu Dhabi, who helped me disentangle the divergent translations provided by Benjamin Slot and Aba Hussein and establish that Freiha was substituted for Deylam by Aba Hussein and an earlier translator (Aghraqja). Unfortunately, the document mentions neither Freiha nor Qatar. The "Khalifat" are probably the Kholaifat, a tribe that eventually migrated permanently to Qatar. Slot, *The Origins of Kuwait*, 2nd ed. (Kuwait: Center for Research and Studies on Kuwait, 1998), 110; A. A. R. Aba Hussein, "A Study of the History of the Utoob," *Al-Watheeka [al-wathiqa]* 1 (1982): 25–42.

28. Gareth Rees, Faisal al-Naimi, Tobias Richter, Agnieszka Bystron, and Alan Walmsley, "Archaeological Excavations at the Settlement of al-Furayḥah (Freiha), North-West Qatar," *Proceedings of the Seminar for Arabian Studies* 42 (2012): 319–30. The investigators indicate that material as early as the sixteenth century may be present, and Aba Hussein considers that the ʿUtub may have been there for as long as half a century, but nothing in the preliminary pottery report indicates anything definitely earlier than the late seventeenth or early eighteenth century. See Agnieszka Bystron, "Freiha Pottery Report," in *Qatar Islamic Archaeology and Heritage Project: End of Season Report 2013—2014*, ed. Sandra Rosendahl et al. (Copenhagen: University of Copenhagen and Qatar Museums, 2015).

29. An early nineteenth-century source, the *Lam' Ash-Shihab*, mentions both towns. See Ahmad Mustafa Abu-Hakima, *History of Eastern Arabia, 1750–1800: The Rise and Development of Bahrain, Kuwait and Wahhabi Saudi Arabia*, 2nd ed. (London: Probsthain, 1988), 71n5.

30. For the dating of the main levels and fortifications of Ruwaida, see Andrew Petersen et al., "Ruwayda: An Historic Urban Settlement in North Qatar," *Post-Medieval Archaeology* 50, no. 2 (2012): 321–49, esp. 327, 332; also Andrew Petersen and Tony Grey, "Palace, Mosque, and Tomb at al-Ruwaydah, Qatar," *Proceedings of the Seminar for Arabian Studies* 42 (2012): 277–89. For Rubaiqa and its historical dating, see Andrew Petersen, "Research on an Islamic Period Settlement at Ras Ushayriq in Northern Qatar and Some Observations on the Occurrence of Date Presses," *Proceedings of the Seminar for Arabian Studies* 41 (2011): 245–56. For Zubara, see, e.g., Alan Walmsley, Hugh Barnes, and Phillip Macumber, "Al-Zubarah and Its Hinterland, North Qatar: Excavations and Survey, Spring 2009," *Proceedings of the Seminar for Arabian Studies* 40 (2010): 55–68; and Tobias Richter, Paul Wordsworth, and Alan Walmsley, "Pearl Fishers, Townsfolk, Bedouin, and Shaykhs: Economic and Social Relations in Islamic al-Zubarah," *Proceedings of the Seminar for Arabian Studies* 41 (2011): 317–32.

31. Other groups of Nejdi origin include, for example, the Dawasir of various Gulf states, the Maʿadhid (the tribe of the Al-Thani family who eventually won control of Qatar), and several tribes of Qatar who along with the Maʿadhid were said to be members of the wider Banu Tamim lineage, including the Al Bu Kuwara (discussed in more detail later). The Arab tribes who populated the coastal towns were not considered bedu, but rather settled (*ḥadar*), despite their frequent migrations in search of new places to settle.

32. The ruling families of Umm al-Qaiwain and Jazirat al-Hamra (now part of Ras Al-Khaimah) were of Huwala origin, and arguably also the Qawasim rulers of Sharjah and Ras Al-Khaimah, though they disavow the

designation. Ras Al-Khaimah was not a new town, having been founded as a successor to Julfar by the early sixteenth century. Ajman was ruled by a branch of the Naʿim, a largely bedu tribe of eastern Arabia. The Al Musallam and Al Bu ʿAinain are examples of longer-term Arab residents of the coast, both being members of the formerly powerful Banu Khaled confederation. The former lost control of Qatar during the eighteenth century, while the latter founded Doha. An example of a tribe originally from Oman can be found in the Sudan, who founded Bidaʿ (later subsumed into Doha), who are now mainly in the UAE, though some remain in Qatar. According to Lorimer, *Gazetteer*, vol. 2, *Geographical and Statistical*, the Suluta tribe may have come from Qatar via Iraq, but this appears uncertain.

33. See entries in Lorimer, *Gazetteer*, vol. 2, *Geographical and Statistical* for a town-by-town breakdown of the demographics of each pearling center, and also entries on the named tribes for their purported origin. Montigny, "Évolution d'un groupe bédouin," 254, refers to Baharna being described as "demi-Persians," a misapprehension still common in local societies.

34. See especially Matthew S. Hopper, *Slaves of One Master: Globalization and Slavery in Arabia in the Age of Empire* (New Haven, CT: Yale University Press, 2015); and Carter, *Sea of Pearls*, 212–13.

35. Hughes Thomas, *Arabian Gulf Intelligence*, 94. This quote is extracted from Lt. Kemball's *Memoranda on the Resources, Localities, and Relations of the Tribes Inhabiting the Arabian Shores of the Persian Gulf* (1845).

36. The Al Bu Kuwara appear to have been most strongly associated with Sumaisma and Fuwairit. For their travels, see Lorimer, *Gazetteer*, vol. 2, *Geographical and Statistical*, 490, 1077; Lorimer, *Gazetteer*, vol. 1, *Historical*, 804–5, 839–40; Abu-Hakima, *History of Eastern Arabia*, 115; Abdullah bin Khalid Al-Khalifa and Ali Aba Hussain, "The Utoob in the Eighteenth Century," in *Bahrain through the Ages: The History*, ed. Abdullah bin Khalid Al-Khalifa and Michael Rice (New York: Kegan Paul International, 1993), 305; Zekeriya Kurşun, *The Ottomans in Qatar: A History of Anglo-Ottoman Conflicts in the Persian Gulf* (Istanbul: Isis, 2002), 71ff, 76n1; Jerome A. Saldanha, *The Persian Gulf Précis*, vol. 5, specifically Colebrook's 1820 report in the *Précis of Turkish Expansion on the Arab Littoral of the Persian Gulf and Hasa and Katif Affairs 1804–1904* (1904; repr., Gerrards Cross, UK: Archive Editions, 1986); Hughes Thomas, *Arabian Gulf Intelligence*, 151; Penelope Tuson, *Records of Qatar, Primary Documents 1820–1960*, vol. 7, *1949–1960* (Slough, UK: Archive Editions, 1991), 25–26; Tuson, *Records of Qatar, Primary Documents 1820–1960*, vol. 3, *1879–1896* (Slough, UK: Archive Editions, 1991), 223, 248, 558; Mohamed A. J Althani, *Jassim the Leader: Founder of Qatar* (London: Profile

Books, 2012), 64; Habibur Rahman, *The Emergence of Qatar: The Turbulent Years, 1627–1916* (London: Kegan Paul, 2012).

37. Letter no. 8 of 1851 from Lt Frederick Erskine Manners, Brigantine Tigris, to Commodore John Patterson Porter, Commanding Indian Naval Squadron, Persian Gulf, British Library, India Office Records and Private Papers (IOR), R/15/1/128, ff 41v–42, accessed at http://www.qdl.qa/en/archive/81055/vdc_100023211499.0x000053.

38. One can also highlight the behavior of an attacking force from Abu Dhabi that took part in the destruction of Doha and Bida' in 1867: after the seizure of the boats and plundering of the houses, they "returned, and, pulling off the roofs of the houses, carried off the rafters and doors, together with date poles [presumably the '*arish* date fronds used for inexpensive housing], and any boats, tanks, and domestic utensils that had been left." See Penelope Tuson, *Records of Qatar, Primary Documents 1820–1960*, vol. 2, *1853–1879* (Slough, UK: Archive Editions, 1991), 117.

39. Montigny, "Évolution d'un groupe bédouin," 273, considers that the most significant bedu participation was in Qatar, and indeed that, apart from the paramount sheikh's immediate family, *all* the Qatari Na'imi bedu appear to have participated directly in the fishery. Montigny also notes that many of the divers in Dubai were Baluch, but that most were Africans of slave descent, with most haulers being slaves in Qatar (254, 256). Of Kuwait, Al-Hijji, *Kuwait and the Sea*, 27, considered that 30 percent of Kuwait's diving force were bedu.

40. Data is derived from the Old Doha Rescue Excavation (ODRE) conducted jointly in winter 2013–14 by Qatar Museums and UCL Qatar's Origins of Doha and Qatar Project (funded by NPRP grant no. 5–421–6-010 from the Qatar National Research Fund). Thanks to Faisal Al-Naimi, Ferhan Sakal, Alice Bianchi, and the ceramics team (especially Francesca Pisano, Tracey Cian, and Huda Abu Amer) for making this data available and helping to record the pottery.

41. Note that the brief lag evident between revenue and manifestation of imported pottery in the archaeological level is expected, as it takes some years for ceramics to pass from purchase to breakage and loss. Total numbers of sherds in each phase assemblage of Area D are as follows: D7: 127; D6: 905; D5: 842; D4: 2,467; D3b: 612; D3a: 1,129). Regarding the high percentage of Global Ceramics in Phase D7, the total assemblage size in that phase is very small, at 127 sherds, so this percentage should be regarded as unreliable.

42. Anita Burdett, *Records of the Persian Gulf Pearl Fisheries 1857–1962*, vol. 2 (Farnham Common, UK: Archive Editions, 1985), 81–82. For a recent study of the urban development of Manama that highlights also the place of pearling in this process, see Nelida Fuccaro, *Histories of City and State in the Persian Gulf: Manama since 1800* (Cambridge: Cambridge University Press, 2009).

43. For expositions of this material, see especially Anthony Grey, "Appendix 1: Specialist Report on Selected Far Eastern and European Imports," in *Muharraq Excavations 2010*, ed. Robert Carter and Javier Naranjo-Santana (Oxford: Oxford Brookes Archaeology & Heritage, 2010), 72–97, online report at http://ucl.academia.edu/RobertCarter/Papers/636240/Muharraq _Excavations_2010; Therese Sundblad, "European Refined White Wares and Japanese Imitations," in *Ceramics of the Qatar National Museum*, Robert Carter (Oxford: Oxford Brookes Archaeology & Heritage, 2011), 20–26, online report at https://www.academia.edu/700174/Ceramics_of _the_Qatar_National_Museum; Timothy Power, "A First Ceramic Chronology for the Late Islamic Arabian Gulf," *Journal of Islamic Archaeology* 2, no. 1 (2015): 1–33; Tony Grey, "Late Trade Wares on Arabian Shores: 18th- to 20th-Century Imported Fineware Ceramics from Excavated Sites on the Southern Persian (Arabian) Gulf Coast," *Post-Medieval Archaeology* 45, no. 2 (2011): 350–73.

44. The literature on late nineteenth and early twentieth century export pottery from Japan and China is scanty. Initial examination of the Chinese literature has failed to throw up any parallels, except for a variety of plain fluted coffee cup (which appears to be present in the Gulf, but is not illustrated here), while the combination of a porcelainous body with painted decoration of various colors, with gold, is characteristically Japanese.

45. Power, "A First Ceramic Chronology."

46. The full study of the Doha pottery is being undertaken in conjunction with Qatar Museums, and will be published in the final reports.

47. Unpublished preliminary report on the Far Eastern ceramics from the Doha excavations, by Dr. Ran Zhang, 2017.

48. Population estimates are derived from Hughes Thomas, *Arabian Gulf Intelligence*, 105, 559; C. Constable and Arthur Stiffe, "The Persian Gulf Pilot, including the Gulf of 'Oman, 1864," in *The Persian Gulf Pilot 1870–1932*, vol. 1, *First Edition, 1870* (Slough, UK: Archive Editions, 1989), 105; Palgrave, *Personal Narrative*, 236; Kurşun, *The Ottomans in Qatar*, 16–17; Lorimer, *Gazetteer*, vol. 2, *Geographical and Statistical*, 489; Tuson, *Records of Qatar*, vol. 3, 248–49; Tuson, *Records of Qatar, Primary Documents 1820–1960*, vol. 5, *1916–1935* (Slough, UK: Archive Editions, 1991), 355; IOR/L/MIL/17/15/141, Military Report on the Arabian Shores of the Persian Gulf, Kuwait, Bahrein, Hasa, Qatar, Trucial Oman and Oman, available also in Qatar Digital Library, http://www.qdl.qa/en/archive/81055 /vdc_100023509623.0x00000b; Tuson, *Records of Qatar, Primary Documents 1820–1960*, vol. 6, *1935–1949* (Slough, UK: Archive Editions, 1991), 560. The 1823 estimate was made by taking Brucks's permanent population of 400 men and multiplying by five (a standard formula used in the region to calculate population size, employed by Lorimer and others). The same method was used to extrapolate from Kemball's 1845 estimate of a

maximum of 700 fighting men. The final figure from 1941 is likely to be an overestimate: the observer considered the population to be somewhere between 5,000 and 10,000.

49. A surge of migration from the Persian shore occurred due to equally harsh economic conditions on that side coupled with the imposition of taxation and unwelcome social reforms by the Qajar state. For an account of simultaneous migration to Dubai for these reasons, see Frauke Heard-Bey, *From Trucial States to United Arab Emirates: A Society in Transition*, 2nd ed. (London: Longman, 1996), 244–45; and Djamel Boussaa, "A Future to the Past: The Case of Fareej Al-Bastakia in Dubai, UAE," *Proceedings of the Seminar for Arabian Studies* 36 (2006): 128.

50. Area calculations were made by Richard Fletcher, based on reconstructions of the historical geography in Richard Fletcher and Robert Carter, "Mapping the Growth of an Arabian Gulf Town: The Case of Doha, Qatar," *Journal of the Economic and Social History of the Orient* 60, no. 4 (2017): 420–87.

51. Kevin H. O'Rourke and Jeffrey G. Williamson, "When Did Globalization Begin?" *European Review of Economic History* 6, no. 1 (April 2002): 23–50; Gelina Harlaftis and Vasilis Kardasis, "International Shipping in the Eastern Mediterranean and the Black Sea: Istanbul as a Maritime Center, 1870–1910," in *The Mediterranean Response to Globalization before 1950*, ed. Sevket Pamuk and Jeffrey G. Williamson (London: Routledge, 2000).

52. Stephanie Jones, "British Indian Steamers and the Trade of the Persian Gulf, 1862–1914," *The Great Circle: Journal of the Australian Association for Maritime History* 7, no. 1 (April 1985): 23–44.

53. Sarah Croucher, "Exchange Values: Commodities, Colonialism and Identity on Nineteenth Century Zanzibar," in *The Archaeology of Capitalism in Colonial Contexts*, ed. Sarah Croucher and Lindsay Weiss (New York: Springer, 2011).

54. As revealed by the project The Black Sea and Its Port-Cities from the 18th to the 20th Century. For example, as witnessed in population growth in Constanta, Romania, in the 1870–90s, see Constantin Ardeleanu, "Romania's Investments in Its Maritime Ports (1878–1914)," in "Port Cities of the Western Black Sea Coast and the Danube: Economic and Social Development in the Long Nineteenth Century," ed. Constantin Ardeleanu and Andreas Lyberatos, Black Sea Project Working Papers, vol. 1, Corfu, 2016, 130–64. See also Constantin Cheramidoglu, "Aspects Regarding Constanța's Economic Life (1878–1914)," in Ardeleanu and Lyberatos, "Port Cities," 165–76. For Burgas, Bulgaria, in the 1870s–80s, see Dimiter Christov, "The Rise of a Port: Socio-Economic Development of Burgas in the 19th c." in Ardeleanu and Lyberatos, "Port Cities," 193–94 and table 7.1.

EIGHT

Enslaved Africans and the Globalization of Arabian Gulf Pearling

MATTHEW S. HOPPER

BEGINNING IN 1938, Australian mariner Alan Villiers spent eighteen months on board the Arab dhow *The Triumph of Righteousness*, sailing from Kuwait to Zanzibar and back. He published his experiences in his classic *Sons of Sinbad*. Some of the most memorable parts of the book are Villiers's descriptions and photographs of pearl divers in the waters of the Arabian/Persian Gulf, many of whom have a distinctly African appearance. Some readers of Villiers's book may understandably be puzzled by the large number of African men among the crews of the Arabian Gulf pearling boats and may wonder whether these African men were visitors, recently arrived migrant laborers, or representatives of a larger African population in the region. In fact, enslaved African men and their descendants may have accounted for as many as a quarter or half of the region's diving crews by the first decades of the twentieth century.

This chapter describes how the significant African presence in the Gulf connects to the region's pearling industry, which expanded substantially in the nineteenth century in response to global economic forces. Although they were not the only divers, Africans were essential to the massive Gulf pearling industry, which by the turn of the twentieth century produced more wealth from pearls than all other regions of the world combined. Pearls had long been a staple of the Gulf economy, feeding regional markets centered on India and the Middle East, but in the late nineteenth century Gulf pearls found new markets in Europe and North America. Changing fashion among wealthy elites in Europe and North America led to exponential growth in pearl imports and a global pearl boom that drove the expansion of pearl diving around the world, from Mexico to Australia. But the increased demand for divers in the Gulf also led to a rise in the slave trade from East Africa. Many enslaved men imported to the Gulf worked in pearling, and, unlike other regions described in this volume, slave divers in the Gulf worked alongside free divers during the annual pearling season.

PEARL DIVING IN THE GULF

In 1863, Sheikh Muhammad bin Thānī, ruler of Qatar, lamented about the economic realities facing the population of coastal eastern Arabia to the traveling European scholar William Palgrave. Sheikh Mohammad explained, "we are all, from the highest to the lowest, slaves of one master, [the] Pearl."[1] The sheikh's comment belies the very real disparity between slave and free in the Gulf, but it demonstrates his grasp of the growing influence of global markets on the region by the second half of the nineteenth century. Even before the Gulf's lucrative pearl export market reached its ultimate peak half a century later, Sheikh Muhammad could detect a growing dependence on global trade. But his remark also illustrates a broader paradox of the late nineteenth century: the era of expanding global markets that followed the abolition of slavery in much of the world also created systems of labor that mirrored slavery or were in fact systems of slavery.

In the late nineteenth century, soaring global demand for pearls sparked a worldwide surge in pearl production, and the Gulf became its epicenter. Pearl diving intensified at pearl banks around the world, but the Gulf was by far the world's leading producer. Between 1873 and 1906, the value of pearl exports from Bahrain increased by more than 800 percent. By 1905, the value of pearls produced in the Gulf exceeded the production of all other parts of the world combined. At the peak of pearl production in the early twentieth century, the Gulf pearl banks were worked by more than 3,400 boats, which employed more than 64,000 men from Muscat to Kuwait.[2] The pearling industry was the largest source of employment in the region, and chronic shortages in labor for diving created demand for slaves. Enslaved divers from Africa became a common sight by the late nineteenth century and were universally regarded as the region's best and most valued divers.[3]

The annual diving season in the Gulf in the era of Sheikh Mohammad was a massive enterprise lasting approximately five months of the year. The waters of the Gulf are too cold between October and April for divers to tolerate long enough to make pearl diving possible without modern diving equipment, so diving was mostly a summer affair. By the end of the nineteenth century, the *Ghaūs al-Kabīr* (the great dive) began in the middle of May and continued for 130 days until the middle of September.[4] The main diving season was the primary source of income for coastal and insular Arabia in the nineteenth century, and involved deepwater diving long distances from shore for weeks at a time.[5] Each diving boat consisted of an all-male crew, including one *nākhuda* (captain, pl. *nawākhida*), and an equal number of *ghawāwīs* (divers, sing. *ghawwās*) and *siyūb* (haulers, sing. *saīb*), in addition to an assortment of *radhafa* (assistants or extra hands, sing. *radhīf*) and *awlād* (boys or apprentices, sing. *walīd*).[6] A captain gathered the crew and paid them at the end of each season, selected the pearl banks to be fished, leased the boat if he did not own it, prepared the necessary provisions for the boat, maintained order aboard, and sold the pearls for the best price possible at the end of the season. Diving began each morning and continued until sunset with only a brief break in the afternoon. Each diver wore only a loincloth and was equipped with only a pair of horn pincers, leather fingertips, and a knife. Gulf pearling depended on the close relationship between the diver and puller, who worked together in pairs. Divers descended to the sea floor with the aid of a heavy stone weight attached to a rope and fitted with a loop to the diver's foot. With the aid of the hauler, the diver would slip his foot into the loop, inhale, and descend rapidly to the sea floor.[7]

Typical dives would take a diver to depths of between fifty and eighty feet and would last between one and two minutes. When a diver reached the sea floor, he kept his foot in the weight's loop and reached and maneuvered himself as best he could to collect as many oysters as possible—rarely more than a few from each dive—using the knife to pry the shells from the rocky surface below. For as long as he could hold his breath, the diver put oysters into a net basket tied to his waist. Before ascending, the diver released the weight, which the hauler pulled back onto the ship, and signaled to the hauler he was ready to resurface by tugging the second rope fastened around his waist. The hauler pulled the diver back to the surface as quickly as possible before his air expired. Divers would rest for only a few minutes before repeating the process.[8]

Diving crews heaped the oyster shells into a pile in the center of the boat and allowed them to sit through the heat of the day and then overnight. Each morning, the crews, under the close supervision of the nākhuda, would pry open the oysters and search them for pearls. Only a small minority of oysters contained any type of pearl (one in five, by one estimate), and most of those found were small. As members of the crew found pearls, they passed them to the nākhuda for safekeeping until the catch could be sold.[9] Pearl banks were spread across the Gulf and varied in yield annually, requiring pearl captains to move from place to place in order to find productive areas. Boats were accordingly kept away from towns for weeks at a time and were unable to return home for the duration of the season. Pearl boats would only come ashore in order to resupply, usually every three weeks. When within reach of a coastal town, they were provisioned by local entrepreneurs who specialized in delivering drinking water and supplies to pearling boats.[10]

When the boats returned to shore at the close of the annual season, the captain set about selling the boat's catch and paying off the crew. If the captain owned the boat he commanded, he had the option of selling the pearls to the pearl merchant of his choice. If the boat was rented, the captain was obligated to sell the pearls to the owner of the boat, usually at a deflated price for payment in kind rather than cash. This system maximized the lender's profits, though thefts did occur as pearls could be concealed in garments and taken off boats. If the captain owned the boat, he took a cut of 20 percent of the gross earnings. The remaining proceeds were split among the crew, with divers receiving three shares and haulers two shares of the remainder. If the boat was leased, the owner kept the 20 percent and the captain received a diver's share. On the Trucial Coast (so-called for its early nineteenth-century anti-piracy treaties with Great Britain, and home today to the United Arab Emirates), the sheikh of the town from which the boat sailed sometimes received a diver's share of the proceeds as well. If the boat was leased, the crew were forced to take their earnings in kind—most often in bags of rice. What could not be used by the crew was sold in the market for cash which was then distributed among the crew.[11]

The lives of pearling crews were hard. Mortality was high and health problems abounded. Ruptured eardrums and blindness were common among seasoned divers. Respiratory ailments, scurvy, and skin problems were widespread. Sharks, stingrays, and, most commonly, jellyfish presented danger. By the early twentieth century, many divers wore tight-fitting cotton suits that could partially shield the body from painful jellyfish stings.[12]

AFRICANS AND PEARL DIVING IN THE GULF

Enslaved Africans and free men of African ancestry accounted for a large number of the pearl divers in the late nineteenth and early twentieth centuries. Although the precise proportions are unknown, the descriptions of several contemporary observers attest to a substantial African presence among Gulf pearling crewmen in this period. Captain E. L. Durand in 1878 noted that, while most haulers in the Gulf were Bedouin or Persians, the divers were generally "sedees" and sometimes "sedee domestic slaves."[13] J. G. Lorimer, in his comprehensive gazetteer of the Gulf published in 1907, stated that the divers were "mostly poor Arabs and free Negroes or Negro slaves; but Persians and Baluchis are also to be found among them, and in recent years, owing to the large profits made by divers, many respectable Arabs have joined their ranks."[14] Paul W. Harrison recalled in 1924 that many divers on the Trucial Coast were slaves, but "they do not number over one-half the divers." "Most of these slaves are Negroes from Africa," he noted. "A few are Baluchees from the Makran coast between India and Persia."[15] Charles Belgrave recalled that, while most divers abstained from eating much during the dive season and were relatively gaunt, "the pullers were stalwart specimens; many of them were negroes with tremendous chest and arm development."[16] In 1929, the senior naval officer in the Gulf estimated that there were twenty thousand slave divers (roughly a quarter of the total) diving in the Gulf in each season.[17] Bertram Thomas reported in 1929 that a significant number of the divers who migrated north each season from Oman were enslaved. He estimated that a fifth of the "army" of thousands of divers that Batinah sent to the diving banks each year were enslaved.[18] Alan Villiers also counted "the huge muscular slave" among the Gulf pearl divers following his visit to the pearl banks in the 1930s.[19]

Enslaved Africans also appear in letters received at the British Residency complaining of instances of piracy and listing slaves among "lost property." Raiders attacked the *bughala* of Ghaīnim bin ʿAli al-Mahairbī at Bidda in the summer of 1876, killing two men and taking MT $400 worth of pearls and one "seedie slave," valued at MT $120.[20] African divers and haulers are also visible in the photographs taken by early twentieth-century photographers like Ronald Codrai, who documented life in Arabia. Photographs of pearling crews and notable pearling singers reveal a significant African presence throughout the industry.[21]

Many slave divers who sought manumission from British officials at Muscat, Sharjah, Bahrain, and Būshire gave personal testimonies of being kidnapped from East Africa as young boys and sent for diving as soon as they reached their early teens. For example, Juma bin Fundi, originally from Mfenesini in Zanzibar, who as a boy had worked as an orderly to a British officer in the East African campaign, boarded a

Figure 8.1. Pearl divers at work, Persian Gulf (ca. 1904). Source: *London Magazine* 11 (January 1904): 717.

dhow from Zanzibar to Mombasa, where he hoped to find work, but the dhow never landed at Mombasa. Juma was kidnapped by the owner of the dhow, Hamid bin Salim of Batinah, and was sold at Dubai to Mohamad bin Ibrahim of Sharjah to work as a pearl diver around 1926.[22] Some divers of African descent worked as free divers, but many others were second-generation slaves who were not brought directly from East Africa themselves but were born into slavery from parents who had been brought previously. An old man named Bashir bin Farajullah appealed to the Political Agency in Bahrain for a manumission certificate in 1934. The agent's staffer estimated that he was about eighty years old and remarked that he "looks like a Negro and talks Arabic." He had been born a slave in Qatar to slave parents serving in the house of Sheikh Abdullah bin Qāsim ath-Thāni, the ruler of Qatar. When he was about thirty years old, the sheikh sold him to a pearl diving captain named Abdullah bin Jābur al-Musallamī of Ghariyah (in Qatar), for whom he served as pearl diver for fourteen years. At the age of forty-four his master took him to Hasa, where he sold him to a man who employed him for three years as a gardener. When his new owner realized that he was not fit for the work, he set him out to earn his own keep, so Bashir returned to Qatar, got engaged as a free diver, and earned a few rupees—enough to get married—and returned to his old master in Hasa with his wife, where he remained into his old age.[23] In his study of the Atlantic world, Kevin Dawson argues convincingly that "slave traders targeted Africans with swimming skills for capture and sale to New World colonies in need of their skills."[24] But it is unclear whether boys in East Africa were similarly targeted specifically for their potential as divers in Arabia. Many were captured when very young and were made to work in date farms in Oman until they reached the proper age to be sent diving—usually their early teens. The demand for their labor appears to have been largely the result of a labor shortage in the Gulf. However, this subject demands further exploration.[25]

THE GULF AND THE REVIVAL OF PEARL FASHION

The rise of pearl fashion in Europe and North America between 1880 and 1930 represented a revival of tastes that had predominated in European royal courts during an earlier "pearl age" between 1524 and 1658. Pearls had enjoyed wide popularity among European royalty following the introduction of massive amounts of pearls from the Spanish and Portuguese conquests of the sixteenth century. The popularity of pearls waned following the mid-seventeenth century upheavals in Europe, through the age of revolutions, until it was revived in the mid-nineteenth century by royal women like Queen Victoria in England and Empress Eugenie in France.[26]

Queen Victoria was a leading force in women's fashion in the early decades of her reign and was in a large part responsible for the revival of European pearl fashion. In her public appearances she was consistently seen wearing a pearl necklace and always wore a four-strand pearl portrait bracelet—a gift from Prince Consort Albert. Following the death of Albert in 1861, Victoria went into a semipermanent state of mourning, limiting her public appearances and wearing black for the remainder of her life. But even in mourning she wore her trademark tasseled pearl sautoir and favorite pearl bracelets. In Paris, Empress Eugenie revived the opulence of the French court with her pearl necklaces, especially black pearls.[27] After the fall of the French monarchy in 1871, Empress Eugenie lost her already contested fashion preeminence in Paris, the Western fashion capital. In the late Victorian era, English women looked increasingly to minor royalty, landed aristocracy, and a growing class of nouveau riche for fashion trendsetting. Fashionable women in Europe and North America looked to actresses like Sarah Bernhardt and professional beauties like Lillie Langtry as role models. Following Victoria's death in 1901, her son Edward VII and his wife Alexandra, princess of Wales, set fashion trends that hastened the growing pearl revival. Alexandra wore a trademark choker necklace made of four rows of pearls to hide a scar on her neck inherited from a childhood disease, but her style of necklace caught on as a popular fashion trend.[28]

At the close of the nineteenth century, the nouveau riche joined the ranks of high society and eventually overtook it in dictating fashion trends in Europe and North America. In the United States, the Carnegies, Vanderbilts, Morgans, and other multimillionaires used fashion to distinguish themselves as part of a new American aristocracy. As wealth replaced lineage as the measure of respectability in Europe and the United States, the bodily display of wealth grew in importance, and pearls increasingly became a vehicle of such display. If America's new aristocracy could not be royalty, they could dress like royalty. William K. Vanderbilt demonstrated as much when he bought a pearl necklace that had formerly belonged to Catherine of Medici and followed with the purchase of a more extravagant necklace of five hundred pearls that formerly belonged to Empress Eugénie as gifts for his wife.[29] Vanderbilt's daughter, Consuelo, who inherited the necklace from her mother, symbolized the rise of the new American elite in 1895 when she married Charles Spencer-Churchill, Duke of Marlborough, becoming the first member of the new American aristocracy to marry into European royalty.[30] Consuelo Vanderbilt's portraits invariably depict her wearing pearls. By the early decades of the twentieth century, pearl necklaces, pendants, earrings, and decorations on brooches dominated women's fashion.

PEARLS AND PROFITS IN THE GULF

The money generated by the Gulf pearl industry primarily benefited the merchants and financiers, many of them from India, who owned the boats and lent them at interest to the nawākhida and in turn took half of the proceeds of the dive. Risk for these investors was comparatively low, and payback was high. The pearls could be sold at high prices to agents with connections and the rice used as payment for the crew could be acquired through connections for less than its local value in cash. The dual sources of income benefited the financiers. Likewise, the ruling families profited from duties levied on the imports. Some of this money was used to build and furnish elaborate houses with modern conveniences.

The main market for Gulf pearls throughout the nineteenth century was Bombay, and the pearl trade was handled largely through Arab and Indian merchants in Bahrain and, later, Dubai. For most of the industry's history, pearls were primarily exported to India, where they were used to make long necklaces, ornamental jewelry, and elaborate earrings and nose rings. Bombay remained the center of Gulf pearl exports until about 1907. During the U.S. Panic of 1907, British creditors who normally extended credit to Gulf pearl traders in Bombay collected on their loans and created a temporary lapse in the Gulf pearl purchasing system, severely limiting exports. One Parisian jewel firm saw the lapse as an opportunity to capture the Gulf's pearl catch, a deliberate attempt to shift the center of the world pearl market to Paris in the face of competition from other areas.[31]

Léonard Rosenthal emigrated to Paris from Chechnya at the age of fourteen, learned French, and scraped together a living as a teenager by working as a petty trader in furniture, antiques, and art. Between 1890 and 1906 he developed a local reputation as a small-time pearl dealer, forming with his brothers the firm Rosenthal et Frères.[32] Pearl exports from the Gulf more than quadrupled in value in the quarter century ending in 1904, and Bahrain saw pearl exports rise in ten years from 3.7 million rupees in 1894 to 10.3 million rupees in 1904. By 1905, jewelers in Europe recognized the great potential of the pearl market, and a few firms contemplated bypassing the Bombay middlemen by traveling directly to the Arabian Gulf. Victor Rosenthal of Rosenthal et Frères traveled to Bahrain in 1906 and purchased 187,000 rupees worth of pearls. He already had substantial knowledge of the market from working in Bombay and spoke Arabic fluently. Victor returned the following year and purchased 350,000 rupees worth of pearls. Then, following the Panic of 1907 in the United States, Rosenthal et Frères took advantage of a great opportunity.

Pearl exports from Bahrain, which had steadily risen since 1900, plummeted from 12.4 million rupees in 1907–8 to 5.5 million rupees in 1908–9 on account of a plague outbreak from April to July 1907 (which killed nearly two thousand people and frightened a large portion of the working population away) and the action of Bombay merchants who recalled advances they had made to pearl traders in response to the panic in the U.S. During this temporary slump in the pearl trade, Léonard and Victor convinced a prominent banker to lend them several million francs. In the following three years, the Rosenthals succeeded in cornering the Parisian pearl market. As it happened, this maneuver was perfectly timed. Values of pearl exports from the Gulf were poised to increase exponentially and enter their peak years, 1910–14.[33] To accomplish this feat, Victor traveled to Bahrain in 1909 and made an ostentatious display of wealth. He converted his money into half-franc silver coins and paraded the cash through Manama in sacks that filled the backs of fifty donkeys to portray his company as the best and biggest in order to secure the year's best pearls. The success of Rosenthal et Frères continued in subsequent years. Victor reportedly purchased pearls valued at 6.4 million rupees in 1911.[34] The *New York Times* reported that Léonard Rosenthal's fortune in 1914 amounted to at least 450 million francs (well over $1 billion in today's terms). Léonard decorated his house in Paris with paintings by Monet, Pissarro, and Guardi.[35] By the start of the First World War, he had begun diversifying his investments by expanding into Paris real estate. By 1928, Rosenthal's real estate profile included twenty-six residential-to-commercial conversions on the Champs-Élysées, which annually netted him over 30 million francs. Maurice de Waleffe estimated Rosenthal's net worth in 1928 at 300 million francs.[36]

DEBT, SLAVERY, AND DIVING IN THE GULF

In sharp contrast to the wealth made by leading European, Indian, and Gulf merchants, the typical pearl diver in the Gulf lived in poverty. The position of the slave diver was even worse than the free diver because slaves surrendered their earnings to their masters. For a typical crewmember, earnings for a season were insufficient to provide subsistence for the remainder of the year, but captains and financiers encouraged divers to accept additional wages on credit in anticipation of higher earnings the following year. Creditors offered cash and goods to divers at the beginning of the pearling season (in order to maintain their families while they were away diving), at the end of the season, and during the off season in order to keep the divers constantly indebted, ensuring they would return to dive the following year. Since nearly all divers were illiterate, they had little power to ensure the paper records of their debt were accurate. Divers also depended on their captains, who arranged the pearl sales in private, to report the proceeds accurately. There was, undoubtedly, much abuse, and many contemporary observers likened the system of indebtedness to slavery or serfdom.[37]

The life of the typical diver was harsh, but the situation was significantly worse for divers who were enslaved, whose earnings went to their masters. Masters sent their slaves diving each year, often with a representative from the master's tribe or locality to ensure the slaves did not abscond. Slaves' account books reflected not only their annual earnings and debts, but often their sale prices as well. While free divers brought bags of rice and cash home from the annual dive and could dream of one day possibly paying off their debts, slave divers had to surrender their earnings and were burdened with the additional cost of their purchase, making it impossible to ever earn their freedom on their own.

The perpetual indebtedness of free divers kept them diving year after year. In many ways the lives of free divers mirrored those of slaves. Like their enslaved counterparts, free divers could be purchased, in effect, from their previous employers by paying the employer the debt amount claimed against the diver.[38] One reason the starting amount in a diver's debt book was so high was that slave owners actually wrote the purchase price of a slave as the slave's starting debt. A forty-year-old enslaved diver named Jumah Kanaidish who appealed for manumission in Muscat in 1936 provided evidence that his master had been indebted to a merchant for 2,200 rupees and, being unable to pay, sold him to the merchant in lieu of cash. Jumah's new master wrote his purchase price in his diving book as his debt. Three years later, Jumah still "owed" his new master 2,216 rupees. Average prices for slave divers ranged by location, age, and skill level. Spotty evidence from 1910 to 1930 includes prices for divers as low as 600 rupees and as high as 2,000 rupees, with averages somewhere between 900 and 1500 rupees.[39]

Perpetual cycles of debt for both enslaved and free divers created relationships of dependency that required divers to work for their captains year after year and limited their mobility. Although many divers may not have been literally enslaved, they had to provide for themselves and their families in an economic environment that placed them in perpetual debt servitude. Enslaved divers were forced to hand over their earnings or advances to their masters, but the masters were, in theory, obligated to provide for their subsistence. The secretary to the political resident in the Persian Gulf noted in 1925 that "their earnings, in the majority of cases are not paid to them entirely and whatever out of same is given them is valued at very low prices. These two are the reasons for which diving slaves run away from their Nakhudas."[40]

During the peak of the Gulf pearl industry in the early twentieth century, some enslaved African pearl divers who brought consistent profits to their masters could negotiate certain aspects of their enslavement. They could expect, for example, their masters to arrange a marriage for them, conventionally around the age of twenty-five. A master's failure to meet this obligation could be justification for desertion. One twenty-five-year-old enslaved African diver in Bahrain, the epicenter of the Gulf pearl industry, ran away from his master for this reason in 1907. Faraj bin Sa'id was near the peak of his career as a diver and had grounds to expect his master to arrange a marriage for him. So, when his master failed to fulfill this obligation, he absconded to the British political agency offices in Bahrain to seek manumission. His master followed to beg his return, promising to provide him with a wife.[41] By contrast, however, many enslaved African divers experienced harsh treatment from their masters, including beatings if they refused to dive. For example, Mubarak bin Nar, an enslaved African pearl diver in Dubai who had been kidnapped from Zanzibar around 1895, was too ill to dive in the pearling season of 1930. His master, who was heavily indebted to some of Dubai's merchants on account of falling earnings, became desperate. He beat Mubarak for refusing to dive, even when he was lying in his sickbed.[42]

THE COLLAPSE OF THE GULF PEARL INDUSTRY

Expanding global markets for pearls in the nineteenth century spurred a dramatic increase in pearl production around the world, especially in the Gulf, and enslaved Africans were essential to the expansion of Gulf pearling. But as quickly as the pearl boom emerged, it also collapsed. The global forces that created new fortunes and drove demand for slave labor would also help destroy the slave-based pearling economy. In 1894, a Japanese noodle-shop owner named Kokichi Mikimoto perfected the ancient Chinese practice of producing cultured pearls by inserting a spherical piece of mother-of-pearl into oyster shells and inducing the oyster to produce a pearl. Mikimoto began producing cultured pearls from oysters grown in cages and received a ten-year patent on the process in 1896. His first crop of pearls was harvested in 1900 by a group of exclusively female employees. The same year, he invited Emperor Meiji's popular cousin, Prince Komatsu, to visit his pearl-growing operation, and when the prince attended the coronation of King Edward VII in 1902 he presented some of Mikimoto's pearls to the royal family, generating headlines in London and Paris. By 1905 Mikimoto had one million oysters planted in his pearl beds. His perfect cultured pearls began to enter the global pearl market in 1908 as global markets were nearing their peak.[43]

Using industrial assembly-line technology, Mikimoto constantly increased production. By 1913, he had perfected the cultured pearl to the point that it could not be distinguished from natural pearls, and he offered his product at a quarter of the market price. Applying the latest in assembly-line technology, he constantly increased production. He was known to say, "I want to live long enough to see the day when we have so many pearls we can sell necklaces for two dollars to every woman who can afford one and give them away free to every woman who can't."[44] By the end of the First World War, cultured pearls made inexpensive pearl necklaces available to working-class women in Western countries. By that time, women had entered the Western workplace in massive numbers and had come to embrace a leaner ideal figure, slimmer lines, and more masculine fashions. In the United States, the "flapper" look of the 1920s came to symbolize the growing independence of women. That look involved the simple black dress popularized by Coco Chanel, the bobbed hair popularized by dance sensation Irene Castle, and the long pearl necklace popular in wealthy circles for more than a quarter century, which was now available at a fraction of the cost. As pearl consumption rose, demand for more expensive natural pearls declined. The decline devastated the Gulf in addition to European dealers in natural ("oriental") pearls. Then the Great Depression was to provide the final blow to the Gulf pearl industry.[45]

Léonard Rosenthal called the Japanese cultured pearl his "worst enemy." He first encountered cultured pearls in 1913 and became concerned that they would devastate Paris merchants. In 1920, Rosenthal brought suit in French courts on behalf of the Chambre Syndicale des Négociants en Diamants et Pierres Fines. The case succeeded in forcing dealers in cultured pearls to distinguish their products as "cultured" rather than "natural" or "oriental" pearls, and the name remains today.[46] When the Nazis invaded Paris in 1940, Rosenthal fled to New York City.[47]

By the 1920s, cheap cultured pearls infiltrated the Gulf, where enterprising pearl merchants began to mix them with locally produced pearls in order to inflate their profits. Recognizing the potential disaster the trend posed for the local industry in the Gulf, the British Persian Gulf Administration worked quickly to stop the flood, encouraging local sheikhs to make examples of corrupt merchants who would knowingly sell cultured pearls as natural pearls. In July 1935, two merchants in Bahrain were sentenced to seven years in prison for selling cultured pearls, but the rules were difficult to enforce.[48] Although the Gulf pearl industry persevered through the rise of cultured pearls well into the 1920s, the value of pearl production declined steadily from 1919 to 1929. Then, with the onset of the global depression in

1929, the pearl industry collapsed. Revenues from pearl exports were reduced to below even mid-nineteenth-century levels, and they never recovered.[49]

THE FORCES OF GLOBALIZATION that helped create vast global markets for Gulf pearls also helped destroy them. Japanese industrial technology and mass marketing undercut the centuries-old pearling enterprise in the Gulf, which had grown dependent on imported slave labor. The collapse of eastern Arabia's export market for pearls contributed to the decline of the slave trade from East Africa. Other factors also contributed, including British anti-slave trade patrols in the Indian Ocean, Portuguese imperial expansion in Mozambique, and the rise of new sources of labor, particularly—after the First World War—from Baluchistan.[50] With the decline in demand for African labor, many enslaved Africans were freed only to be cast out to fend for themselves. Others continued to live in their masters' households and work independently. Some found work with the growing oil industry or in the Gulf's growing cities. Some of these individuals continued to hand over their incomes to their masters, while other former slaves were forced into dependency on their former masters. In 1936, the British political agent at Bahrain reported that one old man, a former slave, believed that his government-issued manumission certificate, which ostensibly attested to his freedom, was in fact a confirmation of his enslavement to his former master, who was obligated to feed him.[51] The expansion of the Gulf pearl industry had thrust many enslaved Africans into the hard life of the enslaved pearl diver, and the collapse of the industry forced enslaved Africans into equally precarious positions. The global economic forces that created fabulous wealth from pearls also helped to create poverty and enslavement. In this regard, Gulf pearling mirrors the experiences of many other regions around the world in the era of the pearl boom.

NOTES

1. William Gifford Palgrave, *Personal Narrative of a Year's Journey through Central and Eastern Arabia, 1862–63* (London: Macmillan, 1883), 387.

2. Matthew S. Hopper, *Slaves of One Master: Globalization and Slavery in Arabia in the Age of Empire* (New Haven, CT: Yale University Press, 2015), 23. This essay is derived from chapters 3 and 6 of this book.

3. George Frederick Kunz and Charles Hugh Stevenson, *The Book of the Pearl: The History, Art, Science, and Industry of the Queen of Gems* (New York: Century, 1908), 80; Léonard Rosenthal, *The Pearl Hunter: An Autobiography* (New York: Henry Schuman, 1952), 66.

4. John Gordon Lorimer, *Gazetteer of the Persian Gulf, Oman and Central Arabia*, vol. 1, *Historical*, part 2 (Calcutta: Superintendent Government Printing, 1915), 2228–29.

5. E. L. Durand, "Notes on the Pearl Fisheries of the Persian Gulf," Appendix A to Part 2, *Administration Report of the Persian Gulf Political Residency and Muscat Political Agency for the Year 1877–78* (Calcutta: Superintendent Government Printing, 1879), 34; Centre for Documentation and Research, Abu Dhabi, ND1/I.

6. Lorimer, *Gazetteer*, 2227.

7. Alan Villiers, *Sons of Sinbad* (New York: Charles Scribner's Sons, 1940), 393–96. See also Saif Marzooq al-Shamlan, *Pearling in the Arabian Gulf: A Kuwaiti Memoir*, trans. Peter Clark (London: London Centre of Arab Studies, 2000), 101–34.

8. Durand, "Notes on the Pearl Fisheries," 32. National Archives (NA), United Kingdom, formerly Public Record Office (PRO), Foreign Office (FO), 78/5108; Lorimer, *Gazetteer*, vol. 1, part 2, 2228–29; and Villiers, *Sons of Sinbad*, 375–78.

9. Charles Belgrave, *Personal Column* (London: Hutchinson, 1960), 43.

10. For an excellent discussion of the operation of the pearling industry, see Yacoub Yusuf Al-Hijji, *Kuwait and the Sea: A Brief Social and Economic History* (London: Arabian, 2010), 25–50.

11. Durand, "Notes on the Pearl Fisheries," 30; Rāshid Al-Zayānī, *Al-Ghaūs wa at-Tawāsha* (Manama, Bahrain: Al Ayam Publishing, 1998).

12. Hopper, *Slaves of One Master*, 89.

13. Durand, "Notes on the Pearl Fisheries," 32; NA, PRO, FO 78/5108. The term *sidi* (also rendered variously as *seedee* and *seedie*), originating in northern India, denoted people of African descent, many of whom were employed in maritime trades. In the wider Indian Ocean context, British officials applied the term to descendants of East Africans, enslaved and free, outside of East Africa. See Janet J. Ewald, "Crossers of the Sea: Slaves, Freedmen, and Other Migrants in the Northwestern Indian Ocean, c. 1750–1914," *American Historical Review* 105, no. 1 (February 2000): 83.

14. Lorimer, *Gazetteer*, 2228.

15. Paul W. Harrison, *The Arab at Home* (New York: Thomas Y. Crowell, 1924), 88.

16. Belgrave, *Personal Column*, 44.

17. Senior Naval Officer, Persian Gulf Division, HMS *Triad*, to Commander in Chief, East Indies Station, September 12, 1929, No. 27G/56/1, British Library (BL), IOR L/PS/12/4091.

18. "Notes on the Slave Trade by Wazir Thomas, August 1929," P. 7418/29, BL, IOR L/PS/12/4091.

19. Villiers, *Sons of Sinbad*, 375.

20. Fatwa of Khalīfa bin Yūsuf bin ʻAli al-Khamīrī, Qādhi of Abu Dhabi, dated 27th Rajab 1293, quoted in W. F. Preideaux to T. H. Thornton, August 31, 1876, enclosure no. 5 in H. W. Norman et al. to Marquis of Salisbury, Secretary of State for India, November 9, 1876, copied in Anita L. P. Burdett, ed., *Records of the Persian Gulf Pearl Fisheries, 1857–1962*, vol. 1 (London: Archive Editions, 1995), 97–110.

21. Ronald Codrai, *The Emirates of Yesteryear* (London: Stacey International, 2001), 50–65.

22. Summary of Declaration of Juma bin Fundi, Swahili, Native of Mfenesini District of Zanzibar, Age Unknown, recorded April 1931, BL, IOR R/15/1/209.

23. Statement of Bashir bin Farajullah, aged about 80 years, recorded at the Political Agency, Bahrain, in Political Agent, Bahrain, to Secretary to Political Resident in Persian Gulf, March 11, 1934, BL, IOR R/15/1/209.

24. Kevin Dawson, "Enslaved Swimmers and Divers in the Atlantic World," *Journal of American History* 92, no. 4 (March 2006): 1339.

25. Hopper, *Slaves of One Master*, 88.

26. See R. A. Donkin, *Beyond Price: Pearls and Pearl-Fishing: Origins to the Age of Discoveries* (Philadelphia: American Philosophical Society, 1998); and Joyce and Shellei Addison, *Pearls: Ornament and Obsession* (New York: Simon and Schuster, 1992), 81, 104. For an excellent discussion of this era of pearl consumption, see Molly A. Warsh, *American Baroque: Pearls and the Nature of Empire, 1492–1700* (Chapel Hill: University of North Carolina Press, 2018).

27. Ki Hackney and Diana Edkins, *People and Pearls: The Magic Endures* (New York: HarperCollins, 2000), 73; Michael Hancock, "The Stones in the Sword: Tennyson's Crown Jewels," *Victorian Poetry* 39, no. 1 (Spring 2001): 14; Otto Charles Thieme, "The Art of Dress in the Victorian and Edwardian Eras," *Journal of Decorative and Propaganda Arts* 10 (Autumn 1988): 21; Elizabeth Wilson, *Adorned in Dreams: Fashion and Modernity*, rev. ed. (New Brunswick, NJ: Rutgers University Press, 2003), 32; Oskar Fischel and Max von Boehn, *Modes and Manners of the Nineteenth Century as Represented in the Pictures and Engravings of the Time*, vol. 4 (London: J. M. Dent and Sons, 1927), 80–174.

28. Thieme, "The Art of Dress," 21; Hackney and Edkins, *People and Pearls*, 73; Barbara Worsley-Gough, *Fashion in London* (London: Allan Wingate, 1952), 14–17.

29. Hackney and Edkins, *People and Pearls*, 68.

30. Consuelo Vanderbilt Balsan, *The Glitter and the Gold* (New York: Harper, 1952); Amanda Mackenzie Stuart, *Consuelo and Alva: Love and Power in the Gilded Age* (London: HarperCollins, 2005).

31. Hopper, *Slaves of One Master*, 91–96.

32. Rosenthal, *The Pearl Hunter*, 21–60.

33. Léonard Rosenthal, *The Pearl and I: The Diary of an Ex-Millionaire* (New York: Vantage, 1955), 112–15; Rosenthal, *The Pearl Hunter*, 66–67.

34. D. L. R. Lorimer, "Report on the Trade of the Bahrain Islands Together with Statements of Imports, Exports and Shipping Returns for the Year 1910–11," in *Persian Gulf Trade Reports 1905–1940*, vol. 5, ed. Penelope Tuson (Cambridge: Cambridge University Press, 1987), 3.

35. Hopper, *Slaves of One Master*, 95.

36. Rosenthal, *The Pearl Hunter*, 163–70; Maurice de Waleffe, *Quand Paris était un paradis: Mémoires 1900–1939* (Paris: Denoël, 1947).

37. Villiers, *Sons of Sinbad*, 376–78.

38. Statement of Account Showing the Debts of Ismail bin Sanqah to Rashid bin Abdullah, May 26, 1924, BL, IOR R/15/1/208.

39. Case of Jumah bin Sanqur, Known as Jumah Kanaidish, Aged 40 Years, October 27, 1936, BL, IOR R/15/1/219: Hopper, *Slaves of One Master*, 103.

40. Secretary to PRPG Bushire, September 27, 1925, BL, IOR R/15/1/208.

41. Hopper, *Slaves of One Master*, 105–6.

42. Hopper, 121.

43. Robert Eunson, *The Pearl King: The Story of the Fabulous Mikimoto* (Tokyo: Charles E. Tuttle, 1965).

44. Eunson, 23–24.

45. Hopper, *Slaves of One Master*, 191–96.

46. Micheline Cariño, "The Cultured Pearl Polemic," *World Aquaculture* 27, no. 1 (1996): 42–44; Micheline Cariño, "The Great Debate: The Cultured Pearl Polemic," *Pearl Oyster Information Bulletin* 10 (August 1997: 49–51; Rosenthal, *The Pearl and I*, 115–17.

47. Rosenthal, *The Pearl Hunter*, 179–93; "Leonard Rosenthal Dies at 83: Authority and Dealer in Pearls," *New York Times*, July 18, 1955.

48. Acting Political Agent, Bahrain, to Political Dept., Government of India, July 25, 1935, BL, IOR R/15/2/346; *Police v. Khalil Ibrahim al-Bakr (Cheating, importing, selling, and being in possession of cultured pearls)*, case no. 398, October 8, 1933, BL, IOR R/15/3/7012.

49. Sarah Abrevaya Stein, *Plumes: Ostrich Feathers, Jews, and a Lost World of Global Commerce* (New Haven, CT: Yale University Press, 2008), 23–26.

50. Matthew S. Hopper, "East Africa and the End of the Indian Ocean Slave Trade," *Journal of African Development* 13, no. 1 (2011): 27–54.

51. Political Agent, Bahrain, to Political Resident, Persian Gulf, January 16, 1936, BL, IOR R/15/1/226.

NINE

Torres Strait in the Moluccas
The Transformation of Pearling in the Residency of Ambon, Netherlands Indies, 1890s–1942

STEVE MULLINS

FIFTY YEARS OF AUSTRALIAN pearling in the Aru Islands, in what was once the Residency of Ambon, now the Indonesian province of Maluku, came to an end on July 30, 1942, when a platoon of Japanese marines from the submarine chaser *Fukei Maru* disembarked at Dobo, the small port in the west of the archipelago that had been the pearlers' base. A Catalina flying boat sent to rescue American oilmen fleeing Netherlands New Guinea already had taken away most of the European civilians, arriving in Darwin the day before 242 Japanese aircraft attacked that port. About eighty Japanese deep-sea pearl-shell divers and their families also had fled Dobo, shuttled off by the *Arafura Maru II* to Palau-based Japanese pearling vessels that worked the Arafura Sea. The few Australians who had remained behind to secure their property left by boat at the last moment for Merauke on the south coast of New Guinea, and from there to Thursday Island in Torres Strait, Queensland. Although a small detachment of KNIL troops (Koninklijk Nederlands Indisch Leger, or Royal Netherlands East Indies Army) had been sent to defend Dobo, the town was taken quickly without resistance.[1]

Notwithstanding its dramatic exit, Australian pearling in the Aru Islands had all but petered out by the start of the Pacific War. Carl Monsted and Harry Jessup were the only Australians still active, and it's unlikely their business would have survived another year, even had the war not intervened.[2] Most of their twenty or so pearling luggers were laid up, unable to compete against the modern, larger, Palau-based Japanese boats that were flooding the world market with pearl shell and driving prices down.[3] Indeed, the Australian industry itself was in deep crisis because of record low prices caused by overproduction and competition from cheaper substitutes for mother-of-pearl.[4] Nevertheless, despite the ignominious end, Australian pearlers, especially those from Torres Strait, had had a profound influence on the industry in the Residency of Ambon.

This chapter describes the expansion of Australian industrial pearling to the Aru Islands, the location of the most productive grounds in the Netherlands Indies. It focuses on the determined incursions of 1893–94 and the 1905 relocation of Australia's largest pearling syndicate from Thursday Island to Dobo. It explores how the arrival of Australian fleets altered the regulation and management of pearling in the Residency of Ambon, assesses its influence on the day-to-day working arrangements of regional and indigenous pearling, and reflects on how it changed local and regional power relations against a backdrop of shifts in the larger framework of Netherlands Indies policy. It also identifies commonalities and contrasts that bring into sharper focus issues that affected the management of pearling in Torres Strait, the northwest of Western Australia, and other pearling regions of the Indian Ocean World.

As Martínez and Vickers explain, after commercial pearling commenced on Australia's northern coasts in the late 1860s, a pearling zone developed that encompassed nearby Indonesian islands. Some of these islands were a source of labor for the Australian industry, which relied on a multicultural workforce drawn from across the Indo-Pacific. Others, such as the Aru Islands, were themselves important pearling regions that Australians eventually would exploit.[5] John G. Butcher, in his landmark history of fishing in Southeast Asia, explains this Australian expansion in terms of the application of new technologies to old grounds, a key process driving nineteenth-century fishing into new territory and ecological strata.[6] He identifies the adoption in the 1870s of the full-dress (hard hat) deep diving suit in Torres Strait as a pivotal moment, but technical innovation on the factory floor in Europe, North America, and Japan was just as important.[7] In this pearling zone the principal product was mother-of-pearl from *Pinctada maxima*, the largest and most valuable species of pearl oyster, used mainly in the manufacture of buttons. Thus, the invention of sophisticated industrial sewing machines in the 1850s, in particular ones capable of stitching buttonholes, was decisive, as were improvements to button-making machinery, from pedal-driven cutters and grinders to the power-driven automatic facing and drilling machines that came into use at the turn of the century.[8] In Australian pearling, industrialization both increased production and stimulated demand, and was a powerful force propelling expansion across colonial maritime boundaries. As we shall see, innovation in on-the-water management practices also was a significant driver.

PREINDUSTRIAL PEARLING IN THE ARU ISLANDS

The Aru archipelago is an ancient pearling region of the Indian Ocean World. On its west coast, where Dobo is located, the sea drops precipitously to great depths, but in the east, the backshore, or *achterwal* in Dutch, a maze of small islands, shoals, and reefs skirt the coast, creating the perfect environment for *Pinctada maxima*. For centuries, indigenous Aruese gathered and traded it, along with the pearls it occasionally produced, to merchants from across the Indies who visited Dobo on the annual monsoon. The Verenigde Oostindische Compagnie (VOC) probably instigated this trade in the late seventeenth century, and when it left during the Napoleonic Wars exports declined, perhaps also because of an increasing demand for trepang (bêche-de-mer), which could be more easily collected in shallow water.[9] There was a revival in the 1850s, stimulated by the growth of Singapore and the declaration of Makassar, Ambon, and Bandaneira as free ports.[10] The English naturalist Alfred Russel Wallace, who was in the Aru Islands for five months in 1857, listed mother-of-pearl as one of the archipelago's principal products, making its way to international markets mostly through Makassar.[11] In 1859, about 200 tons were exported, but this had dropped to an annual 90 to 100 tons by 1890.[12]

The Netherlands Indies government took little direct interest in pearling and there were no ordinances specifically designed to regulate it. It mostly occurred in the "self-governing realms," where local sultans exercised exclusive rights over marine resources.[13] Also, after the demise of the VOC, inter-island trade in forest and marine products was left largely to Indonesians and "foreign Orientals," mainly ethnic Chinese and Arabs (Hadrami). Although the Aru Islands were not part of a "self-governing realm," they were remote from Ambon, the regional capital. Apart from being included in annual rounds of inspection, until the 1880s the inhabitants were left largely to themselves. As Wallace observed, while Dobo acknowledged Ambon's authority, the place was "without the shadow of a government.... Trade is the magic that keeps all at peace, and unites these discordant elements into a well behaved community."[14]

The Australian natural history collector John Cockerell provides a rare glimpse of how Dobo's atomized power relations worked. On arriving off the town in his small schooner in April 1872, he was summoned ashore and interrogated by about fifty of the leading men. "magistrates of Dobbo [sic], captains of the various vessels, supercargoes, Chinese merchants and Macassar traders." They asked him to mark on a map his schooner's track and each day's run. About a dozen merchants spent an hour going over his boat, and he was invited to dine with three Ambonese schoolteachers, who were "much respected by the people of Aru." Cockerell was only free to go about his business when enough prominent men were satisfied about how he got there, where he came from, what he intended to do, where he intended to go, and when he planned to leave.[15]

On the achterwal, indigenous, animistic Aruese exercised communal rights over the pearl-shell beds adjacent to their coastal villages, but some were claimed by west-coast *rajas* who allowed local villagers to exploit them in return for royalties. The raja were Muslim descendants of the seventeenth-century Bandanese diaspora (post-1621) who initially drew their authority over indigenous Aruese from the VOC, and then had it reinforced in the nineteenth century by Ambon. There were four rajas: of Oedjir (Ujir), Wamar, Wokam, and Maikor. Their regions radiated out from Dobo and had been conduits for trade in forest and marine products since VOC times.[16] The achterwal was exposed during the southeast monsoon, when the sea became too boisterous for pearling.

In this season Dobo was almost deserted, but it sprang to life again when traders arrived at the commencement of the northwest monsoon. After making a small payment to the raja of Wamar for squatting rights, they erected temporary stores and negotiated terms and advances with Aruese pearl-shell skin divers. Once these were settled, a sequence of elaborate *adat* rituals were performed in the achterwal villages before divers set out for the pearling grounds.

The anthropologist Patricia Spyer has explained how these rituals were connected to webs of debt that tied divers to traders. Before a season commenced, divers needed to propitiate sea wives, "seductive and dangerous undersea female spirits" who demanded offerings, usually in the form of china plates, which had to be obtained from the traders' stores on credit and paid for in pearl shell.[17] These entrenched asymmetrical trade relations were the source of considerable resentment that occasionally erupted into violence against traders, which sometimes escalated into insurrection against the Dutch, although the millenarian character of these suggest that the root causes went even deeper. Also, violence was exacerbated by the large volumes of arak that were a feature of Aru Islands trade. Nevertheless, Aruese divers continued putting to sea in their specialized beamy, planked, wind-powered craft in a pattern of pearling uninterrupted until the 1890s. By then, however, trade was passing more directly to Makassar (instead of through the wider Bandanese diaspora), Chinese and Buginese merchants had established permanent stores at Dobo, and their agents resided in the achterwal villages themselves.[18]

Australian industrial pearling reached the Aru Islands in the 1880s, but Australians employing skin divers were there earlier. The 32-ton schooner *Jessie* arrived in July 1872, just a few years after commercial pearling commenced on the Australian coast. It was the wrong time of year, the Aruese could not be persuaded to engage as divers, and the *Jessie* left without raising a single pearl oyster.[19] In 1880 and 1881, James Burns and Adam Forsyth, both subsequently directors of the large Australian trading firm Burns Philp & Co., dispatched the 42-ton schooner *Clara Crawford*. It was warned off by the Dutch and the venture collapsed.[20] Following this, Ambon appointed *posthouders*, the most junior rank of colonial field officer, to Dobo and the village of Gomo Gomo on the achterwal.[21] In addition, it closed Dobo and Tual (capital of the nearby Kei Islands) to general trade; indeed, to foreign vessels altogether, except in distress.[22] Although the Treaty of Paris (1784) guaranteed freedom of navigation in the Netherlands Indies, and the Treaty of London (1824) explicitly gave British merchants the right to trade in the Moluccas, the Dutch continued to regard commercial competition in the region as a strategic threat.[23] The most significant consequence of these early pearling incursions was, therefore, to draw colonial government more closely into the Aru Islands.

Australian pearlers continued trying to penetrate the Aru Islands, only to be turned away by the Dutch authorities. But excluding foreigners from the pearling grounds depended mainly on denying them access to the amenities of the port of Dobo, and that stratagem began to unravel in 1893 with the arrival of Thomas Haynes's Pearling and Trading Co. from Western Australia. It employed full-dress helmet divers, but, more significantly, deployed floating stations. This was a mode of production in which a schooner of about 100 tons served as tender to a fleet of pearling luggers, a uniquely Australian type of vessel, at this time varying in burden from about 10 to 15 tons.[24] The key to the system's profitability was that it enabled owners to secure all the pearls divers brought to the surface, thereby increasing earnings by as much as 12 percent. The schooner anchored at a promising spot, often out of sight of land, and the pearling luggers, about twelve to make the system viable, took the big boat as their mark. Each morning a reserve lugger or skiff would do the rounds, collecting the previous day's catch of live oysters, which were then opened on the schooner under management's watchful eye.[25]

The floating station system was first developed by Torres Strait pearlers to facilitate their relocation to newly discovered deepwater beds in the northwest of Western Australia in 1885–86, and, while pearling from shore continued, by the 1890s schooner-based fleets were generally regarded as the most efficient way of working. They enabled the grounds to be picked over systematically and significantly reduced downtime. As the live pearl-shell oysters were collected from the luggers, stores were dropped off, faulty gear retrieved for repair on the schooner, and men were relieved as needs be, thus keeping divers at work and intensifying the fishing effort. Almost unlimited mobility was an obvious advantage, as well as being able to operate well off shore, outside the three-mile limit, to avoid excise duties, royalties, and taxes. In Australia, this practice posed a direct challenge to colonial authority, and Queensland and Western Australia responded by extending their territorial jurisdiction.

In Queensland, legal doubts about jurisdiction over Torres Strait waters were resolved in January 1888, when the Federal Council of Australasia passed the Queensland Pearl Shell and Bêche-de-Mer Fisheries (Extra-Territorial) Act, Australia's first piece of federal legislation. Western Australia followed in 1889, putting a similar act through the Federal Council that extended the colony's jurisdiction over fisheries hundreds of miles into the Indian Ocean.[26]

THE ARRIVAL OF AUSTRALIAN FLOATING STATIONS

The Pearling and Trading Co.'s venture to the Aru Islands was a determined and well-prepared affair. It consisted of two floating stations, the first based on the schooner *Mavis*, and the second on the schooner *Flowerdale*. The firm was heavily capitalized (£50,000) and most of its shareholders were City of London merchants. The director, Thomas Haynes, had been a leading figure in an 1887–89 floating station tax revolt in Western Australia, and although the passing of the extraterritorial act put him on the losing side of that argument, his role in the controversy had earned him an international reputation as an expert on the law of the sea.[27] Anticipating Dutch obstruction, he instructed his fleet managers to work outside the three-mile limit, but not to give way if the Dutch tried to warn them off pearling grounds that lay beyond that limit. He wrote to the British Foreign Office requesting it take precautions in case his boats were interfered with on the high seas, and when the inevitable occurred, he pressed the foreign secretary to intercede on his firm's behalf.[28]

There was a dramatic standoff in the waters off the Aru Islands, as Batavia dispatched HNLMS *Sumatra*, HNLMS *Tromp*, and HNLMS *Pontianak* to patrol the pearling grounds. Diplomatic notes were exchanged between London and The Hague, the British sought assurances that the Australians would not be fired upon, and the Dutch colonial navy kept up a close surveillance. Despite the urging of Ambon, Vice Admiral J. A. Roëll refused to permit his captains to use force against foreign vessels outside the three-mile limit. Instead, he recommended legislation specifically prohibiting foreigners from gathering marine products in Dutch waters, and a diplomatic effort to persuade the British to pressure the Australians to abide by the new regulations. He also suggested a hydrographic survey to establish the three-mile limit exactly.[29] For the British, in June 1894, HMS *Lizard* of the Imperial Gunboat Flotilla was sent from Sydney to the Residency of Ambon to report on the confrontation, and its commander, Lt. Com. Lionel Hancock, concluded that it had been caused by the lack of clear regulations. He wrote that "on the arrival of the Pearling & Trading Company's fleet at the Aru Islands, pearl fishing, except in a very small way by naked divers, was unknown in the Netherlands Indies & consequently that there were no laws & the Dutch officials had no instructions on the subject." He could now add that a new pearling ordinance had been proclaimed, and he forwarded a copy to the Admiralty.[30]

Ordinance no. 261 of 1893 (October 7) left little room for misunderstanding. It outlawed anyone but Indonesians collecting pearl shell or trepang in Dutch territorial waters without written permission from the governor general. Infringement would result in fines of between ƒ10 and ƒ1,000 (£83) and/or imprisonment for between six days and two years.[31] For non-Europeans—that is, practically all Australian pearling lugger skippers—the sentence would be served on a work gang. Product illegally gathered was subject to confiscation, as was the equipment used to commit the offence; indeed, the vessel itself might be forfeited to cover fines and legal costs. As in Australia, the most productive pearl-shell beds in the Aru Islands lay beyond the three-mile limit. Queensland and Western Australia were able to extend their territorial jurisdiction to encompass regional fisheries because the legislation applied only to British-registered vessels. For the Dutch, exercising jurisdiction over British vessels in international waters was out of the question. But a workable solution to the problem was found. Even floating stations had to occasionally send boats to shore for wood and water. Article Three of the ordinance gave authorities the power to search vessels in Dutch waters for pearl shell and trepang, and if those products or the equipment to gather them were found, an offence was deemed to have been committed unless it could be proved otherwise. Proving a negative was difficult, and the penalties were so severe it would be foolhardy to risk even the possibility of infringement.[32]

THE DUTCH REGULATORY RESPONSE TO INDUSTRIAL PEARLING

Ordinance no. 261 did not explicitly prohibit anyone from applying to go pearling, but, as the Pearling and Trading Co. and others discovered, permission was not granted to foreigners. Indeed, even Dutch nationals found it difficult to obtain. Thomas Haynes complained bitterly to

Whitehall about the new ordinance, and others, including the commodore of the Australia Station, Rear Admiral N. Bowden-Smith, and the premier of New South Wales, Sir George Dibbs, considered it a "very unfriendly" law.[33] But in 1886, Western Australia had enacted legislation excluding Chinese owners from the industry there, and in 1898 Queensland would make it illegal for foreigners to own or lease any boat licensed for pearling.[34] The Foreign Office requested a legal opinion, but ultimately would not object to an ordinance which, on the face of it, concerned matters entirely within Dutch jurisdiction.

The Aru Islands were thus effectively closed to Australian pearling, but Ordinance no. 261 already had had a transformative influence. There had been an experiment in industrial pearling in the late 1880s, when the Dutch firm De Bordes & Co. worked in the north of the archipelago using a diving bell, an antiquated and unsuitable technology, and that venture folded.[35] The first pearling permits after the 1893 ordinance went to the Rotterdam firm Blankert & Co., which had been in the Banda spice trade. It started with the small steamer *Enterprise* and a brand-new Fremantle-built pearling lugger called *Marina*, leased for six months from the Pearling and Trading Co. It had six full-dress diving suits, not all of them complete, and later purchased more Australian-built pearling luggers.[36] However, by 1898 Blankert & Co. was in financial trouble and sold out to the Banda Hadrami firm Baädilla Brothers & Co., headed by (Sjech) Sa'id bin 'Abdullah Baädilla. Baädilla Bros. had been pearling since the 1880s, employing Butonese crew and Bandanese skin divers, mainly around the Raja Ampat Islands.[37] The firm also had the rights for waters off Banda and Ternate, and after obtaining permission for the Aru Islands became the largest pearling enterprise in the Netherlands Indies.[38] Within a few years, Baädilla Bros. was operating a floating station based on the small 30-ton schooner *Reliance*, built in Singapore, with 22 boats, about half of them Australian-built pearling luggers. The divers were mostly Australia-trained Japanese and Filipinos working in full dress, and the rates of pay were similar to those pertaining in Torres Strait and the northwest.[39] To all appearances, the *Reliance* floating station was modelled on the Pearling and Trading Co. fleets that had caused such controversy in the region only a few years before.

Ordinance no. 261 gave the Netherlands Indies power over who could gather pearl oysters, but it did not regulate and manage the industry as did legislation in Queensland and Western Australia. Queensland passed its first pearling act in 1881, but the Pearl-Shell and Bêche-de-Mer Fishery Act Amendment Act of 1891 represented a watershed. Drawing on the research of fisheries scientist William Saville-Kent, it provided for closures to enable pearl-shell beds to replenish; imposed a minimum export shell size of six inches (15.24 cm); required that pearl dealers be licensed in an effort to prevent divers from selling illegally obtained pearls, which also discouraged divers from raising undersize oysters in the hope of finding pearls; and, most remarkably, allowed for a system of lease areas for the propagation of pearl shell, as in the table oyster industry. It also contained a number of industrial provisions to better regulate the payment of wages, restricted the availability of alcohol in the pearling fleets, and instituted half-yearly inspections of diving equipment.[40] The licensing of full-dress helmet divers had been introduced in 1881.

The Netherlands Indies adopted a hands-off approach to fisheries management more generally, deriving revenue from salt monopolies and by the simple expedient of an enterprise tax, which applied to all businesses. As Butcher points out, as late as 1905 a major government inquiry dismissed proposals to regulate fishing.[41] However, in 1901 the Netherlands adopted the Ethical Policy, which aimed to promote economic development to improve living standards in the Indies. In keeping with this developmental philosophy, and possibly because it had become apparent pearling's industrial age had arrived, Batavia proclaimed Ordinance no. 4 of 1902 (January 3). While, in the past, pearling had been conducted under a system of official permission (usually called concessions), with royalties often paid directly to traditional owners, this ordinance, applicable outside the self-governing realms, foreshadowed a system of exclusive government leases allocated over nominated, large-scale pearling regions.[42] An Ambon lease, covering a large portion of the residency, would include the Aru Islands.

Why Batavia adopted the lease model, which was so different from Queensland's boat licensing system and Western Australia's boat licensing and royalty payments to government, is difficult to say, but it probably was based on the one recently implemented by the British in the Mergui archipelago.[43] As in the Mergui archipelago, Ordinance no. 4 of 1902 introduced competitive leasing, the main advantage being simplicity and cost-effective administration. Rent was collected from the leaseholder, it was in the leaseholder's interest to prevent poaching, and it was relatively easy to maintain law and order on the pearling grounds. In a region were the number of pearling boats employed was likely to be moderate, a system of competitive leasing might also mean greater returns to treasury. Both the Mergui and Netherlands Indies regulations allowed lessees to legally sublet and included the trepang fishery. Also, neither jurisdiction required royalty payments to government or the licensing of full-dress helmet divers.

On the other hand, in stark contrast to Australian legislation, both Ordinance no. 261 of 1893 and Ordinance no. 4 of 1902 recognized an indigenous right to collect pearl shell. Some Aruese villages claimed ownership of pearl-shell beds lying beyond the three-mile limit, but in 1886 Batavia had ruled otherwise, and even within territorial waters the indigenous right was constrained by the absolute right of the state over all resources.[44] De Bordes & Co., the first government-sanctioned non-indigenous pearler in the Aru Islands, paid a royalty of ƒ750 a year to the Raja of Oedjir (Ujir).[45] The Pearling and Trading Co., even while pearling in defiance of the government, paid royalties to a west-coast raja and, in defiance of the raja, to local *orang kaya*. The resident (governor) of Ambon was instructed to ensure this never happened again, because only the state could cede the right to pearling.[46] Nevertheless, in the spirit of the Ethical Policy, Ordinance no. 4 of 1902 went a step further than Ordinance no. 261 with respect to indigenous rights. Article two stipulated that in territorial waters less than five fathoms deep, Aruese had an exclusive right to gather pearl shell and trepang, and that right was inalienable.[47]

Ordinance no. 4 laid the groundwork for the new leasing system, including who was entitled to apply. Companies registered by foreigners in the Netherlands Indies were explicitly included, with the proviso that senior representatives reside in the lease region. This opened the way for Australian pearlers, although it would be three years before the final regulations were proclaimed. Responsibility for the allocation and administration of leases was shared between the regional authority and the new Department of Agriculture, another outcome of the Ethical Policy, which was not inaugurated until January 1905.[48] While the department's predecessor institution, the Bogor Botanical Gardens, was a world-class research facility, its Visscherij-Station (marine research laboratory) did not open until 1904. Thus, when the pearling lease system commenced in 1905, the Netherlands Indies administration still lacked experience in fisheries management.

To enable pearling to continue while the new detailed pearling regulations were being formulated, Ordinance no. 4 contained transitional provisions. These allowed permits to be issued by regional authorities, in the case of the Aru Islands the resident of Ambon, giving exclusive rights to gather pearl shell in territorial waters more than five fathoms deep. The cost was ƒ37.50 a month for each diving device employed, paid half yearly in advance.[49] Under these temporary arrangements, therefore, it was impossible to obtain a permit unless equipped with modern deep-diving equipment, a clear indication that Batavia was now intent on promoting Australian-style industrial pearling.

THE CLARK COMBINATION ABANDONS TORRES STRAIT FOR THE ARU ISLANDS

Between the proclamation of Ordinance no. 4 of 1902 and Ordinance no. 263 of 1905, which set out the regulations in detail, a Torres Strait pearling syndicate known as the Clark Combination, led by Australia's most prominent pearler, James Clark, made preparations to apply for the Ambon lease. Clark is credited with having developed the floating station system, and Haynes's Pearling and Trading Co. *Mavis* fleet had been acquired from him. He also had been a significant player in the floating station tax revolt in Western Australia. The Clark Combination began to take shape in Torres Strait in 1891, and by 1904 Clark, his brother-in-law George Smith, Edwin Munro, Percy Outridge, and Reg Hockings were its senior partners. It was the largest Australian pearling operation in history, with two shore stations (Friday Island and Goode Island, both in Torres Strait) and six floating stations deploying about 115 pearling luggers. Clark, who from 1891 resided in Brisbane, was the entrepreneurial mind behind the Combination and its public face, but it was a loose confederation of family businesses, each based on the ownership of one or two floating stations, bound together by cross-investment, shared utilities, and agreed strategies on boat acquisition, working and labor hire arrangements, and the marketing of pearls and pearl shell.[50]

The Combination's reasons for abandoning Torres Strait have been addressed elsewhere, with most writers pointing to resource depletion.[51]

There were other significant drivers, however. Clark initiated a first, preliminary Aru Islands venture, the Netherlands India Pearling Co., in 1903. For the previous few years, pearl-shell production in Torres Strait had been steady, at 867 tons in 1901, 910 tons in 1902, and 908 tons in 1903.[52] But since 1901 it had become harder for the Combination to source labor because of stringent immigration controls imposed by the first Commonwealth of Australia government, as it began to implement what became known as the White Australia policy. At the same time, there was intense competition from syndicates of Japanese nationals already residing in Torres Strait, despite the stringent prohibitions contained in Queensland's 1898 pearling act against the leasing or sale of pearling luggers to foreigners: "dummying" was commonly used to evade the act.[53] Also, Clark and his partners had become deeply resentful about the anti-monopoly rhetoric that the labor movement used against them both in parliament and in the press, and had good reason to be apprehensive that the federal government, under pressure from the burgeoning Labor Party, would restructure pearling in ways distinctly unfavorable to their way of working. As Butcher observed, the transformation of the state had a "profound influence on fishing," but it probably was the sensational May 1903 spike in the London price of pearl shell that finally convinced Clark the Aru Islands were worth trying.[54]

Clark's Netherlands India Pearling Co. was a modest family affair. He transferred two small pearling luggers to it and had a Dutch national, a Mr. Bos, write to Ambon for permission to pearl in the Aru and Tanimbar Islands. Crews were signed on before the Dutch consul in Brisbane, and on the evening of May 12, 1903, Victor, his twenty-two-year old nephew, and Bos sailed for the Netherlands Indies.[55] Under the interim provisions of Ordinance no. 4 of 1902, Bos was eligible to apply for permits on behalf of the Netherlands India Pearling Co., but they were exclusive, and those for the Aru Islands already had been allocated to Baädilla Bros.[56] The application was turned down, but Victor commenced work regardless and both his vessels were seized. Out of his depth, he wired Brisbane for help and James Clark left for the Aru Islands to deal with the problem in person. He negotiated the release of the boats and paid Baädilla Bros. f1,000 (£83), the equivalent of the mandated fine for infringements against the 1902 ordinance. After giving a guarantee that the Netherlands India Pearling Co. would in future work outside the three-mile limit, he was granted permission to access the closed port of Dobo to refresh ship and transship cargo, without which the family venture was impracticable.[57]

Clark took careful note of what he saw in the Aru Islands. He traveled on to Makassar, opened a line of credit with prominent local merchants A. & C. Schmid, and purchased pearl shell from them for sale in London as a trial.[58] He then went to Batavia where he met with John Campbell MacColl, a businessman who specialized in introducing foreign firms to the Indies, and learned that the Baädilla Bros. permit would expire in May 1905, when the exclusive lease system was supposed to come into effect.[59] He probably also took advice from MacColl about engaging crew in the Indies, labor recruitment being a large part of his business.[60] Clark was nearly three months away, and when he returned to Brisbane in November 1903 the Aru venture was shaping as something more substantial. If he needed further convincing, a new Queensland Labor-Liberal coalition government lifted a short-lived moratorium on new pearling licenses in Torres Strait, and in 1904 an additional seventy-seven boats drove the average take per boat down to a little over two tons, which was not sustainable.[61] With May 1905 in mind, Clark ramped up the family investment to six boats, conferred with his Combination partners, and then instructed MacColl to register a company in the Netherlands Indies. On November 22, 1904, the Celebes Trading Co. (CTC) came into being, with Clark and Edwin Munro as principals and nominal capital of ƒ750,000 (£62,500).[62]

Ordinance no. 263, gazetted on April 22, 1905, contained the regulations that would govern pearling in the Netherlands Indies. Because it was principally concerned with the management of leases, most of its twenty-seven clauses dealt with contract law: how and by whom the lease plots would be defined; how the leases would be issued; who was eligible to apply and how eligibility would be established; what would happen on the death of a lessee; in what circumstances might the lease be inherited or sold; and procedures governing the management of disputes or appeals arising from the lease allocation process. Beyond these procedural issues, the regulations protected indigenous rights within the five-fathom zone, as foreshadowed in 1902, and required the Ambon lessee to negotiate with traditional owners the distribution of a compensation payment and obtain their consent in writing to work waters outside the five-fathom zone. As also foreshadowed in 1902, it allowed subletting without further application, and set a minimum pearl-shell oyster weight of one *kati* (600 gm), although it did not specify whether this referred to live weight including flesh, the weight of two halves of an oyster, or just one piece. It also established the lessee's right to build facilities ashore.[63]

Ordinance no. 263 was supplemented by Ordinance no. 262 gazetted on the same day. It allowed bona fide prospective lessees to prospect in a lease area in order to evaluate the resource and calculate a bid.[64] Some ten months before, however, in November 1904, Clark had written to Jim Mackenzie, his fleet manager in Torres Strait, to begin preparations to send the Combination's best floating stations, based on the *Alice*, *Wanetta*, and *Ariel*, to the Aru Islands.[65] The *Alice* and nineteen pearling luggers departed on April 1, 1905, weeks before Ordinances no. 262 and no. 263 had been proclaimed.[66] Furthermore, the *Alice* fleet was accompanied by a 165-ton steamer, *Pretoria*, which had been purchased as tender to the Celebes Trading Co. While Clark knew that the Baädilla Bros. permits were due to lapse in May 1905, his apparent foreknowledge of the proclamations and confidence about acquiring the Ambon lease does raise questions about the integrity of the lease-granting process.

Clark relied on MacColl in Batavia for insights into the Indies administration, and the latter seemed to have his finger on the pulse. He lobbied on CTC's behalf and probably entertained Dutch officials. In October 1904, Clark extended MacColl a £2,000 line of credit to "fix the matter up," as he put it, which seems more than was required to register CTC and the boats and make arrangements for the hire of labor.[67] Furthermore, since 1904 Victor Clark had been engaging crew at Bandaneira, the capital of the Banda Islands, and it is unlikely that could proceed without Baädilla Bros. sanction.[68] Banda sailors were Muslims bound to their usual employers by social obligations, if nothing else, and (Sjech) Sa'id bin 'Abdullah Baädilla was the Dutch-appointed Kapitein en Hoofd der Arabieren, that is, leader of the Banda Arab community. While there is no direct evidence, CTC and Baädilla Bros. might have reached a mutually beneficial understanding on the Ambon lease before it went to a sealed-bid auction in September 1905.

The Ambon lease auction was confidential and it is uncertain whether Baädilla Bros. participated. Certainly, the Dutch complained about a lack of competition. But if the Hadrami firm did participate, the odds were decidedly against it. Under the lease system, a company with 115 boats to deploy could easily outbid one with forty, because the larger company had the capacity to gather more than twice the tonnage from the lease. Nevertheless, while the highest bid won the lease provisionally, conditions had to be met before final allocation. The lessee and two guarantors had to demonstrate they were persons of substance and good standing, and that the business was likely to succeed. If judged on merit, these conditions posed no problem for CTC, with its wealthy directors who were well-connected in Queensland and plant that was second to none. The final decision was made on November 8, 1905, when CTC was granted a three-year lease after a bid of ƒ85,300 (£7,100). It also was obliged to pay indigenous pearl-shell bed owners an additional ƒ25,000 (£2,080), despite being excluded from the five-fathom zone that was reserved for indigenous use. The total cost of the lease came to ƒ110,300 (£9,200), or about ƒ34,000 (£2,830) a year, and it was to be in effect from November 1, 1905, to December 31, 1908.[69]

Raising further doubts about the process, all the Combination's floating stations had arrived in the Residency of Ambon before the official decision on the lease was handed down. The voyage from Torres Strait to the Aru Islands took about a week. The *Wanetta* departed Thursday Island on August 31 with fourteen luggers, followed on September 20 by the *Sketty Belle* and *Ariel* with thirty-two luggers. The last to join CTC were the *Aladdin* and *Three Cheers* with twenty-five luggers, setting off on October 3, 1905.[70] By the end of the first season, CTC had six schooners and about a hundred luggers on the lease and was subletting to James's brother John and nephew Victor, who worked the 72-ton ketch *Ruby* and fourteen luggers, and to Baädilla Bros., which had two 35-ton schooners and thirty-five luggers, some of them purchased from CTC. CTC sublet on a pro rata basis, and Baädilla Bros. gave it access to its Kak Fak and Monokwari leases in the Residency of Ternate on the same terms.[71] There were altogether about 150 boats on the Aru Islands pearling grounds, a number that would never be exceeded.

DUTCH DISSATISFACTION WITH THE OPERATION OF THE AMBON LEASE

The arrival of fifteen hundred or so pearling workers at Dobo, as well as an influx of laborers, tradesmen, and hawkers from across the Indies, tested the capacity of the regional administration. A *contrôleur*,

Figure 9.1. The Sketty Belle fleet, Aru Islands, photographed by Ernest Naylor, ca. 1910. Mary E. Mohr, with permission.

the senior rank of regional official, had been appointed to the Aru Islands in 1904, and a police boat was put at his disposal.[72] It patrolled during the pearling season, watching for breaches of lease conditions, and assisted with the maintenance of order at Dobo during the long lay-up, when CTC crews mostly lived ashore.[73] In 1906, local police were reinforced by a sergeant, a corporal, and ten Bandanese soldiers.[74] Although somewhat chaotic, the town soon took on a prosperous look as boarding houses, galvanized iron Singapore-style "go-downs," and brothels sprang up. CTC erected its own offices and commodious bachelor quarters for managers, ships' officers, and clerks, and also built a small hospital that was open to all.

The two key officials administering the lease were the resident of Ambon, Baron A. J. Quarles de Quarles, and Dr. Melchior Treub, longtime director of the Bogor Botanical Gardens and first director of the Department of Agriculture.[75] Quarles was an experienced civil servant, although only recently appointed to Ambon, his first posting as resident. As a general principle, the Dutch held the view that trade drew remote regions into the colonial order and assisted in the maintenance of peace. Sjech Baädilla, for instance, had been honored with the Great

Gold Star for Loyalty and Merit and the Order of Orange-Nassau, not only for services to his own community, but also because his trading and pearling had promoted Dutch authority on the coast of New Guinea.[76] Quarles, in harmony with the Ethical Policy, understood that punitive expeditions alone would not bring order to remote regions. Local authorities needed to engage proactively to create the circumstances that attracted traders and the civilizing influence of commerce.[77] Thus, while he anticipated CTC would cause his regional government inconvenience in the short term, this would be outweighed by the commercial activity it would generate, at a time when the whole of the Indies was being squeezed to meet the cost of military campaigns.

Even so, it was not long before the Dutch were dissatisfied with the operation of the pearling lease. The Batavia and Makassar press reported CTC raking in huge profits, and merchants complained that its floating stations contributed next to nothing to local economies, just as merchants in Australia had done. A submission to the Commonwealth's Dashwood Inquiry into pearling (1901–2) described them as "moveable cities," impeding rather than encouraging settled communities, and therefore injurious to the state.[78] The Dutch authorities were also concerned about resource depletion and speculated that the Australians, with nothing to lose in the final season of their three-year lease, would overwork the pearling grounds. Quarles was instructed to explore ways in which a larger proportion of the yield of the Aru Islands might be returned to government, and Treub sent Pieter Nicolaas van Kampen, a young Visscherij-Station zoologist with a doctorate from the University of Amsterdam, to inspect and report on the workings of the pearling lease.[79]

RENEGOTIATING AND RETHINKING THE AMBON LEASE

While the Dutch were having serious misgivings, in October 1907, more than a year before the lease was due to lapse, CTC decided to seek a renewal, an option allowed under Ordinance no. 262 of 1905. It was motivated by a sense of urgency because it had become apparent Queensland was on the verge of reimposing a moratorium on new pearling boat licenses, which, in tandem with Commonwealth restrictions on the entry of additional indentured nonwhite pearling workers imposed immediately after the Combination left Torres Strait, would make it impossible for its fleets to return.[80] If the Dutch got wind of this, it could severely weaken CTC's bargaining position in any end-of-lease renegotiation. To formulate and submit the extension application, Clark's brother-in-law, George Smith, left Sydney for Ambon on November 7, 1907. He had fewer outside business commitments than either Clark or Munro, and a well-deserved reputation for being shrewd in the business of pearling. Smith arrived at Darwin by the Eastern & Australian steamer *Aldenham* on the 18th and then transferred to CTC's steamer *Pretoria* for the voyage across the Arafura Sea.[81]

Smith met with Baron Quarles in Ambon and requested an extension of the lease to the end of May 1909 on existing conditions, which was only five months, but time enough, he explained, to allow CTC to properly complete 1908–9, the last season of the lease.[82] This probably was a gambit to determine whether the Dutch were at all willing to grant a straightforward extension. Quarles, who shared Batavia's dissatisfaction with existing lease arrangements, informed Smith the government preferred renegotiation. The two men then met a number of times over the following weeks before Smith submitted a formal application for renewal on December 24, 1907.[83] On behalf of his partners and Baädilla Bros., which had agreed to be named, he offered a flat ƒ30,000 per year, inclusive of payments to traditional owners, which the administration should manage itself. He proposed a ten-year lease to dispel fears of overexploitation and addressed some minor issues, such as seeking greater government commitment to the protection of the leaseholder against competition outside the three-mile limit, the adoption of a five-inch minimum size rather than one kati, and the maintenance of existing favorable customs arrangements.[84]

Quarles, who had completely lost faith in the exclusive lease model of management, regarded CTC's offer as entirely inadequate. He was convinced the Australians were making excessive profits on annual pearl-shell production that he calculated at about 850 tons a year (he would not even try to guess the value of pearl production). He also had figures that demonstrated that CTC's contribution to the regional economy was negligible. Its floating stations bypassed local suppliers, from October 1905 to September 1906 importing direct from Britain goods worth ƒ69,132 (£5,760), from Singapore ƒ23,947 (£2,000), from Australia ƒ9,471 (£790), while spending only ƒ4,150 (£346) in the Indies. As a consequence, and because CTC pearl shell was exported directly out of the colony rather than through local firms, Quarles blamed it for a severe downturn in business at Dobo and Makassar.[85]

Just as the labor movement in Australia, both its industrial and political wings, employed anti-monopoly rhetoric against the Clark Combination, so did Quarles. In a June 1907 report to the governor general, he observed that private monopolists were intent on nothing but profit, without a thought for the welfare of the people. His strong preference now was for a fishery owned and operated by the state, but he had to concede that that was at present beyond the administration's capacity. He concluded that the best alternative was a system of individual boat licenses, much as existed in Australia, which would hand back the industry to small producers *and* benefit the local economy.[86] The idea certainly would not appeal to CTC, but Quarles thought that some floating station owners might break ranks with the syndicate to participate. Whatever the case, his confidence in the good sense of an individual boat-license model and its potential economic benefits was such that he began to plan for a new town on Aru's remote achterwal.[87]

Even before arriving in Ambon, Smith was aware the Dutch were contemplating a boat licensing system, and in notes accompanying the Christmas Eve application he was emphatic that, if it were introduced, CTC would quit the Indies altogether.[88] He wrote that he and his partners refused to compete against the Japanese syndicates that inevitably would proliferate under such a system, working on a share basis, paying no wages, carrying few costs, and poaching CTC's best-trained Japanese divers, just as they had done in Australia. In the same vein, he requested that if the lease were renewed CTC's contract with traditional owners should be maintained. It restricted the Aruese to traditional skin diving, not because CTC anticipated villagers would buy pump boats and take up full-dress helmet diving, but to prevent Japanese lugger skippers from using them as fronts in a version of the dummying so prevalent in Australia. In the context of the negotiations underway, this bringing of a likely influx of Japanese nationals so insistently to the government's attention proved to be Smith's masterstroke.[89]

On the day Smith submitted his application to Quarles, Australia's second prime minister, Alfred Deakin, ignoring Colonial Office protocol, sounded out the American consul in Sydney directly about the possibility of President Teddy Roosevelt's Great White Fleet visiting Australian ports. Deakin's biographer, Judith Brett, explains his audacity by reference to Australia's deepening concern about the rise of Japanese naval power, observing that "race was in the air and in the waters of the Pacific."[90] Dutch colonials were just as anxious, and while Quarles might accuse Smith of self-serving exaggeration about the flood of Japanese maritime workers to his residency, it was undeniable that, if pearling was thrown open to individual license holders, the number of Japanese nationals would increase markedly.[91] Quarles certainly was not xenophobic, but Batavia had become seriously concerned about the illegal entry of Japanese mariners, and in December 1907 regional authorities were instructed to do all in their power to stem the flow. Quarles had to concede that this directive put individual boat licensing out of the question.[92]

Quarles and Treub now had to decide whether to renegotiate the existing lease or again put it to a sealed-bid auction. Quarles favored throwing the lease open to auction. Unlike Quarles, however, Treub had always favored the straightforward, administratively efficient lease model of management, although he was alert to the political sensitivities. He knew that Quarles had championed boat licensing because it might restore Aru Islands pearling to Indies hands, a policy that had considerable support both within and outside government. Now that this option was off the table, Treub, consistently inclined toward continuity and administrative convenience, favored renegotiation with CTC because, as Quarles himself had put it in correspondence to the governor general, it was a high-quality, well-managed, and accommodating company that had fully complied with its obligations under the lease.[93]

Ultimately, it came down to the adequacy of the CTC offer. Just as Quarles had done, Treub tried in person to persuade Smith to increase his bid, but the Australian insisted that although CTC's production seemed large, costs were heavy. He agreed to submit the company's financial accounts for scrutiny, a task ultimately undertaken by the auditor-general of the Netherlands Indies himself, but even after adjustments had been made to the underlying assumptions, it was difficult to demonstrate unequivocally that CTC's profits were excessive.[94] To resolve the impasse, Treub conceded there might be merit in accepting an offer from a "genuine" Indies firm, and agreed that the lease be put to auction again.[95] Quarles then embarked on a tour to solicit bids from likely Makassar and Banda merchant houses, including Baädilla Bros., solely or in combination, but while they all were enthusiastic to his face, none submitted formal written offers. They lacked the confidence to compete against CTC, and on August 12, 1908, the Australian-owned firm was granted the lease on its own terms for a period of ten years.[96]

One reason George Smith stubbornly refused to increase the Christmas Eve 1907 offer was that CTC's fleet managers predicted a decline in production. Even as negotiations proceeded, Reg Hockings secretively somehow managed to obtain permission from Queensland and the Commonwealth to return his *Wanetta* fleet to Torres Strait, which took some pressure off the resource. Clark, Smith, and Munro, who were wealthy and ready to retire from pearling, subsequently made numerous unsuccessful applications to also return their boats to Australia.[97]

However, it was not until the Great War threw the Australian industry into disarray that an opportunity arose. In 1915, Jim Mackenzie, James Clark's manager, negotiated a special arrangement with the Western Australia and Commonwealth governments, both anxious about unrest among hundreds of unemployed indentured nonwhite pearling workers left stranded by the war in the northwest, to relocate fifty Clark boats to Broome.[98] This left CTC largely in the hands of Munro and Smith, who owned about sixty pearling luggers. As predicted, production in the Aru Islands decreased, from about 850 tons a season to about 770 tons in 1909 and 380 tons in 1913. In 1917, a considerably reduced fleet raised only about eighty tons, but the take recovered to reach about 160 tons in 1918.[99]

Nevertheless, peace inspired optimism in the future of pearling, with a global backlog of unmet demand and a return to normal shipping. In this atmosphere, Munro and Smith sold CTC to Schmid & Jeandel of Makassar, the successor firm to A. & C. Schmid. It negotiated a lease through to May 1924—which was a version of the boat license system that had been proposed by Baron Quarles—at a charge of ƒ240 (£20) per boat per year, for not less than twenty-five and no more than sixty boats, with exclusive right to the territorial waters beyond the five-fathom zone and no payment to traditional owners.[100] Schmid & Jeandel's pearling arm continued to operate under the Celebes Trading Co. name and was managed by Australians, most of them old CTC staff, including Vince Jessup, Bert Vidgen, William Field Porter, Chum Jardine, and Carl Monsted. In 1935, it still owned the schooner *Ariel*, fourteen motorized luggers, and eighteen smaller, engineless luggers known as the shallow-water fleet. The motorized boats worked deepwater beds discovered off Arnhem Land by the Palau-based Japanese pearlers, but until *Ariel* was lost in April 1936 the shallow water fleet went to the achterwal and operated as a floating station in much the same manner as CTC fleets had done thirty years before.[101]

THE 1930S were a difficult time for pearling everywhere. Sa'id bin 'Abdullah Baädilla was declared bankrupt in 1933 and Baädilla Bros. left the industry altogether soon afterwards.[102] In 1937, Schmid & Jeandel sublet the Aru Islands lease to Carl Monsted, his nephew Neils Preben Monsted, and Harry Jessup (Vince's nephew), who purchased CTC's boats. About six Japanese-owned pearling luggers, along with the occasional Darwin-based pearler, worked the Aru Islands grounds beyond the three-mile limit, and Dobo was a port of call for the Palau-based fleets, which was just enough economic activity to underpin the viability of the town. In such a remote region, colonial authority had always been constrained by the lack of capital and overstretched administrative resources, but the Dutch went on patrolling local waters, now by air as well as sea, to enforce territorial jurisdiction, preserve the integrity of the Aru Islands pearling lease, and restrict the five-fathom zone to indigenous use.

Achterwal villagers never did participate in Australian-style industrial pearling, even to work as crew. Rather, they continued to gather pearl shell in their waters to a rhythm of their own. In 1908, van Kampen reported that CTC's activities were unlikely to harm indigenous pearling.[103] However, the German zoologist Hugo Merton, who was in the Aru Islands at about the same time, observed that some achterwal Aruese had been forced to resort to farming because of pressure on the marine resources.[104] Whatever the case, in the 1930s indigenous production ranged between 150 and 160 tons a season, which more than equaled pre-1890s levels, and their pearl shell, known as "Native Aroe," was highly regarded for its quality.[105] While the CTC fleet was lost in the Pacific War, indigenous pearling persisted.[106] Dogged by recurring outbreaks of pearl-oyster disease and resorting to other sea products in poor seasons and depressed markets, villagers still relied on the income from pearl oysters when the anthropologist Patricia Spyer commenced her residence on the achterwal in 1984, although by then they were gathered live for the cultured pearl industry. Ancient adat rituals were still being performed, underwater "sea wives" still had to be appeased, and

Aruese pearl-shell divers and ethnic Chinese traders were still locked in cycles of debt. However, by then, both the resource and the lifestyle were seriously under threat.[107]

NOTES

1. Author interviews with Pam Ivey (Gold Coast, Queensland, November 10, 1993), Hans Kraal (Brisbane, Queensland, January 22, 1993), and Mores Larway (Dobo, Indonesia, June 12, 15, and 17, 1996). See also Silvano Vittorio Jung, "Wings beneath the Sea: The Aviation Archaeology of Catalina Flying Boats in Darwin Harbour, Northern Territory" (MA thesis, Charles Darwin University, 2001), 49–84.

2. Strictly speaking, Monsted was stateless at the start of the Pacific War. A Dane by birth, he became a naturalized Australian in 1918. In late 1937, he applied for Dutch nationality, but the process was interrupted by the war. Captured by the Japanese in January 1942, he spent four years in captivity. On returning to Australia in 1946, he learned that his naturalization had been revoked in 1938. Carl Anton Monsted file, A435, 1946/3284, National Australian Archives (NAA), Canberra.

3. "Aroe Islands News Items," *Northern Standard* (Darwin), April 25, 1939.

4. J. P. S. Bach, *The Pearling Industry of Australia: An Account of Its Social and Economic Development* (Canberra: Department of Commerce and Agriculture, Commonwealth of Australia, 1955), 180–95.

5. Julia Martínez and Adrian Vickers, *The Pearl Frontier: Indonesian Labor and Indigenous Encounters in Australia's Northern Trading Network* (Honolulu: University of Hawai'i Press, 2015).

6. John G. Butcher, *The Closing of the Frontier: A History of the Marine Fisheries of Southeast Asia, c. 1850–2000* (Leiden: KITLV Press, 2004), 73.

7. Butcher, 125.

8. Grace Rogers Cooper, *The Sewing Machine: Its Invention and Development* (Washington, DC: Smithsonian Institution Press, 1976), 58–62.

9. On the VOC, see *Encyclopaedie van Nederlandsch-Indië*, ed. Jozias Paulus (Leiden: E. J. Brill, 1917), 1:62. On the decline of exports, see D. H. Kolff, *Voyages of the Dutch Brig of War Dourga . . . 1825–1826*, trans. George Windsor Earl (London: James Madden, 1840), 178.

10. Law officers to Earl of Kimberley, March 28, 1894, FO 37/784, National Archives (NA), Kew.

11. Alfred Russel Wallace, *The Malay Archipelago* (1869; repr., Singapore: Graham Brash, 1983), 368.

12. Gerrit W. W. C. van Hoëvell, "De Aroe-eilanden, geographisch, ethnographisch en commercieel," *Tijdschrift van het Koninglijk Nederlandsch Aardrijkskundig Genootschap* 33 (1890), 86–87.

13. John G. Butcher, "Resink Revisited: A Note on the Territorial Waters of the Self-Governing Realms of the Netherlands Indies in the Late 1800s," *Bijdragen tot de taal-, land- en volkenkunde* 164, no. 1 (2008), 1–12.

14. Wallace, *The Malay Archipelago*, 336.

15. John T. Cockerell, "Visit to the Aru Islands: III," *Brisbane Courier*, February 16, 1874.

16. A. G. Weddik, "Report, Consideration and Advice by the Governor of Borneo Etc, Commissioner for the Moluccas, February 1, 1848," Peter Elder Collection, Charles Darwin University Library, Darwin.

17. See Patricia Spyer, "The Eroticism of Debt: Pearl Divers, Traders, and Sea Wives in the Aru Islands, Eastern Indonesia," *American Ethnologist* 24, no. 3 (August 1997): 515–38.

18. Van Hoëvell, "De Aroe-eilanden," 93.

19. J. W. Tyas, "'Pearling' Near the Australian Coast," *Queenslander* (Brisbane), March 22, 1873, March 29, 1873, and April 5, 1873.

20. James Burns to Robert Philp, January 31, 1882, Mrs. Haughton Jones typescript, N115/607, Burns Philp & Co. Papers, Noel Butlin Archives Centre, Australian National University, Canberra; Adam Forsyth to "Select Committee of Inquiry on the Costa Rica Packet Case," *Journal of the Legislative Council of New South Wales* 53, no. 3 (1894–95): 18.

21. Van Hoëvell, "De Aroe-eilanden," 11.

22. Lionel Hancock, "Report on Pearl Fishery in Dutch East Indies, July 1894," FO 37/784, NA.

23. Nicholas Tarling, *Anglo-Dutch Rivalry in the Malay World, 1780–1824* (St. Lucia: University of Queensland Press, 1962), 51–74, 133–78.

24. Initially, Australian pearling was carried on by skin divers in a nondescript variety of boats. By the late 1880s, a generic design began to emerge to facilitate the use of deep-diving technology. These were vessels of about ten meters with two lug-rigged masts. By the mid-1890s, the boats were larger (up to fifteen meters) gaff-rigged ketches. However, they continued to be called "pearling luggers."

25. Steve Mullins, "James Clark and the Celebes Trading Co.: Making an Australian Maritime Venture in the Netherlands East Indies," *The Great Circle: Journal of the Australian Association for Maritime History* 24, no. 2 (2002): 22–52.

26. *Debates of the Federal Council of Australasia*, January 27, 1886, 13; Queensland Pearl Shell and Bêche-de-Mer Fisheries (Extra-Territorial) Act of 1888; West Australian Pearl Shell and Bêche-de-Mer Fisheries (Extra-Territorial) Act of 1889.

27. Haynes self-published three tracts on territorial waters and fishery disputes over the next few years: *Legislation in Western Australia before Responsible Government* (1890), *International Fishery Disputes* (1891), and *Territorial Waters and Ocean Fishery Rights* (1893).

28. Steve Mullins, "Australian Pearl-Shellers in the Moluccas: Confrontation and Compromise on a Maritime Frontier," *The Great Circle: Journal of the Australian Association for Maritime History* 23, no. 2 (2001): 3–23.

29. J. A. Roëll to governor general, July 29, 1893, no. 9851, Ministerie van Koloniën, Netherlands Nationaal Archief, The Hague (NNA); Hancock, "Report on Pearl Fishery."

30. Hancock, "Report on Pearl Fishery."

31. In the period under consideration here, one Dutch guilder was worth about twelve British shillings.

32. Ordinance no. 261 of 1893 (October 5, 1893), Parelvisscherij: Strafbepalingen op het Visschen Zonder Vergunning naar Parelschelpen, Paarlemoerschelpen en Tripang in de Territoriale Wateren van Nederlandsch-Indië door Personen, niet Behoorende tot de Inheemsche Bevolking, in *Staatsblad van Nederlansch-Indië over het Jaar 1893* (Batavia: Landsdrukkerij, 1894).

33. N. Bowden-Smith, "Report of Investigation by HMS 'Lizard' into Alleged Irregular Proceedings in Pearl Fishery, with Revised Information on Dutch Indies, August 11, 1894," FO 37/784, NA; Premier Sir George Dibbs to the NSW agent general, London, May 14, 1894, FO 37/793, NA.

34. "Sharks Bay Pearl Shell Fishery Act of 1886," *Inquirer and Commercial News* (Perth), November 10, 1886; Pearl-Shell and Bêche-de-Mer Fishery Act Amendment Act of 1898 (Queensland).

35. Pieter Nicolaas van Kampen, *De paarl- en parelmoervisscherij langs de kusten der Aroe-eilanden* (Buitenzorg, Dutch East Indies: Departement van Landbouw, Drukkerij van het Departement, 1908), 1–2.

36. Hancock, "Report on Pearl Fishery."

37. Des Alwi, *Friends and Exiles: A Memoir of the Nutmeg Isles and the Indonesian Nationalist Movement*, ed. Barbara S. Harvey (Ithaca, NY: Southeast Asia Program, Cornell University, 2008). See also Clarence-Smith's chapter in this volume.

38. V. I. van de Wall, "Sjech Said bin Abdullah Baädilla: Een Arabier van beteekenis in de Groote Oost," *Nederlandsch-Indië Oud & Nieuw* 15 (1930–31), 347–52.

39. D. K. Holden, "Northern Territory," *Bacchus Marsh Express* (Victoria), November 12, 1904.

40. Pearl-Shell and Bêche-de-Mer Fishery Act Amendment Act of 1891 (55 Vic. no. 29).

41. Butcher, *Closing of the Frontier*, 98.

42. Ordinance no. 4 of 1902 (January 3, 1902), Parelvisscherij: Regelen voor het Visschen naar Parelschelpen, Paarlemoerschelpen en/of Tripang, Binnen den Afstand van Niet Meer dan Drie Engelsche Zeemijlen van de Kusten van Nederlansch-Indië, in *Staatsblad van Nederlansch-Indië over het Jaar 1902* (Batavia: Landsdrukkerij, 1903).

43. See Pedro Machado's chapter in this volume.

44. Government secretary to resident of Ambon, March 20, 1886, cited in J. A. Roëll to governor general, May 1, 1893, no. 4314, Ministerie van Koloniën, NNA.

45. Van Hoëvell, "De Aroe-eilanden," 89.

46. Roëll to governor general, May 1, 1893.

47. Ordinance no. 4 of 1902 (January 3, 1902).

48. Andrew Goss, *The Floracrats: State-Sponsored Science and the Failure of the Enlightenment in Indonesia* (Madison: University of Wisconsin Press, 2011), 87–91.

49. Overgangsbepalingen, Ordinance no. 4 of 1902 (January 3, 1902).

50. For a full account of the Clark Combination, see Steve Mullins, *Octopus Crowd: Maritime History and the Business of Australian Pearling in Its Schooner Age* (Tuscaloosa: University of Alabama Press, 2019).

51. J. P. S. Bach, "The Pearlshelling Industry and the 'White Australia' Policy," *Historical Studies: Australia and New Zealand* 10, no. 38 (1962): 210; Regina Ganter, *The Pearl-Shellers of Torres Strait: Resource Use, Development and Decline, 1860s–1960s* (Melbourne: Melbourne University Press, 1994), 162–64.

52. "Average Take per Boat for Each Year, from 1890–1907," in "Report of the Royal Commission Appointed to Inquire into the Working of the Pearl-shell and Bêche-de-mer Industries" (Brisbane: Anthony J. Cumming, Acting Government Printer, 1908), xlix (henceforth, Mackay Royal Commission 1908). Bach gives 924, 961, and 970 tons: "Production Figures to 1940, Queensland," in Bach, *Pearling Industry of Australia*, 289.

53. "Dummying" was the practice whereby pearling luggers ostensibly owned by British subjects were secretly leased or sold to foreigners, usually syndicates of Japanese pearling workers.

54. "Shell Sales," *Sydney Morning Herald*, April 30, 1903.

55. James Clark to register of shipping, Brisbane, May 15, 1903; James Clark to register of shipping, Sydney, May 15, 1903; James Clark to N. H. Paling, Dutch vice-consul, May 14, 1903, Clark Family Papers (privately held), Brisbane.

56. Overgangsbepalingen, Ordinance no. 4 of 1902 (January 3, 1902).

57. James Clark to Willem Bosschart, November 19, 1904, James Clark Letter Books, OM84, Oxley Memorial Library (OML), Brisbane.

58. James Clark to James Gray, October 29, 1904, James Clark Letter Books, OM84, OML.

59. Overgangsbepalingen, Ordinance no. 4 of 1902 (January 3, 1902).

60. Yoko Hayashi, "Agencies and Clients: Labour Recruitment in Java, 1870s–1950s," CLARA working paper no. 14 (Amsterdam: IIAS/IISG, 2002), 7.

61. Parliamentary debates (Hansard), Queensland Legislative Assembly, vol. 91 (Brisbane: Govt. Printer, 1903), 716–21; "Average Take per Boat for Each Year, from 1890–1907," in Mackay Royal Commission 1908, xlix.

62. *Handboek voor cultuur- en handelsondernemingen in Nederlandsch-Indië*, no. 27 (Amsterdam: J. H. de Bussy, 1915), 863.

63. Ordinance no. 263 of 1905 (April 22, 1905), Parelvisscherij: Reglementen, Verpachtingsreglement voor de Parelvisscherij, in *Staatsblad van Nederlansch-Indië over het Jaar 1905* (Batavia: Landsdrukkerij, 1906).

64. Ordinance no. 262 of 1905 (April 22, 1905), Parelvisscherij: Aanvulling van de Ordonnantie in Staatsblad 1902 no. 4, Betreffende de Parelvisscherij, in *Staatsblad van Nederlansch-Indië over het Jaar 1905*.

65. James Clark to Jim Mackenzie, November 21, 1904, James Clark Letter Books, OM84, OML.

66. *Northern Territory Times and Gazette* (Darwin), April 21, 1905.

67. James Clark to J. Campbell MacColl, December 8, 1904, James Clark Letter Books, OM84, OML.

68. Van de Wall, "Sjech Said bin Abdullah Baädilla," 349.

69. A. J. Quarles de Quarles, "Nota: Betreffende de werking van de pacht op de parelvisscherij in de Residentie Amboina, June 30, 1907," 1 and 27, Ministerie van Koloniën, NNA.

70. "Thursday Island, April 3," *Brisbane Courier*, April 4, 1905; "Departure of a Pearling Fleet," *Brisbane Courier*, August 29, 1905; "Thursday Island: Thursday," *Brisbane Courier*, September 2, 1905; "From the Torres Straits Pilot," *Northern Miner* (Charters Towers), September 21, 1905; "The Pearling Industry: Further Departures from Thursday Island," *Brisbane Courier*, October 5, 1905.

71. J. E. Jasper, "Het een en ander omtrent de parelvisscherij in de Molukken," *Weekblad voor Indie*, May 6, 1906, 37.

72. [E. J. de Rochemont], *De Zuid-West Nieuw-Guinea expeditie, 1904/05: Van het Kon. Ned. Aardrijkskundig Genootschap* (Leiden: E. J. Brill, 1908), 117.

73. A. J. Quarles de Quarles, "Rapport betreffende eene door dan resident van Amboina gemaakte reis naar de Zuid-Molukken speciaal naar de Eilanden Wetter, Babber, Wetan, Teoun, en Nila in de Maand November 1905," 14, Ministerie van Koloniën, NNA.

74. A. G. H. van Sluys, "Dobo-Ervaringen," *Koloniaal tijdschrift* (Vereeniging van Ambtenaren bij het Binnenlandsch Bestuur in Nederlandsch-Indië) 5, no. 1 (1916), 302–3.

75. Goss, *The Floracrats*, 87–91.

76. Van de Wall, "Sjech Said bin Abdullah Baadilla," 349, 352.

77. Quarles, "Rapport Betreffende eene door dan Resident van Amboina," 12-13.

78. Arthur E. Slater to Mr. Justice Dashwood, May 25, 1902, Appendix N, "Report of the Inquiry into the Pearl-Shelling Industry in Port Darwin and the Northern Territory," *Commonwealth Parliamentary Papers* 2 (1901–2), 25.

79. M. Treub to the resident of Ambonia, December 11, 1906, no. 9019, Ministerie van Koloniën, NNA.

80. Parliamentary debates (Hansard), Commonwealth of Australia Senate, no. 44, November, 2 1905, 4453–71 & no. 48, November 30, 1905, 6043–54.

81. "Shipping," *Sydney Morning Herald*, November 7, 1907; "Shipping," *Northern Territory Times and Gazette* (Darwin), November 22, 1907.

82. A. J. Quarles de Quarles to governor-general, January 2, 1908, Verbaal, March 2, 1909, no. 8, file 388 (letter A), Ministerie van Kolonien, NNA.

83. Quarles to governor-general, January 2, 1908.

84. George Smith to A. J. Quarles de Quarles, December 24, 1907, Verbaal, March 2, 1909, no. 8, file 388 (letter A), Ministerie van Kolonien, NNA.

85. Quarles, "Nota: Betreffende de werking van de pacht op de parelvisscherij," 20-21.

86. Quarles, 22.

87. Quarles to governor-general, January 2, 1908.

88. George Smith Codes, Darwin, November 20, 1907, and Soerabaya, January 1, 1908, Clark Family Papers (privately held), Brisbane; Smith to Quarles, December 24, 1907.

89. Smith to Quarles, December 24, 1907.

90. Judith Brett, *The Enigmatic Mr. Deakin* (Melbourne: Text Publishing, 2017), 365–68.

91. Kees van Dijk, *The Netherlands Indies and the Great War, 1914–1918* (Leiden: KITLV Press, 2007), 19–44.

92. Secret Circular no. 407 of December 3, 1907, cited in Quarles to governor-general, January 2, 1908.

93. Melchior Treub to governor-general, January 27, 1908, no. 7, referring to Melchior Treub to governor-general, August 26, 1907, no. 55, Ministerie van Kolonien, NNA.

94. Treub to governor-general, February 17, 1908, no. 10, Ministerie van Kolonien, NNA.

95. Melchior Treub to the governor-general, June 4, 1908, no. 27 (Secret), Ministerie van Kolonien, NNA.

96. Abdullah Baädilla to A. J. Quarles de Quarles, March 31, 1908 (letter Xb); W. G. Werdmuller to A. J. Quarles de Quarles, March 30, 1908 (letter Xa); A. Schmid to A. J. Quarles de Quarles, April 8, 1908 (letter Xc), Verbaal March 2, 1909, no. 8, file 388, Ministerie van Kolonien,

NNA. For the granting of the lease, see Gouvernementsbesluit no. 7, August 12, 1908.

97. See Mullins, "James Clark and the Celebes Trading Co.," 45.

98. James Mackenzie to Hugh Mahon, minister of external affairs, February 5, 1915; James Mackenzie to Atlee Hunt, February 18, 1915; Atlee Hunt, Memorandum for the minister, February 24, 1915; "Luggers and Permits transferred to James Clark & Co.," A1/1, 1923/2606, NAA.

99. C. J. Wiggers, "The Pearl Fisheries near the Aroe Isles," *Sluyters' Monthly*, March 1921, 221–27.

100. A. J. Beversluis and A. H. C. Gieben, *Het gouvernement der Molukken, met een voorwoord van den gouverneur der Molukken L. H. W. van Sandick* (Weltevreden: Landsdrukkerij, 1929), 192–94.

101. "Dobo Items," *Northern Standard* (Darwin), May 8, 1936; "Notes and Extracts from Harry Jessup, 'Drawn from Memory,'" 1976, Clark Family Papers (privately held), Brisbane.

102. Alwi, *Friends and Exiles*, 16–18.

103. Van Kampen, *De paarl- en parelmoervisscherij*, 26.

104. Hugo Merton, *Ergebnisse einer zoologischen Forschungsreise in den Südöstlichen Molukken (Aru- und Kei-Inseln)* (Frankfurt: Senckenbergische Naturforschende Ges., 1911), 150.

105. A. Balk, "Memorie van overgave van de Ondersfdeling Aroe Eilanden, July 21, 1937, Ministerie van Koloniën, NNA; "Aroe Islands News Items," *Northern Standard* (Darwin), April 25, 1939.

106. Carl Monsted to secretary, Department of Immigration, May 1, 1947, Carl Anton Monsted file A435, 1946/3284, NAA.

107. Patricia Spyer, *The Memory of Trade: Modernity's Entanglements on an Eastern Indonesian Island* (Durham, NC: Duke University Press, 2000), 14–27.

PART IV

Life-Stories, Memory, and Experiences

TEN

Pearling Fortunes
Recovering 'Alī al-Nahārī, a Legendary Red Sea Magnate in the Early Twentieth Century

JONATHAN MIRAN

ANYONE FAMILIAR WITH twentieth-century French travel and adventure literature will recognize *Les secrets de la mer Rouge*, published in Paris in 1931, as a classic of the genre. Written by the eccentric adventurer, maverick, and prolific writer Henry de Monfreid (1879–1974), the book is still—some eight decades after its original publication—reprinted and distributed in bookstores across France. Already an immense success in the 1930s and selling fifty thousand copies over the course of that decade, *Les secrets* is a romanticized account of Monfreid's experiences in the Red Sea as a one-time smuggler, wannabe pearl trader, and gunrunner in the 1910s and early 1920s.[1] The book launched Monfreid's career as a popular writer and was promptly translated into English and published in London in 1934. It was subsequently adapted into a film released in 1937, starring France's *monstre sacré*, or star, of the period, Harry Baur (1880–1943), who played the role of "Saïd Ali," an old, exoticized "Arab sheikh" and ultra-rich pearl magnate who was one of the principal protagonists of Monfreid's book. Saïd Ali's character was based on *sayyid* 'Alī 'Abd al-Raḥmān al-Nahārī (or, 'Alī al-Nahārī) (1851–1931), a somewhat cagey and elusive Yemeni-Eritrean pearl merchant whom Monfreid had met briefly in late January 1914 in the Dahlak archipelago off the Eritrean coasts, and who died in the very same year that *Les secrets de la mer Rouge* first appeared in print.

Adopting an approach that marries biography with commodity histories from a global historical perspective, this chapter reconstructs fragments of the material life and romanticized figure of sayyid 'Alī al-Nahārī. Nahārī was possibly the most prominent magnate in the highly lucrative pearling industry in the southern Red Sea during the heyday of the global pearl boom in the early twentieth century. His story is first and foremost tied to a particular luxury commodity whose value skyrocketed between the 1880s and the 1920s.[2] Changing fashion trends among the rich and *nouveaux riches* in Europe and North America spurred a dramatic growth in the demand for fine pearls, which, in turn, propelled extensive pearl diving and trading operations across a growingly interconnected globe. The Persian Gulf was by far the global leader in pearl production in the early twentieth century, producing more pearls than all other world areas combined and providing approximately 80 percent of the fine pearls exported to Western gem trade centers.[3] Though dwarfed by the Gulf, pearls harvested along the African and Arabian banks of the Red Sea—especially around the Farasan Islands, the Dahlak archipelago, and along Djibouti's coastline and the Gulf of Aden—also found their way to the global pearl-trade centers in Bombay and Paris.[4]

Comprising approximately one hundred and twenty-five islands, islets, rocks, and reefs with deeply indented coasts opposite the Eritrean port of Massawa, the Dahlak archipelago was the chief pearl fishery in the Red Sea in this period.[5] We find in the Red Sea principally two pearl-producing bivalve molluscs: the *Pinctada radiata* (known as *bulbul*) and the *Pinctada margaritifera erythreensis* (known as *ṣadof*). Estimates from the early twentieth century—at the apex of the pearl boom—put the number of boats engaged in pearl-fishing activities in the islands at between four hundred and four hundred and fifty, employing about ten thousand men as divers and other crew members. The harvesting and commercialization of pearls and mother-of-pearl from the archipelago involved distinct systems of financing, labor, and trade that brought together an assortment of Red Sea and western Indian Ocean actors. Spikes in demand drew pearling enterprises to the waters of the archipelago from far and wide, making them transregional operations *par excellence*. Sudanese, Afar, Somali, Dahlaki, and other northeast Africans (free and freed slaves) as well as Arabs and Africans (slaves or freed slaves) from the Arabian Red Sea littoral (Hijaz and Tihama coasts), its offshore islands (e.g., Farasan), and the Persian Gulf labored as divers; Gulf, Hijazi, Yemeni, or Dahlaki boat owners handled fishing crews and provided for transportation, whereas Indian and Arab merchants—such as ʿAlī al-Nahārī—financed pearl-fishing enterprises through an elaborate system of credit, debt, and dependency and exported the luxurious marine products, usually through networks of agents, to regional markets and to the global pearl centers in Bombay, Paris, and London. Interacting with a host of local, regional, and global actors—from indigent pearl divers to Indian brokers and global pearl magnates and bankers—figures such as ʿAlī al-Nahārī tied the Red Sea region to global commercial, financial, and consumption systems, involving networks and actors in India, Europe, and beyond.[6]

ʿAlī al-Nahārī's case thus presents an excellent prism through which to explore new spaces between microhistory, transregional history, and global history. This line of inquiry grows out of a broader reflection on how to frame and narrate the relationship between the global, regional, and local in large-scale historical analysis. In an introduction to a special issue on this theme, Bernhard Struck, Kate Ferris, and Jacques Revel wrote that "zooming in and out from grand and large-scale questions to micro analysis, case studies of individuals or small groups" allows for the exploration of new spaces between micro and macro history and brings actors and agency back into the analysis.[7] The study of biographies (biographical fragments, traces) is thus a fitting medium for exploring the spatial purview of highly mobile and/or transregionally connected individual actors that may offer new avenues to thinking and writing both global history and the histories of globalization.[8] Framed in a "global microhistory" perspective, a biographical approach also serves to problematize rigid conceptions of space, boundaries, and mobility; instead, it highlights the fluidity, complexity, and blurredness of a lived and perceived spectrum of individual experiences and hybrid identities, especially in a tangled area such as the Red Sea region in the age of empire.[9]

The grandson of a Yemeni Arab who moved from Hudaydah to Massawa, ʿAlī al-Nahārī was born in the Eritrean port town, married women with family origins from across the Red Sea, unwittingly became an Italian colonial subject, prospered as a merchant-financier in the furtive pearl industry, and entertained intimate business, social, and family relations with members of Red Sea–wide trading and shipping networks (mostly Hadrami) in port towns stretching from Aden to Alexandria. Like some of his counterparts in the Persian Gulf, he traveled to France to directly sell pearls to the world's leading pearl dealers, such as Léonard Rosenthal (1875–1955) and Jacques Bienenfeld (1875–1933), two Jews born in the Caucasus region and Eastern Galicia (Ukraine), respectively, who had immigrated to France.[10] In the 1930s, through the exoticizing and Orientalizing lenses of French literary representations, Nahārī was revealingly characterized intermittently as "an Arab Sheikh from East Africa" and "a great Yemeni lord [Fr. *seigneur*]."

This offers an apropos segue to another dimension of ʿAlī al-Nahārī's story that I address in this essay: the intersection of commodity histories, changing consumption habits in Europe, and the production and consumption of popular culture in France in the 1930s. Pearls possessed an exotic quality that inflamed the imaginations of Europeans and Americans, who already held romanticized perceptions of the East. One of the by-products of the global pearl boom was the proliferation of colorful journalistic accounts, captivating travel literature, and fanciful fiction and film revolving around these exotic gems from the ever-mysterious Orient. And since the world's largest pearl market in the heyday of the boom was Paris, it is no surprise that France was particularly enchanted with pearling tales, real or imagined. Interestingly, significant popular attention was directed toward the Red Sea and, among other figures, ʿAlī al-Nahārī was captured and duly exoticized in the process.

A RED SEA PEARLING FAMILY AND ITS NETWORKS

Various fragments of information allow us to reconstruct aspects of the history of the Nahārī family.[11] Tracing distant origins to the Banū Hāshim clan of the Quraysh tribe of Mecca in the Hijaz, the Nahārīs are *ashrāf*. The distant ancestors of the family are believed to have settled in the Red Sea port of Yanbuʿ from where they traded with the Syrian region (Bilād al-Shām), especially a town by the name of Nahāriyye, from which the family name is drawn. In the eighth *hijri* century (fourteenth century CE), members of the family moved to Hadramawt and from there to Rimaʿ, located on the edge of the Yemeni Tihama coast. The first Nahārī to have crossed the Red Sea from Hudaydah in Yemen, possibly in the early decades of the nineteenth century, was ʿAbd al-Raḥīm b. Muḥammad al-Nahārī (1775–1850, d. in Sawākin). He settled in Gimʿhilé, a small village on Dahlak Kabir Island and a center of pearling activities. After establishing himself in the pearl trade and making a fortune, he moved from the islands to Massawa, married Fāṭma b. ʿUmar b. ʿAbd Allāh Danbar (from the Balaw Yūsuf, a lineage associated with the Eritrean coastal elite), and was appointed *qadi* (judge).[12] ʿAbd al-Raḥīm's son, ʿAbd al-Raḥmān (b. ca. 1820), was also involved in the pearl business. Like his father, he also served as qadi, and by the time of his death in September 1871 he had amassed quite a sizeable fortune. Information gleaned from legal records from Massawa tells us that his estate included "a batch of pearls, parcels of land, money, credits, goods, livestock and boats valued at a total of more than 120,000 Maria Theresa Dollars."[13] ʿAbd al-Raḥmān had four sons and four daughters from at least two wives, Āmna from Harar and Fāṭma b. Ḥasan Mūsā. One of the boys was ʿAlī.

Financing and commercialization arrangements in the Red Sea pearl fishery were quite comparable to those in the Gulf. Elaborate systems of credit, debt, and dependency governed and fueled labor relationships between divers, boat captains, boat owners, merchants, and financiers. Most commonly, Arab and/or Indian pearl-dealing merchants/financiers/boat owners, based on either side of the Red Sea, advanced loans to boat captains and pearling crews (and, sometimes, their families) who were in turn committed to sell them the proceeds of the catch at the end of the fishing season (corresponding to the *salafiyya* system in the Gulf). Under another system, merchants/boat owners financed fishing expeditions by hiring crews and providing them food and other supplies. Based on a five-day working week, divers and captains received the pearls harvested in the first four days, while the catch of the fifth day went to the boat owner (corresponding to the *khammas* or *khumsi* system). The exact modalities of these arrangements varied.[14]

Commercialization was equally elaborate, multifarious, and, in the case of fine pearls, extremely secretive. Sometimes the agents of big firms in Bombay or in Europe sent their representatives to buy pearls directly in fishing waters, but such agents were at times sent to reside for longer periods in port towns such as Massawa, where they bought pearls that they sent either through deftly organized regional networks or directly to Bombay or Paris. Red Sea–based pearl-dealing merchants—such as 'Alī al-Nahārī—sold batches of pearls either received from their boats (owned or sponsored/financed) or bought from more independent captains and smaller traders.[15] Selling could be done in a number of ways (all of which Nahārī employed): (1) Red Sea–based pearl dealers could sell to the resident or itinerant Indian and European agents of Bombay and European-based firms, who expedited them to India and Europe; (2) pearl merchants could also sell to Arab or Indian dealers located in regional Red Sea pearl-trade markets such as Jeddah, Hudaydah, and Aden, who then sent them to Bombay or Paris; or (3) they could also travel themselves to Bombay or Paris and sell directly to the big global dealers.[16]

We may assume that 'Alī and his older brother 'Umar took over the family business after their father died in 1871. This was an opportune moment to be in the pearl trade since increasing global demand for pearls triggered a dramatic ascent in their price in the 1870s and 1880s. 'Alī's acquisition of a building in Massawa in 1884 might suggest the beginning of the materialization of profits and the consolidation of the Nahārī family.[17] The establishment of the Nahārī brothers on Massawa's commercial scene also translated into real estate acquisitions in the port town: in 1889 'Umar bought two stores/warehouses and between 1899 and 1906 'Alī bought two houses, two lots, and a store. 'Alī was also said to have a private mosque, which even among Massawa's affluent elite was not so common.[18] Though he owned (or formally declared) a modest fleet of boats (only four *sanābīq* in 1908), it is clear that Nahārī financed fishing expeditions on boats belonging to other Dahlakis.[19] By the turn of the century, 'Alī al-Nahārī was recognized as the most prominent pearl merchant and entrepreneur in the pearling business in Eritrea.[20] In a brief biographical entry, Giuseppe Puglisi characterized Nahārī's ascent in these words: "he emulated the big Arab and Indian pearl merchants, collecting pearls, financing pearl divers and owning a fleet of boats. He eventually began to trade directly with India and Europe, wriggling the trade from local intermediaries."[21]

Figure 10.1. Photographic portrait of ʿAlī al-Nahārī, early twentieth century. Nahārī family collection, with permission.

What were the underpinnings of Nahārī's success? What qualitative advantage did he have (over Indian merchants, for example), apart from being in the right trade at the right time with the right material and social capital (inheritance and his father's networks), as well as perhaps the personal savvy required of a trader in the singular pearl business? I contend that Nahārī wove a web of social, political, and business networks in coastal Eritrea, the Dahlak, as well as the broader Red Sea zone, that were pivotal to his success. Some of these bonds and alliances were possibly already established by his Yemen-born grandfather, who tied himself through marriage to the Eritrean coastal political elite (which exercised social and moral authority also in the Dahlak). 'Alī's marriages may also reveal a carefully calculated strategy that allowed him to attach himself simultaneously to local and regional structures of authority and power in the Eritrean mainland, the Dahlak Islands, and the Yemeni Tihama. His first wife, Fāṭma al-Amīn Danbar (d. 1945), was from the same potent family that his grandfather married into; a second wife was a Dahlaki (Fāṭima 'Abd Allāh Maknūn); the third a Yemeni (Zaynab Ḥasan), and the fourth a Yemeni from Dahlak (Khadīja Aḥmad Khidr). Taking this a step further, 'Alī's sons' matrimonial alliances reveal a broader marriage pool, if no less strategic. They married into the local coastal elites (e.g., Ṣā'igh, Shīnītī, 'Adūlāy, and Bayt Shaykh Maḥmūd families) and Massawa-based influential Hadrami *sādah* and *ashrāf* families (e.g. Ṣāfī, Ḥayotī, Bā Ṭūq, and Bā 'Alawī) who were tied to a web of transregional commercial and shipping networks in the broader Red Sea and Gulf of Aden.[22]

Hadrami families were especially prominent in Massawa's cosmopolitan commercial elite in that period and, together with Indians and Dahlakis, some were involved in the pearl and mother-of-pearl trade. This included the Ṣāfī and Bā Ṭūq families who were tied in marriage to the Nahārī family.[23] An especially meaningful business and social relationship was with the Bā Zar'a family (though not by marriage). One of the most enterprising families in the broader Red Sea area and the western Indian Ocean from the 1870s, the Bā Zar'as were involved in shipping and trade in sundry commodities, including coffee, hides, textiles, and marine products. They had businesses, agencies, and agents in numerous cities and towns between Egypt, southern Arabia, the Horn of Africa, the Gulf, and India.[24] Nahārī was especially associated with shaykh Muḥammad 'Umar Bā Zar'a, the founder of the Bā Zar'a family firm, who, after having made a fortune in Massawa (starting as a humble porter), left it for Mukalla and Aden in the early twentieth century, but still visited it often (he had houses and families both in Massawa and in Aden).[25] The Bā Zarʿa and Ṣāfī families were involved in the pearling business and were intimately related to Nahārī.[26] Below we will see the involvement of both in the context of ʿAlī al-Nahārī's trips to Europe.

It is important to shed light on another dimension of Nahārī's story: the relationship between the pearling industry off the Eritrean coasts, on the one hand, and the Italian colonial enterprise in Eritrea, on the other. Throughout his life, Nahārī entertained a complex relationship with the Italian authorities. After their occupation of Massawa in 1885, the Italians quickly grew aware of the economic potential that the marine industry in the Dahlak held for them. The global pearling boom was in full swing and voices in the metropole deplored those "foreigners" who were profiting from the colony's natural resources. Indeed, in the last two decades of the nineteenth century fishing boats and crews from the Arabian coasts and the Gulf area continued to operate in the waters of the newly established colony and the number of Banyans in Massawa (many connected to the marine industry) increased exponentially. In the first decade of the colony's existence, industrial entrepreneurs in Italy put pressure on the authorities in Eritrea to control and regulate the lucrative marine industry. The granting of a concession for pearl fishing to the Società Perlifera Italiana in 1898 was unsuccessful due to local pearlers' resistance, and in 1903 the pearling sector was again liberalized.[27] Suffice it to say here that though mother-of-pearl exports would remain important throughout the colonial period, the authorities in Eritrea were never able to tap into the fine-pearl trade, which was based on secretive methods between actors enjoying highly codified and delicately woven trust relations. European travelers who spent months in Massawa reported that one would not suspect the existence of the pearl trade, since it was carried out away from the eyes of customs officials.[28] The high occurrences of smuggling, frequent evasion of the customs authorities—not declaring or under-declaring—and the largely furtive nature of the pearl trade come together to explain why, for example, figures for the exportation of pearls are unreliable. It also explains the checkered and strained relationship that the authorities entertained with Nahārī, who, though present in various colonial sources, seems increasingly elusive and evasive.

NAHĀRĪ'S TWO BUSINESS TRIPS TO FRANCE

Reaching tremendous heights, the value of pearls exported from the Persian Gulf between around 1880 and 1904 more than quadrupled.[29] There is no reason to believe that Red Sea pearl exports did not echo this pattern. Growing demand for the gems in Europe and North America led both European and Indian merchants to make every effort to maximize profits by bypassing intermediaries and gaining direct access to pearl-producing regions. This propelled two concurrent phenomena: it prompted some global pearl firms to send their agents to pearling areas to buy directly from producers, and it also motivated some traders in pearl-producing areas to travel to Europe or Bombay to sell pearls and circumvent regional intermediaries and markets. The presence of Indian agents for Bombay dealers in the Red Sea is well known, but European pearl dealers, too, sent their representatives to buy pearls in the region.[30]

Though the first decade of the twentieth century represented the peak of the boom years, the pearl market was often fickle and volatile. An important turning point occurred when the temporary global market crisis in 1907 allowed Paris to overtake Bombay as the world pearl-trade center. This is the context in which some Paris-based merchants such as Jacques Cartier, but more pertinently Léonard Rosenthal and Jacques Bienenfeld (both dealt with Nahārī), traveled in person or sent agents to the Gulf, the Red Sea, and other fisheries and, as a result, made massive profits.[31] This was also the point at which some Red Sea, Gulf, and Indian pearl dealers traveled chiefly to Paris (usually via Marseille), but also to London and Italy. Some resided there and served as consignees or brokers and others opened gem stores.[32] A member of a well-established family of Kuwaiti pearl traders and fishers, Saif Marzooq Al-Shamlan, provided information about Arab merchants from the Gulf operating in Bombay and in Paris, including other brokers owning stores in Bombay, Bahrain, Paris, and London. More pertinently, al-Shamlan provided fascinating details about pearl traders from Kuwait, Bahrain, Sharjah, and Lengeh (Iran) who traveled to Paris, London, Marseille, and Milan between ca. 1922 and 1932. He reproduced excerpts from the correspondence of several of those merchants, describing, for example, market conditions in Marseille and Paris, as well as providing information on interpreters and brokers.[33] The following subsections offer more-or-less comparable information, this time pertaining to an Eritrea-based Red Sea pearl merchant.

The First Trip (1906–7)

Toward the end of his life, 'Alī al-Nahārī told Italian journalist Renzo Martinelli that he had traveled to Paris and London several times and to Rome once.[34] Since we have evidence of only two trips taken in 1906–7 and 1923–24, both to France, it might be the case that intra-European side trips were undertaken on these two occasions. Of his first trip, the only known evidence is found in an entry in Ferdinando Martini's (governor of Eritrea, 1897–1907) diary and in a letter written by Nahārī and addressed to his son Muḥammad. Most certainly a coincidence, Martini and Nahārī found themselves on board the steamer *Vespucci* on September 11, 1906, as it made its way from Massawa to Aden. Direct ships from Massawa to Italy operated only once a month at that time, and most travelers to Europe had to board a ship in Aden.[35] Martini's entry clearly demonstrates the arcane nature of the fine-pearl trade and the degree to which this commerce was impenetrable to the Italian authorities in Eritrea. It also shows, perhaps, Nahārī's attempts to deflect any attention away from himself. Martini wrote:

> Hot, but not excessively. A pleasant night. Fellow travelers: doctor Paladino, who disembarked at Assab, and a Frenchman who spent three months in Massawa buying pearls worth several hundred thousand lire. He is an agent of the Rosenthal firm in Paris. . . . There is an Arab on board in second class—a rich Arab from Massawa. In addition to a large quantity of pearls—of varying dimensions and quality—he possesses two pearls for which he is asking 80,000 Maria Theresa Dollars. It is the famous Nahari. I talked about him with the Captain and the Rosenthal firm agent and I am convinced that those who estimate the annual pearl commerce in Massawa at two million [lire] are correct. The captain says that this year, or, to be more precise, following the first [pearl fishing] campaign [season] this year, he took two lots of pearls to Aden. One was of a value of 80,000 Maria Theresa Dollars (at a rate of 1 [MTD] to 2.75 lire, [amounting to] 220,000 lire) while the other was 150,000 Maria Theresa Dollars (412,500 lire), a total of 632,500 lire. The agent of the Rosenthal firm says he already sent to Paris [goods] valued at 400,000 lire. That's a total of 1,032,500 lire and he has on board with him more [pearls] valued at 300,000, therefore amounting to 1,332,500 [lire worth] of pearls, without

counting all the rest. Because not all the commerce is concentrated in these areas.³⁶

The only other piece of information that we have about the trip is a letter written by 'Alī to his son Muḥammad on April 25, 1907, on the return from France (seven and a half months after Martini's account on board the Vespucci) and sent from Cairo on the letterhead of "Salem Mohamed Ba 'Abed" (a Hadrami), with a Cairo address. The note strongly alludes to the 1907 crisis. Interestingly, though not surprisingly, it also points to a business-cum-social relationship with Muḥammad Bā Zar'a. After salutations and good wishes, Nahārī writes:

> Yesterday we arrived by ship to Alexandria [from Marseille] and in four days we will be heading towards you [in Massawa]. . . . We inform you that we have not sold any of the merchandise that we brought with us but we left it in a safe deposit box in a bank and we have the key with us. That is, until prices will go up. My son, do not buy pearls. Prices are now low. Send a letter to Walī and to Yūsuf and instruct them not to purchase any pearls. We will tell you more when we meet. If you wish to write to me, send me your letters to Aden to Shaykh Muḥammad Bā Zar'a. There is a good chance that he will come for 'Izz ad-Dīn's ['Alī's son] wedding [in Massawa].³⁷

The Second Trip (1923–24) and Final Years

We know little about 'Alī's specific business dealings between the two trips to Europe. But a yet to be fully decrypted three-page document, possibly drawn from (or summarizing) a double-entry bookkeeping register in Arabic, confirms transactions with dealers in Bombay. The document shows that between 1915 and 1925, 'Alī conducted transactions with, among others, Muḥammad al-Mushārī, a prominent Arab pearl dealer (from Lengeh) who owned a large store in Bombay.³⁸

Sixteen years after the first trip, Nahārī undertook a second business trip to France, this time accompanied by two of his sons, Ṭāhā and Muḥammad. One source suggests that French pearl merchants "urged" Nahārī to go to Paris to sell pearls.³⁹ This trip is better documented and therefore more instructive than the first; it offers detail about the itinerary itself, the identity of brokers and interpreters accompanying the Nahārīs on their voyage, various critical contacts in Aden, as well as details about business dealings in Marseille and Paris. This section is based on excerpts from a travelogue that Muḥammad ('Alī's son) is said to have kept, recording in detail the important "facts" of the trip.[40] Following the wishes of the Nahārī family, I have excluded from this account details pertaining to specific sums of transactions and other financial details.

Accompanied by Karl Linder, a German national who served as a "translator cum broker" [sic], Nahārī and his sons left Massawa on December 20, 1923. They reached Ma'ala (Aden) seven days later, where they were hosted by Muḥammad Ṣāfī and Muḥammad Bā Zar'a, two Hadrami merchants with family and business attachments to Massawa and a host of Red Sea ports (Muḥammad Bā Zar'a was involved in the 1907 trip; see above). Muḥammad noted in his journal that they handed the bag of pearls to (Aḥmad) Muḥammad Bā Zar'a for safekeeping and that during their five-day stay they had bought some *barbari* pearls (possibly from the Gulf) from Shaykh Aḥmad Bā Zar'a, a Port Sudan merchant. They also exchanged some Italian lire for rupees and purchased Aden-Marseille tickets, as well as warm woolen clothes for the European winter. Nahārī had the manager of the Aden branch of the National Bank of India Ltd. prepare a letter addressed to a Paris-based foreign exchange, letters of credit, and securities firm. The letter introduced Nahārī as a "constituent of ours, a Pearl Merchant from Massawah, who is proceeding to Paris via Marseille with a view to obtaining a market for Red Sea Pearls" and informed the money-wiring firm that Nahārī would remit them sums to be transferred to the London office of the National Bank of India Ltd. during his business trip.

Having paid freight on twenty pounds of pearls, the party left Aden on board the steamer *Amiral Pierre* and reached Djibouti for a layover of five hours on the very last day of the year 1923.[41] Joining them there was a broker, Chagganlal Hukamchand (who was possibly a Jain from Bombay or Gujarat). The *Amiral Pierre* sailed northwards for a week, reaching first Port Suez, then Port Sa'id, where the Nahārīs took the opportunity to mail letters to their family in Massawa. Six days later, on January 13, 1924, they arrived in Marseille, where, following some bureaucratic procedures, they collected the consigned pearls. They soon thereafter contacted Jacques Bienenfeld's office in Paris to have the pearl shipment insured for the Marseille–Paris leg of the journey. Two days later they delivered the pearls to the Marseille branch of a Parisian bank to be shipped by train to its main offices in Paris. They also made deposits in two bank branches in Marseille. They reached Paris and checked into the Hotel Cervantes in the 9th arrondissement on the edge of the gem dealers' district. Several days later, after paying customs duties and a fee to the Chamber of Commerce, they finally received the pearls on January 21.

The last section of the diary excerpt relates much more specifically to the business dealings in Paris in the first week of February 1924. The Nahārīs worked through a locally based broker, Amoulek Shah, who mediated between them and several pearl dealers who made bids, including Jacques Bienenfeld and Léonard Rosenthal and his brother Adolphe. After circumspect deliberations, 'Alī al-Nahārī, his sons, and the brokers Amoulek Shah and Chagganlal Hukamchand went to the Léonard Rosenthal et Frères firm, where they closed a deal for a considerable sum of money. The very last details of the diary excerpt note that, after the deal was sealed, Nahārī paid the three brokers (the two mentioned and Karl Linder) a commission of 0.25 percent of the transaction sum. Papers kept with the Nahārī family confirm that proceeds from the transaction in Paris were transferred to 'Alī Nahārī's bank account at the Aden branch of the National Bank of India, Ltd.[42]

Information about Nahārī after his return from France is sketchy and inconsistent. In the mid-1920s his reputation as a rich man was ubiquitous and legendary in Eritrea. Jealousy about the pearl merchant's wealth—and his efforts to conceal it—generated stories, legends, myths, and plentiful anecdotic accounts. After the second trip, his relationship with the Italian colonial authorities was fraught with tension and contradiction. On the one hand, in late 1925 he was awarded the Italian colonial order of knighthood, the Cavaliere dell'Ordine Coloniale della Stella d'Italia.[43] Yet, on the other hand, it appears that the colonial authorities were displeased with their Italian subject, who made millions under their noses and, in the process, humiliated the administration. According to one source, news about the business trip was reported in the French press as greatly vexing the governor of Eritrea, who claimed that Nahārī failed to truthfully declare the value of the pearls that he took with him to sell in France (a claim that can be substantiated by evidence that I have seen). As a result, Nahārī was fined.[44] Then again, unsubstantiated oral accounts claim that in 1928 the Italian authorities borrowed money from Nahārī and that after it was returned it was deposited in foreign banks. The pearl merchant's second trip to Paris produced myriad mysteries around his wealth.

One way to bring Nahārī's life story to a close is to summarize Renzo Martinelli's account of their encounter in Massawa in 1929, two years before 'Alī's death. A reporter for the Florence-based *La Nazione* daily newspaper, Martinelli devoted a short chapter in his book to his meeting with Nahārī. The sarcastic title of the mini-chapter "Il meschino Nahari" (The wretched [alt.: forlorn, miserable] Nahārī) reflects well Martinelli's incredulous, suspicious, and overall somewhat deriding tone throughout. The journalist described the "poor pearl merchant" who kept on moaning how miserable (*meschin*, or *meskin*) he was. But, as Martinelli forcefully announced, the truth that was known to everyone "is that for twenty, thirty, or even forty years, Nahārī has dominated most of the Red Sea pearl trade and, through his agents, these pearls ended up in the windows of the big jewelry shops in Rue de la Paix [in Paris] and in London and New York." Martinelli went on to insist that Nahārī was at pains to conceal his immense wealth, and that after Nahārī was criticized for the fact that, although he was an Italian "citizen" [*sic*], he had placed his money in foreign banks, Nahārī deposited a few hundred thousand lire ("crumbs," Martinelli wrote mockingly) in an Italian bank.[45]

Martinelli visited Nahārī's house and asked to see some pearls. During their conversation, the seventy-eight-year-old told the Italian journalist that his eyesight had been declining and that he had been retired from the pearl business—and any other business—for about four or five years (corresponding to 1924–25). Yet, for a moment, Nahārī reminisced about brighter days: "Oh, [in the past] I have bought and sold pearls. I can say that the most beautiful pearls harvested in the Red Sea and the Gulf of Aden passed through my hands. The Dahlak Islands have been the main place where my divers worked, and with the harvest from those waters I've been able to conduct much trade in the big markets of Arabia. I have been to Paris and London several times, and once to Rome." But when Martinelli was dazzled by the batches of pearls shown to him, Nahārī continued to try to dispel the notion that he was immensely rich. He continued, "and I have many people [a big family], and the savings have been depleted quickly. Now I am very *meschino*.... Soon it will be necessary to sell these pearls [shown to Martinelli] so they [the family] can eat." Martinelli ended the encounter as skeptical as he was when it began, convinced that the old, emaciated man (a photograph of Nahārī and Martinelli is reproduced in these pages) was as wealthy as his reputation suggested.[46] Be that as it may, the encounter between Nahārī and Martinelli occurred only a few months before the 1929 stock market crash, which, following a set of financial crises since the First World War, constituted one of several factors marking the end of the pearl boom and the decline of the natural pearling industry writ large. The introduction of high-quality cultured pearls in the mid-1920s strangulated the pearl industry; by the Second World War, with European markets closed, the industry received a further blow.

'Alī al-Nahārī died on October 19, 1931, in Massawa, leaving two wives, six adult sons and daughters, as well as four minor sons. Muḥammad, the son who had traveled with Nahārī to Paris, was designated legal guardian to the minor offspring and executor of his father's estate.[47] Since the only will that is available to us is dated March 28, 1923 (11 Sha'bān 1341), hence *before* the second lucrative trip to Europe, it is difficult to assess the precise size and nature of 'Alī's entire estate at the time of his death. For example, claims that I have heard over the years about 'Alī's acquisition of real estate property in Paris (perhaps during the second trip in 1924) await substantiation. Notwithstanding, the will details the division of 'Alī's estate among his legal heirs and thus offers information about properties in the form of residential-business compounds, houses, lots, and stores in Massawa, in multiple localities in the Dahlak Islands (Gim'hilé, Derbushet, Deb'ullo, and other sites), and possibly also in the town of Luhayya on the Yemeni coast. The estate also included funds and batches of pearls kept in a bank in France.[48] Other documents kept by the Nahārī family suggest that there may have been various investments in stock. For example, 'Alī was a shareholder in the Mogul Line, Ltd. (formerly the Bombay and Persia Steam Navigation Company), which was founded in 1877 and was, incidentally, much involved in transporting pilgrims to Mecca.[49]

MANUFACTURING "SAÏD ALI":
HENRY DE MONFREID'S PEARLING FICTIONS

As the somewhat skeptical exchange between Martinelli and Nahārī might suggest, in the late 1920s—after the second European trip and toward the end of his life—'Alī's persona took on an increasingly mythical dimension. His presumed wealth was a source of myriad speculations, arousing jealousy. By focusing on the cultural by-products of the global pearl boom, this closing section of the essay tells the story of Nahārī's afterlife, so to speak, the story of the imagined 'Alī al-Nahārī as reflected in the popular writings of Henry de Monfreid (1879–1974). Nahārī was thus captured in one of the cultural products associated with the exotic character attributed to pearls. In some odd way, the lasting mystery and curiosity surrounding Nahārī's wealth in real life was "resolved" by Monfreid in works of fiction. The singularity of French enchantment with pearling tales—real or imagined—was rooted in the role of Paris as the center of the world pearl trade, and Monfreid had a critical role in bringing fantastic stories about the source of these pearls, which adorned the rich and the famous but were increasingly an object of desire for members of the middle class. Pearls connected middle-class desires with the world of the exotic Orient, the frontier for all adventures, dangers (real or imagined), thrills, and dreams of escape and freedom.[50]

Born to an aristocratic family (his father was an Impressionist painter and a friend of Gauguin), Henry de Monfreid did not enjoy much professional success throughout his twenties. In 1911, when he was thirty-two years old, he left France for Ethiopia to work for a French commercial firm dealing in coffee and hides. Disgusted with the European lifestyle in Africa, he quit the job after two years, settled in Djibouti (Côte française des Somalis), and purchased a sailing boat. Determined to launch his life of adventures, Monfreid began his involvement with different activities such as pearl trading, arms dealing, and hashish smuggling. Though altogether, his success in these ventures was quite small, his exploits inspired the dozens of popular accounts that he published between the early 1930s and the late 1960s.[51] Monfreid's persona, experiences, and the spectacular success of his early writings may have captured a collective latent desire for escape from oppressive attachments, conventions (family, community, society, nation), and bourgeois values in interwar Europe. It expressed a longing for adventure and freedom found in powerful and wild natural settings or such "spaces of alterity" as the sea—in this case, the Red Sea (hostile to all but to the most intrepid, pristine, mysterious, and lawless).[52]

Freeing himself from the confines of a social and spatial order, Monfreid the provocateur lived on his boat, immersed himself in "native life," and dressed like a local; he also converted to Islam and adopted the name 'Abd al-Hai. Colonial officials in Djibouti accused him of having "gone native." His *ensauvagement* (going wild), as Joseph Kessel characterized it ("un Français ensauvagé"), manifested a desire for exoticism, the solitary discovery of the authentic, the quest for the unique adventure—in other words, true freedom.[53] In this context, Monfreid might personify the *Exot*, a term coined by Victor Segalen (1878–1919) to separate the scorned figures of the colonial official/settler and the tourist from the superior and enlightened traveler whose sense of individualism is nourished by difference, diversity, the Other. "An *Exot*," Segalen wrote, "is a born Traveler, someone who senses all the flavor of diversity in worlds filled with wondrous diversities."[54] Segalen did not think that it was possible to totally grasp the Other, but the dream of merging and forgetting oneself in another culture is in itself a source of energy and inspiration.[55] Interestingly, Segalen was a close family friend of the Monfreids.

Following unsuccessful ventures in arms dealing, Monfreid's naïve efforts to try his hand in the furtive Red Sea pearl trade began in earnest in late 1913. He headed to Massawa and the Dahlak with the intention to fish and buy pearls. In January 1914, he reached Massawa, where he met Jacques Schouchana, a Frenchman of Tunisian Jewish origins who lived in Alexandria and Massawa six months per year and the rest in France, and who bought pearls for the Paris-based Rosenthal firm. Monfreid learned much about the pearl business from Schouchana and, notwithstanding the occasional anti-Semitic slur in Monfreid's writings, the two became friends and business partners for long years (well after Monfreid's pearling adventures were over in 1916).[56] After four days in Massawa, Monfreid set sail to the Dahlak, determined to meet 'Alī al-Nahārī. The evidence of this one and only meeting (as far as we know) is recorded in his logbook (*journal de bord*) in a laconic entry dated January 28, 1914. "I have been now in Djembeli [sic] for three days and I'm beginning to think that Dahlak is not better than Massawa [for doing business]. There is [here] an ultra-rich Arab named Saïd-Ali who has traveled several times to Paris, who possesses the paraphernalia of a jeweler and who monopolizes all the pearls of the region [sic]. . . . Saïd-Ali shows me a bag of pearls; I am still not confident enough to launch myself [in trading], but I realize that if one is well informed it is possible to make considerable trade with a 30 percent profit margin."[57] This constitutes the only reliable record of Monfreid's encounter with

Nahārī. It is unknown whether he had any other contact with the pearl merchant in the fifteen years that separated the encounter from the first publications coming out in 1930–31.

The next reference to Saïd Ali in print appeared in *Pearls, Arms and Hashish*, a collaboration between Monfreid and the American journalist and author Ida Treat (1889–1978). Published simultaneously in New York and London in 1930, the book records Monfreid's adventures as written down by Treat. This is where Monfreid begins to exercise his talents as a colorful storyteller and where fact and fiction are mixed and inseparable. The book devotes five pages to the encounter with the now-romanticized Saïd Ali, describing his luscious residence in Gim'hilé and the solemn slaves and servants at his service. Monfreid is soon received by the captivating pearl merchant in a room with court attendants.[58] Here, Saïd Ali is "a big Arab, stout and bearded, draped in the folds of a *chamma* [a long cotton robe]." The two men make small talk and exchange information about a merchant in Djibouti and the conflict between the Ottomans and Zayidis in Yemen, before moving on to discuss pearls. Depicted as an impassioned collector of pearls, Saïd Ali tested Monfreid by showing him some plain pearls before moving on to more sumptuous batches. Tempted to try his hand at business, Monfreid is hesitant and unconfident. A deal is almost concluded but Monfreid reveals to the reader that the sum that he whimsically offered for a batch of pearls was beyond his means; he ducks out of the deal and quickly leaves for Djibouti. Though we do not know whether the two men ever met again, some evidence would suggest that information, or hearsay, about Nahārī found its way to Monfreid years after that encounter. In a footnote included in the pages that feature Saïd Ali, Monfreid observed that, following his death, which had occurred "a few years ago" (counting back from 1930), his heirs sold the pearls that Monfreid had seen "over fifteen years ago" (hence around 1914) for five million dollars.[59]

At around the same time, the journalist Joseph Kessel encouraged the idiosyncratic Frenchman to write down his stories. This he did, and with no discernible restraint. Monfreid authored his adventures (autobiographical and experience-based fiction) in a colorful and romanticized form. He wrote about pearl fishing and trading, drug running, arms trafficking, piracy, slave traders, evasions at sea, and sea wrecks "set amidst barren mountains, basaltic cones, coral reefs, isolated moorings, pirate coves, hostile seas, and the practically biblical cities of the Red

Sea, a body of water whose name tones were improbably evocative."[60] It is extremely challenging to separate fact from fiction in Monfreid's accounts, since, as Richard Pankhurst aptly observed, they "contain a mixture of facts, fiction and gossip, the relative proportion of which varied considerably from volume to volume."[61] In a way, under Treat's and Kessel's initial influence, Monfreid transfigured himself from illegal trafficker to adventurer to popular writer—and thus engineered his own legendary reputation.

The publication of *Les secrets de la mer Rouge* (1931) marked Monfreid's debut as a writer. The book became a bestseller in the 1930s and is still considered a classic of the travel and adventure genre.[62] Translations of *Les secrets* have been published in many languages (about ten, as far as I know), including Arabic, Chinese, and Russian. *Les secrets* devotes three chapters—"Dahlak, the Pearl Island," "The Death of Saïd Ali," and "Cheikh Issa's Story"—to the story involving Saïd Ali and develops an intricate plot of conspiracy and intrigue revolving around his wealth and estate against the backdrop of the Red Sea pearl fishery. Here, too, fact and fiction are blended together, though it remains possible that some expendable detail about the encounter between Monfreid and Nahārī is based in truth. In some strange way, speculations and conjecture around Nahārī's presumed wealth came to a climax in Monfreid's fictionalized account of Saïd Ali in the three chapters of *Les secrets*. The mystery in real life was somehow resolved in fiction.

Quite succinctly, the three core chapters of *Les secrets* tell the story of Saïd Ali, the rich pearl magnate in Dahlak (more than fifty boats fish for him; more than a thousand slaves cultivate his land in Arabia), and a conspiracy which targets him. The main plotter is Zanni, a Greek broker-dealer of pearls from Mytilene, who has his eyes on Saïd Ali's treasures. Providing them with cash advances, Zanni manipulates and controls Saïd Ali's sons, especially Omar, in the hopes of entrapping them into selling him their father's treasures following his death, which Zanni is devising to expedite. Saïd Ali suffers from an unidentified chronic disease (the real Nahārī suffered from diabetes, even losing a foot to the disease) and his pain is alleviated by several shots per day. As the story develops, Monfreid grows suspicious of Zanni's meddling with Saïd Ali's medication (prepared in Massawa and sent to Dahlak), suspecting that Zanni is addicting him to morphine. The anguished pearl merchant is made aware of this but insists on relieving his pain by

Figure 10.2. Front cover of *Le film complet du jeudi* (January 6, 1938) featuring *Les secrets de la mer Rouge* (1937), Harry Baur in the role of Saïd Ali. Author's personal collection.

any means possible. In the background to the main storyline, Monfreid meets Saïd Ali and—not unlike the narrative in Treat—the two form a connection through their common passion for pearls ("This terrible old man had such a way of showing his pearls. He cast a spell over me, he found the words and gestures for my undoing. In short, he communicated to me his passion"). Monfreid seems fond of Saïd Ali, who comes across as genuinely passionate about the intrinsic beauty of pearls and their mystique, in contrast to the greedy, scheming, or weak characters that populate the story, including Saïd Ali's own sons. Monfreid positions himself above all that on some rarefied plane, together with Saïd Ali. Unlike in *Pearls, Arms and Hashish*, Monfreid concludes a pearl deal resulting from the meeting with Saïd Ali.

Jacques Schouchana, the pearl-buying agent employed by the Paris-based Rosenthal tycoons and Monfreid's real-life friend, also makes appearances in *Les secrets*. He is said to have a credit of ten million in the bank to enable the acquisition of Saïd Ali's pearls (per Rosenthal's request). At any rate, a climactic point in the story occurs when Saïd Ali dies. Zanni continues his intrigues and Monfreid suspects him of being behind the change in morphine dosage that clearly caused Saïd Ali's

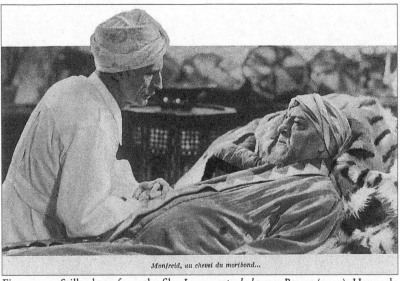

Figure 10.3. Stills photo from the film *Les secrets de la mer Rouge* (1937). Henry de Monfreid (*left*) as himself and Harry Baur (*right*) in the role of Saïd Ali. Source: *Le film complet du jeudi* (January 6, 1938). Author's personal collection.

death. Saïd Ali's attendants prepare his corpse for burial at Seil-Djin, an islet haunted by the *jinn* of the sea. The story goes on to tell how Zanni, the mastermind of the plot to get Saïd Ali's treasures, is tricked into thinking that the rich pearl merchant had all his pearls buried with him on the islet. After multiple twists and turns in the story, and thanks in great part to Monfreid and the trustworthy boat captain Cheikh Issa, the pearls find their way to Saïd Ali's son Omar, who takes the pearls to Aden and then to Bombay, where he meets Schouchana and sells him the greater part of Saïd Ali's prized possessions. Evil Zanni finds his death stranded on the island of Seil-Djin after attempting to dig out the pearls (which were not there) from Saïd Ali's tomb. "Saïd was avenged," the story ends.[63]

Attempting to capitalize on the success of the book, *Les secrets de la mer Rouge* was adapted to film by Joseph Kessel and directed by Richard Pottier in 1937. The plot is based—more-or-less—on the three central chapters of the book relating the story of Saïd Ali that I have described. Monfreid played himself in the film and Harry Baur (1880–1943), one of France's most cherished screen actors in the first half of the twentieth century, played the role of Saïd Ali. Baur's biographer wrote that the role played by the star, "un cheikh Arabe d'Afrique orientale" (an Arab Shaykh from East Africa), was brief and consisted of only three days of shooting. He also strangely added that the French film star claimed to have known "cheikh Said Ali" [sic] personally, a claim that the biographer strongly doubted.[64] At any rate, the film was shot in more than a month in Djibouti and a couple more weeks in the film studios in Paris.[65] News about the shooting was reported in the press and in the major film periodicals. In a brief item in the section of *Ciné-miroir* reporting on current filming locations, the magazine subtitled the item as "Harry Baur est devenu un grand seigneur yéménite" (Harry Baur has become a great Yemeni lord). The recreation of the atmosphere is worth quoting: "Two footsteps from the Champs-Élysées, just beyond the double door of Studio François 1er, [one notices] the immense set reconstituted for *Les secrets de la mer Rouge*, the splendid palace of Cheikh Said-Ali, played in the film by the great Harry Baur. In the hallways, court attendants and Yemeni fishermen wait as the master examines the pearls that they have fished in the depths of the Red Sea, the most beautiful of which will perhaps enrich his fabulous collection."[66] When the film came out in early September 1937, the cover of *Ciné-miroir* and a double-page spread were devoted to *Les secrets*, with large photos and a detailed storyline.[67] All in all, the film was not a great success. The reception by the critics was lukewarm and the entire experience left Monfreid rather discouraged.[68]

IN THEIR CRITIQUE of macro-scale approaches to global history, some historians point to the potential usefulness of several procedures employed by historians associated with the practice of microhistory, including biography. The story of ʿAlī al-Nahārī's life and afterlife displays the intricate intersection between the global history of a luxury commodity, indigenous elite entrepreneurial families, colonial officials, cosmopolitan European and American travelers, and metropolitan markets for both pearls and stories about the exotic. This essay shows how a particular moment of accelerated globalization shaped the trajectory of a Red Sea merchant with respect to a booming commodity and tied a particular producing area—the Red Sea region—with global financing, marketing, distribution, and consumption networks and circuits. In the process, Nahārī interconnected a host of actors separated by space, standing, and even time: for example, pearl divers in the Red Sea, the global gem magnates in Paris, and, ultimately, even European readers of travel adventure books and film audiences.

On a more regional level, the elaborate configurations of labor, financing, and the commercialization of pearls allow us to better understand the Red Sea as an interlaced and tangled historical space, engaging a host of transregional/trans-local actors. Though the Red Sea was divided between several European imperial powers during this period, Nahārī's story underscores how the mobility and circulation of local and regional operators across this maritime space, and between it and the Western Indian Ocean area and Europe, were more fluid than we might realize. Colonial powers were never able to tap into the lucrative and furtive fine-pearl trade, which flourished especially in between and across colonial boundaries. Indeed, Nahārī operated across such boundaries and against the grain of imperial financial interests. This provides a more nuanced understanding of how empires were constrained from below and how operation in the interstices of the European- and American-dominated global capitalist economy offered opportunities for non-Western entrepreneurs. The employment of a transregional/trans-local approach to biography also serves to problematize the question of identity/ies in this period. 'Alī al-Nahārī's case exposes the fluidity, hybridity, and complexity of identities (self-ascribed and perceived) in the southern Red Sea zone in the imperial period before the nation-state rendered boundaries and identities more rigid. Finally, the last part of the essay employs a sort of postcolonial procedure to "de-exoticize" and recover a figure inscribed into the travel-adventure literary genre in France in the 1930s and rescue it from the exotic imaginary.

ACKNOWLEDGMENTS

I would like to thank Cheikh Faisal Bazara, Rob Carter, William G. Clarence-Smith, Alessandro Gori, the late Leila Ingrams, Colleen Kennedy-Karpat, Alain Rouaud, and several members of the Nahārī family for their generous assistance with different aspects of this study. I would like to especially single out Khalid Nahari and thank him for his kind assistance.

NOTES

1. Michael B. Miller, *Shanghai on the Métro: Spies, Intrigue and the French between the Wars* (Berkeley: University of California Press, 1994), 338.

2. A recent volume that deals with luxury commodities from a global history perspective is Bernd-Stefan Grewe and Karin Hofmeester, eds., *Luxury in Global Perspective: Objects and Practices, 1600–2000* (Cambridge: Cambridge University Press, 2016).

3. For the definitive study of the Gulf pearling industry, see Robert Carter, *Sea of Pearls: Seven Thousand Years of the Industry That Shaped the Gulf* (London: Arabian, 2012). See also Matthew S. Hopper, *Slaves of One Master: Globalization and Slavery in Arabia in the Age of Empire* (New Haven, CT: Yale University Press, 2015), 80–104.

4. For brief overviews of pearling in the Red Sea, see George Frederick Kunz and Charles Hugh Stevenson, *The Book of the Pearl: The History, Art, Science, and Industry of the Queen of Gems* (New York: Century, 1908), 139–44; Elisabeth Strack, *Pearls* (Stuttgart: Rühle-Diebener-Verlag, 2006), 142–46; Jean Taburiaux, *Pearls: Their Origin, Treatment and Identification* (Radnor, PA.: Chilton, 1985), 30–34. A reliable Red Sea pearl diving account is Albert Londres, *Pêcheurs de perles* (Paris: Albin Michel, 1931).

5. For the pearling industry there, see a synthesis in Jonathan Miran, *Red Sea Citizens: Cosmopolitan Society and Cultural Change in Massawa* (Bloomington: Indiana University Press, 2009), 99–110. Good overviews

produced across the Italian colonial period are Ambrogio Parazzoli, "La pesca nel Mar Rosso," *L'Esplorazione commerciale* 13, no. 6 (June 1898): 177–90; Giovanni Salvadei, "La pesca e il commercio delle perle e della madreperla in Eritrea," allegato (enclosure) no. 91, in *Relazione sulla Colonia Eritrea del Regio Commissario civile deputato Ferdinando Martini per gli esercizi 1902–1907*, ed. Ferdinando Martini (Rome: Tipografia della Camera dei Deputati, 1913), 3:1157–81; Renato Paoli, "Le condizioni commerciali dell'Eritrea," in Ferdinando Martini, ed., *L'Eritrea economica* (Rome: Istituto Geografico De Agostini, 1913), 181–85); Giorgio Modigliani, "Le perle di Massaua," in *Atti del terzo congresso di studi coloniali, Firenze-Roma 12–17 Aprile 1937*, vol. 8, *VII sezione: Economica—Agraria* (Florence: G. C. Sansoni, 1937): 682–97.

6. See insightful comments on commodities histories from a "bottom-up perspective" ("globalization from below") in Lynn Hunt, *Writing History in the Global Era* (New York: W. W. Norton, 2014), 65–70.

7. Bernhard Struck, Kate Ferris, and Jacques Revel, "Introduction: Space and Scale in Transnational History," *International History Review* 33, no. 4 (2011): 577. See also Francesca Trivellato, "Is there a Future for Italian Microhistory in the Age of Global History?," *California Italian Studies* 2, no. 1 (2011), https://escholarship.org/uc/item/0z94n9hq.

8. See the essays included in the AHR Forum "Transnational Lives in the Twentieth Century," *American Historical Review* 118, no. 1 (February 2013): 45–139. A biographical approach is also employed in the writing of innovative regional and oceanic history. See, for example, Clare Anderson, ed., "Marginal Centers: Writing Life Histories in the Indian Ocean World," special issue, *Journal of Social History* 45, no. 2 (Winter 2011).

9. On the Red Sea as a historical space, see Jonathan Miran, ed., "Space, Mobility, and Translocal Connections across the Red Sea Area since 1500," special issue, *Northeast African Studies* 12, no. 1 (2012); and Miran, "The Red Sea," in *Oceanic Histories*, ed. David Armitage, Alison Bashford, and Sujit Sivasundaram (Cambridge: Cambridge University Press, 2018).

10. Léonard Rosenthal celebrated his success in several autobiographical books, for example, Rosenthal, *The Pearl Hunter* (New York: Henry Schuman, 1952), and Rosenthal, *The Pearl and I* (New York: Vantage, 1955). One can also patch together information about Jacques Bienenfeld in a variety of sources. See excerpts from the periodical, *La Perle*, that he published between 1924 and 1932 in Taburiaux, *Pearls*, 75–88; and William G. Clarence-Smith's chapter in this volume.

11. "Āl al-Nahārī, nasabhum wa-laqabhum wa-'ilmuhum wa-i'māluhum," Nahārī family papers; interview with Maryam 'Umar al-Nahārī, Asmara, March 26, 2000; Giuseppe Puglisi, "Ali El Nahari," in *Chi è? dell'Eritrea 1952: Dizionario biografico con una cronologia* (Asmara: Agenzia Regina, 1952), 11.

12. Somewhat confusingly, one of the most potent families in Dahlak Kabir Island, also involved in pearl fishing, is called Naharāy (as opposed to Nahārī). Suffice it to say here that the Naharāys held political authority, owned boats and houses, and some were pearl dealers, boat captains (*nākhuda*s), and pearl divers. What makes this more confusing is that there is also no doubt that the Nahārīs and Naharāys cooperated in pearling operations. My guess is that Nahārī provided the capital and the Naharāys organized crews. It is also possible that, once pearl prices skyrocketed and the ever-more-lucrative pearl business became ever more hushed, the confusion became "convenient" as a means to confound the colonial authorities. A case in point is the way these two families were tangled in otherwise reliable Italian colonial sources.

13. Massawa Islamic Council (Majlis Muṣawwa'), 1882, sentence of 25 Shawwāl 1299 (September 9, 1882).

14. For financing arrangements in the Dahlak fishery, see Parazzoli, "La pesca nel Mar Rosso," 187; Salvadei, "La pesca e il commercio," 1158; Paoli, "Le condizioni commerciali," 183; Modigliani, "Le perle di Massaua," 685. See also Dionisius A. Agius, John P. Cooper, Lucy Semaan, Chiara Zazzaro, and Robert Carter, "Remembering the Sea: Personal and Communal Recollections of Maritime Life in Jizan and the Farasan Islands, Saudi Arabia," *Journal of Maritime Archaeology* 11, no. 2 (August 2016): 165–67.

15. Pearl traders from Farasan and Jizan, for example, came to Massawa to sell pearls, especially to European buyers. Henry de Monfreid, *Aventures extraordinaires (1911–1921)* (Paris: Arthaud, 2007), 666–70.

16. See a relatively detailed account of pearl trade schemes in Modigliani, "Le perle di Massaua," 689–92.

17. Massawa Islamic Court Records (MICR) 8/61b (5 Dhū al-Ḥijja 1300 / October 7, 1883); 8/73a (4 Rabī' I 1301 / January 3, 1884).

18. *Gazzetta ufficiale del Regno d'Italia*, no. 87 (April 13, 1911): 2030, 2034–36, 2060, 2061.

19. Archivio Storico Diplomatico Ministero degli Affari Esteri (ASDMAE), Archivio Eritrea (AE) 193, "R. Capitaneria di porto di Massaua," Matricola dei sambucchi, January 1, 1908.

20. ASDMAE, AE 349, fascicolo 37, January 3, 1901; and Salvadei, "La pesca e il commercio," 1159. It should be noted that the Nahārīs also traded in textiles and hides.

21. Puglisi, "Ali El Nahari," 11 (my translation from Italian).

22. For the Nahārī family's marriage linkages, see MICR; interview conducted with Maryam 'Umar al-Nahārī, Asmara, March 26, 2000; Miran, *Red Sea Citizens*, 261.

23. Colonia Eritrea, no, 58, *Elenco dei commercianti, industriali, negozianti, imprenditori, appaltatori o fornitori, e degli esercenti professioni,*

arti e mestieri iscritti nel ruolo dei contribuenti della Colonia Eritrea (Esercizio 1912–1913) (Asmara: Tipografia Coloniale M. Fioretti, 1913): 40–47. On Hadrami trade and shipping networks in the Red Sea, see Janet Ewald and William G. Clarence-Smith, "The Economic Role of the Hadhrami Diaspora in the Red Sea and Gulf of Aden, 1820s to 1930s," in *Hadhrami Traders, Scholars and Statesmen in the Indian Ocean, 1750s-1960s,* ed. Ulrike Freitag and William G. Clarence-Smith (Leiden: Brill, 1997); Jonathan Miran, "Red Sea Translocals: Hadrami Migration, Entrepreneurship, and Strategies of Integration in Eritrea, 1840s–1970s," *Northeast African Studies* 12, no. 1 (2012): 129–68; Philippe Pétriat, *Le négoce des lieux saints: Négociants hadramis de Djedda, 1850–1950* (Paris: Publications de la Sorbonne, 2016).

24. Sheikh Faisal bin Hussain Bazara, personal email communications, June 23 and July 18, 2012. On the Bā Zarʻa family, see also Muḥammad ʻAlawī ʻAbd al-Raḥmān Bā Harūn, *al-Shaykh Muḥammad ibn ʻUmar Bā Zarʻa wa dawruhu fī tijārat al-muḥīṭ al-hindī* (al-Ḥāmī [Ḥaḍramawt]: Dār al-Ḥāmī li'l-Dirāsāt wa'l-Nashr, 2013). On Muḥammad ʻUmar Bā Zarʻa in Massawa, see Miran, *Red Sea Citizens,* esp. 240–42; and Renzo Martinelli, *Sud: Rapporto di un viaggio in Eritrea ed in Etiopia* (Florence: Vallecchi Editore, 1930), 35–45.

25. Martinelli, *Sud,* 39.

26. G. R. Millward, "Oysters, Pearls and Pearling in Sudan Waters," *Sudan Notes and Records* 27 (1946): 204.

27. Gian Luca Podestà, *Il mito dell'impero: Economia, politica e lavoro nelle colonie italiane dell'Africa orientale, 1898–1941* (Turin: G. Giappichelli Editore, 2004): 55–58; Massimo Zaccaria, "Italian Approaches to Economic Resources in the Red Sea Region," *Eritrean Studies Review* 5, no. 1 (2007): 113–55; Miran, *Red Sea Citizens,* 101–10.

28. See, for example, Victor Buchs, "Voyages en Abyssinie, 1889–1895," *Bulletin de la Société Neuchâteloise de Géographie* 9 (1896–97): 37; Parazzoli, "La pesca nel Mar Rosso," 186; Salvadei, "La pesca e il commercio," 1181.

29. Hopper, *Slaves of One Master,* 93.

30. For example, Ferdinando Filosa, an Italian resident of Suez employed by the Casa Lattes of Cairo, came to the Dahlak to buy pearls in the early 1880s. ASDMAE, Archivio Eritrea 16, Promemoria from Maissa to Sig. Ammiraglio Noce, June 26, 1885. In the early twentieth century, Léonard Rosenthal sent Jacques Schouchana to buy pearls in Massawa (see more in text) while Jacques Bienenfeld sent his cousin, Simon Lieberman, to the Eritrean port for the same purpose. David Bellos, *Georges Perec: A Life in Words* (London: Harvill, 1995), 23.

31. Carter, *Sea of Pearls,* 165–71; Hans Nadelhoffer, *Cartier* (London: Thames & Hudson, 2007), 125.

32. Carter, *Sea of Pearls*, 168–69; On Paris as the chief world market for fine pearls, see Taburiaux, *Pearls*, 65–70; Louis Kornitzer, *Pearls and Men* (London: Geoffrey Bles, 1935), 56–79.

33. Saif Marzooq al-Shamlan, *Pearling in the Arabian Gulf: A Kuwaiti Memoir* (London: London Centre of Arab Studies, 2000), 164–75. See also Yacoub Yusuf al-Ibrahim, *Les relations koweito-françaises à partir de 1778* (Kuwait: published by the author, 2006) (in Arabic and French).

34. Martinelli, *Sud*, 63.

35. Massimo Romandini, "Le comunicazioni stradali, ferroviarie e marittime dell'Eritrea durante il governatorato Martini (1897–1907)," *Africa* (Rome) 38, no. 1 (March 1983): 94–104.

36. Ferdinando Martini, *Il diario eritreo*, vol. 4 (Florence: Vallecchi, 1947), 585 (my translation from Italian).

37. Letter from 'Alī 'Abd al-Raḥmān Nahārī to Muḥammad 'Alī Nahārī ('Alī 's son), dated Cairo, April 25, 1907, Nahārī family papers. (my translation of a certified French translation of the Arabic original).

38. "Bayān shirā' lū'lū. . . ," Nahārī family papers. I thank Alessandro Gori for assisting me in decrypting this document. Sources note that Muḥammad al-Mushārī had gone bankrupt in 1920 and died in 1922. See Al-Shamlan, *Pearling in the Arabian Gulf*, 164; and Bashār al-Hādī, "[The famous pearl dealer Muḥammad bin 'Abd al-Wahhāb al-Mushārī]" (in Arabic), May 10, 2010, http://bashaaralhadi.blogspot.de/2010/05/blog-post_7231.html, accessed January 10, 2018.

39. Modigliani, "Le perle di Massaua," 693.

40. "The Second Business Trip of Mr. Ali A. Nahari to Paris (1924)," excerpts from the diary of Muḥammad 'Alī al-Nahārī, Nahārī family papers.

41. A receipt for shipping the pearls from Marseille to Paris shows that 11 kg (24 pounds) of pearls were declared, Nahārī family papers.

42. Letters and Statements, National Bank of India, Ltd., Aden branch and Bombay office, Nahārī family papers.

43. 'Alī al-Nahārī's certificate of knighthood decoration, dated December 6, 1925, Nahārī family papers.

44. Modigliani, "Le perle di Massaua," 693–94. Unsubstantiated anecdotic accounts tell how two of 'Alī's sons (Muḥammad and Ḥussein) tried to bribe the governor of Eritrea with pearls and were subsequently jailed. *Sharīfa* 'Alawiyya, a well-known figure in Massawa (a leading member of the Mīrghanī family and the Khatmiyya Sufi order), intervened with the authorities and secured their release.

45. Martinelli, *Sud*, 59–60 (my translation from Italian). In this period in colonial Eritrea, an individual who was not an Italian metropolitan citizen and who did not hold another citizenship, and was an autochthon to the colony, was considered a "colonial subject."

46. Martinelli, 61–65 (my translation from Italian).

47. Court Registration produced in Massawa, October 19, 1931, and signed by Qadi Ḥassen Osman, Nahārī family papers.

48. "Waṣiyya [of 'Alī ibn al-Sayyid 'Abd al-Raḥmān al-Nahārī]," dated 11 Sha'bān 1341 (March 28, 1923), Nahārī family papers.

49. Letter from Turner, Morrison and Co., Ltd., Bombay [Mogul Line], to Said Mohamed Ali Nahari, Massawa, dated December 7, 1934, Nahārī family papers.

50. From the 1930s, the Horn of Africa and the Red Sea area became the object of many journalistic reportages and novels (e.g., by Joseph Kessel, Albert Londres, and Henry de Monfreid), mostly concerned with slavery, pearling, smuggling, contraband, and arms trafficking. See Colette Dubois, "La traite des esclaves dans la littérature coloniale: Exotisme humanitaire ou sordides réalités?," in *Littératures et temps colonial: Métamorphoses du regard sur la Méditerranée et l'Afrique*, ed. Jean-Robert Henry and Lucienne Martini (Aix-en-Provence: Édisud, 1999).

51. A detailed biography of Monfreid is Daniel Grandclément, *L'incroyable Henry de Monfreid* (Paris: Grasset, 1998). See also Alain Gascon, "Henry de Monfreid," *Encyclopaedia Aethiopica*, vol. 3, ed. Siegbert Uhlig (Wiesbaden: Harrassowitz, 2007): 1000–1001.

52. See pertinent observations in Fabienne Le Houérou, "Aventures en Abyssinie: Henry de Monfreid et les 'ensablés,'" in *Littératures et temps colonial: Métamorphoses du regard sur la Méditerranée et l'Afrique*, ed. Jean-Robert Henry and Lucienne Martini (Aix-en-Provence: Edisud, 1999).

53. Joseph Kessel, *Marchés d'esclaves* (Paris: Union Générale d'Éditions 1984), 42–46 (originally serialized in *Le Matin* in 1930).

54. Victor Segalen, *Essay on Exoticism: An Aesthetics of Diversity* (Durham, NC: Duke University Press, 2002), 21, 25.

55. For insightful comments on the "exotic imaginary" in France in the 1930s as manifested in film, see Colleen Kennedy-Karpat, *Rogues, Romance, and Exoticism in French Cinema of the 1930s* (Madison, NJ: Fairleigh Dickinson University Press, 2013). See also Colin Crisp, *Genre, Myth, and Convention in French Cinema, 1929–1939* (Bloomington: Indiana University Press, 2002), esp. ch. 3.

56. Grandclément, *L'incroyable Henry de Monfreid*, 148–54. See also letters and diaries in Monfreid, *Aventures extraordinaires*.

57. Henry de Monfreid, "Journal de Bord: Voyage aux Îles Dahalak: 11 janvier–20 février 1914." Reproduced in Henry de Monfreid, *Journal de bord* (Paris: Arthaud, 1984), 36, and Monfreid, *Aventures extraordinaires*, 335–36 (my translation from French). I have yet to access a second unpublished logbook manuscript recording another trip to the Dahlak: "Journal de bord: Voyage à Dahalak: 28.01.1916–23.02.1916."

58. Henri de Monfreid with Ida Treat, *Pearls, Arms and Hashish: Pages from the Life of a Red Sea Navigator, Henri de Monfreid* (New York: Coward-McCann, 1930), 68–74.

59. Monfreid and Treat, 73. Here, too, fact and fiction are mixed (or facts are inaccurate). Nahārī died in 1931, *after* the publication of *Pearls, Arms and Hashish*. On the other hand, the time of their meeting (over fifteen years before 1929–30) is quite accurate.

60. Miller, *Shanghai on the Métro*, 338.

61. Richard Pankhurst, "Imaginative Writings (Novels, Short Stories and Plays) on Ethiopia and the Horn of Africa," *Africa* (Rome) 40, no. 4 (December 1985): 645.

62. Henry de Monfreid, *Les secrets de la mer Rouge* (Paris: B. Grasset, 1931). This was translated into English by Helen Buchanan Bell and published as Henry de Monfreid, *Secrets of the Red Sea* (London: Faber & Faber, 1934).

63. Other print publications that mention Saïd Ali and that either summarize parts of *Les secrets* or add on to the accounts in that book are Henry de Monfreid, "Pearl Fishing in the Red Sea," *National Geographic*, November 1937, 597–626; Monfreid, *La perle noire* (Paris: Grasset, 2009), first published in 1957 by Éditions Librairie Gedalge, Paris; and Monfreid, *Le trésor du pèlerin* (Paris: Gallimard, 1938).

64. Hervé Le Boterf, *Harry Baur* (Paris: Pygmalion, 1995), 141.

65. On the film, see Grandclément, *L'incroyable Henry de Monfreid*, 329–31.

66. "Du studio à la ville," *Ciné-miroir* 641, July 16, 1937, 466 (my translation from French). Other news items about the shooting are "Le cinéma," *Les annales coloniales* (Paris), May 28, 1937, 8; and "En regardant tourner . . . ," *Le matin* (Paris), July 9, 1937, 4.

67. "Les secrets de la mer Rouge," *Ciné-miroir* 649, September 10, 1937, 592–93.

68. A television series, *Les secrets de la mer Rouge*, was aired in France in 1968 and 1975, consisting of thirteen episodes in each season. It was one of the first series to be broadcast in color on French television.

ELEVEN

Pearling Women in North Australia
Indigenous Workers and Wives

JULIA T. MARTÍNEZ

DURING THE 1860S, when the colonial pearl-shell industry in Western Australia was in its infancy, many pearling masters preferred to employ Indigenous women as pearl-shell gatherers and divers.[1] The same was true of the Torres Strait Islands, located between north Queensland and Papua New Guinea. Allegations of kidnapping and forced labor, however, led to the Western Australian and Queensland governments banning women's employment in 1871 and 1901, respectively. Instead, the industry came to rely on male divers and crew of varied ethnicity. Pearlers retained male Aboriginal, Torres Strait Islander, and Pacific Islander workers, and expanded the workforce by importing indentured labor from Asia. While women may have been banned from working on pearling luggers, there is some evidence to suggest that they did continue to be involved in the industry informally.

Pearl-shell diving, in a global historical context, has been mostly male-dominated. There were some exceptions, such as the women divers of Japan and Korea. As Dolores Martinez observes, the Japanese *ama* were popularly imagined "as strong, tough, and independent women."[2] Traditional diving in other locations was less obviously gendered. In some islands of the South Pacific both men and women were divers.[3] In Australia there is scattered evidence that among Aboriginal and Torres Strait Islanders it was women who excelled in diving as a means of maintaining their marine-based diet. Grace Karskens, in her study of Eora fisherwomen in colonial Sydney, observed that it was women, rather than men, who dominated fishing and diving.[4] Further inland, an 1877 account of the upper Murray River also notes that it was Aboriginal women who went diving for freshwater mussels.[5]

In the northern Australian pearl-shell industry, women's traditional diving led to their being forced to engage in the largely unregulated commercial enterprises that set up in the frontier colonies in the 1860s. Despite their pioneering role in the industry, women divers have only recently come to be recognized in public memory. In the pearling town of Broome in 2010, a bronze statue of an Aboriginal woman diver was unveiled. She is naked and pregnant, rising from the sea with a pearl shell in her hand. The statue was designed to be a poignant reminder of those early years when Aboriginal women were forced to dive.[6]

While it is difficult to uncover detailed evidence of women's working conditions in pearling, we know that pearlers were frequently brutal in their treatment of male Aboriginal workers, even after the industry was regulated. There is also evidence from Queensland of inadequate food, with Torres Strait Islander divers dying of beriberi due to lack of vitamin B.[7] Even in the best of conditions, diving was inherently dangerous, and repeated dives could lead to hypothermia and exhaustion. Thus, when the colonial governments banned women's participation in the pearl-shell industry, it was their intention to protect women from these dangers. But "protection" of Aboriginal and Torres Strait Islander women across north Australia left them with very few legal opportunities for employment. In later years, women who were placed into domestic service—deemed to be appropriate as "women's work"—found that it, too, carried risks of physical and sexual abuse.[8]

There is a dearth of historical literature on women in the pearl-shell industry. Susan Jane Hunt's 1986 *Spinifex and Hessian* canvassed women's connections with the pearl-shell industry, including the Irish and British wives of pearling masters who sailed on board the schooners and the Japanese prostitutes who provided sexual services for the pearling workers of Broome.[9] Ruth Balint has called for greater attention to the role of Aboriginal women, though her emphasis is more on women as wives, or "fishwives."[10] My focus in this chapter is on Aboriginal and Torres Strait Islander women's role in the industry, from Western Australia to Queensland. I consider both their labor as pearl-shell gatherers and divers and their position as wives and as sexual companions to pearl-shell workers.

ABORIGINAL WOMEN DIVERS IN WESTERN AUSTRALIA

In the Western Australian regions of Kimberley, Pilbara, and Gascoyne, there was a long history of Aboriginal pearl-shell collection, well before the arrival of Europeans.[11] The first Europeans to gather pearl shell in this region arrived in Nickol Bay in 1861 on the exploration voyage of the barque *Dolphin*. While waiting for the exploration team to return, the crew became acquainted with the local Indigenous people, who helped them load water and wood, and no doubt helped them to gather an unexpected bounty of £600 of shell plus a quantity of pearls.[12] By the mid-1860s in Nickol Bay, European pearlers were regularly recruiting the labor of Aboriginal women, initially as dry-shellers, gathering shell when the tide was out and then moving to wading along the shoreline. As shelling operations increased and the easy-to-reach shell was exhausted, they began using boats and divers. Shoreline collection did not end. Personal accounts suggest that around the 1920s there was still shell to be gathered by wading. Indigenous Yawuru woman Doris Edgar, interviewed at the age of seventy-four, recalled her childhood in Broome when she and her family collected shell at low tides. They ate the shell meat and traded the shell for flour, tea, and sugar.[13]

The European-owned pearl-shell industry took off quickly after 1868, in which year there were at least ten boats employing Aboriginal men and women.[14] American W. F. Tays is attributed with teaching Aboriginal women (and men) to dive deeper for pearl shell. A 1930 account recalls Tays as an employer who was "generous," providing Aboriginal men and women with "tea, flour, sugar and tobacco" in return for their labor.[15]

The skill of Aboriginal women divers is described in numerous sources. In 1868, master pearler H. Merton, on the 18-ton schooner

Medora, was laid up at Butcher Inlet in Tien Tsin Harbour during the winter off-season.[16] He wrote in a letter that he was feeding the Aboriginal divers on a diet of a pound of flour per day.[17] This limited diet made additional food a necessity, and he was full of praise for the skill of Aboriginal women as they fished, writing, "The Ceylon divers would be far surpassed by our own natives, who in this respect may be called a kind of 'half-fish.' They think no more of swimming five or six miles than I do of walking the same distance, and the women actually dive and catch a sort of schnapper [*sic*] here in two or three fathoms of water."[18] Another report claimed that women could dive to a depth of seven fathoms, or about thirteen meters.[19] But even while Merton was pleased with his working relationships, complaints were being received by authorities about the abduction and harboring of Aboriginal women by pearlers. Concern was expressed, not so much for the fate of the women, but over the increased likelihood of retaliation on "the part of the black."[20] The government resident at Roebourne, Robert J. Sholl, was nevertheless pleased to report that the *Medora* was especially successful in securing pearl shell that year.[21]

By 1870, there were some thirty boats on the northwest coast, employing an estimated 62 white men and three hundred Aboriginal men and women. The Western Australian government banned women's employment the following year in the Aboriginal Natives Pearl Shell Fishery Act of 1871, described as "An Act to regulate the hiring and service of Aboriginal Natives engaged in the Pearl Shell Fishery; and to prohibit the employment of women therein."[22] During the parliamentary debate on the act, Maitland Brown, the infamous leader of the 1865 Lagrange Bay expedition that massacred Aboriginal people, spoke. He favored the registration of workers but also wanted to retain women divers. He challenged the clause preventing "native women being engaged," protesting that the women "were the very best divers, and . . . were as numerous as the men."[23] Newly arrived from British Honduras, Attorney General Robert John Walcott also supported Aboriginal registration. Using the paternalistic language of the time, he asked that Aboriginal people "be treated as children, and be protected as children."[24]

The Pearl Shell Fishery Regulation Act, 1873, which replaced the 1871 act, confirmed the prohibition on the employment of women. Aboriginal men's work was further regulated, being fixed for twelve months, with contracts to be entered into voluntarily. The men were also to be returned to their home district at the end of that period.[25] But despite these new regulations, in 1875 the governor of Western Australia informed the Colonial Office in London that Aboriginal workers were in "a condition little better than slavery."[26]

Despite the ban on Aboriginal women's employment on pearling luggers, the practice did continue. In September 1875, two men were fined for having Aboriginal women on board their vessels. They were Samuel Sustenance, master of the schooner *Game-Cock* (fined 22 shillings and costs), and Edward Chapman, master of the cutter *Edward James* (fined 17 shillings).[27] Aubrey Brown (brother to Maitland) protested that Aboriginal women were even banned from opening shell on shore. He argued that the women "would be deprived of their bread, and immorality would considerably increase," a reference to the increased likelihood that women's sexual services would be offered in return for food.[28] Aboriginal women did, however, continue in onshore work. After journalist Ernestine Hill visited Shark Bay in 1932, the *Sun* published a photograph of Aboriginal women opening pearl shell, described by Hill as an "unpleasant and tedious task, cruel to the hands."[29]

The tendency to represent women as passive observers of men's diving can be seen elsewhere in the literature. North of Australia, across the Arafura Sea, the pearling beds of the Aru Islands in eastern Indonesia have been worked by indigenous people for centuries. While women sometimes gathered the delicacy bêche-de-mer (or trepang) in the shallows, diving for pearl shell was regarded as a male occupation. Patricia Spyer described scenes of joy as the indigenous male pearling crews returned from a day of diving. The cliffs overlooking the harbor were crowded with women, "the wives, mothers, and sisters of the divers together with their children—who wait to greet their husbands and sons and to hear how the divers have fared."[30]

In Western Australia, there is little evidence of such community-based celebrations of pearl-shell harvest. One early pearler's recollection is instead a depiction of women's grief as their sons and husbands set sail for the pearling season. In the Aru Islands, the men left for the day and returned to the families. In north Australia, the pearling season meant an absence of many months.

> I once saw a schooner-load of natives leave Cossack . . . and
> the sight was the most affecting I have ever witnessed. The boys

had just been brought in from the back country, where they had been running wild since the previous season. Although most of them had walked two or even three hundred miles to the port, they were followed by their mothers and wives, who came to see them depart. That night before the schooner sailed, the women were camped on the sandhills where, in unison with the dogs . . . they howled dismally until dawn. They then collected upon the beach abreast of the schooner, an ash-covered, dishevelled, tear-stained crowd, and wailed. Shortly after sunrise the schooner sailed. No sooner did she begin to move than the women broke again into loud lamentations, running the while along the edge of the water, so that they might keep up with the vessel.[31]

In this account it appears that only the men were being taken to work, suggesting that it took place after 1871. Perhaps the women went along hoping that they would be allowed to accompany the men? We cannot assume that the women were happy about the new restrictions. Penelope Edmonds and Lynette Russell, writing on Aboriginal women in the sealing and whaling industries, have cautioned against taking colonial narratives of women's enslavement and protection at face value, noting how antislavery activities often worked against women's agency.[32]

The question of worker's agency was raised in relation to Aboriginal work in pearling at the time. Pastoralist and pearler McKenzie Grant, writing in 1879, protested at the allegations that police were "running in" Aboriginal workers for pearlers, claiming, "Our natives know us, have confidence in us, and know when they are well off, and they are only too glad to engage, in consideration of the many advantages they derive from employment." Grant explained that when summer diving was over, the divers were taken back to their country and their families (which had been provided for in their absence), and "all the winter they are fed and treated like human beings." Grant was feeding around four hundred people at De Grey River, people who, he claimed, thanks to him had "no fear of starvation."[33] In his effort to refute accusations of slavery, Grant revealed the entrenched paternalism under which Aboriginal women were relegated to remaining at home, without their male relations, and increasingly reliant on a white master for their food supply.

The pearl-shell industry in north Queensland was centered in the Torres Strait Islands. Colonial rule over the islands developed alongside the expansion of the pearl-shell industry, with the first official settlement in Somerset being established in 1864. Commercial quantities of shell were taken from Tudu (Warrior) Island (located toward Papua New Guinea) in 1869, which led to a pearl rush over the next two decades.[34]

Historian Regina Ganter explains that the women of nearby Mer (Murray) Island in the eastern Torres Strait regarded diving as a traditional female activity.[35] According to Anna Shnukal and Guy Ramsay, until 1874 both men and women were employed as divers in the Torres Strait.[36] Douglas Pitt from Jamaica had arrived on Murray Island in 1871 and started a bêche-de-mer station with partners Doyle and Bruce. Frank Jardine, an experienced pearl sheller working since 1869, claimed that these "two West Indian blacks" were taking women and forcing them to work on the station. They had married into the local community, which thus enabled them to employ local labor.[37] Murray and Darnley (Erub) Islands were both outside the territorial limits of Queensland until 1879, which meant that the authorities could not intervene. In the first few years of fishing operations, the indigenous population of Darnley Island dropped from four or five hundred to around 130 people.[38]

The London Missionary Society arrived in the Torres Strait in 1871 and, with the aid of the pearl shellers, set up Polynesian missionaries on Murray and Dauan Islands. Complaints were made from Mabuiag Island of raids on women, implicating the new missionaries. Reverend William Wyatt Gill, who visited the Torres Strait in 1872, wrote that "women make excellent divers," but also warned that "women have been kidnapped and compelled to dive."[39] According to Captain Charles Pennefather, writing in 1882, the men of Tudu Island would bury "their women and young girls in the sand with only their noses showing" as soon as a pearling vessel appeared.[40]

The earliest legislation aimed at protecting pearling labor in Queensland related specifically to Pacific Islanders who had been brought to Queensland from nearby islands such as the French colony of New Caledonia, New Hebrides, and Tonga.[41] The Pacific Islanders Protection Act of 1872 (Kidnapping Act) forced ships to register workers and ensure they gave consent.[42] Whether women from the Pacific

Islands were specifically sought for diving is unknown, their labor being even less visible than that of Aboriginal women. As Tracey Banivanua Mar observed, "if Islanders were a subaltern group written out of colonial memory, Islander women were doubly so."[43]

Pacific Islander women's work is considered by historian Steve Mullins, who describes how the term "passenger fish" was used in the Torres Strait fishery to refer to Pacific Islander women workers, "who, under mid-1870s British legislation, were prohibited from being employed at sea on British registered vessels." The term originally referred to sailors illegally joining trading vessels. In the case of women, Mullins argues, they worked for their keep, and even if many were wives, that did not stop them from "gathering, processing and packing" produce.[44] This term also extended to women working on shore processing bêche-de-mer.

The Native Labourers' Protection Act (1884) related specifically to workers in the pearl-shell industry, requiring them to be signed on and off and returned home within twelve months. This act did not apply to Pacific Islanders, who were at this time described as being capable of managing their own employment contracts. Ganter has argued that these restrictions were not welcomed by Aboriginal workers, who were resentful of "being taken far away from home, to Thursday Island or Cooktown, to be signed on and off."[45]

Summing up the role of women, Regina Ganter concludes that they "played only a minor role in the fishery, mainly confined to the sexual companionship of the men engaged in the industry."[46] This she attributes to the ban on women workers, which started as early as 1885 on Thursday Island. Even though the historical evidence for women's work is scarce after 1885, this is not surprising, given that the pearling masters would have kept women's involvement hidden from the authorities so as to avoid a fine or worse. After the bans, more attention is given to reporting women's sexual relations with pearling crews, and the discussion of diving all but disappears. Ganter found surviving accounts of relationships between pearlers and Aboriginal women "too much coloured by moral condemnation."[47] Anna Shnukal similarly describes how Filipino pearl shellers were accused of abducting men and women from mainland Cape York without permission in the 1880s and 1890s.[48]

The subsequent Aborigines Protection and Prevention of the Sale of Opium Act (1897) distinguished between Aborigines and Torres Strait Islanders, allowing pearl shellers to recruit the latter. The argument made by the authorities was that, as Murray Islanders were "quite as intelligent as Polynesians," they would understand the contracts they signed.[49] It is not clear how women workers fitted into this debate. It should be noted that by this period many islands would have had a second generation of Pacific Islander children. According to a 1908 census of the 230 people living on Darnley Island, an estimated two hundred were Pacific Islanders.[50]

John Douglas, the government resident on Thursday Island, would have reason to celebrate the swimming skills of the local Torres Strait women when tropical cyclone Mahina struck Cape York on March 4, 1899, claiming the lives of an estimated four hundred people. The newspapers at the time were full of admiration for the feats of swimming displayed by the so-called "colored women." On the schooner *Tawara*, Captain Jones picked up a Samoan man and an Aboriginal woman who had swum for four days over twenty miles. Another report claimed that "two colored women swam 10 hours with their children on their backs." Around six schooners, sixty luggers, and twenty swimming and diving boats were lost.[51] Despite the ban on women divers, these women would have had permission to be on board luggers under the clause that allowed married women to accompany their husbands.

The married women clause was part of an amendment put through in 1901, inspired by Northern Protector of Aborigines Walter E. Roth.[52] Specifically, Section 10.3 of the Aboriginals Protection and Restriction of the Sale of Opium Acts (1901) banned from boats "any male aboriginal who has not arrived at puberty, or any female aboriginal or female half-caste, unless under a written permit given by a Protector." Written permits to be on board vessels could only be allowed for women who were "tribally" or lawfully married. Section 9 of the act also required permission to be sought for the marriage of an Aboriginal woman to a non-Aboriginal man, presumably to prevent marriages of convenience.[53] In reading the Aboriginals Protection and Sale of Opium Bill in the Queensland Legislative Assembly, Mr. Maxwell expressed the view that it was undesirable for any woman to be on a lugger, adding, "When an aboriginal woman went there they all knew what she went there for."[54] His suggestion of sexual impropriety was rejected by the home secretary, the Hon. J. F. G. Foxton, who stated that

> this clause provided for women who were the wives of the men on the boats. Many a man had his wife with him on board the pearl-shelling

boats in Torres Straits. One of these men might have an aboriginal wife, and it would not be fair to exclude her from being with her husband on the boat.... Moreover, these people, especially on Darnley and Murray Islands, had a high moral sense of the marriage tie. It was very sacred to them, and it would be a great injustice if the wives of these men were not allowed to accompany their husbands. It would mean that these women would have to stay all their lives on the islands, for it was only once in a blue moon that a steamer went there.[55]

Foxton had toured the pearling region in 1899, afterwards speaking out against the supposed abduction of mainland Aboriginal women by "Manilamen" pearling masters. At that time he appeared to challenge the claim that the women were only there to accompany their husbands.[56] Even as Foxton came to express sympathy for the presence of "wives" on luggers, this emphasis on marriage overshadowed women's earlier role as workers. There is no mention in this parliamentary discussion of women divers. If women did continue to dive after 1901, it was apparently done without knowledge or approval from the authorities.

Writing on early twentieth-century Pacific Islander women, Mullins notes that women generally did collect marine produce from 14-foot dinghies after 1910, and by the mid-1930s the term "passenger fish" had been replaced by "dinghy produce." Mullins suggests the protector's office later came to regard the work of these women as coming under its jurisdiction, so they were no longer working off the books.[57]

Women working without permission were occasionally reported in the newspapers. For example, in 1920 Aboriginal women were reported to be living with Japanese men and diving at Cape Sidmouth in exchange for flour and tobacco. There were five or six luggers under the supervision of white pearling master Hugh Giblett. The Protector of Aboriginals on Thursday Island, Ernest Wilby, wondered if the local Protector had sanctioned the employment of Aboriginal workers, and asked, "does he know that females are employed diving"?[58]

PEARLING WOMEN AS SEXUAL COMPANIONS IN NORTH AUSTRALIA

The official position on women's work in the pearl-shell industry was shaped by the notion that women needed to be protected from the moral and health risks associated with sexual relations with pearling crews. Under the White Australia policy, there was the added concern that the north might see an increase in the so-called "half-caste" population. Despite this rhetoric, there was no ironclad anti-miscegenation law. Relationships between Asian pearling crews and local women were publicly discouraged but occasionally sanctioned, and sometimes policed as criminal infractions.[59] Ann McGrath argues in *Illicit Love*, however, that the number of applications approved for marriage between Aboriginal women and Asian pearling workers was nevertheless substantial.[60]

As Japanese men came to dominate the industry, Japanese women also immigrated to the pearling ports to work in brothels, particularly during the 1890s. The *karayuki-san* (a euphemism for sex workers) were said to have invested in pearling luggers, contributing to the dominance of Japanese in the industry.[61] As James Francis Warren demonstrates in his pathbreaking scholarship on karayuki-san, Japanese women during this period were part of a broader Indian Ocean migration that saw Japanese women moving southwards throughout Southeast Asia.[62] In 1900. there were 1,030 male Japanese and 61 female Japanese recorded living on Thursday Island. During the "lay-up" season from December to April, as Yuriko Nagata writes, there were "hundreds of young men with sufficient money to entertain themselves with drink and in the gambling house and brothels."[63] After 1902, further federal immigration restrictions made it more difficult for Japanese women to immigrate to Australia.[64]

Apart from Japanese women, there were a very few Chinese, Filipina, and Malay women living in the pearling ports. A Malay woman was mentioned in the newspapers as having been on board the pearling lugger *Venus* off Port Hedland in Western Australia in 1887 along with four men. If she was a young woman, she may have been the daughter of a Malay man and an Aboriginal mother, but the news item does not provide her name.[65] The 1896 Thursday Island census recorded 626 Europeans, 233 Japanese, 119 Filipinos, 115 Malays, 84 Chinese, 70 Pacific Islanders, 65 Aboriginal Australians, 30 Singalese, and two Javanese. The census also recorded three Malay women and fourteen children along with some 270 Malay men employed in pearling.[66]

Usually it was the more established divers who were able to marry. Japanese diver Yamamoto Tsunematsu, for example, settled down as a merchant in the pearling port of Darwin in the Northern Territory and married locally born Chinese woman Mary Edith.[67] Another pearling family of note was that of Carl Pon, who came to Australia from Kupang (West Timor) in the 1880s and became manager of the Jolly & Co. pearling fleet.[68] He married Kitty, an Aboriginal woman from the McArthur River district who had been raised by a respected white family, the Strettons, and taught Sunday school. They lived on Frances Bay, where the pearling fleet anchored, and had two sons, Herman and Jacob.[69]

Not all families were able to stay together. Writing on the Kimberley region of Western Australia, Sarah Yu tells how some Malay fathers had to leave their children behind because of government deportation policies.[70] Christine Choo has explored the restrictions imposed by missionaries in their effort to curtail contact between Aboriginal women and Malay men.[71]

In the Torres Strait, the descendants of such mixed marriages are well-known today as storytellers of the north, publishing personal insights into pearling history.[72] Ahwang Dai, a Dayak, came from Singapore to the Torres Straits in the 1880s and in 1891 married Annie, a Badu Island girl with whom he had eleven children. Atima, the daughter of Ahwang Dai and Annie, applied for permission to marry a Malay man in 1914, but was refused by Protector of Aborigines William Lee-Bryce. Instead, the couple were married in "Malay fashion." Descendants of this family are the Ah Mats, with branches in the Torres Strait and Darwin.[73] In another case, Cissie Malay, who was "designated as a half-caste Aboriginal woman and under the age of 21," was also forbidden to marry when Drummond Sarawak applied for permission in 1916.[74] In 1922, John McLaren argued that pearling indentured laborers at Thursday Island should not be allowed to marry Aboriginal women because it would practically assure them permanent residence, and this might encourage others to marry in order to secure that right.[75]

Similar restrictions applied in Western Australia, where the Chief Protector of Aborigines in 1903 demanded restrictions on the movement of Aboriginal women into Broome to prevent them from having sexual relations with Asian pearling workers. A Royal Commission on the Condition of Natives in Western Australia was headed by Queensland medical officer Walter E. Roth in 1905 to investigate.[76] Roth reported on the bartering of women for "gin, tobacco, flour and rice" and recommended that the police have the power to order pearling crews back to their luggers, that landing areas be formally reserved, and that a patrol boat be chartered.[77]

The authorities tended to assume their moral right to restrict the freedom of movement of women on pearling luggers, but individual court cases reveal women who actively rejected such paternalism. One case in Broome in 1927 concerned Mercedes Hunter, a married woman of Spanish-Malay-Aboriginal descent who had been found on board the pearling lugger of Captain James Arthur Mulgrue. He was taken to court and fined £10 and costs for having an Aboriginal woman on his vessel. In 1928, Mercedes was again found on his lugger the *Delaware*. He was fined and Mercedes was sent to the Moore River Mission. Two Aboriginal men gave evidence in court saying that they had been forced to go to work for Mulgrue. When they claimed that Mercedes was having sexual relations with Mulgrue, Mercedes reportedly burst out laughing from the back of the courtroom.[78] Her response suggests a woman who was not in need of protection.

Mulgrue himself admitted that he had taken on board three Aboriginal men and three women apart from Mercedes. Before going to Beagle Bay to register two of the male Aboriginal workers, Mulgrue had dropped off one man and the three women along the coast. He then dropped Mercedes off at Bullabullaman Creek for one night, presumably to avoid alerting the police at Beagle Bay to her presence on his lugger.[79] Bullabullaman Creek was well known to authorities as a meeting place where pearling luggers could find shelter and gain access to Aboriginal women. Some years earlier, in 1903, Constable Napier had been there on patrol and reported at length on the so-called "immoral intercourse between coloured crews on pearling luggers and Aboriginal Native women at Sunday Island Mission."[80]

In Darwin, relationships between Aboriginal women and pearling workers were also perceived as illicit. The Northern Territory Aboriginals Ordinance 1918 made it a criminal offence to keep as a mistress or have carnal knowledge of "a female aboriginal or half-caste," with punishments of up to three months in prison. Marriage required the permission of the chief protector.[81] Despite this ordinance, the pearling crews continued to seek out local women for sexual companionship. In 1936, as the number of Asian pearling workers increased in Darwin, one local police officer, Sergeant Koop, complained that "Malay and Koepang divers and crews freely patronise the hotels." He asked that compounds—such as were used in other colonies—be introduced, hoping to restrict their movements.[82] Jack McDonald, secretary of the North Australian

Workers' Union, claimed that the pearling crews, "Koepangers, Malays, Maccassars, Aroe Islanders, Japanese and others," lived in a boarding-house in Cavenagh Street, Darwin, where the "coloured girls" (women of Aboriginal descent) were freely able to visit them.[83]

The interactions between Japanese pearling crews and Aboriginal women on neighboring islands were also under surveillance by the Northern Territory administration. The Japanese had been welcomed in the mid 1890s, when they first helped to open up new pearl-shell beds near Melville Island, but by the 1930s they were treated as unwelcome intruders. Captain Haultain patrolled the islands frequented by pearling luggers. His reports in 1936 include one of finding ten luggers off Buchanan Island. He had information that Aboriginal canoes had been traveling from nearby Melville and Bathurst Islands (Tiwi Islands) to visit the luggers. They boarded one boat and found three Aboriginal women on deck. The women had been given flour, sugar, and tobacco in return for sexual services. Two Japanese divers working for pearling master R. M. Edward were fined for permitting Aboriginal women on board their lugger and threatened with deportation. Constable G. L. Don visited Garden Point on Melville Island, where some two hundred Aboriginal people lived, and found an Aboriginal-Japanese child. He was told that there were other children of Japanese fathers, but their mothers had hidden them, fearing the police would take them away.[84]

Monsignor Francis Xavier Gsell, who had established the Bathurst Island Roman Catholic mission in 1910, had also protested to the minister of the interior in the 1930s about the alleged Japanese exploitation of Aboriginal women for prostitution.[85] In another report of women going out to Japanese luggers from Goulburn Island, the women gave evidence that they had been forced to go by their elders. That these were temporary encounters is suggested by the fact that the women rarely mentioned the Japanese men by name, but called them by their pearling ranks: engineer, diver, second diver, and tender.[86] None of these reports spoke of Tiwi Island women being asked to dive for pearl shell.

THE LATE NINETEENTH CENTURY push to abolish Aboriginal and Torres Strait Islander women's employment in the pearl-shell industry led both to a decline in women's employment and to a shift in the narratives of women's involvement in the industry. The once-lauded skills of women divers were apparently forgotten as Asian men came to dominate the industry. Instead, women connected to the industry were assumed to be either sexual companions or wives to the male pearling masters and their divers and crew. For the most part, the limited evidence only points to women boarding luggers to exchange sexual services for food. This trajectory can be viewed as part of a broader historical movement in which woman were discouraged from a range of supposedly inappropriate employment. In the case of Queensland, where married women were still permitted on board pearling luggers after 1901, there is evidence that they did work at shell-opening, but there is little discussion of diving. Certainly by the 1920s, the authorities viewed women's diving as an inherently fraught activity, but primarily because diving was presumed to coincide with sexual relations between Asian pearlers and Indigenous women.

NOTES

1. Ronald Moore, "The Management of the Western Australian Pearling Industry, 1860 to the 1930s," *The Great Circle: Journal of the Australian Association for Maritime History* 16, no. 2 (1994): 121–38; Mike McCarthy, "Before Broome," *Great Circle* 16, no. 2 (1994): 76–89; Sumi Kwaymullina, "For Marbles: Aboriginal People in the Early Pearling Industry of the North-West," *Studies in Western Australian History* 22 (2001): 53–61.

2. D. P. Martinez, *Identity and Ritual in a Japanese Diving Village: The Making and Becoming of Person and Place* (Honolulu: University of Hawai'i Press, 2004), 29.

3. "Pearl Diving," *Australian Town and Country Journal* (Sydney), December 12, 1906, 67.

4. Grace Karskens, *The Colony: A History of Early Sydney* (Sydney: Allen and Unwin, 2010), 38.

5. "The Upper Murray Blacks," *Riverine Grazier* (Hay, NSW), March 28, 1877, 2.

6. The sculptors were Joan Smith and Charlie Smith. See Vanessa Mills, "Women Recognised for Love and Death in Broome Pearling," *ABC Kimberley*, November, 29, 2010, http://www.abc.net.au/local/stories/2010/11/29/3079734.htm.

7. In 1907–8 there were twenty-one deaths among the three hundred "Papuans" employed, and fifteen were due to beriberi. Report, Lieutenant-Governor J. H. P Murray, Thursday Island, to Minister for External Affairs, February 23, 1909, "Mortality of Papuans," National Archives of Australia (NAA), A1, 1909/11315.

8. See "Employment of Lubras in Mines—N.T.," NAA, A1, 1935/3291. For more on women's employment restrictions, see Alison Holland, *Just Relations: The Story of Mary Bennett's Crusade for Aboriginal Rights* (Crawley, Western Australia: UWA Publishing, 2015), 365. See also Victoria K. Haskins and Claire Lowrie, eds., *Colonization and Domestic Service: Historical and Contemporary Perspectives* (New York: Routledge, 2015).

9. Susan Jane Hunt, *Spinifex and Hessian: Women's Lives in North-Western Australia, 1860–1900* (Nedlands: University of Western Australia Press, 1986), 64.

10. Ruth Balint, "Aboriginal Women and Asian Men: A Maritime History of Color in White Australia," *Signs* 37, no. 3 (Spring 2012): 546.

11. Ruth Balint lists the shell-collecting peoples as "the Bardi, Nyul Nyul, Jabirrjar, Gumball, and Yawuru" in "Aboriginal Women and Asian Men," 546. See also Ben Collins and Hilary Smale, "Uncovering the First 20,000 Years of Australia's Pearling History," *ABC Kimberley*, June 6, 2014, http://www.abc.net.au/local/stories/2014/06/06/4020357.htm.

12. "Mr. F. T. Gregory's Expedition to the N.W. Coast of Australia," *Inquirer and Commercial News* (Perth), November 27, 1861, 3.

13. Kwaymullina, "For Marbles," 53.

14. J. P. S. Bach, *The Pearling Industry of Australia: An Account of Its Social and Economic Development* (Canberra: Department of Commerce and Agriculture, Commonwealth of Australia, 1955), 47.

15. Norman Bartlett, *The Pearl Seekers* (London: Andrew Melrose, 1954), 82; see original in "Pearling Pioneers, Native Divers," *West Australian* (Perth), December 6, 1930, 4.

16. The nearby township was named Cossack in 1872.

17. His cargo manifest some five months earlier had included potatoes and onions. See "Sailed," *Inquirer and Commercial News* (Perth), January 1, 1868, 2.

18. Letter to J. Reilly, Port Walcott, June 5, 1868, quoted in "The Pearl Fishery at Nickol Bay," *Inquirer and Commercial News* (Perth), July 15, 1868, 3.

19. Mike McCarthy, "Naked Diving for Mother-of-Pearl," *Early Days: Journal of the Royal Western Australian Historical Society* 13, no. 2 (2008): 247.

20. "Roebourne, Port Walcott," *Inquirer and Commercial News* (Perth), March 31, 1869, 3.

21. "Port Walcott," *Inquirer and Commercial News* (Perth), November 18, 1868, 3.

22. *Hansard*, Western Australia, Parliamentary Debates, Legislative Council, January 2, 1871, 69; Bach, *Pearling Industry of Australia*, 82.

23. M. Brown in *Inquirer and Commercial News*, December 21, 1870, 2.

24. "Aboriginal Natives—Pearl Fishery," *Inquirer and Commercial News* (Perth), December 21, 1870, 2.

25. Bach, *Pearling Industry of Australia*, 82.

26. Bach, 83.

27. "Cossack," *Inquirer and Commercial News* (Perth), September 22, 1875, 1.

28. "Shark's Bay," *Inquirer and Commercial News* (Perth), October 3, 1873, 2.

29. Ernestine Hill, "Where Streets Are Paved with Pearl," *Sun* (Sydney), September 4, 1932, 17.

30. Patricia Spyer, "The Eroticism of Debt: Pearl Divers, Traders, and Sea Wives in the Aru Islands, Eastern Indonesia," *American Ethnologist* 24, no. 3 (August 1997): 520.

31. Quoted in Bartlett, *The Pearl Seekers*, 83.

32. Penelope Edmonds, "Collecting Looerryminer's 'Testimony': Aboriginal Women, Sealers, and Quaker Humanitarian Anti-Slavery Thought and Action in the Bass Strait Islands," *Australian Historical Studies* 45, no. 1 (2014): 13–33; Lynette Russell, *Roving Mariners: Australian Aboriginal Whalers and Sealers in the Southern Oceans, 1790–1870* (Albany: State University of New York Press, 2012).

33. "The Truth about the North-West," *Inquirer and Commercial News* (Perth), February 12, 1879, 1.

34. The five main ethnolinguistic groups are Miriam Le, Kulkalgal, Saibailgal, Maluilgal, and Kaurareg (who intermarried with Cape York Aboriginal people). Anna Shnukal and Guy Ramsay, "Tidal Flows: An Overview of Torres Strait Islander-Asian Contact," in *Navigating Boundaries: The Asian Diaspora in Torres Strait*, ed. Anna Shnukal, Guy Ramsay, and Yuriko Nagata (Canberra: Pandanus Books, 2004), 33–35.

35. Regina Ganter, *The Pearl-Shellers of Torres Strait: Resource Use, Development and Decline, 1860s–1960s* (Melbourne: Melbourne University Press, 1994), 4.

36. Shnukal and Ramsay, "Tidal Flows," 35.

37. Ganter, *The Pearl-Shellers*, 28; Steve Mullins, "To Break 'the Trinity' or 'Wipe Out the Smaller Fry': The Australian Pearl Shell Convention of 1913," *Journal for Maritime Research* 7, no. 1 (2005), 219.

38. Ganter, *The Pearl-Shellers*, 1920.

39. William Wyatt Gill, *Life in the Southern Isles, or Scenes and Incidents in the South Pacific and New Guinea* (London: Religious Tract Society, 1876), 297.

40. Nonie Sharp, *Stars of Tagai: The Torres Strait Islanders* (Canberra: Aboriginal Studies Press, 1993), 26.

41. "Pearling Near the Australian Coast," *Queenslander* (Brisbane), March 22, 1873, 7.

42. Ganter, *The Pearl-Shellers*, 34–36.

43. Tracey Banivanua Mar, "The Contours of Agency: Women's Work, Race, and Queensland's Indentured Labor Trade," in *Indigenous Women and Work: From Labor to Activism*, ed. Carol Williams (Urbana: University of Illinois Press, 2012), 75.

44. Steve Mullins, "Company Boats, Sailing Dinghies and Passenger Fish: Fathoming Torres Strait Islander Participation in the Maritime Economy," *Labour History*, no. 103 (November 2012), 41.

45. Ganter, *The Pearl-Shellers*, 39.

46. Ganter, 4.

47. Ganter, 4.

48. Anna Shnukal, "A Double Exile: Filipino Settlers in the Outer Torres Strait Islands, 1870s–1940s." *Aboriginal History* 35 (2011): 163.

49. Ganter, *The Pearl-Shellers*, 40; Regina Ganter and Ros Kidd, "The Powers of Protectors: Conflicts Surrounding Queensland's 1897 Aboriginal Legislation," *Australian Historical Studies* 25, no. 101 (1993): 536–54.

50. Ganter, *The Pearl-Shellers*, 26–27.

51. "The Hurricane, A Colored Man's Bravery," *North Queensland Register* (Charters Towers), March 20, 1899, 14.

52. Ganter, *The Pearl-Shellers*, 40–41.

53. Aboriginals Protection and Restriction of the Sale of Opium Acts 1901 (2 Edw VII, No. 1), available at http://www.austlii.edu.au/cgi-bin/viewtoc/au/legis/qld/hist_act/toc-1901.html. The 1901 acts were amendments to the earlier 1897 act.

54. *Hansard*, Queensland Legislative Assembly, September 3, 1901, 613–14.

55. *Hansard*, 614.

56. "Mr. Foxton's Northern Tour," *Morning Bulletin* (Rockhampton), August 11, 1899, 5.

57. Mullins, "Company Boats," 42.

58. Ernest A. Wilby, Protector of Aboriginals, Thursday Island to the Chief Protector of Aboriginals, South Brisbane, October, 30, 1920, "Indented Japanese living ashore with Aboriginals," NAA, A1, 1921/9735.

59. See Regina Ganter, with contributions by Julia Martínez and Gary Lee, *Mixed Relations: Asian-Aboriginal Contact in North Australia* (Crawley: University of Western Australia Press, 2006).

60. Ann McGrath, *Illicit Love: Interracial Sex and Marriage in the United States and Australia* (Lincoln: University of Nebraska Press, 2015), 213.

61. D. C. S. Sissons, "*Karayuki-san*: Japanese Prostitutes in Australia, 1887–1916," pts. 1 and 2, *Historical Studies* 17, no. 68 (April 1977): 323–41; 17, no. 69 (October 1977): 474–88; Noreen Jones, *Number Two Home: A Story of Japanese Pioneers in Australia* (Fremantle, W.A.: Fremantle Arts Centre Press, 2002), 49–62; Raelene Frances, *Selling Sex: A Hidden History of Prostitution* (Sydney: University of New South Wales

Press, 2007), 53–57; Pamela Oliver, *Empty North: The Japanese Presence and Australian Reactions, 1860s to 1942* (Darwin: Charles Darwin University Press, 2006), 14.

62. James Francis Warren, *Ah Ku and Karayuki-san: Prostitution in Singapore 1870–1940* (Singapore: Oxford University Press, 1993).

63. Yuriko Nagata, "The Japanese in Torres Strait," in Shnukal et al., *Navigating Boundaries*.

64. Frances, *Selling Sex*, 60.

65. "Town Talk," *Victorian Express* (Geraldton, W.A.), January 29, 1887, 4.

66. "Pearlshell and Beche-de-Mer," *Brisbane Courier*, November 24, 1897, 5.

67. John D. Lamb, *Silent Pearls: Old Japanese Graves in Darwin and the History of Pearling* (Deakin, Australian Capital Territory: published by the author, 2015), 62.

68. Julia Martínez, "The 'Malay' Community in Pre-war Darwin," in "Asians in Australian History," ed. Regina Ganter, special issue, *Queensland Review* 6, no. 2 (November 1999): 49.

69. "Death of C. J. Pon," *Northern Standard* (Darwin), April 11, 1930, 5.

70. Sarah Yu, "Broome Creole: Aboriginal and Asian Partnerships along the Kimberley Coast," *Queensland Review* 6, no. 2 (November 1999): 66.

71. Christine Choo, *Mission Girls: Aboriginal Women on Catholic Missions in the Kimberley, Western Australia, 1900–1950* (Crawley: University of Western Australia Press, 2001), see chap. 3.

72. See, for example, Samantha Faulkner with Ali Drummond, *Life B'long Ali Drummond: A Life in the Torres Strait* (Canberra: Aboriginal Studies Press, 2007); Sally Bin Demin, *Once in Broome* (Broome: Magabala Books, 2007); and Peta Stephenson, "Keeping It in the Family: Partnerships between Indigenous and Muslim Communities in Australia," *Aboriginal History* 33 (2009): 97–116.

73. Julia Martínez and Adrian Vickers, *The Pearl Frontier: Indonesian Labor and Indigenous Encounters in Australia's Northern Trading Network* (Honolulu: University of Hawai'i Press, 2015); 112; Ganter, *Mixed Relations*, 83–90.

74. Faulkner and Drummond, *Life B'long Ali Drummond*, 6–7.

75. McLaren to Sub-Collector, September 15, 1922, NAA, A1, 1922/19013.

76. D. J. Mulvaney, *Encounters in Place: Outsiders and Aboriginal Australians, 1606–1985* (St. Lucia: University of Queensland Press, 1989), 183–85.

77. Bach, *Pearling Industry of Australia*, 153; See especially pages 10–12, Royal Commission on the Condition of the Natives, Report, Western

Australia, 1905, "General Correspondence Records Commissioner O'Dea," NAA, D4099, 65.

78. "Abo, Blushes with Shame," *Truth* (Sydney), July 1, 1928, 6.

79. "Abo, Blushes with Shame," 6.

80. Journal of Constable Napier (452) 25 February to 3 April 1903 whilst on patrol to Beagle and Cygnet Bays, Item 1903/1618, State Records Office of Western Australia, Perth; See also Henry Reynolds, *North of Capricorn: The Untold Story of Australia's North* (Sydney: Allen and Unwin, 2003), 140–41.

81. Northern Territory Ordinance No. 9 of 1918, *Government Gazette*, October 26, 1918.

82. A. E. Koop, Sgt, to Superintendent of Police, Stretton, Darwin, October 18, 1936, F1 1936/220, NAA Darwin.

83. "V. D. Epidemic Scandal," *Northern Standard* (Darwin), March 2, 1937, 3.

84. Julia Martínez, "Ethnic Policy and Practice in Darwin," chap. 5 in Ganter, *Mixed Relations*, 130–31.

85. Peter Donovan, "Gsell, Francis Xavier (1872–1960)," *Australian Dictionary of Biography*, National Centre of Biography, Australian National University, http://adb.anu.edu.au/biography/gsell-francis-xavier-6502/text11151; "Exploitation of Aboriginal Women," *Northern Standard* (Darwin), October 27, 1936, 3. For details of Gsell's mission, see Regina Ganter, *The Contest for Aboriginal Souls: European Missionary Agendas in Australia* (Acton: Australian National University Press, 2018), 13839.

86. Julia Martínez, "Ethnic Policy and Practice in Darwin," 130–31.

TWELVE

"Pearly Shells," a "Perfect Pearl," and a Guitar in a Pillowcase
Australian Pearling Industry Songs as Community and Personal Memories

KARL NEUENFELDT

THERE IS an important connection between music, memory, and narratives: "Music is vital to the construction of personal and collective cultural memory . . . [and] (re)collective experiences are constructed through narratives."[1] In the case of the pearling industries of the Indian Ocean world, music has played a key but varied role not only in documenting them but also in humanizing them through expressive culture.

Two varying views of pearl-shell divers and their engagement with music, and singing in particular, are expressed by a pair of Japanese interviewees in Australia in the foreword to *Full Fathom Five*, a book focusing on the pearling industry of the northern Australian coastline stretching from the Indian to the Pacific Ocean.

> Diver #1: Yes, I was a diver. I was very frightened for a year. . . . Gradually I lost my fear. I relaxed, I sang; sound marvelous in head-dress [diving helmet]. You are alone and the sea is so beautiful. There is nothing so beautiful above the water.
>
> Diver #2: No, I did not sing. Maybe it was beautiful, but I went down to get shells and get them quickly.[2]

One view is idealistic, almost romantic; the other is dismissive and a reality check about the ultimate goal of the work of pearling: harvesting pearl shells and, if very lucky, maybe finding a natural pearl. They encompass four key historical and contemporary facets of the pearling industry: its work, its economics, its aesthetics, and the expressive culture of its crews. This chapter explores some Australian songs of that industry, analyzing how they are about more than just finding "Pearly Shells" or a "Perfect Pearl."[3] These are but two of many songs, along with novels, films, and photographs, to have entered Australian popular culture and epitomize the romanticizing and exoticizing of the products of the pearling industry, not its labors. However, other songs tell different stories related to the actual work underlying the gathering, processing, and disseminating of those occasionally plentiful pearly shells and those historically rare perfect pearls. It is these kinds of songs and that kind of expressive culture of an Australian maritime workforce that are the focus here. It was a workforce that has been described elsewhere in the Indian Ocean littoral, analogously, as a transnational, trans-ethnic, and common maritime culture of an itinerant workforce.[4] Such a description is also germane in an Australian context.

There is a primary question underlying this exploration of selected songs of Australia's geographically scattered, regionally based pearling industries: what impelled workers to engage in a dangerous and arduous occupation? The unavoidable reality was, as elsewhere in the Indian Ocean, that "the life of a pearl diver was brutal, perilous, and grueling," and, furthermore, that "pearling, a grimly basic industry, served a luxury market."[5] Consequently, the work was not only harsh, but pearl shelling for a living was inherently unpredictable and unstable, always at the mercy of a vast and ecologically and geopolitically complex international commodity trading industry, let alone the whims of fashion.

Although there were diverse economic, social, and cultural motivations across Australia's northern coastline, Lawrence Potter's comments concerning the pearling industry in the Arabian Gulf can be usefully extrapolated to this extensive region: "the prospect of finding a valuable pearl, however improbable, gave hope to the poor pearl divers and sent them back to the pearl beds, year after year."[6] Notwithstanding the substantial role of official and unofficial slavery in the Arabian Gulf's workforce, the observation arguably also holds true historically for maritime workers who toiled in various facets of Australia's pearling industry, sometimes as unpaid, underpaid or indentured labor.[7]

In the Indian Ocean's numerous pearling sites and regions, the great majority in the workforce had to struggle to survive or even ever aspire to better themselves economically. Consequently, they looked to pearling as one of only a few possible work options. However, working in the industry was an option that in Australia as elsewhere could be made cruel by inherent occupational risks, the specter of interminable debt, and the "boom and bust" instability of an international luxury-commodity market based on two highly prized and fetishized objects: pearl shell and pearls.[8]

One answer to the question posed above is that perhaps songs in particular, as intangible yet recognizable cultural artefacts, can reflect aspirational senses of agency and subjectivity. Importantly, it was the multicultural pearling industry workers in Australia who overwhelmingly composed and authored songs and sang them, not the primarily Anglo-Australian or European bosses.[9] (It is worth noting here that pearling business owners and bosses self-designated themselves as "master pearlers," an appellation with arguably master-servant overtones vis-à-vis the rest of the work force.[10]) So, in essence, it can be argued that pearling songs are folk songs of an expendable but nonetheless essential workforce and of work essential to production that led eventually to consumption. Intriguingly, the physical work of the Australian industry is not always foremost thematically or even commented on explicitly. Rather, the songs are usually about the people, places, boats, natural environments, events, and challenges encountered. Thus, while they are undoubtedly chronicles of the working life of a maritime workforce, they are also transgenerational communal songs of "longing and belonging," complementary sites of nostalgia and pride in what was habitually itinerant, hazardous and unpredictable employment.[11]

Figure 12.1. A diver entertains while on his way to the fishing grounds, Thursday Island, Queensland. Frank Hurley, ca. 1920s, National Library of Australia, PIC FH/8583.

PEARLING AND MUSIC

There have been numerous descriptions of the pearl as a prized art and decorative object.[12] There have also have been many accounts and analyses of both the global and regional pearling industries.[13] However, in Australia there has been relatively less attention paid to the expressive culture and intangible heritage of the "crew culture" of the Australian pearling industries, such as its songs (and songs associated with dances).[14] A crew culture can be defined thus: "Crew cultures imply mobile labour cultures, transmitted by experience and custom, but also by the very fluid and migratory nature of terrestrial and oceanic networks and linkages spread across vast spaces."[15] Elsewhere across the Indian Ocean, and in particular the Arabian Gulf region, there are descriptions or recordings of regional music, including pearling and more generally maritime songs. These include research, recordings, and analyses focused on the music of Arabs in general,[16] the Arabian Gulf,[17] the Arabian Gulf and Saudi Arabia,[18] Kuwait and the Arabian Peninsula,[19] Oman,[20] Bahrain,[21] United Arab Emirates,[22] and, less specifically, on the Western Indian Ocean littoral.[23] There is to date less readily available documentation of songs in other Indian Ocean pearling regions such as Sri Lanka and Myanmar. For Australia, there has been similar research, in particular for the Queensland (Torres Strait) and Western Australian industries.[24]

One such description of the Western Indian Ocean's littoral pearling industry demonstrates the significance of music and songs, in this case from the Khaliji culture of the Arabian Peninsula.

> [A] unique marker of Khaliji culture is its music, in which the songs of the pearl divers form an important musical tradition. Each year the great Arab pearling fleets left port to the sounds of this music with its drumming "imbued with mystical, religious and symbolic meanings" and designed to strengthen the will of the divers as they headed off on their hazardous occupation. "In every boat, whether pearling boat or cargo boat, there used to be a *naham*, a chanter. Some shipmasters vie to get first-class *nahams* and pay them well. . . . The *naham* had a great influence on the sailors. They would take up their grueling work with strength and vigour and, if the *naham* was really good, forget about their hardships."[25]

Khaliji music today is important as a Western Indian Ocean cultural form, even though the pearling industry itself is all but extinct apart from a regional touristic focus. What *Khaliji* music signifies, however, is that it retains its power as an expression and reflection not only of an economic activity but also resonates as a reminder of regionally based sociocultural cohesion and musical diffusion.[26]

In Australia, pearling songs also provide an expression of and reflection on its now faded pearl-shelling and natural pearl industries, but they still resonate culturally in some Australian communities. This chapter analyses select songs of the Australian pearling industry as it occurred historically in the nineteenth and twentieth centuries, in the Indian Ocean littoral as well as in the contiguous Timor, Arafura, and Coral Seas along Australia's northern coastline: its "pearl frontier."[27] The songs address directly and indirectly workers' experience of the industry, its challenges, dangers, and delights.

The main geographic focus is on the cities of Broome on the Indian Ocean coast of Western Australia and Thursday Island (known by its initials as T.I.) on the Coral Sea in the Torres Strait region of

Queensland.[28] Both locales have retained repertoires and recordings of historical and contemporary songs about the pearling industry. Darwin was another center for Australian pearling, but retains fewer songs that have, to date, been documented and disseminated via commercial and archival recordings.[29] Although the Torres Strait region and its main entrepôt, administrative center, and port-of-call, Thursday Island, are technically outside the Indian Ocean, the industry in Queensland was inextricably linked to that of Western Australia, the Northern Territory, and elsewhere.[30] Over the lifespan of the pearling industry there were considerable movements of workers, boats, and organizational and technological expertise across northern Australia, as well as into geographically neighboring locales such as the Aru Islands and the Moluccas in the former Dutch East Indies.[31]

Songs, as easily transportable cultural artefacts and intangible social "things," traveled readily with a mobile workforce as a component of the Australian pearling industry's oral traditions.[32] Songs moved back and forth across the pearling frontier, sometimes incorporating elements gleaned from the diverse musical cultures of the industry's workers.[33] Consequently, versions of songs sung on Thursday Island such as "Black Swana," "Old T.I.," and "Nona Manis" were also sung in Darwin and Broome, either to workmates while working at sea or to appreciative local audiences at the informal social gatherings that helped a mobile workforce not only to enjoy entertainment but also to find solace and camaraderie.[34] As Anglo-Australian folksinger Ted Egan has noted about the borrowing and adaptation of songs across Australia's northern pearling regions, "the important thing was that the songs had lovely tunes, so people felt free to put whatever words they wanted to [the melody] as long as the tune was there."[35] Songs provided an eclectic kaleidoscopic soundtrack for what has been termed "a brotherhood of the sea" in the context of the Western Indian Ocean's maritime workforces.[36] In Australia, a shared repertoire of pearling songs is still extant, although predominantly in an elderly generation whose personal lives and those of their home communities were deeply linked to the industry.

As elsewhere in the Indian Ocean, Australian pearling songs are noteworthy as the sometimes generalized and sometimes personalized stories of workers embedded in the impersonal commodity chain of a global industry of "production, consumption and desire."[37] They are also important as community memories preserved and disseminated as part of communal identity narratives.[38] Some songs remain, along with documentary and feature films, art works, and museum exhibitions.[39] However, the historical Australian pearling industry and its workers, boats, and organizational and technological expertise increasingly fade from living memory—thus highlighting the importance of documenting existing songs. Interestingly, there are few if any new songs about what is now Australia's main pearling industry: pearl farming.[40] Perhaps this is because because pearl farming is to a large extent quasi-mechanized and takes place in fixed production facilities, and thus is less perilous, somewhat more predictable, and has a less culturally diverse workforce. Therefore, the previously crucial role of a mobile workforce, and their equally diverse support communities, is now somewhat secondary to the role of technology in the contemporary pearl-farming industry.

The Australian pearling industry songs explored here were recorded either for community-based, essentially archival, albums or by soloists and music groups for commercially orientated albums.[41] The descriptions, contextualizations, and analyses herein focus on some representative songs as personal and collective memories expressed by and within Indigenous and non-Indigenous songs. They are narratives, musical stories that both recall and preserve maritime and sociocultural histories of their regions and places, where there are enduring communal memories of the time when the pearling industry was the economic mainstay.

While pearling songs and dances are links to life and work styles that are now fading from living memory, nonetheless community memories of a maritime past still abide in them. These continue to be documented in contemporary music and dance recording and filming projects, as well as celebrated in casual music performances at house parties and on verandas and in dance performances at community and civic events. They are performed publicly as part of community events in Aboriginal communities such as those of Western Australia's Bardi people of Dampier Peninsula, touristic celebrations such as Broome's recurrent Shinju Matsuri (Japanese for "festival of the pearl") community event, and Torres Strait cultural festivals.[42] Thus the songs (and dances, in some cases) remain the same, or at least recognizably similar, although their contexts, performers, and performances may have changed.

Songs were not specifically a "commodity," but rather a reflection of the multicultural workforce of the Australian pearling industry, which changed irrevocably the sociocultural and political makeup of modern Australia, especially in the northern regions.[43] In the Western Indian Ocean's maritime traditions, music was essential to the organization of work.[44] In the context of the Arabian Gulf, it has been noted, "it is understandable that the crew had little interest or energy for entertainment when the day was done. There was no time for musical merry-making. However, during the day, there was a great need for work songs, as the men longed for musical encouragement to lighten their endless burden of labor. The songs and their lead singer became crucial to most every boat."[45]

In Australia, however, music had a limited role in the daily organization of work tasks. Nevertheless, it had a major role in the organization of the workforce's leisure. There was time for leisure because in Australia, as elsewhere, the phases of the moon, tides, and water conditions determined when diving for pearl shells could and could not be pursued. Music was also, importantly, a part of the cultural baggage itinerant workers would carry with them from afar, along with their meager personal belongings. One Torres Strait Islander ex-diver, Henry Gibson Dan, recalls that, for a fellow maritime worker who had journeyed from

Figure 12.2. Henry "Seaman" Dan diving in Timor Sea off Western Australia, ca. 1955. Henry Dan personal collection.

Queensland to Western Australia, on the opposite side of the continent, with just a change of clothing, "his most prized possession was his guitar in a pillow-case."[46] A pillowcase may afford no protection, especially on a working pearling lugger, but just having a guitar to play and sing songs when at leisure was an entree into the sociality intrinsic to music.

We now turn to explore some contextualized examples of songs of the Australian pearling industry, its workforce, and its crew culture. They are composed, authored, and performed by Indigenous and non-Indigenous Australians. They not only chronicle an industry but can also celebrate and sometimes critique the work of pearling.

"BLACK SWANA" AND "FORTY FATHOMS"—TWO TORRES STRAIT ISLANDER PEARLING SONGS

The former deepwater pearl-shell diver Henry Gibson Dan was born on Thursday Island, Queensland, in the Torres Strait region in 1929. His mixed cultural heritage was common in the multicultural milieu of Thursday Island.[47] Officially recognized as a Torres Strait Islander, he is a descendant of West Indian, Polynesian, and Melanesian migrants who came to the region as maritime workers.[48] Because of his mixed cultural heritage, he himself was not directly "under the act" (Aboriginals Protection and Restriction of the Sale of Opium Act of 1897) and subsequent state and federal race-based legislation. Nonetheless, for much of his life he has lived and worked in a region and society imbued with racial classifications. As of mid-2018, the Queensland state government has only very belatedly been considering Henry Dan and other maritime workers for compensation for the historical underpayment of wages. At 89 years of age, he is one of the few remaining pearl-shell divers and maritime workers who might actually finally be appropriately compensated financially for their decades of work in the industry.

As a child, Henry Dan absorbed the multicultural music circulating in the Thursday Island community, which was later to become an important part of his performance repertoire.[49] As a young man, just after World War II, he began working in the trochus and then pearling industries and acquired his lifelong nickname, "Seaman." Over decades of work in Queensland, the Northern Territory, and Western Australia, he has been variously a trochus and pearl-shell diver, a head diver for a government pearling industry survey vessel, a pearling lugger skipper, and finally a "chicken shell" supplier for the early pearl-farming industry in the Torres Strait region. Along the way he has had numerous adventures, such as avoiding schools of curious sharks as well as stalking gropers, getting "the bends" (decompression sickness), and having a boat capsize in a storm and then bobbing ashore clinging to a kerosene tin.[50]

Seaman Dan has also had the chance to reflect on the evolution of the pearling industry from his childhood recollections of 1930s Thursday Island, with a busy harbor full of luggers and crews, to the industry's brief revival after World War II, and finally to seeing the industry's demise in the 1970s. He then had to take on shore-based employment, similar to many other maritime workers of his generation. Some of those personal memories have been recounted in his recordings and songs, which are simultaneously autobiographical yet also repositories of communal memories.

There are two songs that provide representative examples of two differing types of pearling song Seaman Dan has recorded on his nine albums: those based on community memories and those based on personal memories. The song "Black Swana" is an ode to the *Charm*, a Thursday Island boat in the Farquhar family's fleet of pearling luggers. Japanese shipwrights had built it at Thursday Island in the early 1930s. It was called the *Black Swana* locally because of its easily identifiable black hull and circular white spot on the bow. There are no native swans in the Torres Strait region, so where it got its common name is unknown. The song was originally from the Western Torres Strait islands. It is attributed to the *Charm*'s crewman Kawane Motlop and is sung in the traditional Torres Strait Islander language of Kala Lagaw Ya. When Seaman Dan wanted to record his version, he asked a Torres Strait Islander (Mabuyag Island) linguist and cultural custodian, the late Ephraim Bani (1944–2004), to do an English translation.

"Black Swana"

Ina ngoey *Black Swana* sager gubanu paypa / Dhayal mathaman guba paypa / Matha lugipatalay uzarima / Guthathan maytha thayanu gar / Matha thari ulayke e / Koey koelak sageraw payaya e / This is our boat *Black Swana* / Sailing in the southeast wind / We are sailing, sailing faster / Pushed by the south east wind / Sailing in all its glory / Eastward current turn to flow / We applaud this sailing in the southeast wind[51]

Ephraim Bani had grown up in the Torres Strait region after World War II, at the time of a still-viable pearling industry, and thus was able to capture in his translation the sense of a pearling lugger moving under sail. When it was decided to add a chorus of male singers to the recording, Seaman Dan recruited several Kala Lagaw Ya–speaking ex-maritime workers to recreate as close as possible the vocal music that men on the luggers would have sung for their own entertainment. Luggers were small boats, so there usually was no room for instruments on board, but the Islanders have a long-standing and cherished tradition of unaccompanied choral singing in worship and in casual performances.[52] "Black Swana" celebrates community memories and does so with instrumentation that would have been common in the region's community music, including stringed instruments such as guitar, ukulele, and mandolin and Islander percussion such as *warup/buruburu* drums and bamboo cylinders.

As a noteworthy aside, along with Seaman Dan's version, fully arranged choral versions of "Black Swana" have been recorded, filmed, and uploaded to YouTube, one from Canada and one from Asia.[53] Whether or not the arrangers or members of the choirs are aware of its cultural derivation, the song has obvious musical and aesthetic appeal. "Black Swana" may be from a distant place and have nothing to do with the choristers' personal or community identity, but the music and the lyrics, even if not understood, along with the song's ambience, transcend those sometimes restricting geographical and sociocultural criteria. The musicality of the song is clearly appealing, even if performers do not know its provenance in the Australian pearling industry.

An example of a Seaman Dan song that combines personal memories that can be extrapolated to community memories is "Forty Fathoms." He wrote the song based on his own diving experiences at the Darnley Deep in eastern Torres Strait near to Erub (Darnley Island). It was an important pearling area historically because of its rich but deepwater beds of pearl shells and also its regional role as a nursery for spawned juvenile oysters known as spat. The chorus of the song is based melodically and lyrically on an Australian folk song, "The Arafura Sea," of unknown provenance. It is known across the pearl frontier of northern Australia, encompassing the Timor, Arafura, and Coral Seas, with lyrics adapted to the different locales.

Musically, "Forty Fathoms" features ukulele, harmonica, and Islander percussion, with an intentionally informal male choir on the call-and-response chorus.

"Forty Fathoms"

> Diving down to forty fathoms at the Darnley Deep / Searching for the precious pearl shell the pearls to keep / All aboard the pearling lugger / *Grafton* by name / Crews are waiting for the divers / Praying for some rain / Goodbye to you farewell my love / Soon we'll be sailing to the Darnley Deep / And in your heart please think of me / For I'll come back to you from the Darnley Deep / Diving down to forty fathoms / Down deep below / How to find a precious pearl shell only divers know / I can see the other divers / Working here with me / Getting shells at forty fathoms in the Darnley Deep / Sailing home for dear old T.I. [Thursday Island] / Divers all asleep / So we bid farewell to the Darnley Deep[54]

Seaman Dan was skipper of *Grafton*, one of three luggers working together at the Darnley Deep for the Burns Philp Company. His brothers-in-law, James and Vincent Dorante, skippered *Galton* and *Floria*, respectively. It was at the Darnley Deep that Seaman Dan himself got decompression sickness ("the bends") after diving to depths of around forty fathoms (approximately 240 feet or 73 meters).[55] It and nitrogen narcosis ("rapture of the deep") were feared hazards of diving, ever-present during each dive and compounded by repeated dives. There were numerous pearling-industry casualties in the region and the cemetery at Thursday Island, for example, contains the graves of many divers, Japanese in particular, who perished in the region's treacherous currents, extensive reefs, and deep waters.[56]

After World War II, pearl-shell divers such as Seaman Dan did use Australian Navy decompression-staging tables, but mishaps still happened, even to experienced divers. Consequently, for the divers themselves and for local communities and extended families, the dangers of the pearling industry were ever-present.[57] However, the camaraderie of the crews is an often-remembered and highly valued facet of the work, as is the longing for loved ones back at home. Musical stories such as "Black Swana" and "Forty Fathoms" are cogent examples of songs of "longing and belonging."[58] While audiences, Indigenous and non-Indigenous, may be listening to a particular singer, such as Seaman Dan, they are also listening to a community's memories, which are evocative not only of a time and place but also of a workforce central to Torres Strait Islanders' communal identity as a maritime people.

"ADHAZ OCKINGU": A TORRES STRAIT ISLANDER COMMUNITY PEARLING SONG

An illuminating example of a pearling song deeply embedded in community memory is Badu Island's "Adhaz Ockingu," attributed to the late James Eseli. The song is in the language of Badu Island in the Western Torres Strait, Kala Lagaw Ya, and is sung by a mixed-generation community choir assembled for a recording and filming project to document traditional and contemporary music and dance in the community. The *Badu Nawal* album booklet states that their communal maritime songs "are about Badu Island's pearling and trochus shell gathering boats and the weather. Many are also dances."[59] They were usually composed by members of a lugger's crew and presented to the community at the end of the pearling season. They then became community songs and dances. Sometimes people who were not with the boat would also compose songs based on stories told by the crews.

Badu Island (also known as Mulgrave Island) is the largest Outer Island community, with approximately one thousand inhabitants.[60] It has had a long historical association with pearling, and was economically successful during boom periods in the pearling industry such as the post–World War II era.[61] It is also recognized regionally as a "strong culture island" with outstanding visual, dance, and musical artists.[62]

Musically, "Adhaz Ockingu" features characteristic Torres Strait Islander multipart singing, with shifting harmonies and accompaniment on acoustic guitar and a *warup/buruburu* drum and *lumut/thram* bamboo percussion.

"Adhaz Ockingu"

Adhaz ockingu ngadhe dhobau garka kai ahda thanurima eh /
Parr kadaka nika / Kutau zibazibanu ngoigar naki awayani sanik /
Thaingai adhiya koi gutha thanan thema / Pearl Harbour ka gar /
Muk tharapima inah ngoi *Envy* nah eh

Badu Nawal's booklet provides the following explanation, supplied by the community:

> This song is about the [pearling] boat *Envy* sailing from Badu Ocki, the "working ground," to Pearl Harbour, Badu's harbor. It was like a man when he digs *dhob*, a root type yam that grows deep in the ground. He sits away from it to give himself room to do the work. In the same way, *Envy* did not sail directly to the island but was slowly moving closer. In the afternoon, in the calmer water of Badu, it looked like a pelican pushing through the water—as if it was going to lift off the water towards Pearl Harbour.[63]

Similar to many other Torres Strait Islander pearling songs, "Adhaz Ockingu" mentions places near to the home island, Badu in this instance. As noted in the explanation above, "Badu Ocki" may refer to what is termed the "old working ground," where historically there were productive pearl-shell beds until they were depleted because they were relatively close to the industry based at Thursday Island. The *Envy* lugger was a "company boat," and is also now one of the few, perhaps twenty, remaining former pearling luggers out of what was once a fleet of hundreds.[64] Now renamed *Ise Pearl*, it has been used for sailing charters in the Whitsunday Islands of eastern Queensland. "Adhaz Ockingu" contains facets of pearling's economic and sociocultural history in the Torres Strait region, in Australia, and on one particular island, and reflects music's crucial role in processes of documenting and maintaining community memories.

"FREE DIVING": AN ABORIGINAL COMMEMORATIVE PEARLING SONG

Focusing on the Western Australian coast of the Indian Ocean, the presence of pearl shells had been noted as early as the late 1600s by the British explorer William Dampier.[65] Aboriginal people have decorated and traded them (*riji* and *jakuli*) in networks that stretched across the continent.[66] In 1908, George Kunz and Charles Stevenson remarked on the involvement of women in the global pearling industry, such as in Japan, Polynesia, the U.S. state of Arkansas, and the Indian Ocean coast

Figure 12.3. Commemoration of Aboriginal women in nineteenth-century pearling industry, Broome, Western Australia. Karl Neuenfeldt.

of East Africa, in their *The Book of the Pearl*.[67] In Australia, Indigenous women were directly involved in early regional pearling industries, especially during their initial expansions into unexploited regions along Australia's northern frontier in the 1860s and 1870s. However, accounts of their contributions are poorly documented in the historical record and remarked on only occasionally in general, impersonalized terms in settlers' and administrators' accounts of European colonization.[68] Nonetheless, they had a vital role in northern Australia's economic development. Women were directly and indirectly of considerable importance to the Australian pearling industry in general and also, particularly, the complex multicultural regional communities that arose to service it. The focus here is geographically on Western Australia, although women were also involved in the Queensland and Northern Territory pearling industries centered at Thursday Island and Darwin, respectively.[69]

In Western Australia, starting from the mid-1860s, the involvement of Aboriginal women divers was commonplace for at least two decades. After the early phase of the industry known as dry shelling, when shells could be gathered by hand from shallow waters or reefs, they worked in what has been referred to as "naked diving" or "bare pelt" diving.[70] That is, women and men diving to shallower depths than those that became possible when diving suits, lead boots, bronze helmets, and air compressors were introduced in the mid-1880s. According to Susan Jane Hunt, "Pearlers 'recruited' women from amongst the local coastal tribes or took them in blackbirding [forced unpaid labor] raids from regions further north. In the 1860s, Aboriginal women worked as divers for pearlshell, and it was believed they were more proficient divers than men."[71] John Bailey contends that "women were preferred by the shellers. They were more tractable than the men and, so it was said, could hold their breath longer and had keener eyesight."[72] James Battye records that "in 1868 some ten boats were employed [in the northwest region], the divers being principally natives—many of them women." He also notes that "the treatment of these latter [women] was certainly not in many instances creditable to the white pearlers."[73] Concurring with this last opinion, Perth's *Inquirer* newspaper commented, "the thirst for shells, for pearls, for success, in fact, brutalizes and unchristianises the pearling speculator."[74] The Christian missionary John Gribble railed against the depredations occasioned against Aboriginal people in Western Australia, including women and men working in the pearling industry, that he encountered in the Pilbara region.[75] However, despite Gribble's entreaties, his Anglican superiors in Perth abandoned him for alienating the powerful "squattocracy" of regional pastoralists, some of whom were also pearl shellers and, as members of the colonial elite, helped to support and finance the Anglican Church in Western Australia.[76]

Having Aboriginal women in the workforce was problematic not only for the women themselves, and their families and communities, but also for a colonial government attempting to regulate labor practices amid reports of the widespread economic exploitation noted above. Such economic exploitation was also linked directly to the sexual exploitation and prostituting of Aboriginal women.[77] Bailey suggests women were actively recruited for such purposes, "and the younger the better—to train [as divers] and get used to the ways of their white masters on the boats at night."[78] Western Australia's Pearling Regulation Acts of 1871, 1873, and 1875 attempted to militate against the economic and sexual exploitation and even the presence of Aboriginal women on pearling boats. Stephenson notes, "the hiring and conditions of service of Aborigines employed in the pearling industry were regulated [by the acts], and Aboriginal women were prohibited from working as divers and from boarding vessels."[79]

However, the northwest coast of Australia was remote from the main colonial administration center in Perth in the colony's southwestern region. Such legislation and concomitant regulation, no matter how well intended, was difficult to enforce, due not only to distance but also to the alliance of powerful pastoral and pearling interests, at times with the connivance of resident judicial officials.[80] For example, Mike McCarthy comments on the disjuncture between what local judicial officers in the northwest region of Western Australia claimed and what was the clearly identifiable impetus for legislation: "[Robert John] Sholl, the Resident Magistrate in the North-West of Western Australia claimed in 1871 that 'Native Women, as a rule are not employed as divers.' The use of the phrase 'as a rule,' and the need for legislation prohibiting the employment of Aboriginal women on pearling craft, indicates that the women were used in that capacity however. The act [of 1871] prohibiting their employ was entitled *An Act to Regulate the hiring and service of Aboriginal Natives in the pearl shell fishery and the prohibition of the employment of women therein.*"[81] It is undisputed that vested interests profited from the use of cheap labor, many Aboriginal workers being paid in-kind, if at all. According to Sumi Kwaymullina, "The [Western Australian] pearling industry was built on the exploitation and inhuman treatment of Aboriginal people yet they receive no credit and usually no mention."[82] In this context, "Free Diving" is a song-based form of belated acknowledgement and respect.

Subsequent to the introduction in Western Australia of protective legislation aimed at Aborigines, indentured laborers from Southeast Asia and Japan began to be recruited.[83] For example, some came from the Dutch East Indies, Malaya, and Singapore ("Malays"), West Timor ("Koepangers"), Philippines ("Manila men"), China, and Japan.[84] In 1912, an attempt was made to recruit and make use of British salvage divers and tenders. The intent was to show that white divers could be as successful as "Asiatics," but this failed for various reasons, not least of which were unfamiliar local diving conditions and the incapacitating paralysis or death of many of the British divers.[85] The combination of peoples from such diverse cultures eventually created a multicultural workforce centered at Broome, which was gazetted as a town in 1883. It evolved its own distinctive culture as the major pearling community in the region.[86]

However, it was a workforce not without its own reoccurring intercultural conflicts and reports of ill treatment of Aboriginal women.[87] It was, importantly, also a workforce whose composition evolved during the heyday of Australia's White Australia Policy that specifically targeted Asian immigrant labor and also played on the fear among the European colonizers of creating a community of mixed Aboriginal-Asian descent.[88] The pearling industry, however, was an exception that flaunted the otherwise pervasive White Australia Policy, which began in 1901 and lasted until the 1970s.[89] It was the Australian form of the race-based paranoia, discrimination, and draconian legislation that infused white settler colonies of the British Empire in the nineteenth and twentieth centuries.[90]

As mentioned previously, there is a song that centers on the significant role of Aboriginal women as free divers in Western Australia's early pearling industry: Lorrae Coffin's fictional song "Free Diving" (1998). She is a singer-songwriter from the Nyiyaparli and Yindjibarndi Aboriginal peoples of the Pilbara region, and has been active professionally as a musician, media specialist, and community arts practitioner and administrator. The predations and dislocations occasioned by the early pearl-shell industry directly affected Coffin's ancestors.

"Free Diving"

Heading out to the open sea on a lugger with a colourful crew / Searching for that hidden pearl / Snuggled in a haven of blue / Wave goodbye to my family / Pray I'll return in one piece / Diving down with no tank on my back / Just the air in my lungs to help me / *Chorus:* I'm a long way from home / My country my people I leave / I hear the sea gulls scream / And the voice of the captain telling me to earn my keep / So I'm free diving / Into the waters I go / So I'm free diving / Malay man to watch my back / And a Japanese watching my side / Free diving / The night is warm and the moon is high / But my body feels like ice / Diver's arms wrap around my chest / Saying "Everything is alright."[91]

Although "Free Diving" may be fictionalized, what it recounts remains part of community memories for Aboriginal people of northwestern Australia. It is an example of how songs written generations later by an Aboriginal songwriter can not only mention but also bring credit to the role of Aboriginal women in the pearling industry. In 2006, a sculpture was unveiled on Broome's foreshore of a pregnant Aboriginal woman diver ascending from the sea holding a pearl shell.[92] The cultural significance of the song itself is witnessed by Broome's Magabala Books publishing an illustrated children's book, *Free Diving*, based mainly on the song's general themes.[93] The practice of free diving may have been free of breathing apparatus, but the Aboriginal female (and male) workforce was anything but free. They were economically important but nonetheless a fettered and mostly forgotten facet of Western Australia's early pearling workforce.

"SAYONARA NAKAMURA":
AN ANGLO-AUSTRALIAN PEARLING SONG

After more than seventy years of commercial resource extraction, pearling in Australia all but ceased during World War II, with many luggers impounded by the Australian military or destroyed. The large Japanese workforce was also interned and the majority was then deported after the cessation of hostilities in 1945.[94] However, after World War II there was an increased worldwide demand for pearl-shell products. Australian pearling companies were desperate to revitalize their industry after the wartime closure, so the recruitment of Japanese workers to help harvest the replenished pearl-shell beds was mooted. Even with increasing numbers of Australian Indigenous and non-Indigenous maritime workers, recruitment from Japan seemed a logical step.[95] Given their high level of skills and prior experience, Japanese were considered the preferred workforce. However, Japanese migration to Australia was barred until 1949 and anti-Japanese sentiment remained common, especially in pearling centers because of the bombings of Broome, Darwin, and the Torres Strait (Horn Island) in 1942.[96] An alternative proposal was to recruit workers from the Ryukyu Islands (Nansie-Shotō) southwest of Japan. They had historically been part of the Japanese sphere of influence and were eventually annexed and became the Okinawa Prefecture in 1879. They were the sites of brutal battles in World War II between Allied and Japanese military forces, and the final battle for the islands was the largest of the war in the Pacific. After the cessation of hostilities, they became a Mandated Territory of the United States, with large military facilities built in particular on the largest island of Okinawa. It had been devastated, leaving a population desperate for employment, with some of those being experienced local divers.[97]

Consequently, because of the United States occupation, people from the Ryukyu Islands (Ryukyuans) could technically be said by the Australian government to be not "Japanese." Thus, being designated as Okinawans, they were able to come to Australia as contract maritime laborers to Broome, Darwin, and Torres Strait. Over the relatively short time period Okinawans worked in Australia (ca. 1958–1961), they had varying levels of success. For example, some were repatriated from Torres Strait after a few months because, according to the pearling companies, they had not adjusted to the region's diving conditions and the deeper depths to which they were unaccustomed. This is an accusation that has been disputed: "the facts do not support accusations of incompetence. Any problems the Okinawans had are easily explicable in the context of inappropriate recruiting practices, declining shell resources, language problems and poor labour relations."[98]

One anecdote exemplifies the paradox of Okinawans feigning they were not Japanese. A diver named Nakamura Shohaku recounted, "I felt like shouting loudly: 'Look at the power and the will of the Japanese. I mean Okinawans!' I particularly wanted to say it to the heads of those three [Torres Strait pearling] companies who had sent back our fellow workers after six months. They left Thursday Island in shame."[99] Regardless of the complicated politics and economics of post–World War II designations of nationality, Okinawans contributed to the revitalization of the Australian pearling industry. Nevertheless, the emergence of the widespread use of plastics for buttons, the overexploitation of the resource, and the beginnings of pearl farming led eventually to the historical Australian industry's collapse. There was also a concomitant waning of the need for a large and mobile workforce, although maritime workers were still recruited from the Torres Strait region and elsewhere for emerging pearl farms such as at Kuri Bay in far northern Western Australia, founded in 1956.[100]

The role of Okinawans and Japanese in the Australian pearling industry has been memorialized in "Sayonara Nakamura," *sayonara* meaning goodbye in Japanese. The song is well known in Australia and was written by the Anglo-Australian folk singer-songwriter Ted Egan.[101] It is a fictional story song about the death in the Indian Ocean near Broome of an Okinawan/Japanese diver from decompression sickness ("the bends"). Nakamura is a common Japanese cognomen/family name (*myouji*). For example, there are four men buried at Broome's Japanese Cemetery identified as Nakamura. They are listed as (family name, given name, village, prefecture): Nakamura, Sotaro—Zatsugazaki, Wakayama; Nakamura, Masami—Kamimimochi-gun, Nagano; Nakamura, Jintaro—Kurose, Tomie-mura, Goto, Nagasaki; and Nakamura, Kurakichi—unknown. According to Ted Egan, none of the men buried in Broome directly inspired the song. A reason for choosing the name Nakamura was more prosaic: it partially rhymed with and had the same number of syllables as the words Okinawa and sayonara, and also alliterated with them by repetitive use of the soft *a* sound. Egan says, "I wrote my song in the knowledge of the strong representation [in Broome] from both Taiji [in Higashimuro District, Wakayama Prefecture, Japan] and Okinawa. Okinawa was rhythmically better than Taiji, too. And I knew that one of the most popular Japanese names—it's a bit like Smith, Jones, and Brown among Europeans—was Nakamura." Egan also knew there were several Nakamuras buried in Broome's Japanese Cemetery, and he knew that generally Japanese divers "were young and fit and usually very, very tough blokes, and quite often both flamboyant and aggressive. They used to have sovereign buttons on their

Figure 12.4. Restored gravestone of Jintaro Nakamura, d. 1917. One of four Nakamura persons buried in Japanese cemetery, Broome, Western Australia. Karl Neuenfeldt.

starched suits and they used to light cigars with five-pound notes, that sort of thing."[102]

However, youth, strength, and fitness were no guarantees for longevity in such a dangerous occupation and such an extreme climate. The threat from cyclones and accidents at sea was ever-present for the whole pearling workforce. The Broome Japanese Cemetery alone has over nine hundred graves, overwhelmingly men.[103] Many other pearling casualties from other non-European ethnic groups (e.g., "Malays" and Chinese) were buried in the Broome Cemetery or elsewhere, and still others were either buried or lost at sea.

Egan began writing the song in 1981 while on a holiday in a most unlikely place for a song set on the tropical shores of the eastern Indian Ocean. "I wrote it in the United Kingdom of all places. I was in a great traffic snarl in the north of England. It was freezing cold and I thought, 'what's the opposite of this' and I thought of Broome. I continued to work on it as we drove around the United Kingdom and when we came back to Australia I recorded it."

Along with telling an interesting story, Egan had another reason for writing the song. "I guess I'm very strong on this need for recognition of the [contribution of immigrants to Australia]. You know, I've written songs about Afghan camel drivers and a little old Chinese grandmother in Darwin. I like to put across that I have met these people. And, I'm impressed by these people. They have made a contribution to Australia in their different fields and we are blessed with a pretty relaxed multicultural society. And the more we recognize the things like the contribution made by Japanese divers to the pearling industry, the better we'll be as a nation, I think." As to the song's reception during live performances, Egan has only once encountered a negative reaction: from someone whose family member had been imprisoned by the Japanese during World War II. Nonetheless, response from Japanese people is always noteworthy. "I get amazing reactions from Japanese if they're in the audience and they hear it for the first time. . . . The eyes are, you know, they're full of tears. . . . And I got the translation of the chorus into Japanese from a group of Japanese students one night. So it's probably my best ever song in terms of world recognition. I've got it on iTunes and it's certainly the best earner of any songs of mine on iTunes."[104]

"Sayonara Nakamura" features a common folk song structure (verses and repetitive chorus) and a melody that does not compete with the sequential and detailed lyrical content, but rather escorts it to the narrative's conclusion. Musically and melodically it is not overtly "Japanese" or "Oriental" (that is, in clichéd musical modes), but it is well suited to audience participation, in the sing-along chorus in particular.

"Sayonara Nakamura"

When the luggers all sailed away from Roebuck Bay on that fateful day the diver on the *B-19* was Nakamura / Not yet twenty-one from the Land of the Rising Sun his homeland was the island Okinawa

In the deepest holes of the Lacepede Shoals to fulfill the pearling master's goals went the diver of the *B-19* Nakamura / His quest for the lustrous pearl as strong as his love for the beautiful girl he'd wed when he returned to Okinawa

But it's goodbye now farewell say goodbye to Okinawa / For today they'll bury you in West Australia / And you will never be as one with the Land of the Rising Sun / Sayonara sayonara Nakamura

From the west came a tropical squall then the mercury began to fall forty fathoms deep was Nakamura / Set sail no time to stage for the storm began to rage and they pulled to the surface the diver Nakamura

The agony is in his eyes an old Malay man cries for he knows the bends have got young Nakamura / Helplessly they cursed as the diver's lungs near burst and he died on the deck the boy from Okinawa

To the diver's cemetery in Broome bearing gifts all deep in gloom they walked with the body of the diver Nakamura / Headstones face the west a thousand divers lie at rest and they're joined today by the boy from Okinawa.[105]

While the song is a fictionalized account, it is nevertheless geographically and historically credible and lends credence to the narrative. For example, the places mentioned are all in the general Broome area of Western Australia's West Kimberley coast; cyclones are a persistent threat; a Malay character is included to further reflect Broome's multicultural workforce; and the cemetery verse highlights the fact many divers died from their work in the West Australian pearling industry.[106] Further to this, chronologically, Roebuck Bay lies adjacent to the port of Broome, historically the center of the northwest region's pearling industry from the 1880s. The alphabetical designation "B" (as in *B-19*) identifies the pearling lugger as Broome-based; for Torres Strait the designation would be "A" and for Darwin "D." The Lacepede Shoals and Lacepede Islands mentioned in the song lie approximately 120 kilometers (75 miles) northwest of Broome in the Indian Ocean.[107] The mention of the directional alignment of graves in the cemetery is also correct: the headstones of Japanese face westward, those of Muslims north-south and of Chinese eastward.[108]

Aside from the song's commercial success for Ted Egan and its geographical, historical, and occupational veracity, its significance as an Australian pearling song is arguably in how it highlights the pivotal role of maritime workers from Japan, and Okinawa, across northern Australia. It presents a personalized story of the pearling industry to a wider audience that might not have had any idea of the occupational realities for its workforce, aside from the romanticized and exoticized clichés of films and books.[109] "Sayonara Nakamura" contains facets of the economic and social history of Western Australia's Indian Ocean pearling industry. It reflects music's significance in creating, maintaining, and celebrating personal and community memories—even if the narrative is fictionalized.

AUSTRALIAN SONGS of the pearling industry are about more than just pearly shells and perfect pearls. They are also not only about the work, economics, and aesthetics of the pearling industry, but are also about the social, cultural, and community life of whole regions that historically depended upon it. Such musical connections can be fragile, but the music can still carry memories worth preserving and performing through time.

Beyond the historical and aesthetic values of pearling songs such as "Black Swana," "Forty Fathoms," "Adha Ockingu," "Free Diving," and "Sayonara Nakamura," some pearling songs have recently also assumed an important role unimagined by their originators. Songs have been used successfully in the adjudication of Native Title claims by Indigenous Australians, because a song can help substantiate links of a community to places over time, including where crews harvested marine resources such as pearl shells and pearls.[110] Consequently, songs encompass aspects of culture, commerce, and creativity as well as being accounts of the Australian pearling industry's work, economics, and crew culture.

To paraphrase the quotation that begins this exploration, music is vital to personal and collective memories. Pearling songs are narrative stories rich in history and worthy of research, preservation, and dissemination.

NOTES

1. Jośe van Dijck, "Record and Hold: Popular Music between Personal and Collective Memory," *Critical Studies in Media Communication* 23, no. 5 (2006): 357.

2. Mary Albertus Bain, *Full Fathom Five* (Perth: Artlook, 1982), 11–12.

3. "Pearly Shells (Pupu 'O 'Ewa)," music and lyrics by Webley Edwards and Leon Pober, published by Criterion Music Co., 1962, track 1 on Burl Ives, *Burl Ives Sings Pearly Shells and Other Favorites*, Decca, DL4578, 1964. The song is partially based on the traditional Hawaiian song "Pupu A 'O 'Ewa." "Perfect Pearl," music and lyrics by Henry Dan, track 3 on Seaman Dan, *Perfect Pearl*, Hot Records, HOT1094, 2003. The album won the 2004 Australian Recording Industry Award (ARIA) in the World Music category.

4. Stephen J. Rockel, "Between *Pori*, *Pwani* and *Kisiwani*: Overlapping Labour Cultures in the Caravans, Ports and Dhows of the Western Indian Ocean," in *The Indian Ocean: Oceanic Connections and the Creation of New Societies*, ed. Abdul Sheriff and Engseng Ho (London: Hurst, 2014).

5. "The life of a pearl diver": Lisa Urkevich, *Music and Traditions of the Arabian Peninsula: Saudi Arabia, Kuwait, Bahrain, and Qatar* (New York: Routledge, 2015), 153. "Grimly basic industry": Alan Powell, *Northern Voyagers: Australia's Monsoon Coast in Maritime History* (North Melbourne: Australian Scholarly Publishing, 2010), 180.

6. Lawrence G. Potter, "Introduction," in *The Persian Gulf in History*, ed. Lawrence Potter (New York: Palgrave Macmillan, 2009), 11.

7. On slavery in the pearling industry, see Matthew S. Hopper, *Slaves of One Master: Globalization and Slavery in Arabia in the Age of Empire* (New Haven, CT: Yale University Press, 2015); and William G. Clarence-Smith, ed., *The Economics of the Indian Ocean Slave Trade in the Nineteenth Century* (New York: Routledge, 2013). For an overview of the economics of pearling for its maritime workers in general, see J. P. S. Bach, "The Political Economy of Pearlshelling," *Economic History Review*, n.s.,

14, no. 1 (1961): 105–14. On unpaid, underpaid, and indentured labor in the Australian industry, see, for example, Sumi Kwaymullina, "For Marbles: Aboriginal People in the Early Pearling Industry of the North-West," *Studies in Western Australian History* 22 (2001): 53–61; and Julia Martińez and Adrian Vickers, *The Pearl Frontier: Indonesian Labor and Indigenous Encounters in Australia's Northern Trading Network* (Honolulu: University of Hawai'i Press, 2015).

8. For Australian research on the effects of deepwater diving, see D. H. Le Messurier and Brian Hills, "Decompression Sickness: A Study of Diving Techniques in the Torres Strait," *Hvaldradets Skrifter* 48 (1965): 54–84; and Robert Wong, "Pearl Diving from Broome," supplement to *Journal of the South Pacific Underwater Medicine Society* 26, no. 1 (March 1996): 15–26, available at http:// http://archive.rubicon-foundation.org/xmlui/handle/123456789/6356. For the relationship between pearl-shell divers and debt, see Patricia Spyer, *The Memory of Trade: Modernity's Entanglements on an Eastern Indonesian Island* (Durham, NC: Duke University Press, 2000); Spyer, "The Eroticism of Debt: Pearl Divers, Traders, and Sea Wives in the Aru Islands, Eastern Indonesia," *American Ethnologist* 24, no. 3 (August 1997): 515–38; and Potter, *The Persian Gulf in History*, 11. On pearls and the pearling industry, see Norman Bartlett, *The Pearl Seekers* (London: Melrose, 1954); and Elisabeth Strack, *Pearls* (Stuttgart: Ruhle-Diebener-Verlag, 2006).

9. In Western Australia, these bosses and especially owners also had music in their social and cultural lives, such as Broome's Dampier Orchestral Society (est. ca. 1923), an ensemble featuring European musical instruments and a repertoire of light classical and contemporaneous popular songs and dances. See John DeBurgh-Norman and Verity Norman, *A Pearling Master's Journey in the Wake of the Schooner* Mist (Strathfield, NSW: published by the authors, 2007), 241.

10. The master pearlers' role was commonly entrepreneurial or supervisory and not always hands-on. For accounts, see Richard Ferguson, *Pearls of the Past: A Biography of Captain Frank Biddles, Master Pearler* (Applecross, Western Australia: published by the author, 2001); Rosemary Hemphill, *The Master Pearler's Daughter: Memories of My Broome Childhood* (Sydney: Pan Macmillan, 2004); DeBurgh-Norman and Norman, *A Pearling Master's Journey*; DeBurgh-Norman and Norman, *Broome 1910* (Strathfield, NSW: published by the authors, 2017); Robert Lehane, *The Pearl King* (Brisbane: Boolarong Press, 2014); David Payne, "Walter Reeks, James Clark and the Origins of the Thursday Island Pearl Sheller," *The Great Circle: Journal of the Australian Association for Maritime History* 28, no. 2 (2006): 3–25.

11. Karl Neuenfeldt, "Examples of Torres Strait Songs of Longing and Belonging," *Journal of Australian Studies*, no. 75 (2002): 111–16.

12. For the pearl as a prized art and decorative object, see Neil Landman et al., *Pearls: A Natural History* (New York: Harry Abrams in association with American Museum of Natural History and Field Museum, 2001); Strack, *Pearls*.

13. Some useful sources include Edwin W. Streeter, *Pearls and Pearling Life* (London: George Bell and Sons, 1886); George Frederick Kunz and Charles Hugh Stevenson, *The Book of the Pearl: The History, Art, Science, and Industry of the Queen of Gems* (1908; repr., Mineola, NY: Dover, 1993); Robert Carter, *Sea of Pearls: Seven Thousand Years of the Industry that Shaped the Gulf* (London: Arabian, 2012). For analyses of the Australian industry, see J. P. S. Bach, *The Pearling Industry of Australia: An Account of Its Social and Economic Development* (Canberra: Department of Commerce and Agriculture, Commonwealth of Australia, 1955); Jeremy Beckett, "The Torres Strait Islanders and the Pearling Industry: A Case of Internal Colonialism," in *Aboriginal Power in Australian Society*, ed. Michael Howard (St. Lucia: University of Queensland Press, 1982); Beckett, *Torres Strait Islanders: Custom and Colonialism* (Cambridge: Cambridge University Press, 1987); Regina Ganter, *The Pearl-Shellers of Torres Strait: Resource Use, Development and Decline, 1860s–1960s* (Melbourne: Melbourne University Press, 1994); Mike McCarthy, "Before Broome," *The Great Circle: Journal of the Australian Association for Maritime History*, 16, no. 2 (1994): 76–89; Steve Mullins, *Torres Strait: A History of Colonial Occupation and Culture Contact 1864–1897* (Rockhampton: Central Queensland University Press, 1995); and Sarah Yu and Tanya Edwards, eds., *Lustre: Pearling and Australia* (Welshpool: Western Australia Museum, 2018).

14. Dances are not a focus here, but they are an important part of the expressive culture memorializing Australian community memories of the pearling industry. In Western Australia, the Bardi people of the Dampier Peninsula at One Arm Point (Ardiyooloon) maintain dances based on their community's links to pearling. In the Torres Strait region of Queensland, Torres Strait Islander dances referencing the pearling industry are common, especially expressed visually through dance apparatuses. These include elaborate headdresses depicting pearling luggers or hand-held props featuring aspects of the natural environment encountered by maritime workers, such as wind, waves, and reefs.

15. Rockel, "Between *Pori*, *Pwani* and *Kisiwani*," 97. On the theme of itinerant workforces as "carriers of culture," see Stephen J. Rockel, *Carriers of Culture: Labor on the Road in Nineteenth-Century East Africa* (Portsmouth, NH: Heinemann, 2006), 23–8.

16. Habib Hassan Touma, *The Music of the Arabs* (Cambridge, UK: Amadeus Press, 1996).

17. Nasser Al-Taee, "'Enough, Enough, Oh Ocean': Music of the Pearl Divers in the Arabian Gulf," *Middle East Studies Association Bulletin*, 39, no. 1 (June 2005): 19–30.

18. Waheed Al-Khan, *Laiwa Music of the Gulf* (Qatar: Gulf Cooperation Council Folklore Centre, 2002). For the Arabian coast of the Red Sea, see Dionisius A. Agius, John P. Cooper, Lucy Semaan, Chiara Zazzaro, and Robert Carter, "Remembering the Sea: Personal and Communal Recollections of the Maritime Life in Jizan and Farasan Islands, Saudi Arabia," *Journal of Maritime Archaeology* 11, no. 2 (August 2016): 127–77.

19. For excellent quality recordings and informative booklets, see Hamid Bin Hussein Sea Band, *Kuwait: Sea Songs of the Arabian Gulf*, recorded (2006–12), produced, and annotated by Lisa Urkevich, Music of the Earth series, Multicultural Media, MCM3051, 2014, CD and booklet; and *Bahrain: Fidjeri: Songs of the Pearl Divers*, recorded (1976), produced, and annotated by Habib Hassan Touma, UNESCO series Musical Heritage / Music and Musicians of the World, Auvidis/UNESCO D8046, 1978. Other useful sources include Lisa Urkevich, *Music and Traditions of the Arabian Peninsula: Saudi Arabia, Kuwait, Bahrain, and Qatar* (New York: Routledge, 2015); Yacoub Yusuf Al-Hijji, *Kuwait and the Sea: A Brief Social and Economic History* (London: Arabian, 2010); Saif Marzooq Al-Shamlan, *Pearling in the Arabian Gulf: A Kuwaiti Memoir* (London: London Center of Arab Studies, 2000); and Shihan De Silva Jayasuriya, "Indian Oceanic Crossings: Music of the Afro-Asian Diaspora," *African Diaspora* 1, no. 1–2 (2008): 135–54.

20. Issam El-Mallah, *Music of an Ancient Civilization: The Sultanate of Oman Muscat* (Oman: Ministry of Information, 1994); Majid H. Al-Harthy, "African Identities, Afro-Omani Music, and the Official Constructions of a Musical Past," *World of Music*, n.s., 1, no. 2 (2012): 97–129; Majid Al-Harthy and Anne Rasmussen, "Music in Oman: An Overture," *World of Music*, n.s., 1, no. 2 (2012): 9–41; Anne Rasmussen, "Preface," *World of Music*, n.s., 1, no. 2 (2012): 7–8; Rasmussen, "The Musical Design of National Space and Time in Oman," *World of Music*, n.s., 1, no. 2 (2012): 63–96; Laith Ulaby, "On the Decks of Dhows: Musical Traditions of Oman and the Indian Ocean World," *World of Music*, n.s., 1, no. 2 (2012): 43–62; Dieter Christensen and Salwa El-Shawan Castelo-Branco, *Traditional Arts in Southern Arabia: Music and Society in Sohar, Sultanate of Oman* (Berlin: Verlag für Wissenschaft und Bildung, 2009).

21. Poul Rovsing Olsen, *Music in Bahrain: Traditional Music of the Arabian Gulf* (Moesgaard, Denmark: Jutland Archaeological Society, 2002); Scheherezade Hassan, review of *Kuwait: Sea Songs of the Arabian Gulf*, Hamid Bin Hussein Sea Band, *Yearbook for Traditional Music* 49 (2017): 187–88, 215.

22. Maho M. Sebiane, "Traditional Music Patrimonialization in the United Arab Emirates: State of Play and Stakes of a Cultural Policy in Mutation (1971–2010)," *Translingual Discourse in Ethnomusicology* 2 (2016): 103–16; Sayyid Hamid Hurriez, *Folklore and Folklife in the United Arab Emirates* (London: Routledge, 2016).

23. Hopper, *Slaves of One Master*, 213–15; Rockel, "Between *Pori, Pwani* and *Kisiwani*," 102–4.

24. For the Torres Strait region of Queensland, see Frank A. York, *Children's Songs of the Torres Strait Islands* (Bateman's Bay, NSW: Owen Martin, 1990); Ron Edwards, *Some Songs from the Torres Strait* (Kuranda, Queensland: Rams Skull, 2001); Henry Dan and Karl Neuenfeldt, *Steady, Steady: The Life and Music of Seaman Dan* (Canberra: Aboriginal Studies Press, 2013); Karl Neuenfeldt and Will Kepa, "A Case Study of Indigenising the Documentation of Musical Cultural Practices," in *Antipodean Traditions: Australian Folklore in the 21st Century*, ed. Graham Seal and Jennifer Gall (Fremantle, Western Australia: Black Swan, 2011); Jeremy Beckett, "'This Music Crept on Me by Water': Recollections of Researching Torres Strait Islander Music 1958–1961," *Perfect Beat* 5, no. 3 (2001): 75–99; Philip Hayward and Junko Konishi, "*Mokuyo-to no Ongaku*: Music and the Japanese Community in the Torres Strait (1890–1941)," *Perfect Beat* 5, no. 3 (2001): 34–47. For the Broome, Western Australia, region, see Christopher Lawe-Davies, "Black Rock and Broome: Musical and Cultural Specificities," *Perfect Beat* 1, no. 2 (1993): 48–59.

25. Potter, "Introduction," 12–13, italics and ellipsis in original. Potter is quoting Al-Taee, "Enough, Enough, Oh Ocean," 20 ("imbued with mystical"), and Al-Shamlan, *Pearling in the Arabian Gulf*, 111–12 ("In every boat").

26. William Beeman, "Gulf Society: An Anthropological View of the Khalijis—Their Evolution and Way of Life," in *The Persian Gulf in History*, ed. Lawrence Potter (New York: Palgrave, 2014). For a description of khalijis' music, see also "Africans in the Arabian (Persian) Gulf," February 22, 2007, *Afropop Worldwide*, http://afropop.org/audio-programs/africans-in-the-arabian-persian-gulf.

27. Martínez and Vickers, *The Pearl Frontier*.

28. Bain, *Full Fathom Five*. For Broome as an Indian Ocean pearling center, see Joseph Christensen, "'A Patch of the Orient in Australia': Broome on the Margin of the Indo-Pacific, 1883–1939," in *Subversive Sovereigns across the Seas: Indian Ocean Ports-of-Trade from Early Historic Times to Late Colonialism*, ed. Kenneth R. Hall, Rila Mukherjee, and Suchandra Ghosh (Kolkata: Asiatic Society, 2017), 256–76. On Thursday Island, see Ganter, *The Pearl-Shellers of Torres Strait*; and Mullins, *Torres Strait*.

29. Charles Dashwood, *Pearl-Shelling Industry in Port Darwin and Northern Territory* (Melbourne: Government Printer, 1902); Bach, *Pearling*

Industry of Australia; Craig Wilcox, "The Sanyo Maru and Japanese Pearling in the Arafura Sea, 1934–1938," *The Beagle: Records of the Museums and Art Galleries of the Northern Territory*, Supp. 2 (2006): 1–39. For a post–World War II account of Darwin including the pearling industry, see Maisie Austin, *The Quality of Life: a Reflection of Life in Darwin during the Post-War Years* (Darwin: Colemans Printing, 1992); and for Darwin community music, see Jeff Corfield, *String Bands and Shake Hands: A Tribute to the Life and Music of Val McGinness* (Townsville, Queensland: published by the author, 2010).

30. Steve Mullins, "James Clark and the Celebes Trading Co.: Making an Australian Maritime Venture in The Netherlands East Indies," *The Great Circle: Journal of the Australian Association for Maritime History* 24, no. 2 (2002): 22–52; Martiñez and Vickers, *The Pearl Frontier*.

31. Steve Mullins, "From TI to Dobo: The 1905 Departure of the Pearl-Shelling Fleet to Aru, Netherlands East Indies," *The Great Circle: Journal of the Australian Association for Maritime History* 19, no. 1 (1997): 30–39; Mullins, "Australian Pearl-Shellers in the Moluccas: Confrontation and Compromise on a Maritime Frontier," *Great Circle* 23, no. 2 (2001): 3–23.

32. Arjun Appadurai, "Introduction: Commodities and the Politics of Value," in *The Social Life of Things: Commodities in Cultural Perspective*, ed. Arjun Appadurai (Cambridge: Cambridge University Press, 1988).

33. Steve Mullins and Karl Neuenfeldt, "Grand Concerts, Anzac Days and Evening Entertainments: Glimpses of Music Culture on Thursday Island, Queensland, 1900–1945," in *Landscapes of Indigenous Performance: Music, Song and Dance from Torres Strait and Arnhem Land*, ed. Fiona Magowan and Karl Neuenfeldt (Canberra: Aboriginal Studies Press, 2005); Karl Neuenfeldt and Steve Mullins, "The 'Saving Grace of Social Culture': Early Popular Music and Performance Culture on Thursday Island, Torres Strait, Queensland," *Queensland Review* 8, no. 2 (November 2001): 1–20.

34. Dan and Neuenfeldt, *Steady, Steady*.

35. Ted Egan, interview with the author, May 14, 2017.

36. Alan Villiers, *Sons of Sinbad* (New York: Scribners, 1940). See also Villiers, *Monsoon Seas: The Story of the Indian Ocean* (New York: McGraw-Hill, 1952).

37. Rockel, "Between *Pori, Pwani* and *Kisiwani*," 95.

38. Martin Denis-Constant, "The Choices of Identity," *Social Identities* 1, no.1 (1995): 5–20.

39. For some Australian popular-culture images of the pearling industry in film, see Jane Landman, *The Tread of a White Man's Foot: Australian Pacific Colonialism and the Cinema 1925–1962* (Canberra: Pandanus Books, 2006). For indigenous art works that include pearling motifs, see Bruce McLean, "The Power of Young Men: The Contemporary Torres

Strait Print Movement," in the exhibition catalog *The Torres Strait Islands: A Celebration* (Brisbane: Queensland Art Gallery/Gallery of Modern Art/State Library of Queensland/Queensland Museum, 2011), 74–103; Yu and Edwards, *Lustre: Pearling and Australia*.

40. Clem Tisdell and Bernard Poirine, "Economics of Pearl Farming," in *The Pearl Oyster*, ed. Paul Southgate and John Lucas (Oxford: Elsevier, 2008), 473–96. For a contemporary song about pearl farming, see "The Pearl Farmer," by Karl Erikson (the *nom d'artiste* for this chapter's author, Karl Neuenfeldt), at https://www.youtube.com/watch?v=Tz_dGjAUi8U.

41. The author has been directly involved in co-producing over fifty Australian recording projects and albums, primarily with Indigenous Australian communities and artists and also for archival institutions. He has produced, written for, and performed with one of the informants noted herein, Henry "Seaman" Dan, since 1999.

42. For the Shinju Matsuri event, see Lorna Kaino, "Re-mooring the Tradition of Broome's Shinju Matsuri," *Rural Society* 15, no. 2 (2005): 165–75. For ongoing pearling-based links between Japan and Australia, see Yuriko Yamanouchi, "Migration and Beyond: Continuing Relationship between Kinan Area in Japan and Northern Australia," *Oteman Journal of Australian Studies* 35 (2009): 147–55. On the Torres Strait festivals, see Anna Shnukal, "Torres Strait Islanders," in *Multicultural Queensland 2001: 100 Years, 100 Communities, a Century of Contributions*, ed. Maximilian Brandle (Brisbane: Multicultural Affairs Queensland, Department of the Premier and the Cabinet, 2001).

43. Henry Reynolds, *North of Capricorn: The Untold Story of Australia's North* (Sydney: Allen and Unwin, 2003); Regina Ganter, with contributions by Julia Martiñez and Gary Lee, *Mixed Relations: Asian-Aboriginal Contact in North Australia* (Crawley: University of Western Australia Press, 2006).

44. For comments on the role of music in the crew culture, organization. and synchronization of maritime labor within the Western Indian Ocean littoral, see Villiers, *Sons of Sinbad*; Villiers, *Monsoon Seas*; Agius et al., *Seafaring in the Arabian Gulf and Oman*; Hurriez, *Folklore and Folklife in the United Arab Emirates*, 138–40.

45. Urkevich, *Music and Traditions of the Arabian Peninsula*, 115; and Urkevich's commentary in the booklet to Hamid Bin Hussein Sea Band, *Kuwait: Sea Songs of the Arabian Gulf*.

46. Henry Dan, interview with the author, May 24, 2017.

47. Ganter, *The Pearl-Shellers of Torres Strait*, 99–150; Reynolds, *North of Capricorn*, 85–103.

48. John Singe, *The Torres Strait: People and History* (Brisbane: University of Queensland Press, 1989).

49. Mullins and Neuenfeldt. "Grand Concerts, Anzac Days and Evening Entertainments"; Neuenfeldt and Mullins, "The 'Saving Grace of Social Culture.'"

50. Dan and Neuenfeldt, *Steady, Steady*.

51. Used by permission of Steady Steady Music and the estate of the late Ephraim Bani.

52. Helen Lawrence, "'The Great Traffic in Tunes': Agents of Religious and Musical Change in Eastern Torres Strait," in *Woven Histories, Dancing Lives: Torres Strait Islander Identity, Culture and History*, ed. Richard Davis (Canberra: Aboriginal Studies Press, 2004); and Karl Neuenfeldt, "Assembling a Sacred Soundscape: Choosing Repertoire for Torres Strait Islander Community CDs/DVDs in Australia," in *Austronesian Soundscapes: Performing Arts in Oceania and South East Asia*, ed. Birgit Abels (Amsterdam: University of Amsterdam Press, 2011).

53. Henry "Seaman" Dan's recorded version is at https://www.youtube.com/watch?v=jK7N_i80AO8. Ted Egan's medley of three pearling songs, including "Black Swana," is at https://www.youtube.com/watch?v=ybcEIaGQoA. There are also choral versions by the Hastings and Prince Edward Regional Choir (Belleview, Ontario, Canada) (n.d.), at https://www.youtube.com/watch?v=R7yiIuggUIc, and the Success Choir (possibly from Taiwan) (2010), at https://www.youtube.com/watch?v=3fRHA4mizdo.

54. Used by permission of Steady Steady Music. Henry "Seaman" Dan's version of "Forty Fathoms" is at https://www.youtube.com/watch?v=zK5H6h5yuRg.

55. See Dan and Neuenfeldt, *Steady, Steady*, 52–55.

56. "Thursday Island Cemetery," Torres Shire Council website, http://www.torres.qld.gov.au/thursday-island-cemetery.

57. *The Pearl Shell Divers: Australia's Deadliest Catch: An Oral History on Film*, directed by Garry Kerr (Portland, Victoria, Australia: Garry Kerr DVD Productions, 2010), DVD.

58. Neuenfeldt, "Examples of Torres Strait Songs of Longing and Belonging," 111–16.

59. Liner notes for *Badu Nawul: Traditional and Contemporary Music and Dance of Badu Island, Torres Strait*, Torres Strait Regional Authority, 2008, CD and DVD.

60. "Thursday Island Cemetery."

61. Beckett, *Torres Strait Islanders*, 147–70; "Strait Natives' Good Money from Pearling," *Worker* (Brisbane), October 24, 1949, 7.

62. Beckett, "'This Music Crept on Me by Water.'"

63. Liner notes for *Badu Nawul*.

64. Beckett, *Torres Strait Islanders*, 52–53, 118–19; Mark Smith, email correspondence with author, July 30, 2016.

65. Diana Preston and Michael Preston, *A Pirate of Exquisite Mind: Explorer, Naturalist and Buccaneer: The Life of William Dampier* (London: Corgi, 2005).

66. Kim Akerman and John E. Stanton, *Riji and Jakuli: Kimberley Pearl Shell in Aboriginal Australia* (Darwin: Northern Territory Museum of Arts and Sciences, 1994).

67. Kunz and Stevenson, *The Book of the Pearl*.

68. Bob Reece and Tom Stannage, eds., *European–Aboriginal Relations in Western Australian History* (Nedlands: University of Western Australia, Department of History, 1984).

69. Accounts of Aboriginal women working in the pearling industry appear in Bain, *Full Fathom Five*; Kwaymullina, "For Marbles"; Peta Stephenson, *The Outsiders Within: Telling Australia's Indigenous-Asian Story* (Sydney: University of New South Wales Press, 2007).

70. Michael McCarthy, "Before Broome," *The Great Circle: Journal of the Australian Association for Maritime History* 16, no. 2 (1994): 76–89.

71. Susan Jane Hunt, *Spinifex and Hessian: Women's Lives in North-Western Australia, 1860–1900* (Nedlands: University of Western Australia Press, 1986), 102.

72. John Bailey, *The White Divers of Broome: The True Story of a Fatal Experiment* (Sydney: Pan Macmillan, 2001), 23.

73. James Battye, *Western Australia: A History from Its Discovery to the Inauguration of the Commonwealth* (London: Oxford University Press, 1924), 273, 299.

74. Cited in Raelene Frances, *Selling Sex: A Hidden History of Prostitution* (Sydney: University of New South Wales Press, 2007), 81.

75. John Brown Gribble, *Dark Deeds in a Sunny Land, or Blacks and Whites in North-West Australia* (1905; Crawley: University of Western Australia Press, 1987).

76. Hunt, *Spinifex and Hessian*.

77. Hunt, 109; Frances, *Selling Sex*, 80–82.

78. Bailey, *The White Divers of Broome*, 23.

79. Stephenson, *The Outsiders Within*, 60–61.

80. Chris Owen, *Every Mother's Son is Guilty: Policing the Kimberley Frontier of Western Australia 1882–1905* (Crawley, Western Australia: UWA Publishing, 2016.

81. McCarthy, "Before Broome," 88n30, italics in original, citing Bartlett, *The Pearl Seekers*, 85.

82. Kwaymullina, "For Marbles," 53.

83. Martiñez and Vickers, *The Pearl Frontier*.

84. "Malay" was a general term, ignoring the specific geographical origins of workers who might speak Malay as a lingua franca or an additional language, or come from a contiguous region of Southeast Asia.

85. Bailey, *White Divers of Broome*.

86. On Broome culture, see, for example, Ian Idriess, *Forty Fathoms Deep: Pearl Divers and Sea Rovers in Australian Seas* (Sydney: Angus and Robertson, 1937); Lorna Kaino, "'Broome Culture' and its Historical Links to the Japanese in the Pearling Industry," *Continuum: Journal of Media and Cultural Studies* 25, no. 4 (2011): 479–90; Susan Sickert, *Beyond the Lattice: Broome's Early Years* (Fremantle, Western Australia: Fremantle Arts Centre Press, 2003); and Sarah Yu, "Broome Creole: Aboriginal and Asian Partnerships along the Kimberley Coast," *Queensland Review* 6, no. 2 (1999): 59–73.

87. See Christine Choo, "Asian Men on the West Kimberley Coast, 1900–1940," *Asian Orientations: Studies in Western Australian History* 16 (1995): 89–111; Michael Schaper, "The Broome Race Riots of 1920," *Studies in Western Australian History* 16 (1995): 112–32; and Liz Conor, "'Black Velvet' and 'Purple Indignation': Print Responses to Japanese 'Poaching' of Aboriginal Women," *Aboriginal History* 37 (2013): 51–76.

88. Ruth Balint, 'Aboriginal Women and Asian Men: A Maritime History of Color in White Australia,' *Signs* 37, no. 3 (Spring 2012): 544–54.

89. J. P. S. Bach, "The Pearlshelling Industry and the 'White Australia' Policy," *Historical Studies: Australia and New Zealand* 10, no. 38 (1962): 203–13.

90. Marilyn Lake and Henry Reynolds, *Drawing the Global Colour Line: White Men's Countries and the Question of Racial Equality* (Melbourne: Melbourne University Publishing, 2008).

91. Used by permission of composer-author Lorrae Coffin and Magabala Books.

92. Vanessa Mills, "Women Recognised for Love and Death in Broome Pearling," *ABC Kimberley*, November, 29, 2010, http://www.abc.net.au/local/stories/2010/11/29/3079734.htm. Mills notes, "The bronze statue is of an Aboriginal woman desperately rising out of a wave with a pearl shell in her hand." Western Australian sculptors Joan and Charlie Smith created it after extensive community consultation.

93. Lorrae Coffin, *Free Diving* (Broome, Western Australia: Magabala Books, 2017). See also Lorrae Coffin, "Free Diving," track 5 on *Didj'un: Singer/Songwriters from the Kimberley*, prod. Alan Pigram, Goolarri Media Enterprises (Broome), GMCD001, 1998. A YouTube version of the song sung by Lorrae Coffin, with illustrations from the book by Bronwyn Houston, is at: https://www.youtube.com/watch?v=d8Ha4gt2cbo.

94. David Sissons, "The Japanese in the Australian Pearling Industry," *Queensland Heritage* 3, no. 10 (1979): 9–21. Yuriko Nagata, *Unwanted Aliens: Japanese Internment in Australia* (St. Lucia: University of Queensland Press, 1996).

95. Beckett, "The Torres Strait Islanders and the Pearling Industry," 131–58.

96. Nagata, *Unwanted Aliens*. See Mervyn W. Prime, *Broome's One Day War: The Story of the Japanese Raid on Broome, 3rd March 1942* (Broome, Western Australia: Shire of Broome, for Broome Historical Society, 1992); Peter Grose, *An Awkward Truth: The Bombing of Darwin February 1942* (Crows Nest, NSW: Allen and Unwin, 2009); and Vanessa Seekee, *Horn Island: In their Steps 1939–45* (Horn Island, Queensland: published by the author, 2002), 15–39.

97. Yuriko Nagata, "Okinawan Contract Pearl-Shell Labourers in the Torres Strait: 1958–1961," *Osutoraria Ken Kyu* [Journal of Australian studies] 3 (2017): 61–70.

98. Nagata, 68.

99. Nagata, 66.

100. Shnukal, 'Torres Strait Islanders.'

101. Graeme Smith, "Ted Egan: Bringing it Home," in *Market and Margins: Australian Country Music*, vol. 3, ed. Mark Evans and Geoff Walden (Gympie, Queensland: AICM Press, 2005): 180–202.

102. Ted Egan, interview with the author, May 14, 2017.

103. Hayato Sakurai, "Investigating the Japanese Cemetery in Broome," in *Taiji on Distant Shores: Tales of Immigrants from Taiji and other Towns on the Kii Peninsula* (Taiji, Japan: Taiji Historical Archives, 2014), 87.

104. Ted Egan, personal communication with author, May 14, 2017. Egan's version of the song, with some Japanese language towards the end, can be heard at https://www.youtube.com/watch?v=N57zrGbvGcs.

105. Used by permission of composer-author Ted Egan.

106. Wong, "Pearl Diving from Broome."

107. The Lacepede Islands were used to maroon kidnapped Aboriginal workers, women and men, after "blackbirding" or forcing them to work on pearling luggers. For an account, see Blaze Kwaymullina, "Blackbirding," in *Historical Encyclopedia of Western Australia*, ed. Jenny Gregory and Jan Gothard (Crawley: University of Western Australia Press, 2009), 132–33.

108. Register of Heritage Places (Western Australia). Assessment Documentation Broome Cemetery—Japanese/Chinese/Muslim Section 18, November 20, 2008.

109. For a popular albeit dramatically embellished Australian account of Broome, see Idriess, *Forty Fathoms Deep*. For an analysis of films with a pearling component in the context of Australia's Pacific colonialism and the cinema, see Jane Landman, *The Tread of a White Man's Foot*.

110. See Grace Koch, *We Have the Song, So We Have the Land: Song and Ceremony as Proof of Ownership in Aboriginal and Torres Strait Islander Land Claims* (Canberra: Australian Institute of Aboriginal Torres

Strait Islander Studies, 2013); and Grace Koch and Alexandra Crowe, "Song, Land, and Ceremony: Interpreting the Place of Songs as Evidence for Australian Aboriginal and Torres Strait Islander Land Claims," *Collaborative Anthropologies* 6 (2013): 373–98.

Selected Bibliography

Addison, Joyce and Shellei. *Pearls: Ornament and Obsession*. New York: Simon and Schuster, 1992.

Akerman, Kim, and John E. Stanton. *Riji and Jakuli: Kimberley Pearl Shell in Aboriginal Australia*. Darwin: Northern Territory Museum of Arts and Sciences, 1994.

Albedwawi, Saif. "Pearl Merchants of the Gulf and Their Life in Bombay." *Proceedings of the Seminar for Arabian Studies* 47 (2017): 1–7.

Al-Hijji, Yacoub Yusuf. *Kuwait and the Sea: A Brief Social and Economic History*. London: Arabian, 2010.

Allen, Richard. "Ending the History of Silence: Reconstructing European Slave Trading in the Indian Ocean." *Revista Tempo* 23, no. 2 (May–August 2017): 295–313.

al-Shamlan, Saif Marzooq. *Pearling in the Arabian Gulf: A Kuwaiti Memoir*. Translated by Peter Clark. London: London Centre of Arab Studies, 2000.

Al-Taee, Nasser. "'Enough, Enough, Oh Ocean': Music of the Pearl Divers in the Arabian Gulf." *Middle East Studies Association Bulletin* 39, no. 1 (June 2005): 19–30.

Al-Zayānī, Rāshid. *Al-Ghaūs wa at-Tawāsha*. Manama, Bahrain: Al Ayam Publishing, 1998.

Alwi, Des. *Friends and Exiles: A Memoir of the Nutmeg Isles and the Indonesian Nationalist Movement*. Edited by Barbara S. Harvey. Ithaca, NY: Southeast Asia Program, Cornell University, 2008.

Amrith, Sunil S. *Crossing the Bay of Bengal: The Furies of Nature and the Fortunes of Migrants*. Cambridge, MA: Harvard University Press, 2013.

Appadurai, Arjun. "Introduction: Commodities and the Politics of Value." In *The Social Life of Things: Commodities in Cultural Perspective*, edited by Arjun Appadurai, 3–63. Cambridge: Cambridge University Press, 1986.

Armitage, David, Alison Bashford, and Sujit Sivasundaram, eds. *Oceanic Histories*. Cambridge: Cambridge University Press, 2018.

Bach, J. P. S. *The Pearling Industry of Australia: An Account of Its Social and Economic Development*. Canberra: Commonwealth of Australia, Department of Commerce and Agriculture, 1955.

Balint, Ruth. "Aboriginal Women and Asian Men: A Maritime History of Color in White Australia." *Signs* 37, no. 3 (Spring 2012): 544–54.

Balsan, Consuelo Vanderbilt. *The Glitter and the Gold*. New York: Harper, 1952.

Belgrave, Charles. *Personal Column*. London: Hutchinson, 1960.

Benton, Lauren. *A Search for Sovereignty: Law and Geography in European Empires, 1400–1900*. New York: Cambridge University Press, 2010.

Blussé, Leonard. "In Praise of Commodities: An Essay on the Cross-Cultural Trade in Edible Birds' Nests." In *Emporia, Commodities and Entrepreneurs in Asian Maritime Trade, c. 1400-1750*, edited by Roderich Ptak and Dietmar Rothermund, 317–35. Stuttgart: Franz Steiner Verlag, 1991.

Bolster, W. Jeffrey. *The Mortal Sea: Fishing the Atlantic in the Age of Sail*. Cambridge, MA: Harvard University Press, 2012.

———. "Putting the Ocean in Atlantic History: Maritime Communities and Marine Ecology in the Northwest Atlantic, 1500-1800." *American Historical Review* 113, no. 1 (February 2008): 19–47.

Bose, Sugata. *A Hundred Horizons: The Indian Ocean in the Age of Global Empire*. Cambridge, MA: Harvard University Press, 2006.

Boutan, Louis. *La perle: Étude générale de la perle: Histoire de la méléagrine et des mollusques producteurs de perles*. Paris: Gaston Doin, 1925.

Brewer, John, and Roy Porter, eds. *Consumption and the World of Goods*. Abingdon, UK: Routledge, 1993.

Burdett, Anita L. P., ed. *Records of the Persian Gulf Pearl Fisheries, 1857–1962*. London: Archive Editions, 1995.

Butcher, John G. *The Closing of the Frontier: A History of the Marine Fisheries of Southeast Asia c. 1850–2000*. Singapore: Institute of Southeast Asian Studies, 2004.

———. "Resink Revisited: A Note on the Territorial Waters of the Self-Governing Realms of the Netherlands Indies in the Late 1800s." *Bijdragen tot de taal-, land- en volkenkunde* 164, no. 1 (2008): 1–12.

Butcher, John G., and R. E. Elson. *Sovereignty and the Sea: How Indonesia Became an Archipelagic State*. Singapore: National University of Singapore Press, 2017.

Cariño, Micheline. "The Cultured Pearl Polemic." *World Aquaculture* 27, no. 1 (1996): 42–44.

———. "The Great Debate: The Cultured Pearl Polemic." *Pearl Oyster Information Bulletin* 10 (August 1997): 49–51.

Cariño, Micheline, and Monteforte, Mario. *Une histoire mondiale des perles et des nacres: Pêche, culture, commerce*. Paris: L'Harmattan, 2005.

Carter, Robert. "The History and Prehistory of Pearling in the Persian Gulf." *Journal of the Economic and Social History of the Orient* 48, no. 2 (2005): 139–209.

———. "How Pearls Made the Modern Emirates." In *New Perspectives on Recording UAE History*, edited by Jayanti Maitra, 258–81. Abu Dhabi: Centre for Documentation and Research, 2009.

———. *Sea of Pearls: Seven Thousand Years of the Industry That Shaped the Gulf*. London: Arabian, 2012.

Chang, Wen-Chin, and Eric Tagliacozzo. "Introduction: The Arc of Historical Commercial Relations between China and Southeast Asia." In *Chinese Circulations: Capital, Commodities, and Networks in Southeast Asia*, edited by Eric Tagliacozzo and Wen-Chin Chang, 1–17. Durham: Duke University Press, 2011.

Charney, Michael W. "Esculent Bird's Nest, Tin and Fish: The Overseas Chinese and Their Trade in the Eastern Bay of Bengal (Coastal Burma) during the First Half of the Nineteenth Century." In *China and Southeast Asia*, vol. 4, *Interactions from the End of the Nineteenth Century to 1911*, edited by Geoff Wade, 207–21. London: Routledge, 2009.

Charpentier, Vincent, Carl S. Phillips, and Sophie Méry. "Pearl Fishing in the Ancient World: 7500 BP." *Arabian Archaeology and Epigraphy*, no. 23 (2012): 1–6.

Choo, Christine. "The Impact of Asian-Aboriginal Australian Contacts in Northern Australia." *Asian and Pacific Migration Journal* 3, nos. 2–3 (June 1994): 295–310.

Christensen, Dieter, and Salwa El-Shawan Castelo-Branco. *Traditional Arts in Southern Arabia: Music and Society in Sohar, Sultanate of Oman*. Berlin: Verlag für Wissenschaft und Bildung, 2009.

Christensen, Joseph. "'A Patch of the Orient in Australia': Broome on the Margin of the Indo-Pacific, 1883–1939." In *Subversive Sovereigns across the Seas: Indian Ocean Ports-of-Trade from Early Historic Times to Late Colonialism*, edited by Kenneth R. Hall, Rila Mukherjee, and Suchandra Ghosh, 256–76. Kolkata: Asiatic Society, 2017.

Clunas, Craig. *Superfluous Things: Material Culture and Social Status in Early Modern China*. Honolulu: University of Hawai'i Press, 1991.

Codrai, Ronald. *The Emirates of Yesteryear*. London: Stacey International, 2001.

Comaroff, John L., and Jean Comaroff. *Ethnography and the Historical Imagination*. Boulder: Westview Press, 1992.

Croucher, Sarah. "Exchange Values: Commodities, Colonialism and Identity on Nineteenth Century Zanzibar." In *The Archaeology of Capitalism in Colonial Contexts*, edited by Sarah Croucher and Lindsay Weiss, 165–91. New York: Springer, 2011.

Cushman, Jennifer Wayne. *Fields from the Sea: Chinese Junk Trade with Siam during the Late Eighteenth and Early Nineteenth Century*, Studies on Southeast Asia no. 12. Ithaca, NY: Cornell University, Southeast Asia Program Publications, 1993.

Dakin, W. J. *Pearls*. Cambridge: Cambridge University Press, 1913.

Dalrymple, Alexander. *Oriental Repertory*. 2 vols. London: Ballantine and Law, 1808.

Dan, Henry, and Karl Neuenfeldt. *Steady, Steady: The Life and Music of Seaman Dan*. Canberra: Aboriginal Studies Press, 2013.

Dawson, Kevin. "Enslaved Swimmers and Divers in the Atlantic World." *Journal of American History* 92, no. 4 (March 2006): 1327–55.

De Silva, Chandra R. "The Portuguese and Pearl Fishing off South India and Sri Lanka." *South Asia: Journal of South Asian Studies* 1, no. 1 (1978): 14–28.

De Silva, Colvin R. *Ceylon under the British Occupation, 1795–1833*. 2nd ed. 2 vols. Colombo, Ceylon: Colombo Apothecaries' Co., 1953–62.

Donkin, R. A. *Beyond Price: Pearls and Pearl-Fishing: Origins to the Age of Discoveries*. Philadelphia: American Philosophical Society, 1998.

Edwards, Hugh. *Port of Pearls: A History of Broome*. 2nd ed. Swanbourne, Western Australia: published by the author, 1988.

Ericson, Kjell D. "Nature's Helper: Mikimoto Kokichi and the Place of Cultivation in the Twentieth Century's Pearl Empires." PhD diss., Princeton University, 2015.

Eunson, Robert. *The Pearl King: The Story of the Fabulous Mikimoto*. Tokyo: Charles E. Tuttle, 1965.

Ewald, Janet J. "Crossers of the Sea: Slaves, Freedmen, and Other Migrants in the Northwestern Indian Ocean, c. 1750–1914." *American Historical Review* 105, no. 1 (February 2000): 69–91.

Faroqhi, Suraiya. "Moving Goods Around, and Ottomanists Too: Surveying Research on the Transfer of Material Goods in the Ottoman Empire." *Turcica* 32 (February 2000): 435–66.

Fischel, Oskar, and Max von Boehn. *Modes and Manners of the Nineteenth Century as Represented in the Pictures and Engravings of the Time*. London: J. M. Dent and Sons, 1927.

Fletcher, Richard, and Robert Carter. "Mapping the Growth of an Arabian Gulf Town: The Case of Doha, Qatar." *Journal of the Economic and Social History of the Orient* 60, no. 4 (2017): 420–87.

Flores, Jorge Manuel. "The Straits of Ceylon and the Maritime Trade in Early Sixteenth Century India: Commodities, Merchants, and Trading Networks." *Moyen Orient et Océan Indien* 7 (1990): 27–58.

Forrest, Thomas. *A Voyage to New Guinea and the Moluccas from Balambangan: Including an Account of Mindanao, Sooloo and other Islands*. London: G. Scott, 1779.

Fuccaro, Nelida. *Histories of City and State in the Persian Gulf: Manama since 1800.* Cambridge: Cambridge University Press, 2009.

Fujimoto, Helen. *The South Indian Muslim Community and the Evolution of the Jawi Peranakan in Penang up to 1948.* Tokyo: Gaikokugo Daigaku, 1989.

Ganter, Regina. *The Pearl-Shellers of Torres Strait: Resource Use, Development and Decline, 1860s–1960s.* Melbourne: Melbourne University Press, 1994.

Ganter, Regina, with contributions by Julia Martínez and Gary Lee. *Mixed Relations: Asian-Aboriginal Contact in North Australia.* Crawley: University of Western Australia Press, 2006.

Gerritsen, Anne. "Domesticating Goods from Overseas: Global Material Culture in the Early Modern Netherlands." *Journal of Design History* 29, no. 3 (August 2016): 228–44.

———. "From Long-Distance Trade to the Global Lives of Things: Writing the History of Early Modern Trade and Material Culture," *Journal of Early Modern History* 20, no. 6 (November 2016): 526–44.

Gillis, John R. and Franziska Torma, eds. *Fluid Frontiers: New Currents in Marine Environmental History.* Cambridge, UK: White Horse, 2015.

Hackney, Ki, and Diana Edkins. *People and Pearls: The Magic Endures.* New York: HarperCollins, 2000.

Hanley, Susan B. *Everyday Things in Premodern Japan: The Hidden Legacy of Material Culture.* Berkeley: University of California Press, 1997.

Harrison, Anthony J. *Savant of the Australian Seas: William Saville-Kent (1845–1908) and Australian Fisheries.* Hobart: Tasmanian Historical Research Association, 1997.

Harrison, Paul W. *The Arab at Home.* New York: Thomas Y. Crowell, 1924.

Hassan, Scheherezade. Review of *Kuwait: Sea Songs of the Arabian Gulf,* Hamid Bin Hussein Sea Band. *Yearbook for Traditional Music* 49 (2017): 187–88, 215.

Haynes, T. H. *International Fishery Disputes.* London: published by the author, 1891.

Henare, Amiria J. M., Martin Holbraad, and Sari Wastell. *Thinking through Things: Theorising Artefacts Ethnographically.* Abingdon, UK: Routledge, 2006.

Hill, Ernestine. *The Great Australian Loneliness.* 2nd ed. Sydney: Angus and Robertson, 1963.

Hopper, Matthew S. "East Africa and the End of the Indian Ocean Slave Trade." *Journal of African Development* 13, no. 1 (Spring 2011): 27–54.

———. *Slaves of One Master: Globalization and Slavery in Arabia in the Age of Empire.* New Haven, CT: Yale University Press, 2015.

Hornell, James. *Report to the Government of Madras on the Indian Pearl Fisheries in the Gulf of Mannar.* Madras: Government Press, 1905.

Hunt, Susan Jane. *Spinifex and Hessian: Women's Lives in North-Western Australia, 1860–1900*. Nedlands: University of Western Australia Press, 1986.

Hussin, Nordin. *Trade and Society in the Straits of Melaka: Dutch Melaka and English Penang, 1780–1830*. Singapore: National University of Singapore Press, 2006.

Ivanoff, Jacques, and Thierry Lejard. *A Journey through the Mergui Archipelago*. Bangkok: White Lotus, 2002.

Kopytoff, Igor. "The Cultural Biography of Things: Commoditization as Process." In *The Social Life of Things: Commodities in Cultural Perspective*, edited by Arjun Appadurai, 64–94. Cambridge: Cambridge University Press, 1986.

Kornitzer, Louis. *The Pearl Trader*. New York: Sheridan House, 1937.

Kunz, George Frederick, and Charles Hugh Stevenson. *The Book of the Pearl: The History, Art, Science, and Industry of the Queen of Gems*. New York: Century, 1908.

Kwaymullina, Sumi. "For Marbles: Aboriginal People in the Early Pearling Industry of the North-West." *Studies in Western Australian History* 22 (2001): 53–61.

Latil, Pierre de, and Jean Rivoire. *Man and the Underwater World*. London: Jarrolds, 1956.

Leach, Edmund Ronald. *Political Systems of Highland Burma: A Study of Kachin Social Structure*. London: London School of Economics and Political Science, 1954.

Londres, Albert. *Pêcheurs de perles*. Paris: Albin Michel, 1931.

Lorimer, John Gordon. *Gazetteer of the Persian Gulf, Oman and Central Arabia*. 2 vols. Calcutta: Superintendent Government Printing, 1908, 1915.

MacKnight, Campbell C. *The Voyage to Marege': Macassan Trepangers in Northern Australia*. Carlton: Melbourne University Press, 1976.

Martineau, Harriet. *Illustrations of Political Economy*. 9 vols. London: Charles Fox, 1832–34.

Martinelli, Renzo. *Sud: Rapporto di un viaggio in Eritrea ed in Etiopia*. Florence: Vallecchi Editore, 1930.

Martínez, Julia, and Adrian Vickers. *The Pearl Frontier: Indonesian Labor and Indigenous Encounters in Australia's Northern Trading Network*. Honolulu: University of Hawai'i Press, 2015.

McCarthy, Michael [Mike]. "Before Broome." *The Great Circle: Journal of the Australian Association for Maritime History* 16, no. 2 (1994): 76–89.

———. "Indonesian Divers in Australia's Northern Waters." *The Great Circle: Journal of the Australian Association for Maritime History* 20, no. 2 (1998): 120–37.

———. "Naked Diving for Mother-of-Pearl." *Early Days: Journal of the Royal Western Australian Historical Society* 13, no. 2 (2008): 243–62.
McEvoy, Arthur F. *The Fisherman's Problem: Ecology and Law in the California Fisheries, 1850–1980.* New York: Cambridge University Press, 1986.
Melillo, Edward D. "Making Sea Cucumbers Out of Whales' Teeth: Nantucket Castaways and Encounters of Value in Nineteenth-Century Fiji." *Environmental History* 20, no. 3 (July 2015): 449–74.
Miran, Jonathan. *Red Sea Citizens: Cosmopolitan Society and Cultural Change in Massawa* Bloomington: Indiana University Press, 2009.
Modigliani, Giorgio. "Le perle di Massaua." In *Atti del terzo congresso di studi coloniali, Firenze-Roma 12–17 Aprile 1937,* vol. 8, *VII sezione: Economica—Agraria,* 682–97. Florence: G. C. Sansoni, 1937.
Monfreid, Henri de, with Ida Treat. *Pearls, Arms and Hashish: Pages from the Life of a Red Sea Navigator, Henri de Monfreid.* New York: Coward-McCann, 1930.
Monfreid, Henry de. *Les secrets de la mer Rouge.* Paris: B. Grasset, 1931.
———. "Pearl Fishing in the Red Sea." *National Geographic,* November 1937, 597–626.
Montigny, Anie. "Évolution d'un groupe bédouin dans un pays producteur de pétrole: Les Al-Na'im de Qatar." PhD thesis, Université de Paris V, 1985.
Moore, Ronald. "The Management of the Western Australian Pearling Industry, 1860 to the 1930s." *The Great Circle: Journal of the Australian Association for Maritime History* 16, no. 2 (1994): 121–38.
Mullins, Steve. "Australian Pearl-Shellers in the Moluccas: Confrontation and Compromise on a Maritime Frontier." *The Great Circle: Journal of the Australian Association for Maritime History* 23, no. 2 (2001): 3–23.
———. "Company Boats, Sailing Dinghies and Passenger Fish: Fathoming Torres Strait Islander Participation in the Maritime Economy." *Labour History,* no. 103 (November 2012): 39–58.
———. "James Clark and the Celebes Trading Co.: Making an Australian Maritime Venture in the Netherlands East Indies." *The Great Circle: Journal of the Australian Association for Maritime History* 24, no. 2 (2002): 22–52.
———. *Octopus Crowd: Maritime History and the Business of Australian Pearling in Its Schooner Age.* Tuscaloosa: University of Alabama Press, 2019.
———. "To Break 'the Trinity' or 'Wipe Out the Smaller Fry': The Australian Pearl Shell Convention of 1913." *Journal for Maritime Research* 7, no. 1 (2005): 215–44.

———. *Torres Strait: A History of Colonial Occupation and Culture Contact, 1864–1897*. Rockhampton: Central Queensland University Press, 1995.

Neuenfeldt, Karl. "Examples of Torres Strait Songs of Longing and Belonging." *Journal of Australian Studies*, no. 75 (2002): 111–16.

Nimmo, Harry Arlo. *The Sea People of Sulu: A Study of Social Change in the Philippines*. San Francisco: Chandler, 1972.

Olsen, Poul Rovsing. *Music in Bahrain: Traditional Music of the Arabian Gulf*. Moesgaard, Denmark: Jutland Archaeological Society, 2002.

Palgrave, William Gifford. *Personal Narrative of a Year's Journey through Central and Eastern Arabia, 1862–63*. London: Macmillan, 1883.

Parazzoli, Ambrogio. "La pesca nel Mar Rosso." *L'Esplorazione commerciale* 13, no. 6 (June 1898): 177–90.

Paterson, Alistair. "Unearthing Barrow Island's Past: The Historical Archaeology of Colonial-Era Exploitation, Northwest Australia." *International Journal of Historical Archaeology* 21, no. 2 (June 2017): 346–68.

The Pearl Shell Divers: Australia's Deadliest Catch: An Oral History on Film. Directed by Garry Kerr. Portland, Victoria, Australia: Garry Kerr DVD Productions, 2010. DVD.

Petersen, Andrew. "Research on an Islamic Period Settlement at Ras Ushayriq in Northern Qatar and Some Observations on the Occurrence of Date Presses." *Proceedings of the Seminar for Arabian Studies* 41 (2011): 245–56.

Petersen, Andrew, Faisal Abdullah Al-Naimi, Tony Grey, Ifan Edwards, Austin Hill, Hannah Russ, and Dee Williams. "Ruwayda: An Historic Urban Settlement in North Qatar." *Post-Medieval Archaeology* 50, no. 2 (2012): 321–49.

Puglisi, Giuseppe. "Ali El Nahari." In *Chi è? dell'Eritrea 1952: Dizionario Biografico con una cronologia*, compiled by Giuseppe Puglisi. Asmara: Agenzia Regina, 1952.

Reynolds, Henry. *North of Capricorn: The Untold Story of Australia's North*. Sydney: Allen and Unwin, 2003.

Richter, Tobias, Paul Wordsworth, and Alan Walmsley. "Pearl Fishers, Townsfolk, Bedouin, and Shaykhs: Economic and Social Relations in Islamic al-Zubarah." *Proceedings of the Seminar for Arabian Studies* 41 (2011): 317–32.

Rosenthal, Léonard. *Au royaume de la perle*. Paris: Payot, 1919.

———. *The Pearl and I: The Diary of an Ex-Millionaire*. New York: Vantage, 1955.

———. *The Pearl Hunter: An Autobiography*. New York: Henry Schuman, 1952.

Salvadei, Giovanni. "La pesca e il commercio delle perle e della madreperla in Eritrea." Allegato (enclosure) no. 91. In *Relazione sulla Colonia Eritrea del Regio Commissario civile deputato Ferdinando Martini per gli esercizi 1902–1907*, edited by Ferdinando Martini, 3:1157–81. Rome: Tipografia della Camera dei Deputati, 1913.

Saunders, Nicholas J. "Biographies of Brilliance: Pearls, Transformations of Matter and Being, c. AD 1492." *World Archaeology* 31, no. 2 (October 1999): 243–57.

Seetah, Krish, ed. *Connecting Continents: Archaeology and History in the Indian Ocean World*. Athens: Ohio University Press, 2018.

Sen, Sudipta. *Empire of Free Trade: The East India Company and the Making of the Colonial Marketplace*. Philadelphia: University of Pennsylvania Press, 1998.

Shnukal, Anna, Guy Ramsay, and Yuriko Nagata, eds. *Navigating Boundaries: The Asian Diaspora in Torres Strait*. Canberra: Pandanus Books, 2004.

Sissons, D. C. S. "*Karayuki-San*: Japanese Prostitutes in Australia, 1887–1916." Pts. 1 and 2. *Historical Studies* 17, no. 68 (April 1977): 323–41; 17, no. 69 (October 1977): 474–88.

Sivasundaram, Sujit. *Islanded: Britain, Sri Lanka, and the Bounds of an Indian Ocean Colony*. Chicago: University of Chicago Press, 2013.

Smith, Kate. "Amidst Things: New Histories of Commodities, Capital, and Consumption." *Historical Journal* 61, no. 3 (September 2018): 841–61.

Spyer, Patricia. "The Eroticism of Debt: Pearl Divers, Traders, and Sea Wives in the Aru Islands, Eastern Indonesia." *American Ethnologist* 24, no. 3 (August 1997): 515–38.

———. *The Memory of Trade: Modernity's Entanglements on an Eastern Indonesian Island*. Durham, NC: Duke University Press, 2000.

Stein, Sarah Abrevaya. *Plumes: Ostrich Feathers, Jews, and a Lost World of Global Commerce*. New Haven, CT: Yale University Press, 2008.

Steinberg, Philip E. *The Social Construction of the Ocean*. Cambridge: Cambridge University Press, 2001.

Steuart, James. *An Account of the Pearl Fisheries of Ceylon*. Cotta, Ceylon: Church Mission Press, 1843.

Strack, Elisabeth. *Pearls*. Stuttgart: Rühle-Diebener-Verlag, 2006.

Streeter, Edwin W. *Pearls and Pearling Life*. London: George Bell and Sons, 1886.

Subrahmanyam, Sanjay. "Noble Harvest from the Sea: Managing the Pearl Fishery of Mannar, 1500–1925." In *Institutions and Economic Change in South Asia*, edited by Burton Stein and Sanjay Subrahmanyam, 134–72. Delhi: Oxford University Press, 1996.

Sutherland, Heather. "A Sino-Indonesian Commodity Chain: The Trade in Tortoiseshell in the Late Seventeenth and Eighteenth Centuries." In *Chinese Circulations: Capital, Commodities, and Networks in Southeast Asia*, edited by Eric Tagliacozzo and Wen-Chin Chang, 172–99. Durham, NC: Duke University Press, 2011.

Tagliacozzo, Eric. "A Necklace of Fins: Marine Goods Trading in Maritime Southeast Asia, 1780–1860." *International Journal of Asian Studies* 1, no. 1 (2004): 23–48.

———. *Secret Trades, Porous Borders: Smuggling and States along a Southeast Asian Frontier, 1865–1915*. New Haven, CT: Yale University Press, 2005.

———. "A Sino–Southeast Asian Circuit: Ethnohistories of the Marine Goods Trade." In *Chinese Circulations: Capital, Commodities, and Networks in Southeast Asia*, edited by Eric Tagliacozzo and Wen-Chin Chang, 432–54. Durham, NC: Duke University Press, 2011.

Tarling, Nicholas. *Anglo-Dutch Rivalry in the Malay World, 1780–1824*. St. Lucia: University of Queensland Press, 1962.

Thieme, Otto Charles. "The Art of Dress in the Victorian and Edwardian Eras." *Journal of Decorative and Propaganda Arts* 10 (Autumn 1988): 14–27.

Tuson, Penelope, ed. *Persian Gulf Trade Reports 1905–1940*. Cambridge: Cambridge University Press, 1987.

Ulaby, Laith. "On the Decks of Dhows: Musical Traditions of Oman and the Indian Ocean World." *World of Music*, n.s., 1, no. 2 (2012): 43–62.

Urkevich, Lisa. *Music and Traditions of the Arabian Peninsula: Saudi Arabia, Kuwait, Bahrain, and Qatar*. New York: Routledge, 2015.

van de Wall, V. I. "Sjech Said bin Abdullah Baädilla: Een Arabier van beteekenis in de Groote Oost." *Nederlandsch-Indië Oud & Nieuw* 15 (1930–31): 347–52.

van Hoëvell, Gerrit W. W. C. "De Aroe-eilanden, geographisch, ethnographisch en commercieel." *Tijdschrift van het Koninglijk Nederlandsch Aardrijkskundig Genootschap* 33 (1890): 57–102.

van Kampen, Pieter Nicolaas. *De paarl- en parelmoervisscherij langs de kusten der Aroe-eilanden*. Buitenzorg, Dutch East Indies: Departement van Landbouw, Drukkerij van het Departement, 1908.

Vertrees, Herbert H. *Pearls and Pearling*. New York: Fur News Publishing, 1913.

Villiers, Alan. *Sons of Sinbad: An Account of Sailing with the Arabs in their Dhows, in the Red Sea, around the Coasts of Arabia, and to Zanzibar and Tanganyika: Pearling in the Persian Gulf, and the Life of the Shipmasters, the Mariners and Merchants of Kuwait*. 1940. Reprint, New York: Charles Scribner's Sons, 1968.

Waleffe, Maurice de. *Quand Paris était un paradis: Mémoires 1900–1939*. Paris: Denoël, 1947.

Walmsley, Alan, Hugh Barnes, and Phillip Macumber. "Al-Zubarah and Its Hinterland, North Qatar: Excavations and Survey, Spring 2009." *Proceedings of the Seminar for Arabian Studies* 40 (2010): 55–68.

Warren, Carol. *Ideology, Identity and Change*. Southeast Asia Monograph Series 14. Townsville: James Cook University of North Queensland, 1983.

Warren, James Francis. "Metaphorical Perspectives of the Sea and the Sulu Zone, 1768–1898." In *The Sea: Thalassography and Historiography*, edited by Peter N. Miller, 145–73. Ann Arbor: University of Michigan Press, 2013.

———. *The Sulu Zone, 1768–1898: The Dynamics of External Trade, Slavery, and Ethnicity in the Transformation of a Southeast Asian Maritime State*. 2nd ed. Singapore: National University of Singapore Press, 2007.

———. *The Sulu Zone, the World Capitalist Economy and the Historical Imagination*. Amsterdam: VU University Press/CASA, 1998.

Warsh, Molly A. *American Baroque: Pearls and the Nature of Empire, 1492–1700*. Chapel Hill: University of North Carolina Press, 2018.

Wiggers, C. J. "The Pearl Fisheries near the Aroe Isles." *Sluyters' Monthly*, March 1921, 221–27.

Wilson, Elizabeth. *Adorned in Dreams: Fashion and Modernity*. Rev. ed. New Brunswick, NJ: Rutgers University Press, 2003.

Win, Daw, and Loh Wei Leng. "Regional Links: Yangon, Penang, and Singapore." *Journal of the Malaysian Branch of the Royal Asiatic Society* 82, no. 2 (December 2009): 67–79.

Worsley-Gough, Barbara. *Fashion in London*. London: Allan Wingate, 1952.

Yu, Sarah. "Broome Creole: Aboriginal and Asian Partnerships along the Kimberley Coast." *Queensland Review* 6, no. 2 (November 1999): 59–73.

Yu, Sarah, and Tanya Edwards, eds. *Lustre: Pearling and Australia*. Welshpool: Western Australia Museum, 2018.

Contributors

Robert Carter has long-standing interests in the maritime cultures of the Persian Gulf and globalization in all its forms, with publications ranging from the first trading networks and pearl fishers of the Neolithic period, through to the peak of the historic pearl fishery in the twentieth century. His book *Sea of Pearls* (2012) examines the deep history and formative influence of the pearl fishery in the Gulf. These interests drew him to the archaeology and history of the Gulf towns, nearly all of which began as pearl-fishing settlements. Since 2012, he has investigated the people, archaeology, history, urban life, and architecture of Doha in the pre-oil and early oil period with the *Origins of Doha and Qatar Project*, a multidisciplinary project funded by the Qatar National Research Fund. Apart from revealing aspects of premodern and early-oil urban life in a typical Gulf town, this has given tangible evidence for the integration of Doha and other Gulf towns into global networks of production, consumption, and trade between the eighteenth and twentieth centuries. He has also published extensively on many other periods and aspects of archaeology in the Gulf and Mesopotamia, and is currently Visiting Professor in Arabian and Middle Eastern Archaeology at UCL Qatar.

Joseph Christensen is a Postdoctoral Fellow at the Asia Research Centre at Murdoch University in Perth, Western Australia, where he works in the fields of maritime and environmental history, and a graduate (PhD, BA Hons) of the University of Western Australia. His other publications include the coedited collections *Historical Perspectives of Fisheries Exploitation in the Indo-Pacific* (2014) and *Natural Hazards and Peoples in the Indian Ocean World* (2016).

William Gervase Clarence-Smith is Emeritus Professor of the Economic History of Asia and Africa, SOAS University of London, where he has taught African, Southeast Asian, and world history. He acts as Editor of the *Journal of Global History*, published by Cambridge University Press, and is a Fellow of the Royal Asiatic Society and the Royal Historical Society. Currently, he is researching the trading, processing, marketing, and consumption of pearling products around the world in the nineteenth and twentieth centuries. In relation to the same period, he is working on the history of sponge gathering and whaling, as well as Portuguese fishing enterprises off the coast of northwestern Africa. He also researches the history of tropical agricultural commodities, narcotics, manufacturing in the Global South, diasporas from the West, the Middle East, and South Asia, slavery and other forms of labor, and Islamic attitudes to sexuality. With Ed Emery, he has organized SOAS-based conferences on quadrupeds and marine animals since 2010. Conferences to date have concerned donkeys and mules, war horses, camels, elephants, and sponges. Further conferences are planned on oysters, fishing, and buffaloes. In 2018, they launched the fledgling Interdisciplinary Animal Studies Initiative at SOAS.

Matthew S. Hopper is Professor of History at California Polytechnic State University, San Luis Obispo. His book, *Slaves of One Master: Globalization and Slavery in Arabia in the Age of Empire* (2015), was a finalist for the 2016 Frederick Douglass Book Prize. He received his PhD in History from UCLA, MA in African Studies from UCLA, and MA in History from Temple University. He has been a postdoctoral fellow at the Gilder Lehrman Center at Yale University, a Member at the Institute for Advanced Study, Princeton, and the Smuts Visiting Research Fellow in Commonwealth Studies at the University of Cambridge. He has held fellowships from the Social Science Research Council and Fulbright-Hays, and his writing has been published in *Annales*, *Itinerario*, and the *Journal of African Development*. He is currently writing a history of liberated Africans in the Indian Ocean world.

Pedro Machado is Associate Professor of History at Indiana University, Bloomington. He is the author of several works, most recently *Ocean of Trade: South Asian Merchants, Africa and the Indian Ocean, c. 1750–1850* (2014), "Views from Other Boats: On Amitav Ghosh's Indian

Ocean 'Worlds'" (2016), and *Textile Trades, Consumer Cultures and the Material Worlds of the Indian Ocean* (2018). He is currently at work on a global history of pearl-shell collection and exchange while also developing research on eucalyptus and colonial forestry in the Portuguese empire in the nineteenth and twentieth centuries.

Julia T. Martínez is Associate Professor of History at the University of Wollongong, Australia, in the Faculty of Law, Humanities and the Arts. She was an Australian Research Council (ARC) Future Fellow (2013–17) exploring the policing of trafficking in women and children in Southeast Asia and Australia. She has published broadly in Asia Pacific history on slavery, labor, mobility, and migration histories. Her monograph (co-authored with Adrian Vickers) *The Pearl Frontier: Indonesian Labor and Indigenous Encounters in Australia's Northern Trading Network* (2015) won the 2016 Queensland Literary Award's History Book Award, the Northern Territory History Book Award, and was shortlisted for the 2016 Australian Historical Association's Ernest Scott Prize. She has co-published with Claire Lowrie on male domestic service in Australia and the Philippines in *Gender and History* and *Pacific Historical Review*, and as sole author on Indian domestic service in *Australian Historical Studies*. Her ARC-funded monograph, coauthored with Claire Lowrie, Frances Steel, and Victoria Haskins, is *Colonialism and Male Domestic Service across the Asia Pacific* (2019). She is currently researching for a new ARC-funded project with Claire Lowrie and Gregor Benton on Chinese indentured labor in Asia Pacific colonies after 1919.

Michael McCarthy has for many years written about history and maritime archaeology, publishing many articles, chapters, books, conference proceedings, and compendia. These have included works on the colonial entrepreneur and early pearler in Australia C. E. Broadhurst, which led more broadly to the study of pearl-shell harvesting on the continent's northwest coast and the transition from Aboriginal harvesting methods to diving and the use of diving apparatus during the European phases of the industry. He has curated and co-curated numerous exhibitions and websites as Curator of Maritime Archaeology at the Western Australian Museum. As "Inspector of Wrecks," he headed the Australian Contact Shipwrecks Program, an analysis of the interaction of Indigenous peoples with shipwreck survivors, and the study of indigenous maritime depictions on the Western Australian coast. He has been responsible for the excavation and study of several wrecks, including the Dutch East India Company ship *Zuytdorp* (1711) and the iron hulled *SS Xantho* (1872), and helped pioneer the study of abandoned hulks, aircraft wrecks, and historic submarines in Australia and elsewhere. He has held adjunct appointments at Notre Dame University in Fremantle, Western Australia, and at Texas A&M University in the United States. Since 2013, he has also been coordinating editor of the *Great Circle*, the biannual journal of the Australian Association for Maritime History.

Jonathan Miran is professor of African and Islamic history at Western Washington University in Bellingham, Washington. He was trained in African studies and history at the Institut National des Langues et Civilisations Orientales (INALCO) in Paris and at Michigan State University. He has researched and written about the social, religious, and cultural history of Muslims and their institutions and practices in Northeast Africa, especially Eritrea and Ethiopia. More recently, he has also developed interests in the histories of Northeast Africa and the Red Sea area from broader regional and maritime perspectives that draw on and converse with transregional and global history approaches. Miran is the author of *Red Sea Citizens: Cosmopolitan Society and Cultural Change in Massawa* (2009) and articles in various journals including *Islamic Law and Society*, *Journal of African History*, *Slavery & Abolition*, *Die Welt des Islams*, *International Journal of African Historical Studies*, and *History Compass*. He currently serves as the General Editor of the journal *Northeast African Studies*.

Steve Mullins teaches at Central Queensland University. He is a maritime historian interested in Australia's colonial tropical sedentary fishing industries, mainly pearl shell, bêche-de-mer (trepang), and trochus, and their interconnections across the western Pacific, northern Australia, and Propinsi Maluku, Indonesia. He also researches in Torres Strait history and contemporary issues, Australian South Sea Islander (ASSI) history and contemporary issues, and maritime and coastal environmental history. He has written numerous scholarly books and articles, serves on a number of editorial boards, and is an Honorary Research Fellow at Queensland Museum.

Karl Neuenfeldt trained academically in Cultural Studies (PhD, Curtin University, Australia) and Anthropology (MA, Simon Fraser University, Canada). He is also active professionally as a music researcher, producer, and recording artist. His publications focus on Australian Indigenous popular music and recording studio practice. He is currently doing postgraduate research on the history of Australian pearling songs at Murdoch University, Perth, Western Australia.

Samuel Ostroff is a historian of modern South Asia and the wider Indian Ocean world. His research rests at the intersection of science, environment, culture, and the economy in the context of Dutch and British imperialism between the eighteenth and twentieth centuries. He earned his PhD in History and South Asia Studies at the University of Pennsylvania and holds an MA in Middle Eastern, South Asian, and African Studies from Columbia University. He completed his undergraduate studies at Bucknell University. He is currently revising his dissertation on pearling in the Gulf of Mannar for publication as a scholarly monograph, and is Publications Officer at the Institute for Health Metrics and Evaluation and Affiliate Faculty in the Henry M. Jackson School of International Studies at the University of Washington, Seattle.

James Francis Warren is Emeritus Professor of Southeast Asian Modern History at Murdoch University, Perth, Western Australia. He has held positions at the Australian National University, Yale University, and as a Professorial Research Fellow at the Centre for Southeast Asian Studies, Kyoto University, and the Asia Research Institute, National University of Singapore. He has been awarded grants by the Social Science Research Council and the Australia Research Council and is a Fellow of the Australian Academy of the Humanities. He is currently director of a major Australia Research Council Linkage Project, "Hazards, Tipping Points, Adaptation and Collapse in the Indo-Pacific World." Professor Warren's major publications include *The Sulu Zone, 1768–1898* (1981), *Rickshaw Coolie: A People's History of Singapore, 1880–1940* (1986), *At the Edge of Southeast History* (1987), *Ah Ku and Karayuki-San: Prostitution and Singapore Society, 1870–1940* (1993), *The Sulu Zone, the World Capitalist Economy and the Historical Imagination* (1998), *Iranun and Balangingi: Globalization, Maritime Raiding and the Birth of Ethnicity* (2001), and *Pirates, Prostitutes and Pullers: Explorations* *in the Ethno- and Social History of Southeast Asia* (2008). In 2003, he was awarded the Centenary Medal of Australia for service to Australian society and the humanities in the study of ethnohistory, and, in 2103, the Association for Asian Studies Grant Goodman Prize in Historical Studies.

Index

Page references in *italics* refer to tables/illustrations.
Page references in **bold** refer to the main contribution from each author.

A. & C. Schmid (later Schmid & Jeandel), 294, 302–3
'Abd al-Rahmān, 317
'Abd al-Rahman al-Ibrahim, 42
'Abd al-Rahman bin Hasan Al-Qusaybi, 42
Abdullah bin Qāsim ath-Thāni (Sheik), 269
Aboriginal Natives Pearl Shell Fishery Act 1871, 347
Aborigines, 6, 156–62, 388–89; labor, 18–19, 24, 122, 131, 164–73, 344–63, 377–82, *378*
Aborigines Protection and Restriction of the Sale of Opium Acts, 351–52, 372
abuse, 95, 165–68, 170, 241–42, 273–75, 345, 347–51, 353, 372, 381. *See also* violence
accidents. *See* injuries
Account of the Pearl Fisheries of Ceylon, An (Steuart), 91
Adbdullah bin Jābur al-Musallamī, 269
"Adhaz Ockingu" (song), 376–77
Adur, 165
Africa, 8, 21, 244–45, 263–80, 315
agents, 35–37, 41, 43, 239, 285, 315, 317–18, 322–23
Ahmad Bā Zar'a (Shaykh), 325
Ahmed, Ebrahim, 20, 209, 217
ailments, 6, 11, 66, 150, 152–53, 267, 275, 375
Aladdin, 296
Albert, 159, 164
Albert Ochse and Co., 139
Al-Bīrūnī, 6–7
Aldenham, 299
Aldrich, Fred, 136, 137, 138
Alexandra (Queen), 270
'Alī al-Rahïm bin Muhammad al-Nahārī, 23, 43, 313–43, *319*
Alice, 295
al-Mas'ūdī, 6–7

Amateur, 161
American Baroque (Warsh), 88
Amiral Pierre, 325
Antaki, Elias, 41
Appadurai, Arjun, 10, 59
Arabian Gulf, 7, 21, 23, 32, 119, 122, 263–80, 366–68, 371; terminology, 26n9. *See also* Persian Gulf
Arabian Sea, 2, 87
Arabs, 7, 233, 236–39, 244–46, 267, 315; trade 37, 38, 40, 42–43, 271, 277, 284
Arafura Maru II, 281
Ariel, 159, 295, 296, 302–3
Armenia, 191, 194, 244
Aru Islands, 22, 281, 283–87, 348
Asia, 3,4; labor, 34, 344, 381; trade, 31–34, 37–44, 88, 184–85, 194, 196, 201, 207–8, 218, 220
Australia, 4, 6, 22, 39, 42, 300–301, 364–400; pearl fisheries, 147–79, 187, 193, 198, 201, 204, 206, 213, 218–220, 281–93, 285, 344–63. *See also* Aborigines
Austria, 35, 138, 201

Baädilla Brothers & Co., 289, 293–96, 299, 301, 303
Baboom, Gregory, 191
Bach, John, 120–21
Baharna, 244–45
Bahrain, 232–62, 264–65, 269, 271, 272, 322
Bailey, John, 379–80
Baja California (Mexico), 38–39, 41–42
Balangingi, 69–70, 76
Balint, Ruth, 346
Baluchis, 267, 277
Bandaneira (Indonesia), 283, 284, 289, 295
Bani, Ephraim, 373–74
Banians, 36–37, 37, 40, 43, 239

Banivanua Mar, Tracey, 351
banyaga. See slaves
Barnes, Edward (Governor), 93–94, 100, 103, 106
Bashir bin Farajullah, 269
Batavia (Indonesia), 287, 290–92, 294, 299, 301
Battye, James, 379
Baudin, Nicolas, 156
Baur, Henry, 313, *333, 334,* 335
Bā Zarʻa family, 320–21
bêche-de-mer, 188, 198, 220, 283, 348, 350, 351
Beck, Henry Le, 103
Becker, Hendrick (Governor), 101
bedu, 238, 240, 244–45
Belgrave, Charles, 267
Bengal, Bay of, 3, 13, 87, 183–85, 187, 189, 191, 197, 209
Benton, Lauren, 12
Bertolacci, Anthony, 99–100
Bienenfeld, Jacques, 35, 39, 316, 322, 325–26
Bienenfeld family, 41, 43
birds' nests, 187–89, 191–93, 198
blackbirding, 131, 168, 379
Black Swana (Charm), 373
"Black Swana" (song), 372–76
Blankert & Co., 289
Blurton (boat owner), 161
boatmen, 62, 64–65, 67–70, 95–98, 101, 119
boats, 92–94, 100–105, 157–59, 161, 165, 239; crews, 97–98, 240, 265–67, 367; mother boats, 154, 162, *163,* 218; number of, 98, 124–26, 134, 139, 148, 168, 172, 296, 314
Bolster, Jeffrey, 13
Bombay (India), 33, 34, 36–37, 41–43, 239, 271–72, 314–15, 318, 322, 324
Book of the Pearl, The (Kunz and Stevenson), 193, 379
borders, 56–59, 70, 74, 97, 205–6
Bos (Mr.), 293
Bose, Sugata, 34, 97
Bowden-Smith, N. (Rear Admiral), 289
Boyd, Robert, 106
Braudel, Fernand, 57
Brett, Judith, 300–301
Britain, 245–47, 277, 287–88, 381; pearl fisheries, 37, 88–108, 125–26, 170, 241, 271, 290; trade, 58, 74, 189–98, 201–6, 209, 214–15. *See also* London
Broadhurst, C. E. (Charles), 163–66, 168–70
Broadhurst, Daniel (nephew), 170
brokers, 35, 40, 322, 324–26
Brown, Aubrey (brother), 348
Brown, Maitland, 347
Brucks, George Barnes, 242–44, 243

Bu Kuwara, 246
Burma, 183–231
Burma Fisheries Act, 217
Burma Pearl Fishing and Culture Syndicate (BPFCS), 219
Burns, James, 285
Burns Philp & Co., 285, 375
Butcher, John G., 68–69, 219, 282–83, 290, 293
buttons, 138, 139, 201, 283, 384

Cadell, Francis, 168, 170
Cameron, C. H., 94
Carter, Robert, 20–21, **232–62**
Cartier, Jacques, 322
Celebes Trading Co. (CTC), 294–303
ceramics, 233, 247–51, *248, 249, 250,* 254, 285
Cervantes, 156–57
Ceylon. *See* Sri Lanka
Ceylon Company of Pearl Fishers Ltd., 41, 137–38
Chapman, Edward, 348
Charm (Black Swana), 373
Charney, Michael, 187–88
Charon, 159
Chill (Mr.), 201, 203
China, 6, 7; labor, 34–35, 124, 131, 168, 172, 354, 381; trade, 33, 37–39, 57–59, 70–75, 183–231, 284, 285, 289
Choo, Christine, 355
Christensen, Joseph, 17–18, **118–46**
Clara Crawford, 285
Clarence-Smith, William G., 15–16, **31–54**
Clark, James, 138, 292–95, 299, 302
Clark, John (brother), 296
Clark, Victor (nephew), 293, 295, 296
Clark Combination, 292–96, 298, 300
Cockerell, John, 284
Codrai, Ronald, 268
Coffin, Lorrae, 381
Colebrooke, Henry Thomas, 86
Colebrooke, W. M. G., 94
colors, 32, 34, 35, 122, 137, 170
Comaroff, Jean and John, 60
commission agents. *See* agents
commodities, 10–11, 58–60, 69–72, 187–88, 247, 370; commodity-based history approach, 16, 59–61, 73–75; commodity chain, 15–16, 31–54, 369; prestige, 90, 92
Commutation Act (1784), 190
compressed air, 150–53
Coquette, 165
Cordiner, James, 96, 99, 102–4
crime 35. *See also* fraud; poaching; smuggling; theft

Crisp, James (Captain), 107
CTC (Celebes Trading Co.), 294–303
cultured pearls, 39, 119–20, 140, 219–20, 235, 275, 303, 328; trade in 41, 43–44, 276

Dai, Ahwang, 355
Dalrymple, Alexander, 57, 63, 148–49
Dampier, William, 122, 156, 377
Dan, Henry Gibson, 371–76, 371
Darling (Mr.), 157–58
Dashwood Inquiry (1901–2), 298
Dawson, Kevin, 269
Deakin, Alfred (Prime Minister), 300–301
dealers, 36, 40–43, 276, 290, 316, 318, 322, 326
death. *See* mortality
De Bordes & Co., 289, 291
debt, 271–75, 304, 315
decompression sickness, 152–53, 375
decoration, 6, 156
Delaware, 356
Dibbs, George (Sir), 289
disease, 97, 165, 168, 303
divers, 11, 95–101, 160–61, 172, 263–69, 268, 371; illegal diving, 37, 100–102, 288, 290; payment, 214, 273–75, 289–90, 317, 346; songs, 24–25, 364–400, 367; techniques, 65–68, 105, 149, 151–54, 155, 162–69, 163, 186, 214–20, 240, 265–66, 347; women, 149–50, 162, 166–67, 344–63, 379
diving equipment, 66–67, 105–7, 155, 163–66, 172–73, 265, 289–90; suit or dress, 147–54, 152, 155, 212–13, 215–16, 283, 289, 379
Dolphin, 346
Don, G. L. (Constable), 357
Dorante, James and Vincent, 375
Douglas, John, 352
dummying, 293, 300
Durand, E. L. (Captain), 267
Dutch East India Company. *See* VOC

eardrums, burst, 150, 267
East India Company (English), 58, 63, 85–87, 89–108, 190, 193–95, 214–15
Eaton, Natasha, 10
Edgar, Doris, 346
Edith, Mary, 354
Edmonds, Penelope, 349
Edward, R. M., 357
Egan, Ted, 369, 384–88
Emma, 157–58, 163
Empire of Free Trade (Sen), 90
employment. *See* labor
Enterprise, 289
Envy (Ise Pearl), 377

Eritrea, 321, 326. *See also* Massawa
Eseli, James, 376
Ethical Policy, 290, 291, 298
Eugenie (Empress), 270–72
Europe: fashion, 14, 197–98, 270–72, 314, 316, 322; pearl fisheries, 156–62, 172, 203, 206, 213, 346; trade, 33, 264, 276

Fairy, 159, 164
Faraj bin Sa'id, 274–75
fashion, 6, 14, 264, 269–71, 276, 314
Ferris, Kate, 315
Field Porter, William, 302
fishing pearls. *See* divers; pearl fisheries
Flores, Jorge Manual, 87
Floria, 375
Flowerdale, 287
Forbes, Jonathan, 91, 96
Forrest, John (Sir), 127–28, 130–32
Forrest, Thomas, 57
Forsyth, Adam, 285
"Forty Fathoms" (song), 372–76
Foxon, J. F. G. (Hon.), 352–53
France, 156, 201, 206, 316, 322–28. *See also* Paris
fraud, 67, 96, 103–4, 106
"Free Diving" (song), 377–81
Fujita brothers, 38
Fukai Maru, 281

Gale, Charles Frederick, 134, 136, 138–39
Ganter, Regina, 24, 350, 351
Gazelle, 158
Giblett, Hugh, 353
Gill, William Wyatt (Reverend), 350
globalization, 7–10, 19–22, 32–34, 72, 74–75, 232–80, 315
Grafton, 375
Grant, McKenzie, 349
Great Australian Loneliness, The (Hill), 118–19, 141
green snails, 198, 213–14, 216, 218
Gregory, F. T., 157
Gregory, John (Inspector), 119–22, 136, 140–41
Gribble, John, 379–80
Gsell, Francis Xavier (Monsignor), 357
Guy, John Michael, 242–44, 243

Habib, Albert, 42
Hajji Shah Mahomed Ali, 202
Hamid bin Salim, 269
Hancock, Lionel (Lt. Com.), 288
Hardin, Garret, 126
Harper, Charles, 161
Harrison, Paul W., 267

Index 421

Haultain (Captain), 357
Haynes, Thomas Henry, 204, 286–89, 292
Heere, Gerrit de, 102
Heesterman, Jan, 97, 205
Hepburn, James (Collector), 104
Herdman, William, 108
Hill, Ernestine, 118–20, 141, 348
Hindu Vaniya, 34, 36
Hockings, Reg, 292, 302
holothurians, edible. *See* bêche-de-mer
Hopper, Matthew S., 21, 60, **263–80**
Hovhannes (merchant), 191
Huddleston (Collector), 100–101
Hughan, Allan, 164, 166
Hukamchand, Chagganlal, 325–26, 326
Hundred Horizons, A (Bose), 97
Hunt, J., 66
Hunt, Susan Jane, 345–46, 379
Hunter, Mercedes, 356
Huwala, 238, 244–45

Ibn Battuta, 147–48, 150, 173
Illicit Love (McGrath), 354
Illustrations of Political Economy (Martineau), 85–87
Imhoff, Gustaav Willem van (Baron) (Governor), 94
India, 6, 85–117, 195, 205–10; trade, 33, 39, 43, 194, 218, 239, 244, 271, 315, 322. *See also* Bombay
indigenous peoples, 156–62, 284, 291, 294, 296, 300, 303. *See also* Aborigines
Industry, 164
injuries, 150, 152–53, 166, 267
Iran. *See* Persia
Iranun, 69–70, 76
Ise Pearl (Envy), 377
Italy, 321–23, 326–27
Ivanoff, Jacques, 186

Jains, 34, 36, 37, 39, 43
Jameson, Lyster, 136
Japan, 293, 300–301, 303; labor, 34–35, 172, 218, 281, 289, 353–54, 357, 381–88; trade, 38–39, 41, 43–44, 219–20. *See also* Kobe
Jardine, Chum, 302
Jardine, Frank ,201, 210, 350
Jasim al-Ibrahim, 42
Jawi Peranakans, 208–9
Jessie, 285
Jessup, Harry (nephew), 282, 303
Jessup, Vince, 302
jewelry, 31, 33–35, 40, 196, 270–72, 276
Jews, 39–42, 244
Johnston, Alexander, 85–86
Jones (Captain), 352

Jonville, Eudelin de, 106
Juma bin Fundi, 268–69
Jumah Kanaidish, 274

Kampen, Pieter Nicolaas van, 298, 303
Karskens, Grace, 345
Kemball (Lt.), 245–46
Kessel, Joseph, 330–32, 335
Khoja (trader), 36
Kobe (Japan), 34, 39, 41, 44
Kokichi, Mikimoto, 35, 43–44
Koop (Sergeant), 356
Kopytoff, Igor, 59
Kornitzer, Louis, 35, 40, 41
Kunz, George Frederick, 193, 377–79
Kuwayti, 42, 43
Kwaymullina, Sumi, 381

labor, 35, 85–117, 127, 236–42, 237, 365–66; demand for, 58, 69, 245, 265; sources of, 8, 11, 18–19, 24, 64–67, 165–73, 183, 277, 282, 293; women, 344–63, 380–88. *See also* Aborigines; China; Japan; slaves
Leach, Edmund, 57
Lee, George, 94
Lee-Bryce, William, 355
legislation, 167–68, 287–95, 347–48, 350–51, 356, 372, 380–81. *See also* Sharks Bay Pearl Shell Fishery Acts
Lejard, Thierry, 186
Les secrets de la mer Rouge (Monfreid), 23, 313–14, 332–36, *333*, *334*
Lévy, Émile, 41
Linder, Karl, 325, 326
Little Eastern, 159
Lizard, HMS, 287–88
London (Britain), 33, 35, 40, 315, 322–23
Lone Star, 159
Lorimer, J. G., 234–35, 237–38, 237, 241–42, 267
Loten, Joan Gideon (Governor), 104
Lushington (Collector), 98

MacColl, John Campbell, 294
Machado, Pedro, 1–28, 19–20, **183–231**
Mackenzie (Captain), 249
Mackenzie, Jim, 295, 302
Maingy, A. D., 191–92, 195, 196
Makassar (Indonesia), 38, 189, 283, 285, 294, 301
Malay, 19, 168–72, 192, 207, 215, 217, 218, 354–55, 381
Malay, Cissie, 355
management, 17–18, 94–95, 118–46, 281–310
Mann, Michael, 75
Manners (Lt.), 246

Marakkayars, 37, 38, 208, 215
Marina, 289
marine environment, 13, 61–64, 118–46
marine products, 185–89, 213, 216, 220
markets, 9–11, 31–54, 118–46. *See also* trade
Martineau, Harriet, 85–87
Martinelli, Renzo, 323, 327–28
Martinez, Dolores, 345
Martínez, Julia, 282, **344–63**
Martini, Ferdinando, 23, 323
Mary Ann, 158, 164
Massawa (Eritrea), 43, 314, 318, 320–32
Maung Tun U, 211
Mavis, 287, 292
Maxwell (Mr.), 352
Maxwell, F. D., 211
McCarthy, Michael, 18–19, **147–79**, 380
McCulloch, John Ramsay, 90, 91
McDonald, Jack, 356–57
McDowall, John, 99
McEvoy, Arthur E., 121
McLaren, John, 355
McLeod (Captain), 236
McRae, Duncan, 167
McRae, F., 164–65
McRae, George, 167
medicinal uses, 6, 33, 64, 187, 211
Medora, 159
Melanie, 165
merchants, 11, 35–44, 57–58, 101, 239, 241–42, 271–76, 285, 298, 318, 322. *See also* trade
Mergui archipelago, 19–20, 183–231, 290–91
Mergui Pearling Company, 203, 208
Merton, H., 346–47
Merton, Hugo, 303
migration, 11, 97–100, 242–47, 253
Mikimoto, Kokichi, 39, 275–76
Miran, Jonathan, 22–23, **313–43**
missionaries, 350, 355, 357
Mohamad bin Ibrahim, 269
Moken, 186–89, 193–95, 205–7, 214–18
Monfreid, Henry de, 23, 313–14, 328–36, 334
monopolies, 34, 37, 41, 86–95, 125–28, 141, 204, 206, 210–11, 300
Monsted, Carl, 282, 302–3
Monsted, Neils Preben (nephew), 303
Morning Star, 158, 161
mortality, 11, 152–53, 166, 267, 345, 375, 386, 388
mother-of-pearl, 5, 16, 67, 201, 216, 220, 275, 282, 283, 321
Motlop, Kawane, 373
Moussaieff, Rehavia, 40
Mubarak bin Nar, 275

Muhammad 'Ali bin Zaynal 'Alireza, 42–43
Muhammad al-Mushārī, 324
Muhammad al-Rahmān, 323–25, 328
Muhammad bin Thānī (Sheik), 264
Muhammad Faruq bin Muhammad 'Aqil, 42–43
Muhammad Sāfī, 325
Muhammad 'Umar Bā Zar'a (Shaykh), 320–21, 324, 325
Mulgrue, James Arthur (Captain), 356
Mullins, Steve, 22, 60, 127, 138, **281–310**, 351, 353
Munro, Edwin, 292, 294, 299, 302
music, 24–25, 364–400, 367
Muslims, 36–37, 101, 208, 284, 295
Myanmar, 219, 220

Nagata, Yuriko, 354
Nakamura, 384, *385*
Napier (Constable), 356
Native Labourers' Protection Act 1884, 351
Nattukottai Chettiars, 37, 208
Natural History (Historia Naturalis) (Pliny the Elder), 6
Naturalist in Australia, The (Saville-Kent), 134, 136
Nautilus, 159, 164
Nemchand, Thakordas, 43
Netherlands, 88–89, 94, 98, 100–102, 104, 106, 170–71
Netherlands India Pearling Co., 293
Neuenfeldt, Karl, 24–25, **364–400**
New York (USA), 33, 40
nomadism, 67–69
North, Frederick (Governor), 95, 98, 99, 102–3
North America, 264, 270, 314, 316, 322. *See also* United States of America

objects 6, 9–10, 61
Okinawans, 383–84, 388
Oman, 268, 269
Ostroff, Samuel M., 16–17, **85–117**
output, 294, 302; mother-of-pearl, 220, 283; oysters, 209–11; pearls, 32–33, *32*, *135*, 148, 157–59, 166, 170, 234–35, 266; pearl shell, 122–24, 131, *135*, 293, 299, 303
Outridge, Percy, 292
oysters, 7, 209–12

Pacific Islanders Protection Act 1872, 350
Pacific Islands, 38–39, 165, 168, 189, 344, 350–53
Palgrave, William Gifford, 242, 264
Panama, 41, 150, 153
Pankhurst, Richard, 332

Index   423

Pannâlâl, Amîchand, 36
Paris (France), 33, 35, 40, 42, 43, 271–75, 314–16, 318, 322–28
Parsis (Parsi Zoroastrians), 36, 37, 39, 194
Paviljoen, Anthony (Commander), 99, 100
Pearl, 159, 164
pearl farming, 370, 384
pearl fisheries, *1–4*, 5–28, 61–66, 86, 90–108, 122–24, 196–98, 281–310; auction-lease system, 198–210, 200, 202, 213, 215–18; boundaries, 12, 102–4, 127, 203–6, 286–88, 293–94; cultivation, 129–32, 137–38, 140, 219; floating station system, 286–88, 292, 298, 303; harvesting methods, 7–8, 147–79, *149*, *155*; indigenous rights, 284, 291, 294, 296, 300, 303; leases, 41, 120, 125–34, *133*, 138–41, 289, 290–304; licenses, 37, 90, 104, 122–27, 132, 140, 207, 213–18, 290–302; minimum legal size, 67, 124, 128, 136–37, 290, 294–95; Persian/Arabian Gulf, 232–80, 237; practices, 105, 119, 122–24, 129, 130, 131, 138, 140–41; registration, 101–2, 347, 350–52, 356; rotating closures, 124–34, 129, 290; royalties, 284, 290–91

Pearling and Trading Company, 203, 286–89, 291, 292
Pearls, Arms and Hashish (Monfreid and Treat), 331
Pearls and Pearling Life (Streeter), 66, 162
Pearl Shell Fishery Regulation Act 1873, 167–68, 347–48
pearl shells, 5, 55–82, 156, 183–231, 196–209, 288
Penang (Malaysia), 190–95, 207–9, 209
Pennefather, Charles, 350
Pen-ts'ao kang-mu (Compendium of Materia Medica), 187
Percival, Robert, 105
Persia (Iran), 7, 33, 37, 40, 42, 147, 244–45, 252, 267
Persian Gulf, 2, 7, 13, 20, 22–23, 32, 60, 62, 64, 107, 139, 147–48, 232–62, 263, 268, 274, 276, 314–16, 322; terminology, 26n9. *See also* Arabian Gulf
Philippines, 148, 171, 218, 289, 351, 354, 381
Pillai, Sundaralingam and Muttu, 93
Pilot, 161
Pitt, Douglas, 350
plastics, 119–21, 139–40, 384
Pliny the Elder, 6
poaching, 97, 100–102, 291. *See also* theft
political economy, 11, 85–117, 242
Pon, Carl and Kitty, 355
Pontianak, HNLMS, 287
population, 236–39, 244–45, 251–54, 252, 253

Portugal, 88, 94, 98, 100, 101, 104, 106, 232, 277
Potter, Lawrence, 366
Praag, Joseph von, 42
Premchand Roychand & Sons, 43
prestige goods/commodities, 90, 92
Pretoria, 295, 299
prices: falls, 120, 138–39, 203, 235, 282, 324; surges, 33, 124, 134, 159, 234–35, 271–72, 293. *See also* value
processing, 34–35
profit, 271–73, 276, 299–301, 322
Puglisi, Giuseppe, 318
pumps, 213, 215–16, 218

Qatar, 232–62, 243, 269
Quarles, A. J. Quarles de (Baron), 297–302

Ramsay, Guy, 350
Ranong (Thailand), 195, 206, 217
Red Sea, 2, 22–23, 313–43
regional differences, 148, 169
regional time, 56–59, 74
Reliance, 289
religion, 92–94, 156, 209
Rennell, James, 57
Revel, Jacques, 315
revenue, 119, 134–35, 234–35, 235, 236, 277
rice, 192, 207–9, 271, 273
rituals, 6, 285, 303–4
Roberson, Davey, 99
Rosenthal, Adolphe (brother), 326
Rosenthal, Léonard, 39–41, 272–73, 276, 316, 322, 326, 334
Rosenthal, Victor (brother), 272
Rosenthal et Frères, 272, 323, 326, 330
Roth (Jewish trader) ,42
Roth, Walter E., 352, 355
Royal Asiatic Society, 86
Rubin, Mark, 42
Ruby, 296
Rudmose Brown, R. N., 210
Russell, Lynette, 349
Russia, 33

Sāfī family, 320–21
Sa'id (Sjech) bin 'Abdullah Baādilla, 38, 43, 289, 295, 297–98, 303
Saif Marzooq Al-Shamlan, 322
Salleby, Najeeb, 73
Samal Bajau Laut, 61–68, *62*
Sarawak, Drummond, 355
Sarkies (trader), 191
Saucy Lass, 159
Savant of the Australian Seas (Saville-Kent), 140

Saville-Kent, William, 18, 121–22, 124–25, 128–41, 290
"Sayonara Nakamura" (song), 382–88
Sayyid 'Alï al-Nahārï. *See* 'Alï al-Rahïm bin Muhammad al-Nahārï
Schmid & Jeandel (previously A. & C. Schmid), 302–3
Schouchana, Jacques, 330, 334–35
sea cucumbers (*haishen*), 188, 220
sea nomadism, 67–69
sea wives, 285, 303–4
security, 16–17, 35, 96, 100–105
seed pearls, 195–97, 210–13
Segalen, Victor, 330
Sen, Sudipta, 90
sexual services and companionship, 346, 348–49, 351–58
Shah, Amoulek, 326
Shah, Chandulal, 43
Shark (Sharks) Bay (Australia), 17–18, 118–46, 123, 156, 169–71, 173
shark fins, 220
Sharks Bay Pearl Shell Fishery Acts, 121, 122, 124, 125, 128, 135, 141, 171
Shnukal, Anna, 350, 351
Shohaku, Nakamura, 383–84
Sholl, Robert J., 154, 157, 159, 161–62, 164, 166, 168–69, 173, 347, 380
Sholl, Robert (son), 161
Siam (Thailand), 206, 220. *See also* Ranong
Silva, C. R. de, 106
Simpson, James J., 210
Singapore, 38, 73, 193–94, 207, 283
Sivasundaram, Sujit, 13, 97
Sketty Belle, 296, 297
slave raiders, 8, 69–70, 76
slaves, 8, 11, 58, 67–70, 74–77, 148, 150, 244–45, 263–80, 349, 366. *See also* abuse; labor
Smith, George, 292, 299–302
Smith, Kate, 11
smuggling, 97, 100–102, 321
songs, 24–25, 364–400, 367
Sons of Sinbad (Villiers), 119, 263
Sophia Jane, 159
Spain, 72–73
species, 64, 130, 136–37, 212–13, 314; *Pinctada albina*, 119, 122–24, 128–30, 132, 136, 156; *Pinctada maxima*, 10, 119, 122, 130–31, 136, 138, 156–57, 184, 283
Spencer-Churchill, Charles, 271
Spinifex and Hessian (Hunt), 345–46
Spyer, Patricia, 285, 303, 348
Sri Lanka, 17, 34, 37, 41, 85–117, 148, 150, 195, 204–6, 347
steamships, 105–6
Sterling Comb Company, 139

Steuart, James, 90–91, 103, 106
Stevenson, Charles Hugh, 193, 377–79
Stewart Mackenzie, J. A. (Governor), 94, 106
Straits Settlements (1826), 193
Streeter, E. W. (Edwin William), 63, 66, 150, 162, 166
Stross, Ludwig, 18, 121–22, 124–28, 131–34, 136–41
Struck, Bernhard, 315
Sub Marine Explorer, 153
Subrahmanyam, Sanjay, 88, 138
Sulu Islands, 16, 55–82, 150, 169
Sumatra, HMS, 287
Sunderland, Heather, 73–74
Sustenance, Samuel, 348
Sweet, O. J. (Major), 63

Tagliacozzo, Eric, 190
Tahiti, 220
Taing Shwe Hla, 211
Taiwan, 39
Tamil Marakkayars. *See* Marakkayars
Tamil Paravas, 99, 205, 206
Tavernier, J. B., 148
Tawara, 352
tax-free boats (*mauniam*), 92–94
Tays, W. F., 157–58, 163, 346
tea, 58–59, 70, 74–75, 190
Thailand (Siam), 206, 220. *See also* Ranong
theft, 86–87, 96, 100–104, 266. *See also* poaching
Thomas, Bertram, 267–68
Three Cheers, 296
tin mining, 192, 207, 209, 219
Torres Strait (Australia), 22, 201, 281–310, 344–45, 350–53, 355, 357, 368–69, 372–77, 383–84
trade, 35–44, 88, 156, 185–99, 239, 284–86; consumption and, 247–51, 253–54; cross-cultural, 55–82; free-trade ideology, 90, 254. *See also* globalization; *individual countries*
Treat, Ida, 331
trepang, 188, 189, 198, 283, 288, 291, 348
Treub, Melchior (Dr.), 297–98, 301
trochus shells, 188, 213, 216
Tromp, HNLMS, 287
Tsunematsu, Yamamoto, 354
Tuckey (Mr.,) 158
Turnour, George, 96, 99
turtle eggs, 199, 201–2

United States of America (USA), 14, 138, 156–57, 270–72, 276, 300–301, 383. *See also* New York; North Amercia
U Shwe I, 188, 192–93

Index   425

value, 21, 67, 90, 234–35, 235, 236, 264, 272, 322, 323, 326. *See also* prices
Vanderbilt, Consuelo (daughter), 271
Vanderbilt, William K., 270–71
Vane, George (Superintendent), 95, 103
Venezuela, 41
Venus, 354
Vickers, Adrian, 282
Victoria (Queen), 270
Vidgen, Bert, 302
Vienna (Austria), 35
Villiers, Alan, 119, 263, 268
violence, 11, 76, 95, 131, 161–62, 167, 275, 285. *See also* abuse
Viscoloid Company, 121, 139–40
VOC (Verenigde Oostindische Compagnie), 6, 88–89, 94, 99, 101, 195, 283–84

Walcott, Robert John (Attorney General), 347
Waleffe, Maurice de, 273
Wallace, Alfred Russell, 283–84
Wanetta, 295, 296, 302
Warren, James Francis, 16, **55–82**, 354

Warrington Smyth, Herbert, 197–98
Warsh, Molly, 88, 107–8
wealth, 5–6, 69, 107–8, 264, 270, 272, 326–29, 332
Wellsted, James, 238–39
West, 35, 39–42, 44, 74
White Australia Policy, 118, 293, 354, 381
Whitelock, Henry, 241
Whitmarsh, Hubert Phelps, 172
Wilby, Ernest, 353
Wilson (Colonel), 237
Withnell, John and Emma, 157–58, 160
women, 23–24, 36, 149–50, 162, 166–67, 276, 344–63, 377–82, 378

Xantho, SS, 168, 169

Yasui, Todo, 35
yield. *See* output
Yu, Sarah, 355

Zanzibar, 254
zones, 56–57, 205. *See also* borders